Special educational needs, inclusion and diversity

Second edition

Special educational needs, inclusion and diversity
Second edition

Norah Frederickson and Tony Cline

Open University Press

Open University Press
McGraw-Hill Education
McGraw-Hill House
Shoppenhangers Road
Maidenhead
Berkshire
England
SL6 2QL

email: enquiries@openup.co.uk
world wide web: www.openup.co.uk

and Two Penn Plaza, New York, NY 10121–2289, USA

Reprinted 2010

A catalogue record of this book is available from the British Library

ISBN-13: 978-033-5221462 (pb)
ISBN-10: 0-33-5221467 (pb)

Library of Congress Cataloging-in-Publication Data
CIP data has been applied for

Typeset by RefineCatch Limited, Bungay, Suffolk
Printed in the UK by Ashford Colour Press Ltd, Gosport, Hampshire

The **McGraw·Hill** Companies

Contents

Acknowledgements

We would like to express our thanks to Professor John Morton and Professor Uta Frith for their very helpful comments on an early draft of the version of Chapter 5 that was in the first edition.

The two cases featured in Activity 17.4 were taken from an advanced course which was run at University College London. The accounts were written by Ann Robson, and we are grateful for her permission to use them here.

We would also like to express our thanks to Jane Lang for her excellent support during the preparation of the second edition of this book. Finally, we wish to thank the many colleagues and students who have challenged and stimulated us to keep updating our thinking and knowledge in this field.

Sections of the following chapters were adapted from earlier publications by the authors. We are grateful to the publishers and journal editors who have graciously given permission to use this material. Publishers and details of the original publications are as follows.

Chapter 7: Cline, T. (1998) The assessment of special educational needs for bilingual children. *British Journal of Special Education*, 25(4): 159–63; Cline, T. and Shamsi, T. (2000) *Language Needs or Special Needs? The Assessment of Learning Difficulties in Literacy among Children Learning English as an Additional Language: A Literature Review* (Research Report RR184). London: DfEE. Authorized under individual licence from HMSO (no. C02 W0000128).

Chapter 8: Cline, T. and Frederickson, N. (eds) (1996) *Curriculum Related Assessment – Cummins and Bilingual Children*. Clevedon: Multilingual Matters.

Chapter 9: Frederickson, N. and Cline, T. (eds) (1995) *Assessing the Learning Environments of Children with Special Educational Needs*. London: Educational Psychology Publishing; Frederickson, N. (1990) Introduction to soft systems methodology and its application in work with schools, in N. Frederickson (ed.) *Soft Systems Methodology: Practical Approaches in Work with Schools*. London: Educational Psychology Publishing.

Chapter 10: Cline, T. and Frederickson, N. (eds) (1991) *Bilingual Pupils and the National Curriculum: Overcoming Difficulties in Teaching and Learning*. London: University College London, Department of Psychology.

Chapter 13: Cline, T. and Frederickson, N. (1999) Identification and assessment of dyslexia in bi/multi-lingual children. *International Journal of Bilingual Education and Bilingualism*, 2(2): 81–93. Publisher: Multilingual Matters. Cline, T. and Shamsi, T. (2000) *Language Needs or Special Needs? The Assessment of Learning Difficulties in Literacy among Children Learning English as an Additional Language: A Literature Review* (Research Report RR184). London: DfEE. Authorized under individual licence from HMSO (no. C02 W0000128).

Chapter 16: Frederickson, N. (1991) Children can be so cruel – helping the rejected child, in G. Lindsay and A. Miller (eds) *Psychological Services for Primary Schools*. London: Longman (Pearson Education).

Chapter 17: Cline, T. (1997) Educating for bilingualism in different contexts: teaching the deaf and teaching children with English as an additional language. *Educational Review*, 49(2): 145–52. Publisher: Taylor & Francis Ltd. www.tandf.co.uk/journals.

Permission was also granted for reproduction of the following tables and figures.

Figure 2.1: Chrispeels, J. (1996) Effective schools and home-school-community partnership roles: A framework for parent involvement. *School Effectiveness and School Improvement*, 7(4): 297–323. Reprinted by permission of the publisher (Taylor & Francis Ltd, http://www.tandf.co.uk/journals).

Table 4.2: Baker, E.T., Wang, M.C. and Walberg, H.J. (1994–1995) The effects of inclusion on learning. *Educational Leadership*, 52(4): 33–5. Copyright 2007 by ASCD (www.ascd.org). Used with permission.

Figure 4.4: Mastropieri, M.A., Leinart, A., & Scruggs, T.E. (1999). Strategies to increase reading fluency. *Intervention in School and Clinic*, 34(5), 278–83. Reproduced with permission of Sage Publications Inc.

Figure 4.5: Mathes, P.G., Fuchs, D., Fuchs, L.S., Henley, A.M., & Saunders, A. (1994). Increasing strategic reading practice with Peabody classwide peer tutoring. *Learning Disabilities Research in Practice*, 9(1), 44–8. Reproduced with permission of Blackwell Publishing.

Table 5.1: Sharman, C., Cross, W. & Vennis, D. (2007) *Observing Children and Young People*, 4th edition. London: Continuum. By kind permission of Continuum International Publishing Group.

Figure 5.1: Frith, U. (1997) Brain, mind and behaviour in dyslexia, in C. Hulme and M. Snowling (ed.) *Dyslexia: Biology, Cognition and Intervention*. London: Whurr, with acknowledgement to the British Dyslexia Association.

Figures 5.2 and 5.3: Frith, U. (1995) Dyslexia: can we have a shared theoretical framework? *Educational and Child Psychology*, 12(1): 6–17, with acknowledgement to the British Psychological Society.

Figure 5.4: Frederickson, N. and Cameron, R.J. (1999) *Psychology in Education Portfolio*. Psychology in Education: Assessment in Practice. © nferNelson, 1999. All rights reserved.

Table 5.4: Cline, T. and Baldwin, S. (1994) *Selective Mutism in Childhood*. London: Whurr, with acknowledgement to the British Dyslexia Association.

Figure 5.5: Rutter, M. (1989) Pathways from childhood to adult life. *Journal of Child Psychology and Psychiatry*, 30: 23–51. Publisher: Cambridge University Press.

Table 6.1: Glover, T.A. & Albers, C.A. (2007). Considerations for evaluating universal screening assessments. *Journal of School Psychology*, 45(2), 117–35. With permission from Elsevier.

Table 7.2: Reynolds, C.R. (1980) Differential construct validity of intelligence as popularly measured: correlation of age with raw scores on the WISC-R for blacks, whites, males and females. *Intelligence*, 4(4): 371–80. Publisher: Elsevier Science.

Table 8.1: Black, P. & Wiliam, D. (1998) Assessment and classroom learning. *Assessment in Education: Principles, Policy and Practice*, 5(1): 7–74. Reprinted by permission of the publisher (Taylor & Francis Ltd, http://www.informaworld.com).

Table 8.2: Wiliam, D., Lee, C., Harrison, C. & Black, P.J. (2004). Teachers developing assessment for learning: impact on student achievement. *Assessment in Education: Principles, Policy and Practice*, 11(1), 49–65. Reprinted by permission of the publisher (Taylor & Francis Ltd, http://www.informaworld.com).

Table 8.3: Gavine, D., Auchterlonie, L., & Godson, J. (2006). 'Assessment for learning' and its relevance to educational psychology. *Educational and Child Psychology*, 23(3), 99–108. Reproduced with permission from *Education and Child Psychology*, © The British Psychological Society.

Figure 8.4: Deno, S.L. and Fuchs, L.S. (1987) Developing curriculum based measurement systems for data-based special education problem solving. *Focus on Exceptional Children*, 19(8): 1–16. Publisher: Love Publishing Company.

Figures 8.6, 8.7 and 8.8: Rogers, U. and Pratten, A. (1996) The Cummins framework as a decision making aid for special education professionals working with bilingual children, in T. Cline and N. Frederickson (eds) *Curriculum Related Assessment – Cummins and Bilingual Children*. Clevedon: Multilingual Matters.

Figures 9.2 and 9.3: Design Council (2005). *Learning Environments Campaign Prospectus: From the Inside Looking Out*. London: The Design Council. Reproduced with permission, www.designcouncil.org.uk.

Figure 9.4: Knoff, H.M. (1984) The practice of multi-modal consultation: an integrating approach for consultation service delivery. *Psychology in the Schools*, 21: 83–91. Publisher: John Wiley & Sons, Inc.

Table 9.2: Woolner, P., Hall, E., Higgins, S., McCaughey, C. & Wall, K. (2007). Assigned foundation? What we know about the impact of environments on learning and the implications for Building Schools for the Future. *Oxford Review of Education*, 33(1), 47–70. Reprinted by permission of the publisher (Taylor & Francis Ltd, http://www.informaworld.com).

Table 9.3: Waxman, H.C. (1995) Classroom observations of effective teaching, in A.C. Ornstein (ed.) *Teaching: Theory into Practice*. Published by Allyn and Bacon, Boston, MA. Copyright © 1995 by Pearson Education. Adapted by permission of the publisher.

Table 9.4: Ruiz, N.T. (1995) The social construction of ability and disability: II. Optimal and at-risk lessons in a bilingual special education classroom. *Journal of Learning Disabilities*, 28(8): 491–502. Reproduced with permission of Sage Publications Inc.

Figure 9.8: Checkland, P.B. and Scholes, J. (1990) *Soft Systems Methodology in Action*. Copyright John Wiley & Sons, Limited. Reproduced with permission.

Figure 9.9: Bettle, S., Frederickson, N. and Sharp, S. (2001) Supporting schools in special measures: the contribution of educational psychology. *Educational Psychology in Practice*, 17(1): 53–68. Publisher: Taylor & Francis Ltd., PO Box 25, Abingdon, Oxfordshire, OX14 3UE (http://www.informaworld.com).

Figure 10.1: Crystal, D. and Varley, R. (1998) *Introduction to Language Pathology*, 4th edn. London: Whurr.

Figures 10.2 and 10.3: Bishop, D.V.M. (1997) *Uncommon Understanding: Development and Disorders of Language Comprehension in Children*. Hove: Psychology Press (International Thompson Publishing Services Limited).

Table 10.2: Baker, C. (1996) *Foundations of Bilingual Education and Bilingualism*, 2nd edn. Clevedon: Multilingual Matters.

Activity 10.2: Skutnabb-Kangas, T. (1981) *Bilingualism or Not: The Education of Minorities*. Clevedon: Multilingual Matters.

Figure 10.6: Lees, J. and Urwin, S. (1997) *Children with Language Disorders*, 2nd edn. London: Whurr.

Table 10.5: Cline, T. (1997) Special educational needs and language proficiency, in C. Leung and C. Cable (ed.) *English as an Additional Language: Changing Perspectives* (pp. 53–64). Watford, Hertfordshire: National Association for Language Development in the Curriculum.

Figure 11.3: Framework used in Circle of Friends for thinking about different relationships with people in our lives. Reproduced by kind permission of Jane Turner, Buckinghamshire Educational Psychology Service.

Figure 11.4: Toplis, R., & Hadwin, J. (2006). Using Social Stories to change problematic lunchtime behaviour in school. *Educational Psychology in Practice*, 22, 53–67. Reprinted by permission of the publisher (Taylor & Francis Ltd, http://www.informaworld.com).

Figure 11.5: Center for Effective Collaboration and Practice (2006). Problem Behavior Pathway. Cecp.air.org/fba/problembehavior2/appendixg.htm. Reproduced with the permission of the Center for Effective Collaboration and Practice.

Figure 12.2: Riding, R.J. and Rayner, S. (1998) *Cognitive Styles and Learning Strategies*. London: David Fulton.

Table 12.2: Tomlinson, S. (1988) Why Johnny can't read: critical theory and special education. *European Journal of Special Needs Education*, 3(1): 45–58. Publisher: Taylor & Francis Ltd., PO Box 25, Abingdon, Oxfordshire, OX14 3UE (http://www.informaworld.com).

Table 12.3: Molteno, C., Roux, A., Nelson, M. and Arens, L. (1990) Causes of mental handicap in Cape Town. *South African Medical Journal*, 77: 98–101, with acknowledgement to the South African Medical Association.

Table 12.5: Jensen, M. (2003). Mediating knowledge construction. *Educational and Child Psychology*, 20(2), 100–42. Reproduced with permission from *Education and Child Psychology*, © The British Psychological Society.

Table 12.6: Campione, J.C. (1989) Assisted assessment: a taxonomy of approaches and an outline of strengths and weaknesses. *Journal of Learning Disabilities*, 22(3): 151–65. Reproduced with permission of Sage Publications Inc.

Figures 13.4, 13.6 and 13.7: British Psychological Society (BPS) (1999) *Dyslexia, Literacy and Psychological Assessment*. Leicester: British Psychological Society.

Table 13.4: Gregory, E. (1994) Cultural assumptions and early years' pedagogy: the effect of the home culture on minority children's interpretation of reading in school. *Language, Culture and Curriculum*, 7(2): 111–24, with acknowledgement to the Linguistics Institute of Ireland.

Figure 13.5: Goswami, U. (2006). Neuroscience and education: from research to practice? *Nature Reviews Neuroscience*, 7, 406–13. Reprinted by permission from Macmillan Publishers Ltd.

Figure 13.9: Palinscar, A.S. (1986) The role of dialogue in providing scaffolded instruction. *Educational Psychologist*, 21(1–2): 73–98. Publisher: Taylor & Francis Ltd., PO Box 25, Abingdon, Oxfordshire, OX14 3UE (http://www.informaworld.com).

Table 14.1: Merttens, R. (1999) Family numeracy, in I. Thompson (ed.) *Issues in Teaching Numeracy in Primary Schools*. Buckingham: Open University Press.

Table 14.2: Shuard, H. and Rothery, R. (1984) *Children Reading Mathematics*. London: John Murray. Reproduced by permission of John Murray (Publishers) Ltd.

Activity 14.4: 'Maths phobia' from the University of Hull Study Advice website, http://www.hull.ac.uk/studyadvice/Mathsresources/Mathsphobia.doc. Reproduced with the permission of the University of Hull.

Activity 14.5: Nunes, T. (2004) *Teaching Mathematics to Deaf Children*. London: Whurr Publishers. Copyright John Wiley & Sons, Limited. Reproduced with permission.

Table 15.2: DuPaul, G.J. & Weyandt, L.L. (2006). School based intervention for children with attention deficit hyperactivity disorder: Effects on academic, social and behavioural functioning. *International Journal of Disability, Development and Education*, 53(2), 161–76. Reprinted by permission of the publisher (Taylor & Francis Ltd, http://www.informaworld.com).

Figure 15.5: British Psychological Society (BPS) (1996) *Attention Deficit Hyperactivity Disorder (ADHD): A Psychological Response to an Evolving Concept*. (Report of a Working Party of the British Psychological Society). Leicester: British Psychological Society.

Table 16.1: Caldarella, P. and Merrell, K.W. (1997) Common dimensions of social skills of children and adolescents: A taxonomy of positive behaviours. *School Psychology Review*, 26(2): 264–78. Copyright 1997 by the National Association of School Psychologists, Bethesda, MD. Reprinted with permission of the publisher. www.nasponline.org.

Figure 16.3: Konu, A.I. & Rimpelä, M.K. (2002). Well-being in schools: a conceptual modal. *Health Promotion International* 17(1), 79–87. By permission of Oxford University Press.

Figure 16.4: Dodge, K.A., Pettit, C.S., McClasky, C.J. and Brown, M.M. (1986) Social competence in children. *Society for Research in Child Development Monograph*, No. 213, Blackwell Publishers.

Figure 16.5: Salovey, P. and Sluyter, D.J. (1997) *Emotional Development and Emotional Intelligence*. Reprinted by permission of Basic Books, a member of Perseus Books Group.

Figure 16.6: Lemerise, E.A. & Arsenio, W.F. (2000). An integrated model of emotion processing and cognition in social information processing. *Child Development*, 71(1), 107–18. Reproduced with permission of Blackwell Publishing.

Figure 16.8: Frederickson, N. and Graham, B. (1999) Social skills and emotional intelligence, in N. Frederickson and R.J. Cameron. (1999) *Psychology in Education Portfolio*. Windsor: NFER-Nelson.

Figure 16.10: Webster-Stratton, C., & Hancock, L. (1998). Parent training: Content, methods and processes. In E. Schaefer (Ed.), *Handbook of Parent Training*, 2nd edition (pp. 98–152). Copyright John Wiley & Sons, Limited. Reproduced with permission.

Figure 16.11: Oden, S. (1986) A child's social isolation: origins, prevention, intervention, in G. Cartledge and J.F. Milburn (eds) *Teaching Social Skills to Children*. Oxford: Pergamon Press (Pearson Education).

Figure 17.1: Ridley, J. (1991) The structure of the ear and the hearing system. *Education Guardian*, 25 June 1991: 10, with permission from Guardian Newspapers Ltd. Copyright Guardian News & Media Ltd 1991.

Figure 17.2: Watson, L. (1996) *Hearing Impairment*. Tamworth, Staffordshire: NASEN, with permission from the author and NASEN.

Figure 17.4: Thompson, R.F. (2000). *The Brain: A Neuroscience Primer*. Third edition © 1985, 1993, 2000 by Worth Publishers. Used with permission.

Figure 18.3: Cairney, J., Hay, J.A., Faught, B.E. Wade, T.J., Corna, L. & Flouris, A. (2005). Developmental coordination disorder, generalized self-efficacy toward physical activity, and participation in organized and free play activities. *Journal of Pediatrics*, 147: 515–20. With permission from Elsevier.

PART ONE

Principles and concepts

1

Special educational needs, inclusion and diversity: an integrated approach

---

Objectives

When you have studied this chapter you should:

- be able to explain the implications of describing special educational needs as one aspect of social and cultural diversity;
- be familiar with the way in which this book is structured and the main themes running through it.

Contents

Diversity in society

- A changing society
- Key concepts in charting diversity

An integrated approach

- SEN and educational provision
- Theoretical approaches to SEN

The structure of this book

Diversity in society

A changing society

We have written this book because almost all the books that we read about special educational needs (SEN) and inclusion did not seem to us to reflect adequately the rapidly changing, increasingly diverse nature of the society we live in. What was once a relatively homogeneous and stable population has been transformed. Every aspect of society that affects the treatment of disabilities and learning difficulties has changed radically and continues to evolve – the cultural, ethnic and religious profile, patterns of family organization, economic and occupational structures, the relative status of men and women, and the perception of human rights and social responsibilities.

We will illustrate the pace of change in the UK by outlining two of the dimensions of diversity that have particular implications for those working with children and young people who have SEN. The first dimension is ethnic background. In 1951 the non-white population of Britain was very small, perhaps less than 50,000 (Peach 1982). By January 2007 one pupil in five in England alone was recorded as having an ethnic minority background – 21.9 per cent of pupils in maintained primary schools and 17.7 per cent in maintained secondary schools (Department for Children, Schools and Families (DCSF) 2007c). At the same time there were nearly 800,000 pupils learning English as an additional language (EAL) – 13.5 per cent of pupils in maintained primary schools and 10.5 per cent in secondary schools (DCSF 2007c). While most minority ethnic children and children learning EAL live in urban areas, there has been a good deal of dispersal from the initial areas of settlement:

> All secondary schools in England, and about three quarters of primary schools have at least some minority ethnic pupils. The great majority of teachers across the country may now expect to work with minority ethnic pupils at some point in their career
>
> (Department for Education and Skills (DfES) 2004c: 2)

The second dimension is family organization. Fewer people than in the past spend the whole of their childhood with their biological parents and siblings in a household comprising a traditional nuclear family. Divorce is more common, and more men and women choose to cohabit without marrying. The proportion of children living in lone-parent families in Great Britain more than tripled between 1972 and spring 2004, to 24 per cent (Horton 2005). Adoption by stepfathers is increasingly common: about half of adoption orders made in England and Wales each year are to birth parents (usually mothers) and their spouses (Finch 2003). O'Donnell (1999) reported that in recent years there has been increased appreciation within the law of different family structures and of functional parenthood. But traditional ways of thinking about roles and responsibilities in relation to children have remained a key reference point in our culture. For example, those responsible for academic research and professional services have generally construed lesbian parents in terms of how they are similar to and different from heterosexual parents (Clarke 2002).

It is much more common than in the past for both parents in households with dependent children to be in paid employment. 68 per cent of such families in the UK were in that position in 2004, while the proportion of lone parents in employment rose to 54 per cent in that year (Walling 2005). Parents of children with SEN find themselves under particular pressure. For example, Beresford (1995) found that in a sample of 1000 families of children with physical disabilities:

● household income tended to be lower on average than among families with non-disabled children (although they faced additional costs);

● fewer parents were in full-time employment;

● the family home was often unsuitable for the care of a child with disabilities;

● two-thirds of the parents did not belong to a parent support group, though those who did found them helpful;

● almost half of the parents had not found their relationships with professionals supportive.

The father of a deaf-blind girl who had a rare genetic disorder called

Pallister–Killian syndrome recalled his first vivid memory of contact with professionals like this:

> For many months after Eléonore's birth (in France), we knew that something wasn't right, but nobody, professionals included, could quite put their finger on what precisely was wrong. The first experience that stands out in my mind took place at a children's hospital in southwest France, where Eléonore had been sent for tests. There must have been over a dozen people in her room: a neurologist, ophthalmologist, physiotherapist, audiologist, paediatrician, some medical students and, at one point, the mistress of one of the specialists waiting to take him to lunch. My wife and I were gradually being shunted to the far corner of the room, as being of little importance to the proceedings. When I finally asked the most senior consultant if he knew what was wrong he replied, 'No.' 'But is it serious?' my wife asked. 'Yes, very.' This was how we were informed of the major difficulties we, and Eléonore, would be facing – a very isolating occasion.
>
> (Sigel 2004: 45)

The arrangements for family organization and welfare support which meet the needs of most families in society appear to fall short in relation to families with children who have disabilities. There are good reasons to believe that the difficulties are exacerbated in lone-parent families and among some ethnic and linguistic minority communities (Caesar *et al.* 1994; Beresford 1995; Emerson *et al.* 2004). Any analysis of the education of children with SEN needs to take full account of the increasing diversity of society and the impact this has on the kinds of professional services and educational provision that are required.

Key concepts in charting diversity

As society becomes more heterogeneous, the terms that are used to describe its diversity become themselves a focus of debate and dissent. This applies equally to concepts that are associated with visible markers of diversity such as *race* or *ethnicity* (Ryan 1999) and to concepts that are associated with changing views on diversity such as *handicap* and *disability* (Corbett 1995, 1998). It is important to be explicit and clear about what one means when using such terms. We will attempt to clarify in Chapters 3, 4 and 5 how the concepts of SEN and *inclusion* are used in this book. At this point it is necessary to clarify how we intend to use the terms relating to racial, ethnic and cultural diversity. It is very common for terms in this area to be used loosely. At worst, the effect is demeaning and racist. It may be helpful to have not only working definitions of some of the key terms but also observations on ways of using them that we have tried to avoid in this book.

Race was originally a biological concept categorizing a group of people who are connected by common descent or origin and have some common physical features. This term is often used in a metaphorical and over-generalized way in accounts of the speaker's own group or other groups. Talking in terms of race tends to reinforce traditional stereotypes.

Culture encompasses the learned traditions and aspects of lifestyle that are shared by members of a society, including their habitual ways of thinking, feeling and behaving. The use of this term is often based on an unjustified assumption that there is a high level of cultural cohesion and homogeneity in the social group that is being described (especially when it is a group of which one is not a member).

Ethnicity is a label that reflects perceived membership of, and a sense of belonging to, a distinctive social group. The crucial distinguishing features of an ethnic group vary between different contexts and change over time. They may include physical appearance, first language, religious beliefs and practices, national allegiance, family structure and occupation (Thomas 1994). A person's ethnic identity may be defined by their own categorization of themselves or by how others see them.

The use of terms such as *ethnic group* tends to focus attention on a particular aspect of an individual's identity. But in contemporary society everyone, whether adult or child, has multiple roles and complex identities. It is beyond the scope of this book to explore issues of cultural change and ethnic evolution in detail. We recognize that the definitions that are given here represent just one serviceable way of clarifying the scope of each concept. Fuller discussions of the implications of adopting different definitions may be found in Baumann (1996) and Bhopal (2004).

One reason why it seems important to highlight these dimensions of diversity in a book on SEN is that there is strong evidence of the operation of institutional racism in the delivery of services to children with SEN in many Western societies. Institutional racism has been defined as:

> the collective failure of an organisation to provide an appropriate and professional service to people because of their colour, culture or ethnic origin. It can be seen or detected in processes, attitudes and behaviour which amount to discrimination through unwitting prejudice, ignorance, thoughtlessness, and racist stereotyping which disadvantage minority ethnic people.
>
> (Macpherson 1999: para. 6.34)

When SEN provision began to expand in the West during the post-war period, once ethnically based statistics were collected, it became clear that there were higher than expected numbers of children from some minority communities in some forms of special provision. This was true not only in the UK (Tomlinson 1984) but also in the USA (Losen and Orfield 2002; Harry 2007), in eastern Europe (Gray *et al.* 2003), and in Germany (Powell 2005). For example, in England and Wales in 1972 children from the newly established West Indian communities in many cities constituted only 1.1 per cent of all children in maintained primary and secondary schools, but 4.9 per cent of all children in schools for the educationally subnormal (Tomlinson 1984: 21–2). Over the years the most dramatic forms of over-representation of black pupils in SEN provision in England were reduced, but there remain important areas where anomalies have persisted. For example, African-Caribbean pupils continue to be over-represented in schools for pupils with emotional and behavioural difficulties (Lindsay *et al.* 2006) and among pupils who are excluded from school (DfES 2006j). Bangladeshi pupils are over-represented among pupils identified as having hearing impairment and Pakistani pupils among those with profound and multiple learning difficulties and sensory difficulties (Lindsay *et al.* 2006). Two new groups have emerged in recent analyses of over-representation in English schools among pupils with statements of SEN and pupils with SEN without statements – children with a

Gypsy/Roma or Traveller of Irish Heritage background (DfES 2006d). The overall numbers are small, and data on group differences need to be treated with caution. But the overall trend in the results is consistent.

At the same time some ethnic groups are under-represented in terms of particular types of special need. For example, Chinese pupils and pupils from most Asian groups are less likely to be identified as having moderate learning difficulties or specific learning difficulties (Lindsay *et al.* 2006). A survey of 13 local education authority (LEA) areas in England indicated that children from an Asian background were much less likely to have a formal statement of SEN for autistic spectrum disorders than white children in the same areas (Marchant *et al.* 2006). It has been suggested that, when pupils are learning English as an additional language, it can be difficult to determine whether any academic problems that they encounter in school are caused solely by language differences or have their roots in underlying learning difficulties (see Cline and Shamsi, 2000). The issue of under-representation will be discussed in Chapter 7 below. Lindsay *et al.* (2006) argued that under-representation should be treated as seriously as over-representation and employed the term 'disproportionality' in their review of the issue.

The findings about ethnic disproportionality reflect a more widespread phenomenon: SEN provision reflects a diverse society in uneven ways across a range of dimensions of diversity. For example, boys tend to outnumber girls by a large margin in schools for pupils with emotional and behavioural difficulties, but by only a very small amount in schools for those with profound learning difficulties and hearing difficulties (Riddell 1996; House of Commons Education and Skills Committee 2006: Annex Chart 10). Similarly, children from working-class backgrounds are over-represented among those assessed as having moderate learning difficulties but not among those assessed as having severe learning difficulties (Lindsay *et al.* 2006). These issues are discussed in more detail in Chapters 3, 7, 12 and 15.

Sociologists of education have drawn a distinction between the forms of SEN that are usually identified in terms of apparently 'objective' criteria (e.g. the existence of visual impairment) and forms of SEN where subjective and relativistic judgement has a greater influence on diagnosis (e.g. emotional and behavioural difficulties). It seems likely that the risk of social bias affecting the processes of identification and assessment will be greater when teachers and other professionals are working with children in the second 'non-normative' category (Tomlinson 1982). As in the case of institutional racism, discrimination may occur through 'unwitting prejudice, ignorance, thoughtlessness, and . . . stereotyping'. Those insights and strategies that minimize the risk of institutional racism will also be likely to improve equity and effectiveness in relation to other dimensions of diversity.

Thus, although ethnic and linguistic minorities constitute a relatively small proportion of the country's population, an analysis of SEN in relation to these groups has a significance far beyond their numbers. A key question in every chapter of this book will be whether any analysis or intervention that is described can measure up to the diversity of those minorities and to the challenges of racism that they face. If they pass that criterion, they are likely to stand the test of time with the broader and less heterogeneous groupings that make up the rest of the population. As we saw above, these groupings are themselves becoming increasingly heterogeneous in many ways. We will employ an interactional model in order to ensure appropriate sensitivity to cultural context, and we believe that this will also enhance the analysis of SEN issues for *all* children within a range of educational contexts.

An integrated approach

This book seeks to promote an integrated approach to SEN along a number of dimensions:

- SEN and educational provision;

- theoretical approaches to SEN;

- research and practice;

- multi-disciplinary teamwork to promote effective educatio

The first three of these themes are introduced in this section, and the fourth in Chapter 2. All four are developed throughout the book

SEN and educational provision

SEN are taken to be the outcome of an interaction between the individual characteristics of learners and the educational environments in which they are learning. This means that, if we are to fully understand the learning difficulties experienced by some children, we have to consider the curriculum and learning environment being provided for them. An analysis of learning difficulties in literacy or mathematics, for example, should incorporate a consideration of the curriculum demands and methods of teaching generally employed in these subject areas. Most attention in recent public debate on SEN provision has focused at school level with the question *where should children who have SEN be taught?* There is a case for refocusing the debate at classroom level with the question *how should they be taught?* If an account of a child's SEN is to be pedagogically useful, it needs to be built on an account of their educational environment and of how they have responded to it, and it needs to lead up to an analysis of the implications that might have for differential teaching:

> teaching children with SEN has to be seen in terms of a multi-levelled interacting system in which individual children are nested in the class group, whole school, local authority, regional and central government policies and practices. Classroom pedagogy is nested within teaching programmes that are determined by school and then ultimately national programmes and commitments.
>
> (Lewis and Norwich 2005: 220)

The importance of an integrated approach is widely recognized and advocated. The Code of Practice on the identification and assessment of pupils with SEN advises: 'The assessment process should always be fourfold. It should focus on the child's learning characteristics, the learning environment that the school is providing for the child, the task and the teaching style' (DfES 2001a: para. 5.6).

However, it appears that what has happened in practice has more often reflected a 'within-child' model of SEN. Goacher *et al.* (1988) reported that statements of SEN and the professional reports on which they were based focused largely on deficits within the child in discussing their SEN. They found that very little attention was given to the learning environment. Seven years later a similar conclusion was reached by a working group of educational psychologists set up to review and develop approaches to assessing the learning environments of pupils who have SEN (Frederickson and Cline 1995). A small-scale study of teachers' views on emotional and behavioural difficulties has suggested that many teachers continue to focus solely on within-child and family factors when seeking to explain such problems (Avramadis and Bayliss 1998). These findings have been supported by cross-cultural research in Australia and China which reported that teachers in both countries attributed misbehaviour most to within-child factors and least to teacher factors (Ho 2004).

Throughout this book we discuss ways of integrating SEN identification, assessment and intervention into an analysis of the educational curriculum and the learning environment that is provided. For example, two of the four chapters in Part Two on approaches to assessment of SEN concern assessment for learning and the assessment of learning environments. This is line with the SEN Code of Practice (DfES 2001a) which made it clear that the learning environment, the learning task and teaching style should be assessed, as well as the learning characteristics of individual children. McKee and Witt (1990) suggested that one reason why so much SEN assessment focuses on within-child factors is that professionals lack knowledge and confidence in other forms of assessment. We aim to support readers in developing the knowledge and expertise that are required.

Theoretical approaches to SEN

There are a number of theoretical approaches to SEN that start from different perspectives. Often, different theoretical approaches focus on different aspects so that it is difficult to integrate the insights and ideas that they offer. The definition and explanation of what children and teachers experience as 'learning difficulties' become a site for fruitless debates between theorists and practitioners who adopt incompatible terminology to reflect different perspectives and then cannot engage in a meaningful dialogue. This happened when sociologists of education and educational psychologists studied SEN assessment with different assumptions and when geneticists, neurologists, cognitive psychologists and teachers each tried to understand dyslexia by looking at a different aspect of the phenomenon. For many years the field of emotional and behavioural difficulties was the site of confused debates about the competing insights of behavioural, cognitive, psychodynamic and systemic theories.

In some respects the accounts offered by different theoretical approaches to SEN conflict with each other, but in other respects they may be considered to complement each other. It would appear desirable to be able to draw on different approaches in order both to ensure a comprehensive consideration of the area involved and to capitalize on the relative usefulness of different approaches for different purposes. Morton and Frith (1995) achieved a significant breakthrough in the integration of different theoretical perspectives on problems in child development and SEN. They developed a visual framework in which it is possible to represent different theories so that their commonalities and differences are readily apparent. The framework allows both difficulties of development and hypothesized causal influences to be described in terms of biology, cognition, behaviour and environmental factors or interactions (Morton 2004). In this book we make considerable use of this framework to offer an integrated account of the diverse theoretical formulations that are available for many aspects of SEN.

Research and practice

A further theme that permeates this book is the interplay between research and practice. There has been extensive debate for over a decade about the quality of much educational research and its relevance to either educational policy or classroom practice (Hargreaves 1996; Hillage *et al.* 1998; Tooley and Darby 1998). A central issue has been the extent to which practice can and should be based on research evidence. On the one hand, Hillage *et al.* (1998: 60) recommend that 'more evidence-based decision making should be encouraged where appropriate'. On the other hand, Hammersley (1997: 156) concludes:

> there is much wrong with the quality of teaching in schools … But it seems to me that educational research can only play a fairly limited role in resolving the problems. It can highlight and analyse them, and attempt to provide some understanding. But remedying the failings of schools is a practical business that necessarily depends on professional expertise of a kind that is not reducible to publicly available evidence, even that provided by research.

The proponents of evidence-based practice do not maintain that research evidence is the only knowledge base which will be drawn on in professional practice. However, they do highlight the extent to which other kinds of professional expertise also suffer from limitations. Hargreaves (1997: 411) draws an analogy with medicine which has been much discussed:

> Much clinical work depends on best practice (i.e. what works) derived from tradition and personal experience. Both are potentially deeply flawed, so must be subject to scientific test. When evidence is produced on whether one therapy rather than another makes for a more effective or speedier benefit to patients in certain categories or circumstances, it becomes a valuable component in the matrix of factors considered by a doctor in making a clinical decision. Research transforms individual tinkering into public knowledge that has greater validity and can be shared among the profession as the evidential base for better clinical practice.

Hargreaves argues that teachers also need to make complex decisions and that their decision making could be enhanced by the establishment of a more relevant research base in education. He also identifies a need to establish a culture of accountability in education and openness to new ideas wherein there is an expectation that the best available knowledge on 'what works with whom, under what conditions and with what effects' (Hargreaves 1997: 414) will be sought and utilized. This book aims to support teachers, educational psychologists and others who are seeking to update and develop their knowledge of the research base in key areas of practice for pupils who have SEN.

At the same time, critics of an evidence-informed approach to educational practice have highlighted the dangers of a simplistic view, arguing that 'knowledge cannot be applied, like paint, to a blandly receptive body' (Edwards 1998: 89). In addition, the relationship between research and practice cannot be a one-way street. Research findings may be generalizations drawn from work with representative groups. Or they may be insights drawn from case studies in which the researcher focuses on a unique individual or situation. 'Good practice' that is based on findings from either type of research will not be effective with every child. The only way to learn if an approach is successful in promoting the learning of an individual pupil is through the careful collection of data in monitoring their progress (Good *et al.* 1998). There are many parallels between the process of research and the approach to assessment recommended in the revised Code of Practice and adopted in this text. Such an approach involves:

● generating hypotheses about the difficulties being experienced by a pupil in a particular learning environment;

● collecting a range of data and information from different sources to test out the hypotheses being considered;

● giving careful attention to the reliability and validity of the information collected;

● drawing conclusions about the actions most likely to be effective in promoting the pupil's progress;

● monitoring changes in pupil progress in response to the action taken so that its effectiveness can be evaluated and any further assessment and intervention initiated.

Teachers who undertake extended and repeated cycles of assessment and teaching with pupils who have learning difficulties are actively engaged in a form of investigation of SEN that can contribute to enhancing how we think about the phenomenon in general as well as advancing an individual's learning. Edwards (1998) suggested that such activities can provide a basis for research that is reflexive and conducted on the analogy of a 'conversation' with its participants, where there is the potential for mutually illuminating outcomes. Other researchers who have investigated ways of increasing the contribution of research to the improvement of practice have reached very similar conclusions. Robinson (1993: vii) writes from a New Zealand perspective that:

> Researchers must conduct . . . processes of problem understanding and resolution as a critical dialogue with practitioners, so that competing theories of the problem can be adjudicated and new theories of action learned during the course of the research itself, rather than left to some subsequent process of dissemination.

It seems that the different approaches to research which have been touched on in this section may each have a contribution to make to practice. Selection of strategies may valuably be informed by evidence about what generally is found to work in a specific kind of situation. What kind of evidence will be relevant will depend on the type of question that is posed (Frederickson 2002). The development of an application which is tailor-made for a particular context is likely to require the engagement of those involved in a problem-solving process from which some more broadly generalizable learning is likely also to result. Finally, there will be a need for systematic collection of data that will allow evaluation of the success of a particular application of a specific strategy in relation to the objectives identified for the pupil or pupils involved. In future also the increasing focus on accountability requirements and evidence-based practice in education is likely to fuel demand for systematic evaluation at the organizational level, in schools and local authorities, of local variants of national initiatives (Sebba 2004).

The structure of this book

Throughout this book we attempt to analyse SEN in a way that takes account of the diversity of modern British society and respects the range of individual perspectives and rights of different stakeholders in the education system. We argue for the integration of different strands of theory, research and practice. We also explore the implications of an interactional perspective which, on the one hand, considers the different layers of environmental influence that impact on individual functioning and, on the other hand, recognizes the extent to which such influences are mediated by the meanings that individuals ascribe to them. Ethnic and cultural differences represent important dimensions of diversity along which differences in the ways individuals interpret their worlds may be identified and environmental influences may vary.

Part One is concerned with key principles and concepts that influence work with SEN. Chapters 3 and 4 examine the key concepts of SEN and inclusion. Chapter 5 examines how SEN develop in children's lives and will introduce Morton and Frith's causal modelling framework which allows an integrated consideration of different theoretical perspectives on problems in child development and SEN. This chapter also shows how increasing understanding of genetic factors in development and rapid advances in neuroscience are influencing our thinking about SEN.

Part Two examines how SEN have been identified and assessed. Assessment is seen in its social and cultural context, and the contentious issues of bias and equity are addressed. Chapters 8 and 9 outline key approaches to assessment in educational settings that have particular importance when an interactional approach is adopted but have often received insufficient emphasis in individually focused approaches to SEN assessment – assessment for learning and the assessment of learning environments.

Part Three examines specific areas of SEN, including learning difficulties, literacy and mathematics. A book that attempts to address the challenges of SEN in a multiethnic society must take problems of communication very seriously. Part Three includes a substantial section on communication and interaction (Chapters 10–11). It also includes an examination of the area of need that possibly poses the greatest challenge to the goals of inclusion: behavioural, emotional and social difficulties. There are new chapters in this edition on autism and physical needs, and the chapter on sensory needs now covers visual as well as hearing impairment.

2

Stakeholders in special educational needs and inclusion

Objectives

When you have studied this chapter you should:

- be aware of major changes that have affected the main stakeholders in schools and the relationships between them over recent years, and be able to outline some implications of these changes for work with children who have special educational needs;
- be familiar with the way in which services for children are developing and understand the implications of these changes for work with children who have special educational needs.

Contents

Introduction

Children and young people

Parents

- The changing role and contributions of parents in schools
- Parents whose children have SEN

Schools

Multi-disciplinary teamwork within integrated children's services

---

Introduction

The key stakeholders in education are children, families and schools. If an integrated approach is to be developed towards SEN, it will need to take account of the individual perspectives of each of these stakeholders. Social changes and legal reform have affected their position *vis-à-vis* one another over the last thirty years. In addition, many other professionals play a role in the support of children who have SEN and of their families. The ways in which the services provided by these professionals are organized have evolved with the aim of ensuring that they collaborate more closely and support children and families more effectively. In this chapter we will examine the contributions that a range of stakeholders now make to the education and well-being of children who have SEN. The starting point is the group that has the greatest stake – the children and young people themselves.

Children and young people

In the past children were treated in law in many countries as simply the possession of their parents. Slowly it has been accepted that they should have legal rights as separate individuals and that their views should be taken into account when decisions are being made about them. Article 12 of the United Nations Convention on the Rights of the Child states that:

1   States Parties shall assure to the child who is capable of forming his or her own views the right to express those views freely in all matters affecting the child, the views of the child being given due weight in accordance with the age and maturity of the child.

2   For this purpose, the child shall in particular be provided the opportunity to be heard in any judicial or administrative proceedings affecting the child, either directly, or through a representative or an appropriate body, in a manner consistent with the procedural rules of national law.

(Newell 1991: 44)

The United Kingdom signed up to that convention and has slowly begun to enshrine many of its provisions in UK law. For example, Section 53 of the Children Act 2004 in England requires that, when local authorities determine what services to offer children in need, they must, 'so far as is reasonably practicable and consistent with the child's welfare, ascertain the child's wishes and feelings and give them due consideration (having regard to the child's age and understanding)'. To the dismay of some teachers' representatives, school inspectors have begun to take account of pupils' perceptions of their schools (Shaw 2003). The Department for Education and Skills has issued official guidance to encourage the process (DfES 2004d).

The first Code of Practice on SEN introduced guidance on the issue, advising that schools should 'make every effort to identify the ascertainable views and wishes of the child or young person about his or her current and future education' (DfE 1994a: para. 2: 36). This guidance was considerably strengthened in the revised Code of Practice in which one of five 'fundamental principles' was that 'the views of the child should be sought and taken into account' (DfES 2001a: para 1.5). A whole chapter was devoted to pupil participation on the basis that children with SEN have a right 'to be involved in making decisions and exercising choice' (para 3.1). Subsequent statements of policy have reinforced this emphasis (e.g. DfES 2004c: paras 3.38–3.39). Similar provisions exist in legislation and policy guidance in other parts of the UK (e.g. the Education (Disability Strategies and Pupils' Educational Records) (Scotland) Act 2002) and elsewhere in Europe (e.g. Ireland; see Keogh and Whyte 2005).

Two main arguments were set out in the first SEN Code of Practice:

- *Practical*: children have important and relevant information; their support is crucial to the effective implementation of any individual education programme.

- *Principle*: children have a right to be heard (DfE 1994a, para. 2.35; cf. Gersch 1992: 26).

Davie (1996) has argued that, when schools introduce arrangements for consulting and involving pupils, there is such immediate evidence of the value of the exercise that the principle has 'the characteristic of self-reinforcement'. It is increasingly common to seek pupils' views about their schools (Cullingford 2002; Hoby 2002; Reay 2006) and about other services such as early years settings (Clark and Moss 2005), arrangements for looked-after children (Butler 2006), mental health services (Worrall-Davies and Marino-Francis 2008) and educational psychology services (Woolfson and Harker 2002; Ashton 2007). Researchers have begun to move beyond the basic questions about what pupils think so as to explore teachers' reactions to the ideas that pupils put forward in such surveys (e.g. McIntyre *et al.* 2005) and to investigate how pupils themselves view the methods that are used to investigate their perspectives (May 2005; Hill 2006). In some cases pupils are being given greater control of the agenda about what should be investigated (Thomson and Gunter 2006). Most of this work has been conducted with children who do not have SEN or learning difficulties, and some of the methods of inquiry that have been used, such as lengthy questionnaires or focus group meetings, would not give an effective voice to some children who have learning difficulties.

It is clear that finding out how children and young people with SEN see a situation brings new and illuminating insights for the adults involved. For example, in an investigation of the working of a free-standing SEN unit situated on the campus of a mainstream secondary school, Sinclair Taylor (1995: 263) showed that it was only when the pupils in the unit expressed their views that it became clear that 'the unit, rather than promoting integration, fostered the marginalisation of its pupils'. Similarly, an enquiry into the 'truantist perspective' led Southwell (2006) to propose an approach to thinking about truancy that sees renewed attendance as dependent on addressing unmet educational needs. Researchers working in a range of settings have confirmed the value of children's direct representations for routine planning and management of SEN provision. For example, Watson *et al.* (2007) showed that the evaluation of multi-agency services could incorporate the investigation of the views of children with complex healthcare needs, even those who had no verbal communication. It is potentially a two-way process: Dickinson (2006) showed that an inclusive culture within a voluntary organization can assist in ensuring that information about the way the organization works is shared effectively with young disabled children.

In formal situations, when important decisions are being taken about an individual's future (e.g. in meetings to resolve disagreements about SEN provision) Soar *et al.* (2006) proposed that some kind of child advocacy service might be a way forward. The independence of the advocate would be crucial to the success of such a service. But, outside such formal occasions, could children and young people with SEN not be encouraged to give voice to their own views themselves without an intermediary?

In a study of the participation of pupils with SEN in decision making about their needs in 18 schools, Norwich and Kelly (2006) found that school ethos was the 'outstanding and pervasive' factor that determined how far children's direct participation was supported. Their informants highlighted a range of methods for ascertaining children's views. While talking in formal or informal settings was the most common, adults also sometimes found it helpful to observe non-verbal signs in order to supplement listening, to scribe children's views or to have them draw pictures. They used opportunities while away from school on residential trips to talk and listen, they used picture cards to prompt the expression of views, and adapted questionnaires to make them child-friendly. The researchers' analysis of what different stakeholders considered to be barriers to effective participation indicated that staff and pupils highlighted different problems. The adults were more likely to mention factors within the children themselves such as limited cognitive capabilities, problems in communicating and a tendency to be influenced by their peers' responses. Children, on the other hand, were more likely to mention factors relating to the school or to teachers, such as non-negotiable targets, over-interpreting or misinterpreting children's views, doubts that they would keep pupil's views confidential, and not themselves being in control over what was written about their views.

Many commentators have suggested that the greatest obstacle to effective consultation involving children with learning difficulties lies in a failure to find an appropriate method of eliciting their views. Norwich and Kelly (2006: 269) argued that 'not all limits are a matter of removing obstacles or finding ways and means round barriers to the valued end of participation. It is conceivable that another valued end may conflict with children's participation.' They found that some of the staff they interviewed identified a competing principle of *child protective values* as a constraining factor. Staff expressed concern that making this group of children responsible for giving their views on important matters affecting them might create new threats to their self-esteem and place a burden on them that they would find onerous. In some cases, therefore, a tension was apparent between participation and protectiveness, which would require 'finding a justifiable balance between genuine values' (2006: 269).

It seems likely that, apart from the tensions identified by Norwich and Kelly, a major obstacle to greater involvement of children and young people who have SEN is uncertainty among other stakeholders about how best to enable them to communicate their views and learn the views of others. These concerns about methods of consultation have been addressed in many recent initiatives. Examples include:

- using a questionnaire with cartoons and voice bubbles as a framework for enabling children aged 10+ to present their views in a formal way as part of the SEN assessment procedure (Gersch *et al.* 1993);

- helping children in a 'one-to-one tutorial' to draft written replies about their views to a series of short, open-ended questions as a contribution to the annual meeting at which their SEN statement is reviewed (Jelly *et al.* 2000);

- using a 'graphic facilitator' in a group meeting to discuss a child's views during the annual review of their SEN statement, the role of the graphic facilitator being to record what is being said through drawing simple pictures that capture the main point (Hayes 2004);

- exploring the views of a group of young people with profound and complex learning needs on a drama production in which they had participated, using photographs of the production, including pictures taken during both rehearsals and performance and making additional use of Makaton for one student and of 'Talking Mats' for several others (Whitehurst 2007);

- encouraging students in the middle years of schooling to use photography to formulate and present their views of their school (Moss *et al.* 2007);

- supporting children with a range of SEN in a large scale study to express themselves without interference during individual and small-group interviews through a variety of means, including puppets (of particular value as a quiet confidante), drawing (as a starting point for discussion), 'diamond ranking' (a creative sorting task using sticky notes written or drawn by the interviewer at the child's dictation), and exploring a particular event, recalled by the pupil, in more detail through the support of cue cards (Lewis *et al.* 2005).

Children with less severe difficulties can contribute in larger numbers if questionnaires are adapted to their competence level and if researchers are prepared to read items aloud for them and act as scribes when needed. Wade and Moore (1993) used a sentence completion technique to give children the opportunity to offer open-ended comments on their views, even when they could not manage extended free writing. When the children were asked to complete the sentence 'I get worried in some lessons because . . .', they expressed their lack of confidence in completions such as:

I can't do it very well. (Girl, 7–11)

Sometimes I do not no how to do my work. (Girl, 7–11)

I can't do a lot on my own. (Girl, 12–16)

I think the teacher is going to tell me off. (Boy, 12–16)

Safeguards are required so that children are provided with a listener whom they feel they can trust and in order to ensure that they do not simply say what they assume their listener wants to hear (Dockrell *et al.* 2000). It is important that their understanding of the situation is elucidated: do they feel that they are being interrogated because something is wrong? Do they understand what their views are being collected for and how their contribution will be used? Lewis and Porter (2004) developed guidelines for interviewing children and young people with severe and profound learning difficulties and point out that one of the many challenges involved in this process is the need to explain to participants how and why, after hearing their views, the adults have decided to make (or not make) a particular response.

There may also be problems in interpreting what children intend to say. A strategy that has aroused a good deal of controversy is asking children to draw in order to elucidate their attitudes. This approach has strong advocates (e.g. Dalton 1996) and severe critics (e.g. Dockrell *et al.* 2000). On the one hand, drawing may reflect 'aspects of knowing which exist at lower levels of awareness than that of verbal articulation' (Ravenette, quoted by Dalton 1996). On the other hand, drawings are ambiguous and the factors that determine what a child draws are complex. It is not easy to decide unequivocally for any single drawing what message it conveys about the child's views of the subject: 'A child may draw a person crying for many reasons' (Dockrell *et al.* 2000: 57).

Those who think that problems of interpretation need not eliminate the use of drawing tasks for this purpose altogether, tend to emphasize the value of specific safeguards. These tend to be introduced to prevent investigators imposing their own projected ideas onto their version of what the child is communicating. Most commonly what is advocated is the principle of *triangulation* – seeking confirmatory evidence from other sources, for instance through a 'mosaic' approach that gives young children the time and opportunity to express their views in different ways (Clark and Moss 2005). Multi-method approaches to assessment are advocated throughout this book. Steps can also be taken 'within method' to provide checks on the reliability of the interpretations made. For example, Ravenette (1997, 1999) invited children to construct the opposite of a picture they had created in order to help them to explain or show what they thought the first picture signified (cf. Maxwell 2006). This strategy has its roots in Kelly's (1991) personal construct theory in which people's ideas about their personal world are represented as a continuum between opposites (cf. Salmon 1988; Stoker and Walker 1996). Ultimately, investigating the perspectives of children with SEN simply reflects in a particularly stark form the key dilemmas that face investigators with all children: how can adults learn what children think and feel without influencing and distorting the message?

Activity 2.1   Involving students in the planning of a resource base

It has been agreed that five old-style classrooms on the ground floor of a large secondary school should be converted for use as a 'resource base' for older students with moderate and severe learning difficulties. They are all in one area of a long corridor, and structural changes are being considered. The architects who have been given the commission to design the adaptation wish to see students from both mainstream classes and the existing 'Special Unit' actively involved. Their firm has offered to donate a number of digital cameras for use by students and the time of one of their trainee staff as a source of support. What suggestions and guidance would you give about this project if you were a member of the school staff with responsibility for planning the resource base?

Parents

The changing role and contributions of parents in schools

Over the last 40 years increasing emphasis has been placed on the value of parents' involvement in the education of their children. Initially attention was primarily focused on the negative consequences of mismatches between home and school. From the 1960s onwards a series of official committees and other bodies stressed the importance for schools of encouraging good working relationships with parents and their closer involvement in schools (Cullingford 1985; Vincent 1996: Chaps 1–3). By the end of the century, Kelley-Laine (1998) was reporting on an Organization for Economic Co-operation and Development (OECD) survey that showed widespread encouragement of parental involvement in education across nine countries, including the UK. The following reasons for increasing parental involvement were identified:

- *Democracy*. In some countries parents are considered to have a right to involvement in their child's education.

- *Accountability.* Parental involvement is seen as a means of making schools more accountable to the community that finances them.

- *Consumer choice.* Parents are encouraged to choose the education they want for their child and complain if it falls short of their expectations. This is seen as a mechanism for making schools more responsive to society's requirements of them.

- *Means of raising standards.* Research has shown that high-achieving, well-ordered schools are characterized by good home–school relationships. It is hoped that improving home–school relationships will have a positive impact on standards.

- *Tackling disadvantages and improving equity.* Here the focus is on raising the achievements of individual children by helping their parents to support them more effectively at home. This is seen as particularly important where there are cultural differences between family and school.

- *Addressing social problems.* In some countries school–family programmes are being developed to tackle serious social problems affecting young people (e.g. targeting drug and alcohol abuse, teenage pregnancy or delinquency and violent crime).

- *Resources.* Parents are regarded as a source of extra funds for schools and of unpaid staffing for school trips, sporting activities and additional support in the classroom.

There is thus a wide range of reasons why schools and public authorities endorse effective partnership between home and school. But one goal in particular is emphasized more frequently than any other – the enhancement of student learning. With this goal in mind, Chrispeels (1996) presented an overview of those school practices that have been seen as most effective in this respect, especially in communities where families have few socioeconomic advantages and are likely to be helped by active outreach initiatives from their children's schools (see Figure 2.1).

Reporting on a study of Asian-American, Latino and European-American families, Okagaki and Frensch (1998) highlighted the need to be sensitive to ethnic group differences in parents' beliefs about education and goals for their children. Working in the USA, they pointed out that it cannot be assumed that what works in some family contexts will necessarily work in all. In a series of case studies in the South of England, Abreu and Cline (2005) examined a particular obstacle to easy collaboration between families and school – the existence of a gap between some parents' own past experience of school learning (mathematics in this study) and the curriculum and pedagogy now encountered by their children. Whether parents were successful in supporting their children's learning depended on how they negotiated that gap. This applied to both monolingual and bilingual parents, but for the latter group uncertainties about the use of language for mathematics were an additional concern. It was noted that the children's teachers appeared not to be aware of how important this worry was to the parents. On the basis of other local studies in England more teams of researchers have called on schools to adapt to the specific needs of parents from minority ethnic communities and have challenged the notion that this group is particularly 'hard to reach' (Huss-Keeler 1997; Crozier and Davies 2007).

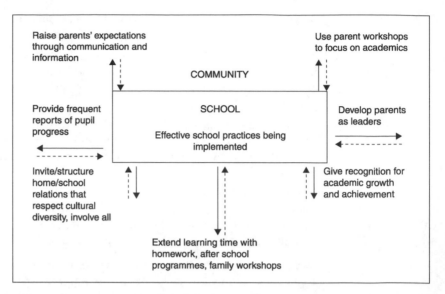

Figure 2.1 Effective school practices for reinforcing parents' efforts to enhance their children's learning
Source: Chrispeels (1996).

Parents whose children have SEN

The involvement in education of parents whose children have SEN should be considered in the context of the general trends in parental involvement that were outlined above. The Warnock Committee suggested that the relationship between parents and professionals be conceptualized as 'a partnership and ideally an equal one' (Department of Education and Science (DES) 1978: 151). However, almost ten years later Wolfendale was to reflect that partnership 'is a slippery concept, probably because it is rarely manifest' (Wolfendale 1989: 107). Cunningham and Davis (1985) suggested that the ways in which parent–professional relationships around SEN have been described over the years might be characterized in terms of three models:

- *An expert model* in which professionals are construed as the source of all knowledge about children who have SEN and where parents are cast in the role of passive recipients of advice from the experts.

- *A transplant model* in which professionals are regarded as the key decision makers and main source of expertise. However, parents are regarded as a valuable resource and source of active support and intervention for their child. Some of the professionals' expertise can be transplanted to the parents who are taught to carry out programmes at home.

- *A consumer model* in which the parent becomes the key decision maker and the professionals offer information and services from which the parent can select according to their needs.

These three models are contrasted with a partnership model in which teachers are viewed as being experts on education and parents are viewed as being experts on their children. The relationship between teachers and parents can then be a partnership which involves sharing of expertise and control in order to provide the optimum education for children with special needs.

(Hornby 1995: 20–1)

More recently, a stronger consumerist ethos in society as a whole has led some commentators to portray the teacher as an *employee* of the parent.

Parents consult us for our knowledge and experience of young children and employ us to support them in advancing their child's educational or other needs. Thus, more than being mere consumers or even equal participants in a partnership with you, parents are actually your employers. They pay considerable taxes for public services and high fees for private services; thus, as with all employers, you are directly accountable to them for your practices.

(Porter 2002: 22)

Following on from the Warnock Committee's advocacy of the partnership model in their 1978 report, the 1981 Education Act on SEN appeared to place new power in the hands of parents of children with SEN. However a review of the implementation of the Act by the House of Lords Select Committee on Education, Science and Arts (1987) after six years highlighted a number of concerns about both access to information and the consideration given to parents' views.

There was evidence that the problems may have been even more acute for parents from black and ethnic minority communities. For example, research carried out by Rehal (1989) in one London borough highlighted particularly poor levels of communication with and involvement of Punjabi-speaking parents. Of the 14 parents interviewed only one was aware that their child had been formally assessed under the provisions of the Education Act 1981 and issued with a statement of SEN. Similar concerns were expressed at that time by agencies working with the Bangladeshi community in London (Chaudhury 1986), by investigators of South Asian communities in other cities (Shah 1992) and by researchers working with the African-Caribbean community (Inner London Education Authority 1985: 69–71). A case study by Grugeon (1992) illustrates vividly the way in which parents and professionals from different cultural backgrounds can misunderstand each other in the course of an SEN assessment. She shows in detail how 'the process . . . has not taken into account the evident disjuncture between the cultural norms of his [the child's] home and community and those of the school' (1992: 92).

It appears that many authorities and schools ignored the official guidance that the formal notification to parents of SEN assessment and the subsequent reporting should be in a language they understood or for which they could obtain an interpreter (DES 1983). Over the years the guidance has been considerably strengthened. For example, where access to interpreters or translated information material is needed in the early years, the revised Code of Practice makes clear that it is for the LEA (and not the parents) to ensure that it is provided (DfES 2001a: para. 2.13). When such arrangements are made, it is essential that there is sensitivity to the position of the parents and children. In some (probably rare) situations what is required is exact, word-for-word translation, while in others the bilingual worker may need to take on a wider advisory and liaison function, helping both the family and the professionals to understand the social and cultural assumptions that each is making (Martin 1994; Shackman 1984). There is evidence that the problems reported in the UK are experienced by parents from minority communities internationally, even in countries where their first language is widely spoken (Salas 2004; Hess *et al.* 2006).

In recent years the perception has grown that professionals and LEAs have generally been slow to embrace partnership in so far as it requires active sharing of information and control. Legislation has increasingly been used to attempt to level out the power imbalance in parent–professional relationships, ensuring that parents are empowered and are not denied their rights. This increasing emphasis on parental rights can be seen in the establishment of bodies independent of LAs to which parents can appeal against LA decisions and turn for information. The establishment by the Education Act 1993 of the SEN Tribunal was a major step in this direction. The *Special Educational Needs and Disability Act* outlined two steps (in Chapter 10, Part I, Sections 2 and 3) which it was hoped would prevent many cases from going to the SEN Tribunal by providing better information and opportunities for negotiation at an early stage. Information on these developments was provided in the revised SEN Code of Practice:

- All LEAs must make arrangements for parent partnership services and are encouraged to work together with voluntary organizations in doing so. The aim of these services is to ensure that parents of children who have additional needs (not just those with statements) 'have access to information, advice and guidance in relation to the special educational needs of their children so they can make appropriate, informed decisions' (DfES 2001a: para. 2.19).

- All LEAs must provide arrangements 'which demonstrate independence and credibility in working towards early and informal resolution of disagreements' (DfES 2001a: para. 2.24). 'Confidence in disagreement resolution arrangements will be greatest when all concerned consider that the service offered is genuinely independent' (DfES 2001a: para. 2.26).

Unfortunately a study in one LEA indicated that some parents experienced the Parent Partnership Services as just a further tier of officialdom that distanced them from the 'real' decision makers, while some schools were seen as absolving themselves of responsibility for partnership with parents once a designated external team is involved (Todd 2003). A larger-scale national survey indicated higher levels of satisfaction, though with considerable variation between services (Rogers *et al.* 2006). Some individual partnerships are strongly committed to overcoming such problems and empowering parents at every stage (P. Jones 2006). But case study reports suggest that many parents continue to have negative experiences of the system (Cole 2004). After a detailed study of the experiences of 14 parents in the London area, Pinkus (2005) suggested four principles for parent–professional partnerships that could overcome at least some of the problems in individual situations:

(i) Establish consensus regarding the purpose of the partnership, e.g. over the roles and responsibilities of the various partners in relation to arranging meetings, applying for assessments, and so on.

(ii) Achieve clarity as to who is in the partnership and why (especially important when many professionals are involved with the family – see the final section of this chapter on multi-agency working).

(iii) Enable equal power relations (e.g. with all having access to key information on issues such as eligibility criteria for services).

(iv) Make special needs procedures as transparent and as accountable as possible.

It is widely recognized that, for these principles to be implemented, there would need to be greater clarity and consistency in policies on inclusion (see Chapter 4) and in arrangements for assessment (see Chapter 6). It would also be necessary for support services and specialist professionals to work in a more coordinated way (as discussed later in this chapter). But, while systemic and organizational changes are necessary, they will not in themselves be sufficient. There is a more fundamental requirement at an individual level for changes in the ways in which many professionals perceive and behave towards parents (Norwich *et al.* 2005).

Activity 2.2 Talking with parents about the possible implications of their child's difficulties at school

Ms Faulkner, an inexperienced teacher who has a class of seven year olds, asks you as the school's special educational needs coordinator (SENCO) for advice. One of the boys in her class, Jason, shows poor motor coordination (e.g. when changing for PE) and is rather isolated within his peer group. In practice tests of maths and English earlier this term his performance indicated that he has made very limited progress in both areas since last tested six months earlier. He is now falling badly behind other pupils in the class. Ms Faulkner is concerned because she will be meeting Jason's mother later today and wants to initiate action to help Jason. However, she knows that he is an only child and that his mother is reported to see only the best in him. The timing means that you will not be able to join Ms Faulkner for the meeting. What advice would you give her?

After you have made some notes on what you would say, review how far your advice would meet Pinkus's principles (i)–(iv).

Schools

Across the developed world the situation of schools has changed substantially in recent years. These changes are perhaps even more radical than the developments affecting the position of children and parents (McLaughlin and Rouse 2000). Previously in the UK the dominant voice in the development of policy on school management and the curriculum was that of professional educators. Schools in the public sector were accountable to governing bodies and subject to inspection, and they worked within a framework of law and regulation that was set by elected politicians. But the democratic touch on the tiller was a rather light one locally and nationally, and it appeared to many observers that the main consumers of the service – the children and their parents – had little influence.

Politicians of the right began to argue against the 'stranglehold' exerted by 'public monopoly' schools. Their case has been summarized as follows:

- Financial support for schools (via taxation) was not linked directly to the satisfaction of their clients.

- The absence of profit or loss motives for school managers led to conservative, self-serving, minimalist survival strategies.

- Schools' decision making was dominated by the pursuit of staff self-interest.

- There were inadequate checks and incentives to foster efficient administration or to force schools to be responsive to parental concerns.

It was argued that these features of the situation allowed educational standards to remain depressed and inhibited any urge to achieve excellence. Furthermore, the fact that schools in the public sector were designed to be similar and that there were restrictions on enrolment meant that parents effectively had no choice and that children's diverse needs could not be met. (This summary has been adapted from Ball 1993: 4.)

The reforms presented as a solution to these problems involved:

- enhancing quality by creating more competition between schools for resources and public support;

- encouraging greater diversity in the organization and funding of schools;

- enhancing parental choice by making enrolment more open and providing more information on which parents could base their decisions about which school would best suit their children;

- giving schools greater autonomy from LEAs in their day-to-day management while making them more accountable.

The overall effect of the changes was intended to be that individual parents would have greater responsibility for the quality of their child's education. There was certainly a considerable reduction in the powers of LEAs. Schools had greater freedom to compete for pupils, and since resources were linked to pupil numbers, a school needed to be popular in order to guarantee its income.

A key lever in the improvement in academic standards was the introduction of the National Curriculum. Schools maintained by LEAs were required to provide for all pupils of statutory school age a basic menu of three core subjects and six foundation subjects (seven in Key Stages 3 and 4 when a modern foreign language was added), plus religious education. Each core and foundation subject would have its objectives and programmes of study specified nationally. All pupils, including those with SEN, would share the right to a broad and balanced curriculum which would be designed to 'promote the spiritual, moral, cultural, mental and physical development of pupils' (DES 1989b: para. 16).

The national specification of the curriculum removed the substantial degree of control that teachers had previously had over what was taught in schools and how it was taught. The reforms went further. At fixed age points (the end of every 'Key Stage' of compulsory education) children's learning would be assessed, and the results for each school would be published. Teachers would thus be accountable for the delivery of the curriculum in a different way than before. The aims were to:

- give a clear incentive for weaker schools to catch up with the best, while the best were challenged to do even better;

- provide teachers with detailed and precise objectives;

- provide parents with clear, accurate information;

- ensure continuity and progression from one year to another, from one school to another;

- help teachers concentrate on the task of getting the best possible results from each individual child.

Parallel changes took place in the Scottish education system, though sometimes with less constraining central control (Riddell and Brown 1995). In Wales, too, there was some divergence after the Education Service became the responsibility of a newly devolved administration. But in England, although there have been substantial developments in the working of the new curriculum arrangements since 1989, the fundamental structures have remained in place. (More recent curriculum initiatives in English and mathematics will be covered in Chapters 13 and 14.)

What impact would these radical changes have on the experience of children with SEN? Offcial documents were optimistic, pointing out that:

> the principle that pupils with SEN share a common entitlement to a broad and balanced curriculum with their peers has taken many years to gain acceptance ... The right extends to every registered pupil of compulsory school age attending a maintained or grant maintained school, whether or not he or she has a statement of SEN. This right is implicit in the 1988 Education Reform Act.
>
> (National Curriculum Council 1989b: 1)

At the same time it was acknowledged that:

> the right to share in the curriculum defined in Section 1 of the Act does not automatically ensure access to it nor progress within it. Some pupils will have physical and sensory impairments which make access into a challenge; others have intellectual or emotional difficulties in learning. Some will meet attitudes and practices in schools which do not actively encourage full participation. Achieving maximum access and subsequent progress for pupils with SEN will challenge the co-operation, understanding and planning skills of teachers, support agencies, parents, governors and many others.
>
> (National Curriculum Council 1989b: 1–2)

Commentators from the SEN field mostly adopted a more pessimistic tone and emphasized that many of the challenges in the new context arose from aspects of the new policies themselves. For example, Upton (1990: 4) reported that many were

> concerned about the relevance of traditional subjects to children who present severe learning difficulties and the effects which the introduction of an apparently narrowly conceived academic curriculum may have on the teaching of cross curricular issues such as social and life skills.

In the event, many of the concerns about the curriculum were soon allayed, and resolute efforts have been made to ensure that there is meaningful access to an appropriate version of the full curriculum for all pupils. (See Chapter 12 for a discussion of what this means in the case of children with profound and multiple learning difficulties.) The most serious challenges for children with SEN and their parents appeared to arise not from the National Curriculum but from other provisions in the reform programme.

The arrangements for greater financial delegation to schools might, in principle, have enabled schools to make more flexible provision for pupils with SEN, because it gave them greater control over resources. But the allocation of funds depended on pupil numbers; schools were ranked on 'league tables' that were to be based on the overall performance of their pupils in National Curriculum subjects. If schools allocated resources to pupils with SEN whose performance might not raise the aggregate achievement level, they were making what would appear in an open financial market a risky investment. Another effect of the changes was to force LAs to delegate a steadily higher proportion of their funds to schools. LAs are now smaller, leaner organizations, and hence cannot provide central services to support schools with SEN in the same way as in the past (Ofsted 2005d). Decentralizing such provision risks the advantages of scale being lost and other priorities swallowing up the available funding at school level (except where there is a statutory safeguard – see Chapter 3).

Irrespective of the impact of the reforms on children with SEN, research across a wide front has challenged claims that they have been effective in achieving their objectives for the bulk of the school population:

● The assessments at the end of each Key Stage have been shown to be so unreliable that approx 32 per cent of the results for Key Stage 2 and approx 43 per cent of those for Key Stage 3 are misclassified by at least one level (Black and Wiliam 2006).

● An apparent rise in standards at Key Stage 2 test scores between 1995 and 2000 was substantially overstated, though there was some improvement (Statistics Commission 2005).

● Because many of the 'failing' schools are in deprived urban areas, the penalties associated with attending them appear to impact disproportionately on minority ethnic and other socially disadvantaged groups (Tomlinson 2000).

● An emphasis on the importance of school inspections and annual tests has well-attested side-effects such as 'window-dressing for inspection' and 'teaching to the test' (de Wolf and Janssens 2007).

As the initial reforms proved to have, at best, only limited success, attention turned to school structures, and new types of school have been introduced – more flexible, more independent of local authority control and, therefore, it was argued, more responsive to parental demands (DfES 2006b). The particular challenge of failing schools in disadvantaged urban areas was tackled through the establishment of new academies – all-ability schools established by sponsors from business, faith or voluntary groups working in partnership with central government and local education partners. The capital and running costs are met from the public purse. Academies are not required to follow the National Curriculum and are expected over time to develop new approaches to the content and delivery of the curriculum. It may be relevant that evidence has accumulated that many schools have responded to the 'high stakes' testing regime by narrowing their curriculum offer or, at least, allocating more time to those subjects that are tested – evidence that has not always been published by the official authorities responsible for collecting it (Mansell 2007).

As the inclusion of pupils with SEN has slowly become a central goal of government policy and the rhetoric of inclusion has been increasingly espoused at every level, schools find themselves caught in a tension between the inclusion agenda and the education reform agenda (tighter curriculum control, the testing and inspection regimes, the pressure to improve 'standards', competition for pupils). There has been a shift of emphasis from some of the market principles that were enshrined in law in the late 1980s and early 1990s. But the pace of education reform has not slowed down, and in England key central features remain, such as aiming to improve standards by publishing assessment and inspection results and by encouraging competition for enrolment between schools. In these circumstances pupils with SEN may not be seen as an asset for a school, and it has been reported that the initial group of city academies refused to teach some children with statements of SEN even when named by the child's education authority as the school best able to meet their needs (Slater 2004).

The pessimism expressed by some of these commentators is to some extent countermanded by other observations about school trends. On the basis of research on school improvement and school effectiveness a number of investigators have pointed out that some of the factors that are found in schools that achieve general improvements in standards are also found in schools with a strong record for inclusion (Ainscow 1995). A large-scale study in England has shown that there is 'a small, but for all practical purposes, insubstantial relationship between inclusion and academic achievement' (Farrell *et al.* 2007: 131). The existence of considerable variation between schools suggested to the authors that there were other factors within the schools' make-up, rather than just the proportion of children with SEN whom they included, that had had an impact on their pupils' results. They concluded that 'mainstream schools need not be concerned about the potentially negative impact on the overall academic achievements of their pupils of including pupils with SEN in their schools'. In a study that used a value-added measure to examine pupil progress within one local authority area, Rouse and Florian (2006) found no evidence that the presence of higher proportions of pupils with SEN in a school lowered the performance of other students in the school. They pointed out that 'many staff in these schools believe that the strategies used by the school for including pupils with SEN contribute to improved achievement for all' (2006: 491) In a detailed study of inclusive practices in 25 English schools, Ainscow *et al.* (2006b: 301) quoted teachers as reporting

> that they had had to develop the responsiveness of their schools to the characteristics of these students (i.e. those with SEN) in ways which promoted students' engagement with learning and their sense of themselves as learners. While these actions would eventually be reflected in the measures for which they were held accountable by government, such holistic developments were, they suggested, valuable 'for [their] own sake', not simply as a means to an end.

Activity 2.3   Collaboration between schools over pupils with SEN

The following extracts are adapted from a 1993 news report (Pyke 1993).

A secondary school . . . has reneged on a 20 year agreement to take children from a nearby school for the partially sighted, according to the Royal National Institute for the Blind . . . For the past two decades the all-age JC School (which provides for pupils with visual impairment) has sent its pupils across the playing field to HP secondary for some lessons. A few partially sighted pupils have been fully integrated. But, after some changes in the governing body, HP is refusing to continue the arrangement unless it receives £26,000 from the LEA plus staff support from JC. The school says it cannot afford this and will have to send the pupils two miles to another secondary school. The RNIB added that HP has refused to integrate a wholly blind girl after a successful first year of partial integration. 'The head told me that, irrespective of financial considerations, he did not believe it right to educate a wholly blind child in a mainstream school,' said an RNIB spokesman. 'Given this comment and the amount of money the school is charging to take the other, partially-sighted pupils, I can only conclude that the head doesn't really want special needs children in the school.' The LEA's Chief Education Officer said: 'Arrangements had worked up to this point, and it's a great pity they are not working now.' HP's headteacher and the school's chairman of governors both refused to comment.

1   On the basis of this report would you agree with a teacher from another secondary school who said that the working relationship between the schools 'appears to be one-sided – not real collaboration'?

2   What features of the overall system might have led the headteachers of the two schools to adopt the positions attributed to them?

3   What changes in the law or in the approach of the LEA or the special school might lead the HP head to revise his view on the prospect of working with selected pupils from JC?

Multi-disciplinary teamwork within integrated children's services

SEN are complex and heterogeneous. It has been recognized for a long time that 'meeting the special educational needs of children requires flexible working on the part of statutory agencies. They need to communicate and agree policies and protocols that ensure there is a "seamless" service' (DfES 2001a: para. 10.1). Yet there have been many obstacles over the years to successful collaboration between colleagues from different disciplines. At an organizational level, 'fragmentation of services between different statutory agencies, competition and tight budgets' (DfEE 1997: 71) have been identified as key problems. At an individual level other factors may impede successful collaboration between professionals from different disciplines:

- They have chosen to work in their field because it interests them and seems important to them. Such preconceptions are often reinforced during their training, so each professional may view the concerns of other groups as having lower priority.

- They are socialized during training to use a particular professional vocabulary.

- Differences in the use of language create problems of communication.

- They often work for different agencies which are funded in different ways and have different priorities.

- Tensions may develop between professional groups because of differences in perceived status, management arrangements or workload.

- Some professional groups have strict codes of confidentiality which make it difficult to share records or information, even if the client agrees.

The greatest imaginable failure for children's services must be when a child dies because of problems in the delivery of the support that they needed. A series of deaths of children at the hands of abusers from Maria Colwell in 1973 to Victoria Climbié in 2000 led to public inquiries that focused, among other things, on the need to ensure that 'services to children and families are properly co-ordinated and that the inter-agency dimension of this work is being managed effectively' (Laming 2003). Plans were already in place to address some of these issues, and urgent concern about what had happened to Climbié galvanized a political will to introduce radical reforms to children's services in England under the slogan *Every Child Matters*. First, all agencies and services were to give priority to achieving *five outcomes* – that every child will:

- be healthy – enjoying good physical and mental health and living a healthy lifestyle;

- stay safe – being protected from harm and abuse;

- enjoy and achieve – getting the most out of life and developing the skills for adulthood;

- make a positive contribution – being involved with the community and society and not engaging in anti-social or offending behaviour;

- achieve economic well-being – not being prevented by economic disadvantage from achieving their full potential in life (www.ecm.gov.uk).

Second, clear guidance was issued on the *sharing of information*, outlining when information should be shared, for what purposes and how that can best be managed (www.ecm.gov.uk/informationsharing). Third, problems of communication about children's needs and strengths were to be overcome by the use of a *Common Assessment Framework* (see Chapter 3). Finally, uncertainty about who should take a lead when a child has complex or additional needs was to be removed by requiring those involved to agree that one of them will take the role of *lead professional* (see below).

Those initiatives are concerned with working practices, and it was recognized that they would only be successful if there were effective arrangements at the organizational level. Education and social services were restructured. Three main ways of organizing frontline multi-agency services were recommended (see Table 2.1). National inspection teams for education and social services were brought together within a single organization (DfES 2006b), and it was made clear that, when evaluating the leadership and the overall effectiveness of service

Table 2.1 Ways of structuring frontline multi-agency services

		Example
Multi-agency panel	Members remain with their agency but meet regularly to discuss children with additional needs who would benefit from multi-agency input. Panel members might do case work or take a more strategic role.	Youth Inclusion and Support Panel (YISP)
Multi-agency team	Members are seconded or recruited into the team with a leader and common purpose and goals. They may still get supervision and training from their home agency, but have the opportunity to work with a range of different services.	Behaviour & Education Support Teams (BESTs) Youth Offending Teams (YOTs)
Integrated service	Different services such as health and education are co-located to form a highly visible hub in the community. Funded by the partner organisations and managed to ensure integrated working, they are often based in schools or early years settings.	Sure Start children's centres and extended schools.

Source: www.ecm.gov.uk/multiagencyworking

providers, including schools, inspectors will consider the contribution the organization is making to all five of the target outcomes for children (Ofsted 2005b). The reforms built on what had been learned from earlier initiatives such as Early Years Development and Childcare Partnerships and are in line with the recommendations for good practice listed by researchers such as Roaf (2002: 87) and Anning *et al.* (2006).

It will be some years before it is possible to evaluate the effectiveness of these changes in terms of their supporting professional teams and individuals towards the achievement of the five outcomes for children. In the short term administrative reorganization inevitably diverts staff attention, at least temporarily, from their central tasks and leads to a preoccupation with concerns about 'being taken over' (Booker 2005). In the longer term the questions that will require close attention in each area include the following:

- How effectively has preparatory work been carried out to clarify roles and responsibilities for service delivery within partner agencies and mainstream services (Robinson *et al.* 2005)?

- Since the Common Assessment Framework had its conceptual basis in the Department of Health's Framework for Assessment, it was necessary to introduce explicit references to learning and to education when it was adapted for a wider purpose. Will the Common Assessment Framework in its final form reflect all aspects of children's experiences and capacities adequately (Booker 2005)?

- Will any improvements that appear be sustained over time? Clearly the inspection regime will help to ensure that they are, but studies of previous local initiatives have emphasized the need for an internal 'systems minder' to monitor and support such developments (Glenny 2005).

- The starting point for the reforms is a concern with effective service delivery to individual children and families. How far will that emphasis prove compatible with a commitment to the kinds of changes in systems and provision that are required if we are to achieve a broader and deeper level of inclusion in education (Todd 2007)?

The reforms require considerable commitment and effort from all those involved. It is perhaps chastening to learn that, while those participating in some earlier initiatives saw many improvements emerging both for their clients and for themselves, they even so anticipated that the ultimate impact of multi-agency working on disabled children and their families would be quite limited (Abbott *et al.* 2005: 155).

Activity 2.4 Drawing a successful multi-agency team

Glenny (2005) described three case studies of inter-agency support for local partnerships of schools. She noted:

> A key theme emerging from the case studies was that of control of the working environment. In the first case study everyone seemed to feel subject to forces outside their control and, as the researcher tracking down possible causes for this, I began to fancifully personify the force as a dragon: it was powerful, it demanded ritual sacrifice which might or might not appease, for example, the procedures for statutory assessment, and yet it was also mythical, because the agency (ability to act) must, in reality, surely be with the human players? So where does the agency lie? How had individuals lost this feeling of control and how might they recover it to enable them to collectively deliver effective services for children? (2005: 167)

Imagine that a school or other organization that you know well is required to work in a coordinated way with another agency to meet children's special educational needs more effectively. Draw a picture or a diagram of how it might be, and label it to show the features that you think would make effective cooperation difficult and those that would facilitate success. Remember it is the latter that are most important. You can use Glenny's image of a dragon if you wish. But you might have other ideas.

3

Concepts of special educational needs

Objectives

When you have studied this chapter you should be able to:

- define SEN and explain how they differ from other additional educational needs;
- evaluate the strengths and weaknesses of two major conceptualizations of SEN, with particular reference to a pluralistic perspective;
- consider the advantages and limitations of applying an interactional analysis to SEN;
- outline the key legislative requirements governing assessment and provision for pupils with SEN.

Contents

Definitions

- Additional educational needs
- Special educational needs
- SEN and AEN

Conceptualizations of SEN

- Focus on individual differences
- Focus on environmental demands

An interactional analysis

- An interactional analysis of SEN
- An interactional analysis of AEN
- The relationship between SEN and AEN reconsidered

The legal context

- The National Curriculum requirements
- The SEN Code of Practice
- Other relevant legislation and guidance

Conclusions

Definitions

In the first section of this chapter we provide definitions of the terms 'SEN' and 'additional educational needs' (AEN). SEN refers to children's learning needs in school. In Britain, as in many other countries, SEN is legally defined and this legal definition is used to decide whether *particular children* are eligible for special educational services. This will be the main focus of this chapter. 'AEN' has been used as an umbrella term to refer both to the needs of pupils with SEN and to the needs which may be experienced by pupils from particular social groups whose circumstances or background are different from most of the school population.

In many ways it is the perception of difference that is central to all definitional approaches to these groups. It is argued that this gives rise to dilemmas – decision situations where each choice is associated with negative consequences or risks. These have been discussed in relation to SEN in particular by Norwich (2008). (For an analysis of paradoxes and dilemmas relating to intersecting differences in SEN, gender and ethnicity, see Artiles 2003.) Norwich (2008) describes the core dilemma as whether or not to recognize and respond to difference, highlighting that 'either way there are some negative implications or risks associated with stigma, devaluation, rejection or denial of relevant and quality opportunities' (2008: 1). In Activity 3.1 you have an opportunity to consider SEN dilemmas relating to identification, curriculum and location that have been used in international research studies. As you read this chapter you might want to record any other dilemmas you can identify.

Additional educational needs

The needs of groups of children whose families are homeless or who speak a language at home which is not the language of instruction at school are often reflected in funding formulae, and are likely to require special consideration by their schools. However, individuals from groups which have AEN may or may not have SEN. This is apparent from the categorization which was developed from a national survey undertaken for the DfES in 2001 (Pricewaterhouse Coopers 2002) and is shown in Figure 3.1.

Although the second category in Figure 3.1 refers to a number of disabilities, a disability may or may not result in a difficulty with learning. The Disability Rights Commission (2002: 28) notes that 'Pupils may have either a disability or special educational needs or both'. While the SEN framework is concerned with provision to meet special educational needs, the disability discrimination requirements, which are discussed later in this chapter, are concerned with preventing discrimination in access to education. More recently the term 'learning difficulties and disabilities' (LDD), commonly used in further and higher education, has become more common in relation to school contexts. For example, in the Ofsted (2006: 21) report on inclusion LDD was used in place of SEN for the following reason: 'The term LDD is used to cross the professional boundaries between education, health and social services and to incorporate a common language for 0–19 year olds. In the context of this report it replaces the term special educational needs'. This is a development which may sit uneasily with the interactionist conceptualization of SEN discussed later in this chapter.

Activity 3.1   The advantages and disadvantages of SEN labels

The following list shows the helpful and unhelpful aspects of the use of labels for SEN as described by Lauchlan and Boyle (2007):

(i)	Diagnosis, or a label, leads to treatment: it opens doors for resources.	A label is applied but there is a lack consideration regarding the nature of intervention.
(ii)	Labelling leads to awareness raising and promotes understanding of particular difficulties.	Labelling leads to stigmatization.
(iii)	Labels reduce ambiguities and provide clear communication devices for professional exchanges of information.	There is no clear agreement amongst professionals about how labels are decided. Moreover, labels lead to generalization of children's difficulties, neglecting specific individualized issues.
(iv)	Labels provide comfort to children and families by 'explaining' their difficulties.	Labelling leads to a focus on within-child deficits and possibly lowered expectations.
(v)	Labels provide people with a social identity: a sense of belonging to a group.	Labelling can lead to teasing, bullying and low self-esteem.

Reflect on how far you think each of these considerations might apply if the following children were attending a primary or secondary school known to you:

(a)   Freddie (aged 7), who is socially isolated in his class and is seen by staff as 'rather odd', is diagnosed at a teaching hospital 80 miles away as having Asperger's syndrome.

(b)   Sarah (aged 11) reads slowly, spells poorly and is badly organized in all her school work. Her response to additional help given during earlier years in primary school has been uneven. Her parents report to the school that an assessment by a private psychologist indicates that she has dyslexia.

(c)   Austin (aged 14) is constantly in trouble at school for inconsiderate and disruptive behaviour. His mother asks his form tutor to show greater under-standing of his problems as he has attention deficit hyperactivity disorder.

(d)   Maria (aged 3), who has Down's syndrome, has help from a learning support assistant for 4 hours each day in the nursery school that she attends.

More recently also a distinction has been drawn between children with additional needs (including SEN) and those with complex needs (including severe and complex SEN), the distinction being based on the need for statutory involvement with individuals. The definition of additional needs in the Common Assessment Framework (see Figure 3.2) focuses on risk status in relation to the achievement of the five *Every Child Matters* outcomes requiring extra support. It is noteworthy that there is no mention here of EAL as an additional need. This relates to the position that provision for children learning EAL should be part of

1. Learning need associated with English as an Additional Language (EAL)

These children require extra support because their capability in English, as a result of it not being their first language, is not sufficient for them fully to access the curriculum. Support might include specialist English language teaching, individually or in groups, in-class support with reading and writing, perhaps provided by a bilingual assistant or a Teaching Assistant, and specific differentiation of lesson content and materials.

2. Particular identified SEN

Children with a barrier to learning related to a particular identified special educational need such as autistic spectrum disorders, dyslexia, dyspraxia, attention deficit/hyperactivity disorder, speech and language difficulties, sensory impairment, physical disabilities. . . . Support might include specific differentiation of lesson content and materials, in-class support from a SENCO or Teaching Assistant, additional input in sessions where the pupil is withdrawn from the classroom, or provision of specialist equipment to allow full participation by the pupil.

3. Other learning need

Children who require extra support because they are struggling to access the curriculum for some reason other than the two identified above. Provision might include in-class support from the SENCO or a Teaching Assistant, additional input in sessions where pupil is withdrawn from the classroom or specially differentiated tasks or materials.

4. Social need

Children who require additional support in school for a variety of reasons associated with their home background and/or their emotional state including behavioural problems. Support may be provided for needs associated with family circumstances, poverty, truancy, traumatic experiences, emotional instability, behavioural difficulties, etc. Support might include activities designed to raise self-esteem or modify behaviour, input from a Learning Mentor, increased communication with family or other agencies, before- or after-school supervision, time spent counselling the pupil or their family, or additional adults in the classroom.

5. Learning need associated with English as an Additional Language and social need

A combination of categories 1 and 4 above.

6. Particular identified SEN and social need

A combination of categories 2 and 4 above.

7. Learning need associated with English as an Additional Language and particular identified SEN

A combination of categories 1 and 2 above.

8. Learning need associated with English as an Additional Language and particular identified SEN and social need

A combination of categories 1, 2 and 4 above

9. Other learning need and social need

A combination of categories 3 and 4 above.

Figure 3.1 Categories of additional educational needs
Source: PricewaterhouseCoopers (2002: 71–2).

Children with additional needs: A broad term used to describe all those children at risk of poor outcomes in relation to the five outcome areas defined in *Every Child Matters*. An estimated 20% to 30% of children have additional needs at some point in their childhood, requiring extra support from education, health, social services or other services. This could be for a limited period, or on a long-term basis. It is the group for whom targeted support within universal settings will be most appropriate. Their needs will in many cases be cross-cutting and might include:

- disruptive or anti-social behaviour;
- overt parental conflict or lack of parental support/boundaries;
- involvement in or risk of offending;
- poor attendance or exclusion from school;
- experiencing bullying;
- special educational needs;
- disabilities;
- disengagement from education, training or employment post-16;
- poor nutrition;
- ill-health;
- substance misuse;
- anxiety or depression;
- housing issues;
- pregnancy and parenthood.

Children with complex needs: Of those children with additional needs, a small proportion have more significant or complex needs which meet the threshold for statutory involvement:

- children who are the subject of a child protection plan;
- looked after children;
- care leavers;
- children for whom adoption is the plan;
- children with severe and complex special educational needs;
- children with complex disabilities or complex health needs;
- children diagnosed with significant mental health problems;
- young offenders involved with youth justice services (community and custodial).

Figure 3.2 Common Assessment Framework: guidance on terms
Source: DfES (2006f).

universal provision available in all schools, supplemented by the additional funding available to schools from the Ethnic Minority Achievement Grant.

As part of this focus on enabling frontline services to meet the needs of children from minority ethnic groups, extensive guidance and training materials have been provided for schools on implementing the primary national strategy with bilingual learners (DfES 2006a). The materials are intended to support all staff in personalizing learning to ensure that every child achieves the highest possible standards and that no group is discriminated against, and specifically to:

- understand and apply the key principles of EAL pedagogy in their daily practice;

- understand the opportunities afforded by the broad curriculum for the development of the additional language;

- explore learning and teaching approaches, including bilingual strategies and the use of ICT, which facilitate access to the curriculum and additional language development for children learning EAL;

- provide conditions for learning which value diversity and promote confidence and a sense of belonging;

- develop effective partnerships with parents, carers, families and communities.

> The member of the leadership team responsible for coordinating provision for EAL will play a critical role in developing and supporting staff expertise and understanding of EAL pedagogy and the use of bilingual strategies in schools.
>
> (DfES 2006a: 13)

In addition, schools are expected to provide strong leadership in this area through the identification of a member of the leadership team responsible for coordinating provision for EAL who can develop staff understanding of EAL pedagogy and support their use of bilingual strategies.

Arguably the most inclusive of the various terms currently in use is that used in Scotland, 'additional support needs' (ASN). These are defined in paragraph 1 of the Education (Additional Support for Learning) (Scotland) Act 2004 as follows:

> (1) A child or young person has additional support needs for the purposes of this Act where, for whatever reason, the child or young person is, or is likely to be, unable without the provision of additional support to benefit from school education provided or to be provided for the child or young person. . . .
>
> (3) In this Act, 'additional support' means –
>
> (a) in relation to a prescribed pre-school child, a child of school age or a young person receiving school education, provision which is additional to, or otherwise different from, the educational provision made generally for children or, as the case may be, young persons of the same age in schools (other than special schools) under the management of the education authority for the area to which the child or young person belongs . . .

The inclusiveness of the new term 'ASN' and its differentiation from SEN is explicated in the summary handout provided by the Scottish Executive Education Department (2004):

> The definition of 'special educational needs' traditionally only applies to children and young people with particular types of learning needs. The new concept of 'additional support needs' refers to any child or young person who, for whatever reason, requires additional support for learning. Add-

itional support needs can arise from any factor which causes a barrier to learning, whether that factor relates to social, emotional, cognitive, linguistic, disability, or family and care circumstances. For instance, additional support may be required for a child or young person who is being bullied; has behavioural difficulties; has learning difficulties; is a parent; has a sensory or mobility impairment; is at risk; or is bereaved.

There will be many other examples besides these. Some additional support needs will be long term while others will be short term. The effect they have will vary from child to child. In all cases though, it is how these factors impact on the individual child's learning that is important and this will determine the level of support required.

The clarity and inclusiveness of the ASN concept presents a contrast to the current situation in England where the use of the term AEN, as we have seen, is rather confusingly used in subtly different ways by different bodies and in different initiatives.

Special educational needs

The past 25–30 years have seen parallel shifts in the UK and the USA in the concept of SEN and the legal framework surrounding its assessment. In the UK, SEN was introduced as a legally defined term by the Education Act 1981, following the advice of the Warnock Report (DES 1978). Prior to 1981 the focus was very much on identifying and making provision for handicapped individuals. There were 12 recognized categories of disability: blind, partially sighted, deaf, partially deaf, physically handicapped, delicate, educationally subnormal (moderate), educationally subnormal (severe), epileptic, maladjusted, speech defects, and autistic.

The Warnock Report recommended that the statutory categories of disabled pupils should be abolished and instead children who required special educational provision should be identified on the basis of a detailed profile of their needs following assessment. This change was recommended for a number of reasons. For example, it was recognized that:

- children often experienced a range of difficulties which meant they could not be fitted neatly into the categories listed above;

- children assigned to the same category of disability may have varied needs in terms of teaching approaches, classroom management, etc.;

- particular children in different categories may have the same educational needs.

The implementation of the Education Act 1981 shifted the purpose of assessment from the diagnosis of disability to the identification of SEN. Figure 3.3 shows the definition of SEN introduced in the Education Act 1981 and maintained in subsequent legislation. It can be seen that the level of need experienced is understood to be the result of a complex interaction between the child's strengths and weaknesses, the level of support available and the appropriateness of the education being provided.

A child has *special educational needs* if he or she has a *learning difficulty* which calls for *special educational provision* to be made for him or her.

A child has a *learning difficulty* if he or she:

(a) has a significantly greater difficulty in learning than the majority of children of the same age

(b) has a disability which either prevents or hinders the child from making use of educational facilities of a kind provided for children of the same age in schools within the area of the local education authority

(c) is under five and falls within the definition at (a) or (b) above or would do if special educational provision was not made for the child.

A child must not be regarded as having a learning difficulty solely because the language or form of language of the home is different from the language in which he or she is or will be taught.

Special educational provision means:

(a) for a child over two, educational provision which is additional to or otherwise different from, the educational provision made generally for children of the child's age in maintained schools, other than special schools in the area.

(b) for a child under two, educational provision of any kind.

Figure 3.3   Legal definition of SEN
Source: Education Act 1996, section 312.

In legal terms, according to the Education Acts of 1981 and 1996, children are said to have SEN if they require special educational provision because they have a significantly greater difficulty in learning than the majority of children of their age or because they suffer from a disability which prevents or hinders them from making use of the educational facilities generally provided for children of their age. In the USA legislation on SEN in the last quarter of the twentieth century also emphasized meeting the individual needs of children and focused on the provision of a match between these needs and the education offered. For example, the Individuals with Disabilities Education Act 1997 defines a student as having a disability if he or she requires 'special education' – defined as 'specially designed instruction'. However, in the USA categories of special educational needs were maintained, although they might be defined differently by different states, notwithstanding the availability of national definitions.

In the UK initially the SEN approach was generally welcomed as an improvement on the 'categories of handicap' approach which it replaced. However, a number of criticisms were raised. The interrelationship between needs and provision embodied in these legal definitions of SEN, where one is defined with reference to the other, was criticized as circular by Goacher *et al.* (1988) in relation to the British Education Act 1981 and by Zigmond and Baker (1995) in relation to the US Individuals with Disabilities Education Act 1997.

More radically, Tomlinson (1982: 173–4) suggested that the real needs being served by this approach are the needs of dominant power interests in society, rather than those of children who experience difficulties in school, in that:

> state special education developed and took the forms it did to cater for children who had been categorized out of the normal education that was offered to the majority of children and that its development had more to do with the 'needs' of an industrialized society which was endeavoring to produce and train a stable, docile, productive workforce, than with the 'needs' of individual children. The smooth running of normal schools and, latterly, their examination-orientated, credentialling functions were impeded by troublesome children who could not, or would not, conform to the requirements of schools, particularly in terms of learning capabilities and appropriate behaviour. Humanitarian ideologies and Christian reformist principles were used to rationalize the removal of the defective, handicapped, or those in need to a special education sector which has expanded continuously.

It has to be acknowledged that categories of SEN have continued to be used over the last 25 years in the designation of special schools, in local authorities and in schools (Wedell 2003), albeit in a subsidiary role to the concept of SEN. The Audit Commission (2002a) found that many LEAs held detailed information on the needs of pupils in their area, but this could not be aggregated regionally or nationally because of a lack of consistency in the categories used and their definition. A new focus on strategic planning based on audit and on stratified analyses of progress achieved by vulnerable pupils led the DfES to amend the Pupil Level Annual School Census return required from schools in 2004 to include the 12 categories of SEN used by Ofsted (and shown in Figure 3.4). A number of concerns have been expressed about this development, both at a conceptual level and in relation to the validity of the data obtained. Gray (2004) reported that schools involved in a pilot found it difficult to assign pupils to categories with any degree of confidence. Florian *et al.* (2004) pointed out that SEN are changeable and very often context-specific, expressing concern that the change may herald a return to within-child conceptualizations of SEN.

However, others have advanced a different view. Warnock (2005) described the original decision to abandon categories as 'a baneful one', elaborating as follows:

> If children's needs are to be assessed in public discussion and met by public expenditure it is absolutely necessary to have ways of identifying not only what is needed but also why (by virtue of what condition or disability) it is needed. It is essential, furthermore, to distinguish needs that radically differ from one another, arising from different disabilities.

(Warnock 2005: 21)

SEN and AEN

This distinction is recognized in one respect in the legislation on special SEN: 'A child must not be regarded as having a learning difficulty solely because the language or medium of communication of the home is different from the language in which he or she is or will be taught' (Education Act 1996, section 312). The fact

---

A. **Cognition and learning needs**
- Specific learning difficulty (SpLD) 7.0%

- Moderate learning difficulty (MLD) 22.2%

- Severe learning difficulty (SLD) 12.1%

- Profound and multiple learning difficulty (PMLD) 3.7%

B. **Behaviour, emotional and social development needs**
- Behaviour, emotional and social difficulty (BESD) 14.3%

C. **Communication and interaction needs**
- Speech, language and communication needs (SLCN) 12.0%

- Autistic spectrum disorder (ASD) 14.6%

D. **Sensory and/or physical needs**
- Visual impairment (VI) 1.8%

- Hearing impairment (HI) 3.0%

- Multi-sensory impairment (MSI) 0.2%

- Physical disability (PD) 7.2%

E. **Other**
- Other difficulty/disability (OD/D) 1.8%

Figure 3.4 Percentage of pupils with statements of SEN by primary type of need in England, January 2007
Source: DCSF (2007c).

---

that this distinction is specifically highlighted reflects the particular problems that can arise where there is confusion between these concepts:

- low expectations of children from ethnic and linguistic minorities may result;

- discrimination against such groups may be fostered;

- provision of the most appropriate educational support may be hampered.

As one aspect of school improvement and a commitment to raising attainment, guidance to schools promotes the need to appraise and address AEN. This is apparent in relation to bilingual pupils (DfES 2006a). The extended schools initiative (DCSF 2007a) represents a further example with particular relevance to social disadvantage. It has long been known that during the summer holidays the achievement test scores of pupils from disadvantaged backgrounds decline. The organization of summer schools and play schemes which have a literacy component has been advocated for ameliorating the effect of poverty on educational achievement in literacy (Cox and Jones 1983).

Activity 3.2   AEN and SEN

1.   Consider the brief case descriptions in the table below. Can you identify any SEN and AEN suggested by the descriptions?

Description	SEN	AEN
Antonio (aged 8) has arrived recently from Spain after his father moved to the UK for work. He has a hearing difficulty and has learned little English so far.		
Jane (aged 14) is depressed, very dependent on her mother and cannot bring herself to get up and leave home in the morning in order to attend school.		
Louisa (aged 10) comes from a small local Travellers' community. Her school attendance is irregular and she is well behind her peers in the development of basic reading and writing skills.		

2.   It is often claimed that there may be undesirable consequences if the terms 'SEN' and 'AEN' are confused. Reflecting on this Activity, or drawing on examples from your own experience, can you identify ways in which confusion between these two concepts may lead to low expectations of children, or to discrimination, or to poor teaching?

Conceptualizations of SEN

There are two conceptualizations of the nature of SEN which are often compared and contrasted. We first describe the view that SEN are best understood by looking at *individual differences* between children. We then describe an alternative approach which argues that SEN arise when inappropriate *environmental demands* are placed on an individual which exceed their current capabilities for meeting those demands. These two approaches are illustrated through the case study of Majid (see Activity 3.3). Throughout it will be important for you to consider the sociopolitical context within which the conceptualization of SEN takes place and to ask questions such as 'What is the purpose of defining SEN?' and 'Whose definition of "normality" or "ordinariness" is being used in identifying an individual as special?'.

Focus on individual differences

In this conceptualization the focus of causation is within the child. This was the view embodied in legislation prior to 1981. The focus in the Education Act 1944 was on 'disability of mind or body'. Individual differences may be considered in a number of domains: biological (e.g. profound hearing loss, cerebral palsy); behavioural (e.g. the length of time the pupil can stay engaged in learning activities); or cognitive (e.g. poorly developed phonological skills, low self-esteem). Factors external to the individual (e.g. quality of teaching) are not considered. Issue has been taken with this approach for a variety of reasons. A number of key issues to consider are outlined below:

- *A focus on individual needs is often based on untested assumptions.* Solity (1993) outlines a number of such assumptions. For example, it is often assumed that children have had appropriate learning opportunities; that their learning experiences have been appropriately matched to their needs; that the teaching available has been effective with their peers but not with them; and that the discrepancy cannot be attributed to starting school with lower attainments than peers or to widely differing preschool experiences.

- *Social and educational contexts are important.* The Special Educational Needs Code of Practice (DfES 2001a: 20) makes this point:

  > It should be recognised that some difficulties in learning may be caused or exacerbated by the school's learning environment or adult/child relationships. This means looking carefully at such matters as classroom organisation, teaching materials, teaching style and differentiation in order to decide how these can be developed so that the child is enabled to learn effectively.

- *Where the educational context contributes to the problem, focusing on the individual will not make a broader contribution to improving the context.* Dyson (1990) argued that the education system is not equally favourable to every child who participates in it and urged that instead of asking how education can change the individual, we should be asking how the education system itself can be changed to accommodate the characteristics of all children, regardless of the degree to which they are atypical. Ainscow (1995) noted a growing recognition that the special needs agenda should be seen as an essential element in the drive towards effective education for all. On this view, those seen as having SEN are regarded as a stimulus that can encourage developments towards a much richer overall environment for learning.

Focus on environmental demands

This approach is situation-centred, rather than person-centred. Proponents hold that SEN 'can only be defined in terms of the relationship between what a person can do and what a person must do to succeed in a given environment' (Deno 1989: 5). Solity (1996b) presents a view that low attainments do not imply a learning difficulty. Rather, children's current attainments are held to reflect the nature and quality of previous learning experiences, and children will learn when taught appropriately. At one extreme, then, the environmentally focused approach holds that there are no children with learning difficulties, only adults with teaching difficulties. While a range of influences are acknowledged, it is typically argued that the most pervasive cause of learning difficulties is that for some children 'the curriculum moves too fast and demands too much in relation to their existing skills. They get further and further behind and are entrenched in a failure cycle' (Gickling and Havertape 1981: 376). The majority of school-related problems are therefore regarded as being curriculum-induced. It must be acknowledged that attributing learning failure to factors such as poor classroom organization, ineffective teaching strategies or inadequate match between task requirements and learner skills at least serves to emphasize the power of the teacher in influencing educational outcomes. This is more likely to stimulate action to help the pupil than an attitude that locates the cause 'within the child'.

Parallels can be drawn with the conceptualization of disability as a source of additional support needs, but not necessarily SEN. Here a focus on environmental demands leads to an analysis of disabling environments and hostile social attitudes, rather than individuals and their different functioning and abilities, which may be played down or even denied (Barnes 1996). Wheelchair users would not be seen as people with a mobility problem. Instead they would be seen as people whose mobility is often hampered by inappropriate building design. Looked at in this way the individual's 'problem' is that they are discriminated against in terms of access. Two key issues to consider are outlined below:

- *Individual differences matter too: different children will respond to teaching in different ways.* A focus on environmental demands attends only to features of the situation and ignores a child's characteristics that may be useful in explaining why they can or cannot perform. Frederickson *et al.* (1991) criticize the view that 'if a child can't read it doesn't matter why they can't read, what they need is to be taught to read'. This is problematic because once one moves on to asking *how* a child should be taught to read then an understanding of the particular nature of their difficulties, their areas of relative strength, their attitudes and interests becomes important. In eschewing individual differences, an environmentally focused approach also fails to account for variability, for the remarkable resilience of many children to learn in spite of teaching which is less than adequate, as well as the remarkable persistence of some children's difficulties in learning despite dedicated and skilful teaching.

- *'Within-child' factors can be influenced by teachers.* The argument that a focus on environmental factors is justified on pragmatic grounds because it encourages the view that teachers can affect outcomes would only be compelling if within-child factors could not be influenced by teachers. However, it is not the case that nothing can be done about 'within-child' factors. To take one example, in Chapter 13 we review recent research which demonstrates that intensive effective reading programmes can change brain functioning.

An interactional analysis

An interactional analysis of SEN

An interactional analysis views the level of need as the result of a complex interaction between the child's strengths and weaknesses, the level of support available and the appropriateness of the education being provided. There is widespread support for this view and for the view that neither individually nor environmentally focused conceptualizations are adequate on their own. Tomlinson (1982: 22) urged that neither 'fatalistic psychological views of individual causality [nor] simple sociological views of environmental determinism' should go unchallenged. Gutierrez and Stone (1997), in discussing a cultural-historical view of learning and learning disabilities, argued that attention must be given to environmental *in addition to* individual variables, not *instead of* them.

Activity 3.3 Case study: Majid

Read the following case study and prepare to take part in a debate. If you have the opportunity to work with a colleague, one of you can prepare notes on (a) below and the other on (b). You can then actually have a debate, where each person argues their case.

(a) Prepare notes on the following case study that will enable you to present the argument that Majid's SEN can best be understood and addressed by adopting a focus on the individual.

(b) Prepare notes on the following case study that will enable you to present the argument that Majid's SEN can best be understood and addressed by adopting a focus on the classroom environment.

For the purposes of this activity be sure to focus on SEN rather than other additional needs (see the previous section for a discussion of this distinction).

Majid (9 years) is causing concern in Flaxfield Primary School due to his low attainments and generally poor progress. In the playground he joins in playing football happily, but in class his teacher describes him as being in a world of his own. He doesn't seem able to follow instructions given to the whole class, although he will usually try to do what the other children are doing. If the task is explained again to him individually he will sometimes seem to understand and be able to complete it. However, in many cases he just doesn't seem to have the basic skills that would allow him to tackle the Year 5 curriculum successfully.

Majid attended a nursery school for one year and then transferred to Collington Primary School for a short time before going with his mother to live in Pakistan for 18 months. He attended school while in Pakistan, where his mother said he had some problems too, and returned to England in the middle of Year 4, when he joined his current school. Majid speaks Punjabi and English at home. His mother has expressed some concerns about his proficiency in Punjabi but considers that Majid is more competent speaking Punjabi than English. A bilingual assessment was completed six months after he started at his present school. It was reported that Majid answered most questions in English and did not talk with confidence in either language.

Majid's parents reported that he has had a lot of problems with his ears. He used to wake up at night in pain, he had constant ear infections and headaches and lost his appetite. Majid had grommets put in both ears about six months after he returned to England and his parents feel they have made a difference. Majid now turns around quickly when his name is called and is more attentive at home. Majid's teacher had not noticed much difference in the classroom but did say that Majid's attendance had improved as he used to have quite frequent absences with ear infections.

One lesson where Majid is doing better in school is in the Literacy Hour. His primary school sets the pupils in each year group. Majid is in the lowest set which is taught by the school's SEN coordinator, supported by a teaching assistant. During the 15 minutes devoted to shared reading and writing at the start of the session the teaching assistant sits with Majid's table. She prompts attention, checks understanding and provides additional explanation as necessary. She reminds the group about work they have covered and encourages their participation. She also works with the group on catch-up programmes focused on objectives at earlier levels that they have not yet achieved.

An interactional position has been acknowledged in government guidance in the UK for almost two decades. *Assessments and Statements of Special Educational Needs: Procedures within the Education, Health and Social Services* (DES 1989a: para. 17) stated:

> The extent to which a learning difficulty hinders a child's development does not depend solely on the nature and severity of that difficulty. Other significant factors include the personal resources and attributes of the child as well as the help and support provided at home and the provision made by the school and the LEA and other statutory and voluntary agencies. A child's special educational needs are thus related both to abilities and disabilities, and to the nature and extent of the interaction of these with his or her environment.

A similar view was embedded in the National Curriculum from the outset: 'Special educational needs are not just a reflection of pupil's inherent difficulties or disabilities; they are often related to factors within schools which can prevent or exacerbate problems' (National Curriculum Council 1989a: para. 5).

An interactional conceptualization is also explicit in the UK government's current strategy for SEN:

> Difficulties in learning often arise from an unsuitable environment – inappropriate grouping of pupils, inflexible teaching styles, or inaccessible curriculum materials – as much as from individual children's physical, sensory or cognitive impairments. Children's emotional and mental health needs may also have a significant impact on their ability to make the most of the opportunities in school, as may family circumstances. We are committed to removing the barriers to learning that many children encounter in school.
>
> (DfES 2004c: 28)

However, despite the fact that an interactional approach has been widely espoused and advocated, it cannot necessarily be assumed that it is widely implemented in practice. In discussing the operation of the Education Act 1981, Goacher *et al.* (1988: 149) argued:

> though the definition proposes an interactive view of children's needs, the implications for the terms in which assessments of needs are made do not seem to have been grasped by many of those involved. Most of the Statements which we have seen in the course of our research concentrated their attention on deficits within the child which led to special needs, with very little attention given to the child's environment, whether at home or at school.

How true is this today? As you read accounts of practice in this book and elsewhere, consider the extent to which they reflect an interactional conceptualization of SEN. You may find more examples of individually focused or environmentally focused approaches than you expect. Activity 3.4 provides an opportunity to examine professional advice for evidence of individually focused, environmentally focused or interactional orientations. If you are working with one or more children who have SEN statements you might want to look instead, or as well, at the professional advice appended to them.

Activity 3.4   Extracts from professional advice about SEN

Below you will find extracts from the professional advice that was attached to the statements of SEN prepared for two quite different children. Can you identify phrases and sentences that:

(a)   focus on the individual;

(b)   focus on environmental demands; or

(c)   are based on an interactional analysis of the child's difficulties?

You may find it helpful to tackle this activity with a partner. Make two copies of this activity and start by working independently. You could each underline what you judge to be (a), (b) and (c) in different colours. Then compare your judgements and, where there are discrepancies, discuss why you each thought what you did. Can you reach a consensus on all the judgements in the end?

John (aged 7)

Extracts from a joint report by the headteacher and class teacher

John is a physically fit and healthy boy. He is tall for his age and derives pleasure from PE (physical education) activities especially when his height gives him an advantage. He generally works and behaves well both in and out of the classroom, he loves PE, games and using the computer. He attends school regularly.

Within the classroom he can be particularly tense when faced with a reading or writing task. He does try his best, but his performance is well below average for his age. At the end of Key Stage 1 his SAT (Standard Assessment Task) scores were all at Level 1, apart from science which was at Level 2. Despite a great deal of work during the Literacy Hour his knowledge of phonics is very weak, and his written letters, particularly p, d, b, are often confused. He still has difficulty remembering many letter sounds, and where he recognizes a letter he will often give the letter name rather than the sound. His unaided written work is now becoming more extensive, but it is still very difficult to understand, and even harder for him to read back. John can spell correctly a few key words and some two- or three-letter words (notably some of the words that are featured in a large display of 'Words we often need' that hangs across the top of the classroom wall above the teacher's desk). When this display was taken down during a test, he made serious errors in words that he has often spelled correctly in the past.

In mathematics John is a little more confident in his approach despite his performance being below average. In a secure, friendly atmosphere John responds well, especially when following predictable tasks. In a changing, unfamiliar situation he quickly becomes unsure of himself and looks to others for help. When reassurance and support are quickly available he can usually tackle the task with some success. Otherwise, he tends to become anxious and tearful and unwilling to attempt the task. His approach to learning and his attitude to language work in particular have improved recently, perhaps because of the amount of school-based support that is offered. However, he remains characteristically nervous and tense about his own performance. When he does a good piece of work and receives praise, he is reluctant to appreciate that the work is good.

John's needs are extensively related to his language development and his self-concept. He needs to improve reading and writing skills and to value himself more. He has a particularly weak memory for letter shapes, sounds and spelling. He has made most progress when given regular daily individual attention following a structured language programme in which he is required to over-learn everything. It is through this regular individual attention that some words have stayed in his memory.

John will require a greater access than other children to the computer, concept keyboard and simple word games.

Peter (aged 6)

Extracts from an educational psychologist's report

I have been involved with Peter for three years since he was in day nursery. The staff there and his mother, Ms T, were finding it extremely difficult to manage Peter's behaviour. They reported that he was 'defiant', 'uncooperative in most adult-directed activities', and 'very distractible'. They felt that his short attention span and difficult behaviour were 'beginning to interfere with his general development and in particular with his learning'.

My most recent involvement with him began this year when he was referred by his school. He had started in a small class of 19 children but found it difficult to settle. His class teacher, Miss F, was concerned about his 'over-activity' from the outset and about his problem of concentration. She said that he seemed not to have difficulties understanding any of the work given, but that he rarely remained on task for more than one to two minutes. We discussed a reward system which involved gradually extending the length of time which Peter was required to be on task. Rewards included time on the computer (which Peter really valued) and extra time with Miss F (which proved to be quite difficult to implement because of the lack of any regular extra help in the classroom). Peter's progress was not consistent in that sometimes he remained in his seat and on task for the required length of time, but at other times he had difficulties doing so. Much seemed to depend on which other children were working at his table and whether they reacted to him in a way that calmed or provoked him. In addition, Miss F reported that his behaviour had rapidly deteriorated to include bad language, disobeying of instructions, fighting with other children, and 'high'/excited behaviour (e.g. screaming, 'karate' movements, etc.) in the playground.

A meeting was held in November with the headteacher, the class teacher, Miss F, and Peter's mother. We discussed a range of strategies for addressing Peter's behaviour. These included:

- the continuation of the reward system for on-task behaviour;

- explaining to Peter (and reminding him of) what was acceptable and unacceptable behaviour both within the classroom and in the playground;

- removing him (temporarily) from the playground or from one area of the classroom to another when conflict occurred or when he used bad language;

- planning activities in such a way as to try to minimize the possibility of conflict (e.g. placing him beside quiet children, making sure that he fully understood what he was required to do, etc.);

- establishing more regular liaison between his mother and the class teacher (i.e. every 1–2 days); and

- awarding him certificates for demonstrated effort to behave or to work well.

In January Miss F left, and over the following six months Peter's class had three changes of teacher. A number of supply teachers were also needed for various periods of time. A further 11 children joined the class, and a primary helper began to work in the classroom in the mornings. Peter's behaviour continued to cause concern, but it proved difficult to implement a consistent programme of behaviour management because of the high turnover of teachers. There were a number of other children in the class whose behaviour caused concern, including one child who was permanently excluded from the school. Peter was suspended for three days in May because of aggressive behaviour towards another child (i.e. grabbing the child's hair and pulling them off their chair).

Strategies implemented by the various teachers in an attempt to manage Peter's behaviour included: praise for positive behaviour; giving stars for good work, effort or behaviour; reminding Peter to work and play nicely; giving him responsibilities (e.g. to distribute worksheets); allowing him to take toys home; encouraging him to bring in work, drawings and models which he had completed at home; allowing him to stay at his desk doing drawing during story time; rewarding him with time on the computer working with another child; certificates/letters home; 'time out' in other classes; working on his own in a corner of the classroom or close to the teacher; working with 'quiet' children; working with the primary helper outside the classroom; noting down his positive and negative behaviours in a 'behaviour book'; and asking Ms T to come into school to work with him in the classroom and to accompany the class on trips. It would appear from speaking to teachers and to Ms T that the most successful of these in terms of Peter producing work and not getting into trouble were the strategies that minimized distractions – that is, those which involved him working on his own or with an adult either within or outside the classroom. Ms T felt that a major deciding factor in Peter's behaviour was his perception of how the teacher viewed him – whether he felt she 'liked' him and treated him in a 'fair' manner, and whether she showed by her behaviour that she valued him as an important member of the class.

An interactional analysis of AEN

In just the same way that the level of SEN experienced by an individual will depend on the responsiveness of the educational environment, so too will this influence the level of special needs experienced by particular groups. For example, the classroom is a unique context that requires special language and interactive skills, some patterns of which may be shared in home and community settings and some of which may not. Whether children are judged to have adequate levels of communicative competence in the classroom will depend both on the opportunities which they have had to develop relevant skills in other contexts and on how classroom events are organized to enable or disable their participation. Children who have attended a well-structured playgroup may initially be more responsive to the style of teacher communication used in their Reception class than children who have started school from home without experience in a preschool setting. The clearer the expectations and the more predictable the Reception class routines, the more quickly children without preschool experience are likely to learn about how to respond and communicate successfully in the Reception class.

The context profoundly affects behaviour, and that behaviour cannot be interpreted without taking into account situational factors. Cummins (1989: 111) argued that academic difficulties may be partially due to the reinforcement by schools of 'the ambivalence and insecurity that many minority students tend to feel with regard to their own cultural identity'. Pupils may become 'disabled' in a manner similar to that experienced by their ethnic communities as they become disempowered or 'disabled' by the dominant group

Cummins (2000) identified three overlapping dimensions along which the attributes important to school effectiveness for pupils with EAL can be located. These are:

- coherent school organization and leadership;

- affirmation of student and community identity;

- pedagogy – balance between meaning-focused approaches designed to promote problem-solving and higher-order thinking and explicit formal instruction designed to develop linguistic and meta-cognitive awareness.

It is argued that minority students can be empowered to the extent that patterns of interaction in school promote their confidence in their personal identity and ability to succeed academically.

Keogh *et al.* (1997) highlight some of the dilemmas involved in attempting to take account of cultural and ethnic diversity in education. They argue that 'on one level the issue is simple: everyone's heritage is due respect and the ideal is to find strength in diversity and to capitalise on rather then stigmatise difference' (1997: 109). However, there is often an unrecognized paradox in well-intentioned efforts to be sensitive to diversity in that individuals may be stereotyped and treated as if they share common traits with all others of a similar background. Ethnic group differences are often treated as markers of cultural differences, but this is usually an oversimplification. It is important to appreciate the social and cultural differences that may exist within groups that share the same cultural background.

Ethnic identity tends to persist though time, whereas culture changes as individuals and groups modify beliefs and practices over time. Consider the differences which may be observed between the lifestyles, expectations and values of new immigrants and those of the second generation to be born in the UK. Keogh *et al.* (1997) therefore argue for carefully distinguishing between ethnicity and culture in educational practice, which allows acknowledgement of variation at three levels: between ethnically defined groups; within ethnically defined groups; and between individuals within ethnic and cultural groups.

The issues of group empowerment and group 'disability' analysed by Cummins (2000) and the concerns about group stereotyping highlighted by Keogh *et al.* (1997) arise in their most intense form when there are racial differences between groups that parallel (or partly parallel) ethnic and/or cultural differences. Racism is a key factor. In this book we will employ a simple educational framework incorporating three perspectives on racism (Inner London Education Authority 1983). These perspectives were seen as developmental in character, the first being the earliest observed in the British education service and the last being the perspective to which the Authority aspired. The implication was that the three perspectives were mutually exclusive. In fact, in most contexts they are likely to overlap to a considerable degree: each is a matter of emphasis, not a separate and exclusive category. The three perspectives highlighted in the model are illustrated in Table 3.1.

Much has changed in the last 26 years, in particular with regard to legislation

Table 3.1   Three perspectives on racism

Perspective on racism	Statements of education policy
Emphasizing mainly assimilation	School curricula should help black settlement by reflecting British traditions, history, customs and culture.
	The first priority for black people is to learn and speak good English.
	Race relations are by and large good. It is counter-productive to try to improve them too fast. The main problems are caused by extreme right-wing groups.
	Racial and cultural differences should not be exacerbated by drawing attention to them.
Emphasizing mainly cultural diversity	Teaching about various cultures will promote a positive self-image among black people and tolerance and sympathetic understanding among white people.
	Educational establishments should make greater efforts to explain their policies and practices to black parents.
	Community languages besides English should be valued positively by schools. Bilingualism should be encouraged.
Emphasizing primarily equality	Black perspectives on world history should be introduced on an equal basis.
	Racism has a central and pervasive influence on all social systems.
	There should be continuous monitoring of policies and provision.
	Positive action is required on employment and appointments.
	Removing discrimination against black people should have a higher priority.

Source: Adapted from Inner London Education Authority (1983).

and central government guidance. Schools have statutory duties under the Race Relations (Amendment) Act (2000) to:

- provide equality of opportunity;

- tackle unlawful racial discrimination;

- promote good relations between members of different ethnic communities.

Extensive guidance and materials have been produced under the aegis of the Primary National Strategy (DfES 2006a) to support improvement in schools where raising the achievement of children learning EAL is a priority. *Aiming High*, the government's strategy for raising the achievement of pupils from minority ethnic groups (DfES 2003a), argues that the needs of minority ethnic pupils should be seen as an integral part of all mainstream policies and programmes, rather than simply an add-on. Nevertheless it addresses directly poorer than average public examination results from black pupils and those from Pakistani and Bangladeshi backgrounds. It is also examines contributing factors from poverty to low teacher expectations and institutional racism.

Activity 3.5   Effective schools for children from minority ethnic groups

The features listed below have been identified as characteristics of schools which have successfully implemented strategies to raise the achievement of children from minority ethnic groups (DfES 2006a: 8–9).

(a) Examine each item and consider whether it appears to be informed by one of the three perspectives on racism.

(b) Comment on the distribution of the items across the perspectives and on any ways in which you feel the perspectives might be developed further.

(c) Think about two schools you know where you consider different perspectives on racism predominate. Identify the main features on which they differ.

- **leadership and management which demonstrates:**

    - a strong and determined lead on race equality;

    - evaluation-led improvement;

    - development of the school as a professional learning community which recognises the benefits of collaboration;

    - a focus on data collected and analysed by ethnicity, gender and first language;

    - ambitious targets for attainment and achievement;

    - data used to inform effective use of resources;

- **an approach to learning and teaching which demonstrates:**

    - a curriculum which is broad and rich, inclusive and relevant;

    - high reliability in teaching the core subjects;

    - a clear focus for developing language across the curriculum;

- appropriately scaffolded and cognitively demanding learning opportunities;

- effective use of assessment for learning;

- effective use of specialist expertise within the classroom;

- use of children's linguistic, cultural and ethnic heritages to enhance learning;

● **a culture and ethos within which the following are demonstrable:**

- everyone feels safe and valued;

- a commitment to tackling underachievement and achieving high standards for all;

- linguistic, cultural, religious and ethnic diversity are valued and celebrated. Diversity is seen as an opportunity, not a reason for underachievement;

- practitioners have high expectations of children and encourage them to have high expectations of themselves;

- children are encouraged to believe in themselves and take responsibility for their learning;

- parents, carers and families are seen as partners and actively involved in their children's learning.

The relationship between SEN and AEN reconsidered

While we have taken care to draw a distinction between SEN and additional education/support needs, it follows that if SEN arise from an interaction between the child's difficulties and the educational environment in which they are placed, then assessing children's SEN must involve a detailed analysis of their learning environments. To take a single example of a group with additional needs (children from a linguistic minority), one of the key elements in their performance in school will be the ethnic and language background of the pupil population of the school. Another will be the attitudes, skills and resources of the staff.

The Warnock Committee (DES 1978: 64) argued that 'any tendency for educational difficulties to be assessed without proper reference to a child's cultural and ethnic background and its effect on his education can result in a category of handicap becoming correlated with a particular group in society'. As there is evidence that certain groups in society are over-represented in particular forms of SEN provision, does this mean that educational difficulties are typically assessed without proper reference to a child's cultural and ethnic background and its effect on their education?

The evidence comes from a variety of sources and, although conclusions differ somewhat, across different contexts there are broad parallels in findings internationally (Mitchell 2004). We will focus here on a recent national study in the UK that was mentioned in Chapter 1. Lindsay *et al.* (2006) report from a DfES-commissioned research study that socioeconomic disadvantage and gender have stronger associations than ethnicity with prevalence of SEN (indexed by receiving support at School Action Plus or through a statement of SEN). Boys were over-represented relative to girls for most categories of SEN: by a ratio of 1.75 : 1 for MLD/SLD, by 2.5 : 1 for SpLD and SLCN, by 4 : 1 for BESD, and by 6 : 1 for ASD. There were no gender differences in sensory or physical needs or PMLD. An association was apparent between socioeconomic disadvantage and most categories of SEN. This was strongest in the case of BESD and MLD significant but lower in the case of SLD, PMLD, PD, MSI, SpLD and SLCN, and weak and non-significant in the case of ASD, HI and VI.

After controlling for the effects of gender, socioeconomic disadvantage and year group, comparisons were made across all SEN categories between pupils from different minority ethnic groups and white British pupils.

● Travellers of Irish heritage and Gypsy/Roma pupils were found to be 2.7 and 2.6 times more likely to have SEN;

● black Caribbean pupils had a similar rate of identification to white British pupils.

● black African, Indian, Bangladeshi and Chinese pupils were less likely to have identified SEN (Pakistani pupils were under-represented but not to a significant extent).

When relative percentages were examined across individual SEN categories a somewhat different picture emerged. Compared with white British pupils,

● black Caribbean and mixed white and black Caribbean pupils were around 1½ times more likely to be identified as having BESD;

● Bangladeshi pupils were nearly twice as likely to be identified as having a hearing impairment;

● Pakistani pupils were 2–2½ times more likely to be identified as having PMLD, VI, HI or MSI;

● other Asian and Chinese pupils were less likely to be identified as having MLD, SpLD or ASD;

● travellers of Irish Heritage and Gypsy/Roma pupils were over-represented among many categories of SEN, including MLD, SLD and BESD.

From a review of the literature, Lindsay *et al.* (2006) also tentatively identify possible reasons for the disproportionalities identified in the national data. In the case of BESD they note that the literature suggests teacher and school factors, including racist attitudes and differential treatment of black pupils, as influential. However as all black pupils (e.g. black African) are not over-represented in this category, they suggest that further investigation of other influences will be important here. For over-representation involving Pakistani and Bangladeshi children the literature suggests a greater incidence of genetic factors related to consanguinity (where parents are blood relations) as an important factor. However, readers are cautioned not to over-attribute developmental difficulties to this factor for these children. It is suggested that the identified under-representation of Asian and Chinese children may reflect difficulties in differentiating learning difficulties from issues associated with learning EAL – separating SEN from AEN. The research base on Traveller groups is more limited. However, their over-representation has been tentatively linked both with factors associated with school (such as negative teacher attitudes, racism and bullying in the peer group, and a curriculum perceived as lacking relevance) and with factors associated with Traveller cultures (such as high mobility, poor attendance and a tradition of early drop-out from school).

The legal context

The National Curriculum requirements

The distinction that has been drawn in this chapter between SEN and AEN is reflected in statutory guidance which also highlights the importance of taking action to address the needs of groups and individuals. The National Curriculum handbooks for primary and secondary teachers (DfEE/QCA 2000; DfES/QCA 2005) set out the legal requirements of the National Curriculum in English schools and offer guidance on its implementation. The statutory inclusion statements contained in these handbooks set out guidance for schools to assist them in meeting their statutory responsibility to provide a broad and balanced curriculum for all pupils. Schools are advised of a range of specific actions that should be taken in all teaching to respond to diverse pupil needs which may relate to gender, disability, social and cultural background, ethnic background (including Travellers, refugees and asylum seekers), linguistic background and SEN. More detailed consideration is given to pupils who have SEN and to two groups of pupils with additional needs – those who have a disability and those who are learning EAL. As was highlighted in Figure 3.3, the Education Act 1996 specifically states that learning EAL must not, of itself, be regarded as a special educational need. The National Curriculum Statutory Inclusion Statement makes a similar point with regard to disability:

> Not all pupils with disabilities will necessarily have special educational needs. Many pupils with disabilities learn alongside their peers with little need for additional resources beyond the aids which they use as part of their daily life, such as a wheelchair, a hearing aid or equipment to aid vision. Teachers must take action, however, in their planning to ensure that these pupils are enabled to participate as fully and effectively as possible within the National Curriculum and the statutory assessment arrangements. Potential areas of difficulty should be identified and addressed at the outset of work, without recourse to the formal provisions for disapplication.
>
> (http://www.nc.uk.net/inclusion.html)

The guidance offered on ways in which schools should respond to pupils' SEN observes that in many cases school-based intervention involving greater differentiation of tasks and materials will be effective in facilitating access to learning. A range of examples are provided to illustrate how help can be provided:

- with communication, language and literacy (e.g. through using visual and written materials in different formats, including Braille, using ICT, translators and alternative and augmentative communication, including signs and symbols);

- in developing understanding through use of all available senses and experiences (e.g. through using play, drama and visits, and diverse materials and resources, including ICT, to encourage exploration of the environment, increase pupils' knowledge of the wider world or make up for a lack of first-hand experiences);

- in planning for pupils' full participation in learning and in physical and practical activities (e.g. through using specialist aids and equipment, adapting tasks or environments and providing support from adults or peers when needed);

- in helping pupils to manage their behaviour, take part in learning effectively and safely, and, at Key Stage 4, prepare for work (e.g. through setting explicit realistic demands, using positive behaviour management and teaching skills for independent and collaborative working);

- in helping individuals manage their emotions and take part in learning (e.g. through setting achievable goals, providing positive feedback, building self-esteem minimizing stress and creating a supportive learning environment).

Further subject-specific guidance is provided by the National Strategies waves of provision for children experiencing different degrees of difficulty in learning. See Chapter 13 for information on these aspects of the National Literacy Strategy. In some cases the school may itself need support in order to take further action:

> A smaller number of pupils may need access to specialist equipment and approaches or to alternative or adapted activities, consistent with school-based intervention augmented by advice and support from external specialists as described in the SEN Code of Practice, or, in exceptional circumstances, with a statement of special educational need. Teachers should, where appropriate, work closely with representatives of other agencies who may be supporting the pupil.
>
> (http://www.nc.uk.net/inclusion.html)

The SEN Code of Practice

The SEN Code of Practice (DfES 2001a) provides guidance to LEAs, school governing bodies, early years' providers and health and social services on their duties under Part IV of the Education Act 1996. The Code also makes reference to provisions in the SEN and Disability Act 2001 and various statutory instruments, including the Education (Special Educational Needs) (Consolidation) Regulations 2001.

The SEN Code of Practice identifies a number of fundamental principles (DfES 2001a: 7):

- a child with special educational needs should have their needs met

- the special educational needs of children will normally be met in mainstream schools or settings

- the views of the child should be sought and taken into account

- parents have a vital role to play in supporting their child's education

- children with special educational needs should be offered full access to a broad, balanced and relevant education, including an appropriate curriculum for the foundation stage and the National Curriculum.

In accordance with the third and fourth of these principles, specific sections of the Code offer guidance on working in partnership with parents and on pupil participation in assessment and decision making.

Guidance on identification, assessment and provision is offered to early education settings and to primary and secondary schools. In accordance with the second of the principles outlined above, it is emphasized that 'all teachers are teachers of children with special educational needs' (DfES 2001a: 44, 59) and that SEN is a 'whole school' issue. The guidance in particular highlights the following aspects. First, the importance of *early identification* and the role of class and subject teachers in monitoring performance in relation to level descriptions in the National Curriculum at the end of a Key Stage and National Literacy and Numeracy Strategy framework objectives.

Second, the importance for *children learning EAL* of considering the child within their home, cultural and community context and utilizing any available community liaison arrangements. Slow progress needs to be carefully examined and it should not be assumed that it can be attributed to the pupils' status as learners of EAL. Early assessment should be made of pupils' past exposure to each of the languages they speak, their current use of them and their proficiency in them. This will provide a basis for identifying and evaluating both pupils' language needs and any SEN they may have.

Third, a *graduated response* is required to the continuum of SEN. Three levels are identified: School Action, School Action Plus and support provided by a statement of SEN. It is emphasized that pupils are not expected to progress through these levels. Indeed, where interventions work successfully the expectation is that pupils will subsequently require *less* help rather than more help. Where teachers or others present concerns supported by evidence about pupils' progress, despite their receipt of differentiated learning opportunities, the *SENCO* should initiate further assessment to identify what school action is needed to help pupils progress.

The SENCO is the member of staff within a school 'who has responsibility for coordinating SEN provision within that school' (DfES 2001a: 206). School action may involve the deployment of extra staff to provide one-to-one or small-group tuition or classroom support; the provision of different learning materials or special equipment; additional staff development and training on more effective strategies; or early advice on strategies or equipment from local authority support services. Parents have to be consulted and informed both about the action taken to help their child and its outcome. The provision made for an individual pupil which is in addition to or different from the differentiated curriculum plan for all pupils should be recorded in *an individual education plan (IEP)*. The IEP should include information about:

- the short-term targets set for or by the child
- the teaching strategies to be used
- the provision to be put in place
- when the plan is to be reviewed

- success and/or exit criteria
- outcomes (to be recorded when IEP is reviewed).

(DfES 2001a: 54)

The guidance also states that IEPs should be crisply written and focus on three or four targets, clearly related to the individual's needs, in key areas such as communication, literacy, mathematics, and behaviour and social skills. It should be noted the IEPs have not been universally welcomed, with some SENCOs describing them as a bureaucratic encumbrance. Tennant (2007) summarizes the continuing debate about the benefits and costs of IEPs, particularly in secondary schools. More recently the DfES has clarified that IEPs *per se* are not a statutory requirement and are only one way of recording provision that is 'additional or different'. (DfES 2005f). It is pointed out that where schools have arrangements to plan individually for all pupils and record progress, IEPs may become unnecessary.

Provision mapping is one strategy that has recently emerged in this context. Provision maps are defined as 'a way of showing "at a glance" the range of provision a school makes for children with additional needs through additional staffing or peer support' (DfES, 2005f: 194). Typically grids are constructed by first showing the additional and different provision being made. Then information may be added showing which children with which targets are accessing what provision and when. Unlike IEPs, a provision map does not have to be rewritten for every child. A provision map for a year group or subject can be highlighted or annotated to show the provision being made for an individual child. Provision maps have been commended as an effective way of demonstrating to a concerned parent/carer exactly what is being provided for their child. They have also been used in demonstrating the range of provision in place for a child to the SEN and Disability Tribunal.

Such developments may go some way towards addressing some of the criticism that the Code of Practice has received, for example that the stages in effect extend the Warnock model of highly individualized assessment and support inappropriately to children in mainstream schools with a much lower level of need (Dyson and Millward 2002). However, others see the main difficulties as residing in later stages of the process.

> the procedural apparatus of identification and assessment which the body of the code is concerned to set out . . . is constructed upon a largely individual-ised model of learning difficulties, in which questions of school organisation disappear from the picture once the graduated assessment process has been set in motion. The focus thereafter is upon monitoring and reviewing the performance of the individual pupil within a system of provision whose prevailing norms are taken for granted.

(Skidmore, 2004: 17)

Where pupils continue to experience difficulties despite an individualized programme and focused support under School Action, external support services may be consulted for more detailed advice through School Action Plus. This may involve external support services offering advice about new IEPs and targets, providing more specialist assessments, advising on specialist strategies or materials, or providing direct support of various kinds. Although the expectation is that the delivery of the interventions recorded in the IEP, or equivalent, will continue to be primarily the responsibility of the class or subject teacher and that the strategies should be implemented as far as possible in the classroom setting, external specialists may be involved in teaching pupils directly for part of the time or in partnership with their teachers. Where a group-based approach to planning and recording is in place in the school, recording in relation to any individualized provision is likely to require a supplementary element.

If a number of alternative intervention programmes have each been implemented for a reasonable period of time without success, the headteacher may consider referring a pupil for *statutory assessment*, detailing information on their National Curriculum levels and attainments in literacy and numeracy, the evidence collected through School Action and School Action Plus, information from the involvement of other professionals, and the views of the pupil and their parents. The pupil should continue to be supported through School Action Plus while the local authority is considering a request for a statutory assessment of their SEN.

Guidance is offered to LEAs on the statutory assessment of SEN. 'An assessment under section 323 of the Education Act 1996 should only be undertaken if the LEA believe that the child probably has special educational needs and that the LEA needs or probably needs to determine the child's special educational provision itself by making a statement' (DfES 2001a: 74). A request for a statutory assessment may be made by a pupil's school, by their parent or by another agency such as an independent school, early education provider, health authority or social services department. Before deciding whether to make an assessment the LEA must notify and inform parents. If the request has not come from the pupil's school the headteacher must be informed and asked for written evidence about the school's assessment of the pupil's needs and the provision that has been made for them. In deciding whether to make a statutory assessment, LEAs are to pay particular attention to:

- evidence that the school has responded appropriately to the requirements of the National Curriculum, especially the section entitled 'Inclusion: Providing effective learning opportunities for all children'

- evidence provided by the child's school, parents and other professionals where they have been involved with the child, as to the nature, extent and cause of the child's learning difficulties

- evidence of action already taken by the child's school to meet and overcome those difficulties;

- evidence of the rate and style of the child's progress

- evidence that where some progress has been made, it has only been as a result of much additional effort and instruction at a sustained level not usually commensurate with usual provision through Action Plus.

(DfES, 2001a: 81)

Guidance is offered on the type of provision that may be required to meet pupils' SEN in communication and interaction, in cognition and learning, behaviour, emotional and social development and arising from physical and/or sensory needs. Where the LEA judges that the child's needs can be met from the resources already available to mainstream schools in their area, the decision will be taken not to make a statutory assessment. The LEA must explain the reasons for their decision to the pupil's parents and their school. Parents may appeal against the decision to the SEN Tribunal.

If the LEA decides to make a statutory assessment they must seek parental, educational, medical, psychological and social services' advice on the pupil's special educational needs plus any other advice considered desirable by the LEA or other relevant bodies. This may include the views of the child. The LEA will consider all this advice in deciding whether they need to make a statement. The LEA has 10 weeks from notifying parents that they intend to make an assessment to writing to parents letting them know the outcome of the assessment.

If, as a result of the assessment, the LEA decide that they do not need to make a statement, they must present parents with a note in lieu, which gives the reasons for their decision, outlines the child's needs and offers guidance on the appropriate educational provision that might be made by the school, possibly with specialist advice, but without being determined by the LEA. Parents may appeal against the decision not to issue a statement to the SEN Tribunal. The operation of the SEN Tribunal is governed by sections 333–6 of the Education Act 1996 and the associated regulations. Appeals to the tribunal are heard by a panel of three people, two of whom should have relevant expertise in SEN and/ or local government and one of whom, the chair, will be legally trained. The SEN Tribunal's 'overriding aim is to consider the needs of the child' (DfEE, 1997: 29).

If the LEA decide they need to issue a statement they will send a proposed statement to the parents. The statement must be set out in the format shown in Figure 3.5 and all sections completed except Part 4, where parents will be invited to express their preferences about the school to be named. The Special Educational Needs and Disability Act places a duty on LEAs and schools to ensure that pupils with SEN are educated in a mainstream setting unless this is incompatible with the wishes of their parents or the efficient education of the other pupils. If LEAs do not name the parents' first choice of school in the final version of the statement they must explain their decision to the parents who have a right to appeal to the SEN Tribunal.

An *annual review* of each statement must be carried out, involving the parents, the pupil, the LEA, the school and all the professionals involved. The purpose of the review is to collect everyone's perspectives on the child's progress, to ensure that desired outcomes are being achieved and, if necessary, to amend the statement to reflect any new needs identified and provision required. The LEA may decide that the objectives of the statement have been achieved and that they should no longer maintain the statement. Where the pupil or their family has EAL the Code highlights the need to:

- translate any relevant documents into the family's mother tongue

- ensure that interpreters are available to the child and family both in the preparatory stages to the review meeting and in the review meeting itself

- ensure that any professionals from the child's community have similar interpretation and translation facilities in order that they may contribute as fully as possible to the review process

The Statement of Special Educational Needs

Part 1. Introduction: The child's name and address and date of birth. The child's home language and religion. The names and address(es) of the child's parents.

Part 2. Special Educational Needs (learning difficulties): Details of each and every one of the child's special educational needs as identified by the LA during statutory assessment and on the advice received and attached as appendices to the statement.

Part 3. Special Educational Provision: The special educational provision that the LA consider necessary to meet the child's special educational needs.

(a) The objectives that the special educational provision should aim to meet.

(b) The special educational provision which the LA consider appropriate to meet the needs set out in Part 2 and to meet the objectives.

(c) The arrangements to be made for monitoring progress in meeting those objectives, particularly for setting short-term targets for the child's progress and for reviewing his or her progress on a regular basis.

Part 4. Placement: The type and name of school where the special educational provision set out in Part 3 is to be made or the arrangements for the education to be made otherwise than in school.

Part 5. Non-Educational Needs: All relevant non-educational needs of the child as agreed between the health services, social services or other agencies and the LA.

Part 6. Non-Educational Provision: Details of relevant non-educational provision required to meet the non-educational needs of the child as agreed between the health services and/or social services and the LA, including the agreed arrangements for its provision.

Signature and date

APPENDICES

All the advice obtained and taken into consideration during the assessment process must be attached as appendices to the statement.

The advice appended to the statement must include:

A   Parental evidence

B   Educational advice

C   Medical advice

D   Psychological advice

E   Social Services advice

F   Any other advice, such as the views of the child, which the LA or any other body from whom advice is sought considers desirable. In particular where the child's parent is a serving member of the armed forces, advice from Service Children's Education (SCE)

Figure 3.5   Format and content of the Statement of SEN
Source: DfES (2001a: 100–101).

- ensure that, if possible, a bilingual support teacher or teacher of English as an additional language is available to the child and family.

(DfES 2001a: 125)

Any annual review held in Year 9 and subsequent years must draw up and review a *transition plan* in addition to reviewing the young person's statement. The aim of the transition plan is to prepare systematically for the young person's transition to adult life and ensure that they receive any specialist help they need during continuing education or vocational or occupational training. Any relevant agencies that may play a significant role in the young person's life during the post-school years should be invited and the 'Connexions' service must be involved.

Other relevant legislation and guidance

Disability discrimination

The Disability Discrimination Act 1995 introduced new measures aimed at ending the discrimination experienced by many disabled people. Circular 20/99 (DfEE 1999c), entitled *What the Disability Discrimination Act Means for Schools and LEAs*, informed schools and LEAs about their new duties in three main areas: employing staff, providing non-educational services to the public (e.g. hiring school rooms), and publishing information about arrangements for disabled pupils. In this last area, governing bodies' annual reports to parents must explain their admission arrangements for disabled pupils, how the access of these pupils will be enabled and what will be done to make sure that they are treated fairly. The guidance points out that failure by the school to comply with their published policy in any individual case could be a central issue in a parental appeal under local admissions appeal arrangements or in an appeal to the SEN Tribunal.

The SEN and Disability Act 2001 extended the Disability Discrimination Act to cover the provision of education. *The Disability Discrimination Act 2005* amended the 1995 Act and placed a duty on all public bodies, including schools, to promote equality of opportunity for people with disabilities. *A person is now defined as disabled if he/she has a mental or physical impairment which has a substantial and long-term adverse effect on their ability to carry out day-to-day activities.* Included in the broadened definition are difficulties resulting from dyslexia, autistic spectrum disorder, diabetes and severe asthma, for example. Not all children who are defined as disabled will have SEN. For example, those with severe asthma or diabetes may not have SEN but may have rights under the Disability Discrimination Act. Similarly, not all children with SEN will be defined as having a disability under the Act. The multi-media resource pack 'Implementing the Disability Discrimination Act in Schools and Early Years Settings' (DfES 2006l) provides a guide to school's duties under the Act and how these fit with SEN duties.

Activity 3.6   Definition of disability

1   Read the following extract from Teachernet (DfES 2005g) about a child to whom the name Tom has been given:

2   Then look again at the three pen pictures of children provided in Activity 3.2:

(a)   Which of these children may have a disability?

(b)   What questions would you need to ask in order to reach a decision in each case?

Is Tom disabled?

Answering the four questions below will help you decide if Tom is disabled.

1   **Does Tom have difficulty with any of the following 'normal day-to-day activities'?**

- *Mobility*: getting to/from school, moving about the school and/or going on school visits?

- *Manual dexterity*: holding a pen, pencil or book, using tools in design and technology, playing a musical instrument, throwing and catching a ball?

- *Physical co-ordination*: washing or dressing, taking part in games and Physical Education?

- *Ability to lift, carry or otherwise move every day objects*: carrying a full school bag or other fairly heavy items?

- *Continence*: going to the toilet or controlling the need to go to the toilet?

- *Speech*: communicating with others or understanding what others are saying; how they express themselves orally or in writing?

- *Hearing*: hearing what people say in person or on a video, DVD, radio or tape recording?

- *Eyesight*: ability to see clearly (with spectacles/contact lenses where necessary), including visual presentations in the classroom?

- *Memory or ability to concentrate, learn or understand*: work in school including reading, writing, number work or understanding information?

- *Perception of the risk of physical danger*: inability to recognise danger e.g. when jumping from a height, touching hot objects or crossing roads?

2   **Is Tom's difficulty caused by an underlying impairment or condition?**

3   **Has Tom's impairment or condition lasted, or is likely to last, more than 12 months?**

4   **Is the effect of Tom's impairment or condition 'more than minor or trivial'?**

Answer:

If you have answered yes to questions 1 to 4, then Tom is probably disabled under the Disability Discrimination Act. If Tom receives medical or other treatment to reduce or remove the effects of his condition, he may still be disabled. The test is whether the effects would recur if he were to stop his treatment.

Looked after children

The Children Act 1989 brought together previously fragmented legislation about caring for, bringing up and protecting children. The welfare of the child was enshrined as the paramount consideration in all decision making. As noted in Chapter 2, children's ascertainable wishes and feelings are accorded importance in that courts must have regard to them. However, the Act also emphasizes the importance of the family – the duty of local authorities being to provide support to children in need and their families. Children are defined as being in need if:

● they are unlikely to achieve or maintain, or to have the opportunity of achieving or maintaining, a reasonable standard of health or development without the provision of services by a local authority;

● their health or development is likely to be significantly impaired, or further impaired, without the provision of such services; or

● they are disabled.

In line with the distinction made throughout this chapter, the SEN Code of Practice acknowledges that 'a child with special educational needs will not necessarily be "in need" as defined in the Children Act 1989' (DfES 2001a: 141).

The concept of parental responsibility was another central element of the Children Act 1989. This applies even when children are unable to live at home, but must be looked after by the local authority. The local authority has a duty to ensure contact with the parents whenever possible for a child looked after by them and a duty to return the child to their family unless this is against their interests. While the interests of the child would require action by a local authority in cases of abuse or neglect in the family, the dangers are highlighted of unwarranted intervention in families which does not positively contribute to the child's welfare. The Act sets out a range of welfare duties for local authorities in looking after children and requires that account must be taken of the child's racial origin and cultural and linguistic background.

There are particular implications for education where a pupil is accommodated by a local authority, is subject to a care order or to an education supervision order (which can be made when a child of compulsory school age is not receiving efficient full-time education – for example, through persistent poor attendance). The Arrangements for Placement of Children Regulations made under the Act require that the childcare plan drawn up in these cases must include information about arrangements for the child's education (the personal education plan). The personal education plan should include information as appropriate from a statement of SEN, annual review or IEP. The Department for Education and Employment/Department of Health (2000) *Guidance on the Education of Children in Public Care* suggests that LEAs and social services departments should consider the advantages of linking their reviews of a pupil's SEN statement and childcare plan in order to ensure an integrated approach to their needs.

Every Child Matters

Ensuring an integrated approach to the needs of children has emerged as one of the major planks of current government policy, together with an accountability focus on ensuring that key outcomes for children are achieved. In response to the

Laming inquiry into the death of Victoria Climbié, the Green Paper *Every Child Matters* (ECM: DfES 2003b) proposed a range of measures to reform the provision of services for children. These focus on protecting children at risk within a framework of universal services which both act preventively and support every child in developing their potential and achieving desired outcomes. Following consultation with children, young people and families the outcomes sought were summarized as follows:

- *being healthy*: enjoying good physical and mental health and living a healthy lifestyle;

- *staying safe*: being protected from harm and neglect;

- *enjoying and achieving*: getting the most out of life and developing the skills needed for adulthood;

- *making a positive contribution*: being involved with the community and society and not engaging in anti-social or offending behaviour;

- *achieving economic well-being*: not being prevented by economic disadvantage from achieving their full potential in life.

These are now commonly referred to as the 'ECM five outcomes'.

In pursuit of these outcomes, ECM identified a number of ways in which existing initiatives would be developed:

- creating Sure Start Children's Centres in the 20 per cent most deprived neighbourhoods;

- promoting full service extended schools open beyond school hours to provide breakfast/after-school clubs and childcare, and have health and social care support services on site;

- developing out-of-school activities for children;

- increasing investment in child and adolescent mental health services;

- improving speech and language therapy;

- tackling homelessness;

- reforms to the youth justice system.

In addition, new proposals for action were presented in four main areas:

- supporting parents and carers;

- early intervention and effective protection;

- accountability and integration – locally, regionally and nationally;

- workforce reform.

It is intended that a coordinated continuum of services will be available to parents and carers (see Figure 3.6). Early intervention and effective protection will be facilitated by improving information sharing between agencies. By 2008 local authorities are expected to introduce a Common Assessment Framework across education, health and social care to assess the additional needs of children and

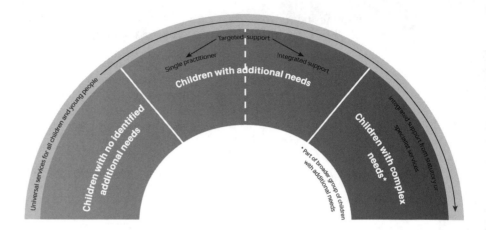

Figure 3.6　Continuum of Needs and Services
Source: DfES (2005g).

young people whose needs are not being met by universal services. Where more than one service is involved a lead professional can be identified to ensure effective coordination. The development of service delivery by multi-disciplinary teams based around schools and children's centres was also advocated as was the integration of key services for children and young people under the Director of Children's Services as part of Children's Trusts which bring together local authority education and children's social services, some children's health services and other services such as Connexions and Youth Offending Teams.

The legislative basis for these reforms was provided by the *Children Act 2004* which established for England:

- a children's commissioner to champion the views and interests of children and young people;

- a duty on local authorities to make arrangements to promote cooperation between agencies and other bodies, such as voluntary and community organizations, ('key partners') in order to improve children's well-being (defined by reference to the five outcomes), and a duty on key partners to cooperate with the arrangements;

- a duty on key agencies to safeguard and promote the welfare of children;

- a duty on local authorities to set up local safeguarding children boards and on key partners to take part;

- provision for common databases to enable better sharing of information about children and young people;

- a requirement for a single children and young people's plan to be drawn up by each local authority (replacing separate education and social care plans);

- a requirement on local authorities to appoint a director of children's services and designate a lead member of the council to take overall responsibility;

- the creation of an integrated inspection framework and the conduct of joint area reviews to assess progress at local level in improving outcomes;

- provisions relating to foster care, private fostering and the education of children in care.

In its strategy for SEN (DfES 2004c), the government explicitly linked the ECM focus on early intervention, preventive work and integrated services for children to meeting the needs of children with SEN and their families. Action programmes are identified in four areas:

- Early intervention – to ensure that children who have difficulties learning receive the help they need as soon as possible and that parents of children with special educational needs and disabilities have access to suitable childcare

- Removing barriers to learning – by embedding inclusive practice in every school and early years setting

- Raising expectations and achievement – by developing teachers' skills and strategies for meeting the needs of children with SEN and sharpening our focus on the progress children make

- Delivering improvements in partnership – taking a hands-on approach to improvement so that parents can be confident that their child will get the education they need.

(DfES 2004c: introduction)

The Education Act 2005 made a number of changes to the framework for school inspections, including new requirements to report on the contribution made by the school to the well-being of their pupils and on the extent to which the education provided meets the needs of the range of pupils in the school, in particular vulnerable pupils, including those with SEN.

Conclusions

In this chapter we have drawn a distinction between the SEN of individual children and the additional needs that may be experienced by particular groups of children whose circumstances or background differ from the majority of the school population. Changes over time in the conceptualization of SEN were tracked and approaches that focus on individual differences and on environmental demands were compared. The advantages of an interactional analysis that brings both of these approaches together were described, and approaches were identified that can be taken by schools to empower groups of students who have additional educational needs. While maintaining the distinction between the terms 'SEN' and 'AEN', relationships that have been found to exist between them were described and possible reasons for these relationships explored. Finally, current legislation and guidance on identifying children's educational and other needs and on making appropriate provision for them were summarized.

4

Inclusion

Objectives

When you have studied this chapter you should be able to:

- outline the development of inclusive education and identify common elements in the concept as described by different authors;
- discuss the main findings of the research which has been conducted in inclusive education;
- describe ways in which inclusion can be promoted and supported.

Contents

What is inclusion?

Segregation, integration and inclusion

'Inclusion' is often defined as a journey or movement away from the kind of segregation described by Bennett *et al.* (1998: 155):

> I arrived at the school at 8.45am. It seemed like a typical suburban primary school. The grounds and school building were well-kept. There was the usual scene of children playing in the yard and arriving at school. The principal had asked me to come to the school before the first class period so that he could introduce me to John's teacher and show me his classroom. He escorted me to a prefabricated building, physically separate from the rest of the school. It was the special class for ten children with mild mental handicap.

Historically, if children had particular difficulties in school they were put together with other children whose needs were perceived to be similar. It was argued that this allowed special facilities and specially trained staff to be made available to children who need them. This solution was also applied to children learning EAL. Putting together groups of children who are thought to have similar needs results in them being segregated from other pupils of their age. This can be stigmatizing. For example, pupils in a special unit in a mainstream secondary school that was studied by Sinclair Taylor (1995: 267) were in no doubt about their image in the school: 'They [mainstream] call us unit kids and provoke us and say we are spastics' (unit pupil, aged 16); 'Main school kids tease you, they see the unit as a place for mental people – less better than themselves' (unit pupil, aged 12).

It can also restrict access to important educational opportunities, as was highlighted when the Commission for Racial Equality (CRE) condemned the segregated arrangements made by Calderdale Borough Council for children who failed an English language screening test for admission to local schools (CRE 1986). The formal investigation found that there was 'indirectly discriminatory practice contrary to the Race Relations Act 1976' (CRE 1986: 5). The investigators noted that 'the range of subjects . . . was narrower than that covered by the mainstream classes . . . [they] had no practical classes, no music, no foreign languages and no specific periods for religious education' (CRE 1986: 12). Such concerns have been important in fuelling a movement away from segregated provision of various types.

The metaphor of a journey is explicitly explored by Clark *et al.* (1999) in their analysis of the attempts of four comprehensive schools to develop in a more inclusive way. Other authors similarly focus on inclusion as a process of change. Reynolds (1989) suggests that inclusion is best regarded as a progressive trend for taking increasing responsibility for educating groups previously excluded from mainstream society. He sees social values about race, ethnicity, language or disability as key influences on exclusion. From this perspective the current debates that will be reviewed in this chapter are set within a historical context where moves in the 1950s to racially integrate schools in the USA had an important influence (Liu 1995). This is also made explicit by Booth *et al.* (2000: 14) writing in a British context:

Racism, sexism, classism, homophobia, disablism, and bullying all share a common root in an intolerance to difference and the abuse of power to create and perpetuate inequalities. Making schools more inclusive may involve staff in a painful process of challenging their own discriminatory practices and attitudes.

The Ofsted (2000: 4) guidance for inspectors and schools on evaluating educational inclusion pays 'particular attention to the provision made for and the achievement of *different groups* of pupils within a school', where the term 'different groups' could apply to:

- girls and boys;

- minority ethnic and faith groups, Travellers, asylum seekers and refugees;

- pupils who need support to learn English as an additional language (EAL);

- pupils with special educational needs;

- gifted and talented pupils;

- children 'looked after' by the local authority;

- other children, such as sick children; young carers; those children from families under stress; pregnant school girls and teenage mothers; and

- any pupils who are at risk of disaffection and exclusion.

In accordance with the purpose of the book, this chapter will focus on inclusion in provision for pupils with SEN in the context of this broader emphasis in inclusive practice.

Inclusion has been seen by many as instrumental in countering prejudice and bias in school and later in society. This is embodied in the Salamanca World Statement issued by the United Nations Educational, Scientific and Cultural Organization (UNESCO 1994: 11) on principles, policy and practice in SEN: 'Inclusion and participation are essential to human dignity and to the enjoyment and exercise of human rights. Within the field of education this is reflected in the development of strategies that seek to bring about a genuine equalisation of opportunity'. The statement was signed by the representatives of 92 governments, including the British government, and 25 international organizations. It calls on governments 'to adopt the principle of inclusive education, enrolling all children in regular schools unless there are compelling reasons for doing otherwise' (UNESCO 1994: 44).

The Department for Education in London expressed support for the principle of inclusion (DfEE 1997). However, at the same time it made clear that the needs of individual children are considered to be paramount. Where individual needs could not be met in mainstream schools, the government made a commitment to maintaining specialist provision as an integral part of overall provision. Alongside this, the aim, wherever possible, was to return children to the mainstream and to increase the skills and resources in mainstream schools. This shift in emphasis from an exclusive focus on the needs of individual pupils to an approach which focuses centrally on the skills and resources available in mainstream schools is an important difference between the earlier concept of 'integration' and the more recent concept of 'inclusion'.

The difference between integration and inclusion

Ainscow (1995) suggested that *integration* is about making a limited number of additional arrangements for individual pupils with SEN in schools which themselves change little overall. On the other hand, *inclusion* implies the introduction of a more radical set of changes through which schools restructure themselves so as to be able to embrace all children. *Integration* involves the school in a process of assimilation where the onus is on the assimilating individual (whether a pupil with SEN or a pupil with a different cultural and linguistic background) to make changes so that they can 'fit in'. By contrast *inclusion* involves the school in a process of accommodation where the onus is on the school to change, adapting curricula, methods, materials and procedures so that it becomes more responsive. Given an inclusive philosophy, pupils with SEN may be a stimulus to development of a richer mainstream learning experience for all.

Despite this conceptual distinction between integration and inclusion, Thomas *et al.* (1998) point out that the terms are often used as synonyms. Where one term is used rather than the other, this may have more to do with the date of publication of the book or article in question than with the educational provision that is being described.

In their study of full inclusion models in five US states, Baker and Zigmond (1995) found that while the term 'inclusion' had different meanings for different people, what was common was the view of inclusion as a 'place' – a seat in an age appropriate mainstream classroom, where a child could have access to and participate fully in the curriculum. It also meant bringing the special needs teacher or assistant into that place to help make it work. In a national study conducted in 1995, the US National Centre on Educational Restructuring and Inclusion defined inclusion as:

> the provision of services to students with disabilities, including those with severe impairments, in the neighbourhood school in age-appropriate general education classes, with the necessary support services and supplementary aids (for the child and the teacher) both to ensure the child's success – academic, behavioural and social – and to prepare the child to participate as a full and contributing member of the society.
>
> (Lipsky and Gartner 1996: 763)

Sebba and Sachdev (1997: 9), writing in a British context, likewise offer a working definition which is prescriptive in suggesting what is needed rather than being descriptive of current practice:

> Inclusive education describes the process by which a school attempts to respond to all pupils as individuals by reconsidering and restructuring its curricular organisation and provision and allocating resources to enhance equality of opportunity. Through this process the school builds its capacity to accept all pupils from the local community who wish to attend and, in so doing, reduces the need to exclude pupils.

The *Index for Inclusion*, which was distributed to all British schools, also emphasizes a process view of inclusion:

> In our view, inclusion is a set of never ending processes. It involves the specification of the direction of change. It is relevant to any school however

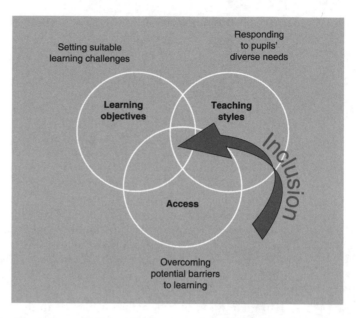

Figure 4.1   The Primary National Strategy model of three circles of inclusion
Source: DfES (2006a: 3).

inclusive or exclusive its current cultures, policies and practices. It requires
schools to engage in a critical examination of what can be done to increase the
learning and participation of the diversity of students within the school and
its locality.

(Booth *et al.* 2000: 12)

Within the *Index for Inclusion* the term 'barriers to learning and participation' is
used instead of 'SEN'. This is intended to focus attention upon an interactional
model of learning difficulties, and upon the role of the school in identifying
barriers and minimizing them through provision of appropriate support. As we
have seen in Chapter 3, this conceptualization is explicit in the UK government's
current strategy for SEN. It is also embedded within the National Curriculum
statutory inclusion statement which sets out key principles for developing a more
inclusive curriculum: setting suitable learning challenges, responding to pupils'
diverse learning needs, and overcoming potential barriers to learning and assessment for individuals and groups of pupils. These principles are incorporated in the
Primary National Strategy model of three circles of inclusion, as can be seen in
Figure 4.1.

Special educational provision

A historical perspective

In the late eighteenth century the first special schools in Britain were set up. At that
time only the children of the upper and middle classes received education. The

special schools were intended to provide for children with severe hearing or visual difficulties who could not learn using the methods and materials available in ordinary schools. As more and more children were brought within the education system in the late nineteenth century, the schools of the day were faced with a wide range of learning and behaviour to which they were not accustomed and which they could not easily accommodate. Increasing numbers of children were excluded. Indeed, there was no incentive to try to include them, rather the reverse. Each year examinations in the 'three Rs' (reading, writing and arithmetic) were conducted by Her Majesty's Inspectors and the performance of each child was combined to determine the bulk of government grant to the school for the following year. Payment by results meant that part of each teacher's salary depended on the rate of exam passes in their classes (Sutherland 1981). The rejection by mainstream schools of slow learning and emotionally disturbed children who were entitled to education under the 1870 Education Act led to the expansion of the special school sector (DES 1978). It has been argued that the introduction of national testing in the last decade of the twentieth century and the publication of league tables of school results has meant that similar factors to those operating a century earlier are again influencing the inclusiveness of educational provision. However, some researchers have found that while the 'standards agenda' may have an undermining effect on inclusion in some respects, it has also required schools to examine closely the progress of groups of pupils who might otherwise be overlooked and to re-examine the practices that appear to be failing these pupils (Ainscow *et al.* 2006a).

Activity 4.1   Influences on exclusion and inclusion: past and present

Thomas *et al.* (1998) argued that the market-orientated education polices introduced by government (e.g. the publication of league tables of test results) have made many schools wary of accepting children whose low attainment or disruptive effect on others' learning may depress examination or SAT scores. They also suggest that the significant increase in exclusions recorded in the 1990s (Ofsted 1996a) was strongly influenced by these new pressures on schools.

(a) To what extent can you see parallels between the factors reported to be influencing inclusion and exclusion in British schools in the late nineteenth century and those which schools are currently experiencing?

(b) Are there other important influences that affect inclusion today but do not seem to have been operating then?

The expansion of the special school sector in the early years of the twentieth century was entirely consistent with the concept of 'handicap' prevalent at the time. Handicap was understood in terms of defect, and physical and sensory impairments were thought to impose limitations on cognitive development. Handicapped children were seen as different in kind from other children, so it made sense to develop a different education system for them. Indeed, it was argued that separate provision should be made in the interests of the children concerned. This view is seen in Cyril Burt's (1917: 38–9) 'tentative suggestions' for special classes for children with learning difficulties:

The ideal arrangement, therefore, would be a series of classes parallel to the customary series, where promotion was slower or the increase of difficulty less. Since backwardness affects scholastic and abstract work more than practical or concrete, the curriculum should include a large proportion of concrete and manual work; and the teaching methods should be similarly adapted ... The classes should be small in number, not only because these children need more individual attention in their work, but also because each class needs close observation and enquiry. Conditions should be systematically analysed; progress systematically tested; and accurate records kept of both in terms of objective facts rather than personal impressions ... Too often when discovered the backward child is merely ignored, or else passed on to another school or class where he is accepted, and his condition has once more to be slowly rediscovered. The feeling that he is not wanted, not understood, not like other children, in short, subnormal and a nuisance, damages the child far more than the subnormality itself.

This concept, of different kinds of education for different types of children, also underpinned the division of the mainstream population at 11 years of age into 'academic', 'technical' and 'manual' which was introduced in most parts of the UK following the Norwood Report (Board of Education 1943) and the Education Act 1944. Prior to the 1960s in many countries the 'handicapped' were considered to be quite distinct from the rest of the population. Ordinary schooling was just not considered to be an option for them. In Britain children with severe learning difficulties – then called 'educationally subnormal (severe)' – were not considered capable of benefiting from education (Hegarty 1993). They did not attend schools run by education authorities. Instead they were provided with health service 'training centres'.

Moves to reverse the separation of 'handicapped' children gathered momentum from the mid-1960s. There was a change in the conceptualization of disability as the result of a broader rights movement in society towards 'normalization'. In this view people with disabilities should have access to the same opportunities and options as other members of society. At the same time, concerns were raised by researchers such as Dunn (1968) about the lack of evidence to suggest that disabled children who were educated in special schools did any better than those who were being educated in mainstream schools by default, due to lack of provision. It was argued that mainstreaming or integration of children with SEN into mainstream schools would facilitate their access to and participation in society, both as children and adults, and that continued segregation could no longer be justified from either a 'research' or a 'rights' perspective.

In Britain the Education (Handicapped Children) Act 1970 removed the legal distinction between those who were and were not educable in school. When this legislation was enacted all children, including those with severe learning difficulties, were entitled to education for the first time. In the USA, similarly, Public Law 94–142 (Education of All Handicapped Act 1975) established the principle of 'zero reject' or entitlement for all in public education. Furthermore, it promoted integration by setting the requirement that children should be educated in the 'least restrictive environment'.

Mittler (1985) drew attention to the way in which the integration movement started as a rallying cry for those with a vision of change in education and within ten years had become the 'new orthodoxy'. The Warnock Committee (DES 1978: 99) identified it as 'the central contemporary issue in special education'. The OECD (1981: 5) considered it 'the dominant policy relating to the organisation of schooling for handicapped children in most of the member countries'. A survey by UNESCO (1988) reported that in 75 per cent of the 58 countries responding, integration was a declared policy.

The continuum of provision and the reform of mainstream education

In the USA the 'least restrictive environment' referred to the educational setting that would best facilitate the educational development of a particular individual child. In order to ensure access for individuals to the least restrictive environment, it was often considered important to ensure that a continuum of services was available. In Britain also the commitment to a continuum of special educational provision has remained a consistent feature over the past 30 years. Figure 4.2

Sample Continuum of Services	(i) Full-time education in an ordinary class with any necessary help and support
Level 1: General education classroom	
Level 2: General education classroom with consultative services	(ii) Education in an ordinary class with periods of withdrawal to a special class or unit or other supporting base
Level 3: General education classroom with supplementary instruction and services	(iii) Education in a special class or unit with periods of attendance at an ordinary class and full involvement in the general community life and extracurricular activities of the ordinary school
Level 4: General education classroom with resource room services	
Level 5: Full-time special education classroom	(iv) Full-time education in a special class or unit with social contact with the main school
Level 6: Special school	(v) Education in a special school, day or residential, with some shared lessons with a neighbouring ordinary school
Level 7: Special facilities, non-public school	(vi) Full-time education in a day special school with social contact with an ordinary school
	(vii) Full-time education in residential special school with social contact with an ordinary school
	(viii) Short-term education in hospitals or other establishments
	(ix) Long-term education in hospitals or other establishments
	(x) Home tuition

Figure 4.2 Special education: a continuum of provision?
Sources: left column, Mastropieri and Scruggs (1997); right column, DES (1978: para. 6.11).

shows how the continuum of special education provision has been conceptualized in the UK and the USA.

Dyson (1991) criticized the conception of the mainstream curriculum which underpins the Warnock Committee's thinking, arguing that it assumes that the curriculum will not change and that certain children will fail without additional resourcing (which in turn is defined as that needed in order to prevent failure). He acknowledged that this might be applicable to some children with sensory or physical difficulties, where they can be given clearly identifiable resources such as technological aids or large-print worksheets to enable them to succeed in a unreconstructed curriculum. However, for the large majority of children with SEN there is a need to look at the curriculum and the way in which it is delivered, and to make substantial revisions.

More recently, Warnock (2005) has agreed with Dyson's analysis and questioned the extent to which mainstream education can be reformed, particularly given the pressures associated with the Education Act 1988 involving raising achievement and league tables. Arguing that some children's special needs will be best met in special schools, Warnock (2005: 22) described the concept of inclusion as 'possibly the most disastrous legacy of the 1978 Report', in particular as it appeared to put the continuing existence of special schools under threat. Warnock argued that the ultimate objective of an inclusive society may be best served by seeing inclusive schooling as involvement in a common enterprise of learning and endorsed the view of the National Association of Head Teachers that the most appropriate educational setting for a child will be 'the one in which they can be most fully included in the life of their school community and which gives them a sense of both belonging and achievement' (Warnock 2005: 41).

The Green Paper, *Excellence for All Children: Meeting Special Educational Needs* (DfEE 1997), attended to the need for mainstream school reform, while remaining committed to the concept of a continuum of SEN provision:

> We want to develop an education system in which special provision is seen as an integral part of overall provision, aiming wherever possible to return children to the mainstream and to increase the skills and resources available in mainstream schools. We want therefore to strengthen links between special and mainstream schools, and to ensure that LEA support services are used to support mainstream placements.
>
> (DfEE 1997: 44)

There has been a trend towards the greater use of mainstream placement, with numbers in special schools falling gradually from 1.5 per cent of children in 1983 to 1.1 per cent in 2004 (DfES 2004c). Considerable variation between LEAs was reported, with the percentage in special schools ranging from 0.1 per cent to 2.4 per cent. However, other trends have also been apparent, particularly for pupils with challenging behaviour of various kinds. Between 2001 and 2003 the proportion of pupils in pupil referral units rose by 25 per cent, and there was a 10 per cent increase in the number of pupils placed in independent special schools, reflecting difficulties experienced by mainstream schools, and some special schools, in meeting severe or complex needs (Ofsted 2004).

In accordance with the focus in the *Every Child Matters* framework on integrated planning and partnership in the delivery of services to meet individual needs, the government's strategy for meeting SEN (DfES 2004c) presented a vision of community partnerships between schools and support services in an area:

- special schools providing for those pupils who have the most severe and complex needs and sharing their specialist skills and knowledge with mainstream schools to enable them to support pupils with less severe needs;

- schools working together and with specialist advice from multi-disciplinary teams of local authority and health service staff to support the inclusion of children from their local community.

In the UK, current government targets encourage further development of inclusive provision, while stopping well short of a commitment to full inclusion.

Tutt (2007) suggests that the debate needs to move on accordingly from a concept of inclusion that involves including all pupils in mainstream schools to one which focuses on including all schools and specialist provision in an inclusive education service. Examples of implementation from across the continuum of provision are provided, including examples of co-located and federated schools. Co-located mainstream and special schools may share the same buildings, but commonly are physically separate, although on the same site. While some long-standing examples can be identified, the Building Schools for the Future programme has provided a new impetus. Federations, which were enabled by regulations introduced with the Education Act 2002, involve bringing together in terms of leadership and operation schools that are usually physically separate. In 'hard' federations the schools involved will have a single governing body and an executive headteacher or chief executive across all schools. In 'soft' federations each school retains their own governing body, although there is a joint governing/ management group. Tutt (2007) gives the following examples of federations involving special schools:

- The Dartington Village Federation consists of a primary, secondary and all-age special school, all under the same roof and with a single governing body and chief executive.

- The West Sussex Federation consists of a secondary school for boys and two special schools (one for pupils with moderate learning difficulties and the other for pupils with behavioural, emotional and social difficulties). The special schools are separated by a few miles but now have a joint governing body.

Inclusion: rights and research

Proponents of inclusion have concentrated on the human rights of children with SEN when arguing their case and have emphasized the social benefits they expect the children to experience. However, the social status and acceptance of mainstreamed children with learning difficulties in different national school systems has generally been found by research studies to be low; see Gresham and MacMillan (1997b) on the USA, Roberts and Zubrick (1992) on Australia, and Nabuzoka and Smith (1993) on the UK. The relevance of such research findings to policy decisions has been challenged by rights advocates – for example, 'Data can be used to evaluate progress towards the goals established by values, but data cannot alter the value itself' (McLeskey *et al.* 1990: 322). The view that inclusion represents an unquestionable moral imperative has been challenged by those who argue that the rights of the child to have maximum access to mainstream education need to be balanced by their right to an effective education, appropriate to their needs. Issues of safeguarding have also been raised. For example, Warnock (2005) specifically cites social rejection and bullying of children with SEN in mainstream schools in arguing for special school placement. Whereas questions about inclusion as social policy tend to have been debated in terms of values and rights issues, questions about the effectiveness of education tend to have been addressed by research and evaluation studies.

There appears to be some agreement at least on the importance of research in monitoring the outcomes of inclusion. Thomas *et al.* (1998: 5–6) pointed out that even if principles cannot be evaluated for their veracity, nor ethics for their truth, 'it is crucial that the principled policy decisions to provide inclusive education are rigorously monitored, especially as recent evidence concerning the academic, social and emotional benefits of integrative programmes [is] nowhere near as clear-cut as earlier evidence promised'. Martin (1995) described his worst fear about inclusion as being that the value of programmes would be judged primarily by teacher and administrator 'feelings', with, in some cases, parent feelings being taken into account. He argues for the importance of careful systematic measurement of child achievement, progress in areas of difficulty, self-concept and socialization, and criticizes the omission in many initiatives of any formal, comprehensive evaluation plan to measure outcomes.

Concerns about outcomes may be challenged by those who argue that inclusive education is of value in itself. However, there are other values which are espoused concurrently with a commitment to maximizing inclusion which may sometimes be in conflict. Hegarty (1987: 9) argued that 'What pupils who have difficulties need is education, not integration. Placing them in an ordinary school is not an end in itself but a means toward the end of securing them an appropriate education'. This would appear also to be the view of the British government: 'The needs of individual children are paramount. Where these cannot currently be met in mainstream schools, specialist provision should be available' (DfEE 1997: 44). So the right of children to an 'appropriate' education appears to be being prioritized over their right to be educated in an inclusive school context. In addition, 'Parents will continue to have the right to express a preference for a special school where they consider this appropriate to their child's needs' (1997: 45).

The Education Act 1996 explicitly required that these rights and others should be given consideration. Section 316 set out the conditions for educating children with SEN in mainstream, stating that this should not be incompatible with:

- parental wishes;

- the children receiving the special educational provision which their learning difficulties call for;

- the provision of efficient education for the children with whom the children with SEN will be educated;

- the efficient use of resources.

The Special Educational Needs and Disability Act strengthened the endorsement of inclusion by revising Section 316 of the Education Act 1996. The second bullet point was removed, so mainstream schools were no longer able to refuse a place to a child with SEN on the basis that the school cannot meet the pupil's needs. In addition, the section was rephrased positively:

> If a statement is maintained under section 324 for the child, he must be educated in a mainstream school unless it is incompatible with –
>
> (a) the wishes of his parent, or
>
> (b) the provision of efficient education for other children.

Although the Act does not specifically mention children's rights, the statutory guidance on inclusive schooling (DfES 2001a) makes specific reference to the United Nations Convention on the Rights of the child in advising that children who are capable of forming views have a right to express an opinion and have it taken into account in any matters affecting them. The SEN Code of Practice advocates that the views of the child (about their needs and how they would like them to be met) should be sought and taken into account as part of statutory assessment (DfES 2001a: 6).

Lindsay (2003) reviews critical perspectives and arguments based on rights and points out that inclusion is only one of several competing values that might be held. It would seem overly simplistic to suggest that there is a clear moral imperative for inclusion, irrespective of all of the other interlinked rights and values considerations. Liu (1995) illustrates ways in which deaf children's educational, cultural or social needs may not be met in inclusive educational settings where the support provided is not adequate to achieve subsequent self-sufficient participation in society. He argues that proponents of full inclusion often make the mistake of pursuing equal treatment at the expense of equal opportunity and urges that the issue should be approached from a cultural pluralism rather than a disabilities perspective. In this regard, he argues, research has an important contribution to make to the ongoing monitoring of socially defined outcomes and to the development of our understanding of the process variables which aid or impede the achievement of these outcomes.

Activity 4.2   Recognizing rights

Read the following case studies of Tom and Jack. We will be revisiting them several times during this chapter. For now we will focus on rights issues.

In each case list what you consider to be the rights of the child and the rights of their parents. Are there any other rights that need to be considered in these cases?

Case study: Tom

Tom is a 7-year-old who has Down's syndrome. His parents are committed to him receiving his education in his local mainstream school. He has attended his local nursery/infant school since the age of 3. He spent the first two years in the nursery class. This year and last year he has been in the Reception class.

Tom's self-help skills (dressing, feeding, toileting) are similar to most of the other children in the Reception class. However, his language skills are more typical of a 3–4-year-old in that he will talk in short (on average, four- to five-word) 'telegraphic' sentences which leave out connecting words – for example, 'Where Lego box?' He has no particular friends, but his classmates (especially Vikki, Emma and Sarah) will include him in their play. He clearly enjoys this interaction, although he is always given dependent and subservient roles – the baby, the patient. His teacher finds him a delightful, friendly child. He loves picture books and will join in appropriately with refrains – for example, 'I'll huff and I'll puff' – when familiar stories are read to him. He does not seem to be aware of the function of print in conveying the story. However, he can recognize his own name. He can also produce simple representational drawings; his 'people' have heads separate from their bodies, from which the arms and legs originate.

His school receives a visit one afternoon per week from a specialist teacher who advises his class teacher and sometimes works with Tom. He has a learning support assistant (LSA) with him each morning, as stipulated on his statement of special educational needs. He has a 20 per cent withdrawal timetable to work in a quiet room with his LSA, mainly on a programme of work devised by the speech and language therapist. He works in the classroom for 80 per cent of the week which includes the Literacy and Numeracy Hours. However, he has his own learning programmes in everything, except project work and PE/games. His teachers fear that he may not be able to make a successful transition to junior school next year. They feel that Tom is making some progress in the Reception class which would probably be disrupted if he were moved to the Year 2 class in preparation for transfer to junior school. They also fear that he may be bullied in junior school and feel that his needs might be best met through placement in a school for children with moderate learning difficulties.

Case study: Jack

Jack is a 10-year-old who has a congenital sensorineural hearing loss. His parents and older sister have profound hearing losses and British Sign Language is the family's first language. However, Jack has a significant level of residual hearing and, with radio aids and developing skill in lip reading, has been able to benefit from the oral/aural approach to education in the hearing impaired resource base attached to his present primary school.

Jack is very well motivated and hard working. Although his literacy skills are more typical of an 8-year-old and he is in the bottom literacy and numeracy group in his Year 6 class, he is continuing to make progress. He currently has two 1-hour individual teaching sessions per week in the resource base working on lip reading and other skills. He and the other resource base child in his class receive 3 hours per week of support teaching in class, focused on literacy. He is a skilful footballer and plays for the school team and a local junior team. His speech is intelligible to familiar adults and peers. His best friend is a hearing pupil with whom he also spends a lot of time out of school playing football and fishing.

His parents' wishes for his secondary education are that Jack should join his sister at a residential school for the deaf where he would be educated through a bilingual BSL/English approach. They think this will give him the best chance of getting qualifications and also fear that otherwise he will be unable to relate in adulthood to the deaf community. The social worker for the deaf, who always translates for Jack's parents when they come to school, strongly supports this view. She is concerned that disabling discourses in the mainstream school have already resulted in substantial alienation from deaf culture and feels that Jack would benefit from counselling to help him come to terms with his identity as a deaf adolescent.

Jack's teachers feel that he could continue his education in the oral/aural unit attached to the neighbouring secondary school, but they also feel that they should support Jack's parents. The resource base teacher knows that the school for the deaf gets very good results with the more able pupils, but is concerned that Jack may not be sufficiently able to really benefit.

Jack wants to go the local school, he does not want to leave his family and friends to go to boarding school. When the issue is discussed he becomes very upset and says he just wants to be normal.

Integration and inclusion: research evidence

Comparative studies

A major research effort, especially in the USA, was initially devoted to examining the efficacy of integrated versus segregated provision. This typically involved comparative studies in which two groups, one integrated and one segregated, were selected for study. Differences in outcomes such as educational attainment, adjustment and self-confidence were measured. Unfortunately these studies suffered from many methodological inadequacies. In particular, children in the 'integrated' and 'segregated' groups were often only matched for age, sex and IQ even though it is highly likely that there were differences between them on other relevant factors. For example, it might be expected that those children with moderate learning difficulties who were sent to special school were more likely to have behaviour problems and very low academic achievement than those who remained in mainstream. Yet these relevant factors were usually not considered.

Important ways in which integrated and segregated placements differed were also often disregarded (Madden and Slavin 1983). For example, the curriculum being followed in each setting was often substantially different, with greater emphasis being placed on academic subjects in mainstream settings and greater emphasis on self-help and social education objectives in special schools and classes. Consideration was rarely given either to the match between the different curricula followed in special and mainstream schools at that time, and the outcome measures on which pupils were compared. Differences between the qualifications and experience of the teachers in mainstream and special placements were rarely examined. Yet these differences were often considerable, particularly in the 1970s when children with severe learning difficulties were first brought into the education system, along with a substantial number of staff who were not qualified teachers but who had worked in the health department training centres previously attended by children with severe learning difficulties. Finally, the most serious methodological difficulty related to the widely differing definitions of 'integration' used in different studies and to sizeable differences in the amount and nature of integration between studies. It could occur only in non-academic classes or in core academic subjects such as reading and could last anywhere from a few minutes to the entire day. As can be seen from Table 4.1, 'segregated' pupils in some studies were integrated for more of the school day on average than 'integrated' pupils in other studies!

In the light of these methodological problems it is not surprising that the conclusions of the majority of reviews of comparative studies tend to be phrased very tentatively. Nonetheless the conclusions reported by studies spanning many years and using a range of different approaches are remarkably consistent. Madden and Slavin (1983) identified a small number of methodologically adequate studies in their review of the literature of the time. From these they concluded that there was no evidence that segregated placements promoted either academic or social progress over that made in mainstream placements. Indeed, there appeared to be some advantage to integrated placements, but only if a suitable individualized or differentiated educational programme was offered.

Hegarty (1993) summarized the OECD/CERI (Centre for Educational Research and Innovation) review of international research literature on integration efficacy studies across countries and different SEN. He reported that the results were generally inconclusive but argued that the absence of a clear-cut advantage supports integration as it is difficult to justify maintaining segregated provision if it is no better.

In addition to these traditional narrative-style literature reviews, a number of meta-analyses have been conducted. A meta-analysis aims to reduce the possibility of reviewer bias by using statistical summary techniques. Baker *et al.* (1994–5) summarize three such studies (see Table 4.2). Effect sizes were calculated to provide a measure of the strength of the findings which allows comparisons to be made across different studies. The positive effect sizes reported indicate a small to moderate benefit of inclusion on both academic and social outcomes.

Table 4.1   What counts as integration?

	School day spent with mainstream peers (%)	
	Integrated group	Segregated group
Kaufman *et al.* (1985)	72	31.7
Taylor *et al.* (1987)	30.5	–

Table 4.2   Effects of inclusive placement – summary of the findings of three meta-analyses

Author(s)	Carlberg and Kavale	Wang and Baker	Baker
Year published	1980	1985–6	1994
Time period	Pre-1980	1975–84	1983–92
Number of studies	50	11	13
Academic effect size	0.15	0.44	0.08
Social effect size	0.11	0.11	0.28

Source: Baker *et al.* (1994–5).

Lindsay (2007) reported a target journal review of published inclusion efficacy studies between 2000 and 2005. Eight journals in the field of SEN were selected and 1373 papers considered. Of these only 1 per cent were found to address efficacy issues, comparing the performance of children with SEN either in special and mainstream settings or in mainstream with typically developing schoolmates. As with the pre-2000 evidence, the weight of evidence from this review was only marginally positive overall. The review concludes that there is a need to research more thoroughly factors that influence optimal education for children with SEN.

A more qualitative approach was adopted by Ofsted (2006). Two-day visits were carried out by specialist inspectors to 74 schools across 17 local authorities and case studies were used to examine the progress of pupils with similar needs in different types of provision. While there was little difference found in overall outcomes across different types of provision, mainstream schools with addition-ally resourced provision tended to get the best outcomes – academic, social and personal. The most important factor associated with progress was found to be quality of provision, not type. Three dimensions of quality in particular were highlighted:

- *Ethos* – a focus on academic as well as personal and social development, use of pupil data to drive improvement and staff–pupil relationships of the highest order.

- *Provision of specialist staff* – who worked directly with pupils, providing a high level of skilled academic and social support, liaised closely with parents and other professionals and carefully monitored the work of teaching assistants.

- *Focus professional development for all staff* – comprising good, continuing, practical training for mainstream staff, including specific training from specialist teachers and outside professionals (where regular). Ready, informal access to specialist colleagues on an ongoing basis was also important.

The efficient education of mainstream pupils

In the UK the law requires that the inclusion of pupils with SEN also takes account of the need to provide efficient education for the mainstream pupils involved. Dyson *et al.* (2004) used information from the UK National Pupil Database to investigate whether there is any relationship between the proportion of pupils with SEN who are included in a school and the educational attainment of the mainstream pupils. Overall it was found that the broad-brush measures of attainment and inclusion used in this study were largely independent, while other factors such as socioeconomic status, ethnicity, gender and first language were found to be much more significantly associated with attainment. Findings were examined at both local authority and school level. At the local authority level, no evidence was found of any relationship between the proportion of pupils with SEN educated in mainstream schools and overall levels of attainment in the local authority when other relevant variables were taken into account. There was some tendency for schools that had higher proportions of pupils at School Action Plus or with statements to achieve lower results in Key Stage tests and public examinations. While a negative causal relationship between inclusion and educational attainment cannot be ruled out, this association could equally be accounted for by the fact that many of these schools were serving disadvantaged populations.

Kalambouka *et al.* (2005) conducted a systematic review of SEN inclusion evaluation studies carried out in other countries (mainly the USA) which reported findings on outcomes for pupils who did not have SEN. Of the 26 studies that met the quality criteria set for the review, the majority had been conducted with primary-aged pupils and focused on academic outcomes. Most findings (53 per cent) indicated a neutral impact of inclusion on academic and/or social outcomes for non-SEN pupils. A positive impact was suggested by 23 per cent of the findings, a negative impact by 15 per cent and a mixed impact by 10 per cent. Further analysis highlighted the following trends:

● Findings were more positive for academic than social outcomes.

● Slightly more mixed outcomes were obtained in secondary schools, where there were very few studies.

● Positive impacts were more often reported from primary contexts where the support offered to pupils with SEN was well managed.

Although the research reviewed was drawn from evaluation studies of inclusion, Kalambouka *et al.* (2005) describe them for the most part as involving 'minimum effort' inclusion, where no specific effort had been made to make the inclusion effective for the non-disabled children or to help them adapt to the presence of their SEN peers. They suggest that specific efforts of this kind might contribute further to positive outcomes.

Factors in successful inclusion

With the consistent conclusion that the quality of the inclusive programme seems crucial, the emphasis in research shifted to identifying the characteristics of effective inclusion. In recent years a range of different studies, conducted in different countries and using different methodologies, have reported conclusions which show substantial overlap (see Table 4.3).

Ainscow (1995) drew on findings from the UNESCO Teacher Education Project 'Special Needs in the Classroom' in identifying conditions necessary within a school if it is to restructure so as to provide effective education for all. McLaughlin (1995) identified five areas necessary for building a flexible and unified restructured school system from interviews with educational administrators and teachers in 67 school districts in the USA that were actively engaged in educational restructuring. McLaughlin (1995) highlighted in addition the importance of flexibility in teaching and student grouping and pointed out that nothing in the vision of a unified school system precludes students from having individualized instruction at some times.

Lipsky and Gartner (1996) analysed the results of the second annual study of inclusive education programmes in the USA which was carried out by the National Center on Educational Restructuring and Inclusion and described factors which appear to be necessary if inclusion is to be successful. Scruggs and Mastropieri (1994) carried out a fine-grained analysis of factors associated with

Table 4.3 Factors in successful inclusion

Identifying author(s)	Factors
Ainscow (1995: 152)	• Effective leadership, not only by the headteacher, but spread throughout the school • Involvement of staff, students and community in school policies and decisions • A commitment to collaborative planning • Coordination strategies • Attention to the potential benefits of inquiry and reflection • A policy for staff development
McLaughlin (1995: 206)	• Clear vision • A set of learner outcomes that can be used for school-wide accountability • Governance structures that promote collaboration and school level flexibility • A curriculum that promotes high expectations for all students • Professional development that builds collaborative work structures, joint problem solving and the sharing of expertise
Lipsky and Gartner (1996: 780)	• Visionary leadership • Collaboration: building planning teams and scheduling time for teachers to work together • Refocused use of assessment – developing methods that allow all students to express their learning • Support for staff and students • Funding models where the funds follow the students • Effective parental involvement • Curriculum adaptation and adopting of effective instructional practice
Scruggs and Mastropieri (1994: 794–803)	• Administrative support • Support from special education personnel • Accepting, positive classroom atmosphere • Appropriate curriculum • Effective general teaching skills • Peer assistance • Disability-specific teaching skills (e.g. for children with hearing difficulties)

mainstreaming success in primary science lessons for students with hearing, visual and physical difficulties. Over a school year evidence was gathered from classroom observation, videotaped records, student and teacher products, curriculum materials and interviews with students, teachers and administrators.

Ofsted (2006) have reported findings which suggest that many of these factors may be important in achieving adequate progress whether pupils with SEN are educated in mainstream or special schools. Key factors for good progress identified were:

- the involvement of a specialist teacher;
- good assessment;
- work tailored to challenge pupils sufficiently;
- commitment from school leaders to ensure good progress for all pupils.

Provision of additional resources to pupils, including learning support assistant time, did not of itself ensure good-quality intervention or adequate progress.

In attempting to identify models and activities associated with inclusive practice and successful attainment, Dyson *et al.* (2004) conducted case studies of 16 schools, all with high proportions of pupils who had SEN, half primary and half secondary, two-thirds of which were high-achieving and one-third low-achieving. Selection of case study schools was made from national data sets and based solely on their relatively high proportions of pupils with SEN. This contrasts with many published case studies in this area which focus on schools identified because of their espousal of inclusive principles.

Clear-cut conclusions proved elusive. Highly inclusive schools, whether higher- or lower-attaining, tend to manage inclusion in similar ways. The proportion of time spent by pupils with SEN in mainstream classes varied from school to school and did not emerge as an important consideration. 'Mainstream' class characteristics also varied, for example in relation to use of 'setting' in secondary or mixed age classes in primary. Classroom observations failed to uncover any significant differences between high- and low-attaining schools in terms of resources, teaching techniques or organization, apart from finding that a higher proportion of classrooms in the high-attaining schools had access to teaching assistants.

While the features of the inclusion models employed seemed to be fairly similar, whether the school was high- or low-attaining, differences were noted in the flexibility with which those features were included in programmes for particular individuals. Flexibility of grouping, customizing of provision to individual circumstances (notably through teaching assistant deployment) and careful individual monitoring, alongside population-wide strategies for raising attainment, were all mentioned. It was concluded that similar activities may be implemented with less sophistication and flexibility in some lower-performing schools. It seemed that high-attaining inclusive schools were characterized by the appropriateness of the approaches used with particular pupils at particular times, rather than by the type of approaches used as such. This is of particular interest as a number of evaluation studies have questioned the extent to which provision intended to be inclusive really is personalized to the needs of individual learners.

Inclusion and individual needs?

Baker and Zigmond (1995) provided case study descriptions of full-time inclusion models for primary-aged children with specific learning difficulties in five states in the USA. A two-day site visit was made to each centre. Classroom observations were carried out and semi-structured interviews conducted with the children, their parents, class teachers, special needs support teachers, heads of special needs and headteachers. It was concluded that students with SEN were receiving a very good general education from enthusiastic class teachers. Special needs teachers were playing roles as coordinator, co-planner and co-teacher and were making it possible for class teachers to feel adequately confident about working with students who have SEN, and for these students to feel adequately confident in their mainstream classes. Class teachers showed a willingness to make changes to help students with SEN, although these consisted of changing an approach for the whole class with the needs of the student with SEN in mind. Very few instances were recorded where adaptations were directed at a single student, and when these did occur they tended to consist of more explicit instructions repeated specifically to the student. Indeed, some teachers expressed the belief that students with SEN had to learn to cope with the world and therefore required them to take the same tests and complete the same assignments as the mainstream students, proudly asserting that they did not individualize or differentiate their work in any way.

Similar conclusions were reached by Pijl (1995) who carried out a study that compared the education of students in a highly segregated system (Netherlands) with that in four other countries (Denmark, England, Sweden and the USA). Data was collected from existing written accounts about the availability and use of resources, and interviews were conducted with experts from the first three more inclusive countries listed. From these investigations Pijl offered the tentative conclusion that teachers working in inclusive school systems did not differentiate more than Dutch teachers working in a largely segregated system.

However, not all studies have reached similar conclusions. In their comparison of eight different model inclusion programmes, Manset and Semmel (1997) report that the programmes that were most effective in promoting the educational progress of pupils with SEN did incorporate curricular modifications, highly structured teaching (particularly of basic skills) and frequent testing. They also provided opportunities to individualize teaching and focus intensively on particular targets through reducing class size, providing additional staff in the classroom or incorporating peer tutoring. It does seem that such strategies are generally necessary, if not always sufficient, to deliver individualization. Moni *et al.* (2007) researched the implementation of differentiated instruction in writing across Years 5–9 and found that, in the absence of well-trained learning support assistants, differentiated instruction was only very rarely observed in classrooms, as were use of group activities or peer support. The effective use of additional adults in the classroom, cooperative group work and peer support are key strategies for promoting inclusion and achievement at classroom level and will be considered in more detail in the next section in addition to whole-school transformation initiatives.

The other conclusion that can be drawn from this section is about the importance of evaluating outcomes. This will ascertain the appropriateness of particular approaches for individual pupils and will allow changes to be made where necessary. The importance of evaluating outcomes has achieved wider recognition as a result of the prominence given in the *Every Child Matters* framework to accountability for the quality of services and their success in achieving outcomes for children. Ainscow (2007) advocates the importance of outcome data in informing change. While there are dangers of focusing on what can easily be measured, rather than what is more broadly valued, it is suggested that careful selection of the evidence to be collected should allow the potential of outcome data as a lever for change to be harnessed. In describing the development with local authorities of an inclusion standard, an instrument for evaluating schools' progress towards becoming more inclusive, Ainscow (2007) places an exclusive focus on pupil outcomes, rather than other variables such as leadership quality or opportunities for participation. While details vary across local authorities, pupil outcomes are commonly assessed in three areas:

- presence, concerned with where pupils are educated, and how reliably and punctually they attend;

- participation, which refers to the quality of their experiences and should therefore incorporate pupil views, for example on the extent to which they feel they belong;

- achievement, which is about the outcomes of learning across the whole curriculum, both inside and outside the classroom.

Particular emphasis is placed on careful monitoring groups of learners who may be at risk of marginalization, exclusion or underachievement, and on taking action as necessary to improve their presence, participation and achievement.

Activity 4.3   Evaluating outcomes: presence, participation and achievement

Refer back to the case studies of Tom and Jack presented in Activity 4.2 and make an evaluation of the success of their current inclusion in the areas of presence, participation and achievement. Is there any further information you would like to have in order to inform your evaluation?

Identify and debate with a partner the priority targets for each child in their current placement and suggest how their achievement could be monitored and evaluated.

Promoting inclusion in a multiethnic society

Promoting a whole-school inclusive ethos

The statutory guidance, *Inclusive Schooling: Children with Special Educational Needs* (DfES 2001b: 2), charges schools with 'actively seeking to remove barriers to learning and participation that can hinder or exclude pupils with special educational needs', through engendering a sense of community and belonging and developing an inclusive ethos. One approach designed to support these endeavours is the *Index for Inclusion* (Booth *et al.* 2000; Booth and Ainscow, 2002). It provides materials designed to be used by schools in their development planning and outlines a process which can involve school staff, governors, pupils, parents and other community members in creating inclusive cultures, producing inclusive policies and evolving inclusive practices in their school. These are designed to minimize barriers to learning and participation related either to SEN or other special needs, and the range of prompt questions contained in the *Index* stimulates reflection across these diverse areas, as the following extract from the *Index* illustrates:

INDICATOR A.1 .1 *Everyone is made to feel welcome*

(i)   Is the first contact that people have with the school friendly and welcoming?

(ii) Is the school welcoming to all students, including students with impairments, Travellers and asylum seekers?

(iii) Is the school welcoming to all parents/carers and other members of its local communities?

(iv) Is information about the school accessible to all, irrespective of home language or impairment, for example, translated, Brailled, taped, or in large print, when necessary?

(v)   Are sign language and other first language interpreters available when necessary?

(vi) Is it clear from the school brochure and information given to job applicants that responding to the full diversity of students and their backgrounds is part of school routine?

(vii) Does the entrance hall reflect all members of the school's communities?

(viii)Does the school celebrate local cultures and communities in signs and displays?

(Booth and Ainscow 2002: 42)

The *Index* has generally been positively received both in the UK and abroad (Engelbrecht *et al.* 2006). Norwich *et al.* (2001) reported that local authority respondents to a national survey were more positive than critical of it as a means of encouraging school development. Vaughan (2002) supported this view, but pointed out that while schools found it could be a very powerful development process, they also highlighted the difficulties of implementing it alongside the many other demands they faced. The materials have also been used in more focused projects within schools, for example in sampling pupil, parent/carer and school staff views in a local authority initiative to help secondary schools be more inclusive of their Year 7 pupils with SEN (Hodson *et al.* 2005). However, in reviewing the uptake and implementation of the *Index*, Rustemier and Booth (2005) suggested that this may have been limited because the values explicitly promoted through the *Index* conflict in some ways with the government's predominant approach.

One area where there has been higher take-up than expected is in special schools. Booth and Ainscow (2002) report that although the *Index* was not initially intended for use by special schools, it had been found useful. A set of special school case studies presented by Tutt (2007) illustrate that changing populations have meant that, like mainstream schools, most special schools have had to adapt in recent years to be able to meet a range of needs not previously encountered. Ofsted (2004) reported a 10 per cent increase since 2001 in the number of pupils placed in independent special schools by local authorities as a consequence of the difficulties that mainstream schools, and some special schools, had in meeting severe or complex needs. It is not only mainstream schools that need to undertake self-review and to develop inclusive practice in relation to the diversity of local cultures and communities.

Promoting an inclusive ethos in the classroom

Cross and Walker-Knight (1997) argue that successful inclusion involves restructuring classrooms to meet all children's individual needs: 'inclusive settings must emphasise building a community in which everyone belongs and is accepted and supported by his or her peers and other members of that community while his or her educational needs are being met' (1997: 269–70). To date there has been comparatively little investigation of the psychological mechanisms under-pinning the formation of accepting and supportive attitudes in inclusive settings. Frederickson and Furnham (2004) drew on social exchange theory in accounting for relationships between children's behavioural characteristics and their peer group acceptance or rejection. In general, children will interact with others where the benefits of interaction (e.g. in terms of interest, enjoyment, access to resources, achievement of success, feeling good about oneself, receiving praise from adults) outweigh the costs (e.g. in terms of compromise, sharing own resources, being the target of undesirable behaviour, risk of peer rejection or exclusion). Different children have different 'comparison levels' or cost–benefit ratios for deciding whether to interact with a specific classmate. This may depend both on expectations based on past experience and on factors such as who is available and whether they are likely to agree to play if asked.

What Frederickson and Furnham (2004) found was that typically developing 9–12-year-old children were judged very much as would be predicted by the theory. Those who were well accepted by peers were rated as high on beneficial behaviours such as cooperation and leadership and low on costly behaviours such as disruption and excessive help seeking. Those rejected as play or work partners showed the opposite patterns of behaviour. However, when judgements were made about classmates with moderate learning difficulties who were receiving part-time withdrawal support a different, reduced, pattern of associations was apparent involving lower expectations of benefits and higher toleration of costs. The conclusion that, at least in some contexts, children set different, more lenient, standards of behaviour for classmates with SEN has been supported by other studies (Nabuzoka and Smith 1993; Roberts and Zubrick 1992).

Children have also been found to treat classmates with SEN more generously when dividing up rewards for work done. Frederickson and Simmonds (2008) gave 10–11-year-olds a task to finish which they were told had been started by one of their classmates, who had done about a third of it. When the classmate was someone they had previously rated as a neutrally regarded acquaintance, children tended to divide stickers with them in proportion to how much of the task each had completed, taking two-thirds themselves and giving their classmate one-third. In contrast, when they were told that the classmate was someone they had identified as a best friend they tended to divide the stickers equally, even though they had 'earned' more. The same tendency to divide the stickers equally was also shown when the classmate was a child with SEN (autistic spectrum disorder, included full-time with in-class support), even though none of the children with SEN had been identified as a best friend of the children involved.

Case studies of relationships between children with SEN and their typically developing classmates also support the view that in many cases these are qualitatively different from relationships between typically developing age-mates. For example, '*Although there is undeniable warmth between the children, most of the comments and non-verbal interactions reflect a helper–helpee relationship, not a reciprocal friendship*' (Van der Klift and Kunc 2002: 22) and 'the *interactions, although tending to be highly positive, had the feel of a parental type of role on the part of the children without disabilities*' (Evans *et al.* 1998: 134). Grenot-Scheyer *et al.* (1998) found that when typically developing early adolescents talked about their friendships generally, loyalty and intimacy were identified as the defining characteristics. However, when they talked about their friendships with classmates who had significant SEN, a caregiving role was usually prominent. Grenot-Scheyer *et al.* (1998) challenge the view that friendships must involve full reciprocity and mutuality. They argue for a broader conceptualization of the reciprocal benefits of friendship. Social exchange theory would suggest that where the perceived benefits of a relationship outweigh the costs for both parties there will be positive motivation to interact, even where the benefits are different for each.

From their observational and interview study of the inclusion of early adolescents with severe learning difficulties Meyer *et al.* (1998) identified six 'frames of friendship':

- *Ghosts and guests*. The pupil with SEN seems either to be 'invisible' or is clearly viewed as an 'outsider'. Language used may draw distinctions between 'them' and 'us' and reflect adages such as 'it's not nice to stare'.

- *The inclusion kid/different friend*. This frame is characterized by different, generally more benign, standards of behaviour and consequences. While the language used tends to highlight difference, even when this is negative (e.g. 'he's weird'), there is agreement that only positive responses are acceptable. So teenagers who tease others in their social circle will draw a line and indicate that it is not nice to tease people with disabilities. Affectionate social interactions, resembling those that might be engaged in with a small child, are common.

- *I'll help*. Language accompanying a range of helping behaviour was often observed where children adopted the manner and voice of a teacher or adult helper.

- *Just another kid/student*. Here expectations were the same (or parallel, with modifications) as for other pupils. Being referred to as 'just another kid' tended to lead to neutrally regarded acquaintance status.

- *Regular friend*. Not a 'best friend', but in the circle of friends just outside that.

- *Best friend*. Inner circle, seen outside as well as inside school. Common attribute: 'I can trust her/him with anything.'

All the constituency groups with whom these frames were discussed – parents, teachers, classmates, university researchers, community activists – saw the 'regular friend' and 'best friend' frames in a universally positive light, whereas the 'ghost/guest' frame was regarded negatively. There were different perspectives on the 'I'll help' frame. Those more distant from everyday life in the classroom tended to view it more negatively. However, it was valued by parents and teachers and was the most common reason given by classmates as to why they named a pupil with severe learning difficulties as a friend. The 'inclusion kid/different friend' was regarded predominately positively by parents and teachers, but also by others when they supported a need for protection over and above that typical for a person's age. 'Just another kid/student' was another category that elicited mixed reactions. This was generally seen as an acceptable status to have with some peers, provided that others showed a more positive and proactive approach (otherwise 'ghost/guest' status became a risk). However, some constituent group members viewed this frame negatively where they felt that being treated differently was needed as an accommodation for the pupil's disability.

Activity 4.4   Frames of friendship

Refer back to the case studies of Tom and Jack presented in Activity 4.2 and identify which of the frames of friendship described by Meyer *et al.* (1998) you think apply to these two children in their current schools.

Would you want to modify the frames you have selected in any way so they better fit these particular cases?

As you read the rest of this section, imagine that it has been decided that Tom will go to the junior school and Jack to the local secondary school next year. Imagine also that you are responsible for planning their induction to their new school. Outline what you would do, and why.

Research informed by attribution theory has shown that how children respond to classmates regarded as 'different' is quite complex. Juvonen and Weiner (1993) summarize a series of studies using the model shown in Figure 4.3. Primary-aged children identified a range of characteristics as 'deviant' (different and undesirable). While some (aggression, anti-social behaviour, obesity) led to rejection, others (shyness, physical disabilities) elicited a more supportive response. What seemed to be crucial was whether the child was regarded as responsible for the characteristic – whether it was considered to be their fault. Typically primary-aged children considered obesity to be a characteristic within their classmates' control, so they judged them responsible and were more likely to report anger and less likely to report sympathy towards them. Obese children

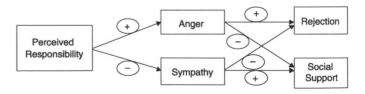

Figure 4.3   The relationships between perceived responsibility, emotions and social responses toward classmate 'deviant' behaviour
Source: Adapted from Juvonen and Weiner (1993).

were more likely to be rejected and less likely to receive social support, a combination particularly likely to put them at risk of bullying. In contrast, children with physical disabilities were typically not considered responsible for their difficulties and so were more likely to elicit sympathy and social support.

This research has important implications for the promotion of inclusion and, in particular, for children with SEN who are less obviously 'disabled'. Where individual children experience personal costs at the hands of others, attributional processes will be triggered. When a goalkeeper fails to move quickly enough to save a goal, when a tactless comment is made about a new hairstyle, when a child pushes their way to the front of the queue, how others respond will depend on much control they perceive the offender to have over the offending behaviour. If these behaviours are attributed to being lazy, unkind and selfish, anger is likely to be elicited and rejection to result. On the other hand, if classmates have been helped to develop an understanding of the problems typically experienced by children with cerebral palsy, Asperger's syndrome and attention deficit hyperactivity disorder and have been told how they can support learning and development, they are less likely to blame the child with SEN.

Psychological process models, such as the attributional model shown in Figure 4.3, help to explain disparaties in the literature where most studies report that children with a statement of SEN are less socially accepted than typically developing classmates (Frederickson and Furnham 2004; Gresham and MacMillan, 1997b), but some report equivalent acceptance, particularly so with pupils who have more severe difficulties (Frederickson *et al.* 2007; Hunt *et al.* 1996). This is of particular interest where studies reporting better social acceptance for pupils with SEN also report particular efforts to influence peer group attitudes. For example, Hunt *et al.* (1996) identified and tested a three-component programme for promoting the social inclusion in primary schools of pupils with multiple difficulties: informing classmates about special needs pupils, using multiple media to stimulate interaction, and supporting social interactions through a range of strategies such as setting up joint activities or buddy systems. Interviews with classmates and teachers provided evidence of the effectiveness of this intervention in increasing positive interaction between the children with SEN and their peers.

The success of a special-school-based inclusion team was evaluated by Frederickson *et al.* (2007). Fourteen pupils (12 of whom had statements for autistic spectrum disorder) who had been supported by the inclusion team in transferring from a full-time placement in the special school to a full-time placement in a mainstream school local to their home were followed up. In the work of the inclusion team good planning and preparation were stressed, with a phased individual inclusion programme being developed according to each child's needs (details of the process and supporting resources are available in 'Practical Pathways to Inclusion', a package of eight booklets and a CD-ROM produced by Kent County Council in 2003). Social and affective aspects were carefully considered throughout, and it was recognized that peer acceptance was an essential feature of an inclusive school. As a result a peer group package was developed for use with mainstream classes prior to and during the early stages of introduction of pupils from the special school. The package included workshop activities led by an inclusion team member, and the class teacher aimed at peer preparation, the provision of information about similarities and differences, and the promotion of supportive pupil interaction. Evaluation of the social and affective outcomes of the programme found that these 8–11-year-old pupils with SEN did not differ from typically developing classmates in peer-assessed social acceptance or self-reported sense of belonging at school.

There is also good evidence of the value of peer preparation for children in the early years. Keller and Sterling-Honig (1993) developed an educational programme for 4–5-year-olds that comprised sessions using stories, videos and doll play on topics such as what it is like to be handicapped, making friends and helping each other. Children who had experienced the programme subsequently showed much higher levels of interaction (seven times higher than children who had not experienced the programme) with preschoolers with SEN who were introduced to their classes. This is an important finding as it is sometimes wrongly assumed that young children either do not notice such differences or are naturally accepting of them.

One concern sometimes raised about peer preparation programmes is that they may have the effect of 'labelling' the child with SEN and that this will have negative repercussions for them. However, this view is not supported by research findings from well-controlled studies which have consistently shown that a label does not have an influence on peer group attitudes over and above the child's behaviour which has a strong influence on attitudes (Law *et al.* 2007). Rather than leave classmates to make their own (often rather negative) attributions for undesirable behaviour, more positive outcomes are likely to result if adults provide advance information, ongoing explanations and appropriately structured and supported opportunities for contact. While peer preparation appears to be helpful in establishing positive social relationships, research has also identified a number of peer-based strategies which can maintain and enhance these while providing ongoing support in the classroom. These are described in the next section.

Evidence-based support strategies in the classroom

Cooperative learning models are among the best-documented approaches for promoting successful inclusion in classrooms where there is substantial diversity in the student group (Nind *et al.* 2004). Cross and Walker-Knight (1997) review studies which have focused on inclusive provision for students who have SEN and describe five attributes common to all cooperative learning approaches:

1   *Common task or learning activity suitable for group work*. The teacher structures a task or activity to accomplish as a group. All members of the group are aware of the task.

2   *Small-group learning*. Small groups (from two to six students), usually heterogeneous, are organized by the teacher.

3   *Cooperative behaviour*. Teachers directly teach students the skills they need to work and learn together.

4   *Positive interdependence*. Teachers structure tasks in such a way that students perceive that they can only attain their goal by working together. Often a team-scoring method is utilized.

5   *Individual responsibility and accountability*. Students are held individually responsible for the learning that takes place in the group.

It is clear from this outline that the teacher has a central role in directing the approach. It is suggested that the teacher should intervene both organizationally, in composing the groups to ensure diversity, and by providing additional instruction – for example, in skills necessary for effective group work, such as giving and receiving criticism, encouraging participation and seeking suggestions/assistance.

Peer tutoring and support strategies place greater emphasis on active involvement and initiation by students. These have been found to be effective in promoting inclusion both with pupils whose primary needs are in cognition and learning (Stenhoff and Lignugaris-Kraft 2007) and with those for whom behavioural, emotional and social difficulties are primary (Spencer 2006). The essential feature of these approaches is that students are paired up, with one acting as tutor and one as tutee. Improvements have been reported in the self-esteem and academic achievement of both tutee and tutor and in their social interactions with others. The consistent finding that tutors also benefit (Cross and Walker-Knight 1997) is important in that concerns may otherwise be expressed by parents of tutors, or by teachers, that the tutors are being 'used' to the detriment of their own learning (Mallon 2000).

In some cases cross-age pairings are established where older students, sometimes students with SEN, tutor younger students. More commonly, in-class pairings are established. In some cases classwide peer tutoring (CWPT) is routinely used to reinforce learning with members of the dyad taking it in turn to play the role of tutor, and in the process gaining points for the classroom team to which each pair is assigned (Maheady *et al.* 2006). This can provide a helpful framework within which particular arrangements for individual pupils involve only small modifications to existing practice for teacher and pupils. The approach has been used with English language learners as well as children with SEN. It has also been used to assist pupils experiencing multiple barriers to learning, alongside their typically developing peers. Saenz *et al.* (2005) worked on reading skills development with 12 classes of 8–11-year-olds containing Spanish-speaking English language learners in the USA. The classes contained pupils with learning difficulties, together with their low-, average- and high-achieving peers. Six of the 12 classes were selected at random to receive CWPT three times a week for 15 weeks. The intervention classes made significantly more progress than those that did not receive the intervention, and the effects were similar across the four attainment groups of pupils.

The primary purpose of CWPT is to increase the time spent by all pupils actively engaged in academic tasks. It also seeks to provide pacing, feedback, immediate error correction and high mastery levels. It has most often been used with literacy learning, but has increasingly been used in a range of other curriculum areas. The guidelines shown in Figure 4.4 involve a focus on reading accuracy and fluency, while the example worksheet shown in Figure 4.5 focuses on comprehension.

Peer tutoring directions for the teacher

1 Group students into pairs. Some researchers suggest ranking students by reading levels from 1 to 20, then matching the 1st reader with the 11th reader, the 2nd with the 12th, the 3rd with the 13th, and so on. This results in each pair having a stronger and less strong reader. You may want to select special tutoring partners for your students with SEN.

2 Teach students how to be both a tutor and a tutee, and provide role-play practice and feedback.

3 Provide special instruction scripts and practice on what you want the tutors to do, including how they should correct errors during oral reading, and how they should record performance and points.

4 Review classroom rules for tutoring.

5 Assign the groups to one of two teams for which they will earn points throughout the tutoring process.

6 Use a timer to tell students to start and stop reading. The stronger reader goes first.

7 Award points for appropriate tutoring and classroom behaviour.

8 At the end of the week, have the students report the number of points earned to determine which team is the winner.

9 Publicly praise both teams for their respective positive performances.

10 At the beginning of the next week, reassign groups to teams.

Peer tutoring directions for the learner

For all learners

1 Pick up your tutoring materials, and go to your tutoring place in the classroom.

2 Follow all tutoring rules, including using a quiet voice and being polite with your partner.

3 Find the place where you left off, and begin reading when the teacher starts the timer.

For the tutee

1 Read aloud continuously for (time to be designated, e.g. 5–10) minutes from the assigned text to your tutor.

2 Read as much as you can without making mistakes.

3 Once you have read for (time to be designated) minutes, switch roles with the tutor.

For the tutor

1 Remember to follow all of the rules for being a good tutor.

2 While the tutee is reading, watch for words missed.

3 If the sentence was read correctly, award (number to be designated) points.

4 If the tutee makes a mistake, point out the word, say it correctly, and have the tutee repeat the word and reread the sentence.

5 Record the reading performance and the appropriate number of points.

6 Once the tutee has read for (time to be designated) minutes, switch roles.

Figure 4.4 Classwide peer tutoring example: reading
Source: Mastropieri *et al.* (1999).

Retell

1. What did you learn first?
2. What did you learn next?

Paragraph Shrinking

1. Name the who or what.
2. Tell the most important thing about the who or what.
3. Say the main idea in 10 words or less.

Prediction Relay ———————————

Predict _____ What do you predict will happen next?

Read _____ Read half a page.

Check _____ Did the prediction come true?

Summarize ___ Name the who or what.

_____ Tell the most important thing about the who or what.

_____ Say the main idea in 10 words or less.

Figure 4.5 CWPT reading comprehension: student prompt card
Source: Mathes *et al.* (1994).

In-class support: extra adults in the classroom

Between 1997 and 2003 there was a 99 per cent increase in teaching assistants (TAs) in schools in England (Blatchford *et al.* 2007). While recognizing that part of this increase was attributable to planned support for the National Strategies and workforce development issues in schools, Howes *et al.* (2003) considered that the rise in mainstream schools mirrored the growing commitment to inclusion and mainly comprised TAs providing support to pupils with SEN. All the available evidence suggests that teachers have very positive perceptions of the support they receive (Giangreco and Broer 2005; Howes *et al.* 2003). Information from inspections of primary schools indicated that the quality of teaching in lessons where TAs were present was judged to be higher (Ofsted 2002c), and that this was most apparent when the TA and teacher worked in close partnership or when the TA was following a tightly prescribed intervention or catch-up programme.

Nonetheless a range of concerns have been raised about the increasing use of TAs to support inclusion in mainstream classrooms of pupils with SEN (see Figure 4.6). In both the USA and the UK the primary response to such concerns has centred on the provision of improved training and supervision. However, attention to systemic issues has also been given in guidance provided to schools. For example, the Secondary National Strategy Guidance to SENCOs and senior leadership teams on ensuring the progress of pupils with SEN emphasizes joint planning between teacher and TA and encourages the assignment of TAs to particular subject departments to facilitate this.

- The least qualified personnel are assigned to provide the bulk of instruction and support to students with the most challenging learning characteristics.

- It is difficult to hire and retain qualified paraprofessionals because they are paid low wages, sometimes without benefits, and report receiving insufficient respect.

- The scope and nature of paraprofessional work are often compromised by inadequate role clarification, orientation, training and supervision.

- Excessive one-to-one paraprofessional support has been associated with inadvertent detrimental effects (e.g. unnecessary dependence, stigmatization, interference with peer interactions, interference with teacher involvement, less competent instruction).

- Virtually no student outcome data exist suggesting that students with disabilities do as well or better in school given paraprofessional supports.

Figure 4.6   Concerns associated with relying on TAs to ensure appropriate education for students with disabilities
Source: Giangreco and Broer (2005).

The final bullet point in Figure 4.6 points to the lack of outcome data, but does not specify the type of outcome being considered. If, however, outcomes in the literature are examined using the framework proposed by Ainscow (2007), comprising presence, participation and achievement, some helpful conclusions can be drawn.

To begin with *presence*, the significant role of TAs in the process of supporting pupils who would otherwise have been excluded or placed in the segregated sector is most clearly seen in the case of pupils with behavioural emotional and social difficulties. From a detailed study of ways in which the role of the TA in supporting these pupils had been developed in primary schools in one English local authority, Groom and Rose (2005) report a strong perception from line managers of TAs in schools that their work made a key contribution to successful inclusion. A range of ways in which TAs supported pupils with BESD were identified: supervising individuals or small groups in class, offering pastoral support to individual pupils, teaching individuals in a withdrawal situation, planning activities for small groups, providing structured aspects of programmes such as Circle Time or Emotional Literacy, running groups aimed specifically at raising self-esteem or enhancing social skills, supporting behaviour management plans, observing and recording behaviour to identify and monitor progress towards targets, liaising with parents and liasing with other staff. In addition, in whole-class situations where pupils with BESD were included they played a broader role in facilitating a calm and purposeful atmosphere: keeping pupils on task, helping pupils with their work, helping pupils to resolve conflicts and disputes.

From a systematic review of the literature, Howes *et al.* (2003) conclude that the strongest evidence of the impact of TA support is on pupil *participation*. This conclusion applied across studies looking at SEN inclusion in a range of different contexts. The results of the review highlighted a link between effectiveness of TA support in promoting inclusion and two other factors: the extent to which TAs were valued, respected and well-integrated members of an educational team and the extent to which they avoided an 'isolated' style of working with the pupil with SEN and instead supported interactions between them, the teacher and other pupils. These conclusions have since been supported by Blatchford *et al.* (2007) who found that the presence of a TA in the classroom resulted in more individualized attention, active and sustained interaction and pupil on-task behaviour.

Howes *et al.* (2003) and Blatchford *et al.* (2007) both reported that the presence of TAs did not have any measurable effect on pupil *attainment* in the classes where they were deployed. Blatchford *et al.* (2007) note that the TAs tended to work directly with only a small percentage of the pupils in the class, in particular those with SEN, low attainment or difficult behaviour. They acknowledge, therefore, that examining outcomes for these pupils, rather than for the whole class, might represent a more appropriate test of the impact of TAs on attainment. However, Muijs and Reynolds (2003) looked at the effect of support in maths from specially trained TAs on the achievement of the low-achieving pupils in Years 1 and 2 who had received support. They matched 180 pupils in the project schools with 180 pupils in comparison schools on variables, including free meal eligibility, prior achievement, special needs, ethnicity and gender, and found no difference in progress in mathematics between the two groups.

A further possibility raised by Blatchford *et al.* (2007) is the high degree of variability in TA deployment and effectiveness that was apparent from their case study data. The impact that deployment of additional adults in the classroom can have is well illustrated by a study carried out by Thomas (1992) which used video recordings to analyse the engagement in learning activities of a class of 10–11-year-old pupils. Learning engaged time, or 'time on task', is consistently found to be significantly related to pupil achievement. Table 4.4 shows the percentage engagement achieved under three different conditions, the last of which involves a version of 'room management'. Room management is an approach which gives each adult in the classroom a clearly defined role. In this study two such roles were specified in detail: the *individual helper* who concentrates on working with an individual on a teaching activity for 5–15 minutes, allowing 4–12 individual teaching sessions to be provided in an hour; and the *activity*

Table 4.4 A comparison of pupil engagement with different models of in-class support

Condition	Mean level of engagement (%)	Standard deviation
A. The classroom functions normally with one teacher without additional adults	57.8	27.1
B. The same classroom functions with one teacher, a learning support assistant and two parents	69.1	25.3
C. The same classroom functions with the same adults as in B but using room management	90.2	11.0

Source: Thomas (1992).

manager who concentrates on the rest of the class, who are normally arranged in groups of between four and eight pupils. The activity manager moves around, keeping the groups focused on their assigned learning activities.

In the Thomas (1992) study two parents and a TA worked as activity managers with particular groups of pupils while the teacher operated as an individual helper. In a given session therefore the teacher was not required to simultaneously manage the class and individualize the curriculum for particular pupils. Essentially the results of the study suggested that having extra adults present was better than not having them present, but that their effectiveness could be significantly enhanced by clearly defining their roles. The other issue that is worth noting from this study is that individual work with pupils was undertaken by the teacher. This relates to the variability identified by Blatchford *et al.* (2007) in TA effectiveness, particularly as TAs were found in a majority of cases to be taking a predominant role in actually teaching the pupils.

The fact that it is mostly the neediest pupils who spend time interacting with TAs raises serious questions. There is something paradoxical about the least-qualified staff in schools being left to teach the most educationally needy pupils, and there is concern over whether this provides the most effective support for the children in most need. Teachers, however, raised very few objections about delegating teaching of particular groups or individuals to their TAs. Rather, they welcome the opportunity that it gives them to deal with the remainder of the class (Blatchford *et al.* 2007: 20).

Giangreco and Broer (2005) likewise found that a majority of TAs reported delivering the primary teaching input for pupils with SEN in mainstream classes and frequently making curriculum and teaching decisions without teacher oversight or input. They suggested that schools should consider alternatives to this extensive reliance on TAs, including cost-neutral exchange of some TA posts for a smaller number of specialist teacher posts and developing peer support strategies.

Conclusions

Lipsky and Gartner (1996) argue that integration cannot be achieved by 'allowing' people of colour (for example) into existing white society, but only by transforming society so that diversity is genuinely valued and normal expectations are not defined by a single group. Inclusive education goes beyond mainstreaming which is founded on the assumption of two separate school systems – a general system and a special system. Also, a restructured inclusive system goes beyond a readiness model which requires that students with SEN prove their readiness to be in an integrated setting, rather than regarding integrated settings as the norm.

Whereas the focus of mainstreaming efforts has been individual students with SEN, the focus in inclusive schooling has been the creation of a school environment supportive of all students and including those at risk of school failure for a variety of reasons: SEN, poverty, homelessness, seasonal migration patterns or sociocultural and linguistic differences (Ball and Harry 1993). Unlike mainstreaming, inclusion is considered not a special education programme, but an outcome of school reform.

Where inclusion is embraced, educational provision carefully structured to meet a diversity of needs, and flexible, personalized programmes delivered, research into social and academic outcomes for pupils with SEN has identified net benefits. Research data have played an important role in identifying ways in which inclusion and learning can be promoted. The importance of evaluation data has increasingly been recognized for monitoring individual students' progress on an ongoing basis in order to ensure that they receive their full rights – an education that is both inclusive and effective.

Activity 4.5   Placement and provision

Refer back to the case studies of Tom and Jack presented in Activity 4.2. Draw up a balance sheet for the placement decision facing each child's parents:

	Mainstream school	*Special school*
Potential advantages		
Potential barriers to learning and participation		
Ways of minimizing the barriers and realizing the advantages		

Can you 'think out of the box' presented above? Are there some novel arrangements of educational support and resources that might present some new possibilities for Tom and Jack?

5

Special educational needs: developmental frameworks

Objectives

When you have studied this chapter you should be able to:

- describe the key dimensions of human development and explain the disadvantages of categorizing SEN solely in terms of these dimensions;
- begin to employ the interactive factors framework to outline the basis of SEN for an individual child;
- recognize the distinctive roles of genetic, biological, cognitive and environmental factors as influences on the development of SEN;
- identify pathways of development for young people with SEN through childhood and into adulthood;
- appreciate the growing contributions that genetics and neuroscience are making to our understanding of the development of SEN.

Contents

Dimensions of development

Case studies of exceptional development

- John
- Mirza
- Janet

The interactive factors framework

- Biological level
- Cognitive level
- Behavioural level
- Environmental influences
- Describing individual needs

Further considerations in using the interactive factors framework

Pathways of development

- The impact of key experiences during childhood
- The interaction between genes and the environment

Neuroscience and special educational needs

Conclusions

Dimensions of development

In any culture, development for most children and young people proceeds in a predictable way that can be traced along five key dimensions: physical development, cognitive development, language development, social development and emotional development (Sharman *et al.* 2007). Table 5.1 shows typical achievements of a 4-year-old on these dimensions in a Western, English-speaking culture. Clearly the precise expression of developmental achievements will vary with cultural and social context, but within each subculture it will be possible to establish norms of development along these dimensions.

Traditionally, SEN have been defined for each child in terms of the developmental dimension which is most obviously or severely impaired. Similar category labels have been used in the past across the world, for example in England and Wales (Brennan 1982), the USA (Haring 1982), the Netherlands (Den Boer 1990) and New Zealand (Department of Education 1981). The category labels that are currently in use in England are mapped onto relevant dimensions of development in Table 5.2. This approach to categorizing SEN appeals to most people's common-sense view of the situation. It seems obvious, for example, that a person with physical disabilities whose mobility depends on the use of a wheelchair will experience their physical impairment as the most salient aspect of their difficulties. However, in an individual case the picture is frequently more complex than the category labels suggest. Most importantly, children may have strengths and personal qualities that dwarf their primary disability. To define their identity in terms of that problem will be misleading as well as demeaning. Apart from that, children with physical or sensory disabilities may well show problems in other dimensions of development too. These may arise in many different ways:

- Problems in other developmental dimensions may be a direct consequence of the syndrome causing the 'primary' impairment. For example, surveys of children with cerebral palsy have shown that, in addition to their manifest physical difficulties, they tend to have a higher than usual risk of visual and hearing difficulties (Stiers *et al.* 2002).

- Problems in other dimensions may also arise as a side-effect of the main difficulties. For example, the obvious problems that children with cerebral palsy experience with the control of movements may also show themselves in speech problems, fatigue and irritability. Speech involves complex motor coordination, and exceptional efforts of motor control exhaust children physically and emotionally.

- A key factor in additional difficulties may be the attitude of parents or families to the child's difficulties. For instance, Stone (1995: 25) described a blind baby girl who, for her own protection, was kept by her parents within the confines of a playpen for most of the day: 'Opportunities to move and explore the environment were very restricted. This child became so fearful of moving that it was some years before she could walk by herself.'

For a teacher, such additional difficulties are of great importance. An educational programme will only be successful if it takes account of the full range of a child's strengths and needs. So it is important to identify each child's strengths and needs across all the dimensions of development. Studying the descriptions of

Table 5.1 Typical achievements of a 4-year-old along five dimensions of development

Dimension of development	Examples of typical achievements in this dimension of a 4-year-old in a Western, English-speaking culture
Physical	Climbs stairs and descends confidently one foot to a stair. Can dress and undress except laces, ties and back buttons.
Cognitive	Builds tower of 10+ bricks and bridges. Dramatic make-believe play can be sustained for long periods.
Language	Speech intelligible and essentially grammatically correct. May still have difficulty pronouncing w, f, th. Continually asking questions: 'Why?', 'When?' and 'How?'
Social	Capable of sharing and taking turns but may cheat in games in order to win. Shows sympathy for friends who are hurt.
Emotional	Becoming more independent and self-willed, which can lead to conflict. Can show sensitivity to other children and adults.

Source: Adapted from Sharman *et al.* (2007: 161–2).

Table 5.2 SEN categories and dimensions of development

Dimension of development	SEN category
Physical	Visual impairment
	Hearing impairment
	Multi-sensory impairment
	Physical disability
Cognitive	Specific learning difficulty
	Moderate learning difficulty
	Severe learning difficulty
	Profound and multiple learning difficulty
Language	Speech, language and communication needs
Social	Behaviour, emotional and social difficulty
Emotional	Behaviour, emotional and social difficulty
Multiple dimensions	Autistic spectrum disorder
	Other difficulty/disability

children in the next section will illustrate this point. You will also note there examples of environmental and social factors that interact with the children's disabilities and learning difficulties in ways that have a substantial impact on their learning. Commentators such as Dyson (2002) and Norwich (2007) in the UK and Truscott *et al.* (2005) in the USA have argued for the replacement of traditional

SEN category systems in order to take account of the range of important influences on children's development more effectively.

Activity 5.1   Identifying dimensions of difficulty for children with SEN

For each child described in the next section identify the major dimension in which they show SEN and also the other dimensions in which they appear to show particular strengths or needs.

Case studies of exceptional development

John

John, who is 6 years old, is described by his mother as 'driving me mad'. He is constantly restless and does not sit still even to watch noisy action movies which he loves. He is the youngest of three children, born when his two sisters were in their teens. 'We hadn't planned him,' his mother says, 'but we were delighted when he came, especially when he turned out to be a boy. My husband dotes on him. But then he's always away driving and doesn't have to put up with his noise and his clumsiness 24 hours a day.' The family live in a neat, three-bedroomed house in a pleasant suburb of a small town in the south of Scotland. The parents both grew up in the town, and their parents live nearby. Their daughters are both now away from home most of the time, one in the armed forces and the other at university. When they come home for a few weeks at a time, they find John's behaviour wearing and frustrating, and the elder one is critical of her parents for not controlling him better. In school John is constantly in trouble with his peers for interfering in their games. The teacher comments that he seems to lack the social skills to negotiate his way out of trouble and that he does not mean any harm but 'somehow causes chaos wherever he is'. He is not aware of how he is seen by others and 'seems a happy child with good self-esteem'. However, he is beginning to be aware that he is falling behind in basic academic skills. His concentration is weak, and he does not appear to have benefited from the school's systematic teaching of literacy and numeracy.

Mirza

During a period when there was extensive fighting in Bosnia, Mirza and her mother arrived in the South-East of England as asylum seekers. After a short time they were placed in a hostel for refugees in a small coastal town, and Mirza was admitted to a school in the area at the age of 10. She had missed a great deal of schooling in the past because of the hostilities. She now appears to have considerable difficulties in settling down into the routines of her new school. She is seen as immature by her classmates and has made very slow progress in learning English, in spite of regular small-group teaching by a school-based teacher from the local English language support service.

The family's first language, which they use together and with one other Bosnian family in the hostel, is Serbo-Croat. Mirza has very poor eyesight, which was not treated until some time after her move to the UK. The cause of the difficulty was macular degeneration. Her mother reported through an interpreter that her vision had appeared normal during her early years. But when she was about 6, it deteriorated first in one eye and then in the other. She could still see out of the corner of her eye quite well and managed without too much difficulty, except when she had to do close work. By that time medical services were limited in the area where they lived, and nothing was done about the problem. The family had other preoccupations when they first arrived in the UK, but once Mirza was referred to a specialist clinic the diagnosis was made quickly and advice on management helped a good deal. The macula is a tiny area in the centre of the retina of the eye. It must have been destroyed by illness or an accident. The family cannot now say exactly when or how that might have happened. The effect is to impair Mirza's fine central vision. Good contrast in the stimulus she is looking at helps her to make it out. So she is not very good with newspapers but manages well with large print books at school. Her class teacher is now trying to ease her slowly towards using smaller print. But her poor progress in learning English as a spoken language inhibits advances in reading as well. The teacher finds it hard to decide whether her problems with books that have normal-sized print are wholly attributable to her visual defect or are partly caused by her limited English vocabulary.

Janet

Janet, who is 10 years old, lives alone with her unemployed mother. They moved a few years ago into a decaying post-war estate on the edge of a small industrial town in the North-East of England. A group of families arrived there together, rehoused from one street in Newcastle when it was demolished for redevelopment.

Janet, like her mother, appears overweight, slow-moving and slow-thinking. There is a question mark about her hearing, as she often seems to look vacant during whole-class sessions in school. But her mother has failed appointments for hearing tests. In the Year 6 classroom Janet rarely speaks unless spoken to. She is teased by most children in her class but protected by a small, lively group of girls whose streetwise leader, Stephanie, is the daughter of a neighbour. In the company of this group, when Stephanie is present, Janet will participate clumsily in playground skipping games and suchlike. But if Stephanie is absent (which is not uncommon), she will often be on her own in the playground.

She made good progress in reading with small-group help during Year 5, though her comprehension lags behind her ability to decode print and read aloud. At this stage most of her attainments are far behind the rest of the class. In maths and in any kind of project work she will sit passively and achieve very little output. Her teacher, an energetic and committed young man, pronounces himself at a loss as to how to break into what he sees as a cycle of self-reinforcing educational failure and increasing social isolation.

The interactive factors framework

As these case studies illustrate, SEN are diverse and develop in many different ways. The main questions to be addressed in this chapter are how individual patterns of SEN develop and whether there is a simple framework that can accommodate the different accounts and explanations that are given. Our starting point is a framework for *causal modelling* which was developed by Morton and Frith (1995). We believe that their approach has a particular advantage in the context with which we are concerned, because it aims to accommodate diverse perspectives on the pathways that development may take.

Morton and Frith aimed to create a simple visual aid to make it easier for people to communicate about developmental problems. Frith (1995: 6) suggested that their graphic schema can act 'as a map, largely white, in unknown territory' which will hint at where to look for landmarks. The framework can be used to represent all theories of development or difficulties in development in a neutral fashion. Morton (2004) has reviewed its use in developmental research. The examples below focus on reading problems, but the framework can be used for any type of difficulty.

Figure 5.1, which is reproduced from Frith (1997), shows a causal model of dyslexia (severe and persistent reading difficulties). It can be seen that the framework uses three levels of description to explain developmental problems: the biological level, the cognitive level and the behavioural level. Arrows indicate a hypothesized causal chain. In addition, the framework recognizes the operation of environmental factors at all three levels, as 'this chain of causal links from brain to mind to behaviour has to be set within the context of environmental and cultural influences' (Frith 1997: 2). These influences may sometimes be of critical importance for exceptional children in a society that is ethnically and culturally heterogeneous.

Biological level

The biological level box can be used to record observations about the brain and about sensory processes such as hearing and vision. In Figure 5.1 an abnormality in the perisylvian region of the left hemisphere of the brain is represented at the biological level. If a brain abnormality is thought to be caused by a genetic factor,

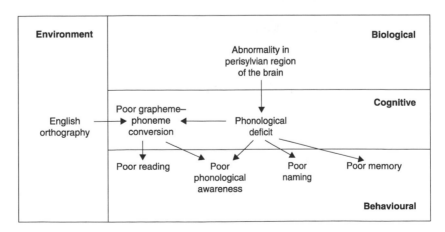

Figure 5.1 Causal model of dyslexia as a phonological deficit
Source: Frith (1997).

this genetic factor can also be shown in the biological level box, and an arrow drawn from it to the brain abnormality. Brain functioning may also be influenced by environmental factors such as quality of nutrition or levels of toxins, and by environmental interventions such as the use of a cochlear implant as an intervention for sensorineural hearing loss. A fuller discussion of processes and influences at the biological level may be found in the sections on genetics and neuroscience later in this chapter.

Cognitive level

Where it is hypothesized that there are within-child causes of poor performance, they are placed in the cognitive level box. Cognitive skills or deficits cannot be directly observed but must be inferred from observed behavioural data. The inferred and hypothetical underlying cognitive deficits are different in different theories. Figure 5.1 shows the central explanatory role given in this theory of dyslexia to what is hypothesized to be a phonological deficit, where difficulties are experienced in identifying and manipulating sounds within words. Morton and Frith (1995) also included affective factors at the cognitive level. An argument could be made for placing affects in the biological level box (as physiological responses) or in the behavioural level box (as facial expressions, voice modulations, etc.). But the cognitive level is crucial in ascribing meaning to affects and explaining their influence on mental activities and behaviour. Again the environment plays an important role. Frith (1997) pointed out that whether a cognitive or affective difficulty will result in literacy problems will not just depend on the nature and severity of the problem but on interactions with environmental factors such as the complexity of the writing system involved. Hence children with dyslexia display different patterns of errors in reading and writing if they are learning to read languages such as German or Dutch, where the process of mapping sounds onto letters, establishing grapheme–phoneme correspondences, is comparatively straightforward, than do those who are learning to read English, which is more complex in this respect (Ziegler and Goswami 2005).

Behavioural level

Observations and facts about poor performance in reading and spelling activities and/or tests are represented in the behavioural level box. We can directly observe behaviour such as incorrect spelling, words read inaccurately or poor performance in naming and memory tests. Of course, any observations and data that are collected will be affected by a range of environmental factors (such as the work ethos in the classroom). In addition, within-child factors other than those directly related to literacy difficulties (such as motivation) are also open to environmental influences.

Environmental influences

Further examples of environmental influences are given in Figures 5.2 and 5.3 (reproduced from Frith, 1995). These figures also illustrate the way in which the causal modelling framework can be used very simply to represent general ideas in

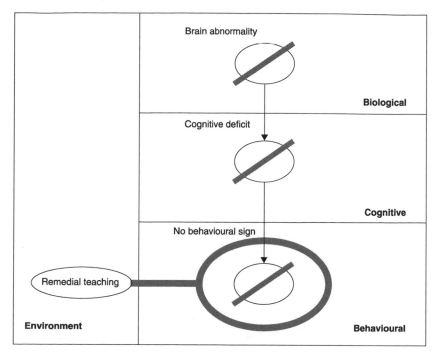

Figure 5.2 Example of compensation
Source: Frith (1995).

outline, without including much detail. In Figure 5.2 you will see that the child had a cognitive deficit that was expected to lead to reading problems, but the provision of remedial teaching was successful and there was therefore no 'behavioural sign' of poor reading. Frith (1995: 8) described this as 'an example of compensation: here remedial teaching is shown to give a protective effect'. In Figure 5.3 a child who shows no problems at the biological or cognitive levels nonetheless is making poor progress in reading. Frith claims that 'more economically than I can do it in words, I can use the diagram to declare just what I assume the critical factors and relationships to be'.

In these theoretical models produced by developmental psychologists and neuropsychologists the contribution of the environment is acknowledged throughout. But that contribution is often poorly specified because of the wide variability that would have to be represented. When one comes to look at individual differences and individual needs, that variability is of crucial importance. Morton and Frith (1995) and Krol *et al.* (2004) suggested that these diagrams could also be used to describe particular individuals. Frederickson (1997) reported that this had been done successfully by educational psychologists in training, Cameron and Monsen (2005) illustrated the process in a case study of a 10-year-old boy who had been referred for a statutory SEN assessment, and Frederickson *et al.* (2008: Figure 1.2) applied it to a 6-year-old with a complex pattern of learning and behaviour problems. A couple of modifications had been made to the framework to facilitate the description of individual children.

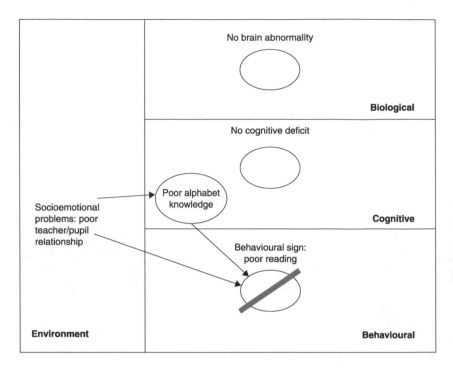

Figure 5.3 Example of poor reading due to emotional causes, not dyslexia
Source: Frith (1995).

Describing individual needs

An example of what is now called the interactive factors (IF) framework is presented in Figure 5.4. Instead of showing the biological, cognitive, behavioural and environmental factors that are characteristic of a specified developmental difficulty, the model for a particular individual represents what is known about the complexity of that individual's particular pattern of strengths and needs. It also shows the environmental and other factors which are thought to be influencing the individual's learning and development. It is often hard to be sure about some of the influences that are identified because any ideas about them will typically be based on a limited amount of information. However, a hypothesis about particular influences can be used to guide intervention. Then an evaluation of the individual's response to intervention will show whether they are accurate and useful. For example, in Figure 5.4 the individual's literacy difficulties are thought to be exacerbated by high levels of off-task behaviour resulting from ineffective classroom management. An intervention to improve classroom management would be expected to reduce levels of off-task behaviour and improve performance on literacy tasks. If subsequent evaluation confirms that this is the case, then the accuracy and usefulness of the model would be supported. However, if the predicted outcomes are not achieved, then further investigation is likely to be needed, leading to a revision of the model.

By comparing Figure 5.4 with Figure 5.1 you can see the slight changes that have been made to Morton and Frith's framework. There is, first of all, much

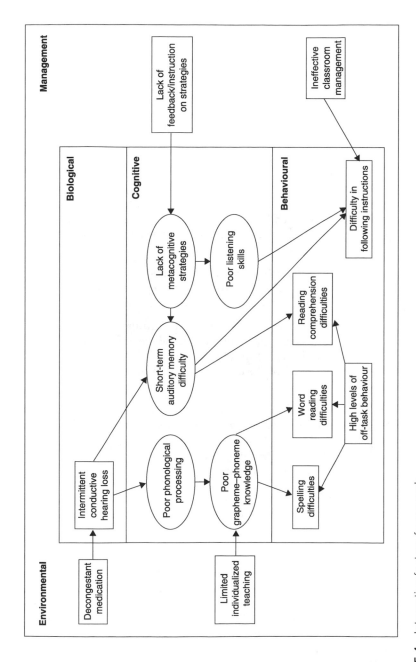

Figure 5.4 Interactive factors framework
Source: Frederickson and Cameron (1999).

greater conceptual space given to environmental factors. This includes the recognition that the environment is also the source of all intervention and management efforts. Figure 5.4 shows that intervention and management strategies might be targeted at all three levels of the framework: decongestant medication at the biological level, instruction in memory strategies and teaching of letter–sound (grapheme–phoneme) correspondences at the cognitive level, and the introduction of classroom management techniques at the behavioural level. Figure 5.4 represents an individual within their environment.

Just as Morton and Frith (1995) suggest that it is helpful to consider different levels of analysis of individual functioning, so Bronfenbrenner (1979: 3) has suggested that it is helpful to conceive of the environment as 'a set of nested structures, each contained inside the next like a set of Russian dolls'. Four levels are identified in this broader and more differentiated conception of the environment in a model which he now terms the *bioecological model* (Bronfenbrenner and Morris 2006):

- A *microsystem* is a pattern of activities, roles and interpersonal relations experienced by a child in a given setting. The home, classroom and playground would all be examples of settings within which children actively participate.

- A *mesosystem* describes the relationships between two or more settings in which a child actively participates – for example, the relationships between home and school, between neighbourhood and peer group.

- An *exosystem* refers to one or more settings that do not involve a child directly as an active participant but which affect or are affected by what happens in settings that do involve the child. Examples of exosystems might be the work setting of the child's parent(s) or the LEA.

- The *macrosystem* refers to consistencies in the other systems that exist or could exist at the level of the subculture or culture as a whole, together with belief systems underlying any such consistencies. Within a given society (e.g. Britain, France, Japan) settings such as school classrooms, restaurants or home–school relationships will share certain features, along which the settings differ across cultures.

Gibbs and Huang (1989) point out that Bronfenbrenner's perspective is particularly relevant in analysing the influence of factors such as poverty, discrimination and immigration on the psychosocial development of children and young people from minority cultural groups. For example, Lynch and Cicchetti (2002) studied links between children's exposure to violence in a low-income urban neighbourhood in the USA and their sense of security in their relationship with their mother inside the family. Children aged 7–13 who reported that they had been exposed to high levels of community violence also indicated that they felt less positive when with their mother, less close to her and more anxious when separated from her. In addition, they reported higher rates of what they saw as negative behaviour on the part of their mother (e.g. taking things away from them if they misbehaved). These correlations may have arisen because the level of community violence in the area had an adverse effect on the caregivers' parenting on account of the stress that it caused them. Or it could be the case that children who felt insecure with their caregivers perceived the external environment as more threatening as a result. Because the design of this investigation meant that the children were not studied over time as they grew up, it was impossible to be sure about the causal pattern. However, their findings support the central idea in Bronfenbrenner's ecological systems theory that children's psychological development is crucially affected by interactions between the different levels in his model. (For a review that used this model to organize research on educational inclusion, see Odom *et al.* 2004.)

A further illustration of these processes arises when families move to another country so that children are exposed to different sets of values and norms in new settings, and there are potential areas of conflicting expectations. Thus one source of stress for Mirza, who was described above, has been the different views on food and diet of her peer group at school and her mother at home. Tensions between home and school values may take many forms within a diverse society. For example, it has been argued that one of the problems faced by Gypsy children in school is that they develop a distinctive spatial awareness in the site environments where they live and then find it difficult to accommodate to the expectations that are imposed on them about how social space should be used in school. A study of Gypsy children attending a small sample of primary schools in the South-West of England showed that 'certain uses of space, which might appear anti-social and disruptive to schools, might equally be perceived as a reflection of behaviour in the home environment'. Examples that were reported to them included pupils from Traveller families crossing boundaries in school at forbidden times to check on younger family members and trying to colonize certain spaces around the school as being 'safe' for their group (Levinson and Sparkes 2005: 768–9).

A further difference between the framework employed in this book and the original framework developed by Morton and Frith (1995) can be seen in the use of slightly different terminology such as 'interactive factors framework' rather than 'causal modelling framework'. While Morton and Frith had emphasized that causal links in the modelling process are not determinant, it was found that use of the word 'causal' could prove confusing when professionals were developing tentative representations of the factors thought to be affecting an individual child. In this age of acronyms, the title 'IF framework' seems particularly apt given that a major purpose is to represent working hypotheses about the nature of children's needs. Professionals working with an individual can ask '*If* the child's learning is being influenced in this way, what are the implications for teaching and management?'. The evaluation of the intervention they design will show whether their working hypothesis is a useful guide to practice. The focus on *interactive* factors is also important, given the points made in the opening section of this chapter about the complex and multi-faceted nature of individual children's needs. On the basis of Figure 5.4 we would not expect an intervention at one level alone to be enough to meet the child's needs. For example, the introduction of more effective classroom management techniques alone would not have a sufficient impact on the child's literacy skills in the absence of appropriately individualized teaching. Similarly, it is unlikely that individualized teaching of letter–sound correspondences on its own would result in improved reading and spelling performance in the classroom unless the ineffective management is also addressed.

In this book we will return to the causal modelling framework in describing different theories of particular developmental difficulties. We will also use the IF framework in describing the complex difficulties experienced by individual children and the ways in which professionals working with them can attempt to understand and meet their needs.

Activity 5.2 Applying the IF framework to individual cases

(a) Reread the account of Janet in the previous section. Can you draft an IF framework to show what her current reading difficulties are and how they may have developed?

(b) Repeat the process for a child known to you professionally or personally.

(c) Show your two diagrams to a friend or colleague and ask them to tell you in words what they think is the nature of each child's difficulties and what lies behind them. Does their verbal account agree with what you would have said yourself?

Further considerations in using the interactive factors framework

Morton and Frith (1995: 359) argued that, when constructing a model of how a serious problem develops, it is essential to 'start with biology'. This will be important even if the precise disturbance to the brain system is not fully understood. For example, when childhood autism was first identified, an influential theory suggested that the family's style of interaction might be a key factor in the development of the symptoms. Over recent years evidence has accumulated that the condition in fact has a biological origin (see Chapter 11). If professionals continue to suggest that a mother's manner in handling her child may be the cause of his or her strange behaviour and social isolation, it is not only misleading and unhelpful, but also potentially very damaging.

Another example is the group of children with problems of attention and activity labelled as attention deficit hyperactivity disorder (ADHD). John, who was described earlier, is an example of a child with this pattern of difficulties. Some educationists treat ADHD as a wholly educational issue. They assume that, if appropriate classroom management strategies are adopted, the children's behaviour will be controlled and their attention will be focused (Cooper 1997). Unfortunately this is sometimes too optimistic: neuropsychological factors make it so difficult for some children to inhibit impulsive behaviour that changing the approach to classroom management will not, on its own, enable them to sustain concentration on schoolwork. If key factors are involved at the biological level it may not be effective to intervene solely at the behavioural or cognitive level.

However, saying that we should 'start with biology' does not mean that we should give attention only to biological factors. The intensity of a child's problems of attention with ADHD may be affected by what they or others think about the causes of their difficulties. So cognitive processes mediate the impact of biological factors. In turn, the views of the child and parents will be affected by external environmental factors such as social and economic pressures on the family and expectations about children's behaviour that are prevalent in the general community.

The impact of environmental factors may operate at a broader level as well as in the subtle ways implied in the example of ADHD. When socioeconomic differences within a society are extreme, the incidence of different types of mental and physical handicap will reflect this. For instance, in a series of studies in the area of Cape Town in South Africa, Molteno and his colleagues showed that the proportion of children developing severe SEN after birth was higher in the African population than in the coloured population and lowest among white children (see Table 5.3). The incidence of postnatal disabilities in the white group was comparable to what had been recorded in other developed countries. It was evident that the higher rates among the other groups in the same area were not linked to some ethnic disadvantage but were a consequence of their worse socioeconomic conditions. For example, children were more likely to develop diseases such as tuberculosis, pneumonia and measles in these groups, and also more likely, once they had these illnesses, to develop secondary cerebral infections leading to disability (Arens and Molteno 1989; Molteno *et al.* 1990; Donald 1994). (For a review of research on early adversity and developmental disorders in Western societies, see Taylor and Rogers, 2005.)

Thus environmental factors may influence development in a range of different ways. We will illustrate this further with an outline framework that was used by Cline and Baldwin (2004) to show ways in which selective mutism can develop in childhood. Selective mutism is the term used to describe a phenomenon in which children who are able to speak and do speak in some situations (e.g. home) persist in remaining silent in some other settings (e.g. school). It appears to develop most often around 3–6 years of age when children are moving out of their family homes into a different kind of setting outside the family, such as a playgroup or nursery or school. (For a fuller account, see Chapter 10.) Table 5.4 presents a summary of how selective mutism may develop. Note that the community (including school) as well as the child and the family may play a part in the process. It is usual to distinguish between three ways in which factors may influence psychological events.

Firstly, there are *disposing factors*, which create a situation that is favourable to the development of the behaviour. At the community level a significant social distance may be maintained between families or groups in a rural community or between ethnic or linguistic groups in an urban community. Within the family some older family members may model shyness or mutism or may encourage these patterns of behaviour, especially in contact with people outside the household. At a personal level the child may have a temperamental disposition towards shyness,

Table 5.3 Proportion of children in Cape Town with mental handicap or cerebral palsy for whom postnatal causes had been identified

Population	Mental handicap (%)	Cerebral palsy (%)
African	21.7	36.1
Coloured	13.6	24.0
White	9.8	13.2

Source: Donald (1994).

Table 5.4 Summary of how selective mutism may develop

Factors	The community	The family	The child
Disposing	Family is isolated or marginalized in the community.	Parents have personal experience and/or a family tradition of silence/reticence.	
		Factors within the family encourage mutism as a reaction to challenge.	Factors within the child favour mutism as a reaction to challenge
Precipitating			The child faces a challenging transition to the outside world (or other stressful challenge) and reacts by withholding speech.
Maintaining	Reactions from adults and peers reinforce mutism.	Reactions from family members reinforce mutism.	The child experiences reduced anxiety and secondary gains.

Source: Cline and Baldwin (2004).

timidity and fearfulness or may have failed to develop the level of independence from one or both of their parents that would be considered appropriate for their age within their culture.

Secondly, there are *precipitating factors*, which trigger the behaviour on the first few occasions when it occurs. For some children these may include starting to attend an institution outside the home such as a nursery, playgroup or school.

Thirdly, there are *maintaining factors*, which encourage the persistence of the behaviour pattern. Adults and peers inside and outside the home (including school) may treat selectively mute children as special and unusual, convey the expectation that they will remain mute and respond to their non-verbal communication readily in such a way that it is reinforced. The children themselves may come to relish their own uniqueness, hold a self-image as a mute person, and become fearful of the consequences of speaking.

It seems most likely that selective mutism will develop when some factors are present at each of the levels – the community, the family and the child. However, it may occur when only two levels (or even one level) are implicated. However, the development of a particular pattern of difficulty is often 'over-determined', i.e. caused by several interacting factors (cf. Figure 5.4). The IF framework is helpful not only in depicting the status of each factor but also in attempting to show how they may have formed a causal chain.

These frameworks do not highlight an important set of factors that have received increasing attention in recent years – protective factors (or sources of 'resilience'). Why is it that many people who suffer potentially very damaging experiences when they are young appear to show no negative consequences in their later development? For example, Collishaw *et al.* (2007) followed up a large group of adults in their early forties who had originally been interviewed as part of a population study of children in the Isle of Wight in 1964. Ten per cent of the sample reported that they had been physically or sexually abused during childhood. Many of those showed increased rates of psychological problems in adolescence or in adult life: they were more likely to report that they had had recurrent depression, had attempted suicide at some point or had become involved in substance abuse. But nearly half of those who had experienced abuse in childhood did *not* report significant psychological problems over a 30-year follow-up period and also demonstrated positive adaptation in other domains (employing diverse measures such as the stability of an individual's relationships over time, their reported involvement in crime and their self-ratings of their health).

What enables some individuals to be so resilient in the face of adversity? Rutter (2007a) has argued that resilience cannot simply be an inherent personality trait and that it is likely to involve:

- the mental sets that individuals have when faced with challenges and the coping strategies that they employ in order to deal with them;

- genetic susceptibility or resistance to environmental risk or more generally to environmental change (perhaps expressed in physiological responses to an environmental hazard, e.g. through neuroendocrine functioning);

- the nature of a person's experiences following exposure to risk (e.g. in their relationships with others both inside and outside the family).

Thus an understanding of resilience requires 'a shift from a focus on external (or for that matter internal) risks to a focus on *how* these risks are dealt with by the individual' (2007a: 207). That advice should be borne in mind as we move in the next section to examine 'pathways of development' in more detail.

Activity 5.3 Analysing factors that underlie Mirza's difficulties at school

Re-examine the account of Mirza that was given earlier in the chapter and decide what might appropriately be written in the cells of this table to summarize factors underlying her current difficulties at school.

	The community	The family	The school
Disposing factors			
Protective factors			
Precipitating factors			
Maintaining factors			

Pathways of development

The impact of key experiences during childhood

Over the last 60 years the prevailing climate of opinion among researchers has shifted more than once. During the period following World War II an image was presented of a high degree of consistency in personality: children were seen as being born with certain fixed characteristics which changed little over time, though very adverse factors in the early years, such as 'maternal deprivation', might impair development. This simplistic view was challenged during the 1960s and 1970s when it became clear that the way people develop was more varied and unpredictable than had been thought (Clarke and Clarke 1976). Commentators such as Mischel (1969) highlighted evidence that behaviour is often situation-specific: a person will behave quite differently in different circumstances. Moss and Susman (1980: 590) summarized indications from longitudinal research as showing that some problems persist and others fade away:

> Severe disturbances tend to be long-standing, whereas isolated symptoms and mild reactions tend to be transitory. This difference in the persistence of severe and mild reactions may be based on the probability that severe disturbances are likely to reflect a fundamental and pervasive personality problem that is tied to the psychobiological history of the individual. Isolated symptoms are more likely to reflect temporary stress reactions to passing situations and ephemeral developmental demands.

In recent years evidence has accumulated that there are both continuities and discontinuities in development. There has been growing interest in analysing *pathways of development* in greater detail to show how both stability and change may be seen in individual cases. Rutter (1989) reviewed a number of factors that may affect vulnerable children over their life span. We will illustrate his analysis by examining one factor in particular – the effectiveness of the school the child attends in early adolescence. The criterion of effectiveness in these studies was not the school's success with a particular pupil but general outcome measures for all its pupils. Figure 5.5 presents a simplified summary of data on the employment record of young people one year after leaving school.

There was no direct relationship between attending one of the less effective schools in their sample and moving into unskilled work or having a poor employment record. But if a child attended one of the less effective schools they were twice as likely to attend poorly, and if their attendance was poor they were twice as likely to leave school early without sitting national examinations. That had an impact on how well qualified they were, which in turn affected their work record.

As the research on resilience at an earlier stage in child development showed, young children are both vulnerable and robust. For example, studies of national and international adoption have shown that, even when children have had deeply damaging early experiences in a maltreating family or a neglectful orphanage, adoption into a new family can lead to substantial recovery in terms of physical growth, emotional security, cognitive development, school achievement, self-esteem and behavioural adjustment (van Ijzendoom and Juffer 2006). That review, which involved the meta-analysis of more than 270 studies, indicated

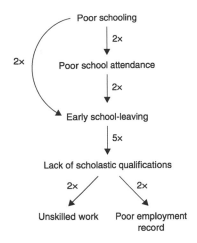

Figure 5.5   Simplified pathway from poor schooling to poor job success; 2x means 'twice as likely to lead to . . .'
Source: Rutter (1989), citing Gray *et al.* (1980).

that this 'catching up' process is likely to be more complete if the child is adopted before the age of 12 months – a finding that suggests that, while there is a surprising degree of plasticity in human development, there are also sensitive periods.

   The notion of 'critical periods' has been recognized in developmental psychology and biology for almost a century. The classic example was the demonstration by Konrad Lorenz of how young geese came to treat him as their mother and follow him around. During a critical (or sensitive) period specific neuronal systems are particularly susceptible to modification by experience. Lorenz's geese went through an imprinting process on him because they saw him during a critical period shortly after birth and did not see any adult geese at that time. Educationists have sometimes applied the concept of a critical period rather loosely to varied kinds of learning without any systematic evidence. There is no doubt that such windows of opportunity exist in specific areas of development (Hensch 2004). For example, human infants are uniquely sensitive to language input, but behavioural observation and brain imaging techniques have shown that their sensitivity to various features in what they hear decreases as they move through childhood.

The interaction between genes and the environment

In human beings genetic instructions for reproduction are handed down from parent to child through the genes that are contained in 46 chromosomes. These chromosomes are inherited as 22 matching pairs with one extra pair, the sex chromosomes, which match in the case of females, who have two X chromosomes, but not in the case of males, who have one X and one Y chromosome. Genetic factors are implicated in many developmental problems, though the causative route has been identified in only a small number of conditions so far. Classic examples of conditions with a well-defined genetic basis are Down's syndrome (where children have an extra 21st chromosome) and fragile X syndrome (where the X chromosome looks as if it has one end breaking off because of an abnormal gene in a particular location). Down's syndrome is not inherited from the parents but occurs because one chromosome fails to divide normally during conception. Fragile X syndrome, on the other hand, is inherited with the X chromosome. Each of these conditions is associated with an increased risk of general learning difficulties (Carr 1988; Dew-Hughes 2004).

Chromosomal abnormalities of that kind are the most widely known types of genetic disorder. That has sometimes led to a deterministic, even fatalistic, attitude to such conditions. Developmental research has increasingly challenged such assumptions:

1   Most developmental problems that have a genetic component cannot be attributed to a single malfunctioning gene. The image of a 'gene for autism' or a 'gene for ADHD' is simply wrong (Kendler 2005).

2   There is increasing evidence of interaction between genes and the environment which undermines a simple, deterministic view of how a genetic disorder may influence development. For example, Taylor *et al.* (2006) studied a non-clinical group of young men and women in California and identified those who might be vulnerable to depression. They each had a genetic predisposition – a short form of the *5-HTTLPR* gene. Earlier research had identified an association between that gene and elevated risk for depression. Those participants in the Californian study who had the gene were significantly less likely to report depressive symptoms as a young adult if they had been brought up in a supportive family as a child. The effects of their upbringing appeared to be successful in protecting them against the risk associated with the gene which they continued to carry.

3   That example implies an impact on the child's development from the family environment that modifies the influence of a genetic predisposition. There is suggestive evidence too of an interactive process that operates in the opposite direction. Ge *et al.* (1996) showed that adopted children whose biological parents had behaved in anti-social ways or had been dependent on drugs or alcohol were more likely to have *adoptive* parents who treated them harshly and were inconsistent in their approach to discipline with them. This appeared to have come about because the children's disruptive behaviour had elicited negative parenting from them. In this case the specific genetic mechanisms have not been identified, but the origins of the children's behaviour appeared to lie partly in their genetic make-up (as indicated in their biological parents' record of anti-social behaviour and addiction).

Recent progress in behavioural genetics has arisen not only through technical advances but also because of a shift in the scientists' theoretical and conceptual grasp of the phenomena they are investigating. Understanding the role of 'nature' and 'nurture' in the development of special educational needs or human intelligence is no longer viewed as a matter of measuring the heritability of different conditions and functions, that is, the proportion of variance between individuals that can be attributed to genetic factors. The task is now seen as not simply identifying genes that make people susceptible to certain problems but as studying the environmental risk factors that are involved and the interplay between genes and the environment (Rutter 2007b, 2007c). This work is in its very early stages, and there are as yet few results from it that have clear implications for education.

But this area of scientific activity has been transformed in recent years, and it can be expected to offer new insights that will inform teaching in the future, for example in the development of more sophisticated strategies for prevention and early intervention.

Neuroscience and special educational needs

There has also been dramatic progress in recent years in scientists' understanding of how the brain works both during the process of learning and when there are obstacles to that process. This progress has been based partly on technical advances in methods of investigation (see Table 5.5). But significant progress is only possible when the application of novel technical expertise is accompanied by conceptual advances. The developing brain is constantly changing so that any apparent 'abnormality' needs to evaluated against an accurate developmental match. The behaviours and competencies that are observed at what Morton and

Table 5.5 Applications of recent advances in techniques of brain imaging

Technique	Focus of attention	Example of its application to SEN research
Structural magnetic resonance imaging (SMRI)	Brain structure	Part of the temporal lobe was enlarged in adults with cleft lip and palate who had had no history of hearing impairment in childhood (Shriver *et al.*).
Diffusion tension imaging (DTI)	Brain structure	Reduced connectivity between the brain hemispheres was shown in boys with Tourette's syndrome (Plessen *et al.*).
Functional MRI	Brain function	Young people's neural response to rewards differed between those with a major depressive disorder and controls (Forbes *et al.*).
Event-related potentials (ERP)	Brain function	Children diagnosed with anxiety disorders showed different maturational patterns from controls in cortical circuitry that is involved in monitoring responses to a stimulus (Ladouceur *et al.*).
Magnetic resonance spectroscopy (MRS)	Brain chemistry	Men with a history of dyslexia in childhood showed both metabolic and morphological changes in the cerebellum compared to controls (Rae *et al.* 2002).

Note: This table draws on information on brain imaging techniques that was presented by Pine (2006) in the introduction to a special issue of the *Journal of Child Psychology and Psychiatry* on neuroimaging. See his article for a fuller account of each technique. The undated examples in the table of applications of these techniques are all taken from papers in the same special issue of the journal.

Frith called the behavioural level may not be caused in a straightforward manner. The picture may be more complex with interactive causative factors operating. C.D. Frith (2006: 979) gave an example of this from autism: if people with autism have an abnormal brain module for recognizing faces, 'this might not be a cause of difficulties in processing faces, but a consequence of a failure in the programme that normally causes infants to seek out faces as a source of stimulation'. He suggests that there are at least three kinds of brain abnormalities associated with developmental disorders:

- *primary* abnormalities that are the primary cause of the abnormal developmental trajectory;

- *secondary* abnormalities that are the consequence of the abnormal experiences created by the primary abnormality;

- *tertiary* abnormalities that are the consequence of compensatory processes designed to overcome the cognitive problems created by the first two kinds of abnormality.

When rapid scientific advances in a complex field appear to have implications for important aspects of people's lives, there is a ready market in the media and the public mind for what, in this field, have been called 'neuromyths'. The general world of education and pedagogy has provided fertile ground for the growth of such myths, which academic neuroscientists have viewed with alarm. They fear not only that the public and professionals will be misled into particular activities that offer no benefit, but also that the potential value of their science will eventually be undermined in the eyes of the world.

- Children are either 'left-brained' or 'right-brained' learners and should be taught accordingly. If their left brain dominates their approach to learning, teachers should emphasize language, logical argument, analysis and the acquisition of factual information. If, however, they are stronger in their right brain, teachers should place greater reliance on forms and patterns, spatial representation of ideas, rhythm, images and pictures.

- Children differ in learning styles, with many learning almost exclusively through either visual or auditory or kinaesthetic modalities. Teachers should test all their pupils to identify their learning styles and then teach to their strengths.

- A simple series of body movements (as prescribed, for example, in 'brain gym') will 'integrate all areas of the brain to enhance learning'. There should be regular intervals of brain gym in every lesson.

Figure 5.6 Examples of 'neuromyths' sold to teachers in the general field of education

---

Goswami (2006), who gave the examples of neuromyths in Figure 5.6 that have been pressed upon teachers, argued that educational prescriptions of this general kind over-extend the application of findings from neuroscience and sometimes misrepresent those findings, but, in spite of that, she believed neuroscience has a great deal of potential for providing guidance to teachers in the future (see also Teaching and Learning Research Programme 2005; Blakemore and Frith 2005).

If that is the position in relation to general pedagogy, what can educators learn from neuroscience about the development of special educational needs? You will find discussions relating to this question in some later chapters, for example on dyslexia in Chapter 13 and on dyscalculia in Chapter 14. As in the case of genetics, the neuroscience of learning difficulties is at an early stage of development and there are few established findings with clear practical implications at this point. However, there is a great deal of activity, and it can be expected that our understanding of the neurological basis of severe difficulties such as autism and ADHD will advance significantly over the next few years. The implications for practice may not involve a simple translation of laboratory findings into prescriptions for pedagogy, however, but rather an indirect analysis of teaching or prevention strategies that might be more successful. For example, one hypothesis about developmental dyscalculia highlights the possibility of damage to the parietal area of the brain. If evidence is found to support that idea, brain imaging studies of young children with early behavioural symptoms of possible number difficulties could identify those who might benefit from a specific teaching programme focused on the problems associated with dyscalculia (Goswami 2006: 4; Blakemore and Frith 2005: 65–6).

Caution is required in this field too. It is understandable that, where children face severe impairments and exceptional challenges in their development, parents and professionals will be attracted to any strategy that appears to offer the prospect of a substantial amelioration in the symptoms or even a 'cure'. Many such strategies have been developed with a neuropsychological explanation of their design but little or no systematic evidence to support their claims. The Son-Rise Program for autism (sometimes known in the UK as the Option Method) is one example. This home-based programme is intended to develop an optimal physical learning environment for children with autism. (For details of the approach see the programme originators' website, http://www.autismtreatmentcenter.org). The evaluation of long-lasting, home-based interventions of this kind is very difficult. For example, many families may implement the programme in ways that differ from what is typically described in the literature (Williams 2006), and there are other technical problems (Charman and Howlin 2003).

Evaluation studies themselves can become the focus of controversy as researchers contest the validity of different strategies for testing the effectiveness of an intervention. The controversy is likely to be exacerbated if the proponents of an approach are seen to be publicizing positive results in the mass media. See, for example, a critique by Rack *et al.* (2007) of an evaluation report on the DDAT programme, an exercise-based programme for dyslexia that is also known by the name of the businessman who developed it, Wynford Dore. The same issue of the journal includes a response from the original report's authors.

Neuroscience promises new levels of insight into fundamental aspects of the development of children who have SEN. But developing a critical understanding of those insights is only the beginning of the task for those who work with the children and their families. The goal of turning them into practicable and effective forms of intervention and teaching will require a different kind of expertise. That is the subject of the next two sections of this book.

Conclusions

The meticulous analysis of environmental factors which characterized much research in the latter part of the twentieth century is now being complemented by increased understanding of genetic factors and improved techniques in neuro-science. Today biological influences can be analysed in much more detail, while the relevance of environmental factors and of protective factors (or resilience) is more fully understood too. A full analysis of the development of children who have SEN will need to take account of the whole range of possible factors that might play a part. It will have to give attention to the timing of significant events in a child's life and the interaction between them. It will also examine how biology, cognition, behaviour and the environment interact to produce the observed out-come. In the rest of this book we will return to these themes constantly as we examine different types of SEN and consider issues of education and management.

PART TWO

Assessment in context

Identification and assessment

Objectives

When you have studied this chapter you should be able to:

- understand key principles and concepts that are used in discussing the identification and assessment of SEN;
- explain key requirements which all approaches to identification and assessment should meet, and analyse the extent to which any particular approach meets those requirements;
- critically examine the broad advantages and disadvantages of the most common approaches to identification and assessment.

Contents

Identification and assessment of SEN in the early years

Identification and assessment of SEN at school

Initial assessment questions

Tests for testers – what standards must assessment meet?

Assessment and the delivery of the curriculum

Approaches to the assessment of SEN

- Focus on the learner
- Focus on the teaching programme
- Focus on the 'zone of potential development'
- Focus on the learning environment

Conclusions

Identification and assessment of SEN in the early years

In Chapter 3 you were invited to compare different ways of thinking about SEN. It will be obvious that, if professionals conceive of SEN as a permanent individual characteristic of a child, they will approach the tasks of identifying and assessing those needs differently than if they had an interactional model of SEN. In this chapter we will consider various approaches to identification and assessment that relate to how SEN are conceived, and we will examine the practical implications of tackling the task in different ways.

It is conventional wisdom that SEN and possible educational disadvantage should be identified as early as possible. The UK government has described early intervention as the 'cornerstone' of the *Every Child Matters* strategy, offering lasting benefits and 'providing a sound foundation for future learning and development'. It 'enables some children to catch up with their classmates and for those who need support on a continuing basis it means that help is available as early as possible, reducing the risk of long-term underachievement and disaffection' (DfES 2004c: 9) Similar principles have been adopted in other European countries (Soriano 2005) and in the USA (Individuals with Disabilities Education Act 1997). On the face of it the logic is obvious. Children who are not given extra help at an early stage will fall behind their classmates at school and will then not be able to follow what is taught. They will be aware of the gap between what they can do and what their peers can do, and as a result may come to see themselves as incapable of school learning. Their motivation for classroom tasks will be undermined, their concentration will falter, and this will feed a negative cycle in which failure leads to further failure. Clearly, early identification of potential difficulties could help parents and teachers to halt this process before it starts.

With a traditional 'wait-to-fail' model for service delivery, students have to experience failure or distress or have to reach a critical juncture in their schooling or development before help is offered to them. If those who are at risk are identified early, it is possible (in theory) to provide 'evidence-based prevention and early intervention services delivered through a multi-tiered intervention approach' (Albers *et al.* 2007: 114). However, the situation is more complex than that scenario makes it appear. With any system of screening or early identification it is inevitable that mistakes will be made. When children are young, their behaviour and performance are more variable than when they are older; they may underperform because of minor differences between the way a task is presented and the way they are accustomed to it at home; they may not be prepared by their early experiences for the activities that are used to assess them; children who are very familiar with the assessment materials may do relatively well initially because of prior practice. As a result, children may be wrongly identified as having serious difficulties when this is not the case ('false positives'), or they may not be identified as having difficulties when they really do ('false negatives'). The aim must be to maximize the number of 'true positives' and 'true negatives' – a task that is more challenging when the children involved are younger. Table 6.1 sets out some of the considerations that might be applied when evaluating a screening instrument with these concerns in mind. Glover and Albers (2007), who produced a fuller version of this table, emphasize that there should be an evidence base for making each decision.

In the UK until recently great reliance was placed at the preschool stage on surveillance by professionals in the health and other services. Before school entry this was seen as the most efficient and cost-effective approach available. Strategies included:

- health screening before and after birth and in infancy;
- monitoring by the health visitor service;
- use of developmental checklists in nurseries, playgroups and other preschool provision;

Table 6.1   Some considerations and sample questions for evaluating universal screening assessments

Appropriateness for the intended use

Compatibility with the service delivery needs	Are the timing and frequency of administration appropriate?
	Are the identification outcomes relevant?
Alignment with constructs of interest	Are the measured constructs relevant for determining an individual's risk status?
Population fit	Is the assessment contextually and developmentally appropriate?

Technical adequacy

Adequacy of norms	Is the normative sample representative, recent, and sufficiently large?
Test–retest and inter-scorer reliability	Is measurement consistent over time and across scorers?

Predictive validity

Sensitivity	Of those *actually* at risk, what proportion is correctly identified?
Specificity	Of those *actually* not at risk, what proportion is correctly identified?
Positive predictive value	Of those *identified* as at risk, what proportion is correctly identified?
Negative predictive value	Of those *identified* as not at risk, what proportion is correctly identified?
Hit rate	What proportion of the total sample is correctly identified?

Concurrent validity	Is the assessment outcome consistent with a criterion measure?
Construct validity	Does the assessment measure the construct for which it is designed?
Content validity	Are the assessment format and items appropriate?

Usability

Balance of costs and benefits	Are the costs associated with the assessment reasonable and commensurate with the benefits that will be obtained?
Feasibility of administration	Are personnel able to administer the assessment?
Acceptability	Do stakeholders appreciate the benefits associated with the assessment?
Infrastructure requirements	Are resources available to collect, manage, and interpret assessment data?
Utility of outcomes	Can stakeholders understand the implications associated with assessment outcomes? Are the outcomes useful for guiding instruction?

Source: Adapted from Glover and Albers (2007).

- priority admission of children at risk into 'opportunity playgroups' and similar facilities where additional support is available.

The problem with such a patchwork of arrangements is that it is not difficult for children to fall through the net (e.g. if their family moves a great deal or does not make use of the services available because of fear or unfamiliarity). There is evidence from the USA as well as the UK that factors that lead to underuse of the relevant services are more likely to affect families from ethnic and linguistic minority communities (Shah 1992; Zhang and Bennett 2003; Denney *et al.* 2007).

Efforts have been made to ensure that services are offered more consistently, are coordinated more effectively and are accessible to the most vulnerable families. In relation to SEN, a statutory requirement was placed on health authorities and NHS Trusts some years ago that they

> inform parents and the appropriate local education authority when they form the opinion that a child under the age of five may have special educational needs. They must also inform the parents if they believe that a particular voluntary organisation is likely to be able to give the parents advice or assistance in connection with any special educational needs that the child may have.
>
> (Education Act 1996, section 332)

Subsequently a National Service Framework was put in place to ensure that, among other things,

> children and young people who are disabled or who have complex health needs, receive coordinated, high quality child and family-centred services which are based on assessed needs, which promote social inclusion and, where possible, enable them and their families to live ordinary lives.

This requires that

> services provide early identification of health conditions, impairments and any social and physical barriers to inclusion, through integrated diagnosis and assessment processes.
>
> (Department of Health 2004: Standard 8)

It is no accident that there was an emphasis on communication and coordination between agencies. The fragmentation of provision for children in their early years has been seen as a major weakness over an extended period (Pugh 1988), even though the statutory, private and voluntary agencies that are involved offer a rich variety of facilities to meet the complex needs of parents and children. They include maintained nursery schools, nursery classes in primary schools, independent schools, day nurseries, family centres, preschool centres, playgroups, childminders, and, for children with SEN, a variety of parent support schemes. This increasingly integrated patchwork now has an additional stimulus to coordination in the form of the government's Early Support Programme, a major initiative to provide training and resources that will foster 'better coordinated, family-focused services for young disabled children' (http://www.early support.org.uk). A new post of Area Special Needs Coordinator for early years settings was established to foster good practice and effective inclusion (DfES 2002b). Detailed guidance was issued for professionals involved with the planning and delivery of services to young disabled children and their families with the emblematic title *Together from the Start* (DfES/DH 2003). The notion of a 'team around the child' has evolved, with the parents being full members of the team (Limbrick 2005).

Research sponsored by the DfES that was completed at around the same time as those initiatives were launched showed that attending preschool provision benefits the cognitive development of children who are identified as being 'at risk' (Sylva *et al.* 2004). They also found that those centres which were within the maintained sector were more likely to have systems in place for identifying children who had SEN. Far fewer private day nurseries and fewer still play groups reported having such systems. They argued that 'this suggests that some children "at risk" of developing special educational needs may go unnoticed and miss the opportunity for early intervention in these forms of provision' (Taggart *et al.* 2006: 43). This is not entirely surprising, since those early education providers which accept any form of government funding are required to have regard to the SEN Code of Practice and to have a written SEN policy. They are expected to monitor individual children's progress and to make a graduated response to any difficulties that arise (DfES 2001b: Section 4). One aim of the recent initiatives has been to spread best practice in this regard throughout the sector.

A distinction can be made between lifelong difficulties with physical manifestations that are typically identified before school entry and school-related difficulties that are typically identified at a later stage by teachers. Concepts such as 'hearing impairment' appear comparatively straightforward – a matter of medical diagnosis from the point when the impairment is established (which may be at birth or following a severe illness such as meningitis during childhood). On the other hand, the position is seen to be different when we consider those forms of SEN that are defined in terms of problems in school, so that they are identified later. Sociologists such as Tomlinson (1982) have pointed out that those categories of SEN which are seen as 'subjective' may be more prone to distortion than those sometimes described as 'objective'. (In fact, even apparently straightforward forms of SEN cannot be understood adequately through focusing on obvious impairments and their amelioration. See the discussion of a social/cultural perspective on deafness in Chapter 17.)

There may still be a problem if a child is correctly identified as having significant difficulties but an important aspect of those difficulties is overlooked. Consider the example of Steven who was identified at the age of 3 as having made a slow start in talking. He lived with his mother and two siblings in a run-down cottage in an isolated rural area. The family rarely left the immediate vicinity of their home, and the older children had poor attendance records at school. Steven's problem was noted by an education welfare officer when he visited the home to follow up an attendance issue with the children's mother. He advised her to 'take the lad to your GP for a check-up'. But she could not afford the expense of having to make frequent bus trips to the local town. In addition, she was scared of getting involved in anything that might further overwhelm the family, especially if it required her to keep all three of her children under control in the presence of others. Steven had an intermittent hearing problem (glue ear) in a serious form, and it was not finally identified and treated until he started school two years later.

So there can be errors in early identification, and the consequences for some children are likely to be negative. What will make errors less likely or their impact less serious? Here are three suggestions that have received wide support and are important well beyond the identification stage. You will find that we come back to them again and again throughout this book:

- *Parents must be fully involved throughout.* Full involvement of parents from the outset will add a crucial dimension to the picture. The intimate knowledge that parents bring is enhanced by their emotional commitment to their child. Of course, if you stand very close to something, you do not always see it in the round. But you will still see things about it that nobody else notices.

- *Everyone who knows the child must collaborate.* Errors will be minimized where there is close cooperation and communication between any health and social services professionals who know a child and the teachers who have responsibility for him or her in school. If views from different perspectives are sought, listened to and reconciled, it is less likely that the child's difficulties will be misunderstood because of one person's (or one profession's) blind spots.

- *Intervention should have a low profile.* Low-profile helping strategies will build on the normal school routine of the child's class group and interrupt and disrupt them as little as possible. The effect will also be to reduce any potentially stigmatizing effect of labelling to a minimum.

During the Foundation Stage of education for children aged 3–5 years, progress towards the targeted Early Learning Goals (QCA 2000b) should be monitored closely. It is pointed out in the Code that this will benefit a wider group of children and not only those with SEN: children making slower progress may include those who are younger, who are learning EAL or who have particular learning difficulties. It should not be assumed that children who are making slower progress must, therefore, have SEN. But such children will need carefully differentiated learning opportunities to help them progress, and careful monitoring of their progress (DfES 2001a: paras 4.5–4.8).

Identification and assessment of SEN at school

Schools in England and Wales had statutory baseline assessment arrangements between 1998 and 2002. This involved assessing each child when they started the reception stage at school using an accredited baseline assessment scheme. Many alternative schemes were available. This framework has been replaced by the *Foundation Stage Profile*, a national assessment scheme that helps teachers to sum up each child's progress and learning needs. For most children, the Profile is completed at the end of the Reception year in primary school. It is based on ongoing observations and assessments carried out during the final year of the Foundation Stage, as well as contributions from parents and from practitioners in settings that children have attended previously. They are required to cover the six areas of learning associated with the Foundation Stage:

- personal, social and emotional development;
- communication, language and literacy;

Activity 6.1   Dilemmas in the identification of SEN

Read the following three pairs of dilemma statements from Norwich (2008: 63) and consider the following questions:

1   To what extent does each pair of statements constitute a dilemma for you?

2   In the research study four broad response alternatives were identified. Which of these best characterizes your response to each dilemma:

(a)   Tension – A hard choice is recognized and experienced but a decision is not reached

(b)   Resolved tension – A hard choice is recognized and experienced but some balancing is carried out and a choice is made

(c)   The validity of the dilemma is questioned by questioning the link between the option and the negative outcome. This may have the effect of moderating the dilemma.

(d)   Other outcomes, whether more negative or positive, are presented for each option. This may have the effect of restructuring the dilemma.

Identification:

- If children experiencing difficulties in learning are identified and labelled as having a disability (needing special education), then they are likely to be treated as different, devalued and stigmatised.

- If children experiencing difficulties in learning are NOT identified as having a disability (needing special education), then it is less likely additional educational resources will be identified and ensured for them.

Curriculum:

- If children identified as having a disability (needing special education) are offered the same learning experiences as other children, they are likely to be denied the opportunity to have learning experiences relevant to their individual needs.

- If children identified as having a disability (needing special education) are NOT offered the same learning experiences as other children, then they are likely to be treated as a separate lower status group and be denied equal opportunities.

Location:

- If children with moderate and severe disabilities (needing special education) are taught in general classrooms, then they are less likely to have access to scarce and specialist services and facilities.

- If children with moderate and severe disabilities (needing special education) are NOT taught in general classrooms, then they are more likely to feel excluded and not be accepted by other children.

- mathematical development;

- knowledge and understanding of the world;

- physical development;

- creative development.

During the consultations that led to the replacement of the previous scheme there was strong support for the inclusion of all children in the new scheme, including those who might have SEN, but there was also a strong view that 'the end of the foundation stage was too late to identify children's special educational or other needs'. The majority 'thought that the new assessment could best serve children with special educational needs by acting as a support or trigger to other specialist assessments' (SMSR 2001: 4).

The views expressed during that consultation were in line with a key requirement that was set out in the Code of Practice in the same year – that there should be graduated response so that the action taken to support a child at risk is no more than what is required to resolve the child's needs. Only where progress continues to cause concern should additional action be taken.

> This approach recognises that there is a continuum of special educational needs and, where necessary, brings increasing specialist expertise to bear on the difficulties that a child may be experiencing. However the school should, other than in exceptional cases, make full use of all available classroom and school resources before expecting to call upon outside resources . . . In many cases the action taken will mean that the child's needs are resolved. Only for those children whose progress continues to cause concern should additional action be taken. For children in the primary phase this Code recommends that when a child is identified as having special educational needs the school should intervene as described below at *School Action* and *School Action Plus*. These interventions will not usually be steps on the way to statutory assessment. Nor are they hurdles to be crossed before a statutory assessment can be made. Some children will require less rather than more help if the interventions work successfully. The interventions are a means of matching special educational provision to the child's needs, and are therefore part of the continuous and systematic cycle of planning, action and review within the school to enable all children to learn and progress.
>
> (DfES 2001a: paras 5.20–5.22)

The School Action and School Action Plus provisions that operate in England and Wales were outlined in Chapter 3. Similar graduated approaches to determining a child's level of need in the light of their response to basic adjustments to teaching have been widely adopted internationally. In the USA this is known as the Response to Intervention (RTI) model (Vaughn and Fuchs 2003). Rigorous evaluation studies of the approach have indicated that it can lead to fewer full individual assessments being conducted and those pupils who are assessed being more likely to prove to qualify for additional special education services. It can adapt to the requirements of diverse groups, including children who are learning EAL (Haager 2007). It is not only less stressful for children and parents but also more cost-effective. VanDerHeyden *et al.* (2007), who reported one of the evaluation studies, argued that there is one critical condition for those outcomes:

the interventions to which a response is evaluated must be an established, evidence-based intervention that is implemented in the way in which it was planned to be intended. Assessment of progress involves a detailed evaluation of the intervention as well as an assessment of the child's performance (Barnett *et al.* 2004). RTI may be cost-effective, but its scope is ambitious and it makes considerable demands in terms of staff training and support.

If the interventions arranged through School Action Plus prove inadequate to meet a child's needs, the local authority is required to arrange a statutory assessment and, depending on the outcome of that assessment, to draw up a statement of SEN so that it can arrange provision that the school could not reasonably be expected to make within its own resources. In January 2006 some 236,700 (or 2.9 per cent of) pupils across all schools in England had statements of SEN (DfES 2006d). This number has been decreasing over recent years, but the graduated system of assessment that determines it has come under increasing criticism from parents (Audit Commission 2002b; House of Commons Education and Skills Committee 2006) and teachers (Brettingham 2007). Ofsted (2002b) questioned what SEN statements are for. Because the LEA has a duty to ensure that the provision specified in the statement is made, and the LEA must make available the resources needed to defray the cost of the provision,

> it follows, therefore, that the statement may be seen, not as an educational assessment and a prescription, but as a key to unlocking resources. Where this occurs, the effects on the LEA may be considerable. The budgetary implications are self-evident, but the impact may be broader, in that a culture may be created in which the main focus of SEN-related activity is the production of statements, not the alignment of resources to needs. The statement becomes an end in itself and not the means to an end, which is to improve the standards achieved by the pupils concerned and to extend the range of opportunities open to them. Such a development is likely to be productive only of bureaucracy and litigation. This is not a climate conducive to 'inclusion'.
>
> (Ofsted 2002b: para. 18)

As we noted in Chapter 3, schools have not, in general, made use of the detailed assessment information attached to statements in order to plan the children's teaching or set IEP targets, and IEPs are not generally seen as useful in supporting effective practice, particularly at secondary level (Tennant, 2007).

The fact that local authorities have specific responsibilities towards children with statements may limit their scope for investing in wider preventive work with children with lower levels of need, at School Action and School Action Plus. The Audit Commission, which made this point in 2002, noted that over the previous three years, authorities in England and Wales had increased their spending on children with statements almost ten times as much as they had increased spending on children with SEN but without a statement. They quoted LEA officers as speaking of 'a "catch-22" situation in this respect: their obligations towards children with statements meant that they were unable to spend more on children at School Action and School Action Plus; but until they did, demand for statements could be expected to continue to rise' (Audit Commission 2002a: para. 38) It has subsequently been argued by the House of Commons Education and Skills Committee (2006) and others that local authorities have an inbuilt conflict of interest because they are responsible both for assessing the needs of the child and for arranging provision to meet those needs.

The government's aim is to reduce reliance on statements by improving the skills and capacity of schools to meet a diverse range of needs. Increasing numbers of local authorities have been delegating SEN funding to schools, reducing the number of statements at the same time. The House of Commons Committee argued that, while this is a positive trend, delegated arrangements 'must be set in a system with much greater clarification and much stronger guidance on minimum standards of provision'. They argued that in the absence of such a system the guidance on reducing reliance on statements had led to inequitable provision and a 'postcode lottery'. They found that the proportion of pupils with statements varied substantially between authorities, for example between Nottinghamshire where 1.08 per cent of all pupils had statements in 2002 and Halton in Cheshire where the figure was 4.83 per cent.

There are thus considerable pressures for changes in the framework for the formal assessment of SEN, but reform has been delayed because there is no consensus about what should replace the current arrangements. In England the debate has focused on a small number of key issues:

- How should the assessment of SEN relate to the 'personalization of learning' for all children? In principle, there could be a continuum of levels of support across the system, including high levels that would be suitable for a child with complex or severe SEN. The Scottish education system has adopted a model of 'additional support needs' that does not separate out 'special educational needs' as a distinct categorical entity (Scottish Executive Education Department 2003; Gibson 2005; Hamill and Clark 2005).

- How should approaches to the assessment of SEN build on the data available through the Common Assessment Framework in such a way that explicit reference is made to the five outcomes associated with the *Every Child Matters* initiative?

- To what degree should those who are centrally involved in the assessment process be independent of the bodies that have financial responsibility for SEN provision? The House of Commons Education and Skills Committee (2007b) argued for full independence, while bodies such as the broad-based Special Educational Consortium have argued that it is important for SEN assessment, like other assessment in schools, to be closely integrated into the fabric of teaching and learning.

Initial assessment questions

The formal arrangements for identification and assessment provide a framework within which the 'real work' of trying to understand a child's strengths and difficulties proceeds. We now move on to examine that work. When a child has been identified as being at risk or as experiencing difficulties, it is necessary to carry out a more detailed assessment. Harlen (1983) has suggested some initial questions that need to be considered when embarking on any assessment in school, whatever the focus. We have added a commentary below to highlight issues that arise in relation to work with different groups of pupils.

What is the purpose of the assessment? For example, checking what has been learned; making comparisons; reporting achievements; diagnosing difficulties; evaluating teaching or the curriculum; monitoring at school, LEA or national level.

What information is required for that purpose? For example, what learning outcomes are to be assessed – knowledge, techniques, problem-solving strategies, creativity, confidence, ability to work autonomously, ability to work with others on solving problems and carrying out tasks? (In the case of children with EAL, it may be important to assess their knowledge of the vocabulary for the subject.)

What methods will provide this information? Any assessment method will have the following components:

● *Ways in which the tasks are presented.* For example, on paper; by demonstration; in a practical situation; through normal class work. (In the case of pupils with EAL, the use of methods that place a premium on language proficiency may mean that they fail to understand the question or task properly, so that their knowledge of the target subject is not assessed at all.)

● *Ways in which pupils can respond.* For example, selection of correct answer from multiple choices; writing; drawing, etc.; constructing; speaking. Note that pupils may differ in their success in responding through different media. For example, there is evidence that boys do better on a test in a multiple-choice format, while girls do better when their knowledge is assessed through an essay-writing task (Gipps and Murphy 1994).

● *Standards or criteria used in judging the response.* For example, comparing with others' performance; comparing with stated performance criteria; comparing with pupil's own previous performance.

● *Ways of presenting the results of assessment.* For example, number of correct answers; grade; qualitative comments.

Together these factors combine to determine whether a method of assessment is *reliable* (consistent, yielding the same results whoever administers it and whenever it is given), and *valid* (accurate, giving results that reflect the reality of the child's abilities or achievements). Specifically, we may want to know whether the assessment has concurrent validity and/or predictive validity (see Table 6.1). It will always be important that a test or assessment is reliable. For different purposes either concurrent or predictive validity may be more important.

How will the results be interpreted and used? While the purposes of assessment will not differ for different groups of children in the same situation, the interpretation of the results may be less certain and more sensitive. For example, if children from a minority ethnic group obtain a low score on average on an attainment test, this may be taken to mean that, as a group, their abilities are lower, or it may be taken to mean that the curriculum is ethnocentric or the test biased. For pupils with EAL concurrent validity could be high if decisions made about the purpose, information and methods of assessment take account of their needs. But predictive validity could still be low. If the interpretation of their results takes account of their (possibly unusual) educational history, predictions about their future progress should be more accurate.

Tests for testers – what standards must assessment meet?

This section will highlight four reasonable expectations of the process of assessment: theoretical integrity; practical efficacy; equity; and accountability (Cline, 1992). The first two of these have regularly featured in accounts of SEN assessment. We will emphasize the equal importance of the last two. As different approaches to assessment are introduced in this book, we will examine them in the light of the questions presented in Figure 6.1

Theoretical integrity

- Is the approach to assessment based on an acceptable model of SEN (or is the model on which it is based reliant on outdated or misleading categories of handicap)?

- Does its implicit model of human development incorporate all aspects of development (or is it based on a narrow view of what is important in development – for example, focusing on intelligence to the exclusion of everything else)?

- Is it based on an acceptable model of the learning process that respects the autonomy and initiative of the learner (or does it appear to assume a top-down, highly structured process for all aspects of classroom learning)?

- Does it explicitly focus on aspects of development that are important for successful learning (or does it emphasize only weaknesses, limitations, gaps in knowledge and what might make for failure)?

Practical efficacy

- Does the assessment draw upon the richest sources of information available (or is it based on thin evidence that comes from a restricted perspective on what the child is like)?

- Does it produce information that can lead directly to improvements in teaching and learning (or is the information it yields of limited value in planning how the child can best be taught)?

- Does the way the assessment is conducted empower children, parents and teachers (or does it place them in a subordinate position so that their observations as stakeholders in the situation are ignored)?

Equity

- Are the rights of children and parents effectively protected?

- Does the process operate without bias with respect to gender, social class, ethnicity, language use and religion (see Chapter 6)?

Accountability

- Is the process and the information it produces open and intelligible to children, parents, teachers, other professionals and educational administrators?

- Are the agreed purposes of the assessment satisfied?

- Is the process cost-effective?

Figure 6.1 Questions to be asked about the process of assessment

---

From time to time professional groups involved in SEN assessment have tried to define a set of principles to guide their assessment practice. The following statement was produced by a team of educational psychologists in the London Borough of Southwark (Shah *et al.* 1997):

Assessment carried out in the Southwark Educational Psychology Service will be underpinned by the following principles:

Psychological   The assessment will be informed by the testing of hypotheses which derive from current psychological theory.

Understandable   The assessment will have a number of audiences. It must be understandable by those audiences and have value for all those audiences.

Beneficial   The assessment must make a difference, and that difference must be a beneficial one, both in terms of the process and in terms of the outcomes.

Equity   The assessment process must promote equity and address the issues of disadvantage and deprivation.

Parents   The assessment should in the majority of cases take place only with the full agreement and involvement of the parents/carers of the child or young person.

Contextual   The assessment must be rooted firmly in a real life context and explore concerns in the context in which they occur. The assessment should acknowledge the maturational, developmental and pedagogical processes that children and young people undergo and take account of those processes.

Accurate   The assessment should be based on fact, and opinion and interpretation presented in the report should be denoted as such.

Reproducible   Another psychologist working with the same hypotheses should be able to reach similar conclusions provided no change has taken place.

Activity 6.2   Defining principles of assessment for your own setting

Consider the principles of assessment agreed by the Southwark Educational Psychology Service in 1997. These were clearly based on the challenge of assessment as it was experienced by a group of people doing a particular job at a particular time in a particular kind of setting. Do all the principles they described apply to the context in which you work? How would you adapt their statement for your situation?

Assessment and the delivery of the curriculum

When teachers assess SEN they work within the context of the assessment procedures their school has in place for all children. In England there is a national system of assessment at the end of each Key Stage – that is, at ages 7, 11, 14 and 16. The results are published school by school, and these arrangements are seen as playing a central role in improving educational standards. Since everyone is able to examine the public 'league tables' of schools' results, there is a strong motivation for schools to present the best possible picture of their achievements. These requirements reflect an international trend towards more systematic assessment of pupils' attainments in school and public dissemination of the results (Rouse and McLaughlin 2007).

The strategies of assessment employed to meet national requirements at the end of each Key Stage have been designed to enable broad-brush information to be obtained across the age group. They are not usually helpful in relation to detailed programme planning for children with SEN. However, while it was statutorily possible to exempt some children with statements, teachers considered from the outset that it was important that all children should be included in the process wherever possible. They argued that this would support their inclusion in the delivery of the mainstream curriculum (Lewis 1995). Special arrangements may be made in order to enable children with SEN to participate. For example, they may be allowed additional time during the test session; material may be presented on audiotape or in Braille or enlarged print; they may use any mechanical and technological aids that they would normally use; and an amanuensis or a reader may be employed. It is important to ensure that the operation of the assessment procedures is as equitable as possible. But this is not the only challenging issue that is presented by the national assessment regime in relation to children with SEN. It is equally important that those who are aware that they have underperformed on the assessments are not discouraged from future effort or made to feel that what they can achieve is of no worth.

The ultimate aim of all assessment in the classroom must be to enable teachers to match their delivery of the curriculum to the needs of each pupil (a process of *differentiation*). In a contemporary classroom that goal must be placed alongside the goal of ensuring that learning experiences are shared across a whole class group as much as possible (a process of *inclusion*). The difficulty of achieving this may be illustrated by examining tensions within some of the guidance that has been given on 'including all children' in England's Primary National Strategy:

> For children working significantly below the level of their class or group, learning objectives related to the aspect on which the whole class is working should be chosen as much as possible. However, they should be right for each child at each stage of their learning and development. If, with appropriate access strategies and support, a child cannot work towards the same learning objective as the rest of the class, teachers may want to track back to an earlier objective . . . Planning for individual children or groups of children based on informed observation and assessment for learning will be informed by knowledge of their priorities. For the majority of the time it will be appropriate for children to work on objectives that are similar and related to those for the whole class. However, at other times you will also have to consider whether the children have other priority needs that are central to their learning, for example a need to concentrate on some key skills.
>
> (DfES 2006c: 14)

There is a significant difference between 'tracking back to an earlier objective' (i.e. aiming to develop the pupil's knowledge and skills using the same route as for others but travelling more slowly) and responding to 'a need to concentrate on some key skills' (where the destination or route may be quite different – for example, when mobility skills are taught to children with visual needs; see Chapter 17).

While responsive pedagogy may be widely seen as good practice, it does not appear to be achieved consistently (see, for example, Simpson 1997). Recent school inspections in England have indicated that, while there is wider acceptance of the principle of inclusion, classroom practice in mainstream schools continues to show shortcomings in 'a high proportion of lessons' (Ofsted 2004). A combination of assessment strategies is likely to be most productive in facilitating effective teaching for children with learning difficulties and disabilities. A review by Davis and Florian (2004: 32–3) suggested that we should focus on strategies which:

- are designed to directly raise attainment (e.g. using task analysis and target setting, with associated guidance, prompts and other supports to reach specified objectives and demonstrate success);

- promote 'active learning' (e.g. through self-assessment and response partner systems);

- promote participation and engagement (e.g. through highlighting settings such as collaborative learning and 'real-life' problem solving as contexts for assessment);

- identify and respond to personalized learning styles and preferences (e.g. visual/auditory/kinaesthetic modes of learning or orientation to study (such as deep/surface approaches).

In later chapters we will discuss strategies of assessment for intervention that are intended to facilitate the three key tasks underpinning successful differentiation within an inclusive classroom:

- setting suitable learning challenges;

- responding to pupils' diverse needs;

- overcoming potential barriers to learning.

Approaches to the assessment of SEN

In this final section of the chapter we will describe four distinctive approaches to assessment that have been or are likely to become influential in the field of SEN. They vary markedly in their value in enabling teachers to plan for differentiation. A framework for locating these approaches in relation to the learner is presented in Figure 6.2. The aims and methods associated with each approach are summarized briefly here. You may read more about them in later chapters where each is featured and explained in detail. For the present what matters is to identify the major emphasis of each approach.

Focus on the learner

Traditionally the assessment of SEN has involved a detailed examination of children with difficulties. The assumption was made that the source of any

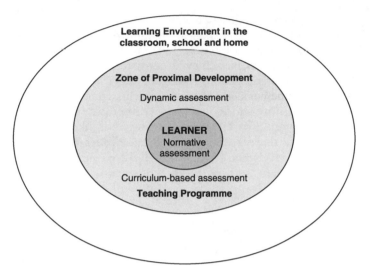

Figure 6.2   Locating approaches to assessment in relation to the learner
Source: Adapted from a figure developed by Sandra Dunsmuir and Jessica Dewey of the University College London Educational Psychology Group.

problems would lie within the children: they must suffer from a disability or impairment of learning ability compared to most children of their age. The assessment task was thought of as similar to medical diagnosis. The aim of assessment was to determine what category of disability the children suffered from. Their performance was compared to norms for their age group. There were a series of assumptions behind this approach. It was assumed that:

- individuals' traits and abilities are relatively permanent characteristics;

- they show a pattern of strengths and weaknesses in learning resulting from these characteristics which can be identified through educational assessment;

- this pattern of strengths and weaknesses is the prime cause of the child's poor classroom performance, with other factors having less importance;

- a teaching programme which remediates weaknesses and builds on strengths can lead to improvement in performance.

This approach has been particularly associated with arranging provision for children with SEN in separate schools or units. (Approaches to assessment within this paradigm will be discussed in more detail in Chapter 12.)

Focus on the teaching programme

Over the last 40 years assumptions relating to a focus on the learner have frequently been attacked, and other approaches have been explored. To some extent the new approaches have been associated with the parallel movement in the direction of inclusive education in mainstream schools. The first new approach to attract attention on a large scale as an alternative to the focus on the learner was a focus on the teaching programme. The underlying assumption here is that the curriculum presented in the classroom is not well suited to the current learning needs of the child. It is necessary to match work on the curriculum more closely to the child's existing skills and knowledge. The educators' task is conceived within a framework of classical learning theory. The immediate challenge is to analyse learning tasks within the curriculum into a hierarchy of component skill elements. Because these elements are thought to be organized hierarchically, it is assumed that they will best be approached in incremental steps. It is possible to determine which elements the child has mastered and which require further work. For children with SEN the incremental steps can be made smaller or otherwise modified so that the challenge that is faced at each stage is less formidable. Thus it is assumed that:

- the school curriculum can be analysed into tasks that can be expressed in the form of smart targets;

- these tasks can be arranged into pedagogically viable sequences;

- by checking frequently on a child's attainments within one of these sequences, teaching can be matched closely to the learning stage the child has reached;

- through a method of instruction that is very firmly under the teacher's control, children can be led to acquire new skills, perform them with fluency, maintain them after teacher support is withdrawn, use them in new contexts, and adapt them to different challenges (Solity and Bull 1987).

This approach to assessment will be discussed in more detail in Chapter 8.

Focus on the 'zone of potential development'

A third approach focuses on the 'zone of potential development' as conceptualized by the Russian developmental psychologist, Vygotsky (Daniels 1992). Suppose the performance of two boys on a traditional test is at the same level – for example, a level equivalent to an average 8-year-old's performance. They are then retested with some adult help – for example, in the form of standard questions prompting them towards the correct solution of problems they could not solve before. One child now attains a score that is just a little better than before, while the other now reaches a level that is associated with much older children. Vygotsky saw the difference between what children can achieve by themselves and the level they can reach with adult help as an operational definition of the 'zone of potential development' (ZPD). Those two children have the same zone of actual development (ZAD) but a very different ZPD: the latent learning ability of one was markedly superior.

Supporters of this approach argue that traditional (static) tests establish current levels of performance but usually tell us little about the processes that underlie that competence. They also ignore functions that have not yet matured but are in the process of maturing. They focus on the 'fruits' of development rather than its 'buds' and 'flowers'. They are retrospective rather than prospective (Vygotsky 1978). Observing embryonic (nascent, emerging) skills closely would provide a better estimate of individuals' potential for proceeding beyond their present level of competence (Campione 1989) and would offer more useful guidance on the kind of teaching that will help them realize that potential. Children are invited to carry out standard tasks that are at the limit of their capabilities. They are given adult assistance to help them to success, and the assistance is monitored closely. Thus the focus of the assessment is on both the children's performance and on the amount and kind of help they required to achieve it. This approach to assessment is discussed in more detail in Chapter 12.

Focus on the learning environment

A fourth approach shifts the focus onto the learning environment provided by the school. The assumption is made that SEN are relative and that, for individual children, a full understanding of their SEN can only be developed if one evaluates the learning environment that is provided for them. Perhaps the learning environment in which a child experiences difficulties fails to provide conditions that will facilitate success. The assessment may involve classroom observation, diary records, questionnaires and/or interviews with both children and teachers. The purpose of the analysis is to determine whether there are factors in the learning environment that may cause or exacerbate the child's learning difficulties (Frederickson and Cline 1995). This approach to assessment is discussed in more detail in Chapter 9.

Activity 6.3 provides an opportunity for you to consider how these approaches to assessment might be employed in practice. This activity introduces

---

Activity 6.3   Why is this bilingual pupil not making the progress I would expect? Evaluating some possible hypotheses

The question you are asked to address in this task is: Which of the approaches to assessment featured in this section would be most useful to evaluate each of these hypotheses? Remember that they focus on a child who is learning to speak EAL. The list of hypotheses was developed by a team of psychologists and teachers in Surrey (Wright 1991). They suggested different reasons why a bilingual child might be underperforming and examined the implications of each explanation for how teachers might aim to help. Indicate in the right-hand column whether the focus of investigation should be:

(a) the individual learner;

(b) the teaching programme;

(c) the zone of potential development;

(d) the learning environment.

Hypothesis	*Suggested focus for assessment*

---

1   The child is learning more slowly than others because the ethos and curriculum of the school are experienced as challenging and alien, rather than welcoming and accommodating

2 The child is not learning because the child's good level of conversational English has misled the teacher into setting tasks that are too abstract for the child's current language level

3 The child is learning at an appropriate rate, and just needs more time to get used to the demands of working in their second language

4 The child has not attained a basic language proficiency in any language, because neither language has been given adequate opportunities to develop

5 The child is failing because of a preoccupation with stress that is affecting their family or their community

6 The child has a general difficulty in learning compared to other children of the same age

7 The child is failing because of a specific language disorder

another way of thinking about the process of assessment – as a hypothesis-testing process. Wright (1991) and her colleagues regarded assessment as being like a piece of detective work. There was a situation to be explained. They thought of various hypotheses that might provide a satisfactory explanation. In the activity you are asked to suggest what kind of evidence should be collected in order to decide whether any of these hypotheses is justified.

Conclusions

While much emphasis is placed on early identification and assessment of SEN, there can be dangers associated with this as well as benefits. We have reviewed a range of measures which should be taken to maximize the likelihood of positive outcomes. These include: parental involvement; multi-disciplinary collaboration; and utilizing the least intrusive intervention approach available. Current arrangements in England for formal assessment of SEN have been subjected to widespread criticism, and there is ongoing debate on possible changes.

A major focus in this chapter was on the critical examination of assessment practice. A guiding framework was proposed within which the purpose of any assessment is carefully considered as a first step. Thereafter the information required for that purpose and the methods that can be used to obtain the necessary information can be decided. It was suggested that a series of questions be asked about the proposed plan of the assessment – questions relating to equity and accountability issues as well as questions concerning the theoretical integrity and practical efficacy of the process. Finally, we considered four distinctive approaches to assessment which relate to the different ways of conceptualizing SEN introduced in Chapter 3. Each of these approaches will be described in further detail in later chapters and has both advantages and disadvantages in relation to the questions posed for a critical examination of identification and assessment practice.

Bias and equity in assessment

Introduction

In Chapter 1 we saw that on both sides of the Atlantic there has been a tendency for higher than expected numbers of children from some minority communities to be admitted into some forms of special educational provision. In England and Wales in the early 1970s there were over four times as many children of West Indian immigrants in schools for the 'educationally subnormal' as would have been expected from their overall numbers in the child population (Tomlinson 1984). Although the over-representation of African-Caribbean pupils in these schools has been reduced over the years, relatively high numbers continue to be admitted to schools for pupils with emotional and behavioural difficulties. In Chapter 1 we also drew attention to other group differences in admission to SEN provision – between boys and girls and between children from working-class and middle-class backgrounds. Such group differences in outcome must arise at some point in the process of identification and assessment. It could be that there are uneven patterns of referral that arise from real group differences in how many children require help and how severe their needs are. In relation to gender, for example, it could be that males are more vulnerable to the effects of trauma and illness than females or that males externalize their feelings in schools more openly than females and in so doing make themselves more likely to be identified and consequently labelled (OECD 2004). There may, in addition, be a mismatch between the pedagogy of the school and the educational needs of male students (Skårbrevik 2002).

In relation to season of birth, the way in which admission to school is organized may lead to unfavourable outcomes for children who are comparatively 'immature' within their year group. In England the academic year runs from 1 September to 31 August, so that a child born on 31 August may start school up to a year earlier than a child born only one day later, on 1 September. Both local and national studies have shown that autumn-born children are markedly less likely to be placed on a school's SEN register or to have a full SEN statement than those born later in the school year, and therefore younger within their age group (Greenwood and Ayre 2005; Crawford *et al.* 2007). Group differences of this kind tend to be attributed to wider cultural and systemic factors so that fairness is thought of as 'a sociocultural, rather than a technical, issue' (Stobart 2005: 275).

Many commentators, however, have emphasized bias in referral processes and bias during formal assessment as key sources of inequity in SEN provision. For example, one of the writers who first highlighted the over-representation of black children in schools for the 'educationally subnormal' in England (Coard 1971: 15) wrote that, when IQ tests were used, a range of biases operating

> against the West Indian child . . . apply just as much to the *actual questions asked on the IQ test* administered to the children, and the very nature of '*the test situation*'. The vocabulary and style of all these IQ tests is white middle class. Many of the questions are capable of being answered by a white middle-class boy, who, because of being middle class, has the right background of experiences with which to answer the questions – regardless of his real intelligence. The black working-class child, who has different life experiences, finds great difficulty in answering many of the questions, even if he is very intelligent.

The Californian federal judge, R.F. Peckham, who banned the use of IQ tests with black children at the end of the 1970s, stated:

> We must recognise at the outset that the history of the IQ test and of special education classes built on IQ testing is not the history of neutral scientific discoveries translated into educational reform. It is, at least in the early years, a history of racial prejudice, of social Darwinism, and of the use of the scientific 'mystique' to legitimate such prejudices.
>
> (Baca and Cervantes 1989: 16)

For Howitt and Owusu-Bempah (1994: 28), tests of intelligence were 'nothing other than weapons of subordination when used with society's disadvantaged'. Similar, though less extreme, concerns have been expressed about other forms of test. (For a full discussion, see Gipps and Murphy 1994; Moss *et al.* 2008.)

There is, however, another way of looking at the situation. In this view an advantage of using tests for assessment is that the decision-making process is transparent. If bias is operating in the content of the tests or in the use made of the results, at least it is possible to trace what is happening. Some decisions in education may be affected by bias in a way that is hidden from gaze. One example

Table 7.1   Proportion of secondary pupils from different ethnic groups allocated to remedial sets for English and mathematics in a Midlands town

	West Indian	Indian	Non-minority
Remedial English	17% (30/176)	12% (23/188)	5% (13/239)
Remedial maths	19% (42/216)	12% (26/224)	8% (25/304)

Source: Adapted from Scarr *et al.* (1983) and Roberts (1984).

would be decisions on the placement of pupils when classes are streamed. An early analysis of the educational careers of the children of immigrants in a UK Midlands town showed that they were two to three times as likely as their white peers to be placed in the remedial stream of a secondary school (see Table 7.1). HMI have observed that it is still the case that, where schools emphasize tight setting, some groups learning EAL (notably pupils from the Bangladeshi and Pakistani communities) are likely to be placed disproportionately in low sets, especially in English (Ofsted 1999a).

Some schools employ standardized attainment tests to profile the educational achievements and needs of groups of children and use the results for planning purposes. The observations of HMI have suggested 'that it is in those schools with the best ethnic data that the performance of the minority ethnic pupils has improved most strongly' (Ofsted 1999a: 16). Inspectors considered that analysing performance on a test such as the Cognitive Abilities Test (Thorndike *et al.* 1986) could assist teachers to plan the organization of a cohort of pupils into groups or to identify students with unused potential by comparing ability with attainment. Focusing specifically on the situation of bilingual pupils, Cline and Shamsi (2000) commented:

> It is common for pupils learning EAL to obtain scores for nonverbal reasoning that are higher than their scores on L2 language and attainment tests (Valdes and Figueroa, 1994, Table 4.1). Analysing the profile of scores on this type of test battery can help to counter the low expectations that are sometimes held of children in the early stages of learning English.

But they added a note of caution:

> If standardised tests are used for guiding even minor decisions about individuals learning EAL, particular care will always be needed. The appropriateness of the decision may be monitored by seeking confirmatory evidence from earlier school records, if available, or by reviewing any new arrangements or provision after an agreed fixed period on the basis of further teacher observation.
>
> (Cline and Shamsi 2000: 39)

Similar analyses have highlighted the role of social class in differential outcomes. For example, Sacker *et al.* (2001) reanalysed earlier national longitudinal data and showed that, while more children whose parents worked in manual occupations had received extra help in school compared to children from professional homes, there was a surprising shift in the balance of the figures when reading, mathematics and psychosocial adjustment scores were taken into account. If that was done, the children from professional homes were more likely to have received help: a child from a professional home was one and a half times more likely to receive help than a child from an unskilled occupational background with the same test scores. Commenting on the use of written examinations for selection purposes, Stobart (2005: 278) recognized the possibility that two apparently contradictory viewpoints can be held simultaneously. 'I can argue that public tests are important as a means of equalizing opportunities and as a necessary corrective to patronage, while at the same time understanding that tests may be biased in favour of one particular gender, social or ethnic group.'

In this chapter we will examine definitions of bias, consider its sources at various points in the assessment process and outline strategies for reducing the impact of bias to a minimum. It cannot be expected that bias will be eliminated altogether. It is not possible (or desirable) to develop methods of educational assessment that are culturally neutral or entirely 'culture-free'. Child development and school education are embedded in a cultural context which is often unfair (DeBlassie and Franco 1983). The result of any assessment is likely to reflect, in part, the pattern of opportunities that exists. Equity in the assessment of SEN requires us to recognize sources of bias and try to reduce them. It is not helpful to pretend that this area of education can operate independently of the inequalities that characterize other aspects of society and schooling.

Activity 7.1   Access, curriculum and assessment questions in relation to equity

Stobart (2005) did not have SEN assessment in mind when he produced the table below. He was concerned with educational opportunities in general. Building on the work of earlier commentators, he argued that fair assessment in education cannot be separated from questions about fairness in access opportunities and in what the curriculum offers. Discuss how far the questions that he developed in relation to educational assessment in general apply to the particular case of assessment of special educational needs.

- Are his questions relevant to SEN assessment?

- Are there other questions in this field that should be considered under the headings of access, curriculum and assessment?

Access questions	Curricular questions	Assessment questions
Who gets taught and by whom?	Whose knowledge is taught?	What knowledge is assessed and equated with achievement?
Are there differences in the resources available for different groups?	Why is it taught in a particular way to this particular group?	Are the form, content and mode of assessment appropriate for different groups and individuals?
What is incorporated from the cultures of those attending?	How do we enable the histories and cultures of people of colour, and of women, to be taught in responsible and responsive ways?	Is this range of cultural knowledge reflected in definitions of achievement?
		How does cultural knowledge mediate individuals' responses to assessment in ways which alter the construct being assessed?

Bias in test content

What is *bias* and what is *fair assessment*? The answers to these questions are sometimes based on confused assumptions. It may be thought that if, say, a test item is more difficult for boys than for girls, that item must be 'unfair to boys'. But an assessment may still be 'fair' even if, on average, one group of people consistently obtains higher scores on it than another group. The first group may really be superior at whatever task the assessment is measuring. Williams (1971, 1975) devised a vocabulary test that would be 'fairer' to black Americans living in northern US cities than the conventional vocabulary tests in published IQ scales. His 'Black Intelligence Test of Cultural Homogeneity' (the 'BITCH' Test) was a multiple-choice vocabulary test comprising 100 items drawn from urban black culture. It was a culture-specific test highlighting the world of the inner city and covering elements of black slang. Two items from the test are:

> *Boot* refers to (a) a cotton farmer, (b) a black, (c) an Indian, or (d) a Vietnamese citizen.
> *Yawk* is (a) a gun, (b) a fishing hook, (c) a high boot, or (d) a heavy coat.

Williams showed that this test favoured black children, while conventional tests favoured white children. Both tests appear to be biased – *if* the criterion of bias is that tests should not discriminate between groups in terms of outcome. Jensen (1980) described this criterion as 'the egalitarian fallacy' – assuming that all human populations are essentially identical or equal in whatever trait or ability the test purports to measure.

The purpose of an assessment is to make predictions about the people who are being assessed. In relation to *bias* the key question then must be whether a test makes equally accurate predictions about all groups of children. In psychometric jargon, a test is biased if it is 'differentially valid for members of different groups' (Wood 1991). From this viewpoint what matters is whether a test predicts performance on a criterion measure with equal validity for each social or ethnic group: 'Bias is a kind of invalidity that harms one group more than another' (Shepard *et al.* 1981).

One technical method that can be used to investigate this is person-fit measurement where the response patterns of a group of examinees are evaluated against a psychometric model of the test. How 'unexpected' (according to the model) is the group's characteristic response pattern? For example, do they often give surprisingly correct responses to difficult questions or surprisingly incorrect responses to easy questions? For an example of the use of this strategy, see a study by Lamprianou and Boyle (2004) of the performance of minority ethnic pupils and pupils learning EAL on National Curriculum tests in mathematics in England.

Another method is the constant ratio model (Thorndike 1971) which tests the assumption that those who do best on a test will prove to be those who do well in the comparison task that requires the use of the abilities that the test is intended to measure. For example, with children it is normally expected that ability test scores will increase with age. This has been the basis of a developmental version of the constant ratio model. The question asked is whether the relationship between test scores and chronological age is the same for children in different ethnic or social groups. This can be illustrated with data on one of the versions of the most widely used individual intelligence scale, the Wechsler Intelligence Scale for

Table 7.2   Correlation of IQ with age on WISC-R Scale

	White males	Black males	White females	Black females
No. of children (6–16 years)	938	137	927	153
Correlation of IQ with age:				
Verbal IQ	0.84	0.83	0.84	0.81
Performance IQ	0.81	0.81	0.82	0.82
Full-scale IQ	0.85	0.86	0.85	0.84

Source: Adapted from Reynolds (1980).

Children (WISC). Table 7.2 shows the correlation of IQ with age across ethnic groups analysed from the standardization data for the test by Reynolds (1980). If there had been an exact one-for-one matching between IQ and age, the correlations would have been 1; if there had been no relationship at all they would have been 0. All the correlations shown are much closer to 1 than to 0 (at a level that could not have arisen by chance alone). The correlations are no higher for the white children than they are for the black children. Reynolds concluded that the relationship between IQ scores and age was consistent across ethnic groups (even though the scores of black males were lower than those of other groups on average). As far as he was concerned this evidence 'fails to support armchair claims of test bias . . . with regard to intelligence tests' (Reynolds 1980: 378). Such confidence might be increased by evidence that various revisions of the WISC predicted scores on tests of educational achievement equally well for African-American, Hispanic and white children (e.g. Reynolds and Kaiser 1990; Weiss and Prifitera 1995).

This robust defence of a general intelligence scale does not address the criticism that bias operates in the way such tests are *used* and *interpreted* (Helms 2006). In addition, it is important to recognize that the correlation of overall score with age is a broad-brush measure of bias in test content. Problems may occur with a whole test and the way it is conceived, but they may also occur at the level of an individual test item or task. For example, Ribeiro (1980) found that some test items in the WISC-R proved easier than expected for one particular minority group in the USA. Portuguese children coped well with two questions in an advanced section of a test where they were failing most other items: 'What is the meaning of "migrate"?' and 'Why does oil float on water?'. The explanations were simple: migration was a feature of the recent family history of many of the children, and they were used to seeing oil float on water in an altar lamp in their Catholic church. On the other hand, Pollitt *et al.* (2000) found that a 16-year-old student (MS) who had recently arrived in England as an immigrant from Pakistan had a surprising profile in a mathematics test in which he 'underperformed' on some items. One example was this question:

> It is claimed that in Florida there are eleven lightning strikes every minute. How many is this in a day?

In his first language, Urdu, there are separate words for a 12-hour *day* ('din') and a 24-hour *day-and-night* ('dinraath' – literally 'day and night'). MS chose to use a 12-hour unit for his calculation, which was not what was expected.

In a classic study of O-level English language exams, Wood (1978) found a similar phenomenon in relation to gender differences. Boys did better than girls on items relating to a passage about a man looking back to a boyhood spent near a railway, while girls did better than boys on a passage about a girl's ordeal at a dance. On another test he found girls doing better on a passage about a 14-year-old girl and boys doing better on a passage about the Crimean War (Wood 1991: 169).

Responsible test developers make a formal commitment to addressing the issue of content bias. For example, in its *Code of Practice for the Development of Assessment Instruments, Methods and Systems* (1998) the National Foundation for Educational Research (NFER) stated that in order to produce fair assessments, NFER developers would:

- review and revise questions, items or tasks and related materials to avoid potentially insensitive content or language;

- enact procedures that help to ensure that differences in performance are related primarily to the knowledge, skills, aptitudes or attitudes being assessed rather than to irrelevant factors;

- investigate the performance of people of different ethnic, gender and socio-economic backgrounds when institutions helping with trials are willing to provide this information and when samples of sufficient size are available;

- carry out the investigation of performance of different groups using data provided on the first actual administration of the assessment;

- provide (where feasible) appropriately modified forms of the assessment procedures for people with disabilities.

Braden and Athnasiou (2005) evaluated the fairness of non-verbal measures of intelligence against a set of criteria that has some overlap in terms of its requirements regarding test development procedures and test characteristics but also some additional requirements:

- The theoretical basis of the instrument should cover multiple abilities and emphasize 'fluid abilities' (i.e. those that are not reliant upon prior formal learning).

- The test development process should have included an expert review of item content for the detection of sources of bias.

- The way in which instructions for any test task are presented and the mode of response that is required should not disadvantage test takers from different backgrounds.

- Time limits should not be imposed (or time credits awarded) in such a way as to penalize those from backgrounds where speed of response tends to have a low value.

- There should be practice/teaching items that enable test takers to learn the nature of the task and what is required of them.

- The test development process should include an analysis of possible evidence of bias in the results, for example individual items that have a different profile for test takers from different backgrounds or variation in the factor structure of the results between groups (cf. Sireci *et al.* 2006).

If a test or assessment task is developed within a school, it is possible to employ less formal, school-based review strategies for checking on possible item bias. The list of questions given here was adapted for an earlier report (Cline and Shamsi 2000) from Berk (1984) and Tindal and Marston (1990). These authors designed a method of reviewing to assist in the identification of test items which may reflect gender, cultural, racial, regional and/or ethnic content bias and stereotyping. Although there is a form for this purpose, the essential process can be followed through without elaborate form-filling. It is most effective if a number of people examine the test with the checklist in mind and if they come from a range of backgrounds. The review team should include sufficient people from the target minority groups to enable it to predict significant patterns of response accurately. They should each complete the task independently and only compare notes afterwards. Their first task is to identify any individual items to which they feel they cannot give an unequivocal answer 'yes' for each of the following questions:

1 Is the item free of offensive gender, cultural, racial, regional and/or ethnic content?

2 Is the item free of gender, cultural, racial, regional and/or ethnic stereotyping?

3 Is the item free of language which could be offensive to a segment of the examinee population?

4 Is the item free of descriptions the content of which could be offensive to a segment of the examinee population?

5 Will the activities described in the item be equally familiar (or equally unfamiliar) to all examinees?

6 Will the words in the item have a common meaning for all examinees?

Note that the questions that are to be asked are specific, focused and explicit. If a more general question is asked (e.g. 'Would this item be likely to favour white children over black children?') it is not likely that reviewers would accurately identify items that actually discriminate between ethnic groups (Hieronymous and Hoover 1986).

After looking at the individual items separately the reviewers should consider the test as a whole. Each item may have little wrong with it in itself, but the cumulative effect of the test as a whole may still be biased against a particular subgroup of candidates. So, when the task of examining the items separately has been completed, it is necessary to consider the overall balance of the paper or tasks as a whole: even if few individual items cause problems, what about the overall balance? Some researchers have argued that achieving a satisfactory overall balance and heterogeneous range in a test is much more important than eradicating individual biased items (Roznowski and Reith 1999). Sometimes test developers may retain items that they know to be biased because they appear to make a valuable contribution to the predictive validity of the test. For example, Smith and Whetton (1988: 257) wrote of a test they had developed to support occupational selection:

Of the items used in the final test only three had any evidence of bias, and in each of these the evidence was only slight. These three were left in the test because their other psychometric properties were particularly valuable. Since each of them slightly favoured a different group (whites, non-whites, females), it is unlikely that any noteworthy bias was introduced by their inclusion.

In addition to having groups of people from different backgrounds inspecting test items for content bias, a test developer can carry out a statistical investigation. This will aim to find out 'whether any questions are disproportionately difficult for a particular group once that group's overall test performance has been taken into account' (Gipps and Stobart 1993: 60). Other statistical checks are possible both on individual items and on the test as a whole (Reynolds and Kaiser 1990).

It is not only aspects of content such as offensiveness or stereotyping that can give rise to bias. There may also be biasing factors in the nature of the tasks that are set. For example, a timed test may favour groups who are culturally prepared for working against time or a rating scale may be used differently by respondents who are culturally prepared to commit themselves to extreme responses and those whose upbringing has made them more 'modest' or 'neutral' in their use of a scale (Arce-Ferrer 2006). Work on gender bias has shown that the format of a test or exam may also have a differential impact between groups. It has been found both in the UK and the USA that boys tend to do better on multiple-choice exams while girls tend to do better on exams that involve writing essays (Wood 1991; Gipps and Murphy 1994; Willingham and Cole 1997). Various explanations have been offered as to why this happens. Perhaps girls' essays are evaluated more favourably simply because they are more fluent in their writing and produce longer answers (Pomplun and Capps 1999). Perhaps girls underperform in the multiple-choice format because they are more likely than boys to omit an item when they are unsure of the answer, while boys tend to guess answers more often (Hanna 1986; Linn *et al.* 1987). Whatever the explanation, the most frequently recommended solution remains valid both for general educational assessment and for SEN assessment: use a variety of methods of assessment so as to minimize the bias associated with any one format (cf. Murphy 1982). At the end of it all an additional check is recommended by Watson *et al.* (1987) – carry out a post-test interview with the children to check on how they experienced the test's demands.

Activity 7.2   Evaluating a novel test

Du Bois (1939, cited by Norman, 1963) developed a 'Draw a Horse' test for use with Pueblo Indian children. He had found that tests that involved drawing a person were not effective for measuring cognitive abilities with this population.

(a)   What assumptions do you think he made when developing this test?

(b)   How would you find out whether using it will lead to unbiased assessment?

Other sources of bias and inequity

Discussions of bias and inequity in assessment usually concentrate on the content of tests. But test content is only one of many possible sources of bias. Testing takes place in a social context. Whether the child is in a classroom group or working alone with an adult, it is possible to think about the situation in terms of one of three models. In the examples given below we have assumed that a specialist teacher is testing a child's educational attainments on their own in a quiet corner of a classroom.

- A *psychometric model*. The teacher proffers a test stimulus; the child responds; the teacher measures the child's response.

- A *psychological model*. The teacher explains the task and offers a test stimulus; the child makes sense of the task and responds; the teacher assesses the child's understanding of the task and also the child's response.

- A *social psychological model*. The child compares the situation she or he is in with other familiar situations. The teacher explores the child's understanding of the situation and observes his or her responses to it. The tasks that the teacher gives the child are seen by both as a special feature of their encounter but not its only feature.

The social psychological model seems to reflect what we know about this situation most satisfactorily. A key concept is 'intersubjectivity': speakers take account of what they think their listeners are thinking as they choose what to say and how to say it; they monitor their own speech to make sure that its content and form are such that their listeners can 'tune into' it; listeners try to reconstruct what they think the speaker is intending to make known. Thus it is important to explore a child's understanding of the assessment situation and address any misapprehensions.

In the light of the social psychological model it is necessary to examine the overall assessment process. Each phase of that process may be a source of bias:

- defining the purpose of the assessment;

- briefing the staff who undertake the assessment and deciding what preliminary information they require;

- selecting the activities that are to be assessed;

- choosing appropriate test materials, if required;

- interviewing, testing, examining or observing children;

- evaluating children's responses;

- interpreting their performance;

- deciding on the action to be taken as a result.

In addition, bias may affect the initial identification by teachers of pupils who may have SEN. For example, there are many more boys than girls identified as possibly having dyslexia (Riddell *et al.* 1994). It is often assumed that this is because biological factors predispose boys to be at greater risk for all language-related disorders. Arguing from a different perspective, Benjamin (2003) suggests that the lower rate of referral of girls may arise because girls with SEN are more adept at seeking help for themselves in less obvious and disruptive ways than the boys. However, there is some evidence that *schools and teachers* play a role in this outcome. In a study in Connecticut, when teachers were asked to identify children with learning disabilities, there was a preponderance of boys in the sample they selected. When tests were used alone to identify children at risk and the opinions of teachers were not sought, this male preponderance was reduced (Shaywitz *et al.* 1990). Similar data were reported by Wadsworth *et al.* (1992) with samples of children with reading disabilities in other areas of the USA and in the UK. Cline and Reason (1993) noted that in Shaywitz's study children who were identified as having a reading disability by the schools but not by the research team's tests were more likely to show behaviour problems at school. The subgroup numbers in this study were small, and it would be wrong to place too much reliance on a single finding. But the hypothesis must be: if children are a bit of nuisance in the class-room, it will be more likely that any learning difficulties they have are identified and action taken. Hill (1994) has shown that, when teachers and others describe children in the formal SEN assessment procedure, there is a tendency for gender stereotypes to appear. As the studies summarized in Figure 7.1 illustrate, the same behaviour may be interpreted differently in a boy and a girl.

How can we reduce the risk of initial identification and assessment in schools being influenced by gender or other bias? Structured observation schemes with

---

Condry and Condry (1976) had subjects (a sample of college students) view a videotape of an infant responding to emotionally arousing stimuli such as a teddy bear and a jack-in-the-box. They found that the students' ratings of the type and intensity of the emotions the child displayed varied depending on whether they had been told the child was a boy or a girl. All the students saw the same child responding to the same stimuli. But those who thought the child was a boy were more likely to rate an ambiguous negative response to one of the stimuli as anger, whereas, if the same child was thought to be a girl, 'she' was seen as displaying the emotion of fear in this situation.

In a later study by Condry and Ross (1985), another sample of students was shown a videotape of two preschool children playing roughly in the snow. Their snowsuits disguised their actual gender, and the investigators systematically varied the gender labels used to describe the children. The students were asked to rate the degree of aggression and affection shown by one of the two children. They tended to rate the target child as significantly less aggressive when they thought she or he was a boy playing with another boy than when they thought he or she was a girl or a boy playing with a girl. This effect was particularly strong among participants with more experience with children. It appeared that they probably expected a higher general level of aggression in play between boys than in the other conditions. Condry and Ross suggested that this may have led them either to discount the aggressiveness they observed on the videotape if they thought the participants were boys or to inflate it if they thought they were girls or both: 'It may not be fair, and it certainly is not equal, but from the results of this study it looks as if boys and girls really are judged differently in terms of what constitutes aggression'.

Figure 7.1   Interpretations of the same behaviour in a boy and a girl

well-defined subheadings make it less likely that behaviour that is not expected will be overlooked. Schemes that ask specific questions about the frequency and severity of particular types of incident make it less likely that vague assertions about extreme behaviour will be made without qualification.

In this situation, as in others, there are many advantages to drawing upon multiple sources of evidence. Sometimes, for example, it can be helpful to have a second adult observing the work of the classroom for a short time with a specific brief to investigate what happens from the perspective of the target pupil. When this was arranged in a Year 5 class by Williams (1996), another teacher interpreted various episodes during a reading activity quite differently from the class teacher. The target pupil was Harry, a mainstream pupil with language-related learning difficulties. Here is a record of the same episode as seen by the teacher and by the colleague who had agreed to observe the lesson by 'pupil shadowing' (Galloway and Banes 1994):

> *Class teacher:* Harry was asked an open-ended question which he struggled to answer and he fidgeted. To avoid focusing attention on Harry's difficulty it was passed to another child in the group.

> *Observer:* Harry needed more time to answer an open-ended question. When someone else was asked to answer the question he was left muttering.

Activity 7.3 Approaches to recording observations of children's learning style

Below are two examples of published frameworks for observation relating to learning style in the classroom. They contrast in that the first is intended solely to provide headings under which a teacher will record comments, while the second aims to help teachers discriminate between different levels of severity by suggesting specific mini-scenarios that illustrate each level.

(a) We think that the *format* of the first approach may be more liable to the risk of observational bias. What reasons might there be for that view?

(b) On the other hand, the *text* of the second example includes many vague and value-laden phrases which could, in themselves, encourage a biased approach to the observation task. Can you suggest ways of rewording the two items in the second example so as to reduce that risk?

This extract is taken from an account by Reid (1997) of a strategy for the assessment of dyslexia in the classroom. This section concerns observational assessment. The framework is not intended to be a checklist 'but a guide to the type of factors which should be observed in identifying learning strategies, strengths and weaknesses' (p. 75).

Attention /concentration   *Comments*

Focus on task

Major sources of distraction

Concentration span in different tasks

These items are taken from a 'Guide to the Child's Learning Skills' developed by Stott (1978). For comparison with the extract above, items relating to concentration and distractibility have been selected.

E: He/she is easily distracted

Somewhat: Allows himself to be distracted to the extent that he doesn't get on with the job in hand.

Definite: Creates frequent distractions for himself and others; behaves in a silly clowning way or creates disturbances.

Severe: Flits rapidly from one momentary interest to another without ever doing anything productive.

N: He/she seems to try to attend, and is not hyperactive or distractible, but cannot concentrate.

Somewhat: Seems to try hard but cannot keep his mind on the task, and gets things wrong that he was getting right.

Definite: As soon as he is asked anything his mind flies off at a tangent.

Severe: Cannot be induced to focus his attention on anything.

When observing and recording children's academic achievements, pupil profiling systems have many advantages over repeated testing on the one hand and unstructured observation on the other (Sheil and Forde 1995). A profiling system, such as the English *Foundation Stage Profile* (QCA 2003a), normally comprises three elements:

- *Indicators*. Statements describing pupils' achievements that are normally linked to the objectives of the curriculum.

- *Levels/bands*. Indicators are grouped together within what is thought to be the same broad developmental level or band of achievement. A pupil's performance is rated as a whole across indicators so that a summary statement can be made about the level reached.

- *Assessment tasks and contexts*. Special assessment tasks may be set for the purpose, or the assessment may be based on portfolios of pupils' work or notes of observations made by teachers during everyday classroom activities.

Where there are groups of children of whom teachers' expectations tend to be low (e.g. many minorities) or whose performance tends to be variable (e.g. recently arrived refugees), a system of this kind may have additional benefits, quite apart from any advantages that apply to all pupils. The significant advantage is that in these schemes performance is rated *over time* and teachers' judgements are made in *a range of curricular contexts*. The effect is that, if a child underperforms on one occasion because of problems with the language or content of a particular task, this will be compensated for on another occasion if the foundation of competence in the subject is really established at the target level. In relation to reading, it was found in one study that teacher ratings on a reading scale of this kind were less affected by the fluency in English of children learning EAL than were scores on the London Reading Test given at around the same time (Hester *et al.* 1988).

When external specialists become directly involved in advising on a child, they will initially be reliant on the information supplied to them by those who have been working with the child previously, particularly teachers. Where schools have successfully followed the procedures set out in the revised *Code of Practice*, there will already be careful records of the child's earlier IEPs and response to them. It will be possible, in the words of the Code, for external specialists such as educational psychologists to look at 'the pupil's records in order to establish which strategies have already been employed and which targets have been set and achieved' (DfES 2001a: para. 5.57). If they have not previously been involved, the first impressions that they gain from the records at this point may have a significant effect on their approach to the assessment process. How far will the reports they read give them a biased view of the situation? What range of information will they receive? How far will the discussions and the paperwork at this stage be open and accessible to the child and parents? What provision will be made for interpreters to attend meetings and for documents to be translated where the family will otherwise be excluded from the process? The answers to such questions will determine to what extent there are effective safeguards against bias during this phase of assessment. Activity 7.4 will enable you to evaluate some examples of the kinds of summary reports that have been written for such purposes in the past.

Activity 7.4   Analysis of teachers' reports on children causing concern

Read the following three reports carefully.

(a) Circle any phrases that seem to you to be based on a stereotype about the group to which the child belongs and therefore liable to contribute to a biased impression.

(b) Underline any information or description that seems to you vague or imprecise. Note how it might have been presented more exactly, taking into consideration whether the advantages for the SEN assessment process would justify the extra time that would be required of the person preparing the report.

(c) To what extent do these descriptions 'identify which strategies have already been employed and which targets have been set and achieved' (DfEE 2000a: para. 6.16)? What additional information would need to be obtained in each case?

Rushana (aged 8) is the eldest of four children in her household. She lives with her parents, who both came to the UK from the Sylhet area of Bangladesh a few years before she was born. She herself visited Sylhet once two years ago to see her family. I think her grandmother was ill at the time. She did not attend school there and missed two terms of Year 2 in this school. Otherwise her attendance has been regular since she was first admitted to the part-time nursery class at the age of 4. She speaks fluent English now, though her only language on entry to the nursery class was Sylheti. It is reported that she uses Sylheti in almost all conversations with her parents and adult relatives at home. At school she is seen as a successful English speaker who does not need support from the part-time teacher of EAL. She used to enjoy bilingual support sessions with a visiting Bengali teacher, especially traditional singing. But unfortunately these sessions are no longer available. Now in Year 4 she is presenting with serious learning difficulties in the classroom. She can make out most of the words in the reading book she has (which I would judge suitable for a Year 3 child), but her fluency is appalling, and she does not seem to take in much of what she reads. She lacks confidence as a writer and has very poor spelling. In cooperative group work she has a strong tendency to allow others to take all the initiatives.

Jean-Paul was 10 when he arrived in the UK two years ago from Mauritius to join his mother. I understand that he attended school in Mauritius regularly, though he himself seems to have only very hazy memories of that (in contrast to his memories of his grandmother's home there which seem to be vivid and happy). He now speaks the French dialect of Mauritius at home with his mother and communicates with his white, UK-born stepfather in English, a language he is still learning. Because there are very few children from linguistic minority families in this area, the school has no extra provision for meeting his language needs. It is his second school in the UK, and when he arrived here four terms ago he had enough English to get by in the classroom. There is increasing concern about his fighting with other children in school (where he says people call him names) and his bullying of his younger half-brother and half-sister at home. While he is certainly not making good progress in school subjects either, our primary concern is the problems with his behaviour. He has not responded well to a structured intervention by the Behaviour Support Teaching Service. We have not seen his mother at school. His stepfather seems to think we should take a stronger line with him and finds it hard to accept that we do not use corporal punishment at all.

Everton (aged 13) has been a cause of concern to us for about two years. He tends to be sullen and aggressive and disrupts lessons. He has a very violent nature and has been violent to other boys on several occasions. Recently he was charged with thefts outside school and is due to appear in court in a month's time. We estimate his general ability to be about average. He has shown some flair in English and gets on well with his English teacher. But other subject teachers say he could do well but spoils himself with bad behaviour. He is disrespectful to teachers and a bully with his classmates. The one subject he seems to find really difficult is mathematics, and he often skips maths lessons. Otherwise his attendance is very good. He is resentful of any kind of authority and hence finds it difficult to do the work that is set. I have written to his parents three or four times and sent them progress reports going back over a year. But in and out of class he constantly causes trouble – sometimes with violence. His father says that at home he is quick tempered and cannot have his leg pulled. Both parents are very concerned about him. They come from Jamaica and are leading members of the Pentecostal church on the High Street.

Who can be fair?

Some commentators have argued that all children should have professional support from the same background as themselves. For some black people it seems 'quite obvious that many black parents and pupils will be at a serious disadvantage ... in the absence of black psychologists ... and other black professionals' (Haringey Black Pressure Group on Education 1984: 9). During the 1970s there was some indirect research evidence that seemed to support that view. For example, Strickland (1972) found that black children in her sample trusted a black interviewer more than they trusted a white interviewer. However, it is impossible to rely totally on indirect evidence. When researchers tried to show directly that the race of an examiner would affect the scores children obtained in tests, their results were inconsistent (Jensen 1980; Graziano *et al.* 1982). Many other factors seem to be involved. For example, the age of the pupils, the region where they live and the nature of the assessment task may each affect whether or not performance changes with the race of the examiner.

In any case, in a multiethnic and multilingual society where children in a conurbation such as London may speak more than 300 languages at home, it will never be possible to offer ethnic and linguistic matching to all children who may require SEN assessment. The matching would need to cover not just language but dialect, and not just ethnic background but culture and regional area of origin. This would be impossible. In addition, there is a danger of placing those psychologists and teachers who speak minority languages in a professional ghetto working mainly with people from the same communal background and having restricted opportunities for wider responsibility.

An alternative strategy (Cline 1998) is to lay an obligation on trainers, employers and the psychologists and teachers themselves to ensure that all professionals are competent to work effectively with all ethnic and linguistic groups in their area. There is a major challenge for services and for university departments in establishing the necessary training as a normal element of all initial and in-service professional training. In some LA services a crucial contribution has been made by the creation of various kinds of liaison and advisory posts (e.g. Rogers and Pratten 1996). The role of workers from ethnic and linguistic minority communities remains critical not only to support effective communication with families (DfES 2004a), but also to contribute to the raising of multi-faceted cultural awareness within the staff group. What is being argued here should not take away the pressure for trainers and employers to ensure that the personnel in professional services reflect the composition of the communities they serve more closely. The argument simply concerns what the personnel should be doing once they are appointed and how they should be trained to do it (cf. DECP 2006).

The following list of some of the key areas of expertise that are required is based on recommendations made by an American Psychological Association Task Force on Cross-Cultural School Psychology Competencies (Rogers *et al.* 1999). The text refers to psychologists throughout but would equally apply to all other advisers and specialists working with children with SEN, including specialist teachers. The expectations held up for school psychologists by this task force include the following elements.

Ethical issues

- They will be aware of the unique ethical challenges and complex ethical issues faced when delivering services to racially, ethnically, culturally and linguistically diverse individuals in schools.

- They will uphold ethical standards. The example is given that, if asked to assess the language and cognitive skills of a non-English speaking child without adequate resources, materials, interpreters or training, the psychologist will not personally fulfil the request. Instead they will seek out the assistance of an appropriately trained person who is skilled in the language and culture of the child.

School culture and educational policy

- They will be well informed and aware of the systemic issues associated with cases referred to them for services. So, in this case, they will be knowledgeable about institutional racism, cultural misinformation and other systemic issues affecting the education of students from culturally and linguistically diverse populations.

- They will provide advice and support to develop systems interventions to support the educational success of culturally and linguistically diverse learners.

- When working with racially, ethnically, culturally and linguistically diverse children and their families, they will have an ethical and professional responsibility to assess whether problems presumed to reside within the student may be manifestations of systemic biases in the institution(s) serving the child. So they will rule out systemic factors as causal influences in the student's situation before proceeding with individually focused assessment or intervention.

Psychological and educational assessment

- They will ensure that the assessments in which they are involved comprise a comprehensive process of gathering information about students that explicitly takes account of the impact of sociocultural, environmental, political, experiential and language-based factors.

- They will consider cultural sources of information about students and search for culture-specific confirming data. Thus, when conducting observations, they will use appropriate comparison group members so that, for example, a second language learner would be compared to another second language learner.

- They will develop expertise in assessing the student's biculturalism and will be supportive of it. When conducting an assessment, they will take into account language and other behaviour considered to be socially appropriate in the culture of the child.

- They will incorporate cultural and linguistic information in their verbal advice and written reports.

- They will recognize the limitations of standardized instruments and the ramifications of using such instruments in the assessment of racially, ethnically, culturally and linguistically diverse students. For example, if tests are used for a group or individual for which appropriate norms do not exist, they will report any findings in a descriptive and qualitative manner.

Consultation

- They will aim to become skilled in developing a multicultural consultation model which reflects an understanding of cultural values and the implications for working with culturally diverse families.

- They will develop culturally sensitive verbal and non-verbal communication skills and an awareness of how their own cultural background and biases may influence their ability to communicate effectively with culturally diverse students, school personnel and family members.

- They will learn about the characteristic family structures, hierarchies, values and beliefs of the communities with which they work. They will aim to be knowledgeable about the main features of the communities, their history and their resources. For example, where a culture structures social interactions hierarchically and prescribes gender roles within the hierarchy, they will initiate working contacts with families taking these expectations into account.

- They will develop strong community networks with culturally knowledgeable practitioners. They will be aware of institutional barriers that may prevent minority group members from accessing services and will be prepared to make different arrangements to facilitate access.

If all specialist teachers and psychologists in multiethnic communities can develop expertise along these lines, then calls for all children to be assessed by professionals from the same background as themselves will be seen as unnecessary. The more desirable and practicable aim must be that, whatever their own background, those responsible become knowledgeable about and sensitive to the key features of the children's culture and languages. Similar principles apply also when those involved in SEN assessment are working across other, less dramatic gaps, such as those of social class and gender. The training requirements represent a major challenge. It is not just a matter of generating the accretion of some new items of factual knowledge. A professional who will be sensitive across the range of diversity found in contemporary schools is likely to have needed to go through a process of restructuring many of their key attitudes and beliefs (Causey *et al.* 2000). Ultimately, the key to reducing assessment bias in practice lies in the principle set out by Watson *et al.* (1987): *know yourself, and the task, so that you can know the child.*

Conclusions

The goal of equity in the support given to children who may have SEN requires constant vigilance and regular review. The population profile of pupils with SEN statements remains quite different from the profile of the school population as a whole. It is possible that some aspects of this mismatch reflect the impact of genetic and environmental factors on the development of SEN, as illustrated in Chapter 5. However, there is a good deal of evidence that it may also have been influenced by the operation of systematic bias in procedures for the identification and assessment of SEN.

In this chapter we have examined different ways in which processes of bias can affect the judgements that are made during assessment. Test bias is important and can be reduced significantly, even if it cannot be altogether eliminated. But test bias is not the only source of distortion during the assessment process. Testing takes place in a social context, and assessment involves several stages apart from any testing that may be included. Each phase of the process may be affected by bias. We gave particular attention to how bias can be reduced in initial identification processes in school. Ultimately the greatest safeguard against bias will be if the assessment draws upon multiple sources of evidence. When this is done, the viewpoints of more than one observer are likely to be taken into account.

In the last section of the chapter we asked the question that is implied by that strategy – who can be fair? A response to the challenge must involve appreciating the areas of expertise that are needed in a diverse society and developing the necessary arrangements for initial training and continuing professional development. Working towards a reduction in the bias affecting assessment is a task for services and systems as well as for individuals.

8

Assessment for learning

Objectives

When you have studied this chapter you should be able to:

- explain why there has been increasing interest in assessment for learning (AfL) in recent years;
- describe key strategies for implementing AfL in the classroom;
- discuss ways in which AfL can be extended for children with SEN by more structured and intensive approaches, such as precision teaching;
- outline ways in which AfL can be extended for children learning English as an additional language through use of the Cummins quadrant.

Introduction

In Chapter 6 the following distinctive approaches to the assessment of SEN were outlined:

- assessment focused on the learner;
- assessment focused on the teaching programme;

- assessment focused on the zone of potential development;
- assessment focused on the learning environment.

This chapter is devoted to the second of these, assessment focused on the teaching programme. In the 1980s assessment approaches focused on the teaching programme gained prominence in the work with children who have SEN. Over the past decade in the UK, assessment for learning (AfL) approaches have been advocated as of key importance in raising attainment for all children.

Assessment focused on the teaching programme for pupils with SEN

Gickling and Havertape (1981: 376) argued that the most pervasive cause of learning difficulties was that for some children 'the curriculum moves too fast and demands too much in relation to their existing skills. They get further and further behind and are entrenched in a failure cycle.' They argued for the importance of eliminating this instructional mismatch through the identification of the child's entry skills in relation to the curriculum, which would allow appropriate tasks and materials to be selected accordingly.

A number of different terms have been used to describe this approach to assessment, of which the most common in Britain are curriculum-based assessment (CBA), curriculum-related assessment, curriculum-based measurement and assessment through teaching. In this chapter we will use the term CBA to refer to this body of research, mainly conducted with pupils who have SEN, and will adopt the definition proposed by Tucker (1985: 200): 'Curriculum based assessment properly includes any procedure that directly assesses student performance within the course content for the purpose of determining that student's instructional needs.' In CBA the pupil's performance is compared in an ongoing way to each new set of curriculum demands as they are presented in the classroom.

Gickling and Thompson (1985) reported that without CBA relevant adjustments were rarely made by teachers for children whose performance deviated significantly from the norm expected for their age. Individualization and differentiation rarely happened and children, increasingly unable to do assigned work, tended to get further behind and become entrenched in a cycle of 'curriculum related failure'. Another important influence on the shift towards CBA in the 1980s was a growing appreciation of the extent to which norm-referenced tests commonly used in making special education placement decisions were affected by cultural and social bias. As illustrated in Chapter 7, cultural bias is apparent in tests where a significant proportion of the items may be outside the cultural experience, customs or values of particular groups of children. The use of norms was another contentious issue as few of the standardized norm-referenced assessment measures which were commonly used in the assessment of children's SEN at the time reported the systematic inclusion of minority children in their standardization samples. It was recognized also that even those measures which had been standardized on populations including proportions of children from minority ethnic groups might not be applicable in communities where there was a different ethnic mix.

However, concerns were also raised about the validity of substituting informal teacher observation and identification for standardized tests. As was pointed out in Chapter 7, at least the extent to which standardized tests are biased can be ascertained. This led some school districts in the USA (in Louisiana, for example) to set a requirement for systematic and structured pre-referral data to be collected by teachers using CBA in order to counter discriminatory practices in referral to special education services. The attorney for the plaintiffs in an influential court case (*Luke* v. *Nix*) quoted research which showed teachers to be biased in their judgements about children's attainment of teaching objectives in a way which underestimated the achievements of children from black and minority ethnic communities. In a scathing attack upon 'the subjective and chaotic referral methods of individual teachers', the attorney pointed out that 'evidence abounds that regular teachers initiate referrals without documenting that alternative instructional strategies have been attempted and evaluated', and concluded that 'teachers have manifested a pervasive propensity to refer students who "bother them". The result is a haphazard, idiosyncratic referral method whereby different teachers refer different types of students because different student traits bother them' (Galigan 1985: 290).

In England and Wales the main purpose of assessment as presented in the SEN Code of Practice is to allow decisions to be made about the adequacy of progress: 'a school's system for observing and assessing the progress of individual children should provide information about areas where a child is not progressing satisfactorily even though the teaching style has been differentiated' (DfES 2001a: 30). It is only when professions from outside the school are consulted at School Action Plus that there is mention of assessment for teaching in addition, where it is suggested that they may 'provide more specialist assessments that can inform planning and the measurement of a pupil's progress' (DfES 2001a: 55). Later in this chapter we will focus in particular on one such approach, precision teaching.

Activity 8.1 Potential advantages of assessment focused on the teaching programme

Here are some of the potential advantages which have been claimed for CBA with pupils who have SEN. As you read this chapter, keep a running record of any evidence that supports these claims. Consider also and note the extent to which each point could equally be claimed as an advantage of AfL for all pupils.

Potential advantage	*Supportive evidence*	
	for CBA and pupils with SEN	*for AfL and all pupils*
It is not necessary to take a lot of 'time out' for assessment since assessment, teaching and monitoring of progress are combined.		
It can provide information that is of direct and immediate use in the classroom on which specific skills and knowledge the child has and has not mastered.		

Potential advantage	Supportive evidence	
	for CBA and pupils with SEN	*for AfL and all pupils*
It offers an immediate check on the appropriateness of particular tasks and materials for particular children. Even 'graded' books and sets of worksheets contain substantial variation in level of difficulty from page to page and task to task. If a low-achieving child is performing erratically it may well reflect constant fluctuation between instructional and frustration level tasks.		
It enables teachers to chart small steps in progress towards the achievement of major curriculum objectives or National Curriculum attainment targets. Step size and pacing of individual programmes can be justified.		
Progress can be communicated in a way which is comprehensible to parents and children.		
It generates detailed assessment information which can be readily appreciated by other professionals who may be consulted about a child's special needs.		
It fulfils the school's responsibilities for assessment, intervention and evaluation and will provide a convincing basis for any case made for the provision of extra resources.		
The approach is based on the optimistic assumption that all children can make learning progress given appropriate teaching. Where difficulties are encountered it is the teaching programme, not the child, that is labelled problematic and targeted for change.		

Assessment for learning

AfL is defined in DfES publications as 'the process of seeking and interpreting evidence for use by learners and their teachers to decide where the learners are in their learning, where they need to go and how best to get there' (Assessment Reform Group 1999). It has been embraced by the government in England, made central to their core principles for teaching and learning and identified as a key element of the thrust towards 'personalized learning', which aims to differentiate teaching to engage and fully develop all learners. Detailed guidance on implementation strategies are provided for primary (DfES 2004b) and secondary schools (DfES 2006g).

In Scotland also AfL has been adopted as a central strand in effective teaching. It forms part of a national initiative, Assessment is for Learning. 'Assessment for learning focuses on the gap between where a learner is in their learning, and where they need to be – the desired goal. This can be achieved through processes such as sharing criteria with learners, effective questioning and feedback' (Learning and Teaching Scotland 2007).

DfES publications (e.g., DfES 2007c) differentiate the purpose of AfL from the purpose of end-of-year or Key Stage National Curriculum assessments:

- Assessment *for* learning (also known as *formative* assessment) is any assessment activity which *informs* the next steps to learning.

- Assessment *of* learning (also known as *summative* assessment) is any assessment which *summarizes* where learners are at a given point in time – it provides a snapshot of what has been learned.

In addition, Wiliam and Thompson (2008) identify a third purpose of educational assessment: *evaluative* assessment which focuses on the appraisal of the quality of educational institutions or programs.

The recent development of interest in the use of formative assessment has been identified as an important example of research-driven change at national level in the UK (Watson 2006). The acknowledged source of this impetus was an article (Black and Wiliam 1998a) which reviewed 250 published research studies in order to address the question whether there is evidence that improving formative assessment raises standards. They concluded that the answer to this question was a clear 'yes'. Most significantly, they then followed up this research journal article with a pamphlet summarizing their findings which was aimed at teachers and policy makers (Black and Wiliam 1998b). Four years later they were able to report the quite spectacular attention the pamphlet had attracted, with sales of over 20,000 copies and wide quotation of its conclusions and recommendations (Black *et al.* 2002).

In examining reasons for the success of this publication in bringing research findings to public attention, the quantitative evidence cited is one factor identified by one of the authors:

> The significant impact of that review, notably on some subsequent policy shifts in the UK, but also in supporting other work on formative assessment in other countries, owes much to its emphasis on the warrants for the claims of such work provided by the quantitative evidence of learning gains.
>
> (Broadfoot and Black 2004: 16)

However, of even greater significance may be the way in which technical quantitative findings about the effects of formative assessment initiatives on pupil learning outcomes were illustrated by reference to the potential impact they could have on the achievement of current educational goals of schools and national governments. Figure 8.1 provides an example of the way in which this was done. The effect sizes quoted are from a meta-analysis (highly structured quantitative review) conducted by Fuchs and Fuchs (1986), leading proponents of CBA, of 23 studies, most involving children with SEN. This allowed the further conclusion to be drawn that 'Some of these studies exhibit another important feature. Many of them show that improved formative assessment helps the (so-called) low

The formative assessment experiments produce typical *effect sizes* of between 0.4 and 0.7: such effect sizes are larger than most of those found for educational interventions. The following examples illustrate some practical consequences of such large gains:

● An effect size of 0.4 would mean that the average pupil involved in an innovation would record the same achievement as a pupil just in the top 35 per cent of those not so involved.

● A gain of effect size 0.4 would improve performances of pupils in GCSE by between one and two grades.

● A gain of effect size 0.7, if realized in the recent international comparative studies in mathematics (TIMSS; Beaton *et al.* 1996), would raise England from the middle of the 41 countries involved to being one of the top five.

Figure 8.1   Illustrating the potential impact of formative assessment
Source: Black and Wiliam (1998b).

attainers more than the rest, and so reduces the spread of attainment whilst also raising it overall' (Black and Wiliam 1998b: 4).

Black and Wiliam (1998a) identify CBA as a formative assessment approach and note that 'many of its features would be essential in any incorporation of formative assessment into a learning programme' (1998a: 45). However, they identify a number of distinctive features of CBA, such as sharply focused specially designed test probes and the use of these frequently to gives graphs of performance against time. Later in this chapter we will give consideration to one specific approach which has these features, precision teaching, and will consider whether the inclusion of such features may be particularly important for pupils experiencing substantial and complex learning difficulties. Drawing on the work of Shinn and Hubbard (1992) who advocate curriculum-based measurement and a problem-solving approach to assessment for children with SEN, Black and Wiliam (1998a) argue for a similar paradigm shift in the predominant approach in schools to assessment for all children (see Table 8.1). They suggest that this table be read alongside the research findings on strategies in order to identify the essential elements of any AfL initiative. In the next section of this chapter these essential elements and strategies will be described and key research findings highlighted.

Implementing assessment for learning

Key strategies

AfL can be conceptualized as comprising five key strategies and one 'big idea' (Wiliam and Thompson 2008). The 'big idea' is that evidence about a pupil's learning should be used to adjust the teaching they receive in order to better meet their needs. The five key strategies are:

1   Clarifying and sharing learning intentions and criteria for success.

Table 8.1   Different questions arising from a paradigm shift in assessment in schools

Dimension	Current assessment paradigm	Problem-solving paradigm
Purpose	Do assessment results spread out individuals facilitating *classi-fication/placement* into groups?	Does assessment result in socially meaningful *student outcomes* for the individual?
Test validity	Does the assessment device measure what it says it measures? Criterion-related validity: Does the test correlate with other tests purporting to increase the same thing? Construct validity: Does the test display a stable factor structure?	Are the *inferences* and *actions* based on test scores *adequate* and *appropriate* (Messick 1989)? Treatment validity: Do decisions regarding target behaviours and treatments based on knowledge obtained from the assessment procedure result in *better student outcomes* than decisions based on alternative procedures (Hayes *et al.* 1983)?
Unit of analysis	Groups: Probabilistic statements about individuals: Do students with similar assessment results *most likely* display similar characteristics?	Individuals: Does assessment show that *this* treatment is working for *this* student?
Time line	Summative: Does the assessment indicate whether or not the intervention *did* work?	Formative: Does the assessment indicate that *this* treatment is working for *this* student?
Level of inference	Does the assessment provide an *indirect* measure of an unobservable construct?	Does the assessment *directly* measure important target behaviours or skills?
Locus of the problem	Does the assessment identify relevant *student characteristics* that contribute to problem etiology?	Does assessment identify relevant *curriculum, instruction and contextual* factors [that] contribute to problem solution?
Focus	Problem certification: Does assessment accurately identify *problems*?	Problem solution: Does the assessment accurately identify *solutions*?
Test reliability	Are test scores stable over time? Are scores based on different behaviour samples, obtained in different contexts/settings consistent?	What factors account for the variability in student performance?
Context	Does the assessment provide a comparison with students receiving a nationally representative range of curriculum and instruction?	Does the assessment provide a comparison with students receiving comparable curriculum and instruction?
Dimension of dependent variable	Does the assessment provide information regarding the *level* of pupil performance?	Does the assessment provide information regarding the *level* of pupil performance and the *slope* of pupil progress?

Source: Black and Wiliam (1998a).

2   Engineering effective classroom discussions, questions, and learning tasks that elicit evidence of learning.

3   Providing feedback that moves learners forward.

4   Activating students as instructional resources for one another.

5   Activating students as the owners of their own learning.
(Wiliam and Thompson 2008: 64).

These key strategies are elaborated in the subsections below, drawing on ideas proposed, findings reported and research reviewed by Black *et al.* (2002), DfES (2004b, 2007c), Leahy *et al.* (2005) and Wiliam *et al.* (2004).

Clarify and share intentions and criteria

This involves teachers sharing their intended learning outcomes for a lesson with the pupils, using appropriate language and/or examples to ensure understanding. The evidence suggests that learning is more effective when pupils understand what they are trying to achieve and why. The learning outcomes make clear what the pupils should know or be able to do by the end of the lesson. Specifying success criteria for each learning task will enable the teacher and pupils to judge how well each outcome has been achieved. Circulating work examples that a previous year's class has completed and having exemplar material on display are suggested as ways of supplementing oral and written descriptions of intended learning outcomes. In addition, they can provide a focus for identification, discussion and clarification of success criteria.

Engineer effective classroom discussion

The element of discussion that has received most attention is questioning. Traditionally most teacher questions seek information from pupils that is already known to the teacher: 'correct' answers to factual questions about content already taught. Often each question is answered by just one pupil, someone who has put up their hand because they think that they know the answer. If a pupil does not give the answer the teacher is looking for the teacher will usually call on one or more additional pupils until the desired answer is obtained. This approach fails to provide information about what most pupils in the class know about the topic and is generally not used to investigate and correct misconceptions. It may provide or reinforce knowledge of a specific fact for those pupils attending to the answer.

In contrast, in an AfL approach a question is only considered worth asking if it provides information that is used to adjust the teaching provided. Examples of such question types are:

● Questions to reveal what pupils know at the start of a lesson so that a judgement can be made about where to begin teaching – 'range-finding' questions.

● Questions to check understanding during the lesson, providing 'hinge points' where the teacher can take different routes through the content and learning activities depending on the pupils' responses.

● Questions that require all pupils to respond – for example, questions that are asked in a multiple-choice format, where each pupil is provided with a set of cards: A, B, C and D. The teacher will use this information to decide which pupils to ask to discuss the reasons for the option they have selected. All pupils are encouraged to maintain engagement as they know they may be called on to contribute to the discussion – they can no longer opt out by not raising their hand.

To encourage pupils to think carefully about teacher questions, teachers are advised to allow several seconds of 'wait time' before selecting a pupil to contribute. A further strategy designed to promote engagement and support less confident pupils is 'talk partners', where pupils are asked to share their ideas in pairs before the teacher selects someone to share their ideas with the whole class.

Provide feedback that moves learners forward

Recommendations are offered on written feedback (marking) and on oral feedback in the classroom. Both psychological theory and research evidence suggest that giving marks or grades to a pupil's work is not merely ineffective in promoting learning but may have counterproductive effects on both learning and motivation. If a teacher provides written feedback and a grade, most pupils will focus on the grade and disregard the written feedback. 'Comment-only' marking is now widely advocated as an AfL tactic.

However, to be effective in promoting learning the comments provided have to provoke thinking. Generally encouraging comments ('Your poem works brilliantly, very well done') are unlikely to be sufficiently specific in order to:

- identify what has been done well in relation to the desired learning outcomes and what still needs improvement;

- give guidance on how to make necessary improvement.

It is additionally advised that opportunities should be provided for pupils to read and follow up comments and to make recommended improvements to their work.
It is recommended that oral feedback should:

- be constructive and informative in order to help pupils take the next steps in their learning;

- consciously model the language that pupils can use in giving feedback to their teacher and peers;

- be developmental, recognizing pupils' efforts and achievements and offering specific information on ways forward in relation to the desired learning outcomes;

- say when an answer is wrong to avoid confusion or reinforcing misconceptions.

In addition, as can be seen from Figure 8.2, staff are cautioned to reflect on unintentional negative messages that may be conveyed by the language used to talk about difficulty with learning.
Children's sensitivity to such messages was well illustrated by a series of studies reported by Graham (1984). Sympathetic teacher responses toward a pupil who had failed at a task led both the pupil themselves and their peers to conclude that the teacher did not consider them sufficiently able to succeed, and subsequently led to a decline in the pupil's expectations for success on the task. By

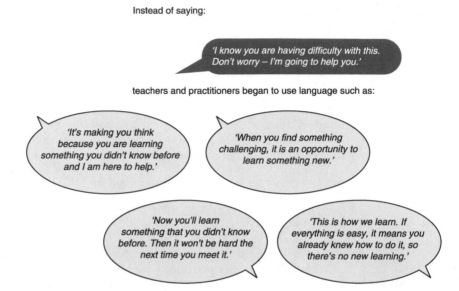

Figure 8.2 Language for talking about difficulties to maintain positive expectancies while providing appropriate support
Source: DfES (2004b).

contrast, an angry response from the teacher was more likely to be interpreted as indicating the teacher believed that the pupil could succeed but had not tried hard enough. Paradoxically, a sympathetic teacher motivated by a desire to protect the self-esteem of a student experiencing difficulties might unwittingly use language that undermines both the pupil's self-esteem and expectations for success. However, this should not be taken to imply that angry responses to pupils experiencing difficulties are preferable! Georgiou *et al.* (2002) found that while anger was associated with a perception of insufficient effort, it was also associated with tendency for teachers to give up efforts to help the pupil improve. This was particularly so when the teacher had a lower sense of efficacy and was unwilling to accept part of the responsibility for the pupil's failures. The AfL approach, which regards the teacher and pupils as being engaged in an ongoing process of working together to achieve desired learning outcomes, provides a context for a more productive set of attributions from both.

Activate students as owners of their own learning and instructional resources for one another

In addition to ensuring that pupils understand what they are expected to achieve, it is argued that they need to be enabled to have responsibility for their own learning and to learn strategies and skills needed to identify their learning needs and judge their success in achieving desired learning outcomes. With regard to the identification of learning needs, a popular strategy is to distribute 'traffic light' cards which pupils can hold up to indicate their level of understanding (green for 'I can do this', amber for 'I am reasonably confident', red for 'I need assistance'). The following anonymous practical adaptation was posted on a website for teaching ideas (http://www.teachingideas.co.uk/more/management/trafficlightselfassessment.htm):

> In Maths we use a traffic lights system. At the end of each lesson the children draw a circle and write:
>
> - G (green light – understand this very well),
> - O (amber light) – need a bit of support but understand the basics or . . .
> - R (red light – help I don't understand).
>
> When I mark the books and feedback to the children or parents it is really useful to know how they feel about the topic and helps me target children more effectively in class. If the letters G, O, R are written rather than coloured it means the children's assessment is still visible if the work is photocopied.

In AfL pupils are also involved in marking their own work and that of their peers using agreed success criteria. Skills in self assessment can be more difficult to acquire than skills in peer assessment, so attention is usually given to developing the latter first. To develop peer and self assessment in the classroom, it is recommended that teachers plan peer and self assessment opportunities in lessons for pairs or small groups of children and train pupils over time to assess their own work and the work of others and to provide constructive, supportive feedback to their response partners (DfES 2004b).

Activity 8.2 No hands-up

During 2007 articles appeared in popular newspapers responding critically to a DfES publication on pupils who fall behind in Key Stage 2. This was based on a survey of 39 schools. In the *Daily Mail* on 1 June 2007 an article appeared entitled 'Why teachers "should stop pupils raising their hands" '. Ministers were reported as saying that teachers should stop asking pupils to put their hands up to answer questions in class. It was argued this practice disadvantages quiet and retiring pupils. Instead teachers were advised to choose children to respond to questions so that the keener ones who always put their hands up do not get all the attention. In addition, it was reported that teachers were advised to give 30 seconds of 'thinking time' before expecting pupils to answer their questions. Asking the children to discuss a question in pairs before answering was also suggested.

Many struggling pupils were said to try to avoid attracting the teacher's attention. Other 'invisible children' were described who were 'on the comfort zone' or anxious about being seen to get things wrong. Their work was neat and they were generally well behaved, but they were not being stretched by whole-class teaching of the traditional kind. A spokesman from the Education Department was reported as insisting it was not 'banning' hands-up in class and 'would categorically never prescribe what teachers do in their own classrooms'.

In fact the official publication did not actually contain any advice to teachers about stopping pupils raising their hands. What was recommended was the introduction or revision of AfL policy in schools.

Why do you think a 'no hands-up' strategy might be advocated as a suitable tactic in AfL?

If you were going to explain the strategy to parents so that they could appreciate its place in an overall assessment policy, how would you go about it?

Supporting teacher development of AfL

There is evidence of a substantial need to support teacher development in this area. The conclusion that formative assessment is not well understood by teachers and is weak in practice comes both from Ofsted reports and from research studies. For example, Ofsted (2003b: 4) makes the following observations:

> Although all schools set numerical targets at the end of Key Stage 2, many still do not set effective curricular targets that focus on what pupils still need to learn, which are then followed through into teaching. Even where the targets focus on pupils' weaknesses, teachers' planning seldom refers to what they are going to do to tackle the weaknesses or how they will monitor progress against the targets.

Clarke (2003) reported that teachers tended to focus in their planning on the activities they would provide for pupils, as opposed to the learning they intended to result from these activities – to the extent that they sometimes responded to questions about learning intentions with descriptions of learning activities. While changes to marking practices are sometimes constrained by school policies, Mavrommatis (1997) found that in primary classrooms in Greece teachers persisted in giving grades on written work after this policy had been statutorily discontinued. Parent and pupils expectations, together with pragmatic constraints of time and class size, were cited as reasons.

However Wiliam *et al.* (2004) have shown that it is possible to provide a feasible professional development programme that can enable teachers to implement AfL in secondary schools in a way that results in educationally significant improvements in summative pupil assessments, such as end-of-key-stage tests. The starting point for this study was that significant changes in practice were unlikely to be produced by a set of 'tips from the research' too specific to be applicable across a range of subjects and classes. On the other hand, general principles were considered unlikely to be taken up by most teachers where they were left alone with the daunting task of translating the principles into everyday practice in busy classrooms. Instead the researchers provided a series of whole-day and half-day training sessions over a period of 16 months, which introduced the teachers to the principles of AfL and provided supported opportunities to develop action plans and share experiences and outcomes over time. In addition, researchers visited schools to make classroom observations and discuss ideas with the teachers about how their action plans were being put into practice.

The research design authentically involved each of the 12 headteachers making their own decision about which two teachers to involve and each teacher deciding which class to involve in the intervention. Teachers were also free to decide which elements to incorporate into their action plans and, as can be seen from Table 8.2, there was considerable variability in this. Use was made of whatever outcome measures each school normally administered or had available. However, the researchers also sought to incorporate aspects of experimental design that would allow meaningful comparative data to be generated from which some valid generalizations could be drawn. Describing their approach as 'local design', the researchers identified a comparison class for each intervention class and treated each of the teachers involved as their own case study, analysing the results obtained from the pairs of classes. Comparison classes could be parallel

Table 8.2 Frequencies of activities in the lesson plans of 24 teachers

Category	Activity	Frequency
Questioning	Teacher questioning	11
	Pupils writing questions	8
	Existing assessment: pre-tests	4
	Pupils asking questions	4
Feedback	Comment-only marking	6
	Existing assessment: re-timing	4
	Group work: test review	4
Sharing criteria with learners	Course work: marking criteria	5
	Course work: examples	4
	Start of lesson; making aim clear	4
	Start of lesson: setting targets	1
	End of lesson: teacher's review	1
	End of lesson: pupils' review	4
	Group work; explanation	2
	Involving classroom assessment	2
Self-assessment	Self-assessment: traffic lights	11
	Self-assessment: targets	5
	Group work: test review	6
	Self-assessment: other	7
	Pupil peer-assessment	5
	Group work: revision	1
General	Including parents	1
	Posters	1
	Presentations	1
Total		102

Source: Wiliam *et al.* (2004).

classes taught by the same or different teachers or historical data could be used in making comparisons with similar classes taught the previous year. Clearly the variables controlled for are different with different comparison groups. A parallel class taught by the same teacher controls both for teacher effects and factors impacting on all classes in a school during the intervention. Historical data from a similar class could control for aspects of the former factor, but not the latter. Data from a parallel class taught by a different teacher could control for other factors impacting on the school during the intervention, but not teacher factors. This study illustrates that the complexities of real-world research are no excuse for abandoning the effort to apply a rigorous approach.

Overall this study reported a mean effect size of 0.32 which the authors interpreted by equating it to approximately one-half of a GCSE grade per student per subject. While acknowledging that this might sound small, the authors point out that it would be sufficient, if replicated across a whole school (admittedly a big 'if'), to raise the performance of a school at the 25th percentile of achievement nationally into the upper half. Of the 25 teacher level comparisons made, only four effect sizes were negative. Data from classroom observations provided some support for attributing the effects on attainment to the quality of AfL.

While the study by Wiliam *et al.* (2004) is helpful in guiding the implementation of AfL and encouraging as to potential impacts, it also highlights variability in outcomes and associated factors such as quality of implementation. Pupil diversity is another potential source of variability and it receives a little specific attention in the guidance on AfL. Advice on pupils learning EAL is offered in one place in DfES (2004b: 43):

> During discussion, EAL learners may articulate their learning in their first language. Where appropriate, bilingual adults who share the children's language have a vital role to play in assessing understanding. When this is not possible, discussion between children in their first language will still support learning.

The whole-school training materials on AfL for secondary schools contain an alternative first unit ('Assessment for Learning in Everyday Lessons') for teachers of pupils who have SEN. However, differences do not extend beyond the video material and advice on modes of communication. It is stated that the essential elements of AfL are the same for all sectors of education, although the approach adopted will depend on individual pupils' strengths and barriers to learning. The next section of this chapter will consider specific approaches for pupils with SEN, and the final section will look at some specific issues in AfL with pupils learning EAL.

Assessment for learning and pupils with SEN

In their account of the Fuchs and Fuchs (1986) meta-analysis, which formed such an important part of the evidence base for their conclusions about AfL, Black and Wiliam (1998a) report some information about associations between pupil diversity and intervention impact. For example, most of the studies were focused on children with SEN and involved assessment activities carried out between twice and five times per week. With this level of implementation mean effect sizes were high overall, slightly higher for pupils with SEN (0.73) than for typically developing pupils (0.63). Of greater significance were the findings on variations in approach and intervention impact. In about half the studies, where teachers worked to clear procedures about interpreting the assessment data and taking action based on it, a large mean effect size of 0.92 was obtained. However, when these elements were left to the judgement of individual teachers the mean effect size was considerably smaller (0.42). In those studies where teachers used routine graphing of progress with the pupil to guide subsequent action higher mean effect sizes were obtained (0.70 as compared with 0.26).

If pupils with SEN are to close any attainment gaps that exist between them and their typically developing peers it seems likely that the AfL approach being advocated for most pupils will need to be supplemented with more regular, highly specified and structured approaches. Precision teaching is an approach which incorporates the key features highlighted as leading to improved outcomes for pupils with SEN. It also is highly congruent with the basic principles and elements of AfL, as Table 8.3 illustrates. Table 8.3 also draws parallels between AfL and dynamic assessment, further information on which can be found in Chapter 12. Precision teaching is described in the next subsection.

Introduction to precision teaching

The confusingly named 'precision teaching' is not an approach to teaching but to assessment and monitoring. It offers a set of strategies for carrying out brief, focused, daily assessments of pupil performance and for recording progress in a way that enables decisions about its appropriateness to be made on a very regular basis (typically weekly). In precision teaching the teacher records how quickly a child can respond to questions as well as whether or not the answers are correct. Thus precision teaching focuses on fluency as well as accuracy. Binder (1993) reviews evidence suggesting that establishing fluency in addition to accuracy is of great value. If a skill is well practised so that we can perform it without hesitation, we are less likely to forget it, are more likely to be able to perform it reliably in distracting or demanding situations and are better able to apply it flexibly in a range of contexts. This can be appreciated by comparing the gear-changing skill of a learner driver and an experienced driver. The experienced driver gives little conscious attention to changing gear, is unlikely to stall when the unexpected happens and quickly adapts to driving an unfamiliar car. When fluency is established as well as accuracy there are improvements in pupils' *resistance to distraction* when using a skill that they have learned, in their memory for and *maintenance* of the skill over time, and in their ability to *generalize* the skill and use it appropriately in a variety of circumstances.

Lindsley (1992) reports that *rate of response or fluency measures* (e.g. number of words read correctly per minute) are very much more sensitive to changes in environmental conditions or drug dosages than are *accuracy measures* (such as percentage correct). He also reports that involving the pupils themselves in daily

Table 8.3 Comparison of components across assessment approaches.

Formative assessment	Precision teaching	Dynamic assessment
Establish prior learning	Pre-teaching probe	Pre-test (assessing performance without help)
Establish learning intentions	Target skill	Mediation of goal seeking, setting
Discuss success criteria	Criteria	Mediation of goal seeking, setting
Highlight gap between current and intended levels	Precise feedback on gap between performance and criteria (verbal and visual)	Mediation of goal monitoring
Provide feedback on closing the gap	Precise feedback on improvement (verbal and visual)	Mediation of feelings of competence

Source: Gavine *et al.* (2006).

assessment, marking and charting of performance increases the effectiveness of learning and their motivation. By training pupils to work together in pairs, the time that needs to be spent by the teacher on the mechanics of monitoring can be greatly reduced.

Precision teaching involves five steps:

1   Specify the desired pupil performance in observable, measurable terms.

2   Sample and record the performance on a daily basis.

3   Chart the performance on a daily basis.

4   Record the teaching approaches in relation to pupil performance.

5   Analyse the data to determine whether:

   (a) the programme is satisfactory;

   (b) changes are needed in the teaching approach.

Merbitz *et al.* (2004b) note that the motto of precision teaching is 'The learner is always right' – underlining the concept that it is what the learner *does* that informs and guides teacher action.

Precision teaching: a case-study example

Claire is 7 years 3 months. Her class teacher, Mrs Wallace, has been becoming more concerned about her reading during the autumn term. She is in a reading group with five other children who were all behind at the end of Year 1. Whereas the other children in her reading group have been making steady progress and catching up on the group above, Claire seems almost to be going backwards and becoming more hesitant and less confident in her reading.

At Step 1 the desired pupil performance must be stated clearly. The target level of fluency or success criterion will often be identified by averaging the scores of two or three pupils who are performing at an expected level for their age or who are making satisfactory progress. In this case Claire and the two pupils from her reading group who are making best progress were asked to read for a minute from Claire's reading book. The number of words per minute they each read correctly and incorrectly was recorded. The scores of the other two pupils were averaged to produce the following objective, or statement of desired pupil performance, for Claire:

> Claire will read aloud from her reading book at a rate of 70 words correct per minute with no more than five errors.

At Step 2 the child's accuracy and rate of performance in the area being targeted are sampled on a daily basis using a short test that typically lasts for a minute. This allows the teacher to monitor progress towards the objective that has been set. The short test is called a 'probe' and can take a number of different forms. A probe designed to monitor performance on a programme to develop sight vocabulary in reading might consist of a grid containing the ten new words being learned that week presented seven or eight times each in random order. However, probes can also be taken directly from learning resources used in class. Deno (1985) reviews extensive research indicating the reliability and validity of

1   Select a passage which the pupil will read during their next session and make a photocopy for yourself.

2   Say to the pupil: 'When I say "start", begin reading aloud at the top of this page. Try to read each word. If you wait for a word too long, I'll tell you the word. You can skip words that you don't know. At the end of one minute, I'll say, "stop".'

(Give pupil 3 seconds before supplying words.)

3   Turn on the stopwatch as you say 'Start'.

4   Follow along on your copy, circling with a pencil words that were read incorrectly (omissions, substitutions, mispronunciations, insertions).

5   At one minute, say, 'stop' and turn off the stopwatch.

6   Place a slash after the last word read.

7   Count the number of words correct and the number of errors.

8   Involve the pupil in recording both correct and incorrect scores on a graph.

9   Repeat steps 1–8 at least three times per week. A different passage can be selected each day as the pupil progresses through the book.

Figure 8.3   Administering a probe from a pupil's classroom reading text

using extracts from the books being read by the child in their classroom reading programme as probes. Deno reports that the number of words per minute read correctly and incorrectly from reading scheme readers (using the kind of procedure shown in Figure 8.3) reliably and validly discriminates growth in reading proficiency through the primary school years.

So it seems that Mrs Wallace made a good choice in selecting this kind of probe for Claire. Deno reports that his data show a close relationship between the number of words read aloud from the text in one minute and measures of pupil comprehension, but he does advise teachers that specific checks should also be made on children's comprehension. So this will be one of a number of aspects of Claire's literacy skills that Mrs Wallace will continue to address using the same approaches she uses for all the children. It is only Claire's progress on the specific reading accuracy and fluency objective that will be monitored using the precision teaching approach. Similarly, Claire will continue to participate in the same literacy programme as other members of her group while receiving some additional input focused on her specific reading accuracy and fluency objective. Typically a pupil would receive an additional 10–15 minutes per day structured teaching, with two of those minutes being devoted to assessment of progress using the probe and graphing at Step 3.

Figure 8.4 illustrates the central role of graphing in this precision teaching approach with individual pupils. The number of words read correctly each day is charted with a dot and the number read incorrectly is charted with a cross. Techniques devised by White and Haring (1980) are used to make decisions about whether progress is satisfactory or when a change in the child's programme should be made. Initially, Claire read 37 words correctly and 8 incorrectly per

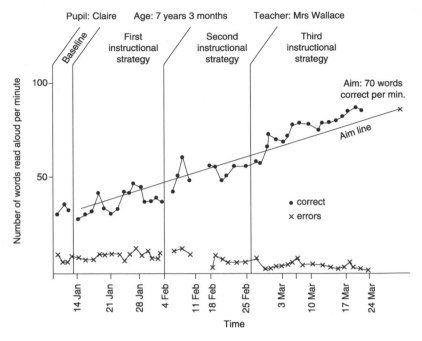

Figure 8.4   Precision teaching ('reading book') chart
Source: Adapted from Deno and Fuchs (1987).

minute. The two classmates from her reading group averaged 70 words read correctly and 5 words incorrectly. It was decided to aim to help Claire achieve this rate by the end of the spring term. An aim line was drawn by Mrs Wallace to help her monitor the rate of progress being made and decide whether or not it was on track. An IEP was drawn up and a specific teaching programme focusing on key phonic skills was devised. This was to be implemented by a learning support assistant during the Literacy Hour. A set of probes was developed to monitor Claire's progress in learning the phonic skills taught each week and the results plotted on her 'sounds chart' showed that the progress being made was very good. However, looking at Claire's 'reading book chart' (Figure 8.4) it can be seen that while some progress was made using this first instructional strategy her perform-ance was quite variable. Nevertheless, the programme was applied consistently until the point in early February when Claire's performance had been below the aim line for four consecutive days. Fuchs *et al.* (1993) advised that if four consecutive scores fall below the aim line a change in the pupil's programme should be introduced to try to increase their rate of progress.

Mrs Wallace planned the introduction of the second intervention. This involved, in addition to the session with the learning support assistant, a computer game which provided speeded practice in applying phonics skills to text. Claire was absent on Monday 11 February when this programme was due to start, as can be seen in Figure 8.4 by the break in the line joining the daily dots and crosses. Claire initially responded very well to the introduction of the computer program, but after the half-term break she did not do so well when left to use the program on her own. A further adjustment in her programme was required. Mrs Wallace included the second lowest performing pupil in Claire's reading group in the ten-minute daily computer session, after which the learning support assistant administered the probe with Claire. In addition, both Mrs Wallace and the learning support assistant made a point of reminding both pupils to apply the skills being practised in the computer sessions in their other reading activities.

Three weeks after the implementation of the third instructional strategy Claire attained her objective for the first time. The probe was administered and Claire's performance charted until the target rate of words correct and incorrect had been achieved for three consecutive days. Mrs Wallace planned to continue the programme after Easter for the first few weeks of the new term, as performance typically shows a decline following a break of this kind. If Claire did not reach her objective by the target date, Mrs Wallace would have to decide whether to extend it. If steady progress was being made which could not be accelerated despite a variety of programme modifications then it would be likely that the initial target was too ambitious and that an extension to the time period was necessary. Alternatively, a less ambitious programme with smaller steps and a more modest target could be developed.

This example illustrates precision teaching's sensitivity to progress and indicates the way in which it can directly inform teaching decisions. It illustrates that the onus is on the teacher to find a strategy that works, and it can provide a very clear indication of the level and type of additional resources that a particular pupil requires to learn successfully. It also indicates how some meaningful norm referencing can be achieved. This is likely to take on particular significance in assessing children from minority ethnic groups in that a particular child's reading performance could be referenced against that of classmates having the same first language and similar educational histories.

Precision teaching: issues in implementation

Although the approach has a basis in behavioural psychology, Lindsley (1992: 52) argues that precision teaching is compatible with a wide range of curricular approaches, 'except those so anti-structure that they cannot permit a counter, timer or chart in the classroom'. The extent to which precision teaching is used by educational psychologists and teachers in Britain has waxed and waned over the years. In the 1980s many articles were published describing applications of the approach (Booth and Jay 1981; Raybould and Solity 1982; Williams and Muncey 1982; Booth and Jewell 1983; Jewell and Feiler 1985; Goddard 1988). Kessissoglou and Farrell (1995) observed that very few studies were published in British journals in the early 1990s, although continuing active interest had been apparent in American journals. However it now appears that this may simply have been a slowing in the pace of publications on a topic that was no longer, of itself, considered novel. Publications on the use of precision teaching in British mainstream schools have continued to appear at intervals on a range of subject areas: spelling (Brooks 1995); maths (Chiesa and Robertson 2000); and reading (Downer 2007). Recent studies have also recorded positive results across a wide range of SEN groups: traumatic brain injury (Chapman *et al.* 2005); autism (Kerr *et al.* 2003); and attention deficit hyperactivity disorder (McDowell and Keenan 2001).

In Hasbrouck *et al.* (1999) a US teacher discusses frankly some of her initial concerns upon being introduced to a CBA approach and outlines her reasons for becoming committed to it. Initially she had taken it up reluctantly when the school district in which she worked made it a requirement that all special education teachers had to use CBA and graphing three times per week. One concern related to increased accountability where the graphs would offer concrete documentation of the effects of her teaching on the progress of those pupils with SEN with whom she was working. There was also an expectation that pupil's CBA graphs would be shared with parents, other teachers and the headteacher in informing decision making about the pupil.

Ainscow (1988) suggested that teachers may find it difficult to organize the implementation of the approach in large-class situations, and teachers in Hasbrouck *et al.*'s (1999) study reported that implementing CBA did reduce instructional time. However, they considered that the resulting greater efficiency in the use of instructional time outweighed the relatively minor cost in time and paperwork. They also identified the following specific advantages:

- The graphed results provide a powerful communication tool and evidence of positive progress – for teachers, pupils and parents.

- When progress is not being made teachers are alerted to this at once and can prepare to implement a programme modification to address the problem.

- The success of a programme change can be quickly evaluated.

Feasibility of implementation of precision teaching is assisted by the availability of resources on the internet to support all stages of the process (see Merbitz *et al.* 2004a). For example:

- www.johnandgwyn.co.uk provides an Excel spreadsheet that randomly generates from the first line a whole probe for sight word recognition, number bonds or phonics targets. It is well used by educational psychologists in the UK.

- www.aimchart.net is run by Charles Merbitz of the Illinois Institute of Technology. It allows teachers to set up pupils on the system with passwords so they can enter their own data which can be seen and/or accessed by the teacher and other authorized people (e.g. parents) as appropriate.

Hasbrouck *et al.* (1999) also describe the implementation of precision teaching on a school-wide basis. In the autumn term all pupils are assessed three times on unpractised age-appropriate reading passages and the median score is used as a baseline for comparison with a second assessment in the spring to see if the pupils are benefiting from the school's reading programme. Any pupils identified as being at risk of reading failure are assessed using weekly CBA measures, and graphs are kept of their progress. CBA only tells a teacher that the progress is not satisfactory, not why. An analysis of the processes being used and errors made by the pupil is then undertaken and the information used to design adaptations for the pupil. Sometimes the intervention may be as simple as a change in seating arrangements in the classroom to reduce distractions. At other times 5–10 minutes daily on focused practice of a targeted skill with a learning support assistant may be needed, or the teaching session may need to be organized so that the teacher can spend a few minutes with the pupil previewing or reviewing the content of a lesson.

Ainscow (1988) also suggested that a focus on analysing specific tasks for individual pupils may result in a narrowing of perspective so that insufficient attention is given to other important contextual factors that may be impeding learning – related, for example, to the curriculum in general, classroom organization or interpersonal relationships. These potential dangers appear much reduced when CBA approaches, such as precision teaching, are implemented in the broader context of a whole-class focus on AfL.

Assessment for learning and pupils learning EAL

The Cummins quadrant

When children are learning EAL there is also often a need to adapt learning tasks and sequences in order to facilitate their access. Figure 8.5 shows a two-dimensional model developed from the work of Cummins (1984) into an assessment framework by Desforges and Kerr (1984) and working groups of educational psychologists at University College London (Cline and Frederickson 1996; Frederickson and Cline 1990). In this framework the *horizontal dimension* is used to indicate the degree of contextual support that is provided. At the context embedded end of the dimension language would be embedded within a meaningful context and gesture or expression cues would be likely to be present. On the other hand, at the context reduced end of the dimension the only cues to meaning would be linguistic ones. To provide a concrete example: if the child was asked to read the sentence 'Tom went to the shop' presented to them as one of the sentences in a sentence reading test, this would be an example of the use of written language in a context reduced situation. On the other hand, if the child was asked to read the same sentence just after it had been written by the teacher to the child's dictation under a picture which they had drawn of their brother, Tom, then this

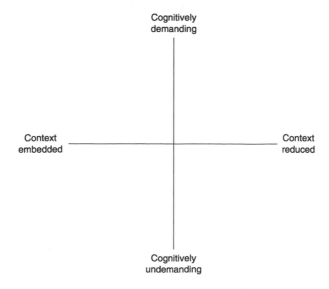

Figure 8.5   Cummins' (1984) two-dimensional model of language proficiency

would be an example of written language use embedded within a context that was meaningful to the child.

The *vertical dimension* indicates the level of cognitive demand placed upon the child by language used in any particular task or situation. Cummins regards cognitive demand as depending on both external and internal factors. External factors refer to those such as task complexity – where one could agree, for example, that addition is an easier and less complex mathematical operation than multiplication. Internal factors refer to the familiarity and acceptability of the task to the child as well as the child's current proficiency. This highlights the point that tasks which are relatively cognitively undemanding for a native speaker of English may be highly cognitively demanding for a second language learner. This model therefore attempts to incorporate knowledge of what the child brings to the learning situation over and above their entry skills on the task in question.

As Desforges and Kerr (1984) pointed out, the model also suggests how classroom activities may be modified in a way which maximizes the access of bilingual children to the curriculum. Typically, if a child is experiencing difficulty with a particular activity the teacher may respond by making that activity easier – that is, by reducing the level of cognitive demand. However, second language learners may well be able to cope with the cognitive complexity of the task but simply not yet have developed the language skills necessary for access. To reduce the complexity of tasks in this situation would result in the children being provided with inappropriately easy work which does not stretch them intellectually. The use of the Cummins quadrant is recommended in government guidelines (DfES 2006a) on planning for children learning EAL. In conducting AfL it can also be helpful to locate on the matrix those tasks where the child is able to succeed and those tasks where success cannot yet be achieved. It is then possible to build up a picture of the child's strengths and weaknesses in terms of the level of cognitive demand they can handle with confidence in particular curriculum areas, and to establish the level of contextual and other support required for success in a range of different situations.

Cline and Frederickson (1996) provide accounts of the use of the model in primary and secondary schools by a range of education service professionals with bilingual children working in a variety of community languages, including British Sign Language. The general conclusion is that it is an attractively simple as well as versatile model. However, a number of potential limitations have been identified. The most obvious of these is the assumption that the cognitive and contextual dimensions are distinct and readily separable. In observing and analysing classroom tasks, instructions and performances it has sometimes proved difficult to disentangle the 'cognitive' fully from the 'contextual'. In some cases, movement along the contextual dimensions has actually been represented on the model as a diagonal shift, as it was found in practice that making tasks or instructions more context embedded also made them somewhat less cognitively demanding. Similarly, changes in cognitive demand may result in tasks actually being presented which are embedded in context to a greater or lesser degree.

It is also important to remind ourselves of what the framework does *not* do:

● It does not analyse the child's cognitive strategies (e.g. preference for rote learning) or learning style (e.g. preference for working independently).

- It does not provide the teacher with the information about the child's cultural background that is required to 'embed' the task.

Thus, ironically, the framework can only be meaningful for the teacher when it, too, is 'context embedded' – that is, the teacher is clear about the aims of the lesson, knows the child's background well and has tried to match the task to the child's learning style and interest.

Solity (1993) had expressed concern that the classifications offered for determining task difficulty (cognitively demanding/undemanding and context embedded/reduced), and the way these are related to the cultural background of children make assumptions and predictions about children's learning which may create differential expectations based on ethnicity. While this is always a danger, the approach encourages teachers to consider for each pupil how their language proficiencies and their familiarity with particular materials and tasks may interact with the planned curriculum activities to increase or decrease the level of difficulty of these activities. The ultimate effect, therefore, should not be to create differential stereotypical expectations based on ethnicity, but to encourage those working with children in a classroom to be sensitive to the *individual* differences that are associated with linguistic and cultural diversity.

At worst, stereotypical underexpectation of children from minority linguistic and ethnic groups will lead teachers to substitute less cognitively demanding tasks (moving vertically down in the framework) if difficulties are encountered, as is suggested by a traditional approach to task analysis. With this approach teachers are encouraged first to move horizontally (left across the model) to ascertain whether the child is able to demonstrate success when given greater contextual support to their developing proficiency in English. In this way the model based on the Cummins framework offers a new dimension to the CBA of bilingual children.

Using the Cummins quadrant in differential assessment

This section describes the use of the Cummins framework approach to CBA in addressing a key question in working with bilingual children for whom the language of instruction is not their preferred language: when does poor learning performance indicate a special need and when does it indicate a need for further support in learning the language of instruction? This decision between the identification of learning needs and language needs is often fraught with difficult political and ethical considerations. If it is mistakenly decided that a child has a learning need then the child may be provided with insufficiently challenging learning experiences and be subject to inappropriately low expectations. Decision errors of this type may also lay the professional involved open to charges of racism or of employing culturally biased assessment procedures.

However, difficulties are also created by mistaken decisions that a child has a language rather than a learning need. In this case the child is likely to receive a language support programme to which they cannot respond because its pace is too fast and it is structured in learning steps which are too large. In subsequent assessment, therefore, they will continue to present as having language needs, so it may be several years before it is finally recognized that their difficulties with learning language are not responsible for their slow academic progress but that problems in both areas reflect general learning difficulties. Maintaining the 'language difficulties' hypothesis until the evidence for 'learning difficulties' becomes overwhelming avoids the political pitfalls for professionals outlined above. However, it can present serious ethical problems if the children concerned do not receive the special learning support they need.

The CBA framework can be used to structure diverse assessment information, aiding its analysis and interpretation. Essentially the approach involves using the Cummins framework to map the tasks at which the child can succeed and those which they are unable to do. For the latter, further assessment involves increasing the level of contextual support as a first step. This may entail increasing non-verbal cues (such as those gained from demonstration) to support the verbal message. Learning experiences may also be contextually embedded by supplementing the language of tuition with explanation or examples in the child's preferred language.

Figures 8.6 and 8.7 provide schematic snapshots of the kinds of profile which may be interpreted as indicating learning and language needs, respectively. Figure 8.6 shows a profile indicative of a child with learning needs. Providing increasing degrees of contextual embedding does not assist the child in achieving success. However, reducing the cognitive demand of the task (i.e. making it easier) does allow the child to succeed. By contrast, Figure 8.7 shows a profile indicative of a child with language of instruction support needs, for whom increasing degrees of contextual embedding allow success to be achieved. Typically, however, those bilingual children who have learning needs will also present with language needs because their general learning difficulties will also affect their learning of the language of instruction – at least their acquisition of cognitive academic aspects of language proficiency. Hence, Figure 8.8 shows a profile likely to be indicative of a

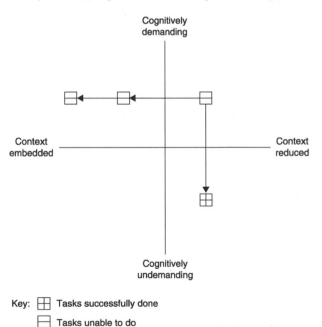

Figure 8.6 A child with learning needs
Source: Rogers and Pratten (1996).

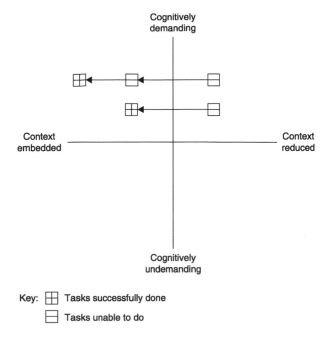

Figure 8.7   A child with language of instruction support needs
Source: Rogers and Pratten (1996).

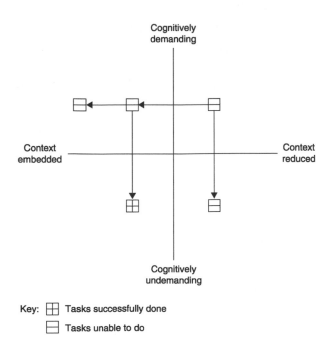

Figure 8.8   A bilingual child with learning needs
Source: Rogers & Pratten (1996).

bilingual child who has learning needs. For these children to achieve success they will need to be provided both with tasks at an appropriate level of difficulty in respect of their learning needs and with tasks which are appropriately contextually embedded in respect of their language needs. This points to the importance of learning and language specialists working effectively together.

Activity 8.3   Differential assessment case studies

Read the following case studies (from Rogers and Pratten 1996) of children referred for advice to an integrated LEA support service.

(a)   For each child use a copy of the CBA framework to map the tasks which the child can and cannot do.

(b)   Decide whether there is a closer match with Figure 8.6, indicating a learning need, or with Figure 8.7, indicating a language need.

Case study A

A 6-year-old boy from a Gujarati-speaking family who has no preschool educational experience. Reason for referral: to establish whether the child has learning difficulties that require formal assessment.

Current targets:

●   naming different rooms in the home;

●   three initial letter sounds to be taught;

●   drawing and naming shapes.

The baseline is that the child only knows the initial letter sound 'a'.

In the Cummins framework these targets would be cognitively demanding and not context embedded. Working with the class teacher, the bilingual support teacher observed that the theme in the lessons was all about the home. The bilingual support teacher provided an activity book with acetate peeling stick drawings. This was used as the medium to provide context embedded experiences for the child to name the objects and to make him aware of the initial letter sounds. In English, the bilingual support teacher found that the child did not know the word 'cooker'. In Gujarati, the bilingual support teacher found that the child identified the item from the question 'Where does your mum cook?'. Only when she had made a home visit did the bilingual support teacher discover that the family used the word 'gas' to describe their cooking appliance. Many families would associate the word 'cooker' with a pressure cooker rather than a stove or range. In discussion with the mother, the bilingual support teacher now uses vocabulary used within the home setting. The work of teaching the initial letter sounds was reinforced at home by the mother using games such as 'I Spy'.

Having context-embedded the material appropriate to the culture and environment, the bilingual support teacher was able to demonstrate that this child's rate of learning was such that he did not require formal assessment. The child was able to identify the common shapes found within his own home, name the different rooms and initial letter sounds, and therefore it was demonstrated that he did not have a significant learning difficulty.

Case study B

An 11-year-old boy from a Punjabi-speaking family.

Reason for referral: learning difficulties in the first year of secondary school.

Previous experience: early schooling in India.

Language of instruction: Hindi.

Dropped out of school because of learning and behavioural difficulties. Mother remarried a Gujarati-speaking husband and the family came to England. The child had not spoken English before he was 11 years old. A bilingual teacher initially worked both in Hindi and Punjabi to establish the following targets.

Current targets:

- to write first name;
- to develop work recognition skills;
- to use common nouns in English.

The last target was addressed first. Initially the child was taught solely in Hindi. Through stories from his own experience the bilingual support teacher introduced a basic vocabulary in English. After the teaching sessions it was demonstrated that the boy was capable of learning, though at a much slower rate than his peers even with a high level of contextual embedding. Use of the Cummins grid in this case indicated that it was not possible to ensure the child's success with an age-appropriate learning task simply by moving horizontally across the framework and providing more contextual support. Rather it was necessary first to move vertically down the framework in identifying easier small steps to the target. In addition, it was still found necessary to ensure that these easier tasks were well embedded in context.

Conclusions

In this chapter we have examined approaches to assessment that are focused on the teaching programme. In these approaches the outputs of the assessment process are changes to the content and/or delivery of teaching programme so that it enhances learner engagement and achievement. Prior research in the use of curriculum-based assessment with children who have SEN has provided an important basis for the current emphasis on AfL in the UK as an approach of key importance in raising attainment for all children. The core strategies of AfL were described and issues in teacher training and implementation discussed. Questions were raised about the need for more structured and intensive AfL strategies to be used with children who have SEN and one such strategy (precision teaching), which has a strong evidence base, was described in detail. The chapter concluded by suggesting ways in which the Cummins quadrant might be used to enhance AfL for pupils learning EAL.

9

Learning environments

Objectives

When you have studied this chapter you should be able to:

- explain the reasons why a greater emphasis has been placed in recent years on assessing the learning environment;
- outline different theoretical models of the learning environment;
- describe the strengths and limitations of commonly used methods for assessing learning environments and designing interventions.

Contents

Introduction

- Influences from legislation
- Influences from research

The learning environment: theory and practice

- Theoretical models of the influence of the learning environment
- The gap between theory and current practice

Methods for assessing learning environments and designing interventions

- Observational measures
- Pupil perceptual measures
- Multi-perspective measures
- Qualitative ethnographic assessment methods
- Soft systems methodology

Conclusions

Introduction

In Chapter 6, four distinctive approaches to the assessment of SEN were outlined: assessment focused on the learner, assessment focused on the teaching programme, assessment focused on the zone of potential development, and assessment focused on the learning environment. This chapter is devoted to assessment focused on the learning environment. Ainscow and Tweddle (1988: 18) wrote: 'In the 1960s we were preoccupied with analysing the individual child; in the 1970s the emphasis was switched to analysing tasks within the curriculum; and now we believe we should be focusing on the learning environment.'

It has been suggested that there are a number of advantages in focusing on 'at-risk school environments' rather than 'at-risk' students (Waxman 1992). Definitions of the at-risk student tend to focus on student characteristics, such as poverty, drug abuse, sexual activity, race, ethnicity, SEN, and first language other than English. There are concerns that this could be stigmatizing and may produce the 'Matthew effect'. The Matthew effect, a biblical reference, involves the rich getting richer and the poor poorer – or in this case, those who start off with advantages in learning making above average progress and those who start off with lower achievements than their peers falling ever further behind. There are a number of ways in which this effect might be magnified. For example, if Shama starts the year behind her peers in maths, her maths teacher may expect less of her, give her easier work or less of it and only call on her to answer low-level questions in class. These strategies effectively restrict Shama's learning opportunities and she falls further behind her peers who are being given a broader range of more challenging opportunities to develop their knowledge and skills.

Waxman (1992) argued that it would be more productive to identify those 'at-risk' school environments that:

- alienate students and teachers;

- provide low standards and a low quality of education;

- have differential expectations for students;

- have high numbers failing to leave school with a minimum level of qualifications;

- are unresponsive to students;

- have high rates of truancy and disciplinary problems;

- do not adequately prepare students for the future.

This kind of emphasis is apparent in the approach to school inspection introduced in Britain in the 1990s. A system of regular independent inspection of all schools was implemented with the purpose of reporting on the quality of education provided by the school, the educational standards achieved, the efficient management of financial resources and the spiritual, moral, social and cultural development of pupils (Department for Education (DfE) 1992). The law relating to school inspections has since been revised. Where a school is considered to be failing to give its pupils an acceptable standard of education it can be placed in 'special measures' or, if it has demonstrated the capacity to improve, given a notice to improve. These are essentially 'at-risk' designations and schools are required to produce an action plan to address the matters raised in the inspection report. The local education authority is expected to comment on the school's action plan and to outline the steps it proposes to take to support the school which will be subject to termly monitor visits by Ofsted and a further inspection.

The focus on these 'at-risk' schools has steadily intensified, as is illustrated by the following quotation from *The Guardian* newspaper on 28 September 2007:

Andrew Adonis, the schools minister, said: 'Over the last decade there has been an unrelenting focus on raising standards.

'We have seen significant improvements in results since then ... But we must press on and reduce even further the numbers of weak and failing schools.

'Our reforms to turn around failing schools demand radical action from the school and local authority. A school in special measures has to turn round in 12 months, otherwise the school could face closure.'

A number of other influences which have contributed to increasing interest in the learning environment can be identified, both from legislation and from research. These are discussed next.

Influences from legislation

In the past, SEN legislation focused exclusively on disabilities within the child. Over the last 20 years more attention has been given to the learning environments of pupils who have SEN. Section 323 of the Education Act 1996 defined SEN in terms of the interrelationship between a child's learning difficulty and the educational support which they are receiving: 'A child has special educational needs if they have a learning difficulty which calls for special educational provision to be made for them'. The *Code of Practice* on the identification and assessment of pupils with SEN (DfES 2001a) goes further. Rather than simply recognizing that the learning environment will have an influence and should be considered, the revised guidance requires the assessment of pupils who have SEN to include assessment of their learning environment. Likewise in devising interventions, changes to features of the learning environment should be considered (2001a, para. 5.6):

> The assessment process should always be fourfold. It should focus on the child's learning characteristics, the learning environment that the school is providing for the child, the task and the teaching style. It should be recognised that some difficulties in learning may be caused or exacerbated by the school's learning environment or adult/child relationships. This means looking carefully at such matters as classroom organisation, teaching materials, teaching style and differentiation in order to decide how these can be developed so that the child is enabled to learn effectively.

Other guidance and training documents also place emphasis on the importance of attending to the learning environment. DfES (2005e) provided training materials to assist staff identify key factors in the environment which help to promote behaviour for learning. Four categories of factors that make up the learning environment are suggested:

- *Physical* – the layout of the school and classroom, its facilities and the resources children use.

- *Relationships* – how people in the school behave towards each other, care about and look after one another.

- *Structures and expectations* – expectations we hold about children's behaviour, and the school and classroom rules and routines.

- *Language and communication* – the way that relationships, structures and expectations are manifested through verbal and non-verbal communication in the school.

In the guidance provided by the DfES (2006e) on using the learning environment as a tool for learning, particular emphasis is placed on the first of these aspects, the physical environment. It is argued that the physical environment has a significant influence on learning through the messages it gives children about the extent to which they and their learning are valued. Later in this chapter we will be looking more closely at the conclusions of available research on the effects of the learning environment on academic and social outcomes. The DfES (2006e) guidance places emphasis on the role of the learning environment in supporting independence in learning. For example, the concept of 'working walls' is advocated, which shifts the use of some classroom wall space from its traditional use for displaying completed work produced by the children. Instead working walls are used by the teacher to support learning of literacy or numeracy targets on which the children are currently working. This involves prominently displaying the curricular target and success criteria, together with modelled examples showing the steps in the learning sequence and providing the relevant vocabulary.

Influences from research

School effectiveness research

School effectiveness research has had a major impact in education over the last 25 years. Prior to that there was a widespread belief that 'schools make no difference'. However, researchers in this area are now expressing the view that 'we have been instrumental in creating a quite widespread, popular view that schools do not just make *a* difference, but that they make *all* the difference' (Reynolds 1995: 13). In fact, Reynolds reports that only 8–15 per cent of the variance in pupil outcomes is usually found to be due to school and classroom factors – which are not therefore as influential as family and community factors. However, the influence of school factors is big enough to make the difference between educational success and failure for many pupils.

From a review of school effectiveness research between 1979 and 2002, Rutter and Maughn (2002) report that the following factors have been found to be associated with school effectiveness:

- *Contextual features* – balanced intake in terms of pupil characteristics. It is also suggested that community support, political support and adequate resources (which have been less systematically studied) may also be important.

- *School organization and management* – good leadership that provides strategic vision, staff participation with a shared vision and goals, appropriate rewards for collegial collaborative working, attendance to staff needs and rewards, and effective home–school partnership.

- *School ethos* – an orderly atmosphere, an attractive working environment, appropriate well-conveyed high expectations, the involvement of pupils in taking responsibility, positive rewards with feedback and clear fair discipline, positive models of good teacher behaviour, a focus on achievement and good behaviour, and good teacher–pupil relationships in and outside the classroom.

- *Effective monitoring* – regular measurement of pupil performance across a range of domains, appropriate assessment of teacher efficiency, and the evaluation of overall school performance in relation to a range of indices.

- *Group management in the classroom* – efficient organization of lessons (or non-classroom activities), clarity of purpose, and appropriately structured lessons.

- *Pedagogic qualities* – good engagement of pupil interest, effective classroom teaching, maximization of learning time, good subject knowledge by the teacher, encouragement of independent work by pupils, and appropriate parental involvement in children's learning.

While these broad generalizations are well established, it must be acknowledged that because many of the study designs are correlational, it is not possible to establish whether a causal relationship exists such that developing these attributes would actually lead to enhanced pupil achievement (Griffith 2003). A number of other questions about research in this area remain:

- How consistent is school performance across different outcome measures?

- Are schools equally effective for all pupils or subgroups?

In relation to the first of these questions there appears to be considerable variation. Mortimore *et al.* (1988) found that those junior schools that came out high on academic effectiveness were not necessarily high on social effectiveness and vice versa. School differences in emotional/behavioural outcomes were less marked than variations in academic attainments. Rutter and Maughn (2002) drew similar conclusions for adolescents from a range of studies that examined outcomes including interest in learning, non-attendance, delinquency, drug use, psychological stress/well-being and self-confidence. However, there is also some evidence of associations with broader social outcomes. For example, Ainley (2006) found that an engaging school climate, whether identified as such by pupils or teachers, was related to students regarding social outcomes connected to interdependence as being important to them in their lives. It is hypothesized that developing a sense of connectedness to others in the school community is part of the process of developing a sense of interdependence with others in a broader social community.

In relation to the second question (are schools equally effective for all pupils or subgroups?), Nuttall *et al.* (1989) argued that there can be different school effects for children of different ethnic groups, ability ranges and gender within the same school. Using examination performance at 16 years as the outcome measure, a study conducted over three years revealed substantial differences between boys and girls, pupils of high and low attainment on entry to secondary school and pupils of Caribbean backgrounds, as opposed to those from English, Scottish, Welsh or Irish backgrounds. Doubts were raised about the meaningfulness of the concept of overall effectiveness and it was suggested that it may be more meaningful to describe differences between schools for different subgroups. This also seems to be the case in some primary schools. In a research study conducted by

Mortimore *et al.* (1988) in London primary schools, gender differences in reading progress were compared. It was found that most schools were equally effective, or ineffective, in promoting the reading progress of boys and girls. However, in 30 per cent of schools differences were found, two-thirds showing positive effects for boys but negative effects for girls.

Semmel *et al.* (1994) reported results from a longitudinal school effectiveness project focusing on primary and secondary schools in California. There was no evidence that schools that did well in terms of general academic achievement also did well with regard to the academic performance, self-esteem or school adjustment of pupils with SEN. Indeed, in primary schools a significant negative relationship was found between the reading performance on state assessments of a school's pupils with SEN and school-wide reading achievement. The authors suggest that pressures on these schools to increase academic standards under conditions of reducing resources may have led to the development of strategies to improve reading performance overall which had a negative impact on the reading progress of pupils with SEN.

The influence of class size on pupil outcomes is an aspect of the learning environment which has been much debated. Rutter and Maughn (2002) concluded that variations within the 25–35 range make little difference, possibly because teaching and classroom management style tend to be similar within this range. However, Nye and Hedges (2000) reported that very small classes (8–15 pupils) may be beneficial, especially for younger children, children with special needs and those from economically disadvantaged backgrounds.

The classroom learning environment

Reynolds (1997) identified the study of classroom or instructional processes as a gap in current British research on school effectiveness. Criticisms of a lack of intersection between school and classroom level effectiveness research were levelled by researchers in the USA at the research base in that country (Bickel 1999). This is an important area for further work as many studies show that a great majority of the variance between pupils is due to factors at the classroom level, not the school level (Rutter and Maughn 2002).

There is a substantial literature which demonstrates that characteristics of the classroom learning environment account for appreciable amounts of variance in a number of important outcome measures such as examination results, standardized test scores, inquiry skills, school attendance, attitudes, interest and anxiety (Fraser 1986). Haertel *et al.* (1981) conducted a meta-analysis of data from 12 studies involving 17,805 students in 823 classes across four countries and reported that better achievement was consistently found in classes perceived as having greater cohesiveness, satisfaction and goal direction, and less disorganization and friction. While it is acknowledged that much research has still to be done in this area, other researchers too have reported results which suggest that student attitude as well as student achievement might be improved by creating classroom environments with more of these positive features (Fraser *et al.* 1989; Burden and Fraser 1993).

An important aspect of research on classroom environments is its international and cross-cultural character. For example, the International Association for the Evaluation of Educational Achievement classroom environment study

(Anderson *et al.* 1989) was conducted in eight countries: Australia, Canada, Hungary, Israel, Korea, the Netherlands, Nigeria and Thailand. This promotes confidence in the cross-cultural applicability of consistently emerging findings. However, to date much of the research has been descriptive or correlational in nature. Waxman and Huang (1996) highlighted the need for longitudinal and, especially, experimental studies which would be important in informing intervention. Urging researchers to examine specifically how aspects of the classroom learning environment can be changed in order to serve a protective function for pupils in at-risk school and community settings, they also argued for the importance of examining the data for differential effects of pupil characteristics such as sex, ethnicity and age.

Figure 9.1 shows the classroom-level variables which affect learning that were identified from a literature review conducted by McKee and Witt (1990). It should be noted that this review focuses on studies carried out with general populations

---

A. Physical setting of the classroom

1   Classroom design, furniture arrangement, seating positions

2   Spatial density and crowding

3   Noise and lighting

B. Classroom organization and management

1   Teacher's classroom management skills

  ● 'With-itness'; overlapping; signal continuity; momentum

  ● Group alerting and accountability in lessons

2   Procedures for establishing effective management

  ● Rules and procedures for everyday classroom life

  ● Procedures for student accountability

  ● Managing inappropriate behaviour

C. Quantity and quality of instruction

1   Quantity or amount of instruction

  ● Allocated time; engaged time

  ● Time spent on tasks on which students have high success rate

2   Quality of instruction

  ● Daily review and checking of homework

  ● Presentation of material to be learned

  ● Arrangements for guided student practice

  ● Feedback and correctives on students' performance

  ● Independent practice; periodic reviews

Figure 9.1   Classroom variables which affect children's learning
Source: Based on a literature review by McKee and Witt (1990).

of schoolchildren, rather than those with SEN. It cannot be assumed that the same variables will have equal salience for different groups of children. For example, Rossmiller (1982, cited in Berliner 1987) found that 'engaged time' had a different significance for high- and low-achieving pupils. Engaged time is the amount of classroom time during which pupils are engaged with instructional tasks. In this study, engaged time accounted for 10 per cent of the variance in reading and maths achievement for high-achieving pupils but, in the case of low-achieving pupils the percentage of variance accounted for was 73 per cent.

There is some further support for the view that the learning environment may play a different and relatively more important role in the educational progress of children with special needs as compared to their mainstream peers. Table 9.1 reports the findings from Kaufman *et al.*'s (1985) extensive evaluation of a major reintegration programme for primary-aged children with moderate learning difficulty (MLD) in Texas. What emerges most strongly is the greater importance for both pupils with special needs and their mainstream peers of a focus on environmental as opposed to individual variables.

There is evidence that pupils with learning difficulties are treated differently by teachers. However, this is not always advantageous for them. Slate and Saudargas (1987) found that teachers were more likely to leave pupils with learning difficulties alone when they were engaged in academic work than when they were engaged in other activities. On the other hand, teachers were more likely to interact with students with learning difficulties when they were out of their seats or interacting with other children. Teachers' differential attention to off-task behaviour was only found with pupils who had learning difficulties, not with their classmates. Alves and Gottlieb (1986) found that teachers directed fewer academic questions and less extended feedback towards pupils who have learning difficulties, although teachers did interact with them more frequently overall than they did with other pupils. The authors suggested that this evidence of lower academic input may reflect perceptions on the part of the teachers that

Table 9.1 Percentage of variance in academic achievement and anti-social behaviour attributable to individual and environmental variables for mainstream and integrated MLD pupils

		Type of variable (%)	
		Learner background (individual, family, home)	Environmental (classroom composition, socioemotional climate, instructional conditions)
Academic achievement	Integrated MLD pupils	13	27
	Mainstream pupils	33	45
Antisocial behaviour	Integrated MLD pupils	5	28
	Mainstream pupils	11	21

Source: Kaufman *et al.* (1985).

socialization, rather than academic learning, represents the primary goal of main-streaming for pupils who have learning difficulties. Cooper and Valli (1996: 156) argued that a very different approach is in fact required: 'classroom organization for poor children of color and for children with learning difficulties must account for individual and cultural differences in knowledge construction by providing well-scaffolded, culturally responsive and socially mediated instructional activities'. Thus, those reporting and commenting on research have supported

Table 9.2   Features of the school physical environment and effects on pupil outcomes

	Attainment	Engagement	Affect	Attendance	Wellbeing
Improvement of environmental element leads to improvement	Light (daylight) Build quality (pathways and positive outdoor space)	Low ceilings (pupil co-operation vs. perceptions of crowding) Colour (contrast walls) Storage (open shelves, more time on task)	'Beautiful' spaces High ceilings (teacher satisfaction) Display (pupil self-esteem)		
Equivocal evidence	Room arrangement (depending on goal of lesson/ interaction)	Ergonomic furniture Noise (learned helplessness) Temperature, ventilation, air quality (distraction of air conditioning) Desk arrangement	Colour Lighting Noise (mood) Build quality (renovation)	Temperature, ventilation, air quality (disputed) Build quality (ownership vs. short-term 'wow' factor) Lighting (disputed)	Ergonomic furniture
Poor quality environmental elements have detrimental effect	Air quality Noise Safe, healthy surrounding	Air quality Noise	Noise (context dependent) Overall build quality	Air quality Safe, healthy surroundings	Air quality (esp. asthma) Storage (open shelves, dust, allergens) Lighting (eyestrain, headaches) ICT (lighting, posture)

Source: Woolner *et al.* (2007).

the official guidance emphasizing the importance of the learning environment of a child who has (or may have) SEN.

There has been a recent increase in interest in physical features of classroom environments in the UK. This relates to the announcement of a significant schools building programme 'to create world-class, 21st century schools – environments which will inspire learning for decades to come and provide exceptional assets for the whole community' (Building Schools for the Future 2004). Woolner *et al.* (2007) note that when government ministers discuss this development their comments often seem to imply that the effect of the physical environment of the school on pupil learning is obvious. However, as can be seen from Table 9.2, available empirical evidence is indicative rather than conclusive on many features of the physical environment. One feature that has been well researched is the arrangement of desks. When individual assignments are to be completed, rows as opposed to groups of desks are found to increase time on task (Wheldall *et al.* 1981). The effect has been found to be particularly marked for pupils with SEN (Wheldall and Lam 1987). Of course not all classroom activities may be facilitated by desks in rows – whole-class discussion and group work may benefit from a different arrangement. Activity 9.1 presents an example of an innovative classroom design project undertaken by a Design Council Team with a school in Liverpool where the focus is on flexibility.

Activity 9.1   Innovative design of the physical learning environment

In this activity you are asked to read the following information about an innovative classroom design project and to consider (and, where possible, debate with a colleague) the likely strengths and limitations of the new design as compared to the traditional classroom layout in the school which is shown in Figure 9.2.

Figure 9.2   A traditional classroom design
Source: Design Council (2005).

This project was carried out by a Design Council team working with staff and pupils at St Margaret's boys' secondary school in Liverpool. Their starting point was the development of a brief for improvements to the learning environment that could raise boys' achievement. They came up with a brief for a 360-degree flexible classroom. Figure 9.3 and the text below describe the classroom design produced by Forpeople (the design agency whose concept won the commission).

Figure 9.3   Innovative classroom design
Source: Design Council (2005).

The concept centres on the 'heart', a secure and mobile multimedia projection module at the centre of the room. The combined table/chair reduces the footprint of a traditional desk and chair, leaving space for the teacher to circulate around the 'racetrack' and so access each student individually. The flexibility of the table/chair means it can also be moved by the students to support individual, paired and group work, while the whiteboards around the walls can be removed (to reveal additional display space) and placed onto the tables to facilitate group work. The aluminium window blinds move individually to control light and air flow and can also be used as whiteboards to provide additional display and projection space, meaning that in the final plenary session of a lesson the teacher can refer to a vivid learning 'trail' that has been built up around the four walls. Finally, the 'utility belt' around the walls allows vital shared storage space.

(Design Council 2005: 32)

The learning environment: theory and practice

Theoretical models of the influence of the learning environment

There have been a number of influences on the thinking about a systematic approach to the assessment of children's learning environments, most notably Lewin's (1936) field theory, Bandura's (1977) concept of reciprocal determinism and Bronfenbrenner's (1979) ecosystems approach. Lewin developed the formula $B = f(P, E)$ to represent the idea that behaviour (B) was a function of personal characteristics (P), environmental factors (E) and the interaction between the two.

Bandura hypothesized that behaviour was determined by reciprocal interactions, continuously occurring between behavioural, cognitive and environmental factors. Bronfenbrenner developed a systems model of the multiple influences on child development that was introduced in Chapter 5. From these theoretical approaches a number of specific models of the influence of the learning environment on pupil performance in school have been developed. Three of these will be described in more detail, one relating to each of these theoretical frameworks.

The Project PRIME (Programmed Re-entry Into Mainstream Education) taxonomic model (Kaufman *et al.* 1985), some results from which are shown in Table 9.1, was developed to guide a major integration study in the USA. Paralleling Lewin's formula, the desired outcome (or 'output'), learner competence, was viewed as a function of the learner performing a specific role within an environment defined by a specific setting. It was represented mathematically by the equation $C = f(Lr, Es)$, where C is competence, L is learner background, E is the environment, r stands for role and s stands for setting. The model analyses each term in the equation into subcomponents. For example, learner competence is further subdivided into academic competence and social competence. Learner background variables include: age, sex, socioeconomic status, IQ, attitudes and previous school experience. Aspects of the learning environment are considered under three headings: classroom composition (peer characteristics and teacher characteristics), socioemotional climate (teacher leadership and peer cohesiveness) and instructional conditions (content and teaching approaches). These were used in the study to analyse three types of learning environment: mainstream class, segregated special class and a resource base (part-time withdrawal). Irrespective of placement a similar profile of classroom environment features was associated with academic progress for pupils with SEN:

- A classroom environment characterized by teacher directed and supervised activities calculated to actively involve the learner.

- Instructional engagement which occurred as a result of teacher activity with the student: teacher querying and student response, supervision, monitoring, feedback.

- Harmony within the classroom, which seemed to enhance peer exchanges, positive teacher–pupil interaction, increased attention to task, and the acceptance and assimilation of the learner with SEN into the regular classroom. Learning was optimized when non-handicapped and peers with SEN cooperated.

- The teacher's ability to create such a classroom environment was shown to be associated with their training and experience (Kaufmann *et al.* 1985: 360–1).

Figure 9.4 shows an updated version of Knoff's (1984) ecomap applying Bronfenbrenner's multi-approach. Originally Bronfenbrenner's (1979) classic model focused on the inter-related real-life environmental contexts in which development occurs. However, over time, the model has been redefined as 'bio-ecological', rather than 'ecological' and the underlined elements in italics added. Bronfenbrenner explains these change as follows:

> For some years I harangued my colleagues for avoiding the study of development in real-life settings. No longer able to complain on that score, I have

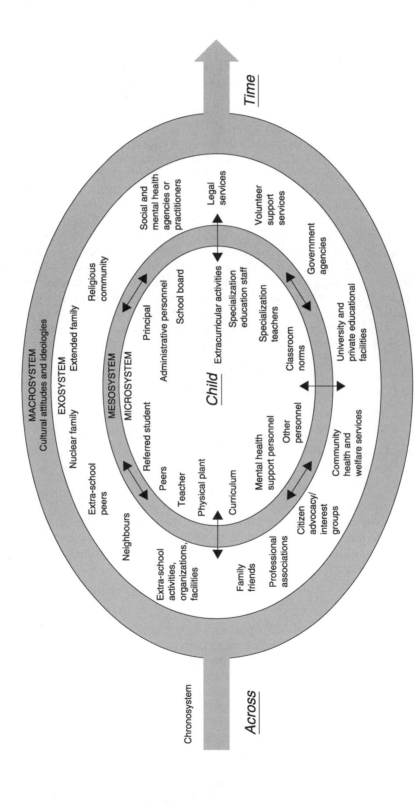

Figure 9.4   Bronfenbrenner's bioecological model
Source: adapted from Knoff (1984).

found a new bete noir. In place of too much research on development 'out of context' we now have a surfeit of studies on 'context without development'.
(Bronfenbrenner, 1986, reported in Bronfenbrenner and Morris 2006)

As a consequence the child (the biosystem) is now formally represented at the centre of the *bio*ecological model. In addition, the chronosystem represents changes in all systems across time. Development is understood in terms of individual-level changes over time resulting from processes of interaction between the individual and the environments within which they are embedded.

Ysseldyke and Christenson (2002) drew on the work of Bronfenbrenner in identifying features of the environment that provide support for learning in the microsystems of both home and school as well as at the mesosystem level of interaction between home and school. Three key types of feature were identified from a review of the literature as both amenable to intervention and important to pupil engagement and learning in school. The first set of features, which occurred in school, was described as indicating 'instructional support'. Examples included instructional expectations, cognitive emphasis, motivational strategies and relevant practice in the classroom. The second set of features could be observed at home and was seen as indicating 'home support'. Examples included the parents' orientation towards discipline, their participation in their children's learning and the 'affective environment' of the home. Finally, there was a set of features that spanned home and school ('home–school support'). These included the sharing of standards and expectations, positive trusting relationships and cross-setting of learning opportunities. A full list may be found in Ysseldyke and Christenson (2002: 4).

The influence of Bandura's work, in particular on the role of self-efficacy, can be seen in the model developed by Patrick *et al.* (2007), which is shown in Figure 9.5. This is a model of ways in which classroom social environment factors can influence student engagement and performance. It was developed from research with Year 6 pupils in maths lessons in the USA. The study showed that engagement and, through engagement, achievement were influenced by individual pupil motivational factors (feelings of efficacy and focus on mastery). These motivational factors in turn were influenced by the extent to which pupils felt emotionally supported by their teacher, academically supported by their peers, and encouraged by their teacher to discuss their work. Task-related interaction, in the form of pupil discussions about maths, was related significantly to maths achievement, over and above their attainment in maths the previous year. This 'value-added' finding reflects the considerable literature on positive effects of pupil discussion on learning. The authors of this study caution against analyses of learning environments which focus solely on academic aspects and highlight the importance of also considering the impact on engagement and learning of the social context of the classroom.

The gap between theory and current practice

Many of the findings discussed so far have broad applications for developing school and classroom learning environments to benefit pupils generally. At the same time there are particularly important practical implications for assessment and intervention practice with pupils who have SEN. Ysseldyke and Christenson

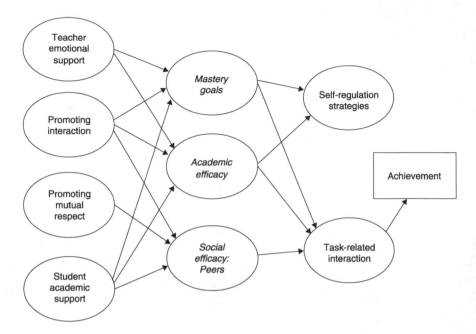

Key:

Classroom Social Environment

Teacher emotional support – pupils' perceptions that their teacher cares about and will help them.

Promoting interaction – teacher encourages pupils to interact and exchange ideas with each other during lessons.

Promoting mutual respect – perception that the teacher expects all pupils to value one another and their contributions, requires students to be considerate of others' feelings, and prohibits students making fun of each other.

Student academic support – pupils perceive support from their classmates with respect to their academic learning.

Mediating Motivational Beliefs

Self-efficacy – individuals' contextually specific judgements of their capabilities to perform tasks successfully. Individuals hold self-efficacy beliefs with respect to different domains, such as for *academic* subjects and *social* relationships.

Mastery goals – this orientation involves a focus on personal improvement and gaining understanding or skill, with learning being seen as an end in itself.

Student Engagement

Self-regulation strategies – these include planning, monitoring, and regulating cognition, and their use is a central aspect of self-regulated learning.

Task-related interaction – includes suggesting ideas and approaches during whole-class lessons, explaining thoughts or reasoning and discussing alternatives with others during small-group activities, and sharing ideas or informally giving help during individual work.

Figure 9.5 Perceptions of the classroom social environment, motivational beliefs, engagement and attainment
Source: adapted from Patrick *et al.* (2007)

(1987: 20) urged teachers and educational psychologists to give more attention to environmental factors in their work with children who have SEN in order to improve outcomes:

> the purpose of any assessment is intervention. Since a student's performance is a function of classroom variables, it is necessary to analyze the learning environment to design effective interventions. We believe that educators should not categorize or label a student without considering the role instructional factors play in the student's learning difficulties. Both student characteristic data and learning environment data should be considered by child study team members engaging in educational and placement decisions.

Similarly, Sattler (1988), in his classic text on assessment of children and young people, advocates environmental assessment as an important component of a comprehensive assessment and argues that it should be conducted before undertaking an individual assessment.

However, the following quotations, taken from UK government-sponsored reports, highlight attention to the environment as an area of weakness in statements of SEN:

> Most of the Statements which we have seen in the course of our research concentrated their attention on deficits within the child which led to special needs, with very little attention given to the child's environment, whether at home or at school.
>
> (Goacher *et al.* 1988)

> Statements generally identify provision in such vague terms that, contrary to the intention of the 1981 Act, they cannot guarantee a specific level of provision.
>
> (Audit Commission 1992)

Activity 9.2 provides an opportunity to consider accounts of learning environments in statements of SEN.

Activity 9.2   How useful are accounts of the learning environment in statements of SEN?

These extracts are taken from a selection of statements of SEN. How useful do you think each of the accounts would be to parents, psychologists and future teachers of the children concerned?

Jonathan, aged 11 (specific learning difficulties in literacy)

Educational advice

'Reason for formal assessment': Although Jonathan has been supported by the literacy support service for five terms at B centre and four terms at H school his progress has been extremely slow . . .

'List strategies employed and outcomes achieved': The literacy support service has employed a multi-sensory approach to reading, writing and spelling. He has received individual and small-group tuition on a regular basis. This has resulted in limited progress in literacy but considerable improvement in self-organization and in his attitude to coping with difficulties. In the classroom Jonathan's programme of work is individualized with work supporting the literacy support programme.

Psychological advice

'Relevant information about this child and the learning environment': Jonathan has been supported by the literacy support service for five terms at B centre and four terms within H middle school.

Sharon, aged 10 (severe anaemia, problems of motor control, learning difficulties)

Educational advice

Sharon has been receiving support from a learning support assistant since September last year. The support has been either in class, helping her cope with instructions and develop some independence, or withdrawal support, going over curriculum content that Sharon has found difficult. She had use of a laptop computer and was given some instruction. The present programme of work is: (a) in close liaison with her class teacher, discussing objectives and targets, exploring the extent of her difficulties and planning future lessons; and (b) encouraging Sharon to talk about her work and explain what she has to do, and getting her to verbalize her ideas. The laptop computer was only a partial success as Sharon was only able to grasp and sequence the most simple of procedures. She was heavily dependent on the learning support assistant to check and print out her work. If she was to have this facility again, she would need a teacher to be trained and designated 'on-site' as an adviser, maintainer and print operator.

(Support teacher)

'Brief description of school organization and child's place in it': National Curriculum year 5 mixed ability class in the first year of middle school.

'Has special attention already been provided in school, e.g. group teaching methods or remedial teaching in school or elsewhere?': Work in all subjects needs modification to meet Sharon's needs as she finds many concepts difficult to grasp even with extensive use of practical equipment. For example, she seemed unable to comprehend the idea of millilitres and litres even after considerable work with water and measuring equipment.

(Class teacher, SEN coordinator, headteacher)

Psychological advice

This advice refers to the learning support assistant support and to the provision of a laptop computer but gives no details or comment.

Adam, aged 8 (severe emotional and behavioural difficulties)

Psychological advice (after a previous meeting)

Mrs L, Adam's class teacher, was advised to build on Adam's strengths in class – for example, his organizational ability and desire to help. Efforts were to be made to continue to give him 'important jobs' to improve his self-esteem and status within the class. I gave Mrs L details of self-recording as a means of boosting self-esteem and to modify Adam's behaviour. When a review was carried out a year later more concerns were being expressed about Adam's academic progress rather than his disruptive behaviour. The SEN support service team was then involved in providing support. Four months later the situation had deteriorated considerably and Mr R, the headteacher, requested 25 hours' welfare assistance per week for Adam, as his attention-seeking behaviour was felt to be detrimental to the rest of the class. (I assessed Adam in school.) I observed him in class during a session where children share their 'treasures' with their teacher; when called out to show his valued object, he stood in front of Mrs L with his back to the children, physically blocking their access to the teacher. He was determined to have Mrs L's attention and was not interested in sharing with his peers.

I subsequently recommended Adam for attendance at the school D learning support department. Fortunately a place was available and he started almost at once. He also had psychotherapy involvement increased from one to two sessions per week. Although progress was made in the unit (e.g. in settling to simple tasks on his own), Adam still found it difficult to share. He continued to have considerable difficulties in the mainstream classes in school D.

I reviewed Adam's progress six months later. In the classroom, I noted that Adam would only work under the close supervision of his teacher. She had to physically sit at his table in order to keep him on task. At a meeting in school it was accepted that while Adam was calmer in school, his emotional needs were still such that he required a great deal of attention to stay on task, more than could be provided within the resources of a mainstream school.

The existence of a gap between theory and practice was also identified by McKee and Witt (1990: 821) who suggested 'There exists in school psychology a lack of congruence between, on the one hand, our data-based assumptions and beliefs concerning the importance of the environment, and on the other hand, our practice where environmental variables are seldom seriously considered for the purpose of designing interventions'. These authors went on to suggest that this discrepancy between educational psychologists' beliefs and behaviours may relate to two different sets of problems:

- *Social and political problems*: related to entering the teacher's domain and presuming to have the right and knowledge to target instructional variables for assessment/intervention.

- *Technical problems*: related to lack of knowledge about what to assess, how to assess it and how to communicate the information to teachers in a way that is helpful and enabling.

The next section of this chapter provides information, in relation to the second point, on measures of the classroom learning environment. These have proved to be of value to educational psychologists in supporting greater involvement in prevention and early intervention, offering consultation and systems-based approaches (Burden and Fraser 1993). The importance of such approaches is highlighted by current moves to reform services for children which require 'consideration of the complex interaction among environmental influences in multiple contexts, those in which children learn and develop' (Reschley *et al.* 2007: 148).

Methods for assessing learning environments and designing interventions

Frederickson and Cline (1995) identified the three most commonly used strategies as follows: (i) direct observation; (ii) investigating pupils' perceptions (e.g. through questionnaires); and (iii) investigating teachers' perceptions. Other approaches are: (iv) investigating parents' perceptions; (v) investigating the perceptions of support staff in the classroom; (vi) examining work completed by pupils and discussing it with them and with their teachers; and (vii) examining teachers' written lesson records.

Frederickson and Cline (1995) suggested that one perspective alone would provide a limited view and that exploring a number of perspectives on the learning environment would be more informative and valid. Fraser (1987), who has been very influential in developing pupil perception measures, acknowledged that the richest information about the classroom environment is likely to come from the use of both observational and student perceptual data, rather than from the use of either technique alone. Waxman *et al.* (1997: 57) also advise on the desirability of a multi-method approach: 'In order to capture all the processes and nuances that occur in classrooms, educators should use triangulation procedures to collect data from multiple perspectives'. They suggested using multiple measures of classroom processes, together with student and teacher self-report survey and interview data in addition to more qualitative ethnographic data from field notes. This section examines in turn the following approaches: observational measures, pupil perceptual measures, multi-perspective measures and qualitative ethnographic assessment methods. Finally, we will take a more detailed look at a methodology derived from systems theory that has been applied to issues in SEN by educational psychologists and teachers in Britain.

Observational measures

Frederickson and Cline (1995) summarized the relative advantages of observation as a method as follows:

- It is a very effective way to gather detailed information directly about how a child is interacting with the whole environment – teacher, peers, learning materials.

- Observation makes it possible to examine the teacher's expectations of the target child – in practice rather than theory.

- One can collect verbatim records of what the teacher, the target child and other children actually say to each other.

- A variety of structured techniques are available which allow detailed 'objective' information to be obtained which will assist in interpreting 'high inference' output such as individuals' accounts of how they see things.

- It is possible to analyse patterns across several situations – what is offered and the child's response to it.

It is important also to bear in mind some potential limitations of observational techniques. For example, there is a possibility that the very presence of an observer may affect the behaviour of teachers and pupils. This can result in reactive effects such as socially desirable responding. As observations are conducted for limited time periods it is also important to consider whether the periods used are sufficient to obtain a reliable and valid sample of the interaction(s) of interest. The collection of data may be time-consuming. Isolated incidents may be focused on, without properly considering the preceding and subsequent events that may provide information about context and meaning.

Many observational techniques have been developed with the purpose of conducting research on features of classrooms and classroom processes – see Good and Brophy (2008) for details of a range of methods and guidance on the use and interpretation of classroom observations. In this subsection we focus on observational approaches that can be used to assess the learning environment of a pupil who has SEN with the purpose of designing appropriate interventions. The Classroom Observation Schedule (COS), developed by Waxman *et al.* (1988; see also Waxman and Padron 2004) is a systematic observation schedule which is designed to record pupil behaviours with reference to a number of aspects of classroom learning environments:

- pupil interactions with teachers· and/or peers and the purpose of these interactions;

- the settings in which observed behaviours occur;

- the types of material with which pupils are working;

- the specific types of activity in which they engage.

The COS has six headings:

1 *Interaction*: describes the type and purpose of any interaction a pupil may have with other pupils, the teacher or support staff.

2 *Selection of activity*: identifies who has decided that a pupil will be working on a particular assignment during the observation period.

3 *Activity types*: possibilities here include watching or listening, working on written assignments and social interaction.

4 *Setting*: identifies the grouping arrangements.

5 *Manner*: describes the pupil's behaviour in relation to the classroom context and activities being observed.

6 *Language used*: identifies the language(s) which the pupil is using for oral and written communication.

The COS, which has been published in Britain (Frederickson and Monsen 1999), has been used in primary and secondary schools in the USA, most notably as one of the key instruments in a five-year research programme being conducted by the National Research Center on Education in the Inner Cities. In a number of studies the COS has been used to examine the classroom instruction and learning environment in effective and ineffective schools in the USA, for pupils generally and for African-American pupils in particular (Waxman and Huang 1997; Waxman *et al.* 1997). Waxman and Huang (1997: 10) argued that 'one of our most serious educational problems continues to be the underachievement of African-American students in urban schools' and reviewed research that suggested the importance of effective classroom learning environments in enabling African-American and other students at risk of failure to achieve success in school.

Waxman (1995) describes the use of the COS in a formative way to provide feedback to school staff and stimulate discussion about improvements. Observations were carried out across a whole school district and Table 9.3 shows an example of the profiles fed back to schools, allowing each school to compare their mean percentages on each category with the averages across the district. The profiles were considered at staff meetings and their implications discussed. In the case of the example shown in Table 9.3, Waxman reported that teachers' concern focused on the amount of time their pupils spent watching or listening (61 per cent), particularly as it was above the district average (53 per cent), and they discussed strategies for raising the amount of active pupil engagement in lessons.

Table 9.3   COS example feedback profile for a primary school

A   Interactions

Variables	Your school mean (%)	All primary schools aggregated mean (%)
1 No interaction/independence	52.73	59.48
2,3,4 Interaction with teacher	39.07	33.40
5 Interaction with support staff	0.00	0.02
6,7 Interaction with other students	8.08	7.06
8 Interaction with others	0.10	0.01

B and C   Activity selection and types

Variables		Your school mean (%)	All primary schools aggregated mean (%)
B1	Teacher-assigned activity	99.76	99.85
B2	Student-selected activity	0.23	0.34
C1	Working on written assignments	9.52	19.55
C2, C3	Interacting	5.00	6.74
C4	Watching or listening	60.83	53.03
C5	Reading	3.45	8.82
C6	Getting/returning materials	1.90	2.77
C7	Colouring, drawing, painting, etc.	1.07	0.46
C9	Working with manipulative materials/equipment	10.83	4.55
C12	Presenting/acting	1.42	0.78
C13	Tutoring peers	0.00	0.18
C14	Not attending to task	3.33	4.08
C16	Other	4.04	3.21

Note: More than one activity may be coded during one observation.

D Setting

Variables	Your school mean (%)	All primary schools aggregated mean (%)
1 Whole class	80.23	78.19
2 Small group	13.09	12.20
4 Individual	6.66	9.60

E Manner

Variables	Your school mean (%)	All primary schools aggregated mean (%)
1 On task	95.11	94.48
2 Waiting for teacher	0.23	0.30
3 Distracted	2.97	3.45
4 Disruptive	1.19	0.84
5 Other	0.47	0.90

Source: Waxman (1995).

The COS can also be used to monitor or evaluate the effectiveness of interventions or the effects of other changes by comparing differences between the percentage observations recorded in particular categories before and after the change was introduced. Particular teachers or groups of teachers may be interested in comparing the characteristics of the classroom environment they provide across different subjects (primary) or different groups of pupils (secondary). Teachers and schools may be interested in examining the data for any differences linked to gender, ethnicity or SEN.

Waxman (1995) argued that many teachers, even those with substantial experience, are sometimes unaware of the nature of their interactions with individual pupils and that one of the most important purposes of systematic classroom observation is to improve teaching practice. There is growing evidence that feedback from systematic observations can be used to improve teaching (Stallings and Freiberg 1991). This may be particularly important where some groups of pupils are being treated differently. For example, many studies have reported gender differences in teacher–pupil interactions, with boys often receiving both more praise and more criticism in the classroom than girls (Good and Brophy 2008). Waxman (1995: 80) suggested that an important purpose for classroom observation is to investigate questions such as: 'Are some pupils being treated differently in the classroom, and does that explain why some pupils learn more than others?' The answers to such questions may have crucial policy implications for schools in raising the achievement of all pupils.

A number of studies have provided information on the validity of the COS categories in differentiating between effective and ineffective schools (see Waxman and Padron 2004). For example, Waxman and Huang (1997) designed a study to examine the classroom instruction and learning environment in effective and ineffective schools for African-American pupils. The primary schools studied were in urban districts that had predominately African-American students from economically disadvantaged families. Schools were classified as effective or ineffective on the basis of pupil scores on state-wide assessments of academic skills. Four schools were randomly selected from those classified as effective and four from those classified as ineffective. The COS was used in 15 randomly selected classrooms in each school during reading or mathematics classes.

The results of this study showed that pupils from the effective schools more often worked individually, whereas those from ineffective schools were taught as a whole class for a higher proportion of the time. Pupils from the effective schools also spent relatively more time interacting with their teacher and working on written assignments, while in ineffective schools more time was spent working with manipulative materials, reading and interacting with others. Although pupils in both types of school were on task for a very high proportion of the time (more than 90 per cent), the level of active involvement and intellectual demand was lower in the ineffective schools where a typical lesson would involve the teacher lecturing to the whole class and merely asking the pupils a few knowledge-type questions near the end of the lesson. Furthermore, students from the effective schools were observed interacting with their teacher almost twice as much as those from the ineffective schools.

The findings of this study are consistent with a range of other findings from the literature:

- that amount and quality of teacher–pupil academic interactions are two of the most important educational variables that promote student outcome (Wang *et al.* 1994);

- that over-reliance on whole-class instruction is detrimental to student outcomes because teachers often have difficulty in maintaining an instructional pace that is appropriate to all (Walberg 1995).

In addition it is reported that small-group instruction and cooperative grouping are especially effective for pupils from minority groups and lead to improved pupil outcomes (Allyn and Boykin 1992; Walberg 1995).

Thus the COS has been shown to identify dynamic influences in the classroom that are also revealed by other research methods. But all observation schedules have a degree of bias in that they concentrate on factors perceived to be important by their authors. Alternative classroom observation schedules with different emphases can be found in the Immediate Learning Environment Survey (ILES) (Pielstick 1987) and the Functional Assessment of Academic Behaviour (FAAB) (Ysseldyke and Christenson 2002). The ILES is a survey instrument which covers four broad domains: physical conditions; social conditions; instructional materials and procedures; and psychological/learning factors. The FAAB is designed to gather information relevant to a concern about the learning of an individual pupil, assessing instructional needs and supportive learning conditions with the purpose of designing interventions. Instruments are provided to support information collection through teacher, student interview and parent interview as well as classroom observation.

Pupil perceptual measures

Among the advantages of using pupil perceptual measures are the following:

- There is evidence that they account for more variance in achievement than directly observed (low inference) variables (Fraser 1991).

- They avoid giving inappropriate weight to events because of their frequency (quality or intensity may matter more than quantity).

- They are based on pupil experiences over many lessons rather than being restricted, as observation normally is, to a small number which may be atypical.

- With group methods the conclusions that are drawn are based on the pooled judgements of all pupils rather than data from a single (though trained) observer. With pooled judgements any individual biases are likely to cancel each other out.

- They directly assess learner perceptions of events which are as likely to determine learner behaviour as the actual events, if not more likely. The classroom environment experienced by the student may be quite different from that which is observed or intended.

- This method facilitates the direct comparison of pupil and teacher perceptions. Fraser (1984) reported that teachers tend to perceive their classrooms more favourably than their pupils.

- Pupil perception measures respond to demands for accountability because information is obtained about the preferences and reactions of consumers.

- They are more economical than observation techniques.

A number of potential limitations should also be kept in mind. The following were reported by a group of British educational psychologists (Frederickson and Cline 1995), from initial trialling of one measure that had been developed by Fraser. First, some children seemed puzzled by the apparent repetition of questions (very similar questions typically make up each scale). Second, the reading level was too high for some pupils. Although this was overcome successfully by reading the items aloud to the children, this made the whole process less clearly 'private' between the individual child and the page. Third, some of the language used proved problematic for some pupils with learning difficulties (e.g. the use of double negatives). Finally, some children expressed uncertainty about generalizing on some questions (e.g. in response to 'In my class everybody is my friend' some children indicated that they would have liked to have a midpoint between 'yes' and 'no' in the response options).

Fraser (1998) provided a review of available pupil perceptual measures and highlighted the strong theoretical influence on their development of the work of Moos (1973), who proposed that diverse psychosocial environments can be classified using three types of dimension:

1   Relationship dimensions which identify the nature and intensity of personal relationships, involvement and support within the environment.

2   Personal development dimensions which assess the directions along which personal growth and self-enhancement tend to occur.

3   Systems maintenance and systems change dimensions which refer to orderliness, maintenance of control and clarity of expectation.

The scales from the two measures described in detail in this subsection can all be classified according to Moos's scheme (Fraser 1998). The two measures that have been selected are those that have been most used and are readily obtainable in Britain. They both involve short pupil questionnaires which are easily scored and summarized in a diagrammatic form which teachers find meaningful and useful. The My Class Inventory (MCI) is designed for primary-aged pupils, while the Individualized Classroom Environment Questionnaire (ICEQ) is designed for secondary-aged pupils and focuses in particular on aspects of the learning environment (e.g. individualization and differentiation) found to be particularly important in promoting the successful inclusion of pupils who have SEN (Madden and Slavin 1983).

Both measures are completed by pupil and teacher participants in the learning environments that are assessed and include an 'actual' and a 'preferred' form. The actual form asks students to rate aspects of their current learning environment, while the preferred form asks how students would ideally like their learning environment to be. Item wording is almost identical in the actual and preferred forms. For example, the statement 'Different students do different work' in the actual form of the ICEQ is changed in the preferred form to 'Different students *would* do different work'. The questionnaires can be administered on a whole-class basis or individually to pupils and teachers. If there are concerns about the reading ability of members of the class it is acceptable for the teacher to read out the questions with time given for the children to mark their questionnaire.

The short form MCI (MCI-SF) consists of five scales, each containing five items. The meanings of the scales are defined as follows:

● *Cohesiveness*: the extent to which students know, help and are friendly towards each other.

● *Friction*: the extent of tension and quarrelling among students.

● *Difficulty*: the extent to which students experience difficulty with the work of the class.

● *Satisfaction*: the extent to which students like their class.

● *Competition*: the extent to which students perceive an atmosphere of competition in a classroom (Fraser 1982; Fraser *et al.* 1982; Fraser and Fisher 1986).

On the MCI-SF the children answer each of the 25 questions by circling YES or NO. When both are used the actual and preferred forms of the questionnaire are usually completed on the same occasion, with the actual form being completed first.

The MCI-SF has been shown to be as reliable and valid a measure of classroom environment as more time-intensive and costly measures, such as direct classroom observations (Fraser 1991). Wright *et al.* (1991) conducted a study in ten primary schools in Surrey from which they reported that the MCI discriminated significantly among the classrooms surveyed and was considered to be useful by the teachers and educational psychologists who participated in the research. From their study of primary mathematics classes in Singapore, Goh and Fraser (1998) reported better student outcomes when classrooms were perceived as having more cohesion and less friction – a predictable finding that tends to support claims for the validity of the instrument.

The MCI has found a wide range of applications. These include a study of ways to improve instruction in multicultural classrooms (Diamantes 2002), an investigation of changes in pupil perceptions across the transition from primary to secondary school (Ferguson and Fraser 1999) and a number of studies focused on SEN and inclusion which are reviewed at the end of this section of the chapter.

The ICEQ was developed by Rentoul and Fraser (1979) to measure how secondary-aged pupils' perceptions of traditional classrooms differed from classrooms which included more inquiry-based and individualized approaches. Interest in these kinds of approaches originally came from research on investigator-based science curricula. Their importance has also been highlighted by research showing that pupils who have SEN tend to make better educational and social progress in integrated mainstream school placements, but only if a suitable individualized or differentiated educational programme is offered (Madden and Slavin 1983). Fraser (1987) suggested that the ICEQ can also be completed by the teachers of the groups of pupils being surveyed and differences in perceptions between pupils and teachers examined.

The short form of the ICEQ was produced by Fraser and Fisher (1986) in response to research and teacher feedback that the original measure provided a very useful assessment of the classroom environment but was time-consuming to administer and score. The short form consists of 25 items, five items in each of five scales. The five scales are interpreted as follows (Rentoul and Fraser 1979):

1 *Personalization*: emphasis on opportunities for individual students to interact with the teacher and on concern for the personal welfare and social growth of the individual.

2 *Participation*: extent to which students are encouraged to participate rather than be passive listeners.

3 *Independence*: extent to which students are allowed to make decisions and have control over their own learning and behaviour.

4 *Investigation*: emphasis on the skills and processes of inquiry and their use in problem solving and investigation.

5 *Differentiation*: emphasis on the selective treatment of students on the basis of ability, learning style, interests and rate of working.

Lim (1995) conducted a study using the ICEQ with students aged 15–16 years attending nine secondary schools in Singapore. As in most studies a gap was found between students' ratings of their preferred and actual classroom environments, with more positive and favourable ratings being given to the preferred environment. Fraser (1982) reports that a similar gap is also found in teachers' ratings of their preferred and actual classroom environments. In addition, teachers tend to rate the actual classroom environment more positively than the pupils. Lim found that in schools achieving better GCSE results, students generally viewed their actual classroom environment as having greater emphasis on personalization, independence and differentiation. Reliability studies in Australia (Fraser and Fisher 1983b) and England (Burden and Fraser 1993) have reported similar satisfactory data for the ICEQ.

There is good evidence for the validity of the ICEQ as a measure of classroom climate. Wheldall *et al.* (1999) found only a small component of school-level influence and a relatively large component of class-level influence on ICEQ scores. The instrument has been used in research on aspects of the classroom learning environment associated with self concept as a learner and 'deep' approaches to learning (which focus on meaning and understanding, as opposed to 'surface' approaches that focus on memorizing and getting by in tests). Dart *et al.* (1999) found that classroom learning environments which were perceived to be high on personalization, participation and investigation were associated with deep approaches to learning. High personalization was also associated with high self concept as a learner.

A valuable practical feature of the ICEQ and the MCI is that they are intervention orientated. Pupil perceptions of both their actual and preferred classroom environments can be assessed in order to identify discrepancies and assist teachers in implementing strategies aimed at reducing them. Fraser and Fisher (1983a) reported person–environment fit research which suggested that students achieve better results when the classroom environment closely matches their preferred environment. Activity 9.3 provides an illustration of the way in which assessment information from these measures can be used as a basis for reflection, discussion and systematic attempts to improve classroom environments.

Activity 9.3   Case study: use of the ICEQ in a secondary school

Fraser (1987) described a study involving a class of 31 boys aged 12–13 years who were studying English, maths and history with the same teacher. As you read about the study consider these questions:

(a) What interventions might be worth trying to increase personalization and participation?

(b) Can you think of any situations in your work where an assessment/intervention approach like this using the ICEQ would be useful?

The following steps were taken:

1   *Assessment*: administration of the actual and preferred forms of the ICEQ-SF.

2   *Feedback*: to the teacher of a profile showing the discrepancy between the actual and preferred class mean scores on each of the five scales. See Figure 9.6, where the 'pre-test' line shows the discrepancy between the actual and preferred class mean scores on each of the five scales of the ICEQ before the intervention.

3   *Reflection and discussion*: as a result of which the teacher decided to introduce an intervention aimed at increasing the levels of personalization and participation.

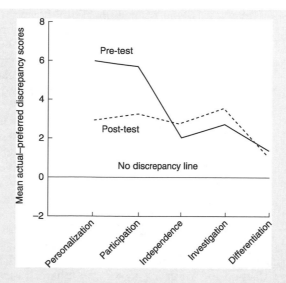

Figure 9.6 Profiles plotted pre- and post-intervention to show the discrepancy between pupils' preferred and actual classroom learning environment
Source: Fraser (1987).

4 *Intervention*: over the course of a month the teacher attempted to increase personalization by moving around the classroom more, making a conscious effort to praise students and demonstrate an interest in them. The organization of more group work and the reduction in teacher as opposed to student talk were the strategies adopted in an attempt to increase participation.

5 *Reassessment*: the actual form was readministered. The 'post-test' line in Figure 9.6 shows the scores after the intervention. The differences between the pre- and post-assessments suggested (and statistical tests confirmed) that success had been achieved in reducing the actual–preferred discrepancy, specifically in the aspects of the classroom environment that had been targeted by the teacher's intervention strategies.

Burden and Fraser (1993) pointed out that as the feedback to teachers comes from the students themselves its impact is likely to be considerably greater than if it was provided by a detached observer. They described, as a development of this process, a case study where desired changes were discussed with a class of secondary school pupils and they were involved in the design and implementation of changes. Reassessment four weeks later indicated significant reductions in the preferred/actual discrepancy on four of the five scales.

Pupil perceptual measures can also be used to investigate whether pupils with SEN, those of different genders and those from different ethnic or cultural groups perceive their classroom environment differently and are affected in different ways by particular intervention approaches. Some initial research suggests that these might be relevant questions to address. Knight (1991) reported differences between African-American and Hispanic students in their perceptions of their classroom environment in the USA. In the UK, Frederickson and Furnham

(1998b) used the MCI among other measures to assess the extent to which environmental factors and individual characteristics each contributed to the social inclusion and peer group acceptance in mainstream classes of pupils who had MLD. They found that both sets of factors made an important contribution. In particular, the perceived cohesiveness of the classroom peer group, as assessed by the MCI, had a significant effect both in supporting inclusion and preventing rejection.

In a study of 30 classrooms in Swedish schools using scales adapted from the MCI, Westling Allodi (2002) found that classes containing a pupil with disabilities were higher on cohesiveness and lower on friction and competitiveness than other classrooms. Levels of friction and competitiveness were also lower in culturally heterogeneous classrooms. The authors suggest that diversity might be associated with processes that heighten acceptance and respect for difference. However, other factors, such as teacher attitude, might also be implicated. An investigation of New Zealand teachers' attitudes to inclusion also reported differences on the MCI (Monsen and Frederickson 2004). Classes taught by teachers with more positive attitudes to inclusion of children with SEN reported higher levels of satisfaction and lower levels of friction than classes taught by teachers whose attitudes were less positive.

One question that arises about pupil perception measures of the classroom learning environment concerns the extent to which pupil perceptions are influenced by their individual characteristics, as opposed to characteristics of the classroom. Walker and Plomin (2006) reported data on 3,020 pairs of 9-year-old identical and fraternal twins (part of the Twins Early Development Study). A classroom environment questionnaire was analysed to estimate the genetic influence, the shared environmental influence and the non-shared environmental influence. They found that non-shared environment explained the majority of the variance in scores, whereas shared environment made almost no contribution. So even when identical twins shared the same home and class contexts, they perceived their classroom experiences in distinctive ways. However, genetics was found to play a modest role in mediating children's perceptions of their classroom environment. Walker and Plomin (2006) point out that this finding, essentially that identical twins consistently perceived their classroom characteristics more similarly than fraternal twins, was open to several possible interpretations. For example, it may result from genetic influence on personal characteristics that affect perception. Alternatively, it may be that the greater physical and behavioural similarity of identical twins may elicit more similar responses from teachers and peers.

Multi-perspective measures

A number of measures are available which collect information on the classroom learning environment from more than one source. The Student Classroom Environment Measure (SCEM), the Teacher Classroom Environment Measure (TCEM) and the Observer Classroom Environment Measure (OCEM) are three related measures developed by Midgley *et al.* (1991) which draw on the three most commonly used sources of information about classroom learning environments. These measures have the advantage that published data are available on their psychometric properties and interrelationships (Frederickson and Monsen

1999). They have been used to study the transition from primary to secondary school, so the SCEM is appropriate to older primary as well as secondary-aged pupils. It consists of nine scales, grouped into three dimensions. The relationship dimension contains the Involvement, Affiliation and Teacher Support scales; the personal growth/goal orientation dimension contains the Task Orientation and Competition scales; and the system maintenance and change dimension contains the Order and Organisation, Rule Clarity, Teacher Control and Innovation scales. In a study of secondary school pupils in New Zealand, Anderson *et al.* (2004) found that positive interactions among students, as assessed by the Affiliation scale, were positively associated with teacher ratings of participation and with a measure of task completion.

The TCEM and OCEM can be used by teachers and observers working across the primary and secondary age range. The TCEM is designed to sample teachers' perceptions of their general teaching and marking practices, discipline techniques, reward strategies, opportunities for student autonomy and cooperative inter-action in the classroom. The OCEM is designed to sample observers' perceptions of aspects of task organization within the classroom, opportunities for student input, competition, cooperation and interaction among students, teacher fairness and friendliness and informal relations between teacher and students.

The FAAB (Ysseldyke and Christenson 2002) provides schedules to assist in collecting information through classroom observation and structured teacher, pupil and parent interview. An Instructional Environment Checklist is also provided to assist in prioritizing and planning interventions to meet pupils' needs, to enlist home support for these and to facilitate effective home–school collaboration.

Qualitative ethnographic assessment methods

Fraser (1998) highlighted the desirability of including both qualitative and quanti-tative strategies in the evaluation of learning environments. Used along with quantitative strategies, qualitative strategies can provide contextual information which assists in the interpretation of quantitative data and can help to generate hypotheses about influences and relationships in the situation. Fraser described the use of interpretative research methods involving classroom observation, inter-viewing of students and teachers, the construction of case studies, use of student diaries and analysis of students' written work.

Observation can also be used to collect quantitative data (as we have seen) and observation, interviewing and diary analysis can be used, albeit differently, in qualitative and ethnographic studies. What mainly distinguishes an ethnographic study is its purpose, described by Uzzell (1995: 303) as 'cultural description'. An attempt is made to understand and describe the situation from the perspectives of the participants. The focus is not on the researchers' questions or theories but on those elements which guide the actions of the participants in the environments under study.

Ruiz (1995) described an ethnographic study conducted as part of the Optimal Learning Environment (OLE) project, which aims to describe effective instructional contexts for bilingual students who have been identified as having general language difficulties. Students' language and literacy skills were observed over a period of 20 months and compared across different classroom events that

Table 9.4   Contextual features of classroom events associated with the upper and lower ranges of children's language and literacy abilities.

Upper range	Lower range
Emphasis on communication, not language forms	Syntactic and lexical constraints
Topic choice	Topic constraints
Increased student initiations	Few student initiations
Student-directed discourse	Teacher-directed discourse
Functional use of language	Language use for teacher evaluation
Whole texts	Fragments of texts
Centred on students' experiences and knowledge	Centred on prepackaged curricular materials

Source: Ruiz (1995).

ranged from teacher-structured formal class sessions to peer-structured socio-dramatic play. Particular contextual factors were found to be associated with enhanced student performance while others were associated with communicative breakdowns and problems with literacy tasks. These are shown in Table 9.4.

Ruiz and Figueroa (1995) reported that at the start of the project teachers tended to see the source of students' academic difficulties as the result primarily of internal processing deficits, whereas towards the end of the study they appreciated the important role of the instructional context in producing effective or ineffective behaviour.

Thick ethnographic description of this kind that includes detailed and extensive observation has an important limitation – the considerable time required for both data collection and analysis. Also, as Rivera and Tharp (2004) point out, the approaches advocated are rarely practical to implement 'live' in classrooms. They ask: '*Can these rich concepts be thinly assessed or is the field of soiocultural research doomed to expensive, impractical ways to measure its conceptual richness?*' (Rivera and Tharp 2004: 205–6). Drawing on activity theory, they present a framework, the Activity Setting Observation System (ASOS), which provides a 'thin' method of description that is:

> (a) based on the essential principles of sociocultural theory, (b) reliable across observers, (c) practical for the live and accurate description of a typical classroom or similar setting, (d) subject to meaningful quantification, and (e) eligible for simultaneous, more detailed, thicker annotation.
>
> (Rivera and Tharp 2004: 206)

In this system the unit of analysis is the activity setting, which is defined by its product, whether tangible (an externally observable outcome or artefact that integrates a series of actions) or intangible (some achieved physical, psychological or social state that integrates a series of actions). For each activity setting observation of the the following features is prompted:

- student initiative or choice in generating or joining the activity setting;

- joint productive activity or collaborative interaction that leads to a single product;

- modelling or demonstration;

- teacher–student dialogue, involving at least two speech turns each;

- responsive assistance by teacher and students, which includes monitoring or informal testing of understanding and consequential adjustment or modulation of the assistance provided;

- contextualization, which involves eliciting student knowledge from outside the classroom or school and actively incorporating it into the activity setting;

- connectedness, which involves incorporation by the teacher into the activity setting of students' previous classroom/school knowledge, experience or products.

Soft systems methodology

Reynolds (1995) reported that schools have been slow to implement the findings from school effectiveness research, while Gallimore (1996: 234) suggested that there may be important cultural forces operating to maintain the status quo:

> Lots of colleagues tell me that they've tried again and again to present to teachers research findings that could improve classroom practice. Many are frustrated that teachers do not share their enthusiasm. Even if told that other schools successfully tried new research-based practices, teachers may still reject what's offered. 'It's different at our school,' they'll say. 'Maybe it worked at those other schools, but your findings are not relevant to our situation, in our school, with our students.'
>
> This insistence on the distinctiveness of the local situation is a tip off that cultural processes are at work. The local routine of classroom activities and how they are perceived are taken for granted as reality itself. They are the way things are, the way they are supposed to be. They are not recognised as evolved adaptations to the challenges of teaching at a particular school . . . If pressed, teachers defend them as unique, essential, and rational. Otherwise, they are so taken for granted they are seldom noticed and almost never examined. Asking that they be given up raises questions in the minds of teachers about the researcher's grasp on reality.

Frederickson (1993) argued that many problematic situations and issues in education are characterized by substantive differences in the perceptions and intentions of those involved. In these cases it is not possible to embark on a classical problem-solving approach because it is not possible to agree on a definition of the problem or achieve consensus on the objectives of any change. In such situations there is a need for an explicit approach which can represent the range of views held without requiring that they be reconciled in order for progress to be made. 'Soft systems methodology' (SSM) is a systematic approach which can be used to guide intervention in the kinds of ill-structured real-world problem situations common in the field of special needs. It aims to bring logical analysis to bear without oversimplifying the real complexities of the situations studied or underestimating the impact of human perceptions and interests in effecting or resisting change.

SSM was developed through a programme of over 100 action research consultancies in commercial and service environments, including health and social service contexts (Checkland 1981; Checkland and Scholes 1990). It does not focus on the problem but on the situation in which there is perceived to be a problem – or an opportunity for improvement. The initial task is not to converge on a definition of a problem to solve, but to build up the richest possible picture of the situation in question, drawing on the disparate perceptions of those involved. The essential nature of SSM is summarized in Figure 9.7. In overview, it consists of some stages which involve finding out about and developing a representation of reality, some stages which involve developing one or more models of systems which might be relevant to changing/improving reality and, finally, some stages where comparisons are drawn between the model(s) and the representation of reality in order to generate improvement suggestions/recommendations for action.

For descriptive purposes SSM consists of the seven stages which are represented diagrammatically in Figure 9.8. Stages 1 and 2 involve finding out about a particular problem situation, collecting information and identifying important themes and issues. Information may be collected by a number of different means (e.g. interviewing, observation). These are practical activities where something is done in the real world.

In Stages 3 and 4 aspects of systems theory are used to analyse the problem situation and to build models of systems which may be relevant to improving it. Notice the words used. A model relevant to improving a problem situation does not purport to be a model of a problem or a problem situation. These activities are purely logical/theoretical. The defining characteristics of systems theories are explained in Chapter 15, while detailed discussion of different strands of systems theory and their application in schools can be found in Frederickson (1990a).

At Stages 5 to 7 possible changes to the real-world situation are suggested so that those directly involved can debate the desirability and feasibility of the suggestions and, if appropriate, implement them. (The last three stages again involve practical activities, such as meetings and feasibility studies which would need to be carried out in the real world.)

Note the distinction which is drawn between Stages 3 and 4, the 'below the line' stages, and the other five stages, the 'above the line' stages. Stages 3 and 4 are theoretical in that they involve formal systems thinking, whereas the other five

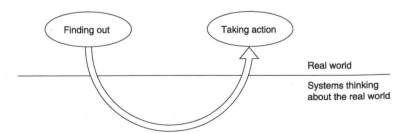

Figure 9.7 The essential nature of SSM
Source: Checkland (1986).

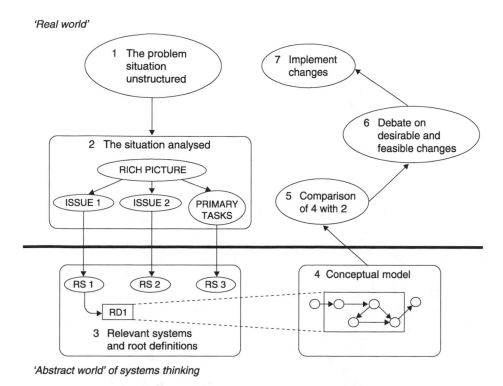

Figure 9.8 The conventional seven-stage model of SSM
Source: Adapted from Checkland and Scholes (1990).

stages are practical in that they involve activities which are carried out in the real world.

The information collected in Stage 1 is used in Stage 2 to express, represent or describe the problem situation – to build up the richest possible picture of the situation. This may be a 'pen picture', but it is often found to be more useful to express the information diagrammatically or indeed pictorially. A rich picture is defined as an evolving diagram that collects together and portrays key information and impressions about a complex situation in a loosely structured and evocative way. Figure 9.9 contains an example of a rich picture which was used by educational psychologists supporting a primary school in special measures, to collate and feed back information from staff interviews (Bettle *et al.* 2001). Figure 9.10, on the other hand, contains an example of a rich picture developed by a project group of secondary school staff working with two educational psychologists to consider how the needs of the large number of demanding pupils in the school could be addressed while ensuring that the rights of the majority of 'undemanding' pupils were also respected.

This kind of picture can helpfully highlight particular features of the environment under consideration and these can be selected as problem themes. Such a picture is also usually capable of being viewed from a variety of different perspectives. At Stage 3, consideration of these different viewpoints and problem themes can help identify systems likely to be relevant to the debate about the

Figure 9.9   Rich picture used by educational psychologists working with a primary school in special measures
Source: Bettle *et al.* (2001).

problem situation, with a view to bringing about improvement. For example, consider the following notional systems which proved relevant to the resolution of a particular parent–school conflict over the school's homework requirements. The viewpoint which suggested each of these systems as potentially relevant is noted in parentheses:

- A system to consolidate pupil learning (teachers).

- A system to enhance the school's academic reputation (headteacher).

- A system to cover exam coursework which is not covered in class because the teachers cannot keep order (pupil).

- A parent undermining system (objecting parent).

In naming possible relevant systems there is no attempt to imply that any of these different perspectives is right or more accurate. In SSM a system is a hypothetical construct which is used to think about some real-world activity from a particular perspective (such as the four perspectives listed above). The purpose in naming relevant systems is to attempt to find some potentially useful or insightful ways of viewing the problem situation.

> **Activity 9.4** A rich picture
>
> Choose a learning environment familiar to you where you feel there are problems or opportunities for improvement. Write a description of the situation that identifies key issues within it (maximum length: one side of A4). Now draw a rich picture to represent what you know about the situation and to capture key issues from your point of view.
>
> Can you identify any differences between writing and drawing in:
>
> - The clarity, accuracy and completeness of the representation produced?
>
> - The amount of time taken to produce it?
>
> - The sensitivity of the matters that can be represented?
>
> - The number of different issues and their interrelationships that can be represented simultaneously?
>
> - Sequences of events or changes over time?
>
> - The sorts of issues that emerge?
>
> - Your willingness to share your representation of the learning environment in question with a colleague?
>
> - The ease with which colleagues can pick up key issues from the description/picture?
>
>   (You might like to check out with a colleague your ideas about this.)
>
> - Your willingness to share the representation with key staff in the learning environment in question?

Having identified a number of relevant systems, some can be selected for further development. This selection is made on the basis of subjective judgement and experience. An element of trial and error is involved and the first attempt at analysis may fail to yield a useful outcome. It will usually be necessary to cycle through Stages 3, 4 and 5 a number of times in order to identify changes that are likely to bring about improvements in the problem situation. The rest of Stages 3 and 4 will involve the logical development of the relevant systems that have been selected. The relevant systems are first defined more clearly. This is done through producing a root definition of each, which describes its basic nature in a way designed to be revealing to those in the situation. The value of root definitions is not judged in terms of their correctness, but in terms of their usefulness in illuminating ways in which aspects of the problem situation can be helpfully changed.

In order to provide a clear definition of what the system under consideration is, the root definition should contain the following six elements:

C   Customers (victims or beneficiaries of the system)

A   Actors (who carry out the activities of the system)

T   Transformation process (what the system does to its inputs to to turn them into outputs)

W   *Weltanschauung* (the view of the world that makes this system meaningful)

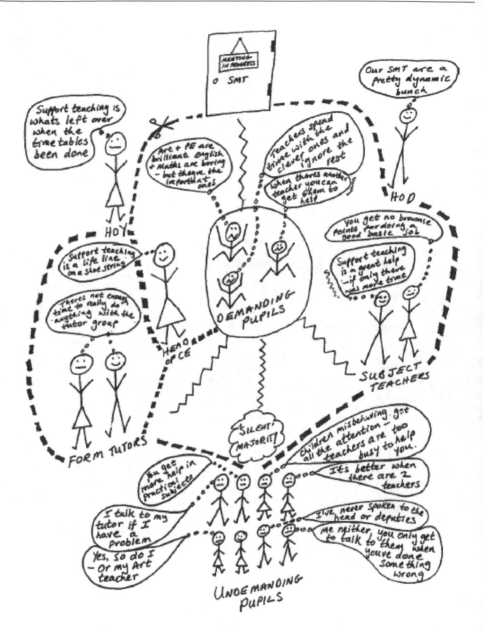

Figure 9.10   Rich picture developed by a project group of secondary school staff

O   Owner (who could abolish this system)
E   Environmental constraints (what in the environment this system takes as given).

Here is an illustration taken from Frederickson (1990b). One of the relevant systems selected on the basis of the rich picture shown in Figure 9.10 was: 'A system to provide effective access to the curriculum through support teaching in the school'. The CATWOE analysis which was selected was as follows:

C All pupils

A Support teachers and subject teachers

T Need for effective access to the curriculum – that need met through support teaching

W 'It's a good thing to maintain pupils with special needs in the mainstream, but important to ensure that the education of other pupils does not suffer'

O Headteacher

E School staffing levels, large proportion of pupils with special needs in a secondary modern school, attitudes of some staff, skills of some support teachers.

The corresponding root definition (Root Definition 1) was: 'A headteacher-owned system, staffed by support teachers and subject teachers which provides for all pupils that support deemed necessary to enable them to gain effective access to the curriculum despite the presence of a large proportion of pupils with special needs in the class and the constraints of current staffing levels, attitudes and skills'. No root definition can claim to be objective. Rather, each is written from a particular viewpoint, which is largely reflected in the 'W' selected. However, there are other components of the root definition on which opinions may differ. In this case there was much debate as to who should be considered to be the customer of the system – other candidates for the role being 'special needs pupils' and 'the subject teachers'.

The root definition describes what the system *is*. In order to describe what it *does* it is necessary to build an activity model of the system. This model will be conceptual in that you must strive to make it a purely logical representation of the activities which would necessarily have to happen in the system described by the root definition. No attempt should be made either to model what really happens or what might ideally happen. Your model is only a relevant intellectual construct to be used to help structure debate. In work at this stage, comments are often made about the advantages of involving an 'outsider' whose greater distance from the real-world situation helps to retain an appropriate focus on the logical and conceptual nature of the model building.

The crucial components of the model will be activities, represented on paper as verbs. The task is to assemble in a logical order the minimum number of activities required to operate the human activity system described by the root definition. The conceptual model shown in Figure 9.11 was developed from the root definition of the system to 'provide effective access to the curriculum through support teaching in the school' which was described above.

In considering the issue of evaluation, Checkland argues that five different aspects need to be considered: efficacy, efficiency, effectiveness, ethicality and elegance (Checkland and Scholes 1990). In evaluating efficacy one needs to ask whether the system is in fact functioning, whether the transformation is being carried out, whether the means selected actually work. In evaluating efficiency one needs to ask whether the system is operating with minimum resources, including time. The evaluation of effectiveness involves asking whether the transformation at the heart of the system is the right activity to be doing in the first place. You should notice that questions about effectiveness can only be answered from outside the system in question, by reference to larger systems of which it is a part.

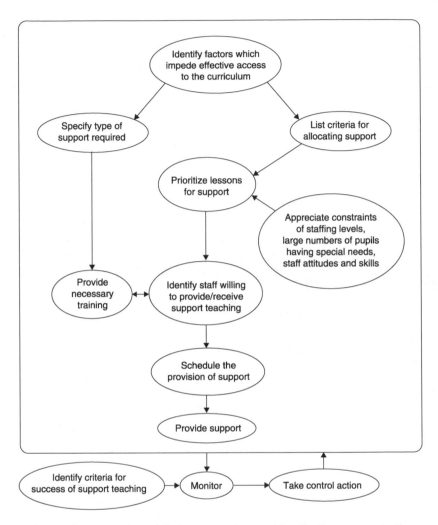

Figure 9.11 Conceptual model of a system to provide effective access to the curriculum through support teaching

Considerations of ethicality require us to consider whether the transformation is a moral thing to do, while the evaluation of elegance would focus on the extent to which the transformation is parsimonious and apt.

At Stage 5 the conceptual models which have been produced during Stage 4 are compared with the real world (the problem situations expressed in Stage 2). This comparison may reveal mismatches:

- Are some logically necessary stages simply left out of the process which operates in real life?
- Is operational effectiveness being reduced by the inclusion of unnecessary stages?
- Are activities happening in an illogical order?
- Are the activities being performed well?

In the above example the way in which support teaching was being provided differed radically from the conceptual model of the activity. The most obvious difference was the sequencing of stages. The conceptual model shown in Figure 9.11 indicated that prioritization of sessions for support should precede the deployment of staff, so ensuring that top priority sessions were effectively supported. In reality, however, support teaching had been described as 'what is left over when the timetable has been done'. Whatever their assessed need for support, sessions could only be allocated a support teacher if a teacher able and willing to provide support happened to be free at that time.

The identification of mismatches at Stage 5 is used at Stage 6 to structure a debate among those who inhabit the problem situation about possible changes which could improve the situation. The debate aims to identify changes which meet two criteria: they must be systemically desirable, as indicated by the outcome of the conceptual modelling activity; and they must be culturally feasible, given the characteristics of the situation and the people in it. As a result of the debate about support teaching a new approach to planning and prioritization was introduced so that support teaching for the top priority periods was formally timetabled for the first time, thus ensuring that it would in future be provided where it was most needed. The formal timetabling of support teaching had a positive effect on its perceived status. This was in addition to the practical advantage that support teachers were no longer called away at short notice to cover for absent colleagues. That had sometimes happened when they had essentially been using a 'free' period to provide support teaching.

The influence of *cultural feasibility* was seen in the decision for the SENCO to engage in a fairly time-consuming face-to-face process of liaison and consultation with department and year heads in identifying priority lessons for support. She could instead have drawn up a set of criteria and generated a list of prioritized sessions on this basis. Staff wished to avoid overtly listing criteria, as this would have involved formally recognizing, for example, that certain departments were more successful than others in supporting pupils with special needs, or that some staff had particularly poor classroom management skills. Such information was widely known informally, but it was felt to be culturally unacceptable to have it recorded formally.

Stage 7 involves the implementation of the changes which have been agreed. This may be straightforward or it may generate other difficulties which can in turn be tackled using the methodology in further cycles. Although the methodology has been described in stage by stage sequence, in the interests of clarity of exposition, Checkland (Checkland and Schole 1990) emphasizes that much repetition of stages and flexible movement between them is expected and indeed desirable. For example, in selecting relevant systems at Stage 3 it may well be useful to test out various possibilities by quickly looking ahead to Stages 4, 5 and 6 and seeing what kind of models might follow from the root definitions considered and what kinds of changes are likely to be generated in the comparison stage. Also, at Stage 5, the attempt to make comparisons between the models that have been generated and the real world frequently highlights the need for more data gathering, where the information needed to make key comparisons is lacking.

Checkland points out that the methodology should not be regarded as a once-and-for-all approach to something sharply defined as a problem, but as a general way of carrying out purposeful activity which gains from the power of some formal systems thinking and results in those involved 'learning' their way to the development of an improved situation. Hence the methodology deals with fuzzy real-world messes, whereas many alternative approaches require clearly defined problems/objectives. Such 'hard' approaches also typically produce ideal systems, modelled by experts, which are imposed on the situation and the people within it as solutions. Burden (1978), having applied the hard systems approach developed by Jenkins (1969) in a number of organizational-level projects in schools, questioned its appropriateness and suggested that a more flexible approach may be preferable. By contrast, SSM seeks to identify systemically desirable and culturally feasible changes to the existing situation, these changes having been selected by those who live in the situation.

SSM has been applied to a wide range of issues in education. Examples include: supporting schools in special measures (Bettle *et al.* 2001), tackling high rates of exclusion (Miller 2003), inclusion of pupils who have special educational needs (Frederickson 1993), establishing a school-based SEN screening programme (Gersch *et al.* 2001), school lunch reform in the light of child obesity data (Suarez-Balcazar *et al.* 2007), strategic planning and quality assurance in schools (Kowszun 1992) and professional development in higher education (Patel 1995). Also of relevance in the light of the move to multi-disciplinary working in Children's Trusts are the applications to complex multi-disciplinary working (Gibb *et al.* 2002), decision making (Cook *et al.* 2001) and professional education (Rushton and Lindsay, 2003) in health and social care contexts.

Conclusions

The emphasis on assessing the learning environment has steadily grown in recent years. Research on school effectiveness and on features of the classroom environment that can facilitate learning has been influential. Legislation and guidance on the identification of SEN has increasingly incorporated a focus on the learning environment, alongside the traditional focus on the learner.

There are a number of well-developed theoretical models of the influence of the classroom and/or school environment on student learning. However, practice with pupils who have SEN has lagged behind the theory and has tended to remain focused on the individual child. In this chapter it was argued that many education service professionals need to develop their knowledge about assessment and intervention approaches that more adequately reflect the importance of the learning environment. Current lack of knowledge may represent one of the most significant problems to be overcome if the gap between theory and practice is to be closed. There are implications also for team working, decision making and professional development in complex multi-disciplinary team contexts, where professionals working with children who have SEN will increasingly be located.

Activity 9.5   A Classroom-level SSM case study

Figure 9.12 shows a rich picture that was drawn by the educational psychologist and SENCO shown in the top right-hand corner of the picture. They were concerned about the learning environment being provided for Alex, a 9-year-old child with a statement of SEN on account of his significant visual difficulties. Alex received additional provision of 10 hours per week from a visiting specialist

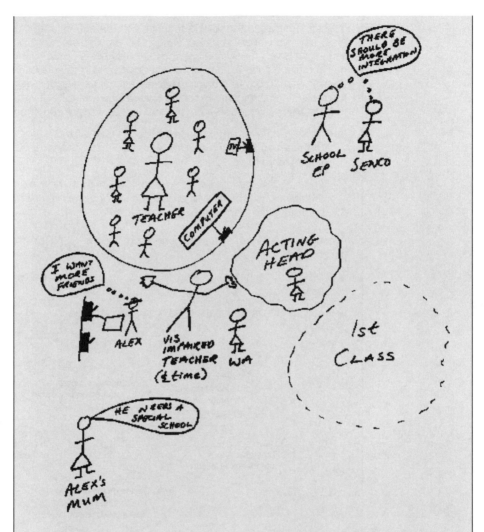

Figure 9.12 Rich picture of the learning environment being provided for Alex

teacher and had 20 hours per week from a learning support assistant. Alex only spent the first 40 minutes of each day in the class of which he was nominally a part. Once the visiting teacher for pupils with visual difficulties arrived at the school, Alex was withdrawn to an alcove in the corridor outside the classroom where he worked with her in the morning and with the non-teaching assistant in the afternoon. This arrangement was said to be necessary so that Alex would have easy access to an electrical socket into which to plug his Brailler. The two sockets in the classroom were 'occupied' by the computer and the television! In addition, the noise of the Brailler was considered by the class teacher to be too distracting for the other children in the class.

Alex had joined the school at the start of the present school year, following a family move, and initially been placed in a parallel class. The teacher of this first class had been unhappy that Alex was notionally a part of her class but was withdrawn for so much of the school day. Four weeks into the first term, following a meeting between the visiting teacher and the acting head, Alex moved classes. Alex, who had been included almost full-time in the classroom in his previous school, feels very lonely and unhappy. His mother is upset by the change in him, as he used to be such a happy boy who loved going to school. Now he sometimes doesn't want to go. She has always feared that as he got older it would be harder for him to stay in mainstream school and wonders whether it would be better for him to go to a special school where he could at least make some friends.

(a) Make a note of any suggestions you have at this stage for ways in which the learning environment for Alex could be changed so that it meets his needs more fully.

(b) Look at the rich picture and consider in turn the perspective of each of those involved in order to produce a list of systems that might be relevant to improving the learning environment for Alex.

Among the relevant systems generated by the SENCO and the educational psychologist were:

● a system to help Alex find his way around familiar environments without assistance;

● a system to increase the time Alex spends in class.

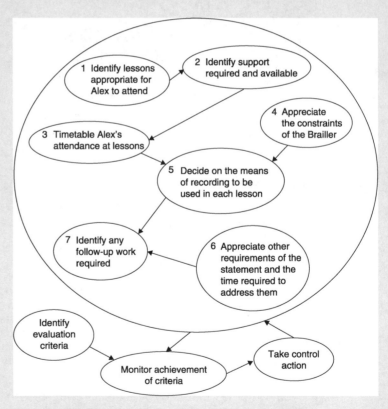

Figure 9.13   A conceptual model of a system to increase the time Alex spends in class

The CATWOE analysis produced for the second of these was as follows:

C   Alex

A   SENCO, class teacher, educational psychologist, learning support assistant

T   Alex in class very little > Alex in class 50 per cent of school day

W   Alex's social and academic needs will be better met if he can spend time in the class

O   Acting headteacher

E   Noise of the Brailler? Availability of learning support assistant and other support time. Appropriateness of class lessons for Alex? Other needs specified on Alex's statement (e.g. learning to use the Brailler fluently)

Figure 9.13 shows the conceptual model produced for this system.

(c) Compare the conceptual model with the rich picture and make a note of any mismatches you can identify. Can you think of any systemically desirable changes whose cultural feasibility you would want to discuss with those involved? For example, have the use of other forms of recording in the classroom been considered? Could Alex use a pocket dictating machine some of the time?

(d) Finally, compare the ideas you generated in (a) with those you generated in (c). What initial conclusions can you draw about the advantages and disadvantages of using SSM to structure thinking about the learning environments of pupils who have SEN?

A number of methods for assessing learning environments and designing interventions were described and their applicability to pupils who have SEN were illustrated. While multi-perspective measures and those involving direct observation typically involve a substantial time commitment, pupil perception measures may take little more than an hour to administer and score. The time taken to implement qualitative ethnographic approaches or SSM will vary with the scope of the investigation. However, all of these approaches offer a potentially high return on the time invested as environmental changes may have a broader preventive impact and benefit other pupils with similar difficulties. Evaluation of attempts to change the learning environment can readily be carried out and corresponding changes in the achievement of different groups of pupils examined. In this respect the approaches introduced in this chapter are likely to have relevance to many more aspects of schools' development plans than those relating specifically to pupils who have SEN.

PART THREE

Areas of need

10

Language

The knowledge and skills involved in language proficiency

Language and communication

Language is central to human experience – a key vehicle for thought and for social contact. Human beings are mutually dependent. Effective communication between them requires that:

- they know the forms of the language they share – how the words sound and how they go together (competence in phonology and syntax);

- they are able to use those forms to convey meaning and can understand what others mean when they use them (competence in semantics);

- they understand the social conventions that determine how people use language to each other, so that they appreciate another speaker's intentions in speaking and can communicate their own intentions to a listener (pragmatic competence);

- they can vary their style of communication and the language they use to suit the needs of different listeners in a conversation (conversational competence);

- they understand how language use and language conventions vary with the social and cultural context (sociolinguistic competence).

These competencies ensure that speakers can each play their full part in a complex 'communication chain'. This involves drawing on interdependent processes of decoding and encoding in which many areas of the nervous system are ultimately involved. Figure 10.1 shows a simplified form of the communication chain.

Children with SEN may have problems in mastering some or all of these areas of competence even when their difficulty is superficially not related to language at all. It is necessary to analyse individually for each child the challenges that are

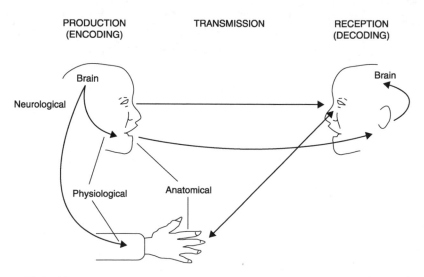

Figure 10.1   The communication chain
Source: Crystal and Varley (1998).

involved in the acquisition and use of language. Consider, for example, observations that have been made about the development of semantic competence by Susan who has been blind from birth and is now aged 4. When she adds to her vocabulary by learning new words for objects (nouns), she seems to be less likely than a sighted child of the same age to extend the nouns immediately to other situations (e.g. generalizing the use of the word 'soap' from the bathroom to the kitchen or the supermarket). Similarly, when she learns a new word for an action (verb), it will typically refer to an action which she has taken herself or an action by someone else that has directly affected her. She seems to be slower than most sighted children to use the new verb in an extended way to refer to an action by a third person that does not affect her (e.g. appreciating that an actor 'shouting' to another in a radio play is using the same action as a neighbour's child 'shouting' to her in the street). Some commentators have suggested that this slowness to generalize (which is not uncommon among children who have been blind from birth) implies that they show egocentricity and a lack of creativity (Dunlea 1989). More recent analysts have argued that it is simply that blind children need longer experience because they lack visual information regarding surrounding objects and events (Pérez-Pereira and Conti-Ramsden 1999: 80).

It is possible to portray what happens when we listen to a statement such as 'The fish is on the table' as a sequential series of transformations of sound waves into meaning (see Figure 10.2). However, this model fails to take account of the way in which listeners' perception of the context and their general knowledge influence their interpretation of what they hear. Bishop pointed out that the statement 'The fish is on the table' will be interpreted differently in different circumstances. For example, the meaning will not be the same if it is uttered by the person doing the cooking at dinner time or by a child whose parent is letting the cat into a room when she is cleaning out a tropical fish tank (Bishop 1997: 14). Figure 10.3 illustrates a model of verbal comprehension that takes account of these effects.

In research and clinical work in the past, most attention was given to the first two types of competence – knowledge of language forms (phonology and syntax) and knowledge of its meaning (semantics). But it is increasingly being recognized that children who have problems in other aspects of language competence, such as pragmatic competence, are just as impeded in communicating effectively with other people as they would be if the sounds of their speech were distorted or their vocabulary was limited (Olswang *et al.* 2001). John, a London child who has been assessed as having an autistic disorder, illustrates this point. When he speaks, he uses the intonations and the words of his parents. But he rarely looks at the person he is talking to. In fact it is sometimes difficult to tell whether he is talking to another person at all. He seems to be choosing his words without reference to what people have said and without following any conversational thread. His mother reports that he constantly reverts to the same few favourite themes and often uses the same pet phrases to talk about them. He makes the journey to school each day by car, but when he arrives he usually lists a series of London Underground stations as though talking about the journey. The list accurately reflects the route from his family home to his grandparents' house, but has nothing to do with the district where the school is located. (See Chapter 11 for a fuller account of the language and communication difficulties associated with autistic spectrum disorders.)

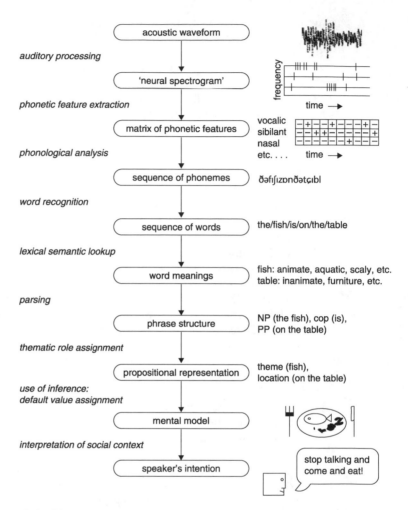

Figure 10.2   Model of the stages of processing involved in transforming a sound wave into meaning when comprehending the utterance 'The fish is on the table'
Source: Bishop (1997: 3).

Language diversity

Difficulties may also arise not because a child has failed to acquire the language and social conventions to which they have been introduced, but because they have grown up with a different set of conventions from those that they encounter at school (Frederickson *et al.* 2008: Chapter 5). It may be that they speak a different language at home, or a different variety of the same language, or that they use different non-verbal signals for communication (e.g. when demonstrating agreement or deferring to another person). At school they are expected to comply with the social code of the classroom and to extend their linguistic repertoire to encompass the accepted standard language of their society (e.g. standard English).

In England, when working with children who make poor progress, this requirement has to be interpreted alongside an apparently unrelated principle in

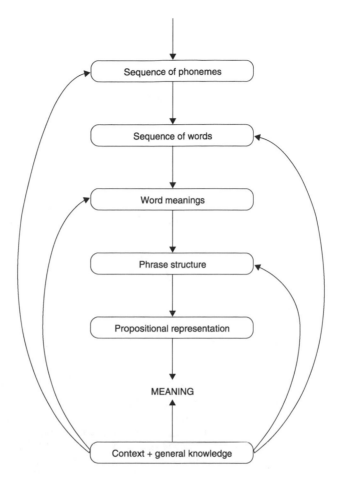

Figure 10.3 Modified model of stages in comprehension from phonological representation to meaning, showing top-down effects of context and general knowledge on earlier stages of processing
Source: Bishop (1997: 14).

the law about SEN: 'A child is not to be taken as having a learning difficulty solely because the language (or form of the language) in which he is, or will be, taught is different from a language (or form of a language) which has at any time been spoken in his home' (Education Act 1996, Section 312). This provision in the law is intended to provide protection so that children are not stigmatized as having SEN when they are simply in the early stages of learning EAL. This protection is important, but it has significant limits. For example, it does not mean that the language or dialect spoken in a child's home will necessarily be treated with respect in the classroom (Creese 2005).

The value of having mastered another language may be seen mainly as providing a route to learning standard English. Monolingual teachers often feel ambivalent about their pupils using dialect or another language in the classroom to talk to each other. In Activity 10.1 you are asked to consider how your own experience bears on this issue. There is now good evidence that teaching in a child's first language strengthens their performance in school in their second language (Thomas and Collier 2002), although 'quality of instruction' may be as important as 'language of instruction' (Parrish *et al.* 2006). Qualitative studies involving classroom observation and interviews with key participants have suggested that the advantages of encouraging children to use their first languages in school learning include that it can:

● foster a full sense of multicultural identity;

● support the maintenance and development of the first language;

● enhance skills in conceptual transfer and translation between languages;

● develop a more sophisticated metalinguistic awareness that is based on the full range of languages in the children's repertoire;

● encourage children to draw on the full range of their cultural knowledge (Pema and Pattinson 1991; Kenner *et al.* 2007).

On the basis of an earlier observation study, Bourne (2001: 103) has argued that, whether it is officially accepted or not, 'where bilingual children are present in classrooms, so are their languages, and those languages are put to use in their learning'.

Activity 10.1   Encouraging pupils to use additional languages in the classroom

In the two columns below we have set out arguments that are sometimes used in the debate about encouraging language diversity in the classroom. Discuss the arguments with a colleague one by one. What personal observations can each of you recall that either illustrate the validity of each assertion or suggest it is invalid?

Reasons given for insisting that only English is spoken in the classroom (teacher quoted by Ryan 1999)	*Reasons given for encouraging pupils to speak together in other languages if they wish*
It makes for better order and control and prevents covert subversion	When teachers affirm students' developing sense of their own identity and show respect for their home language and culture, it is more likely that they will apply themselves to academic effort (Cummins 1996)
It helps pupils for whom English is an additional language to learn it more quickly and successfully	When classroom activities on word-meaning encourage bilingual pupils to draw on their first languages, they learn the second language more effectively and are helped to gain a richer appreciation of ways in which they can make use of each language effectively in their own lives (McWilliam 1998)

Reasons given for insisting that only English is spoken in the classroom (teacher quoted by Ryan 1999)	Reasons given for encouraging pupils to speak together in other languages if they wish
	Children in the early stages of learning the majority language will suffer less stress and fatigue and will have better access to the curriculum (Skutnabb-Kangas 1981; Baker 2006)
It fosters ethnic and cultural integration by discouraging the development of separate, language-based working groups	It makes the break between home and school as small as possible (UNESCO 1953, quoted in Baker 2006)

Among speakers of English, the majority of children – white and black – use different language registers or dialects in different situations; see Willis (2002) for an illustration of this from the African-Caribbean community in an English city. It is possible for a range of dialects to be respected in the classroom while children are helped to access and use the standard version for some purposes. Problems arise when the privileging of the standard dialect is managed in a way that belittles others and when children's personal language difficulties make 'bi-dialectalism' a challenging goal for them. Grossman (1998) summarized US evidence about some of the difficulties associated with this approach, ending with a strong statement of the objections:

- Efforts to teach students to speak standard English are ineffective. For most pupils there are only marginal increases in their adoption of standard forms in the classroom, much less outside school.

- Teaching pupils standard English before they are completely fluent in their original dialect may stunt their language development.

- Disparaging non-standard dialects damages the self-esteem of those who speak them, and it is not possible to encourage the replacement of one set of forms with another without appearing to disparage the first.

According to Grossman (1998: 50):

Teaching standard English to nonstandard dialect speakers is a form of cultural subjugation. Nonstandard English speaking students and their teachers often have different perceptions of the implications of standard English. Teachers tend to view it as a way to learn more effectively and get ahead in the real world; many students view it as talking white, denying their heritage, and giving in to the European American power structure.

Bilingual language proficiency

The term 'bilingual' is used in many different ways. Throughout this book a bilingual child is taken to be one who regularly needs to understand or use more than one language (e.g. at home and at school). There is no implication that the child is yet (or will necessarily ever be) equally competent in both languages. Bilingual status for educational purposes is taken to be regular exposure to situations where dual competence would be desirable. Children will develop different versions of that dual competence in listening, speaking, reading and writing depending on the demands made of them and their ability to learn. Baker (2006: 3–4) listed a number of other dimensions of bilingualism and multilingualism in addition to competence. Those most relevant to children and adolescents are the following:

- Domains of use: where each language is acquired and used (e.g. home, school, street, TV).

- Balance: the degree to which one language is dominant in an individual's repertoire.

- Age: whether two languages are learned from birth ('simultaneous bilingualism') or one is learned first and then another later, e.g. when they start school ('sequential bilingualism').

- Development: whether competence in a language is just beginning ('incipient') or steadily growing ('ascendant') or decreasing or even being lost over time because of a change of circumstances, e.g. after migration ('recessive').

- Culture: the degree to which the acquisition of competence in another language is accompanied by increasing familiarity with the culture associated with that language.

- Contexts: whether the person is living in a bilingual or multilingual community where two or more languages are used regularly on an everyday basis (not necessarily on an equal basis) or in a monolingual society where they use another language for communication with relatives or friends or work contacts in another language community elsewhere.

In Activity 10.2 you are invited to reflect on the different reasons there are for children to develop bilingual or multilingual language proficiency and the implications they may have for the learner.

Activity 10.2   Analysing the varied circumstances of bilingual learners

The notes tabulated below summarize how Skutnabb-Kangas (1981) described the circumstances of the main groups of bilingual learners in her native Scandinavia at that time. Reflect on the circumstances of three people (children and adults) who are known to you professionally or personally and who come from different backgrounds. How well do Skutnabb-Kangas's categories fit their circumstances? Taking account of the headings listed by Baker (2006), how would you revise these categories to fit the languages situation in the area or networks with which you are familiar today?

	Social circumstances	Typical motive for learning second language	Investment in learning second language
Elite bilingual	Parent works in high-status occupation away from home country (e.g. diplomat, business person)	Cultural enrichment; communication with local people, including servants	Modest – success will bring some advantages, failure will incur few costs
Majority bilingual	Parents speak a high-status language in a country where a second language is widely spoken (e.g. English in Quebec)	Political requirement to be able to speak second language for entry into many occupations	Success will offer significant economic advantages and will have some social cachet
Family bilingual	Mother and father from different language backgrounds (e.g. father originally Greek-speaking and mother originally English-speaking)	Parents wish child to be able to communicate with all members of extended family	Success likely to be valued highly by family
Minority bilingual	Parents are refugees or immigrants from a developing country	Social and economic necessity	Failure will restrict employment opportunities and social status very considerably

The proficiency of a bilingual speaker is best understood if all five of the aspects of language competence that were introduced at the start of this chapter are taken into account – they all complement each other. A speaker's proficiency is not made up simply of knowledge of their languages and skill in understanding and speaking them. It also involves attitudes and feelings about the situations in which each language is used: a proficient bilingual speaker requires not only competence but also confidence across a wide range of situations – a wider range than a monolingual speaker will normally face. This is ignored when bilingual language use is described simply as a technical task in terms of a cognitive dimension alone. This overlooks the emotional, social and cultural significance that is usually associated with becoming bilingual. A simple framework of three dimensions has been proposed for describing people's associations with the languages in their repertoire:

- *expertise*: degree of proficiency in a language;

- *affiliation*: affective relationship with a language;

- *inheritance*: membership, by birth, of a family or community with a particular language tradition (Rampton 1990; Leung *et al.* 1997).

Grosjean (1985) has emphasized the different views that are often held of bilingual language proficiency. Across the world, monolingual speakers are in the minority and in many societies bilingual – even multilingual – proficiency is the norm. But traditionally in much of the West the monolingual nation state has become what most citizens see as 'normal'. What effect does that have? Grosjean analysed the assumptions behind the monolingual ('fractional') view which takes monolingualism as the norm and treats bilingualism as a possibly risky deviation. A bilingual speaker is seen simply as the sum of two monolinguals. Bilinguals are described and evaluated in terms of the fluency they have in their two languages and the balance they maintain between them. Language skills in bilinguals are appraised in terms of monolingual standards. Research focuses on what are feared to be the possibly negative effects of bilingualism. Will it damage a child's prospects of normal cognitive development? Will it lead to phonetic or syntactical confusion? The contact between the bilingual's two languages is seen as accidental and anomalous.

Grosjean contrasts with that set of assumptions a bilingual ('wholistic') view. From this perspective bilingual speakers are celebrated for maintaining a flexible communicative competence through different situations and in the face of changing demands on their two languages. There is more to bilingualism than understanding and speaking two languages: bilingual people have a unique and specific linguistic configuration which combines their knowledge of each. The analogy Grosjean uses is of a high hurdler. A sprinter can run faster on the flat and a high-jumper can jump higher, but neither of them has the unique combination of skills that enables a hurdler to race so fast over obstacles. Bilinguals use their languages – separately or together – in different domains of life for different purposes with different people. They switch between languages flexibly to meet the needs of those with whom they are talking or to convey emphasis or intimacy or private meanings when talking to members of their own bilingual language community. Any evaluation of their proficiency needs to focus on this communicative competence rather than on mastery of the forms of each language. Language learning and language forgetting arise in response to new communicative needs. Grosjean suggested that if there were more bilingual researchers (and more bilingual teachers) the holistic view of bilingualism would have greater support.

A perspective of that kind and a social model of language development may have implications for how teachers think about their pupils' abilities. Bourne (2005: 3) has criticized school language policies in which:

Speaking and listening are most often presented as individualised skills or competences. This perspective is emphasised by current assessment regimes, which grade learners at different levels of competence – for example, the Early Learning Goals, the National Curriculum statements, EAL stages. A similar perspective is also dominant in second language acquisition theories which construct speaking and listening as individual competences. I want to re-address this balance. In contrast, I want to focus on speaking and listening as a social and collective practice rather than as a neutral skill; to look at learning as socially situated rather than as an individualised, 'internal' developmental process. From this perspective, learning is about social participation in the practices of different social communities; participation in which the learner is also active in constructing an identity in relation to that community.

She questioned how some pupils come to be seen 'either as competent or incompetent members of the community of practice which is the school, and what they might be learning when they don't learn what it was we were expecting them to learn'. The risk was that those currently thought of as 'less able' on the basis of an unreliable assessment of their language skills would be 'corralled into narrow, impoverished forms of learning', would lose the opportunity to gain access to more productive expansive teaching methods (Bourne 2005: 8–9). At worst there is the risk that low expectations are set for some children who are learning EAL because their language needs are mistaken for learning difficulties in the sense in which that term has been used for SEN (Cline and Shamsi 2000).

Assessment of language proficiency

The importance of assessing language proficiency

Signs of language difficulties in the classroom

The need for early identification of speech and language difficulties has been emphasized in official guidance and in research reports and handbooks on professional practice (DfE 1994a: para. 3.85; Botting *et al.* 1998; Crystal and Varley 1998). Children with severe problems will usually be identified before school entry, but less obvious difficulties are difficult to identify with certainty. Norm-referenced assessment tools and simple questionnaires for parents or professionals are not sufficiently reliable with young children for screening purposes (Dockrell 2001). So some language and communication difficulties only become apparent when a child is faced with the challenges posed by school. Simple delays in the development of language proficiency may reveal themselves if the pupil speaks like a younger child, or shows limited understanding of complex sentences, or uses a limited vocabulary compared to most children of the same age (Hayden and Jordan 2007).

A less common phenomenon, 'specific language impairment', which is described in more detail below, leads to problems in processing grammatical forms and abnormalities in the way children speak as well as limitations in their vocabulary. In school the children may:

- have difficulty keeping track of conversations;

- produce odd grammatical structures when speaking or writing;

- fail to fully understand words that make logical connections such as 'because', 'so', 'if–then', 'however', 'although';

- have a poor memory for information that has been presented through speech or writing;

- talk in a roundabout or vague way, often not completing sentences and often repeating themselves;

- start to avoid tasks and situations that involve using language;

- appear slow to respond to instructions in a group and depend on seeing what other children are doing.

This list of signs has been adapted from more detailed lists presented by Beveridge and Conti-Ramsden (1987) and the Association for All Speech-Impaired Children (1990). When some or all of these signs are observed, it is essential that a full assessment is made of the child's development of language proficiency. Children showing such signs in severe form are unlikely to overcome their difficulties without additional support.

Children with EAL

Because the use of language is central to the educational process, the assessment of language proficiency will always be important in a full assessment of SEN. While this will be true for any child with learning difficulties, in the case of bilingual children it is obviously crucial. The draft revised *Code of Practice* for SEN assessment (DfEE 2001: para. 5.16) emphasizes this:

> At an early stage a full assessment should be made of the exposure they have had in the past to each of the languages they speak, the use they make of them currently and their proficiency in them. The information about their language skills obtained in this way will form the basis of all further work with them both in assessing their learning difficulties and in planning any additional language support that is needed.

It may appear self-evident that this would be important, but the few studies that have been conducted in the UK indicate that such information may often not be collected or recorded. This was indicated, for example, when Curnyn *et al.* (1991) studied the records of need for 35 children with MLD and EAL attending Glasgow primary and secondary schools in 1990. A content analysis of the case papers showed that the assessment report completed by the school mentioned language in describing the child's difficulties in only about half the cases, and bilingualism was referred to in the language assessment in less than a fifth of the cases. One might expect the assessment reports of the psychologists to be more meticulous. But they mentioned the child's bilingualism or EAL status in only two-thirds of the cases and they indicated that the child's first language had been assessed in only half of the cases. It might be expected that professionals would qualify their overall assessment in such cases by indicating that it should be interpreted in the light of the child's bilingual or bicultural status. That was done in less than a fifth of the cases examined. Findings of a similar kind were reported by Cline (1991) and Desforges *et al.* (1995).

Focusing specifically on referrals to a speech and language therapy department, Stow and Dodd (2005) found a similar pattern with evidence that bilingual children with speech disorders were under-reported and that the languages spoken by bilingual children were frequently misreported. It is easy to see that there were deficiencies in the professional practice covered in those studies. It is not so easy to determine the most effective way to put those deficiencies right.

Language competence is complex and multi-faceted. How can we best assess children's language development, and how can we report on that assessment most effectively – whether the children are monolingual, or bilingual, or multilingual?

Investigating a child's previous experience of language

The first questions to be resolved are not about proficiency but about opportunities. What exposure have children had outside school to the main language used for teaching and learning in school, and what exposure have they had to other languages in their homes or neighbourhood, or in a religious setting? In Activity 10.3 you will find a long list of questions that might need to be asked. This list was collated from a sample of booklets and notes of guidance issued by

---

Activity 10.3 Determining the information that is needed about a child's language experience in different situations

Below you will find a long list of questions that have been proposed in guidance notes about SEN and bilingualism. They are not given in any particular order.

Mark with *A* those questions that you think primary school class teachers and secondary school form tutors should know the answer to for every child in their class.

Mark with *B* those questions that you think these teachers should be able to answer in the case of all EAL pupils.

Mark with *C* those questions that you think should be checked if a child shows some of the signs of difficulty listed on pages 249–50.

Mark with *D* those questions that you think need only be checked if a child has difficulties with literacy learning.

1 What language(s) are used by the child and to the child at home and in the community?

2 What is the family's religion? Do the parents wish their religious affiliation to be taken into account at school in connection with diet, religious education teaching, participation in acts of worship, participation in other activities?

3 In what ways is the language with which the child is most familiar different from English – the direction in which the script is written, the alphabet, the symbols used for numerals, intonation and stress patterns?

4 What language(s) are spoken by the child to

● mother

● father

● siblings

● grandparents?

Do any of these family members use a different language some or all of the time when speaking to the child? If so, give details.

5 How long has the child been living in this country?

6   What moves, changes or interruptions might have affected the child's learning of each language to which they have been exposed?

7   Has the child attended school overseas? If so, where, between what ages, for how long, what kind of school and what language was the medium of instruction?

8   Does the child attend any school/class in the community? If so, is the focus of the work home language and/or culture or religious tradition and practice, or support for mainstream school learning?

9   What is the child's reported rate of progress in any community language class that they attend?

10   Is the child learning to read/write any language in addition to English? If so, give details of the language, any formal arrangements for teaching, and an estimate of the child's progress.

11   What access has the child had to first language support in school? What kind of support was provided:

  ● Exclusively with learning activities; exclusively with assessment activities; both?

  ● Through bilingual teachers, bilingual assistants, peer support, dual language materials?

12   Is an interpreter needed for effective communication with the parents about schooling?

LEA staff to teachers and schools. (For a fuller analysis of the coverage of these documents, see Cline and Shamsi 2000.) Activity 10.3 asks you to select from this list the questions appropriate to a particular situation. It is not suggested that an answer to each question is needed in every case.

The list of questions in Activity 10.3 does not probe in detail about aspects of the *school context* that are particularly relevant to children from ethnic and linguistic minorities. Figure 10.4 lists some supplementary questions that may be relevant. The assumption here is that it is not enough to focus on questions about language provision. A full appreciation of the educational setting in which a child's bilingual communicative competence is being developed must go much further.

Approaches to language assessment

Once information has been gathered about a child's language background, it is possible to place any findings about their use of language at school and at home in context. When it becomes evident that there is a significant problem, the first challenge is to determine how to sample children's use of language in more detail. Alternative options (starting with the most 'artificial') include the following:

● Set children a formal language test individually or in a group.

● Arrange meetings with children on their own and record the language they use. This may include creating a contrived situation designed to elicit particular types of language.

- Is their first language widely shared by other pupils at the school?

- Are there adults in the school who share their first language?

- Is there a whole-school languages policy that covers bilingual pupils?

- What resources/teachers are available to meet unique needs of bilingual pupils?

- Are there books, tapes, posters and displays in their first language?

- What flexibility of provision is there beyond what they now receive?

- Is a multicultural approach to teaching emphasized and valued by staff?

- Is there an explicit and effective school policy on racism and on racial harassment that is known to all staff, including support staff?

- Is there effective liaison with parents from their community?

- Is spoken/written information available to parents in their first language if needed?

- What efforts are made to ensure that parents understand what the school is aiming to do for their children and to learn their views on what it ought to do?

Figure 10.4   Relevant information about the school context of bilingual pupils
Source: Cline and Frederickson (1991).

- Collect audio or video samples of the child's language (or written records) in everyday situations, repeating this over time to show progress or repeating it in different situations and with different company to show range.

- Make a written summary record of language use in an everyday situation, selecting only examples of particular interest or significance.

- Conduct enquiries through questionnaires or structured interviews with adults who live or work with the child to record their observations of the child's comprehension and use of language. (This may also involve asking children themselves for a self-report.)

Language tests

The first option in the list, language testing, appears to have many advantages. There is a standard setting and standard materials, making comparisons simpler and more objective. At best, tests can be more systematic, more focused, more transparent and quicker than alternative options. But for more than 30 years there has been widespread criticism of formal tests as a method of language assessment. The main criticisms are that tests:

- force the analysis of a rich, complex, context-dependent communicative competence into a simplistic framework of narrowly defined and unintegrated 'verbal skills';

- assess competence in phonology, syntax and semantics in preference to pragmatic, conversational and sociolinguistic competence;

- often privilege monolingual proficiency in a standard dialect as the ideal with which the performance of all speakers should be compared (Milroy and Milroy 1985: Chapter 8);

- often lack adequate standardization data for the youngest ages when systematic identification of language difficulties is particularly important (Howlin and Cross 1994);

- risk that numerical scores will be treated with undue respect because they appear precise;

- assume wrongly that language production and use in a highly structured exchange dominated by an adult will be a valid sample of how a child might use language in 'real communication' in everyday life.

But, in spite of all these criticisms, structured and standardized tests continue to be used extensively for the assessment of language proficiency in relation to SEN (Dockrell 2001). Some examples of tests that are commonly used with children in the UK are described briefly in Figure 10.5. All were developed in the UK or have been trialled or normed there. They may be used in SEN assessment by speech and language therapists, educational psychologists or clinical psychologists. For all its limitations, test evidence has the advantage that it is cost-effective to collect and can readily be replicated. The most important question about test data is whether they are a valid reflection of what they claim to measure. The inferences that are drawn need to be checked against information from other sources. Are they compatible with the reports of parents and teachers and concurrent measures of educational attainment?

General language scales

Reynell Developmental Language Scales III – The University of Reading Edition (RDLS III) (Edwards et al. 1997). While based on the earlier versions of the scale, this revision is effectively a new instrument. This is a norm-based test for children aged 18 months to 7 years comprising an expressive scale and a comprehension scale. Toys and a picture book are used in both scales. The comprehension scale examines a range from responses to single words (the child points to toys named by the examiner) to drawing inferences (the child points to people in a complex picture of a burger bar in response to questions such as 'Who's being naughty?' and 'Whose daughter is having a birthday party?'). The expressive scale also starts with single words (the child names familiar objects which the examiner presents one at a time). The scale ranges up to advanced language skills where, for example, the child is required to retell a story and is scored for using complex sentences (i.e. at least one main clause plus one other clausal structure). The scales were intended to 'reflect current knowledge about normal language development and language impairment and the way in which language may be conceptualised' (Edwards *et al.* 1997: 2). Because they are more finely differentiated than earlier versions of the same scale, they were judged on publication to offer some potential as an outcome measure for educational or therapeutic intervention (Law 1999). However, there are other general language scales that offer more fully developed psychometric support for producing an analytic profile of a child's language subskills, e.g. the *Clinical Evaluation of Language Fundamentals* (Semel *et al.* 2006).

Speech development and discrimination

Auditory Discrimination and Attention Test (Morgan-Barry 1988). This test aims to assess the ability to discriminate between sounds. The child is presented with a series of pictures that illustrate pairs of words that differ in a single phoneme. After some preparation the examiner says one of the two words, and the child has to indicate the relevant picture.

Diagnostic Evaluation of Articulation & Phonology (DEAP) (Dodd et al. 2006). An initial five-minute 'diagnostic screen' suggests specific areas of articulation and phonology that may need more detailed assessment. The pack includes materials for assessing phonology, oro-motor ability and error patterns in greater depth. There are national UK norms and also some standardization data on bilingual children speaking in English and in Punjabi.

Listening (receptive) comprehension

British Picture Vocabulary Scale (BPVS) (Dunn et al. 1997). In this test of listening vocabulary the child is presented with a series of pages on which four line drawings are shown. For each page the examiner says a single word that names the object or action depicted in one of the drawings. The child is required to point to that drawing. There are separate norms for children who are learning English as an additional language.

Test for Reception of Grammar (TROG-2) (Bishop 2003). Another test in which each item requires the child to select one out of four line drawings. The examiner reads a sentence, and the child has to understand a targeted grammatical construction in order to choose the correct illustration. The complexity and difficulty of the grammatical contrasts increase steadily across 20 blocks of items.

Expressive language

Renfrew Language Scales: Bus Story Test (Renfrew 1997). This is a norm-referenced, screening test for children aged 3–8 years. It evaluates children's narrative speech: 'the ability to give a coherent description of a series of events'. The examiner tells the child a story about a naughty bus which runs away from its driver, showing a booklet of pictures that illustrate the story. The child is then required to retell the story referring to the pictures as they go. A tape of the session is scored for information, sentence length and subordinate clauses.

Pre-verbal language development

Symbolic Play Test: Second Edition (Lowe and Costello 1988). This test is designed to assess early (pre-verbal) concept formation and symbolization by children aged 1–3 years. The child plays with miniature toys that represent everyday objects. An evaluation is made of their level of thinking about the symbolic meaning of the toys, and this is the basis of an estimate of their language potential.

Figure 10.5 Selected examples of language tests used with children with SEN in the UK

Meetings and interviews

If meetings are arranged for the purpose of language assessment (the second option in the list at the beginning of this subsection), there are choices as to how they will be conducted. A meeting can be set up as:

● a 'natural' conversation;

● an interview in which the adult takes the initiative most of the time; or

● an examination in which there is a repeated pattern of the adult initiating, the child responding, and the adult evaluating that response.

It is often assumed that an unstructured interview will generate a more authentic sample of a person's language than a 'formal' or structured interview, or a test. However, it has been shown that even an unstructured interview obtains only a limited sample of a person's linguistic repertoire (Perrett 1990). It may sometimes provide satisfactory data for the assessment of a person's competence in phonology and syntax (though there is evidence that children may produce syntactically more complex language in other situations – e.g. Kenner *et al.* 1996). It may enable a judgement to be made about the ability to use words to convey meaning and to understand what others mean in a limited context (competence in semantics). But it is an atypical social situation, and it will not provide useful information about pragmatic competence, conversational competence or sociolinguistic competence. For example, it is not normally possible to use an interview to assess a person's ability to control conversation, to initiate topics or to assume responsibility for the continuation of a verbal exchange. Suggestions to interviewers about conducting the process more sensitively 'cannot address those unchanging and unchangeable characteristics of the interview as a cultural event in which there is an uneven distribution of power and control' (Perrett 1990: 236).

Thus, if interviewing has a role in language assessment, it is a limited role. Specific examples include an interview task in which a child is required to retell a story, such as the Bus Story Test (see Figure 10.5). Such tasks may have a diagnostic value, since problems with the organization and sequencing of narrative material have been shown to be characteristic of children with pragmatic language impairment (Adams 2001). A short structured interview using culturally appropriate stimulus material was employed by Pert (2006) to study code switching by young bilingual Mirpuri–English speakers in the town of Rochdale in England. He argued that in a population where code-switching is common, a child who does not switch between the two language codes to which they have access may be showing signs of grammatical impairment (specific language impairment – see below). The principles and methods of dynamic assessment (see Chapter 12) were adapted by Snell (2002) and others to facilitate the assessment of non-verbal communication skills of children with profound and multiple learning difficulties. Gutiérrez-Clellen and Peña (2001) applied the same principles to the assessment of bilingual children. Bishop (2006) has highlighted the possible value of dynamic assessment methods in measuring the extent to which language abilities can be modified in response to different kinds of intervention.

Observation and recording of the use of language in 'natural' settings

For the reasons given above, there is a good deal of support for the collection of language samples in 'natural' settings, for example through systematic observation over time during everyday activities and tasks (Martin and Miller 2003). There are then further issues to be considered about the context. Will it be the classroom, elsewhere in school, the neighbourhood or the child's home? Will it be a formal or informal setting? Will the conversant(s) be familiar or unfamiliar to the child, and will they be other children, or adults, or both? There is a good deal of evidence that contextual factors of this kind have a major impact on the amount, the quality and the maturity level of a child's expressive language (e.g. Kenner *et al.* 1996). Everyday classroom language is often dominated by the teacher and takes the form of a stylized exchange of questions and answers (Edwards and Westgate 1994; Jefferies and Donlan 1994). This tends to elicit a restricted sample of a child's language repertoire. For example, the length of children's utterances may be reduced by as much as two-thirds (Shields and Steiner 1973). In an inner-city nursery class, Kenner *et al.* (1996) demonstrated that a 4-year-old girl whose first language was Gujarati showed a more mature command of language in 'pretend play' with a friend than in a conversation about a colourful picture book led by a familiar teacher. Similar findings have been reported by many other investigators – for example, Tizard and Hughes (1984) who contrasted young girls' extensive conversations with their mothers at home with more restricted exchanges with adults in a nursery.

Two concerns seem to impinge on teachers, leading them to dominate and inhibiting them from creating a more productive/fertile environment for a two-way conversation. One factor is a concern to educate – to extend children's knowledge of the topic being discussed and to help them towards formal correctness. The other concern is to maintain control. A more open approach to classroom talk might, it is feared, put at risk the teacher's ability to deliver planned thematic material, to keep the session to time and to maintain expected forms of order within the group.

Working in six Primary 2 classes in Scotland, Jefferies and Donlan (1994) have shown that even small changes in what a teacher says can lead to a doubling of children's verbal responses (see Table 10.1). However, some have argued that changes of this kind will not be enough. The development of a culture of conversation requires a more radical rethink of classroom conventions at least for some of the time (Clay 1998: Chapter 2). Some of the 'rights' that a teacher may choose to give up are suggested by Edwards and Westgate (1994):

- to begin and end the encounters;

- to ask the questions and evaluate the answers;

- to allocate all the turns at speaking which they do not claim themselves;

- to provide a framework within which both they and their pupils operate.

Their approach to the study of classroom talk envisages:

> the possibility that more 'open', untraditional patterns of communication may be recognised in the extent to which they [children] move towards the conversational end of the continuum of speech systems. The point is not that

Table 10.1   The impact of different types of question or comment from a teacher on children's verbal responses

Type of initiation	Mean length in words of child's utterance
Asking children to project into situations or predict outcomes	2.3
Questions on the overt content of the material used (e.g. books, play materials)	2.4
Asking children to give information or knowledge from outside the class	3.2
Questions on the implicit content of the material used	3.3
Asking children to recall personal experiences	5.1
Asking children to clarify what they have said	5.1
Offering children an opportunity to contribute	6.1
Asking children to give an opinion	6.8

Source: Adapted from Jefferies and Donlan (1994).

> classroom talk 'should' resemble conversation, since most of the time for practical purposes it cannot, but that institutionalised talk (such as talk for instructional purposes) shows a heightened use of procedures which have their 'base' in ordinary conversation.
>
> (Edwards and Westgate 1994: 116)

One of the occasions when this approach will be desirable in a classroom will be when speech samples are being sought to evaluate the language proficiency of a child at risk. The key principles are that:

- the language should be sampled as unobtrusively as possible in situations that occur naturally in the classroom (or, if necessary, in contrived situations that *feel* natural);

- the context and the participants in the conversation should be familiar to the child;

- the language that is used should relate meaningfully to the situation and conform to the manner in which that language is normally used.

As a result, the assessment will be based on the child's use of language for 'real, purposeful communication'. Working with young children, Kenner *et al.* (1996) recognized that large-scale taping and transcription would be an impossible addition to teachers' workloads. They advocated spending short stretches of time in the role-play area with a pocket audiorecorder. With this approach it is important to make brief notes of the context at the time, as the tape can be difficult to interpret without them. Those working with older pupils have recorded talk in working groups without an adult present (Edwards and Westgate 1994). It may also be important to evaluate children's listening comprehension under different conditions, for example by observing them in a noisy room and in a quiet place, and in structured and unstructured situations (Martin and Miller 2003).

The collection of samples of children's language is only the first stage of assessment. It is then necessary to evaluate what these samples show about whether their language is developing uniformly and in line with their developmental stage. At best the analysis should provide a basis both for comparison with developmental norms and for identifying areas of difficulty and planning intervention. The Bristol Language Development Scales (Gutfreund *et al.* 1989) exemplify a (relatively) teacher-friendly approach to this task. The scales were based on longitudinal studies of the language at home of 128 children between the ages of 15 months and 5 years. The analysis requires a sample of about 100 representative utterances (e.g. 30 minutes' language in six 5-minute periods) with accompanying commentary on the ongoing situation in which they occurred. The analysis (which is supported by thorough guidance in the manual) covers pragmatic, semantic and syntactic competence. A more specialized approach to the analysis of children's syntactic competence may be found in the Language Assessment, Remediation and Screening Procedure (LARSP) described by Crystal *et al.* (1989). Two questions arise with such materials:

- Is the model of language development that is used valid and relevant for the purposes for which the assessment is planned – for example, will it lead to helpful suggestions for intervention?

- Will the analysis be reliable – for example, would two different examiners obtain closely similar results (cf. Ball 2000)?

Drawing on the observations of those who live and work with the child

It seems, then, that for many purposes test situations elicit too limited a sample of a child's language repertoire, while the language recorded in natural settings offers so rich a sample that it is time-consuming and complex to analyse. Would it be a more effective and economical strategy if language assessment drew on the observations of those who live and work with the child? In this, as in other areas, it has been shown that parents can be reliable reporters about their children's development (Cunningham and Sloper 1984). The accuracy of the reporting of parents (and of those who work with a child regularly, such as care workers and class teachers) will increase if the questions they are asked are precise and systematic. The most effective strategy appears to be to use a structured interview that focuses on current developmental changes. An example is the Pragmatics Profile of Everyday Communication Skills designed for children aged 0–10 years (Dewart and Summers 1995). Separate sections concern:

- a range of communicative functions that children may express, such as requests for an object or for information;

- the way they react and respond to communication from others;

- the way they interact with other people and participate in conversation;

- the way their communication varies depending on context.

Bishop (1998) developed the Children's Communication Checklist for use with teachers and speech and language therapists. Her aim was to offer a tighter assessment framework than is provided in the Pragmatics Profile of Everyday Communication Skills, with full information on reliability and validity. The diagnostic utility of this checklist has been confirmed in subsequent reports (e.g. Geurts *et al.* 2004). It will be evident that all such materials depend crucially on the observation skills and memory of the informant and the interviewing skills of the individual who is collecting the information: the record is at two removes from the child.

Evaluating the language proficiency of children learning EAL

When a child is bilingual, the question arises as to which language is dominant, that is which one they are more proficient in or which one they prefer to use. In some states of the USA questions about 'language balance' or 'language dominance' have had great practical importance, because there has been a mandatory requirement that a child should be educated through their dominant language at least for a transitional period. In these circumstances it has been common to use a test to determine language dominance. For example, investigators will try to discover whether children give word associations more quickly in one language than in the other. The major problem with such tests is that a person may be more proficient with their first language in some domains of conversation (e.g. talking about cooking or about family relationships) and more proficient with their second language in other domains (e.g. talking about science or national history). Particularly for children moving between one language community at home and another language community at school the concept of language dominance may oversimplify the picture of their use of languages across settings (Valdes and Figueroa 1994; Baker 2006).

It is possible to obtain a more complex picture of children's patterns of language use by making enquiries of those who live and work with them in different settings. It is also possible to ask the children themselves. Beech and Keys (1997) developed a Language Preference Questionnaire for research purposes, while Baker (2006: 32–3) proposed a more comprehensive set of questions which do not ask about the child's preferences but about what actually happens. He added friends to the list of family members who are commonly identified as potential informants (cf. Activity 10.3). He also discriminated among many different settings, as Table 10.2 shows. Note that, compared to the abridged version shown in Table 10.2, there are seven other categories of person and seven other categories of situation in the full tables. The language alternatives would be varied to suit the individual child.

How should such data be analysed? A simple counting approach can be misleading. Baker and Hinde (1984) pointed out that, even if many items are ticked for a particular language (Welsh, for example), that language might still be used infrequently. This could happen if, for example, the child's mother who is there all the time speaks English but her father who is regularly away at sea speaks Welsh, as do other relatives on his side of the family whom the child sees rarely. In the Bilingual Language Assessment Record, which was developed in Leeds, Haworth and Joyce (1996) focused on children's observed skills in using their two languages as well as the frequency of their exposure. Since then there has been a good deal of development work on school-based strategies for the direct assessment of children's knowledge and use of community languages (Cline 2005).

What is the most effective way of evaluating children's development of EAL? There have been some attempts to develop standardized tests that evaluate

Table 10.2   Extracts from Baker's Language Background Scale

In which language do the following people speak to you?

	Always in Spanish	In Spanish more often than English	In Spanish and English equally	In English more often than Spanish	Always in English
Friends in the classroom					
Friends in the playground					
Friends outside school					

Which language do you use with the following?

Watching TV or videos					
Religion					
Cassettes/ CDs/records/					
Earning money					
Shopping					

Source: Baker (2006).

verbal ability across languages, such as the Bilingual Verbal Abilities Test (Muñoz-Sandoval 1998), but the main effort has gone into producing structured schedules that draw on the observations of those who have regular contact with the target child. Some have argued for the use of English language scales that are specifically designed for this purpose. This is the norm in many states of Australia and the USA where more resources have been put into achieving consistency and clear links to the school curriculum and classroom practice (Scott 2006). The official English view in recent years has been that it is possible and preferable to integrate the assessment of children learning EAL with that of all other children by assessing their progress in English within the framework of the National Curriculum English levels (Ofsted 1997a; QCA 2000a). A key issue must be whether the language assessment information that teachers gather can be used formatively to lay the foundation for effective teaching (Gravelle 2003).

Whatever strategy is adopted for pupils learning EAL in general may not necessarily fully meet the needs of those showing learning difficulties. In their case assessment has to be sufficiently detailed and precise to discriminate well within the early stages of progress and to highlight uneven patterns of development. The information available through statutory National Curriculum English assessment and unstructured classroom observation is not likely to achieve these objectives. Cameron and Bygate (1997) have argued that the most effective strategy would be to construct SATs and procedures around regular classroom tasks. They consider that this would strengthen the relationship between assessment and classroom activities, and between assessment results and classroom performance. Gardner and Rea-Dickins (2002) have proposed an economical strategy of classroom-based language sampling for this purpose. This is likely to be too great a commitment for a mainstream class or subject teacher on their own, but collaboration with an EAL support teacher might be possible.

A curriculum-related approach has many advantages over those approaches which explicitly or implicitly make comparisons with age-related monolingual norms. In Chapter 8 we introduced an approach to CBA that involves analysing, among other things, how far classroom talk is 'context-embedded' or 'context-reduced'. Examples of the application of this framework to evaluating children's responses to different types of linguistic demand are given in Godfrey and Skinner (1995), Robson (1995, 1996) and Barrados (1996).

If there is disagreement around the assessment of children's progress in EAL, the situation regarding the assessment of children's home languages is even more problematic. There was until recently little published work on the assessment of home language for children learning EAL who have learning difficulties (Cline and Shamsi 2000). Some local authority initiatives have now begun to bear fruit in the form of practicable, if under-researched, assessment instruments (see accounts from five areas in Cline 2005). However, while these approaches have significant advantages over the casual methods that are more commonly used, none of them is based on a programme of systematic research, and none takes full account of the range of language varieties encountered in UK schools. Barden (2003) showed in a case study that, while mother tongue assessment is important, it needs to be 'read' alongside full information about a child's history and experience if the data it yields are to be interpreted constructively. Landon (2005) has argued for a holistic approach which treats learners who are potentially plurilingual as such:

> Their whole language repertoire will be developed and used, with code-switching and code-mixing as strategies to cross and exploit complex patterns of dominance, and with the development of multilingual methodologies for teaching and learning. Assessment will probe and monitor each individual's multilingual development, to identify shifting patterns of dominance and to clarify where strengths and weaknesses lie.
>
> (Landon 2005: 31)

Thus the assessment of the full bilingual language competence of children with EAL who appear to have learning difficulties can be seen to have many facets. While progress has been made with some aspects of the task, there is substantial outstanding development work in other areas needed.

Problems that occur in the development of communication skills

There is no certainty about how many people may experience speech and language difficulties during childhood. A number of surveys have been carried out but they have used different definitions of what constitutes a problem, have surveyed different professional observers and have sampled different age groups (Webster 1988; Winter 1999; Law and Tamhne 2000). As a result estimates vary greatly. It is agreed that preschool children show a relatively high incidence of problems and that the rate drops by school entry. Law and Tamhne (2000: 42) drew a number of conclusions from an extensive review of the literature:

- Conservative estimates are that 1–2 per cent of children have communication difficulties at some stage, but 'well-designed studies suggest that as many as 7 per cent of children may have difficulties which warrant attention'.

- Children whose communication difficulties are still in evidence at the time when they start school entry are at risk of subsequent educational problems, but the position is much less clear for younger children.

- While it is true that a large number of children who show early speech and language difficulties overcome them without specialist intervention, early delays should still be considered 'a risk factor both for subsequent speech and language difficulties and for other schooling and social problems, a risk which needs to be taken seriously'.

Webster (1988) focused on the (less common) severe and specific language problems and concluded that they develop in about 1 child per 1000. Boys are twice as likely to experience problems as girls (Donaldson 1995). Possible sources of difficulty include physical impairment, neurological impairment and social and emotional factors. The potential problems are diverse, and there has often been controversy about how they can most usefully be classified (Crystal and Varley 1998: Chapter 5). For example, it is common to differentiate between *receptive difficulties* (where the problems mainly arise when children are trying to understand what is said to them) and *expressive difficulties* (where the problems mainly arise around speaking and writing). But, as will be shown below, these two major processes are linked, and children with severe difficulties often have problems in both areas – receptive and expressive. The association of pragmatic difficulties with other symptoms is even more problematic. To what degree do the obstacles to effective communication in a child with specific pragmatic difficulties overlap with the problems faced by a child with autism when interacting with other people? Conti-Ramsden *et al.* (2006) showed that young people with a history of specific language impairment have a risk of developing autism that is ten times higher than would be expected from the general population. Clearly traditional diagnostic categories in this field cannot be treated as straightforward indicators for planning intervention or education.

In a study of professionals' perceptions of children attending language units, Crutchley *et al.* (1997b) employed a simple strategy of functional description. Teachers and other professionals who worked regularly with the children were asked to state whether or not their pupils had each of the following types of difficulty:

- *Articulation* – problems with pronunciation which appear to have a physical basis (e.g. poor muscle control).

- *Phonology* – problems with pronunciation which do not appear to have a physical basis.

- *Syntax* – Problems in putting words together to form multi-word sentences or understanding complex sentences.

- *Morphology* – problems using inflections and forming a word by derivation from another word.

- *Semantics* – difficulties with word meaning.

- *Pragmatics* – problems over the use of language in social contexts.

The classification of specific language impairment is complex and controversial, but those headings reflect major areas of concern. For example, they closely overlap the chapter headings on typology adopted by Verhoeven and van Balkom (2004) where more detailed accounts of specific areas of difficulty may be found. It should be noted that the sample of teachers surveyed by Crutchley *et al.* was associated with language units. The level of confidence they showed in describing their pupils' language skills is not usually echoed by mainstream teachers (Dockrell and Lindsay 2001). The inclusion of children with specific language impairments is challenging for mainstream teachers in part because they present complex combinations of difficulties in a field where teacher education in the past has been particularly weak (Mroz 2006).

In this section we will discuss three patterns of speech and language difficulty in more detail:

- the difficulties that develop in association with other disabilities;

- specific language impairment;

- problems of communication deriving from emotional and social difficulties.

Difficulties of language acquisition that develop in association with other disabilities

Speech and language problems are often found when a child has another disabling condition. Infants learn language by hearing it used by others, seeing and understanding the context in which it is used, and experimenting with the sounds they can make themselves. In Chapter 17 we will discuss how that process is affected when children cannot adequately hear what is said to them. The development of language will vary with changes in other elements in the process too. Examples include:

- if the language input children receive is limited (e.g. in conditions of extreme deprivation or neglect);

- if they are congenitally blind and so cannot draw on the visual clues that most infants use to make sense of the speech they hear;

- if they have severe physical disabilities and so cannot use their vocal apparatus to make the sounds they wish to try out.

The variability in the process does not necessarily mean that children in these situations operate to a different set of principles of language acquisition. It may rather be that the normal processes of learning become adapted to meet their needs. They will exploit the resources and mechanisms that they have at their disposal (or are given by adults) and use them to compensate for any deficiency in the input they receive or in their ability to use the strategies open to most children.

We will illustrate this with two examples from work with blind children and one example from work with children with physical disabilities.

The first example concerns research on delays in phonological development in some blind children (Mulford 1988; Mills 1993). Pérez-Pereira and Conti-Ramsden (1999: 70) summarized the conclusions reached in this line of research as follows: 'blind children may be slightly delayed in learning those sounds that have clear visual articulation. However, older blind children show normal use of speech sounds, suggesting that blind children in due course can make use of acoustic information to correct their substitutions and to achieve standard adult pronunciation' (see Table 10.3).

Consider a second example relating to blind children. A distinctive feature of the early language development of blind children is a tendency to imitate whole phrases from others and use them for some time in a stereotyped form before analysing and segmenting them into their constituent parts. All young children do this, but blind children appear to do it more often than most and for a higher proportion of the language input they hear. Some commentators (e.g. Brown *et al.* 1997) have interpreted their style as 'autistic-like' and have suggested that it may arise because congenitally blind children are denied visual clues to other people's attitudes towards the world they share. Unlike autistic children they do eventually overcome this obstacle, but it takes them longer to do so than most unimpaired sighted children. Other commentators have rejected analogies with autism and stressed that the children 'arrive at a similar endpoint following different routes' (Perez-Pereira and Conti-Ramsden 1999: 134). This highlights the challenge for researchers and teachers of interpreting differences between patterns of language development shown by children with SEN and the patterns shown by the majority of children.

For some children with very severe physical disabilities the option of tracking a normal developmental pattern is not open. They do not have the necessary motor control to generate intelligible speech. In the past there was a tendency for children in this position to slip into a role of a passive spectator and never learn to communicate actively with others. Recent developments in *augmentative and alternative communication systems* (AAC) have created the opportunity to prevent this happening. Various codes such as Rebus and Bliss symbols have been evolved, and technological advances allow children who can manage only the slightest of movements under conscious control to communicate successfully. So there has been a tendency to think of the challenge simply as a physical one (what kind of apparatus can the child operate?) and an intellectual one (what kind of code can the child learn?). But, like other language users, those employing AAC need also to develop versions of pragmatic and conversational competence. Light

Table 10.3 Errors in initial consonants of words spoken by young blind children

	Sounds with visible articulation	Sounds without visible articulation
% errors of 3 blind children	41	51
% errors of 3 sighted children	21	52

Source: Adapted from Mills (1993).

(1989) suggested that AAC users need eventually to develop four aspects of communicative competence:

1   *Linguistic competence* – adequate mastery of the native language (vocabulary and grammar) plus the code (e.g. signs or symbols) required to operate the augmentative communication system.

2   *Operational competence* – mastery of technical skills required to operate the system, that is, the motor and cognitive skills required to signal a message or to operate specific device features (pointing, signing, visual scanning, operating switches, controlling cursors, editing, etc.).

3   *Social competence* – knowledge and skill in the social rules of communication (e.g. making appropriate eye contact, sharing the balance of talking and listening) and using communication for a range of different purposes (social chat, making requests, responding to others, contradicting people, etc.).

4   *Strategic competence* – flexibility in order to adapt communicative style to suit the receiver (e.g. signing more slowly to strangers, turning up the volume on the communication aid in a noisy room) or learning how to correct misunderstanding or to extend the conversation (e.g. if a child cannot explain something clearly on his touch talker he might have a message that says, 'Please hold up my Bliss chart. I'd like to explain something').

Later work has confirmed the value of thinking about communication with AAC systems in terms of a broad sociolinguistic model of development (Von Tetzchner and Grove 2003). This can lay the foundation for an effective approach to practical support, for example with the task of acquiring the literacy skills that are needed to make effective use of the systems (Smith 2005).

Specific language impairment

Some children achieve normal milestones in most aspects of development but show specific difficulties in relation to speech and language – specific language impairment (SLI) or language disorder. In the past this was often diagnosed by excluding other possible causes of language difficulty one by one. A child's difficulties might be described as SLI if it could be shown that they were *not* caused by:

- hearing loss;

- general learning difficulties;

- environmental factors;

- emotional problems (Lees and Urwin 1997: 14).

In this respect the category bore some similarities to dyslexia (see Chapter 13). For example, the operational criteria adopted by one research team included 'performance IQ of 85 or above' (Stark and Tallal, cited by Bishop 1997).

Recent studies have emphasized that SLI can be associated with a wide range of factors. The course of its development and the patterns of behaviour associated with it are both complex and heterogeneous. It has therefore been argued (as in the case of dyslexia) that it is more helpful to define it by inclusion. In the example given in Figure 10.6, Lees and Urwin (1997) build on their account of exclusionary definitions cited above.

Recent research has thrown doubt on the value of another distinction that was traditionally given weight in the analysis of SLI – the distinction between expressive disorders and receptive disorders. The problem is that, first, most children with SLI turn out to have comprehension problems if assessed carefully and, second, those comprehension problems turn out to be complex and heterogeneous. So distinguishing between children with SLI who have an expressive-type disorder and children with SLI who have a receptive-type disorder does not take one much further forward (Bishop 1997: Chapter 2). However, increasing attention has been given to a subgroup of children with SLI who present a distinctive profile in everyday life and appear to have distinctive outcomes in education and therapy – children with semantic-pragmatic difficulties (SPD). They speak fluently in sentences that are well formed syntactically, using the phonological system accurately. Yet they do not communicate well, because what they say does not follow on from what came before in the conversation. When young they often simply echo what is said to them. They seem to understand short phrases and individual words but not connected discourse. This pattern of difficulties is clearly recognizable in the classroom but progress in response to therapeutic intervention is found to be very slow.

Speech and language therapists play a key role in interventions for children with SLI, often working closely with teachers or psychologists (for discussions of strategies for collaboration, see Wright and Kersner 1998; Dunsmuir *et al.* 2006). Current educational provision (which generally caters for a heterogeneous group of children with language difficulties) ranges from integrated teaching in mainstream classes through part-time, on-site language units to residential special schooling. The latter option is now generally restricted to the children with the most extreme difficulties, and follow-up studies in adulthood show variable outcomes (Haynes 2000). For the children with less extreme problems who attend language units in mainstream schools the aim is usually to make a successful transition to full-time attendance in an ordinary class within a specified period. Yet in a recent survey, Botting *et al.* (1998) showed that nearly two-thirds of monolingual children in language units in Key Stage 1 continued in a language

---

A language disorder is that language profile which, although it may be associated with a history of hearing, learning, environmental and emotional difficulties, cannot be attributed to any of these alone, or even just the sum of these effects, and in which one or more of the following is also seen:

1. a close, positive family history of specific difficulty in language development;

2. evidence of cerebral dysfunction, either during development or by the presence of neurological signs;

3. a mismatch between the various subsystems of language in relation to other aspects of cognitive development;

4. a failure to catch up with 'generalized' language help.

Figure 10.6 Defining language disorder by inclusion
Source: Lees and Urwin (1997: 15).

unit after the end of Year 2. It is important to plan carefully for the transition from such units to full-time attendance in mainstream classes (Nelson 1998). Activity 10.4 gives you the opportunity to consider what plans you would make to prepare for a particular child's transition. A follow-up report on a cohort of young people with a history of specific speech and language difficulties indicated that, while their primary educational challenges in secondary school revolved around literacy, they continued to have subtle communication problems with peers and teachers. These put them at risk of behavioural, emotional and social difficulties (Dockrell *et al.* 2007).

Activity 10.4   Planning the future of a child attending a language unit

Peter (aged 6) was born prematurely. His development has been normal except for language skills. His motor coordination is good, and he relates to other children and to adults in a friendly and trusting way. The only concern about his social adjustment is that, when he is frustrated over a communication problem, he will sometimes have a temper tantrum. Comparing him to his older sister and brother, his mother says: 'He is no different from them really. They used to have tantrums sometimes at his age. But he has them more often because he gets frustrated more often.' In the language unit the tantrums are closely monitored and controlled. The staff take avoiding action when they can see frustration building up. The learning support assistant says: 'We can usually head it off.'

The language unit is located in an infant school, and, like all the pupils there, Peter is a member of an ordinary class as well as of the unit. He starts each day in his Year 2 classroom where he sits quietly through circle time in a state that the class teacher describes as 'all right but disengaged'. He has made progress in comprehension and use of language since entering the unit. He now follows almost all procedural instructions from teachers without relying on checking what other children are doing. He will respond to questions with one- or two-word answers in a group setting and can often produce fuller sentences in conversations on his own with adults in the unit. He has a small word recognition vocabulary in reading and a basic grasp of number concepts. He has not participated in the Literacy and Numeracy Hour routines in the ordinary classroom.

Peter's parents wish him to transfer at the end of Year 2 to the school near their home which his siblings attend and where his mother is a governor. They do not want him to transfer to the junior school unit which is located in a school at the other side of town, distant from his home. It is planned that he will soon begin to spend each morning in a Year 2 class in the school requested by his parents. His time will gradually build up so that by the end of Year 2 he should be attending that school full-time with continued support from a speech and language therapist. At this stage funding has been approved for a learning support assistant to work with him each morning in his new school.

How would you suggest that the unit teacher, the class teacher and the new learning support assistant plan for these changes? What are the key challenges to be addressed? What preparations will facilitate a good start, and what continuing support will build on the progress that has been made at the unit?

Language difficulties among children learning EAL

The only language difficulties experienced by most bilingual children arise simply because they are living in a mainly monolingual society. Their competence in their first language does not help them to communicate with most of the people whom they meet, yet there is only limited provision for supporting them to learn their second language. They do not have SEN, and readers who wish to learn more about how they can best be supported are referred to other sources (e.g. those accessed through the NALDIC website supporting initial teacher education: http://www.naldic.org.uk/ITTSEAL2).

Even so, it is inevitable that just as some monolingual children have severe difficulties over speech and language, a small minority of bilingual children will experience similar difficulties. There would have been problems even if they had only been learning one language. Almost certainly there are significant problems in their first language as well as in their second. But in their case the recognition of the problem in a nursery or at school may be delayed because of confusion among those working with them (Ofsted 1997a). Ethnic differences in rates of referral for language delay have varied over time. Local surveys reviewed by Winter (1999) suggest that children from linguistic minority backgrounds have tended to be referred to speech and language therapists when they are older, on average, than monolingual children with the same problems (Winter 1999: 86; cf. Stow and Dodd 2005). In a national survey of children in language units, Crutchley *et al.* (1997a) found that bilingual pupils in the units tended to have more severe difficulties than their monolingual peers and to progress less quickly. For a long time there was relatively little coverage of ethnic, linguistic and cultural diversity in the literature on language difficulties and disorders. Gradually textbooks have begun to reflect the significance of this issue for those working in the field (e.g. Martin and Miller 2003).

One source of potential confusion is that some children develop their first language (L1) normally until they start to learn their second (L2). There may then be arrested development of L1 or even some language loss as they use L2 more and more for everyday purposes as well as at school. Children can be misdiagnosed as having specific language impairment if they are then perceived as having difficulties in both languages. Schiff-Myers (1992) argued that this error will be avoided if enough is learned about their early language history. In line with commentators quoted above, she suggested that this should include:

- a description of the form and nature of the language(s) used in the home both by caretakers and by the child;

- the age and conditions under which the child began to learn L2 (probing to check whether this might have occurred before proficiency in L1 was fully established);

- the ages at which the child achieved linguistic developmental milestones in the L1 before being exposed to L2;

- family contacts with their country of origin;

- the motivation to become or remain proficient in each language (which will be affected by attitudes in the home, the school and the community towards the child's home language and culture).

A further source of uncertainty is that phonological and linguistic demands vary between languages. This means that something which would not be problematic if a child were learning one language may lead to difficulties if they are learning another. For instance, a Chinese child who confuses tones will experience semantic and syntactic confusions that would not occur in English, because Chinese is a language in which syntax is partly signalled by tonal variations, whereas English is not. For example, a tone can change a noun to a verb in Chinese (e.g. 'seed' to 'plant') or determine the direction of an action (e.g. between 'buy' and 'sell') (Zubrick 1992: 135). Any speech difficulties in a child's community language may be overlooked by monolingual professionals who do not speak it (Stow and Dodd 2005).

The planning of provision for children with SEN who are learning EAL must take account of their language learning needs. For all children learning EAL, support for their language learning will always be crucial to future educational achievement. The need for support will be greater if the child's acquisition of a second language is impaired by SEN. In the past, IEPs have often overlooked this issue. Sometimes, in fact, the arrangements made for special educational provision have moved children away from those areas of the education service in which provision for the teaching of EAL was available. For example, the pupils may have transferred from a primary or secondary school with EAL provision to a special unit that does not have access to specialist EAL staff. It is essential that intervention for SEN is planned in such a way that a child's language needs and cultural needs are fully taken into account. A number of options are illustrated in Table 10.4.

Table 10.4 Additive and interactive teaching options

Option A (additive)	Teaching in L2 of the general school curriculum adapted to meet the child's SEN.
Option B (additive)	Teaching in L2 of the general school curriculum adapted to meet the child's SEN *plus* teaching of L2 on a withdrawal basis or through in-class support.
Option C (additive)	Teaching in L2 of the general school curriculum adapted to meet the child's SEN *plus* teaching of L2 on a withdrawal basis or through in-class support *plus* part-time teaching in L1 of one or more aspects of the general school curriculum.
Option D (additive)	Teaching in L2 of the general school curriculum adapted to meet the child's SEN *plus* teaching of L2 on a withdrawal basis or through in-class support with adaptations to meet the SEN.
Option E (additive)	Teaching in L2 of the general school curriculum adapted to meet the child's SEN *plus* teaching of L2 on a withdrawal basis or through in-class support with adaptations to meet the SEN *plus* part-time teaching in L1 of one or more aspects of the general school curriculum with adaptations to meet the SEN.
Option F (interactive)	Teaching of L1 and L2 through teaching in L1 and L2 on a systematic basis all aspects of the general school curriculum with adaptations to meet the child's SEN.

Source: Cline (1997b).

Options C, E and F involve some teaching in L1 as well as L2. Option F, 'bilingual special education', has been developed in the USA but not in the UK. To date, options B and D are much more common, but, where a bilingual language assessment suggests that it is warranted, schools might reasonably aspire to provide options C and E – at least for children from their largest local community language groups. Gadhok (1994) has argued that the choice of options for a particular child should take account of the *parents'* command of L1 and of English.

It should be recognized that all of the options in Table 10.4, except option F, represent an 'additive' approach: something required by a minority of children with SEN is added onto the provision that is made for the majority with SEN as a separate extra. Cline (1997b) argued that there are significant risks that the children's experience of school will be fragmented and that opportunities for enhancing learning through consolidation and through the planned interplay of different elements of experience will be lost. The teaching of EAL generally takes that principle into account. But the principle can easily be overlooked in work with bilingual children who have SEN because expertise is often not shared across the SEN and EAL fields. More joint training may overcome this, and structural changes in schools and LEAs may also lead to improved communication between the two groups. As a result it is to be hoped that other 'interactive' options will be developed to add to option F – options that are practicable in the UK context and achievable by existing staff.

Problems of communication deriving from emotional and social difficulties

Children with SLI can find it extremely frustrating that they cannot communicate easily with the people around them. In the early years they present a higher incidence of behaviour difficulties (Drillien and Drummond 1983). It has been shown by Farmer (1997) and others that the problem is also reflected in difficulties in relationships with peers and that these are most acute in the children with the most severe language difficulties. Farmer (1997: 43) argued that 'children with lower levels of competence with language should be allowed to receive the benefit of positive social interactions in familiar situations and . . . there is a specific need for the development of programmes which concentrate on the development of language skills for social interaction with peers'.

In general, these are secondary difficulties that arise from the child's SLI. Some children, however, develop language skills successfully but are unable to use those skills in the expected way because of emotional and social difficulties. The most distinctive pattern of development of that kind is *selective mutism*. Selectively mute children are able to speak and do speak in some situations (e.g. home), but persist in remaining silent with some other people in some other settings (e.g. school). They often develop effective non-verbal strategies for communicating their needs and getting their own way. While some may appear shy and sensitive, they are often also seen by adults as watchful, stubborn and devious. It is possible to behave in an assertive, even a bold fashion while still not speaking. Adults, including teachers, quite often react with strong feelings of frustration and anger when children in their charge refuse to speak to them. Selective mutism is most frequently reported to develop around 3–5 years as children manage the transition from their family homes to organizational life outside the family in a playgroup, nursery or school. There is sometimes an insidious development of shyness from an early age culminating in persistent selective mutism.

This pattern of development is unusual among language-related problems in that girls become selectively mute at least as frequently, if not more frequently, than boys. However, the phenomenon is rare overall. The best estimate of incidence (Kolvin and Fundudis 1981) is 0.8 per 1000 children. The incidence is probably a little higher in urban areas where there is a high proportion of immigrant or ethnic minority families and in rural areas where there is a high proportion of families living in isolated situations (Cline and Baldwin 2004: Chapter 1). Early reports suggested that selective mutism is strongly resistant to traditional therapeutic strategies and classroom management strategies. But later case studies and reviews have indicated that behavioural methods have a much greater rate of success (Kratochwill 1981; Cunningham *et al.* 1983). 'Stimulus fading' appears to be of particular value (Labbe and Williamson 1984). For example, it might be used to help a young child who talks readily to her mother at home but not to her class teacher at school. She might be helped to develop communication with the teacher by playing with (or reading to) her mother in school. After a number of sessions in which she becomes used to communicating with a familiar person in an unfamiliar setting, the teacher may gradually be 'faded in', and eventually the parent may be 'faded out'. A full account of a linked strategy of assessment and intervention based on stimulus fading may be found in Cline and Baldwin (2004).

Conclusions

In this chapter we have analysed the knowledge and skills that are involved in language proficiency and shown that forms of SEN that are superficially unrelated to language may have a significant effect on how it develops. It is important to identify speech and language difficulties as early as possible, but, precisely because language permeates so much of our thinking and our social interactions, the assessment of language proficiency is a complex task and may proceed by a variety of routes. We outlined different ways in which the development of language and communication may go awry, including SLI and problems of communication deriving from emotional and social difficulties. Under each heading the challenges increase when a child comes from a multilingual background. In the case of children and young people with speech and language difficulties, as in the case of those with SEN generally, the learning environment at school may play a crucial role in facilitating or inhibiting progress.

11

Autistic spectrum disorders

Contents

Introduction

> I am an Advisory Teacher for autistic spectrum disorders (ASD), working for the Local Authority. I work with teachers, and deal with issues relating to the inclusion of children with ASD into mainstream classrooms. Teachers can be very stressed, particularly by the challenges presented by some of these children and the fact that they are able to cause such chaos in the classroom by swearing, banging, shouting and generally disrupting. They can also be very demoralised by these children because although they do a lot of planning for the class, one child can wreck an entire lesson in five minutes. Alongside that they get very concerned that their ability to teach is being undermined and that they are losing their skills. Some teachers are very experienced and when they meet their first child with autism they lose confidence completely, because everything that they have relied on for many years, that has worked brilliantly with all the other children just simply does not work for this child. They may even think about leaving teaching. They also feel that they don't want the child in the class. Without the correct support the child ends up failing and the teacher ends up very upset that they have let the child down.
>
> (Dunsmuir and Frederickson 2005)

Why do teaching techniques that work well with other children fail to work for children with autistic spectrum disorders? Tutt *et al.* (2006) argue that this is due to a fundamental mismatch between teacher skills and expectations and the responses of children with autism. They characterize teaching and learning in school as *'essentially a social interactive event – the transmission of sociocultural knowledge in a largely social dimension'*. However, the difficulties experienced by children with autism make it particularly difficult for them to engage with this process. These difficulties are often described as a 'triad of impairments': in reciprocal social interaction, verbal and non-verbal communication and imagination (Wing and Gould 1979). In this chapter we will consider how these mismatches can be reduced both by increased understanding of the ways in which children with ASD see the world and by strategies and programmes that support their effective engagement with social learning situations.

Definitions

The term 'autistic spectrum disorders' is used to refer to autism and a number of related medical diagnoses such as Asperger's syndrome, Rett's disorder and 'pervasive developmental disorder – not otherwise specified'. What they have in common is a set of diagnostic criteria based on the triad of impairments in social interaction, communication and imagination, now redefined as a lack of flexibility in thinking and behaviour (American Psychiatric Association 2000; World Health Organization 1995). Current government guidance in the UK (DfES 2002c) is likewise based on the triad, describing those with ASD as having impairments in their ability to:

- understand social behaviour, which affects their ability to interact with children and adults;

- understand and use non-verbal and verbal communication;

- think and behave flexibly, which may be shown in restricted, obsessional or repetitive activities.

Different medical diagnoses within the spectrum emphasize different elements of the triad. For example, a diagnosis of Asperger's syndrome does not require abnormalities in the development of language below 3 years of age, as would be required for a diagnosis of autism. However, as they grow older children with diagnoses of Asperger's syndrome become increasingly difficult to distinguish from high-functioning children with autism on the basis of their behaviour, their performance on neuropsychological assessments and the educational outcomes they achieve. The general term 'autistic spectrum disorders' is therefore increasingly used (Ozonoff and Rogers 2003).

The idea of a spectrum also captures the wide individual variation within each element of the triad both in severity of difficulties and the way they are manifest. For example, social behaviour may be characterized either by passivity and unresponsiveness or by very frequent socially inappropriate approaches to others. Here are some examples:

> When Ben first came into nursery he never approached the other children and if any of them came over and started to speak to him he would close his eyes, cover his ears and begin rocking and humming loudly.

> Alex didn't seem to notice the other children were there. I had to make sure the carpet was clear before I said 'you can play with Lego now', because if children were sitting on the carpet looking at books he would just walk straight over them to get to the Lego.

> Suzi is fascinated by long hair. At every opportunity she will run up behind children or adults and bury her face in their hair. She doesn't usually pull the hair but it is sometimes difficult to get her to let go which can be distressing for the children concerned and disconcerting for visitors to the school.

> Simon knows all the bus routes in the area and interacts with people in the playground by approaching them and telling them how to get to certain places by bus. He will describe the route in great detail, barely pausing for breath. The other 6-year-olds just run away when he starts but some of the older girls will humour him or even approach him with a place name or route number and he will respond by describing a relevant route.

Identification

There is no diagnostic test for autism. Guidelines for identification, assessment, diagnosis and access to early interventions for preschool and primary school children with ASD have been developed by the National Initiative for Autism: Screening and Assessment Working Group (NIASA 2003). These guidelines emphasize the need for everyone professionally involved with children and young people to be aware of autistic spectrum disorders. While it is possible to recognize and diagnose ASD by the age of 18 months, Howlin and Moore (1997) report that, in practice, the diagnosis is rarely made until after the age of 24 months and the average age is 5 years. Teachers and other professionals may therefore encounter children with ASD who have not yet been diagnosed. Such pupils may be performing academically at an age appropriate level at least in areas such as reading accuracy, mathematics and ICT. They may show impressive memory for facts while appearing unable to follow normal classroom routines. Engagement in inappropriate social behaviour may have been identified and considered indicative of social, emotional and behavioural difficulties by teachers. Parents, on the other hand, may interpret special interests and precocious vocabulary, where these are present, as indicative of giftedness, and attribute teacher reports of behaviour problems to boredom at school.

NIASA (2003: 28–9) highlight the following features in children of primary school age as being ones that should alert staff to the possibility of ASD and trigger discussion with parents about referral for further assessment:

1   *Communication impairments:* Abnormalities in language development including muteness, odd or inappropriate intonation patterns, persistent echolalia, reference to self as 'you' or 'she/he' beyond 3 years, unusual vocabulary for child's age/social group. Limited use of language for communication and/or tendency to talk freely only about specific topics.

2   *Social impairments:* Inability to join in with the play of other children or inappropriate attempts at joint play (may manifest as aggressive or disruptive behaviour). Lack of awareness of classroom 'norms' (criticising teachers; overt unwillingness to cooperate in classroom activities; inability to appreciate/follow current trends e.g. with regard to other children's dress, style of speech, interests etc.). Easily overwhelmed by social and other stimulation. Failure to relate normally to adults (too intense/no relationship). Showing extreme reactions to invasion of personal space and extreme resistance to being 'hurried'.

3   *Impairment of interests, activities and behaviours:* Lack of flexible, cooperative imaginative play/creativity, although certain imaginary scenarios (e.g. copied from videos or cartoons) may be frequently re-enacted alone. Difficulty in organising self in relation to unstructured space (e.g. hugging the perimeter of playgrounds, halls). Inability to cope with change or unstructured situations, even ones that other children enjoy (such as school trips, teachers being away etc.).

4   *Other factors:* Unusual profile of skills/deficits (e.g. social and motor skills very poorly developed, whilst general knowledge, reading or vocabulary skills are well above chronological/mental age). Any other evidence of odd behaviours (including unusual responses to sensory stimuli (visual and olfactory); unusual responses to movement and any significant history of loss of skills).

So far the focus has been on primary aged pupils. There are concerns that at secondary level pupils whose ASD has not been recognized may be categorized as having learning difficulties or social, emotional and behavioural difficulties. There are concerns also about the adequacy of provision for older pupils, especially those who are higher functioning who may not easily be integrated within local mainstream provision (Connor 2005; Batten *et al.* 2006). This is illustrated in Activity 11.1, which presents an interview with a secondary school SENCO about Peter who is in Year 9.

Assessment

Once a concern has been identified, NIASA (2003) recommend a three-stage assessment framework. Stage 1 is *general multi-disciplinary developmental assessment* (GDA). This is a general health-based assessment for any child with a possible developmental problem and comprises: a clear identification of concerns, a developmental history, a full medical examination and appropriate further tests. The local authority will be notified at this stage if special educational needs are suspected.

Stage 2 is *multi-agency assessment* (MAA). It is recommended that a named key worker should be appointed at the beginning of the MAA process and that the multi-agency, multi-disciplinary team involved should be drawn as appropriate from the following key personnel, all of whom should have received specific ASD training:

- psychological (educational and/or clinical psychologist);
- educational (specialist teacher, or early years professional and/or educational psychologist);
- linguistic/communication (speech and language therapist);
- developmental/medical and psychiatric (community paediatrician, child and adolescent psychiatrist);
- occupational therapy, physiotherapy, access to dietician and nutritionist advice;
- ASD family support worker;
- social services (involvement in the care planning and implementation of appropriate early support).

A complete multi-agency assessment should involve:

- focused observations taken across more than one setting;
- assessment of functioning in an educational setting (for school-aged children);
- a communication assessment, including speech and language competences where needed, by a speech and language therapist with ASD training;
- evaluation of mental health and behaviour, given that additional mental health and behaviour problems are common;
- a cognitive assessment, performed in an appropriate setting by either a clinical or an educational psychologist with ASD training.

Activity 11.1   Indicators of autism

Read the following account of an interview with a SENCO about Peter, aged 14, and identify which of the indicators of ASD are present.

Peter, aged 14 years, has a diagnosis of Asperger's syndrome. He has significant difficulties with social interaction and communication, but is an extremely able learner in subjects he enjoys such as science, IT and electronics. His cognitive ability has been assessed as above average and he is able to read well, but is only motivated to read for factual information in his key areas of interest. He has rewired his parents' house, using his father as a labourer. Likewise, he connected the computers in the home into a functioning network. He takes apart electronic equipment, catalogues all the components and uses them to construct novel devices.

As a preschooler Peter attended a mainstream nursery but his parents had to withdraw him due to violent outbursts against other children and staff. This pattern was repeated at various intervals throughout his primary education, including a number of 'voluntary exclusions' until, when he was in Year 5, he was placed in an ASD unit attached to a mainstream primary school. Here he managed to cope with the demands of schooling more effectively, but required a highly individualized approach to his learning and development of his social skills. However, he continued to have major difficulties with other children, often involving aggression. At secondary transfer the choices were special or mainstream school as no unit provision was available.

In secondary school Peter's social skills are an area of significant difficulty. He has great difficulty interpreting facial expressions and in recognizing the emotions of others. From an early age Peter has been an eloquent and polite communicator, although his language patterns have always been more reminiscent of adult than child speech. He is unable to interpret sarcasm or understand other non-literal communication such as jokes. Peter assumes that other people know what he knows and can become extremely frustrated when others do not follow his thoughts or behave as expected. Similarly, he interprets other peoples' behaviour as purposefully directed at him, even if it is not. As a result, an accidental knock from a peer, if not immediately accompanied by an apology, is likely to be interpreted as a purposeful attack. The consequences are that such actions can be met with a vengeful outburst from Peter. Unfortunately these situations are increasingly often complicated and exacerbated by the intentional taunts of his peer group.

Peter has a very low tolerance of crowds and noise, often becoming very distressed in public places. The busy social environment of a secondary school presents him with problems as his anxiety becomes raised in this setting. Even in the classroom Peter can sometimes become violent, upsetting tables and throwing things across the room in an uncontrollable manner. Behaviour plans, Social Stories™, modifications of classroom and curriculum in a whole-class setting have not proved successful in combating his more extreme behaviours. Anger management sessions provided by the NHS do not seem to have helped much either. Now that Peter is a large, strong Year 9 pupil, the headteacher is becoming increasingly concerned about the risk posed to staff and students at the school.

(Adapted from Dunsmuir and Frederickson 2005)

This last recommendation is further discussed as it has sometimes been suggested that formal cognitive assessments for this group of children are not appropriate. However, Howlin (2000) reports that where suitable tests can be used the findings are both valid and highly reliable, often over many years. It is further argued that the pattern of functioning shown by the child in different areas is valuable in identifying particular educational needs, and that children's responses during psychometric testing can provide valuable information on their approach to novel and/or challenging stimuli, behaviour and cooperation in one-to-one structured settings: motivation and persistence on the one hand, and perseveration and resistance to change on the other.

It is recommended by NIASA that a stage 2 assessment should be completed and feedback given to the family within 17 weeks from referral to the MAA team, while recognizing that a final diagnosis may not be possible at this stage. Nonetheless, the child's needs and specific recommendations should be identified and a family care plan (FCP) drawn up for their family. At this stage genetic implications may also be considered.

Stage 3 involves *referral to a tertiary ASD assessment*. The local area team may wish to seek a second opinion, or access to additional specialities if not available at stage 2, such as paediatric neurology, gastroenterology, metabolic medicine, neuropsychiatry or specific advice about treatments including psychological and pharmacological treatments and other specialist therapy services.

Throughout the assessment process recommended by NIASA the importance of working effectively with families is emphasized. In particular, the following elements are identified:

- There should be a two-way information exchange throughout the process. This involves providing parents/carers with high-quality, accurate information which is accessible and begins as soon as difficulties are recognized. It also involves listening to families and recognizing that their views, and the information they provide is central to the assessment process.

- The assessment process should be transparent, with written information provided where appropriate.

- There should be training for carers (parents and others) following identification of the child's needs.

- The views of the child should be incorporated where possible and an advocate used where necessary.

- Cultural differences should be recognized and acknowledged. This involves a commitment to meeting the needs of families from all cultural backgrounds and a recognition that cultural differences may exert a profound impact for families with a child with ASD.

Cultural issues in autism have been recognized as an under-investigated area (Brown and Rogers 2003). However, it is likely that areas of difference identified by cross-cultural research in families of normally developing children will be relevant. For example, parenting styles and their association with child outcomes have been found to differ in different cultural groups. For example, research in the

USA has found that while 'authoritarian' styles of parenting have been linked with negative outcomes in white middle-class families, this association is found less often in African-American families (Lamborn *et al.* 1996; Bates *et al.* 1996). To what degree is the impact of setting clear boundaries for a child who has autism affected by cultural factors?

In relation to core features of ASD, encouragement of attention to persons versus objects in infants and patterns of affective and social interaction have also been found to differ across cultural groups (Garcia-Coll 1990). So the nature of the difficulties in autism is likely to be perceived differently in different cultural contexts, and the characteristics of standard early intervention programmes may appear more appropriate in their focus and approach to some families than to others. While failing to recognize culture as a relevant aspect to explore is problematic on the one hand, Brown and Rogers (2003) caution that making assumptions based on racial identity or socioecomonic background is also likely to be ineffective and unhelpful. A commitment to discussing these issues with individual families is crucial.

Prevalence

Early population studies of autism indicated an occurance rate of 4–5 per 10,000 (Wing and Gould 1979). However, as has been widely reported in the press (see the newspaper reports in Figure 11.1), more recent studies have reported substantially increased prevalence estimates. Chakrabarti and Fombonne (2001) reported rates of 17 per 10,000 for strictly defined autism, and rates of 60 per 10,000 for all autistic spectrum disorders. More recently still, a study carried out in London reported the prevalence of strictly defined autism as 39 per 10,000, with 116 per 10,000 for all autistic spectrum disorders (Baird *et al.* 2006). This is comparable to the prevalence level of 0.9% among the school-age population identified by the Office for National Statistics (2005).

The changes in classification that have occurred since the 1990s might be expected to have had an effect on incidence figures. However, can they really account for 'skyrocketing' numbers of children diagnosed with ASD in the UK, the USA and elsewhere (Fombonne 2003)? In addition to broader classification systems, increased awareness among practitioners, better identification and more sensitive assessment instruments are all thought to have contributed to the increase (Wing and Potter 2002). Much concern has been caused by reports that the measles, mumps and rubella (MMR) vaccination might be responsible for the increased prevalence of autism. However, further research has failed to find any evidence of changes in incidence of ASD following the introduction of the MMR vaccine. There is also no evidence of increased incidence of ASD in vaccinated as opposed to unvaccinated children (Taylor *et al.* 2002; Fombonne and Chakrabati 2001).

There is still much about the causes of autism that is not known. While it is now well established that autism is a neurodevelopmental disorder with a biological basis in which genetic factors are strongly implicated, it has also been proposed that environmental risk factors may interact with genetic susceptibility, possibly involving several different genes, to trigger ASD or affect its severity (Medical Research Council 2001). However, neither the specific genes nor the environmental risk factors have yet been identified. Although prevalence has

---

California cries '273% Increase in Autism and We Don't Know Why!'

A new state report released today raises troubling questions about why California's developmental services system is experiencing a large unexpected increase in the numbers of children with autism, announced by State Senate President pro tem John Burton and Senator Wesley Chesbro, chair of the Senate Select Committee on Developmental Disabilities and Mental Health.

'In the past 10 years, California has had a 273% increase in the number of children with autism who enter the developmental services system – 1,685 new cases last year alone,' Burton said. 'What is generally considered a rare condition is increasing faster here than other developmental disabilities. We need to find out why.' 'The number of children with autism greatly exceeds the numbers you'd expect from traditional incidence rates,' Chesbro said. 'The findings and conclusions of this report show we need to take action now to figure out where this increase is coming from, what the causes of autism are and what we as a state can do.'

(*Los Angeles Times*, 15 April 1999)

New help for teachers to deal with autism crisis
Gaby Hinsliff, chief political correspondent

Teachers are to be given new guidance on dealing with autistic children amid warnings of a 'timebomb' building in Britain's schools.

The number of affected children has soared in the past decade, fuelling fierce debate over the causes of autism – and leaving many parents angry and frustrated at the lack of expert help.

Campaigners say there is only one place in a specialist unit for every six children who need it. Virginia Bovell, the former wife of novelist Nick Hornby and founder of the autism pressure group Pace, said many teachers in mainstream schools had had barely a few hours' training in handling the disorder.

Yet inappropriate teaching could lead frustrated autistic children into aggressive behaviour, with one in five likely to be excluded during his or her school career.

(*Observer*, 21 July 2002)

Figure 11.1   Is there an autism epidemic?

---

increased overall, patterns across samples are consistent in indicating a biological and strongly genetic basis. For example, prevalence does not differ significantly between different geographical locations, ethnic groups or socioeconomic status levels (Dyches *et al.* 2001). However, there appear to be differences across ethnic groups in assessment and provision. In England and Wales children from minority ethnic groups are under-represented in terms of referrals for diagnosis and attendance at support groups and workshops (DfES 2002c), while a survey of 13 local authorities found under-representation of Asian children among pupils with SEN statements for ASD (Marchant *et al.* 2006). ASD is very much more common in boys than girls, and a ratio of 3 or 4:1 is typically reported. Proportionally more boys are identified at higher intelligence levels (Volkmar *et al.* 2004), so that among those with high functioning autism and Asperger's syndrome the ratio of boys to girls may be as high as 15:1. By contrast, in groups of children who have severe learning difficulties as well as autism the ratio of boys to girls may be as low as 2 : 1. The reasons for this gender imbalance and interaction with intelligence are not yet known.

Understanding autistic spectrum disorders

The *Good Practice Guidance* on ASD (DfES 2002c) highlights the importance for all staff involved in the education of pupils with ASD of developing their knowledge and understanding. Knowledge of the characteristic features of the learning style of pupils with ASD is considered important in structuring situations in ways that will promote learning. An understanding of the challenges that can be presented by having an ASD is regarded as crucial in preventing misinterpretation of a child's behaviour and informing appropriate responses. In addition, it is recognized that although children with ASD share difficulties described by the triad of impairments, these can be manifest in widely differing ways between individuals. Staff will therefore need flexibility and resourcefulness in applying this knowledge and understanding to problem-solving for particular pupils with ASD in specific educational contexts.

While DfES (2002c) recommends the development of knowledge and understanding as an essential training requirement for all staff, not just teachers, a lack of this very element had been identified as a key problem with much existing in-service training. Writing about some of the most widely available such training, associated with the TEACCH programme (see below), Jordan (2001: 12) commented: 'Too often in the UK such training reduces to single short courses, not backed by any understanding of autistic spectrum disorders and resulting in teachers performing rituals without understanding and with no ability to adapt and adjust to meet individual needs or circumstances.' G. Jones (2006) points out that knowledge of the principles underlying interventions provides staff with the basis to modify their approach in response to changing needs and circumstances. Psychological research over the last 20 years has made a particularly important contribution in developing knowledge and understanding of children with ASD. This has been especially so in relation to the development of cognitive theories of ASD. These are outlined in the next section of this chapter and feature prominently in most current in-service training initiatives for staff in schools, for example the ASD Toolkit for Teachers (Warwickshire County Council 2005).

Frith (2005) uses the causal modelling framework (see Chapter 5) to illustrate the way in which a cognitive theory of ASD can be used to understand relationships between multiple biological influences on the one hand and multiple behavioural manifestations on the other. The theory of autism depicted in Figure 11.2, the 'theory of mind' or 'mentalizing' deficit hypothesis, is one that has proved particularly influential and relevant in education. This is the theory that will be described first in this section. However, as Frith (2005) points out, the framework can readily be used to model other theories and associated areas of difficulty or relative strength. Indeed, Morton (2004) reports that the causal modelling framework was originally created to provide a means of making sense of what was known about ASD and illustrates how it can be used to compare and contrast different theories and their predictions.

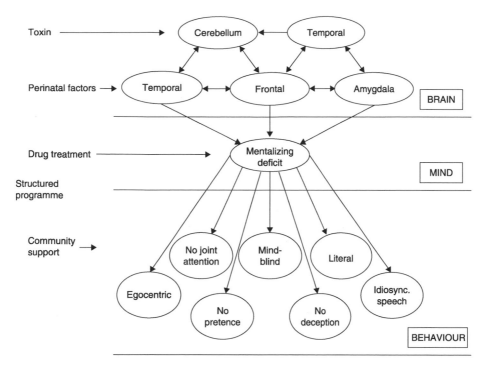

Figure 11.2 A causal model of ASD
Source: From Frith (2005).

Theory of mind

Theory of mind refers to the ability to 'mind-read' or attribute mental states to others. This 'mentalizing' ability allows us to implicitly attribute beliefs and motives to others. Baron-Cohen *et al.* (1985) were the first to suggest that many of the social and communication difficulties characteristic of autism may stem from an impairment in mentalizing ability. This theory has received strong support from many studies using different types of tasks. Prominent among these have been 'false belief tasks' which test whether children can understand that others could have a false belief, and use that understanding to predict behaviour. For example, in the Smarties task young children are shown a Smarties tube by an adult who shakes it so the child can hear it rattling. The child is then asked what is in the tube, but when they say 'Smarties' they are shown that the tube only contains a pen top. Then another child comes into the room and the adult quietly asks the first child what the new child will say if asked what is in the tube. By around 4 years of age typically developing children will say 'Smarties' as they can understand that before the new child has seen the pen top inside the tube they will have a false belief about the tube's contents. However, most children with ASD will say 'pen top'. They seem to have a particular difficulty in understanding that others can have different beliefs from themselves, something which is not difficult for children of similar intellectual development with other developmental difficulties, such as Down's syndrome.

However not all children with ASD fail simple false belief tasks, such as the Smarties task, and many higher-functioning children will eventually be able to pass these tasks although this will usually be 5 years later than is the case with typically developing children (Happé 1995). Even for those children with autism who eventually succeed with simple mentalizing tasks, more complex tasks can continue to present difficulties. Happé (1994) found this with a series of stories that required second-order theory of mind abilities. Here is an example of one of these 'strange stories':

> One day Aunty Jane came to visit Peter. Now Peter loves his aunt very much, but today she is wearing a new hat, which Peter thinks is very ugly indeed. Peter thinks his aunt looks silly in it, and much nicer in her old hat. But when Aunty Jane asks Peter, 'How do you like my new hat?' Peter says, 'Oh, it's very nice.'
> Q1: Is it true what Peter said? (Answer: No)
> Q2: Why did Peter say that?

First-order theory of mind tasks, such as the Smarties task, require the child to understand what another person in a situation thinks. Second-order theory of mind tasks, such as the strange stories, require the child to understand what one of the characters in a situation thinks about the thoughts or beliefs of a second character. Brain imaging studies conducted with adults who have high-functioning autism indicate differences from typically developing adults in the pattern of brain activation elicited by tasks involving mentalizing, including Happé's strange stories (see Frith 2003: Chapter 11). It seems that individuals with autism may be able to compensate to some extent for the lack of a mentalizing mechanism by learning alternative strategies – for example, applying explicit procedures and rules.

If we examine the range of tasks on which difficulties are experienced and compare them with those on which difficulties are not experienced, we see that there are specific problems with mentalizing, rather than other, extraneous features of the situations. For example, children with ASD are able to use instrumental gestures (signalling 'be quiet' or 'come here') much better than expressive gestures (signalling embarrassment or goodwill) (Attwood *et al.* 1998). Likewise children with ASD had no difficulty using sabotage to win a game, but did have difficulty using deception (Sodian and Frith 1994). In the game, use of sabotage required them to padlock a box containing a sweet when a thieving wolf was about. The use of deception involved lying to the wolf about an unpadlocked box when asked from a distance 'Is the box locked or open? I am not bothering to come all that way if the box is locked.'

Even in the first year of life normally developing children show implicit mentalizing abilities, 'joint attention' skills, that are absent in children with ASD (Sigman *et al.* 1986). Joint attention involves looking where another person is looking or pointing. As young as 8 months of age, normally developing babies will pause in approaching an unfamiliar object to look at their mother and are more likely to continue in their approach if her expression, when looking at the object, shows pleasure rather than apprehension. This requires an ability to discriminate basic facial expressions and, more impressively, an implicit awareness both that other people's focus of attention can be inferred from direction of gaze and that others have different knowledge and feelings that have to be ascertained. It is sometimes assumed that a failure of mother–child attachment is at the root of these difficulties, rather than problems with mentalizing. However, this is not the case. In classic attachment test situations when mothers briefly leave their child with a stranger and then return, children with autism show the typical response. This involves an increase in distress when the mother leaves followed by increased interactions directed towards the mother on her return (Dissanayake and Crossley 1996). But in studies of 'joint attention' at the same age children with ASD do *not* show the typical response.

From around 10 months of age, infants also begin to engage others in joint attention when they point to 'show' objects to them. Caregivers will typically acknowledge the child's communication and the shared understanding implied, for example by commenting, 'Yes, that little boy has a Thomas the Tank Engine just like yours'. Children with autism tend not to engage in this protodeclarative pointing, although they will engage in instrumental pointing when they want an object they cannot obtain themselves. Joint attention skills in infancy have been found to be important precursors of later theory of mind abilities and language skills (Charman *et al.* 2001). Likewise, exclusively instrumental use of pointing is often followed by use of language for instrumental purposes (e.g. to obtain food, to avoid a disliked activity), rather than for communication and the development of social relationships. One reason for discussing these very early features of development in autism is to illustrate how much of the implicit learning and tacit knowledge acquired by young normally developing children is not available to children with ASD but has to be explicitly taught and systematically reinforced across different situations at school and at home.

Activity 11.2

Reread the case study of Peter presented earlier in Activity 11.1.

(a) Which of the problems reported by the SENCO might be attributable to 'theory of mind' problems or 'mind-blindness'?

(b) Which appear difficult to account for using this theory?

Now read on with the points you have noted under (b) in mind. Can any of these unexplained features be accounted for by either of the other theories reviewed in this section: executive dysunction and weak central coherence?

Executive dysfunction

There are some characteristics of ASD which are not easily explained by delayed or absent mentalizing abilities. These include restricted, repetitive behaviours, activities or interest, inflexibility and a lack of foresight and planning. It has been proposed that deficits in *executive functions* can help understand these characteristics of children with ASD (Ozonoff 1997). Executive functions are the abilities involved in preparing for and carrying out complex behaviour. These include planning, prioritizing, monitoring several tasks and switching between them, inhibiting inappropriate impulsive actions, generating novel approaches to a situation and weighing consequences for alternative course of actions. A common feature of these behaviours is the capacity to disengage from the immediate context and direct behaviour instead by mental/internal processes (Shallice 1988).

Executive dysfunctions are very often present in children with ASD but are not unique to them and are also common in children who have attention deficit hyperactivity disorder (ADHD) or traumatic brain injury (Pennington and Ozonoff 1996). Executive dysfunction is very often assessed by means of the Wisconsin Card Sorting Test. On this test children are first asked to sort cards and are given feedback on whether they are sorting correctly according to an undisclosed rule (e.g. number, shape, colour). Once the child has achieved 10 correct card sorts the sorting rule is suddenly changed and the number of perseverative responses is noted, that is, responses that use the old sorting rule despite feedback that it is wrong. More recently, measures have been developed that tap everyday behaviour indicative of executive dysfunction. Gioia *et al.* (2003) describe a study using the Behavioral Rating Inventory of Executive Functioning (BRIEF), a questionnaire completed by parents or teachers of children and young people aged 5–18 years. It is composed of 86 items, organized into eight scales the definitions of which are given in Table 11.1.

The study carried out by Gioia *et al.* (2003) investigated the profiles of 151 typically developing children and 150 children who had a range of special needs, including groups of children with specific reading difficulties, ADHD and traumatic brain injury, as well as a group with ASD. The pattern of results supported the validity of the instrument in that the group of children with combined inattentive and hyperactive ADHD was characterized by frequency and severity of problems with inhibition, while the ASD group was distinguished by problems with flexibility. Gioia *et al.* (2003) stress that the BRIEF is not diagnostic in its own

Table 11.1   BRIEF scales and definitions

Scale	Definition
Inhibit	control impulses, appropriately stop own behavior at the proper time
Shift	move easily from one situation, activity, or aspect of a problem to another as the situation demands, solve problems flexibly
Emotional control	modulate emotional responses appropriately
Initiate	begin a task or activity; independently generate ideas
Working memory	hold information in mind for the purpose of completing a task
Plan/organize	anticipate future events, set goals, develop appropriate steps to carry out associated tasks or actions
Organization of materials	keep work space, play areas, and materials orderly
Monitor	check work; assess performance during or after finishing a task to ensure attainment of goal; keep track of the effect of own behaviour on others

right with individual children and its appropriate use is as part of a broadly based assessment. However, Goodlin-Jones and Solomon (2003) highlight it as a particularly useful tool for assessing the impact of executive dysfunctions on 'real-world' performance in order to inform intervention planning and modifications to the educational environment.

Frith (2003) suggests that the lack of 'top-down' control of attention associated with executive dysfunction may also account for unusual sensory responses, which are frequently reported in children with ASD. These may include hypo- or hypersensitivity, or unusual responses to sensory stimuli of various kinds, preoccupations with the sensory features of objects or perceptual processing problems (Baranek 2002). Where individuals lack top-down control of attention and so do not know what is worth attending to in their environment, incidental features can become the main focus of attention. While flexible control of attention is problematic for children with ASD, there is often great ability to sustain attention. So having focused on an incidental detail, a child with ASD may then fixate on it so that it is difficult to redirect their attention. Although there are individual differences, problems in processing transitory auditory stimuli are often noted, while visual-spatial processing tends to be identified as an area of relative strength (Baranek 2002).

Central coherence

Neither executive dysfunction nor problems with mentalizing can account for relative strengths or special abilities shown by some children and young people who have ASD. One example would be Peter's talents reported in the Activity 11.1 case study, which included the ability to rewire a house to the satisfaction of a local authority building control officer. Even some children who achieve very low overall scores on tests of general intellectual functioning show surprising areas of strength or 'savant' skills. Such skills are quite frequently reported in memorizing by rote. In addition, around 10% of children and young people with ASD have special skills in areas such as drawing, playing an instrument, calculating and being able to give the day of the week for any date in the calendar (Hermelin 2001). Frith (1989) proposed that these kinds of patterns of relative strengths among difficulties can be explained by weak central coherence. Central coherence refers to an in-built propensity to integrate information across stimuli to form coherent 'wholes' and to generalize across contexts where possible. Most people will automatically seek to perceive connections and make 'sense' of disparate inputs.

Frith (1989) suggested that in people with autism this capacity for coherence is generally weak and that this can sometimes have advantages. For example, children with ASD tend to show relatively better performance on the Block Design subtest of the Weschler Intelligence Scale for Children. This involves assembling 4 or 9 cubes so that the top surfaces match a printed pattern. Shah and Frith (1993) hypothesized that typically developing children found it difficult to overcome the tendency to see the pattern as an integrated whole and this made it harder to select the individual blocks needed to reproduce it. This hypothesis was supported by the finding that segmenting the pattern into single cube components greatly helped typically developing children. It also helped children with learning difficulties improve their performance. However, the performance of children with autism was similar whether or not the pattern was segmented, suggesting that they were not affected by the strong drive to cohesion experienced by other children.

Happé *et al.* (2001) suggest while there are group differences between people with and without autism in central coherence, it may be most appropriate to think of central coherence as a cognitive style that varies both in the normal population and among people with autism. Using laboratory tasks such as the embedded figures task (which involves detecting a hidden figure within a larger meaningful line drawing), they found a higher rate of weak central coherence in parents of boys who have autism than in parents of normally developing boys or of boys with dyslexia. There were parallel differences between these groups in every-day life, for example involving special interests, attention to detail, insistence on routines and intolerance of change (Briskman *et al.* 2001).

The idea of weak central coherence as a processing bias rather than a deficit, where local detail is preferentially attended to rather than global connections, receives support from an authoritative review of experimental research in the area (Happé and Frith 2006). It has not received the same level of vehement criticism from the ASD community as the theory of mind hypothesis (Smukler 2005). The idea of central coherence may find greater acceptance in this community in time because it recognizes associated strengths as well as weaknesses and focuses on difference rather than deficit when discussing comparisons between people with ASD and those without ('neurotypicals'). The point is well made in a parody website where characteristic problems of neurotypical (NT) individuals are discussed: for example, NTs find it difficult to be alone, to give sustained attention to detailed information or remember it precisely, when with another person they find it difficult to communicate directly and frequently tell lies, when in a group they feel compelled to imitate each other and agree with the group consensus, even when it is obviously wrong (http://www.autistics.org).

There are many implications of weak central coherence for education, especially involving incidental learning, generalization and the use of context. With regard to generalization and incidental learning, children with ASD will rarely make connections between learning tasks or situations commonly perceived to be similar or between others' behaviour in particular situations and how they might be expected to behave. This means that children with ASD should not be expected to apply previous learning in new situations without training, or at least specific prompting. They should also not be expected to learn from observing others: they will need to be told to 'watch what Sam does when he comes in and do the same – he hangs his coat on the peg under his name, brings his bag into the classroom and sits on his chair ready to listen to the teacher'. Furthermore, in teaching this sequence it may well be necessary to go through it step by step on several occasions, with Sam modelling each step at first and the teacher prompting thereafter without a model.

Problems with the use of context in reading were investigated by Happé (1997) using homographs – words with identical spelling that differ in meaning and pronunciation. For example, the pronunciation of 'tear' is determined by the context in the sentences 'There was a big tear in her eye' and 'There was a big tear in her dress'. In both of these cases the context needed to determine the pronunciation of the word comes after the word. Happé also included sentences where the relevant context came before the homograph, for example 'Charlotte was very happy, but in Sallie's eye there was a big tear'. Compared to younger typically developing children, children with ASD failed to make much use of the context when it came before the word. When the context came after the word and indicated that it had been mispronounced, children with ASD were less likely to self-correct than the typically developing children. This built on earlier work by Frith and Snowling (1983) who found that children with ASD had significantly lower scores on tests of reading comprehension than on tests of reading accuracy. Even when able to decode words well, children with ASD may not read for meaning or use meaning routinely, although in many cases they can extract information from texts on areas of special interest.

Approaches to education

Placement decisions

The educational placement of children with ASD in UK local authorities varies (Jordan *et al.* 1998; NIASA 2003). A child with ASD might attend:

- a mainstream school with support from a specialist outreach advisory and teaching service and/or a learning support assistant;

- a mainstream school with a specially resourced provision or unit where staff provide small-group teaching and/or support for inclusion in mainstream classes;

- a special school for children with learning difficulties, with or without a specific unit for pupils with ASD;

- an autism-specialist day school;

- a residential school offering a consistent programme across and beyond the school day.

Some children with ASD, particularly in the early years, may be educated at home, possibly following programmes such as Lovaas or Option (see the section on language intervention below).

The first two of these placement options may be regarded as inclusive provision and there has been particular debate in recent years regarding the appropriateness of inclusion for pupils with ASD. For example, Warnock (2005: 1), in reappraising the recommendations of the Committee of inquiry into SEN which she had chaired some 25 years earlier, controversially concluded:

> There are some needs (for example those of children suffering from autism and those of many children in care) which are more effectively met in separate institutions, where the children are known well by their teachers and are not as vulnerable to bullying as they inevitably are in mainstream schools.

There is some evidence to suggest that, even if it is not inevitable, children with ASD are more at risk of bullying than their mainstream peers. Little (2002) conducted a survey of parents of children with Asperger's syndrome or non-verbal learning difficulties recruited via the internet and found that 75 per cent reported that their children had been bullied by siblings or peers in the previous 12 months.

Children with Asperger's syndrome were particularly likely, in addition, to be identified as shunned by peers (as assessed by not being invited to birthday parties, being picked last or nearly last for teams in school and having to sit alone at lunchtime in school). In the UK the National Autistic Society conducted a survey of parents where bullying specifically at school was reported by almost 60 per cent of those whose children had Asperger's syndrome or high-functioning autism and by 40 per cent of those whose children had more severe difficulties (Reid and Batten 2006).

However, bullying and peer rejection in mainstream school are not inevitable. Frederickson *et al.* (2007) followed up 14 children, 12 of whom had ASD, who had transferred from a full-time special school placement to a full-time mainstream school placement with the support of an outreach inclusion team from the special school. All pupils had been in mainstream for at least 18 months at the time of the study and were in Years 3–6. Information on willingness to work with classmates and peer reports of bullying were collected from questionnaires administered to whole class groups. The former special school pupils were found to be just as well accepted as workmates as their typically developing classmates. Peer reports of bullying were slightly, but not significantly, higher – on average former special school pupils were reported to be victims of bullying by 17 per cent of classmates, as compared with 9 per cent for typically developing pupils. It should be noted, however, that peer acceptance was regarded by the inclusion team in this study as an essential feature of an inclusive school. As a result a peer group package had been developed which included workshop activities carried out with the mainstream classes aimed at promoting supportive pupil interaction.

These findings fit with Jordan and Powell's (1995) contention that success is only documented in relation to well-supported situations, where professionals are trained, and that mere placement (even with one-to-one support of an untrained teaching assistant) does not guarantee either inclusion or the meeting of needs. There is likewise no guarantee that designating a provision as 'autism-specific' necessarily makes it so. UK schools and other special provision, including autism-specific provision, generally adopt an eclectic approach. It is very unusual for a school to focus on only one approach or intervention (Jordan *et al.* 1998). Indeed, it is widely agreed that clear research evidence on the outcomes of different educational approaches for children with ASD is currently lacking (Jordan *et al.* 1998; Charman and Howlin 2003).

Jordan *et al.* (1998) carried out a detailed review for the DfEE of available research evidence on the range of approaches in use at that time. They reported that there was some positive outcome evidence of effectiveness for a range of approaches, although in no case could the research be regarded as entirely satisfactory. Indeed, they found that the scientific quality of this research was highly variable. It ranged from very weak evidence – for example, a few case studies reported by advocates of the approach – to controlled studies using objective assessment measures and incorporating long-term follow-up measures. A systematic review of interventions for ASD being used in the USA which was conducted by the New York State Department of Health (2000) was also highly critical of the quality of available research. It concluded that the majority of studies did not even provide adequate descriptions of the treatments or children involved, so it would not be possible for researchers to replicate the studies or for practitioners to implement the interventions.

In the absence of clear-cut research findings in many areas, government advice on how best to work with the rising numbers of pupils who have a recognized ASD has relied substantially on expert advice (G. Jones 2006). This *Good Practice Guidance* (DfES 2002c) is described next. Following that a number of specific approaches are described in more detail. Approaches have been selected which are cited in the guidance as examples of good practice, which can readily be implemented in a range of school contexts and on which there is some promising evidence of effectiveness.

Good Practice Guidance

NIASA (2003) recommend that within 6 weeks of diagnosis *preschool children* should have access to a trained professional skilled in ASD in each local area who can set up an IEP at home/nursery to develop communication, social and cognitive skills in liaison with parents and staff who will be implementing the plan. It is concluded from a review of early intervention studies that there is good evidence for the efficacy of behavioural approaches in leading to positive improvements. While there is no clear evidence to support any one specific approach over another, there is general agreement that quite intensive programmes are needed. In the UK, NIASA (2003) recommended that 'autism-specific' programmes be provided for around 15 hours a week by specifically trained staff while, in the USA, a review by the National Research Council (2001) identified 25 hours per week as the desirable programme intensity level. Both reports support the use of a structured approach to teaching and the involvement of parents, particularly with regard to generalization and maintenance effects. A focus on ongoing monitoring and evaluation of progress is also commended by both groups.

For *school-aged children* it is recommended that local area services should have a specialist teacher who can contact the parents and visit a child in school within 6 weeks of diagnosis and contribute to the IEP (NIASA 2003). The Code recommends that IEPs should be crisply written and focused on three or four individual targets, chosen as appropriate from the key areas of communication, literacy, mathematics, behaviour and social skills. For a child with ASD, it is likely that the IEP will concentrate on targets relating to the development of communication, social understanding and flexibility of thought and behaviour. The IEP might also include some important targets for developing independence skills and widening the child's range of activities and experiences.

Activity 11.3 *Good Practice Guidance*: a whole-school approach

The DfES (2002c) Autism Working Group argued that a whole-school approach is the most effective way of meeting the needs of children with ASD:

- It is important that all staff are aware of the particular needs arising from ASD. They need to understand the reasons for the child's response to classroom tasks and for their behaviour during lessons and breaktimes. If staff do not know about ASD, then a child might be incorrectly perceived as difficult or uncooperative.

- Staff can do much to prevent challenging behaviour through arranging the environment appropriately, analysing behaviour and managing children sensitively.

> ● Considerable emphasis must be placed on whole-school awareness, training and planning (involving parents, pupils and all adults who work in the school), as the concept of an 'autism-friendly' school is developed.
>
> ● There is a need to pay particular attention to the less structured times, such as break and lunchtimes and lesson transitions.
>
> ● In addition to involving all staff in contact with the child, programmes of active peer support are suggested, such as 'buddy' systems and 'circles of friends' (see below).
>
> ● Explicit and clear rules will be helpful and most peers will be able to appreciate the appropriateness of flexibility in imposition of sanctions.
>
> Access one or more accounts of mainstream school-based provision for pupils with ASD and analyse the extent to which these aspects are stressed in the information the schools make available on their websites or in their prospectuses.
>
> (a) If you know of a school locally that has this provision, you might want to look at its website. You might want to look at the website of a local mainstream school that does not have this provision for comparison.
>
> (b) If you do not know of a school locally that is resourced (e.g. with a unit or department) to support pupils with ASD, you can analyse the website information of the following specially resourced primary schools:
>
> Newbold Verdon Primary School, Leicestershire (http://www.newbold verdonprimaryschool.co.uk/index.php) and Carrington Infants School, Buckinghamshire (http://www.carrington-inf.bucks.sch.uk/index.html).

The DfES Autism Working Group (DfES 2002c: 18) advises that effective programmes for individual children appear to be characterised by the following:

● a programme with a focus on communication, regardless of the language ability of the child

● a programme which involves social interaction, play, leisure and life skills

● access to the academic curriculum in ways that do not depend on social or communicative skills and take account of the particular difficulties of children with ASDs in learning how to learn. These may emphasise structure, visual learning and modelling of activities and behaviours

● an approach to managing behaviour which involves assessing the function of a behaviour and teaching an acceptable alternative to achieve the same result.

Interventions to address these aspects are considered in turn below. In terms of overall approach it is worth noting that the *Guidelines* recommend building on strengths rather than teaching to deficits. For example, teaching reading need not be delayed until a child is competent in retelling a story or sequencing pictures. Many children with ASD tend to be hyperlexic, that is, their reading accuracy is good while their reading comprehension is weak. In these cases their good decoding skills can be used as a starting point in building understanding of language. Focus is also placed on reviewing classroom learning environments and adapting them where necessary to ensure they are facilitatory. Adding more structure to the environment and modifying learning tasks by using visual forms of instructions are likely to be important. It is also recommended that 'escape routes' should be provided for the child if retreat to a quiet space is sometimes necessary. Use of ICT may be important in enabling access to academic achievement while managing the amount of social interaction required. If a support assistant is provided for the child it is recommended that they should receive training in ASD and have some employment security so that the expertise developed can be available as a resource locally. Finally, ongoing liaison between school and parents/carers is advocated to ensure consistency of approaches.

Language and communication

Language functioning is strongly predictive of broader outcomes for children with ASD (Venter *et al.* 1992). Mastergeorge *et al.* (2003) report that 75–95 per cent of young children with ASD have been found to be able to develop useful speech through a range of very different language interventions, provided they are specific and intense. Goldstein (2002) notes that much of the research in the area of language intervention with children who have ASDs has focused on children with the most severe difficulties or who are at early stages of development and has targeted quite rudimentary language skills. These strategies will be considered in this section, and will be outlined relatively briefly as many of them are primarily home-based interventions where developing language is a central aspect of a broader intervention focus. More advanced pragmatic and social communication skills are commonly considered alongside more general social skills which are addressed in the next section.

Early language intervention programmes vary along two major dimensions:

- whether they focus on interactions led by the child with ASD or on interactions led by others;

- whether they are delivered in controlled training settings or in naturalistic play or nursery settings.

The Lovaas (1987) approach, perhaps the best known of the home-based early intervention programmes, is an example of an adult-led approach delivered in controlled training sessions. It uses behavioural techniques and discrete trial teaching involving highly structured presentation of tightly defined antecedent–behaviour–consequence sequences. Tangible, usually edible, rewards are used in the early stages of skill acquisition, alongside praise. There is good evidence of effectiveness in developing spoken language in previously non-verbal children and, in the longer term, some evidence of better progress in the development of social and cognitive skills in comparison to children who have not received the programme (Smith *et al.* 1997, 2000). However, claims that engagement in the programme can result in essentially normal functioning have not been widely supported (Gresham and MacMillan 1997a; Rutter 1996). Questions have also been raised about stress placed on families as these programmes involve 27+ hours per week and about generalization of the language learned, with additional programming being considered necessary to achieve this (Goldstein 2002).

Some programmes combine behavioural techniques with approaches that emphasize using response to child initiation in everyday settings. Incidental or gentle teaching (McGee *et al.* 1987) is an example of this kind of approach. Developmental-pragmatic approaches, such as that of Rogers and Lewis (1989), attempt to motivate the child to communicate and, through location in a pre-school setting, to create situations where communication with others has naturally rewarding consequences. The Picture Exchange Communication System (Bondy and Frost 1994) teaches children without functional communication skills to give a picture of a desired object to another person in exchange for that object. The focus is on communication – requesting rather than labelling, requiring inter-action with others from the outset and encouraging initiation of communication. Concerns that access to such communication systems may reduce motivation to use spoken language are not supported by available research. On the contrary, there is some evidence that gaining understanding of symbolic communication through use of symbols or signs may support the learning of speech (Mastergeorge *et al.* 2003).

At the other end of the 'child-initiation' continuum to Lovaas, the Option/ Son-Rise approach (Kaufman 1994) prioritizes entering the child's world, putting them in charge, following their lead and enticing them to engage with the facilita-tor. In order to create an intensely interactive and totally accepting environment, the approach involves segregating the child, possibly for periods of months, from outside distractions and disturbances beyond the facilitators with whom they interact. There has been little outcome research on this approach. By contrast, a number of other programmes emphasize inclusive preschool contexts and peer mediation, for example, Learning Experiences: an Alternative Programme for Preschoolers and their Parents (LEAP: Strain and Cordisco 1994) and the Walden preschool programme (McGee *et al.* 1994). In the UK, early intervention pro-grammes offered to children with ASD and their families are likely to be eclectic both in their focus and in terms of the strategies used (NIASA 2003). As the needs of the children are very diverse and there is no clear evidence that any one approach is superior, careful assessment of needs and ongoing evaluation of progress should allow the construction of tailored programmes that draw appropriate strategies from different approaches.

Promoting socialization

McConnell (2002) summarizes recommendations for education from the research on interventions to facilitate social interaction for children with ASD. It is recom-mended to:

- Assess social interaction in naturalistic settings – at home and in the class-room, in interactions with both adults and children, in planning interventions to meet identified needs.

- Organize the environment to prompt and support social interaction. In par-ticular, to ensure that there is an overall pattern to the day that is predictable and appropriate for social interaction, that there is access to typically develop-ing peers who have preferably been trained to initiate social interaction and that there are arrangements in place for transfer to other settings (e.g. home).

- Teach specific social skills to children with ASD and typically developing peers, providing *in situ* intervention to prompt social interaction. Typically developing peers often need to extend their social skills in order to interact successfully with a peer who has ASD. However, Lord and Magill-Evans (1995) demonstrated that daily exposure even to untrained but motivated peers produced benefits in terms of social engagement, responsiveness and constructive play.

- Fade direct intervention over time and transfer prompting for social interactions to natural occurring contingencies (e.g. school reward or recognition systems) or self-monitoring by the child with ASD and/or their peers.

- Extend intervention throughout the day and to other activities. Ensure that the use of skills learned is not confined to the social skills session.

- Monitor the effects of interventions and developments in social interaction over extended periods of time.

Three specific approaches will now be described. They are ones that have been noted in reviews of interventions in this area (Rogers 2000) and have, in particular, been highlighted for their relative ease of implementation in mainstream settings (Greenway 2000). Two of them, social skills training and Circles of Friends, are described in detail in Chapter 16, so only their particular application with children who have ASD will be outlined here. The third approach, Social Stories, has been developed specifically for children with ASD.

Social skills training

In a survey of over 1,000 parents of school-aged children with ASD in England and Wales conducted for the National Autistic Society, social skills training was most often identified as a gap in existing provision:

> Social skills training came top of the list when we asked parents if there were other forms of support they felt their children needed, but were not getting. 35% of parents say this is the area of greatest need, particularly parents of more able children, including those with Asperger's syndrome.
>
> (Batten *et al.* 2006)

Social skills training programmes for children who have significant learning difficulties in addition to ASD tend to use behavioural approaches. Modelling has been successfully used to teach skills in a range of areas such as spontaneous greetings, cooperative play, conversational speech and self-help skills. Research has found that the children or adults acting as the models need to demonstrate target behaviours at an exaggeratedly slow pace and that the use of videotaped models appears particularly effective (Charlop-Christy *et al.* 2000). It is important to use prompts reminding children to pay attention to the model and it is thought that the advantage of videotaped models may relate directly to the problems experienced by children with ASD in regulating attention. The camera can be used to zoom in on the important elements of the model's performance, cutting out extraneous features on which the children may otherwise fixate.

For higher-functioning children cognitive-behavioural techniques are most commonly used in training social problem-solving and emotional understanding as well as social interaction skills. Bauminger (2002) described the school-based delivery of such a programme with peer and parent involvement. The programme used training scripts from Spivack and Shure's interpersonal problem-solving model, described in Chapter 16, adapted for the age and language skills of the child. It focused on 13 key competencies such as initiating a conversation, comforting a friend and sharing experiences with a peer. In each area three vignettes were written, for example:

> Initiating Conversation – Tom went out at break time and saw Harry sitting alone. Tom would like to start a conversation with Harry, but he doesn't know how.

These vignettes then formed the basis of the following sequence of work with the child:

1   Defining the problem. The teacher helps the child clarify the social goals.

2   Discussing of the emotions that may be elicited.

3   Identifying of the social alternatives that could be implemented in the situation.

4   Considering the possible consequences of each of the alternatives identified.

5   Deciding on the best alternative for this situation.

6   Practising this alternative with the teacher in role play.

7   Receiving homework to practise with a peer partner.

8   Reviewing peer practice homework with the teacher.

The programme ran for 7 months, and was specified in the Individual Action Plan. It involved 3 hours per week work in school with the child's main teacher. The child met with their typically developing peer partner twice a week, one day after school and during one breaktime. Encouraging results were reported with children across the age range (8–17 years) in terms of improvements in their social behaviour and reduction in repetitive or ritualistic behaviours. There was also some evidence of partial cognitive compensation for problems in social cognition in that more relevant alternatives for action were sometimes suggested by the children following training for social situations that had not been discussed during the training programme.

Circles of Friends

Circles of Friends (CoF) is used in schools to support the inclusion of pupils with social, emotional and behavioural difficulties (Newton *et al.* 1996; Pearpoint and Forest 1992), and other special educational needs (Forest and Lusthaus 1989). Commonly employed components of the approach are a whole-class meeting through which classmate support for a pupil is enlisted and a volunteer, special group or 'circle' of friends established who meet weekly with the pupil and an adult facilitator to help set and review weekly targets and devise ways of helping the pupil to achieve them. A small number of studies to date have investigated the use of the approach to support the inclusion of pupils who have ASD.

Haring and Breen (1992) modelled their circles on the work of Forest (1987). Circles were formed to support two pupils with SEN, one of whom was a 13-year-old boy with autism called Chris. Chris was included with typically developing peers in a small number of mainstream lessons and in unstructured sessions at lunch and breaktimes where he was observed to be socially isolated. The circle was established by inviting the participation of two girls who had some contact with Chris in that, like him, they played trumpet in the school band. These girls agreed to take part and invited two boys they knew to join also. A meeting of the circle of friends was held once a week until key targets had been achieved. In addition, training of specific social skills was conducted by the peers between classes and at lunch, and by a member of staff twice per week for 15 minutes in the special education classroom. In the weekly meetings the adult facilitator prompted, supported, reinforced, and directed the discussion when necessary but sought to encourage peer leadership of the session as far as possible.

The purpose of the weekly meetings included:

- discussion of the previous week's interactions;

- analysis of peer data on assigned and independent interactions with Chris;

- identification of skill areas in need of peer and/or adult instructional support;

- discussion of strategies for the areas identified for social skills intervention;

- role play or modelling of strategies to be applied;

- seeking solutions to specific problem interactions or behaviour;

- assessing group member satisfaction and reinforcing their involvement.

Recording of interactions involving Chris by peers and adult observers indicated that his targets had been achieved in around 6 weeks. After that, during a two-month maintenance phase, when fortnightly meetings continued on a more informal basis, there was good maintenance. Following the start of the intervention Chris also started to be invited occasionally to circle members' houses for meals or on day trips with their families. His mother reported that this had not happened for him before. Finally, when members of his circle moved to high school at the end of the year they recruited other pupils to take their places in meeting with and supporting Chris.

In contrast to Haring and Breen, Gus (2000) describes the use of an adaptation of the whole-class meeting, but not the small-group circles, to support Adam, a Year 10 pupil with autism, who was feeling rejected in a mainstream school. The whole-class meeting usually asks classmates about the strengths and difficulties of the pupil who is the focus of the intervention, following appropriate briefings about consent and confidentiality. The framework for thinking about people in our lives shown in Figure 11.3 is then presented and pupils are asked to consider how they would feel if the only people in their lives were the people at home and people paid to look after them. They are then asked how they might behave if they felt as they had described and parallels are drawn with the behaviour they have reported from the focus child. Finally, their support in offering friendship to the focus child is sought in helping them to change their behaviour. The whole-class meeting conducted by Gus included discussion of the effects of autism, rather than a lack of friends, in eliciting support from the other pupils. Gus reported an

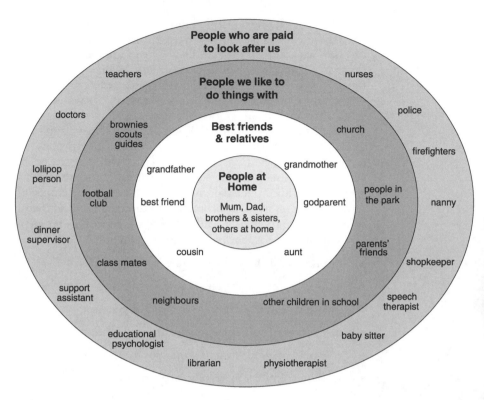

Figure 11.3 Framework used in Circle of Friends for thinking about different relationships with people in our lives
Source: Adapted from Pearpoint and Forest (1992).

improvement in the attitude of Adam's peers towards him, even though they did not consider that there had been any changes in Adam's behaviour.

Whitaker *et al.* (1998) reported a study where both components of the CoF approach (the whole-class meeting and the small-group 'circle' phase) were used with six pupils with ASD in mainstream schools and one in special school. The whole-class meeting and the first six circle meetings were led by a member of the autism outreach team with a member of the school staff. Subsequent circle meetings were run by the school. Positive reports were given by members of the autism outreach team, parents, the school staff and circle members. The positive impact of the introductory session with the whole class was particularly high-lighted. Also at one-year follow-up all the circles were reported still to be running with only occasional consultative support from the outreach team. While 40 circle members reported working, playing or spending time in school with the pupils with ASD, only three referred to them as a friend and only one pupil with ASD had been invited home by a circle member.

Frederickson *et al.* (2005) investigated the impact of the whole-class meeting and the small-group circles. Fourteen primary-aged children, each from a different school, were referred to the programme by educational psychologists. The children had a range of special educational needs, and there was one child with ASD. The whole-class meeting was found to be effective in increasing the social inclusion (as measured by a sociometric technique; see Chapter 16) of all the focus children with SEN. However, the weekly CoF meetings produced no measurable further improvements for 12 out of the 14 children. One of the two exceptions was the child with ASD. In seeking to explain this difference, a number of modifications to the way in which the whole-class meeting was conducted were noted. The children in this class were first given an age-appropriate explanation of the inherent difficulties that children with ASD frequently experience with communication and social interaction, and how these difficulties influence their behaviour. This additional step, in line with the modification employed by Gus (2000), was included in recognition of the difficulty that children with ASD have in modifying their behaviour and the need, therefore, to prepare the children joining the CoF to have appropriate expectations and to take on a somewhat more directive, as opposed to a purely supportive, role in helping the child to achieve the behavioural targets agreed in the weekly meetings.

McConnell (2002) cautioned that CoF was an approach whose popularity was running ahead of its empirical support. There is some limited evidence from controlled and systematic, though small-scale, studies with children who have social, emotional and behavioural difficulties (Frederickson and Turner 2003). There is still less systematic evidence on its use with pupils who have ASD. While the small-scale case study reports which have been reviewed in this section are encouraging, they also suggest that modifications should be made to both the whole-class meeting and the small-group circles phase when aiming to help a child with ASD.

Social Stories

The Social Stories approach was developed to assist individuals with ASD make sense of specific social situations (Gray and Garland, 1993; Gray, 1998). Social Stories are short personalized stories, usually written by teachers, speech therapists or parents. They are designed to provide information which people with ASD find difficult to infer: about the perspectives of others, relevant social cues and expected social behaviour. The stories are usually constructed about social situations that a child with ASD finds, or may find, challenging or confusing. They can be used both to teach children with autism how to manage their own behaviour in such situations and to minimize anxiety by providing a clear description of what will happen, where, when and who will be participating. However, it is recommended that Social Stories should also be used to acknowledge achievement and it is suggested that written praise of this kind may be more meaningful than verbal praise for children with ASD (Gray Center 2006).

Howley and Arnold (2005) describe how the Social Stories approach addresses aspects of effective interaction in social situations identified by psychological theory and research as particularly problematic for children with ASD. Difficulties with theory of mind are addressed by explicitly providing information about others' perspectives and beliefs. Weak central coherence is addressed by linking together into a story features of a situation and information about the people in it that the child with ASD may not otherwise appreciate are related. Emphasis is placed on using different types of sentences to serve these different purposes when constructing Social Stories. Four sentence types are distinguished:

- *Descriptive* – these offer factual statements about the situation and the actions of people in it.

- *Perspective* – these provide information about others' thoughts, feelings or beliefs and offer explanations for their actions.

- *Directive* – these seek to direct the child's behaviour by describing desired responses in the social situation.

- *Affirmative* – these provide information about shared values or expectations within a given context, community or culture.

Gray (2000) advises that for every directive sentence there should between two and five descriptive and/or perspective sentences.

An example of a Social Story which contains each type of sentence, or partial sentence, is shown in Figure 11.4. Given the tendency of children with ASD to interpret language literally, sentences are phrased carefully using 'some', 'sometimes', 'I try', for example to avoid conveying the impression that certain features will always be present and to prepare the child to deal with a number of variations. Howley and Arnold (2005) provide detailed guidance on the production of Social Stories and the use of accompanying visual representations and prompts. The development of cartoon strips based on the same principles is also described.

Reviews of research on the effectiveness of Social Stories (Ali and Frederickson 2006; Nichols *et al.* 2005; Reynhout and Carter 2006; Rust and Smith 2006) have concluded that the approach shows promise. However, all these reviews identify a need for further research that is more rigorously designed than that

---

Things to do at lunchtime

The school bell for lunch goes at ten past twelve. It rings three times. (Descriptive.)

That means we go to our seats and sit down. (Descriptive.)

When all my table is waiting our teacher tells us to go. We can wash our hands in the small sink if we have been doing art or messy stuff. (Descriptive.)

The cloakroom is busy with lots of children. Some get their lunch boxes. (Descriptive.)

Some children are talking to each other. (Descriptive.)

I try to walk past them and into the dining room. Sometimes I say 'excuse me' and wait for them to move. (Directive.)

My seat is on table number three by the door. (Descriptive.)

Eating lunch is good. (Affirmative.)

Then it is time for play. Playtime is a good time to get rid of my energy that builds up when I am sitting. (Descriptive and Affirmative.)

In the play ground the children run and shout. They are loud because they are having fun. (Descriptive and Perspective.)

Figure 11.4 Social Stories – an example
Source: Toplis and Hadwin (2006).

conducted to date. The vast majority of existing studies present a number of individual cases, yet often the strongest types of single case design are not used. In addition, in many published accounts neither the individuals involved nor the various additional interventions they are receiving are adequately described. It is also recommended that further investigations are carried out to determine which components of the approach are critical for its success and to study how best its effects can be generalized across situations and maintained over time.

Supporting curriculum access

Although rarely applied in its entirety as a comprehensive approach, TEACCH (Treatment and Education of Autistic and Communication Handicapped Children; Schopler and Mesibov 1995) has been very influential in the UK in schools and units both mainstream and special. It has been drawn on as a source of techniques for structuring and organizing the learning environment and of materials for promoting engagement and supporting curriculum access. Key features of the approach include:

- providing a transparently structured environment with a focus on labelling of different areas and equipment;

- use of visual timetables showing the sequences of events and activities across a whole day or week;

- incorporating individualized, mainly visual structure and cues into the presentation of curriculum information and specific tasks or activities;

- work systems which use explicit prompts, reminder notes and clear signalling of changes in activity (the aim is to ensure pupils know what work they should be doing, how much is required, how they will know when they have finished and what happens after that).

Mesibov and Howley (2003) describe in detail how these fundamentals of the approach can be used to help pupils with ASD access the UK National Curriculum.

There is a general emphasis on the use of positive strategies of behaviour management, the teaching of functional skills from the start and the development of good work habits to maximize independent functioning within the structured and predictable environment provided. The approach was developed from experience of working in different types of environments with children who have ASD, rather than from any explicit theoretical basis. However, as Tutt *et al.* (2006) point out, the key features of the approach are likely to be of great help to people with executive dysfunction or weak central coherence. It aims to provide a 'prosthetic environment' where such difficulties can be circumvented so that learning and participation are maximized and stress and anxiety minimized.

Jordan *et al.* (1998) noted that although TEACCH is one of the longest-established programmes, there has been little outcome evaluation research. Mesibov (1997) reported research evidence for the rationale of the approach and positive evaluations based on parental reports of satisfaction. While these are also important aspects, they do not obviate the need to assess outcomes for children. Panerai *et al.* (2002) reported better progress by eight children with autism who were following the TEACCH programme in weekly boarding placement in Italy than was made by a comparison group of eight children who were included in mainstream schools on the Italian inclusion model with part-time support teaching and access to relevant therapy inputs. However, these children all also had very significant intellectual difficulties. Further research on applications of key features of the approach in mainstream schools would be valuable.

Potential advantages of information and communication technology (ICT) in supporting curriculum access and participation by pupils with ASD have been highlighted. For example, Murray (1997) identifies the following helpful features of computers:

- visual presentation of information;

- interactive, but do not make social demands;

- enable pace of work to be individualized;

- offer a high level of predictability;

- use of cues and reinforcement can be built in.

Hardy *et al.* (2002) examine how the qualities of ICT relate to the particular needs of pupils with autism and recommend practical strategies and resources across the curriculum. Jones (2002) points out ways in which ICT can be used to overcome barriers to communication. Word processing can help pupils whose written work is hampered by fear of making mistakes. Communication by e-mail and discussion groups, which does not require rapid processing of facial expression and other non-verbal cues, is less confusing and anxiety provoking for many people with ASD than face-to-face communication. Lively internet discussion fora have developed within the ASD community (Dekker 2000; Brownlow and O'Dell 2002). Internet access can assist in using pupil special interests as vehicles for learning and may provide a vehicle for fostering social communication and cooperation without the additional challenges of face-to-face interaction.

Peer tutoring, in particular *classwide peer tutoring* (CWPT; see Chapter 4), is a technique that has been shown to be successful, both in supporting learning in the curriculum and in improving the social inclusion of pupils with ASD. Kamps *et al.* (1994) compared the effects of CWPT and traditional reading instruction on reading skills and social interaction time for three 8–9-year-old high-functioning pupils with ASD and their typically developing classmates. CWPT sessions lasted 25–30 minutes and involved pairs of pupils working together on a highly structured set of activities. The CWPT sessions were followed by unstructured free-time sessions lasting 15–20 minutes. CWPT was found to increase reading fluency, correct responses to reading comprehension questions and total duration of free-time social interactions for all three children with ASD and for the majority of their classmates.

A range of strategies for promoting access and participation, informed by available research and understanding of the needs of pupils with ASD, are reviewed by Jones (2002), writing in the UK context. Myles (2005) presents an edited collection, containing good practice guidance, resources and practical strategies specifically aimed at promoting successful inclusion for pupils with Asperger's syndrome. Although written for teachers in the USA, there is much that is of broader relevance to this section in the chapters on environmental modifications, academic modifications and assistive technology supports.

Functional behavioural assessment and management

Behavioural approaches have long played an important role in the design of interventions aimed at reducing problem behaviours of some children with ASD such as screaming, tantrums, self-injury, physical aggression and property destruction. Systematic reviews of existing research have identified the process of functional behavioural assessment as being central to the design of successful interventions (Horner *et al.* 2002). This approach is based on the assumption that the problem behaviour is serving some function or purpose for the child. Examples of functions that may be served by problem behaviours include:

- communication of needs and wants;
- social attention;
- escape from difficult or boring tasks;
- access to preferred activities and sensory stimulation.

In conducting a functional assessment a psychologist would typically carry out the following four stages:

1 Identify and clearly describe the problem behaviour.

2 Develop hypotheses about the antecedents and consequences likely to trigger and maintain problem behaviour.

3 Test the hypotheses.

4 Design an invention based on supported hypotheses and monitor the child's behaviour.

Stages 1 and 2 might involve interviews with the child's teachers and/or classroom observations. The hypotheses would often be tested by asking school staff to conduct systematic observation and recording of behaviours, antecedents and consequences over a number of days or weeks. The objective would be to ascertain the function the behaviour is serving for the child and to seek to identify alternative, more adaptive behaviours that could be acquired by the child through altering environmental contingencies. For example, it might be observed that hand biting occurred mainly on the days when a particular classroom assistant is present, their response being to distract the child with a favourite toy. The hypothesis might be that the consequence of obtaining the toy is maintaining the hand-biting behaviour and that the function served by the behaviour is to obtain the toy. This could be tested by observing and recording the frequency of attempted hand biting in the presence and absence of the toy, with and without the particular assistant being present. If the hypothesis is supported, an intervention might be designed where the child is taught an alternative behaviour for obtaining the toy, such as pointing to a picture of it, while hand biting is responded to by moving away from the child for a brief period and not providing the toy, an extinction procedure.

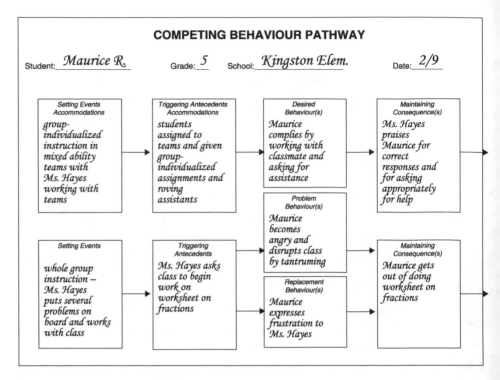

Figure 11.5 Problem behaviour pathway
Source: Center for Effective Collaboration and Practice (2006).

The ultimate goal is not always to teach an alternative, more positive, behaviour that serves the same function. As is illustrated in Figure 11.5, in some cases the function served (escape from challenging learning activities) may be limiting other aspects of the child's learning or development. In such cases the substitution of an alternative behaviour may be seen as an intermediate step while

---

Activity 11.4 Programme plannning for pupils with ASD

Consider the needs either of Peter (the secondary school pupil with ASD described in Activity 11.1) or of a child with ASD known to you. Consider also the recommendations of the DfES Autism Working Group (DfES 2002c), discussed earlier, that effective programmes for individual children should comprise:

- a focus on communication, regardless of language ability;

- a focus on social interaction, play, leisure and life skills;

- strategies to assist children with ASD access the academic curriculum;

- a behaviour management approach which considers the function of behaviour and teaches alternative responses.

You are asked to write three IEP targets and outline in not more than five sentences for each target the main strategies that you would use.

the situation is restructured so that an escape function no longer needs to be served. A useful source of information about the use of functional behavioural assessment is the information module available on the website of the Interactive Collaborative Autism Network, a programme sponsored by the US government (http://www.autismnetwork.org/modules/assessment/fba/index.html).

Conclusions

Increased identification of children with ASD in recent years has required both mainstream teachers and those who support their work, such as advisory teachers and psychologists, to develop further their knowledge and skills in working with these pupils (Williams *et al.* 2005). In this chapter we have examined definitions of ASD, issues in identification and national recommendations on assessment. Cognitive theories of autism have been examined, along with supportive evidence and implications for practice. Good practice guidance on whole-school approaches to support pupils with ASD was reviewed. Finally, characteristics of effective individual programmes were examined and evidence-based strategies described for developing communication skills, supporting social integration, promoting curriculum access/achievement and managing behaviour.

12

Learning difficulties

Objectives

When you have studied this chapter you should be able to:

- outline how thinking about intelligence, learning abilities and learning difficulties has developed over the last century;
- analyse the role of social factors in the development and definition of learning difficulties;
- explain the rationale for different approaches to the assessment of intelligence and learning abilities, and analyse their advantages and disadvantages;
- identify and evaluate a range of options in curricula and pedagogic methods for children with learning difficulties.

Introduction

The concept of *learning difficulties* is at the centre of the law on SEN. The relevant section of the Education Act 1996 opens: 'A child has "special educational needs" for the purposes of this Act if he has a learning difficulty which calls for special educational provision to be made for him'. The definition of a learning difficulty is that the child 'has a significantly greater difficulty in learning than the majority of children of his age' or 'has a disability which either prevents or hinders him from making use of educational facilities of a kind generally provided for children of his age in schools within the area of the local education authority' (section 312). Thus the definition is either normative (greater problems than the majority of age peers) or functional (needing special facilities). It is a broad and inclusive definition which embraces the whole range of SEN.

However, the theme of this chapter is *general learning difficulties* in the narrower sense employed in the guidance quoted in Figure 12.1 (DfES 2005b). The scope of the term as we are using it here may be seen in that figure. *Specific learning difficulties*, in which problems of learning are restricted to a particular area of development or the curriculum, are discussed in later chapters. Here we are concerned with general problems that affect all aspects of children's learning at school or, in more severe forms, all aspects of their development. Work in this area has been strongly influenced by the way in which thinking about the nature of intelligence and learning abilities has developed over the years. The chapter opens with a discussion of these issues before turning to a detailed consideration of learning difficulties.

Learning abilities

Intelligence and abilities

In the past the word *intelligence* was used among professionals concerned with SEN as a convenient shorthand for describing a child's learning abilities. As a catch-all term it was intended to provide an overview of a person's mental abilities – conventionally summarized in the intelligence quotient (IQ) obtained on a general intelligence scale. In relation to people with general learning difficulties, the IQ was used traditionally as a simple indicator of an individual's overall level of intellectual functioning. It is now substantially discredited as a tool for that purpose (Frederickson *et al.* 2008: Chapter 2), though its influence appears to linger on in many ways.

A general intelligence scale comprises a wide range of intellectually challenging tasks that are presented in a standard way to the person being tested. During the development of an intelligence scale for children a large, representative sample of children will have been given these tasks, and data will be available on the average scores of children at each age level and on the spread of scores around the average. When individuals are given the scale subsequently, their performance can be compared to the norms for the original 'standardization' sample. Thus the IQ measure is norm-based. This is a quite different approach from those associated with 'assessment for learning' that were described in Chapter 8. On the face of it, a norm-based measure seems suitable for use in identifying general learning difficulties, since they have tended to be defined primarily in terms of a deviation from normal development. But the use of a general, norm-based instrument to identify and differentiate among children with learning difficulties has been controversial for many years. Those who favoured

Specific learning difficulty (SpLD)

Specific learning difficulties is an umbrella term which indicates that pupils display differences across their learning. Pupils with SpLD may have a particular difficulty in learning to read, write, spell or manipulate numbers so that their performance in these areas is below their performance in other areas. Pupils may also have problems with short-term memory, with organizational skills and with coordination. Pupils with SpLD cover the whole ability range and the severity of their impairment varies widely. Specific learning difficulties include dyslexia (which is discussed in Chapter 13), dyscalculia (which is discussed in Chapter 14) and dyspraxia (which is discussed in Chapter 18).

Moderate learning difficulty (MLD)

Pupils with moderate learning difficulties will have attainments well below expected levels in all or most areas of the curriculum, despite appropriate interventions. Their needs will not be able to be met by normal differentiation and the flexibilities of the National Curriculum. Pupils with MLD have much greater difficulty than their peers in acquiring basic literacy and numeracy skills and in understanding concepts. They may also have associated speech and language delay, low self-esteem, low levels of concentration and underdeveloped social skills.

Severe learning difficulty (SLD)

Pupils with severe learning difficulties have significant intellectual or cognitive impairments. This has a major effect on their ability to participate in the school curriculum without support. They may also have associated difficulties in mobility and coordination, communication and perception and the acquisition of self-help skills. Pupils with SLD will need support in all areas of the curriculum. They may also require teaching of self-help, independence and social skills. Some pupils may use sign and symbols but most will be able to hold simple conversations and gain some literacy skills. Their attainments may be within the upper P scale range (P4–P8) for much of their school careers (i.e. below level 1 of the National Curriculum). (Further information about P scales will be given later in the chapter.)

Profound and multiple learning difficulty (PMLD)

Pupils with profound and multiple learning difficulties have severe and complex learning needs; they also have other significant difficulties, such as physical disabilities or a sensory impairment. Pupils require a high level of adult support, both for their learning needs and also for personal care. They are likely to need sensory stimulation and a curriculum broken down into very small steps. Some pupils communicate by gesture, eye pointing or symbols, others by very simple language. Their attainments are likely to remain in the early P scale range (P1–P4) throughout their school careers (i.e. below level 1 of the National Curriculum).

Figure 12.1   The definition of cognition and learning needs in official guidance
Source: DfES (2005b).

this strategy tended to emphasize that, with the investment of very little time, it makes it possible to:

- provide a reasonably reliable estimate of general mental ability or potential which is stable over time;

- draw upon extensive normative information that cannot be accessed without the use of tests;

- screen for areas of weakness in thinking and information processing;

- provide a baseline index against which to measure future development or learning.

Critics of the strategy have argued that:

- the IQ is a less reliable measure than test constructors claim;

- it gives a misleading impression of scientific precision by presenting an individual's position on a distribution of summarized scores as a single summary number;

- norm-based instruments are only valid for the population on which they have been standardized, yet they are often used for individuals who come from a different cultural or social background;

- knowing a person's measured intelligence does not give enough information on which to base a special education programme for them.

A fundamental problem with defining learning difficulties in terms of intelligence is that it is not clear what is meant by 'intelligence'. Different proponents of the strategy gave a different interpretation. Here are three early definitions of intelligence from Gross (1987: Table 27.1):

(1) An individual is intelligent in proportion as he is able to carry on abstract thinking.

(2) The aggregate of the global capacity to act purposefully, think rationally, to deal effectively with the environment.

(3) Innate, general, cognitive ability.

It will be clear that each of the psychologists who wrote these definitions had something subtly different in mind when using the term. If the quotations are set in context, it is not difficult to see why they saw the concept in different ways. Lewis Terman, the author of (1) in 1921, was conducting a longitudinal study of talented and gifted people and emphasized the feature of their intellectual make-up that distinguished this group from others (Terman 1925). David Wechsler, the author of (2) in 1944, was employed in a veterans' hospital in the USA during World War II. He was responsible for advising on the rehabilitation and employment prospects of ordinary men who had been injured in the war. His concern, above all, was to help guide them towards independence in their everyday lives. Cyril Burt, the author of (3) in 1957, was involved in debates about the impact of heredity and the environment on children's development. He had advised the UK government committee that refined the use of intelligence tests for selection for secondary education (Hadow Committee 1924). Each of these pioneers in the scientific study of intelligence was influenced in his thinking about the concept by the purposes for which he was using the term and by the ideology prevalent in his society at the time.

Activity 12.1   What is 'intelligence'?

1   Think of someone you know who you consider to be 'intelligent'. They can be a child or an adult. If you had to explain to a friend what that individual does that makes you think of them as intelligent, what points would you choose to emphasize? Note down three points that occur to you before reading more about this activity. Then examine the list in the next paragraph.

2   Here are some answers that teachers in various countries gave to Adey *et al.* (2007) when they were asked that question about their pupils: going beyond the given; seeing connections between different ideas; seeing patterns in data; applying concepts to new contexts; thinking logically; applying knowledge from one context to another; demonstrating deep understanding of a concept.

3   To what extent did your answers overlap with that list? What did you add? What did you omit?

4   Reflect on what that suggests about your mental image of 'intelligence'. Can you identify how the context in which you encounter the person you described may affect the notion of intelligence that you use when thinking about them? Bear in mind the account given above of how the contexts in which Terman, Wechsler and Burt were working had an impact on their ideas about intelligence.

Terman made his assumptions explicit as follows:

The essential difference, therefore, [between the moron and the intellectual genius] is in the capacity to form concepts to relate in diverse ways, and to grasp their significance ... One may, of course, question our grounds for designating any kind of mental activity as 'higher' or 'lower' than another. Why, it may be asked, should certain types of mental processes be singled out for special worship? In fact, it is frequently intimated that the individual who flounders in abstractions but is able to handle tools skilfully, or play a good game of baseball, is not to be considered necessarily as *less* intelligent than the individual who can solve mathematical equations, acquire a huge vocabulary, or write poetry. The implication is that the two individuals differ merely in having different *kinds* of intelligence, neither of which is higher nor better than the other. It is difficult to argue with anyone whose sense of psychological values is disturbed to this extent.

(Quoted by Heim 1970: 7)

As the twentieth century progressed, there was increasing support for the kind of 'disturbance' that Terman scorned. In theoretical work on intelligence, two developments in particular affected how theorists responded to diversity in the human condition. The first development was the explicit recognition that there are cultural differences in what is judged to be 'intelligent'. For example, speed of response may be more highly valued in some cultures than in others. Also the context in which a task is presented will affect performance, depending on what is culturally familiar (Ortiz and Dynda 2005).

The second development to challenge the values expressed by Terman has been the introduction of an explicit theory of *multiple intelligences* (Gardner 1993). This approach places less emphasis on the fact that all measures of mental abilities correlate (suggesting that there is a general factor of intelligence). More emphasis is given to the fact that they do not correlate perfectly (suggesting that there are separate abilities that are best thought of as distinct from each other). For Gardner, intelligence is 'the ability to solve problems, or to create products, that are valued within one or more cultural settings' (Gardner 1993: xiv). An ability could be described as an 'intelligence' if there was evidence that in some way it develops separately from other aspects of people's functioning. For example, there may be individuals who lose this ability after brain damage when other areas of functioning are unimpaired, or retain it when others are lost.

The exercise of the ability is likely to rely on an identifiable core mental operation or set of operations. Examples of what Gardner had in mind include:

- *linguistic intelligence*, used in reading, writing, understanding what people say;

- *logical-mathematical intelligence*, used in solving maths problems, checking a supermarket bill, logical reasoning;

- *spatial intelligence*, used in reading a map, packing suitcases in a car so that they all fit;

- *musical intelligence*, used in playing a musical instrument, appreciating the structure of a piece of music;

- *bodily-kinesthetic intelligence*, used in imitating gestures, dancing, running;

- *interpersonal intelligence*, used in relating to other people (e.g. in understanding another person's behaviour or feelings);

- *intrapersonal intelligence*, used in understanding ourselves and how we can change ourselves.

This is not a definitive list, and Gardner added to it later (Gardner 1999). He argued that 'there is not, and there never can be, a single irrefutable and universally accepted list of human intelligences' (Gardner 1993: 59). He saw these distinct abilities as functioning somewhat independently of each other. But when we observe intelligent behaviour, it is usually the result of an interaction between intelligences.

Others have given more emphasis to this aspect of cognitive functioning. Sparrow and Davis (2000: 117) used the metaphor of a family to make this point:

Although these (cognitive) subsystems may differ in their degree of independence or coverage, it is suggested that each unit operates differently and through unique underlying principles. For example, as in a family, each individual member has unique characteristics. To fully understand the functioning of each individual, however, it is essential to learn about the family system. Similarly, to fully understand comprehensive cognitive functioning, one must comprehend the performance of the individual components as well as their integrated or gestalt functioning. Individuals may outperform the sum of their component processing abilities as they develop the capacity to compensate for relative weaknesses by relying on their areas of cognitive strength.

Gardner's ideas have been used as the basis for an approach to the school curriculum that aims to take account of individual differences, allowing pupils to enter through what he called different 'doors or entry points' (Chen and Gardner 2005). He argued that it is necessary for teachers to combine different forms of experience and stimulation in order to meet the needs of pupils with a wide range of intelligences. It will be evident that a theory that emphasizes the possibility of developing distinct intelligences or areas of ability, if it is supported by research evidence over time, must become a threat to an approach to defining learning difficulties that relies on locating individuals along a single dimension of general intelligence. This particular theoretical approach has been the subject of damaging criticism on the grounds that:

- the psychometric assumptions on which it is based are invalid (Brand 1996);

- its key constructs are so broad that they cannot offer a basis for useful classroom planning;

- it relies on ideas about children's abilities that are just as static and fixed as those in traditional factorial theories of intelligence (Klein 1997);

- the criteria and evidence base for defining the separate 'intelligences' are inadequate (White 2004).

However, in spite of its evident weaknesses, Gardner's approach has had considerable influence. This may be because it is in harmony with a vision of *personalized learning* that has attracted increasingly widespread support among political leaders in education (e.g. Knight 2007). However, those who have sought practical ways of expressing that vision in schools, such as Gilbert (2006), have not necessarily been drawn to either traditional views of intelligence or a notion of multiple intelligences as a source of inspiration. As we will see in the next section, an alternative focus of attention has been the analysis of children's learning strategies and learning styles.

Learning strategies and learning styles

Much of the passion in debates on individual intelligence has centred on claims that it is genetically determined and therefore fixed and unmodifiable. A proponent of this pessimistic view was Jensen (1969) who suggested that there are two main forms of intelligence: Level 1, involving simple mental acts of an associative and reproductive nature (e.g. learning the order of a series of familiar objects or pictures); and Level 2, involving complex transformational and abstract mental processes (e.g. learning new concepts, solving problems where the answer is not immediately clear). He argued that we will best educate those with Level 1 type intelligence if we teach to their particular pattern of abilities and, effectively, set them distinct and limited educational goals. A particular problem with his stance was that he appeared to accept that group differences in test performance meant that some groups, such as African-Americans, would be more likely to need to be treated in this way.

Opponents of that position argued that ability is modifiable and that any individual can develop a wide range of learning strategies if given appropriate support. They thought that 'it is more appropriate to regard genetic factors as producing variations in the level of responsiveness of the individual to learning situations that may require corresponding variations in the quality and quantity of investment necessary for growth' (Feuerstein 1979: 8). These authors do not accept any fixed limit on what learning can take place. They argue that it is necessary to examine the situation from the opposite perspective and ask how learning can best be facilitated. That may present a greater or smaller challenge to the teacher, depending on what the learner brings to the task. Even so, the conditions for learning, including the support available, will make a crucial difference. As Chapter 3 showed, this view is much closer to contemporary ideas about SEN.

The notion of intelligence and 'general ability' refers to stable differences between individuals in their competence in a wide range of learning tasks. We might draw on these ideas when answering questions such as 'can he do this?' and 'does he know that?'. But the same ideas appear less useful when we ask other questions that have obvious relevance to the teaching task, such as 'how does he go about this?' and 'what approaches does he prefer when learning?'. With questions of this kind notions such as 'learning style', 'cognitive style' and 'learning strategy' may be more helpful. Identifying children's preferences among possible approaches to learning might enable us to match our teaching strategies to their individual needs more effectively than crude differentiation in terms of general mental ability. This line of thinking has proved both popular and fertile over the last 20–30 years and has had a significant influence on strategies for inclusive education at the classroom level.

Three principal constructs have been employed – learning styles, cognitive styles and learning strategies. The distinction between the first two of these is often blurred. *Learning styles* have been defined as 'qualitative differences among individual students' habits, preferences or orientation toward learning and studying' (Klein 2003: 46) and 'a mode of learning – an individual's preferred or best manner(s) in which to think, process information and demonstrate learning' (Pritchard 2005: 53). Examples might include showing a preference for (and achieving more success through) learning through a particular modality, e.g. visual or auditory or kinaeshetic modes. *Cognitive styles* have been described, in contrast, as involving 'central processes such as reasoning and memory rather than peripheral ones such as perception' (Klein 2003: 47). Alternatively, the distinction may be made by defining cognitive style in terms of an individual's characteristic approach to particular cognitive tasks such as problem solving or information processing. Often the terms are used interchangeably or in combination (Cameron and Reynolds 1999). The third term, *learning strategies*, has a more clearly differentiated definition – habitual ways in which individuals tackle a learning task. Learning strategies are thought of as more malleable and changeable than learning styles and cognitive styles. They are affected by learning style and cognitive style but may also adapt to the learning environment or the demands of the learning task and will be influenced by what and how we have been taught.

Much of the research on *learning and cognitive styles* has focused on adult learners rather than children, and constructs that were developed in studies of adults are often applied to children of school age without empirical evidence of their validity and reliability with that age group. A recent example of a model of learning style is the cognitive control model of Riding and Rayner (1998). They hypothesize that two key dimensions influence how a person approaches the task of dealing with information that is presented to them:

- the *wholist-analytic* dimension – whether they tend to *organize* information in wholes or parts;

- the *verbal-imager* dimension – whether they are inclined to *represent* information during thinking, verbally or in mental pictures.

Riding and Rayner also presented a model of how these dimensions might be related to other aspects of an individual's experience and functioning (see Figure 12.2). Notice that they assume a person's memory of their past experiences plays a significant role in the development of their characteristic learning style.

As might be expected, there is some evidence of cultural differences in learning styles at school level (Hickson *et al.* 1994) and in adult learners (Yamazaki 2005). It is not clear what implications this may have for teaching. Earlier research in this field yielded inconsistent results when attempts were made to evaluate the impact of matching teaching methods to pupils' assessed learning styles (McKenna 1990). Initial results with a questionnaire based on the cognitive control model were more promising (Riding and Rayner 1998), but, while the theoretical coherence of this model has been widely praised, there have been consistently damaging reports on the low reliability of the computerized version of the questionnaire used for assessing an individual's scores on the wholist-analytic and the verbal-imager dimensions (e.g. Rezaei and Katz 2004; Peterson *et al.* 2007). Reviews of studies conducted in further education (Coffield *et al.*

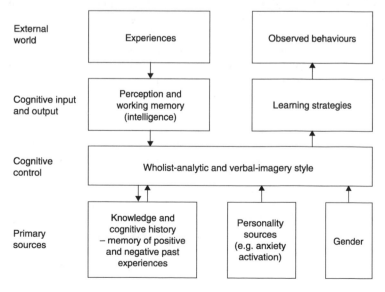

Figure 12.2   Cognitive control model
Source: Riding and Rayner (1998).

2004) and in schools (DEMOS 2005) have indicated that this is a widespread problem with the measures of learning styles that are available to educators. Coffield *et al.* (2004: 59) described the evidence base as 'small-scale, non-cumulative, uncritical and inward-looking'. The proliferation of concepts, instruments and pedagogical strategies was seen as symptomatic of 'conceptual confusion . . . and the absence of well-grounded findings, tested through replication' (Coffield *et al.* 2004: 54).

While their tone was more measured, the DEMOS Working Group agreed that the evidence base for learning styles was 'profoundly unsatisfactory' (2005: 12) and pointed out that the whole question of the validity of the research base is often ignored in the texts that are written for teachers. They were concerned not just that the assessment of students' learning styles is uncertain but also that there is often little evidence that using individual profiles of learning styles will enhance the way individuals are taught so as to improve learning. They saw significant risks in any approach that treats learning styles as largely fixed and innate, as it could:

> lead teachers to label students as having a particular learning style and so to provide materials and sources that are appropriate to that style. Students may then come to internalise this label and think of themselves as a certain type of learner who should concentrate on this diagnosed style. In our view, this is poor professional practice that can damage a student's learning and development. Whilst it may be true that some learners have a dominant learning style, a good education does not limit them to that style or type, but ensures that students have opportunities to strengthen the other learning styles. Whereas bad professional practice restricts opportunities and narrows intellectual development, good practice uses these schemes as ways of expanding opportunities and widening ways of learning. In misguided hands, learning styles could become not a means of personalising learning, but a new version of general intelligence that slots learners into preconceived categories and puts unwarranted ceilings on their intellectual development and achievement.
> (DEMOS 2005: 11)

However, the Working Group did endorse one aspect of classroom practice associated with this paradigm. This is where a model of learning styles is used as a framework to encourage students to reflect on how they learn and thus develop their metacognitive capacities.

The learning styles paradigm is applied more convincingly in work with children who have SEN where the assessment strategy depends on continuous observation, the teaching response is tailored to individual needs and the whole process is treated with some caution. Thus, for example, the assumption that all children with dyslexia will benefit from visuospatial approaches to learning is not supported by the evidence (Mortimore 2005), and a more circumspect and individualized approach is required. Recent research findings have challenged generalized views about the learning styles associated with other forms of SEN, for example the notion that children with Down's syndrome learn most effectively in social partnerships (Wishart 2005). (See also the discussion in Chapter 15 on ADHD.)

The third of the concepts introduced above was *learning strategies*. This appears to have greater potential than *learning styles* for informing effective teaching with children who have learning difficulties. As noted above, it is more clearly defined and is thought to be more readily influenced by methods of teaching. Thus, for example, children who do not generally succeed with academic tasks can be taught more effective memorizing strategies (Male 1996; Bristow *et al.* 1999). However, when children have specific memory problems that have a neurological basis, they may require specially designed classroom interventions that go beyond simply teaching them new learning strategies (Hood and Rankin 2005).

A key generalizable strategy may be the habit of *metacognition* – reflecting on one's own thought processes (how am I thinking about this?) and developing a degree of conscious control over those processes (would it be better if I thought about this differently?). In addition to the direct teaching of metacognitive strategies, the increased use of target setting and self-assessment has played a significant role in general primary and secondary teaching. Porter and Ashdown (2002) demonstrated how concrete materials and visual images may be used to make these approaches accessible to children with severe learning difficulties.

Learning difficulties

Historical background

When the Elementary Education Act 1870 established compulsory elementary education on a national basis in England and Wales, no children could be overlooked just because they found school work difficult. Within 20 years the Education (Defective and Epileptic Children) Act sanctioned the provision of classes and schools specifically for what were then called 'mentally defective' children. These were enabling powers, which could be ignored by local authorities and, in many cases, were. However, by 1913, without statutory compulsion, 175 education authorities had made some provision for 'defective' children, of whom there were 12,000 in 177 schools. But it was decided that a statutory duty should be placed on education authorities to ensure more even provision across the country. In a further revision of the law, education authorities were given the duty to ascertain which children in their area aged 7–16 were mentally defective. They also had to decide which of these were incapable of education in special schools. Responsibility for them was passed to medical authorities, while the education authorities had to provide schooling for the others. As Table 12.1 illustrates, the 1913 law introduced careful distinctions between three terms that had been used inter-

Table 12.1 Official terminology for describing children with learning difficulties

Year	Notional IQ range		
	0–25	26–50	51–70
1913	Idiot	Imbecile	Feeble-minded or high-grade defective
1944	Educationally subnormal (severe)		Educationally subnormal (mild)
1981	Severe learning difficulties		Moderate learning difficulties

changeably up to the last decades of the nineteenth century: 'idiot' and 'imbecile', regarded as ineducable; and 'feebleminded', for whom schooling was to be provided (Pritchard 1963). As that terminology indicates, these establishments offered their students protection and safety at a cost that included marginalizing and stigmatizing them within a paternalistic regime. For a case study of one such regime, see Dale (2007).

Children with moderate learning difficulties

At the end of World War II the 1944 Education Act placed special education on a firmer footing. LEAs were required to ensure that 'provision is made for pupils who suffer from any disability of mind or body by providing, either in special schools or otherwise, special educational treatment, that is to say, education by special methods appropriate for persons suffering from that disability' (Ministry of Education 1946). The regulations issued in connection with the Act included in the list of disabled pupils a category of the educationally subnormal 'who, by reason of limited ability or other conditions resulting in educational retardation, require some specialised form of education, wholly or partly in substitution for the education normally given in ordinary schools' (Ministry of Education 1945). The terms 'mentally defective' and 'feebleminded' were displaced. This 'educationally subnormal' (ESN) group was divided into a 'severe' category and a 'mild' category, abbreviated as ESN(S) and ESN(M).

Provision mushroomed in the period after World War II so that by 1963 special schools were catering for more than 37,000 ESN pupils – more than three times the number that had been identified 50 years earlier (DES 1964). However, this substantial expansion did not have the confidence of all commentators. When the Warnock Committee reviewed the position a decade later, they recommended, among other things, that the terminology should be revised again. They argued that the phrase 'educationally subnormal' was 'imprecise'. It assumed 'agreement on what is educationally normal with regard to ability and attainment', and 'suggests an intrinsic deficiency whereas often the deficiency has been in his [the child's] social and cultural environment'. They advocated the use of the term 'moderate learning difficulties' (MLD) because 'it gives more indication of the nature of the child's difficulties' and 'is less likely to stigmatise the child' (DES 1978: para. 3.26). A study by Hastings *et al.* (1993) showed that a sample of college students did indeed evaluate the term 'learning difficulties' less negatively than terms such as 'mental subnormality' and 'mental handicap'. Norwich (1999) obtained similar results when comparing it to terms such as 'deficit', 'impairment' and 'disability' with three professional groups in education. Kelly and Norwich (2004) interviewed a sample of young people with MLD in the South-West of England and again found that relatively few evaluated the term 'learning difficulties' negatively compared to some other terms that are used.

Traditionally, MLD was defined in terms of measured intelligence – those whose IQ falls within the range 50–69 (see Table 12.1). This approach was discredited at an early stage when studies of special schools for pupils with MLD during their period of rapid expansion in the 1960s showed that the IQ range of their pupil population was significantly wider than the official range. A substantial proportion of pupils had IQs of 70+: for example, 25 per cent in a special school in the Isle of Wight studied by Rutter *et al.* (1970) and 38 per cent in schools in

South Wales studied by Chazan (1964). When Yule (1975) analysed the Isle of Wight data more closely, less than half of those with IQs in the relevant range were actually to be found in the designated special schools. What differentiated the children with low IQs who were in ordinary schools from those in special schools was that the latter had low reading ages. Similarly, the children with relatively high IQs in special schools showed depressed reading skills. It appears that sustained low educational attainment may have been the key factor – a position with parallels in current practice. In a more recent population survey in a London borough only 15 per cent of the children whose measured IQ was below 70 had a statement of special educational needs or attended a school for moderate learning difficulties. It was not low educational attainment as much as behaviour difficulties (particularly problems of social communication) that predicted identification of moderate learning difficulties in the school system (Simonoff *et al.* 2006).

An additional factor in the discrediting of measures of intelligence as criteria for discriminating among levels of general learning difficulties was the accumulation of evidence that groups of children who differed in overall IQ did not show distinctive patterns of intellectual functioning. Those with lower IQ performed specific mental tasks in a similar manner and with the same degree of overall success as younger children who had higher IQ scores, but they did not differ consistently in their performance profile on measures such as verbal working memory (Van der Molen *et al.* 2007).

The growing disquiet about the use of an IQ measure to define MLD did not initially lead to the complete disappearance of the practice. When Cline (1991) studied the SEN statements of 26 children admitted to one inner-city MLD school over an eight-month period, the analysis showed that, for professionals working in that area, measured IQ remained the crucial defining feature of children placed in an MLD school: 'the working model employed for moderate learning difficulties in the Statements is a version of the original model of educational subnormality that has been only partially reconstructed' (Cline 1991: 99).

In spite of such doubts, the number of children assessed as having MLD remains high, constituting almost a quarter of all children with statements of SEN in 2006 (DfES 2006d). However, while they still form the largest single group within the population of children with SEN, the proportion has been dropping from around half in the 1980s and early 1990s (Kysel 1985; Audit Commission 1992). A number of LEAs have closed or amalgamated special schools for children with MLD as part of their move towards a more inclusive SEN strategy, and a survey of local authority officers has indicated that the proportion of pupils with MLD who are being educated in special schools may be falling (Norwich and Kelly 2005). An earlier survey by Male (1996) of 54 special schools for this group indicated that their population was changing. Over 90 per cent of the headteachers in Male's sample felt that some of their pupils had SLD rather than MLD. She calculated that about 1 in 10 of the pupils in the schools were considered by headteachers to have SLD. One factor in the shift is parental choice (with parents of children with SLD preferring these schools to schools in which children with profound and multiple learning difficulties were placed). Such a choice was not available at all until a little over 30 years ago. But there remains a great deal of uncertainty about the future use of special schools in this field. As far as the overall provision is concerned, Norwich and Kelly (2005) reported that the only general trend highlighted by the local authority officers whom they surveyed was a continuing momentum to enhance links between mainstream and special schools.

Children with severe learning difficulties

Until 1970 children with SLD were excluded from the education system altogether and were the responsibility of health departments. A very influential early physician in this field, A.F. Tredgold, had written that 'the essence of mental defect is that it is incurable, and by no "special" education, however elaborate, can a case of amentia [literally, mindlessness] be raised to the normal standard' (quoted by Potts 1983: 186). In the post-war period many children attended junior training centres run by local authorities. By 1967 there were over 18,000 children under 16 on the rolls of these centres (National Association for Mental Health 1969). But there was increasing resistance to the exclusion of these children from the education system. Only 17 per cent of the staff in training centres had taken a short training course designed for the purpose, and just 2 per cent were qualified teachers. Over two-thirds had no relevant professional qualifications at all (Kirman 1972: 128). There was an outcry against this form of provision as well as against the large hospital institutions in which many of the children lived.

In 1970, through the Education (Handicapped Children) Act, responsibility for the education of *all* children passed to LEAs and there began a series of radical changes which were to continue over the next thirty years (Mittler 2002). By the mid-1980s teachers were writing in terms that would have been unthinkable to Tredgold:

> Of central importance is our emphasis on enabling a child to be capable of setting his own goals and having the necessary flexible adaptive behaviours to achieve them. We are concerned with the child's ability to create order from the chaos of the real world. A world which, unlike the classroom, is inconsistent and which brings a wide variety and differing intensity of stimuli and consequent demands on the child . . . The child must not be encouraged to view himself as completely dependent on other people, but to make choices and decisions and, hence, control his own environment. Because we cannot, and would not, wish to account for every situation that the child will encounter, achievement of the skill of generalisation is crucial. This is reflected in the need to avoid placing undue emphasis on the learning of specific skills, or indeed, even in sequences of behaviour, and instead to concentrate on providing learning strategies and opportunities for their use.
>
> (Coupe and Porter 1986: 6–7)

This text and others like it expressed radically different ways of thinking about the educational potential of children with SLD. The terms of discussion had been transformed. However, the ideas of writers such as Burt and Tredgold and the preoccupation with a static, generalized notion of intelligence have continued to influence the way in which many contemporaries think about the education of children with learning difficulties.

The tension between these two views will be one of the themes of this chapter. It can be illustrated with reference to the group of children who have profound and multiple learning difficulties:

> Pupils with profound and multiple learning difficulties who in some respects appear to be functioning at the earliest levels of development and who additionally have physical or sensory impairments. Some of these pupils may be ambulant and may behave in ways that either challenge staff and other pupils or result in their isolation, making it difficult to involve them in positive educational experiences. Most experience difficulties with communication.
>
> (School Curriculum and Assessment Authority 1996: 8)

In public debate there continues to be a vocal strand of opinion that virtually denies that children with PMLD have a full human character – for example, advocating measures such as surgical or hormonal interventions to stunt growth and reduce 'risks' (Hogg 2007). Meanwhile policies on inclusion have led to a shift in the composition of special schools for children with SLD. As we noted in relation to schools for those with MLD above, headteachers of SLD schools report that the proportion of children with PMLD in their schools has increased (Male and Rayner 2007). With improvements in health care the number of children with PMLD is likely to continue to increase (Department of Health 2001). There have been major curriculum developments for this group that offer grounds for optimism about the future (see below). Yet at the same time few children with PMLD themselves benefit from the opportunities that inclusion policies have opened up for many children with SEN in mainstream provision (Male and Rayner 2007). It is more common than it used to be for them to be placed within a special school in a classroom together with children who have less severe learning difficulties. But observational case studies in schools for those with SLD have indicated that the children with the greatest levels of difficulty may effectively be segregated and inactive in heterogeneous class groups for extended periods of time (Simmons and Bayliss, 2007). It is possible for parents to come to think in terms of two different ways of characterizing their child, a negative picture of 'needs' and difficulties (for professionals) and a positive picture of personality traits, communication strategies, and likes and dislikes (for family and friends) (Fitton 1994, cited by Jones 2005).

In the USA, when an IQ-based definition of 'mental retardation' was replaced, attention was paid to children's *adaptive behaviour* – 'the performance of the daily activities required for personal and social sufficiency' (Sparrow *et al.* 1984). The latest authoritative definition of mental retardation put out by the American Association on Intellectual and Developmental Disabilities (2002) referred to 'a disability characterized by significant limitations both in intellectual functioning and in adaptive behavior as expressed in conceptual, social, and practical adaptive skills'.

In the UK, in contrast, an educational focus was adopted and a notion of *curriculum need* was given more prominence. The shift in fundamental educational aims can be illustrated most vividly in relation to children with SLD (see Figure 12.3). The official English definitions in Figure 12.1 invite teachers to draw on classroom observation and assessment and their knowledge of expected levels of performance within the National Curriculum as key reference points. The P scales are a downward extension of the National Curriculum targets, below

Special training was the main remedy put forward when attention was first drawn to the requirements of the defective. In those days the problem seemed comparatively simple. We had only to count up the number of defectives and provide the requisite number of special schools; and the majority would eventually emerge, fitted and equipped for the duties of after-life. Further experience has revealed the error of these ingenuous hopes. We now realise that no amount of training will 'cure deficiency'. The special school may improve behaviour, implant decent habits, and teach the elements of useful knowledge; but it cannot convert a feeble-minded child into a normal adult.

(Burt 1937: 103)

The general aims of education and training for ESN(S) children with IQs roughly above 30 usually include enabling the children:

(a) to acquire certain self-care skills (e.g. dressing, eating, toileting);

(b) to protect themselves from common dangers in home and neighbourhood;

(c) to communicate orally in a limited way;

(d) to become socially adjusted at home and in the neighbourhood, learning to respect property and cooperate in the family unit; and

(e) to become economically useful at home or in the community, in many cases in a sheltered environment under supervision (Kirk, 1957, quoted by Chazan, 1974).

More specific curricular aims include the mastery of motor skills such as walking, running, climbing and dancing; developing visual and auditory discrimination; the learning of simple number concepts; learning to participate in group activity, for example of a musical kind; and the acquiring of certain occupational skills, such as running errands, using the telephone, setting the table, dusting and sweeping.

(Chazan, 1974: 179)

The purpose of education for all children is the same; the goals are the same. But the help that individual children need in progressing towards them will be different.

(DES 1978)

The Qualifications and Curriculum Authority . . . has adopted five key principles which will underpin its work and promote the highest standards of achievement by all learners . . . By applying these principles, QCA aims to ensure that appropriate learning opportunities are developed for all, and unnecessary barriers to achievement are not created.

General principles
In all aspects of its work, including advice to the Government, QCA will seek to ensure:

● the appropriate inclusion of all potential learners at relevant levels of activity;

● opportunities for continuity and progression for all learners;

- the achievement of the highest possible standards for all learners;

- the recognition of the attainments for all learners;

- the provision of easily accessible advice and guidance relevant to all learners.

With the review of the National Curriculum ... the intention is to enable teachers to provide appropriately challenging work for pupils with special educational needs within a new curriculum framework. The guiding principle will remain that the curriculum should represent real entitlement for all pupils.

(Wade 1999: 80)

Figure 12.3   Stages in the evolution of thinking about the aims of the curriculum for children with SLD

their initial starting point at age 5 years. They provide a framework for planning teaching and assessing progress where pupils are functioning below a 5-year-age equivalent level. Initially introduced on a voluntary basis, they have now become a standard part of the overall National Curriculum assessment framework. Schools have to provide data on pupils' performance against the P (Performance) scales when they are aged 5–14, have SEN and are working below level 1 of the National Curriculum. There are P scales covering all national curriculum subjects and Religious Education, PSHE and Citizenship (QCA 2007b). Attempts have been made to refine these materials with more finely graded assessments so that small amounts of progress can be identified and recorded more often (Martin 2006).

Much of the language that has been used in defining learning difficulties throughout the period reviewed above has been based on a premise that the difficulty is *within the child*. Booth and Ainscow (1998: 239–40), among others, have argued that a *social* view of difficulties in learning would be preferable:

On such a view learning difficulties are not something students have, but arise in a relationship between students and tasks and the resources available to support learning ... the insights we gain in understanding the learning of some students, for example those traditionally designated as the ones with learning difficulties, can be applied to the learning of other students not so designated ... We suggest that an emphasis on the social nature of difficulties in learning and disabilities can be signalled by the concept of 'students who experience barriers to learning'.

Hart (1996: 94) also rejected the terminology of 'learning difficulties'. Her concern was to empower teachers to make the adaptations that are needed to their own practices and their classrooms:

prevailing ways of thinking about and making sense of children's learning – or failure to learn – undermine teachers' sense of their own power to make a difference to the outcomes of education. Determinist ideas about ability and educability continually present us with the possibility that limitations of existing attainment might be a reflection of ceilings of innate or acquired ability determined by factors largely beyond teachers' control. The language of learning difficulties and special needs creates the impression that there exists a distinct group of children whose capabilities and needs are different from those of the majority. They raise doubts in teachers' minds about the relevance of their own expertise and resources . . . That is why I believe that we need to set aside once and for all the language of learning difficulties and special needs if we are to become able to exploit more fully the scope available to us for enhancing children's learning.

Social ecology

There were, in addition, other disadvantages to some of the early approaches to defining learning difficulties. As noted in earlier chapters, the social profile of the special schools in this field gives cause for significant concern. Compared to ordinary schools and to special schools for children with SLD, special schools for those with MLD tend to have higher proportions of:

- boys;

- pupils aged 11;

- pupils whose parents are in unskilled occupations;

- pupils whose parents are unemployed;

- pupils from families with four children.

These characteristics of the population have been stable over an extended period (Stein and Susser 1960; Chazan 1964; Kysel 1985; Richardson *et al.* 1986; Male 1996). Recent national data has continued to show a strong association between MLD and socioeconomic disadvantage (Lindsay *et al.* 2006). It is notable that the preponderance of lower socioeconomic groups is not found in those forms of special provision that carry less of a social stigma, such as classes for children with specific learning difficulties (Riddell *et al.* 1994).

Tomlinson (1988: 47) analysed this situation through the perspective of critical theory:

> Critical theorists of education systems are concerned to map injustices and inequalities. They see a sharp contrast between liberal humanitarian rhetoric that education is a force for 'good', for progress, and for equality, and the reality that education systems often mirror, or contribute to, an unequal, competitive, uncaring society. They have noted the way in which education often helps to reproduce the children of minorities, the working-class, and handicapped children, into inferior, powerless social positions. They do not see terms such as 'ability', 'achievement', or 'failure' as objective or disinterested terms, but as social categories, socially constructed by groups who have the power to label others as failures, and they examine processes of labelling and categorisation, as events which usually serve the vested interests of particular groups.

In an earlier report Tomlinson (1981: 10–11) had highlighted the lack of agreement among professional groups in education when asked to give an account of educational subnormality. Their disparate explanations were analysed using the framework that is shown in Table 12.2 (Tomlinson 1988). Tomlinson

Table 12.2 Why Johnny can't read

Level 1 Personal/ interpersonal	Because he's thick
	He can't concentrate
	He doesn't like his teacher
Level 2 Environmental/ institutional	He's got a disadvantaged background
	He lives in an inner-city area
	The school hasn't got the right staff/resources/methods to teach reading
Level 3 Structural/societal	He's black and working class
	Schools help to reproduce cultural, social and economic inequalities

Source: Tomlinson (1988).

pointed out that teachers and psychologists have tended to use Level 1 and Level 2 explanations and that critical theorists have tried to move the focus to Level 3 'in which educational problems can be located in wider structural, historical and ideological contexts' (Tomlinson 1988: 49). Thus, for example, Armstrong (2003: 121) argued that the notion of SEN can become 'a convenient tool for legitimizing discrimination, racism and the lack of opportunities generally for young people'.

Even that sociological analysis cannot do justice to the global complexity of an outstanding major issue in the social ecology of learning difficulties – the impact of ethnicity. Coard (1971), who first drew attention to the issue in the UK, reported that Inner London's day special schools for pupils with ESN had nearly 34 per cent immigrant children on roll at that time, while the ordinary schools in the area had only 17 per cent. He noted that 'three-quarters of the immigrant children in these Educationally Subnormal schools were West Indian, whereas West Indians are only half of the immigrant population in the ordinary schools' (Coard 1971: 5) Subsequent local and national surveys have indicated that the over-representation of African-Caribbean children has been substantially reduced (ILEA 1985; Lindsay *et al.* 2006). When Male (1996) surveyed 54 headteachers of MLD schools, only one respondent considered that black pupils were over-represented in their school. However, a quarter of the respondents expressed the view that Asian pupils were now over-represented in their school compared to their numbers in ordinary schools in the area. This dramatic shift has not been confirmed in more recent national data (Lindsay *et al.* 2006). But it remains a highly sensitive issue. Male (1996: 40) observed that 'this question, alone among all other questions in the survey, was the one that some headteachers (11%) chose not to answer. Of these, a number deleted the question and some inserted comments such as "not relevant" or "not known" . . . Clearly past evidence has indicated that such data *are* relevant and *should* be known'.

Analyses of the composition of 'remedial streams' and 'statemented provision' in secondary schools over the years have confirmed that similar patterns of ethnic over-representation occur. Daniels *et al.* (1999a) investigated SEN provision in 35 primary and secondary schools in two LEA areas. In line with earlier work, they found that black children (a group that included African-Caribbean and 'Black Other') appeared more likely to be allocated to the category 'general learning difficulty' than 'reading difficulty' when compared with their white peers. They were particularly interested in gender and observed that gender differences varied as a function of ethnicity. For example, the male/female ratio was close to 1.0 in the African-Caribbean group and above 2.0 in the white English and Irish groups. In addition, there was considerable variation between schools. Like Male (1996), Daniels *et al.* argued for more detailed monitoring of the way in which resources are allocated. When this has been done in the USA, it has emerged that the form of special help given to black students who were seen as having SEN tended to be outside the regular classroom more often than was the case with comparable white students (Harry 2007: 79).

There has been some evidence that children from ethnic minority communities are less likely to be over-represented in provision for severe learning difficulties. But the review by Lindsay *et al.* (2006) indicated that there is some over-representation in the SLD group of Travellers of Irish heritage and Gypsy/Roma pupils and in the PMLD group of Pakistani pupils. The aetiology of SLD and PMLD is complex (see Table 12.3). Problems may have a genetic basis and arise before birth; they may develop perinatally as a result of problems during birth; and they may emerge later as a result of serious illness or brain damage. In many cases the problem is described as 'idiopathic' because no specific cause is identified. Within any given population the relative importance of each type of cause in SLD/PMLD is affected by social conditions as well as by environmental factors that have an influence on general health. There is often, of course, a link between such factors and ethnic background. In the recent past this has been seen in a particularly stark form in South Africa. Table 12.3 presents data on the causes of mental handicap as reported by Molteno *et al.* (1990) for children born in the area of Cape Town between 1974 and 1986.

Molteno *et al.* (1990) observed that the number of children with mental handicap in the various ethnic groupings was in line with what would have been expected from the birth rates of these groups. However, the distribution of causes of mental handicap was quite different. As can be seen from the table, prenatal causes were identified far more often for the white children than for the black children. On the other hand, the handicap in black children was more

Table 12.3   Causes of mental handicap in Cape Town by ethnic group

	White (N = 122)		Coloured (N = 745)		Black (N = 267)	
	No.	%	No.	%	No.	%
Prenatal	57	46.7	289	38.8	60	22.5
Perinatal	26	21.3	97	13.2	54	20.2
Postnatal	12	9.8	101	13.6	58	21.7
Idiopathic	21	17.2	177	23.8	49	18.4
Unknown	4	3.3	76	10.2	45	16.9
Mixed	2	1.6	5	0.7	1	0.4

Source: Molteno *et al.* (1990).

often associated with a postnatally acquired disease, or else the cause was unknown. The profile of causes for the coloured children was somewhere in the middle between those for the white and black groups. Institutionalized racial discrimination may have an impact on the incidence of learning difficulties not just through assessment bias but also through the impact of broader socio-economic factors. However, data from a recent national study (Lindsay *et al.* 2006) suggest that this impact may be modest in societies where racial differences map onto social advantage in a less extreme way than in the South African regime of that period.

Activity 12.2 Explaining the difficulties experienced by Ambreen and Paul

First, read the reports on Ambreen and Paul below and analyse what you learn about each of them and their situations in two ways:

(a) Draw a diagram using the IF framework (see Chapter 5, in particular Figure 5.4).

(b) On a separate sheet make three lists under the headings used to explain 'why Johnny can't read' (see Table 12.4). How would Ambreen's/Paul's situation be explained using Level 1, Level 2 and Level 3 explanations as described by Tomlinson (1988)?

Then review the two accounts you have produced. What does each tell you that the others do not? Do you agree with the view that both approaches contribute to producing a *full* account of an individual's SEN?

Extracts from a head of year's report from a girl's secondary school located on a run-down estate on the edge of a large industrial town

Ambreen (Year 8), whose first language is Punjabi, is the fourth child (second girl) in a large family. Her school attendance was irregular in primary school, we were told. It improved when she first started at this school but has not been good this year. Often she takes her younger siblings to school and is then late here. Her father speaks little English and her mother none. We usually communicate with the parents through her elder sister. We do not have many Pakistani families in this area, and there is no one on the staff who speaks their language.

Ambreen is functioning academically well below the level expected of her year, especially in maths. We have seen very little progress since she transferred here. She is receiving classroom support in subject lessons for nine hours a week along with other girls who have SEN in the class. She seems quiet and shy with everyone, except one other girl who I think is a member of her extended family. We have been told that she is uncooperative with her parents at home. Her father is a very strict Muslim who expects his children to keep themselves separate from pupils from western cultures. A medical report has indicated that her hearing is satisfactory, as is the vision in her right eye. The vision in her left eye is assessed as weak.

Extracts from the multi-disciplinary advice attached to a statement for a boy attending the Reception class of his local primary school with additional support

Paul is a 5-year-old white boy both of whose parents are described as of limited intelligence. He is the third of four children in the family. Two others are attending special schools. They are both on the non-accidental injury register and are fostered out. Paul is not on the non-accidental injury register.

At a medical examination when he was 2 years old he presented as 'profoundly physically and mentally retarded'. He was admitted to an opportunity group for children with severe learning difficulties within a local day nursery where he made unexpectedly rapid progress. His general health was good, and he showed no sensory impairment. His physical development was slow but normal – though he was 'uncoordinated and unsteady on occasions'. There are inconsistent reports as to whether he was toilet trained by the age of 4. In the classroom he was 'very persistent and lively'. At times he would become uncooperative and have temper tantrums if prevented from continuing to do something he was enjoying. The teacher reported: 'He has made steady consistent progress in all areas of development. He is well motivated and seems to find activities interesting for their own sake and not to please others. He enjoys mastering a new skill and being given the opportunity to practise this new skill over and over again. His level of play has matured, and he is beginning to enjoy playing in the home corner cooperatively with other children, though finding it difficult to share toys'.

At the age of 4½ he was reassessed by an educational psychologist who used selected tasks from a developmental scale and stated that he was 'functioning generally at around the level of a typical 2½- to 3-year-old'. It was recommended that he be given a trial in the Reception class of the local infants school, where he receives ten hours' individual support each week from a special needs support assistant. The school has set out these educational goals:

- the continued development of language skills and attention control;

- helping Paul to improve his social skills in collaborative activities with other children;

- establishing closer home–school links and supporting his parents to ensure that Paul builds up age-appropriate self-help skills.

Learning difficulties: assessment for intervention

Traditional approaches to the assessment of intelligence

We reviewed above and in Chapters 6 and 7 a number of damaging criticisms of traditional approaches to the assessment of intelligence, especially when applied in work with a multicultural population. Yet long after these criticisms were made, such tests have continued to be used regularly for learning difficulties assessment both in the UK and the USA (Woods and Farrell 2006; Haney and Evans 1999). Those who see a continuing role for these methods have emphasized that:

1   While early intelligence scales such as the Stanford Binet and Wechsler series were developed pragmatically and not based on detailed theories of what intelligence and cognition comprise, a number of authors in recent years have produced tests that are carefully based on sound theoretical models. A short list of some major scales for which this claim is made can be seen in Table 12.4.

Table 12.4 Some recently published tests of intelligence and cognition that are claimed to have a strong theoretical base

Test	Theoretical base
Cognitive Assessment System (CAS) (Naglieri 2005)	The PASS theory of intelligence in which human cognitive functioning is seen to be based on four key processes: planning, attention, simultaneous processing and sequential processing.
Kaufman Assessment Battery for Children II (KABC-II) (Kaufman and Kaufman 2004)	The Horn–Cattell theory of intelligence which distinguishes between crystallized abilities (concepts and skills that are acquired through schooling and acculturation) and fluid abilities (involving tackling new and unfamiliar problems).
Universal Nonverbal Intelligence Test (UNIT) (McCallum and Bracken 1997)	A model in which reasoning and memory are seen as central features of intelligence that can be measured without the use of language, by either the examiner or the examinee.

2 Children's performance on a broad-based scale can be analysed to identify a profile of strengths and weaknesses rather than a single overall measure such as the IQ.

3 In clinical practice it is possible to draw upon recent advances in neuro-psychological research in order to move beyond the simplistic models of cognition implicit in many traditional intelligence scales that just distinguish between verbal and non-verbal abilities. Sparrow and Davis (2000: 118), for example, advocate the 'independent evaluation of (1) attention; (2) auditory, visual, and tactile perceptual functions; (3) verbal and language functions; (4) spatial/constructional processing abilities; (5) memory and learning; and (6) executive functions (conceptual reasoning, problem solving, planning, flexibility in cognitive strategies and implementing cognitive plans)'. They argue that different rates of development across functional domains may 'lead to a wide range of configurations in the cognitive system. Such outcomes may have adaptive or maladaptive significance for a person's functional adjustment.'

4 The experience gained by regularly observing children carrying out standard tasks gives a psychologist a sound basis for noting and interpreting an individual's test-taking behaviour and problem-solving strategies during those tasks.

5 In schools the analysis of children's profiles of scores on verbal and non-verbal tests can help to counter the low expectations that are sometimes held of pupils in the early stages of learning English (Ofsted 1999a). They will often obtain scores for non-verbal reasoning that are higher than their scores on attainment and other tests using their second language (Valdes and Figueroa 1994: Table 4.1). A battery that is widely used for this purpose in secondary schools is the Cognitive Abilities Test (Lohman *et al.* 2001).

Those who remain sceptical of normative approaches have replied to each of these numbered claims:

1 Most new scales have not been standardized for use in countries outside the USA and do not directly relate to learning objectives in the school curriculum.

2. Many instruments that aim to make it possible to identify a profile of strengths and weaknesses are not sufficiently reliable for the purpose. Early reviews indicated that, when a profile is used as the basis of a teaching programme that is designed to remedy weak abilities, the results are generally unimpressive (Arter and Jenkins 1979). Later reviews of attempts to use subtest analysis diagnostically (see Frederickson 1999) have drawn overwhelmingly negative conclusions. For example, 'this evidence, both historic and current, suggests that WISC-III subtest analysis should be abandoned' (Watkins *et al.* 1997: 317).

3 If the aim is to obtain diagnostic information on functions such as attention and perception in order to inform teaching methods and the planning of the learning environment, criterion referenced assessment and structured observation are likely to be more effective approaches to obtaining information than norm-based methods.

4 It may be possible to develop satisfactory levels of inter-observer agreement if a simple system is used for categorizing the observed behaviours (Douglas *et al.* 1972). But reliability is not sufficient in itself. There is uncertainty about the validity of the procedure: observations in the setting of a test interview may not successfully predict children's behaviour style or problem-solving strategies in other settings (Glutting *et al.* 1989).

5 If standardized tests are used for any purpose with individuals learning EAL, particular care will always be needed. At the least, confirmatory evidence should be sought from other sources. It will also be important to review any new arrangements or provision after an agreed fixed period on the basis of further teacher observation. As will be seen below, a cycle of assessment–planning–teaching–review is commonly advocated without the use of normative tests.

There is one feature of normative methods of assessment that places an absolute limitation on their value in an educational context and cuts across the specific criticisms just listed. This is that the act of comparing children's performance to an age-related norm cannot help teachers to identify what they have already learned or what they need to learn next. So the information the tests give is of little value in planning an educational programme. The approaches to assessment that were described in Chapter 8 and most of the approaches described below attempt to address that challenge more directly.

Dynamic approaches to assessment

Dynamic approaches to assessment are based on a social constructivist view of child and adolescent development. In this view, deriving from Vygotsky's ideas, higher-order mental processes develop on the basis of cooperating with other people, only later becoming 'inner, individual functions of the child itself' (Vygotsky 1978). Thus other people, notably parents, peers and teachers, are seen as playing a crucial mediating role in stimulating children's learning from infancy:

In this view learning is constructed jointly through social interaction, and understanding can be enhanced by the appropriate amount of assistance, finely tuned to what children know and can do. The emphasis is on potential rather than maturation and readiness, and the role of the 'more knowledgeable other' person is immensely important.

(Watson 2000: 135)

'Static' tests such as IQ tests evaluate what a child has learned in the past – their zone of actual development (ZAD). It is seen as more useful to assess what Vygotsky called their zone of potential development (sometimes known as the zone of proximal development or next development – ZPD). For this purpose 'dynamic' measures are required. Suppose the performance of two boys on a static test is at the same level (e.g. equating to the average for an 8-year-old). They are then retested with some adult help (e.g. in the form of standard questions prompting them towards the correct solution of problems they could not solve before). One boy now attains a score typically associated with children aged 9, while the other reaches a level associated with 12-year-olds. Vygotsky saw the difference between the ZAD (what children can achieve by themselves) and the level they can reach with adult help as an operational definition of the ZPD. In this example one boy has markedly more extensive emerging skills and knowledge than the other: his assessed ZPD suggests that there is greater scope for immediately enhancing his attainments (Vygotsky 1978: 85–6).

With this perspective a further criticism is added to the list of concerns about static tests: they establish current levels of performance but usually tell us little about the processes that underlie that competence (Campione 1989). They ignore functions that have not yet matured but are in the process of maturing. To use a favourite analogy of Vygotsky's, they focus on the 'fruits' of development rather than its 'buds' and 'flowers'. Even if they are intended to form the base for prediction, the process of assessment itself is essentially retrospective rather than prospective. Observing embryonic (nascent, emerging) skills closely would provide a better estimate of individuals' potential for proceeding beyond their present level of competence and would offer more useful guidance on the kind of teaching that will help them realize that potential. Table 12.5 outlines the key contrasts that have been drawn by those involved in developing dynamic assessment.

In the West particular claims have been made for dynamic approaches to assessment in relation to children from ethnic and linguistic minorities. Static tests are seen to penalize children who have had limited opportunities to learn whatever is being tested (Feuerstein 1979). By building coaching or training for the assessment task into the process it was hoped that dynamic assessment would offer a counterbalance to inequalities in experience and thus be less prone to bias (Hamers *et al.* 1996; Hessels 1997).

Different workers in dynamic assessment have different aims in view. For Budoff (1987) the main aim has been to classify children more accurately for special education placement. On the basis of a standard procedure he categorized children as:

- *high performers*, who perform well without support and improve their scores only marginally with coaching;

Table 12.5 Change models vs. stability models

	Change models	Stability models
Assumptions	Human functioning is plastic and modifiable.	Human functioning is stable and predictable in a linear fashion.
Model of learning	Learning embedded in context and culture. So in assessment situations students work interactively with a trained examiner.	Learning is an isolated, individual act. So in testing situations students work alone and unaided.
Primary concerns	• The development of knowledge construction functions • The discovery and remediation of learning problems • Diagnosis and prescription • 'Autoplastic': oriented to relatively active modification	• The identification of rank relative to a referent group • Classification and prediction • 'Alloplastic': oriented to relatively passive acceptance
Model of knowledge construction processes	Theoretical analysis focuses on *processes* of learning and thinking	Theoretical analysis focuses on *products* of learning and thinking
Outcomes of the assessment	• Scores acquire meaning from comparing them pre- and post-mediation • Can be used to develop learning efficiency	• Scores acquire meaning from comparing them to standardization norms • Can be used to inform decisions on eligibility, classification and placement

Source: Adapted from Jensen (2003: Table 1).

- *gainers*, who initially perform poorly but make gains after coaching;

- *non-gainers*, who initially perform poorly and gain little from coaching.

There was a particular interest in identifying children and adolescents who had been classified as of limited intellectual ability but proved to be 'gainers' in these tests. But some later researchers have failed to replicate Budoff's striking results (Lauchlan and Elliott 2001). In any case it seems unlikely that reclassification is the best use of these methods. Higher priority might be given to a different goal – using dynamic assessment in order to plan instruction (or mediation) as effectively as possible (cf. Chapter 8).

There is a range of procedural options in dynamic assessment. The assessment may involve long-term learning with, say, daily training sessions over a week, or only short-term learning may be involved (e.g. when the pre-test, training and post-test phases all occur in a single session). The core of the method is the training phase. There are many different options possible for training:

- simple feedback on correct performance;

- demonstration of the correct solution to a problem (with or without an explanation of its rationale);

- prompts or hints in the form of questions.

Sometimes different forms of training will be combined in a standardized sequence.

A critical issue is whether or not the training is to be standardized and the same for all children or tailored to the needs of each child individually. Feuerstein (1979) advocated and practised a high degree of individualization of the training phase. So did Gallimore *et al.* (1989) in the Hawaii KEEP project in which reading skills were taught through an 'assisted performance' programme. Critics of individualized training highlight the risk that this strategy will make decision-making subjective in both test administration and interpretation. It takes a long time to train in Feuerstein's methods; it takes a long time with each child to use them; inter-tester reliability is untested and suspect (Missiuna and Samuels 1988). One option for future development is to draw upon computer technology for adaptive testing (Guthke *et al.* 1997). Another is to subject this approach to the kind of systematic, controlled evaluation that, as we saw in Chapter 8, has had such an impact on classroom-based assessment for learning. Elliott (2003: 24) has suggested that the agenda for such a research programme might include examining the extent to which:

> dynamic assessments can: (a) result in recommendations for intervention that are (b) meaningful to, and will be employed by, practitioners (parents, teachers, therapists) and which (c) subsequently demonstrate meaningful gains that are unlikely to have been achieved in their absence. Such studies will be complex and problematic yet may be necessary if the claims of advocates of the approach are to be taken up on a widespread basis.

What exactly is measured in dynamic assessment? With a conventional intelligence test the final score recording an individual's performance is usually a quotient formed by comparing the sum of items passed with age norms. With learning ability or learning potential tests based on the dynamic paradigm there is a wide variety of possible ways of measuring performance.

Post-test score

Using this score (rather than a score on a one-off test) gives children the advantage of practice or training. It is thought to reduce the bias that might arise because they are unfamiliar with the task or with test procedures or solution strategies, or because their initial performance is depressed by fear of failure. Using this measure still involves focusing on achievement rather than ability to learn. In theoretical terms it represents an improvement within the conventional psychometric tradition rather than a radical departure. There are examples in the Kaufman Assessment Battery for Children (Kaufman and Kaufman 1983).

Difference score

This score (sometimes called the change score or gain score) is calculated by subtracting the pre-test score from the post-test score. This type of score presents many problems:

1   There is a negative correlation between score on the pre-test and gain score – an artefact that arises because it is statistically more likely that low scorers will gain. This is particularly important for those concerned with SEN because the children they work with will often perform at a low level initially. So they will be more likely to appear to improve their scores, and their difficulties may be underestimated.

2   A difference score draws on two other scores. So, if it is to be reliable, it is essential that the pre-test and the post-test each separately have very high internal reliability (consistency). Otherwise any error component will be magnified.

3   Difference scores are confounded by memory effects (children may do better on the second test simply because they remember aspects of the task from their experience of the first), and by floor and ceiling effects (children may not have the scope to improve their scores with learning because the test overall is too easy or too difficult).

Some of these problems, but not all, can be overcome by constructing a 'residualized change score'. The statistical procedure to calculate this score takes pre-test score differences into account so as to eliminate problem (1). A more sophisticated solution is to apply item response theory (e.g. Sijtsma 1993).

Measures based on the training itself

Typically what is recorded is the amount and/or level and/or kind of training or help that a child needs to solve a problem or reach criterion performance on a task. Examples include:

●   number of items in a standard set on which help is given;

●   number or type of hints given at the child's request.

In this case it is the *cognitive process* that leads to difference scores that is of interest.

Which measure is chosen will depend on the aims of testing. It is suggested that, in general, educationists will find measures based on the training itself more practicable and useful than difference scores. Campione (1989) has proposed a helpful way of classifying the range of approaches in dynamic assessment along three dimensions (see Table 12.6).

It has been argued that some of Vygotsky's concepts have been misunderstood in the West because of problems of translation and cultural distortion (Daniels 1992). A central notion in Vygotsky's thinking about dynamic assessment was *obuchenie* which used often to be translated as 'instruction' but is more accurately seen as referring to both teaching and learning as part of the same interdependent process. For a successful outcome the learner must make active efforts of construction (what Valsiner 2000 calls 'the individual component') and others must

Table 12.6   Classifying approaches to dynamic assessment

Dimension	Ranges between
The focus of the assessment	Assessing by direct observation of improvement and assessing the operation of processes that underlie the improvement.
The type of interaction during the assessment	Standardized interaction (measured quantitatively) and clinical interaction (perhaps measured qualitatively).
The target	Domain-specific skills (e.g. reading text) and general skills (e.g. non-verbal reasoning).

Source: Campione (1989).

guide those efforts in a desired direction ('the teaching component'). Psychological functions that are fully established are the basis on which new ones can emerge. Within the ZPD there is more than one way in which actual learning can occur. Valsiner shows the possibilities as branching routes out of the present: 'Which of these directions will actually be taken would depend upon the co-ordination of circumstances – the decision by the developing person, the guidance of "social others". It is here where social suggestions play their "guiding role"' (Valsiner 2000: 44).

Thus, in seeking to develop dynamic assessment, it may be necessary to stop thinking in terms of a paradigm that has been firmly established in SEN practice in the West in the past – the separation of the processes of teaching and of assessment, as exemplified by the IQ test. In this view, efforts to develop valid learning ability *tests* such as those of Hessels (1997) are unhelpful. Good practice in dynamic assessment will require a constant assessment–teaching–assessment cycle. An alternative view seeks to combine the advantages of assisted (dynamic) assessment with the psychometric standards of the best traditional tests. Ultimately the selection of an assessment approach for a particular purpose must depend on what will best inform intervention and lead to more successful learning.

There are practical issues too. Dynamic assessment takes longer than static assessment (and requires more extensive and sophisticated training). Are the improvements in the information that it offers sufficiently valuable in a particular case to justify allocating those resources? Can these methods be used cost-effectively? Vye *et al.* (1987) have proposed a 'continuum of assessment services' in which assessment may begin with the simplest of screening procedures and continue through a graded series of methods to the most intensive of individualized dynamic methods.

How will the findings from such methods be followed up? Dynamic assessment with an individualized prompt procedure will lead to (or may be part of) an individualized teaching programme. Is it realistic to expect that such programmes will always be practicable in busy classrooms, granted the other pressures and demands made on teachers and the time and particular skills required to put such programmes into effect? Missiuna and Samuels (1988: 21) rephrase the previous point: 'Is the additional time and expense of a dynamic assessment only worthwhile if adaptive instruction is available?' Brown *et al.* (1992) showed that the potentially valuable information that is generated by dynamic assessment is not always utilized by teachers. Elliott (2000) observed that, in addition to the challenge of making time in a busy classroom, there is uncertainty over how much systematic knowledge teachers require of the underlying theory and associated concepts in order to make sense of the tasks they face with this approach.

At the same time, reports of work on *reciprocal teaching* (e.g. Brown and Campione 1996), *instructional conversation* (Tharp and Gallimore 1988), and *collaborative learning* (Meadows 1998) give ground for optimism. Watson (2000) summarized the advantages of these kinds of teaching approaches as promoting learning experiences in which:

- the learner is active;

- the teacher is responsive to pupils' interests and existing understanding;

- educational talk, focusing on the task in hand, is emphasized;

- social experiences are integral to learning and highly valued;

- teachers build on and extend pupils' thinking;

- through scaffolding and mediation, teachers encourage cognitive restructuring;

- pupils' awareness of their own learning is assisted;

- transfer is facilitated;

- challenging tasks indicate that teacher expectations are high;

- pupils are gradually helped to become self-directed, self-aware learners, who are in control of their own learning;

- confidence and self-esteem are raised.

Curriculum and pedagogic issues

As ideas about the nature of learning difficulties have changed, thinking about the aims of education has evolved. Figure 12.3 illustrates four stages in this evolution. What has this really meant for pupils with high levels of difficulty who need to develop basic skills as a central element of their learning at school? Sometimes working towards an inclusive ideal seems to have involved little more than a token attempt at 'redescription'. The teaching of developmental or functional skills that are relevant to the needs of the pupils was redescribed as teaching a National Curriculum subject. Grove and Peacey (1999: 83) parodied such attempts: 'Thus sensory exploration may be described as Science; eating skills as English or Personal and Social Education; tracking objects as Mathematics; and signs of anticipation as History'. An alternative approach which they recognized – and which Byers (1999a) suggested is more commonly pursued in schools – is to take subjects as contexts of experience. With this approach a group of pupils with diverse needs and interests may participate in the same activity and take different things from it. Sebba *et al.* (1993: 21) illustrated the strategy with a piece of work designed to address what was then an attainment target in science at Key Stage 3:

To illustrate some of these issues, consider an activity designed to address the effects of water on the Earth's surface (science, Key Stage 3). This can be successfully presented at a wide range of levels, through, for example, watering plants in the school grounds, observing hard rain on a mud slope compared with on the tarmac path, etc. Some pupils may learn something of this process and hence will achieve within this area of science even if the school staff could not have predicted they would do so prior to the session. Other pupils may be able to work on current individual priorities within the context of this activity. For one pupil this teaching context might be used to practise wheelchair mobility skills while another is encouraged to produce the signs for 'rain', 'down' and 'on'. Hence, some pupils may achieve science skills, some mobility or communication skills and some nothing at all (but not necessarily predictably so).

What it means to achieve an attainment target is now widely understood, but 'experiencing' a learning activity is not as well defined. Byers (1999a) proposed that there might be a continuum of pupil outcomes in relation to educational experiences. At one end this would involve *encountering* (being present during an activity) and *awareness* (noticing that something is going on); and at the other end would be *involvement* (active participation, doing, commenting) and *attainment* (gaining, consolidating or practising skills, knowledge, etc.) (Byers, 1999a: 186). At any rate the range of experience that is offered through school is much wider than it was. For example, a narrow focus on the sight words of 'functional literacy' has been replaced by a broader approach to practices that mirror the skills of a literate person with an emphasis on effective communication and a readiness to draw on multi-modal strategies (Byers and Fergusson 2003). A further example is the slow evolution of sex and relationship education as a serious commitment for those teaching these groups. Drama may be used as a context in which students not only practice skills that they may need (including saying 'no') but are also able to build up their confidence in and understanding of the implications of different situations (Sex Education Forum 2004).

Key issues in the curriculum for children with MLD have been different. Here the need for a distinctive interpretation of the curriculum is not so clear. In fact many have questioned whether the existence of a separate 'category' is required at all (Norwich & Kelly 2005). A review of the literature on the pedagogic needs of the group by Fletcher-Campbell (2005: 187) concluded that there was evidence that:

- This group of learners can follow a programme of work broadly similar to their age-peers: for example, they have access to written language, can record their own work in conventional ways, can manipulate numeric symbols.

- This group of learners can follow a common programme without particular technical aids: for example, the benefits of drafting work on a computer will be qualitatively similar to the benefits for other pupils in an age-related teaching group.

- Differentiation for these learners as a group rests on focusing on earlier stages of the learning path which their peers have travelled rather than traversing a different path. Thus, these learners will have less complex texts and tasks, and be required to engage in more straightforward analysis of situations (for example, in history) than their peers.

- These pupils do not need a supplementary curriculum (unlike, for example, those needing mobility training . . .) unless they have associated learning difficulties in another area.

- These pupils, as a group, are rarely discussed in terms of benefiting from other specific therapies, interventions or medication even if these may benefit individual pupils within the group and the group may benefit to a similar extent to any group of age-related peers.

For an extended period within the last half century teaching methods for children with learning difficulties were strongly influenced by behavioural principles. The adaptations that were made in order to respond to children's learning difficulties were a very considerable advance on earlier practice. For example, well-defined objectives were set for teachers and pupils, and systematic methods were available to work towards them. In schools which took these principles on board there was a purposeful ethos with a clear focus on the educational task (Ainscow and Tweddle 1979; McBrien and Foxen 1981). However, critics have argued that there were disadvantages too (Watson, 2000):

- *Teachers* became more directive, reduced their expectations of the pupils, set undemanding tasks and neglected to foster metacognition, learning strategies and generalization of learning.

- *Pupils* became more passive, showed low levels of engagement and low self-esteem, sought a good deal of reassurance and pretended to understand more than they really did.

- *Curricula* were highly organized and tightly planned, yet lacked intellectual coherence or intrinsic interest.

- *Tasks and activities* were often solitary with little demand or opportunity for joint or collaborative working.

Activity 12.3   Making effective use of a multi-sensory room

A multi-sensory environment (MSE) is an environment designed to stimulate the senses through light, sound, touch and smell. Typically an MSE room contains a collection of devices or objects such as ball pools, bubble tubes, optic fibre tail lights and musical effects in one place. These facilities may be used for leisure purposes but have been put into schools for educational use with pupils who have PMLD. The notion is that multi-sensory experiences will heighten participants' levels of alertness and will encourage basic interaction. However, studies with adults (Vlaskamp *et al.* 2003) and children (see review by Hogg *et al.* 2001) have provided little evidence for an increase in activity levels or communication simply as a result of giving individuals time in an MSE. Taking account of the points that are made in the text below about teaching and communication methods with children who have PMLD, reflect on how the facilities in such an environment might be used in a structured way to greater educational effect.

As a result of these concerns there was a reaction against behaviourist methods. This can be exemplified from developments in the teaching of communication skills to children who have PMLD. Those methods had succeeded in teaching simple unrelated sub-skills and keywords, but children were not helped to become active participants in a conversation or to use those skills effectively in everyday situations. If they were to learn to communicate in a responsive way with the capacity to convey meaning intentionally, a different strategy was required. One approach, *intensive interaction*, built on the model of what happens 'naturally' between a caregiver and an infant. An emphasis was placed on key processes such as sharing control and synchronizing movements. These were developed during one-to-one interactive games between a student and a member of staff. A key motivating factor, as in the development of communication in early infancy, was mutual enjoyment. Children were drawn to develop communication skills because they needed and wanted to (Nind and Hewett 2005). Case study evidence of the efficacy of the approach is slowly accumulating (e.g. Kellett 2003). Questions have been raised about the adaptation of the technique to take account of cultural diversity, for example where parents use different communication styles with their children from those commonly adopted by white European parents (Fergusson and Duffield 2003). It has been argued that more could be done to exploit the full potential of music (Ockelford *et al*. 2002) and of enhanced physical contact – with safeguards (Hewett 2007) as media for communication with children whose verbal skills are limited. How best to take that forward for an individual pupil will probably best be planned on the basis of a 'meaning audit' (Goss 2006) – a systematic analysis of what appears to be most meaningful to the child drawing on reports from parents and carers as well as the teacher's own observations. Reflect on the task set in Activity 12.3 about multi-sensory environments in the light of this suggestion.

As we have noted throughout this chapter, low expectations that have deep historical roots continue to influence thinking about the education of children with learning difficulties. But there is an increasing tendency for their SEN to be discussed in terms of an analysis of their rights instead of an acceptance of their apparent limitations. Activity 12.4 gives you an opportunity to consider what that might mean in practice in the classroom.

Activity 12.4   What have you done this week . . .?

The following list of questions for a parent, carer or teacher is based on a manifesto on the civil rights and responsibilities of those with learning difficulties developed in Wisconsin (quoted in Wood and Shears 1986). Imagine that you are the mainstream Year 3 class teacher of a child with SLD aged 8 who has recently been admitted to your class for three afternoons a week (spending the rest of her time in an SLD unit in a junior school nearby). At the end of one term you are asked these questions on a Friday afternoon. What would you hope to be able to answer?

(a)   What have you done this week to convey to this young person that she is a valued member of the classroom community who is taken seriously?

(b)   What have you entrusted her to do which challenged her sense of responsibility?

(c) How have you enabled her this week to demonstrate fresh self-confidence, courage and initiative?

(d) In what settings has she been enabled to cooperate actively on a valued task with others who have learning difficulties, and with others who do not?

(e) On what occasions and over what issues have you sought her views and acted in a way that shows that you respect them?

(f) How has she been enabled to act unselfishly for the benefit of others?

Conclusions

There have been radical changes over time in the way in which learning difficulties are conceived. These changes have mirrored shifts in theorizing about the nature of intelligence and abilities. It is increasingly appreciated that successful performance may depend, in part, on effective learning strategies and on a learning style that is well matched to the way in which information is presented. This means that a learning difficulty is partly determined by the learning context and cannot solely be understood as a fixed characteristic of the learner. For some commentators this has led to the rejection of the term *learning difficulties* altogether.

Concerns about separate educational provision for children with learning difficulties were fanned by the recognition that those most likely to be identified tended to come from low-status social groups and ethnic minority communities. The analysis of assessment techniques, curriculum issues and pedagogic methods each showed a shift over recent years in the direction of approaches that are compatible with inclusive principles. These principles pose new and uncomfortable challenges. The themes that have emerged as significant in relation to learning difficulties will reappear in various guises in the chapters that follow on other areas of SEN.

13

Literacy

Objectives

When you have studied this chapter you should be able to:

- describe ways in which pupils with SEN and those learning EAL can derive maximum benefit from the Framework for Teaching Literacy;
- appreciate the range of theories that have been developed to account for learning difficulties in literacy and evaluate different approaches to the identification and assessment of dyslexia;
- describe methods for assessing reading accuracy and fluency, the appropriateness of the literacy learning opportunities that have been provided, and pupils' learning progress in literacy;
- outline strategies that may be of value for teachers and other professionals working with pupils experiencing learning difficulties in literacy, including pupils learning EAL.

Contents

The literacy curriculum

The National Literacy Strategy and the National Primary Strategy Framework for Teaching Literacy

The National Literacy Strategy (NLS) has been described as one of the most ambitious national initiatives for change that primary education in Britain has seen (Ofsted 1999c). It developed from dissatisfaction with both the standards being achieved by pupils and the methods of teaching commonly adopted in primary schools. Hearing individual children read was identified as the major approach used by many primary school teachers in the past to develop literacy skills. By contrast, the NLS required teachers to place a major emphasis on teaching reading skills directly to the whole class and to small groups.

The NLS was implemented in primary schools in September 1998. Its declared purpose was to improve literacy standards so that, by 2002, 80 per cent of 11-year-olds would reach the level expected for their age in the Key Stage 2 National Curriculum tests. While this target was not reached, the 75 per cent of children who reached Level 4 in 2002 represented a substantial increase over the 63 per cent of children reaching it in 1997. In addition, a Canadian external evaluation team concluded that the National Literacy and Numeracy Strategies had substantially narrowed the gap between results in the most and least successful schools and LEAs. They also concluded that teaching had improved substantially (Earl *et al.* 2003).

The NLS initially consisted of two components:

- the *NLS Framework of Learning Objectives*, which provided details of *what* should be taught;

- the *Literacy Hour*, which specified *how* teaching should be organized and delivered.

The Framework covered the statutory requirements for reading and writing in the National Curriculum. The relevance and contribution of speaking and listening were recognized, although these elements were not separately identified in the Framework. A major emphasis was placed on learning to use a *range* of strategies to access the meaning of a text. Four types of strategy were identified and depicted as a series of searchlights, each of which sheds light on the text. This 'searchlights' model is shown in Figure 13.1. It was noted that teachers had often given less emphasis to phonic strategies and the importance of directly teaching these skills was emphasized in the Framework, particularly in the early stages of learning to read and write (DfEE 1998c).

The purpose of the Literacy Hour was to promote the direct teaching of key strategies. It was delivered in four sections:

- shared reading and writing as a whole class (15 minutes);

- word-level work (phonological awareness, phonics and spelling) as a whole class (15 minutes);

- group and individual work, independent or teacher guided (20 minutes);

- plenary for consolidation and monitoring as a whole class (10 minutes).

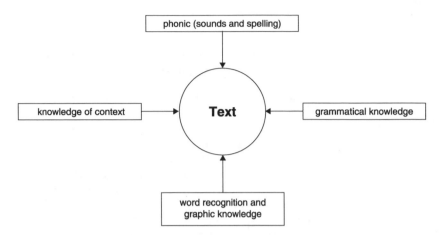

Figure 13.1 The 'searchlights' model of reading strategies
Source: DfEE (1998c: Section 1, p. 4).

Activity 13.1 Maximizing the effectiveness of daily literacy teaching for all pupils, including pupils with SEN/learning EAL

In contrast to the optimistic and inclusive thrust of the initial government guidance, a number of authors expressed reservations about the value of some features of the NLS as originally introduced.

(a) Consider the concerns listed below. It has since been suggested that many of them were not realized in practice (e.g. Wall 2003). What is your view? To what extent do these concerns relate to your knowledge/experience of the operation of the Literacy Hour in schools?

(b) What are the implications for developing the daily teaching of literacy to meet the needs of pupils with SEN and/or pupils learning EAL with whom you are working?

(c) As you read on and consider the PNS Revised Framework for Literacy, introduced in 2006, decide to what extent these concerns have been addressed.

- Solity *et al.* (1999) argued that research in instructional psychology indicates that teaching should initially focus on letter sounds, together with skills in segmenting words into phonemes and in blending phonemes into words. By contrast, they pointed out that the NLS also teaches other things early on: letter names, initial and final consonant clusters and the segmentation of words into onsets and rimes (e.g. c/at, sk/ip). It is suggested that this is a lot of information to remember and that teaching different ways in which words can be segmented (into phonemes and into onset/rime divisions) is potentially confusing.

- Solity *et al.* (1999) also argued that research in instructional psychology indicated that it is more effective to teach children through distributed rather than massed sessions. They recommended three 10–15-minute literacy sessions per day, rather than an hour-long session (see also Seabrook *et al.* 2005).

- After reviewing research evidence on the impact of teaching phonics, Wyse (2000) proposed that, while there is some justification for the work on phonics in Years 1 and 2, the NLS Framework should be rewritten 'to remove the phonics objectives from Years 3 and 4'. He pointed out that much of the evidence on the value of extended work on phonics 'has been collected in the context of struggling readers' (Wyse 2000: 362).

- Byers (1999b: 11) highlighted a number of challenging questions that had arisen in discussions with teachers of children with learning difficulties. They included: 'Will the focus upon literacy and numeracy skills facilitate the process of inclusion (ensuring enhanced access, perhaps, to an increasingly inclusive society for school leavers) or lead to a hardening of the boundaries between those pupils who can "catch up", thereby helping the Government to meet its challenging literacy target, and those who cannot?'

- Pietrowski and Reason (2000: 52) suggested that it will be valuable that 'the common language of the NLS . . . enables class and support teachers to work together [as] support teachers now have a central role in preparing children for classroom activities through their assessments, targets and additional teaching as necessary. The information provided by support teachers enables class teachers to adjust their teaching to individual needs . . . This way of working assumes, of course, that we have the pre-requisite teacher time, expertise and resources'.

- 'Like their predecessors, they [New Labour] have repudiated all socioeconomic explanations for low achievement in literacy, preferring to point to the variation between schools serving similar populations, rather than to the much more substantial variation between the mean scores of schools serving populations of different socioeconomic levels' (Dombey 1998: 36).

- 'Why do we read and write? In addition to more mundane purposes, we read to enlarge our understanding of the world and our place in it, to explore other lives, to take pleasure in the virtual reality which we conspire with the author to create, and the language which gives it life. We write to shape our thoughts, to put them in a form which makes them communicable to others, to put our mark on the world. Such conceptions do not inform the Literacy Framework: formalism rules' (Dombey 1998: 39).

Analysis of the behavioural skills needed by pupils to participate successfully in the Literacy Hour – such as maintaining attention, waiting their turn to speak, staying on task and/or in seat, cooperating in a group (Gross *et al.* 1999) – initially led to concerns that children with SEN might have substantial difficulties in participating. However, the 2002 report of the Chief Inspector of Schools confirmed that almost all pupils with SEN were included in the Literacy Hour (Ofsted 2002a). The report highlighted a different problem. It indicated that the pressure to achieve literacy and numeracy targets and publication of school results had led to the desired focus on these areas being achieved and warned of a 'serious narrowing of the primary curriculum' in most schools (Ofsted, 2002a: Primary Schools, para. 37).

The government responded to a range of criticism such as this by announcing a new National Primary Strategy that placed emphasis on both *Excellence and Enjoyment* (DfES 2003d). Incorporating the NLS, it advocated a rich and varied curriculum to develop children in a range of ways, and teaching that was exciting and creative as well as successful in promoting high achievement. There was recognition that rigid adherence to the Literacy Hour structure could constrain creativity and learning, and teachers were encouraged to be flexible in their organization of the daily teaching of literacy to meet children's needs. In a subsequent evaluation of the impact of this initiative, Ofsted (2005e) reported that while headteachers welcomed the vision for primary education set out in *Excellence and Enjoyment*, little immediate response was apparent and schools' focus on the Literacy Hour and daily mathematics lesson had been largely unaffected. Ofsted also reported that day-to-day assessment to improve pupils' learning continued to be weak. Too many pupils were given work that was not matched well enough to their needs and too many pupils received additional support that did not meet their needs well enough. A need for better assessment for learning was highlighted.

The new Primary National Strategy's (PNS) Framework for teaching literacy, issued in 2006, reinforced both these aspects. While it continued to promote the daily teaching of literacy, there was greater emphasis on the use of a range of approaches, on the effective application of literacy skills across other subjects and on planning for progression across longer sequences of lessons. A teaching and learning cycle was promoted, comprising the steps shown in Figure 13.2. The cycle may be implemented in a lesson or across a teaching sequence.

A further development has been a greater focus upon teachers using their assessment to personalize learning:

> There will be different sparks that ignite learning, making it vivid and real for different children. All children need teaching tailored to their needs – those with special educational needs (SEN), those who are gifted and talented, those learning English as an additional language (EAL), or those whose needs have not been attended to well will need their teachers to pay particular attention to tailoring teaching to meet these needs.
>
> (DfES 2006c: 9)

Two main purposes of assessment are identified: assessment of learning (summative assessment) and assessment for learning (formative assessment). The role in assessment of informed observation and effective questioning, which help the teacher note what children can do and what they need to do next, is highlighted.

The second significant influence on changes to the PNS Framework for teaching literacy was the Rose (2006) report on the teaching of early reading. This report recommended the replacement of the 'searchlights' model of reading strategies with a different conceptual model: the 'simple view of reading' (Gough and Tunmer 1986), as shown in Figure 13.3. This model identifies two components of reading: 'word recognition' and 'language comprehension'. Both sets of processes are deemed necessary for reading, and the report reviewed research findings supporting their independence. Given evidence that the same language comprehension processes underlie spoken and written language comprehension, it is argued that greater attention should be paid to the development of children's

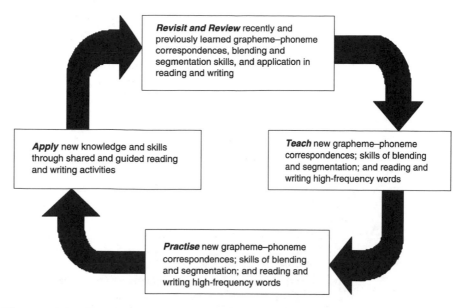

Figure 13.2 Teaching and learning cycle
Source: Adapted from DfES (2007b).

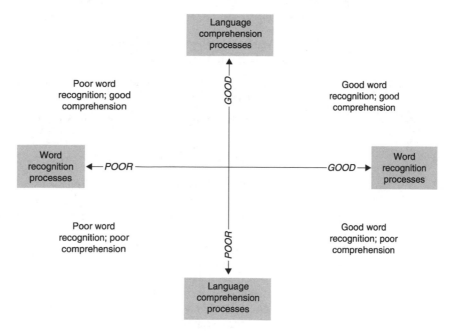

Figure 13.3 The simple view of reading
Source: Gough and Tunmer (1986).

speaking and listening skills. To simplify the structure of the objectives and to incorporate speaking and listening, 12 strands of learning are identified in literacy. These give a broad overview of the curriculum for English in the primary phase.

Accordingly, the revised Framework for Literacy includes guidance on developing spoken English which was not mentioned at all in the original. Speaking and learning objectives have been included and the structure of the objectives simplified into 12 strands, four of which relate to National Curriculum Attainment Target 1 speaking and listening, three to Attainment Target 2 reading, and five to Attainment Target 3 writing.

The specific kinds of teaching required by each of the components of reading is detailed and a different weighting is proposed as children become increasingly fluent and accurate readers. It is argued that children need to acquire and practise certain skills in the early stages of reading in order to develop fluent automatic word reading (*learning to read*) and that this should be time-limited, whereas the abilities to understand and appreciate written texts (*reading to learn*) continue to develop throughout life. Key to the development of fluent and automatic word reading skills are the acquisition and use of phonic knowledge, and there is a focus on teaching phonic knowledge and skills as the prime approach to the teaching of early reading.

High-quality phonic work is defined in the Rose report in terms of both process and content. In process terms, the importance of systematic phonics teaching is emphasized where there is good planning, reinforcing and building on previous learning and discrete and daily teaching which is engaging and multi-sensory. It is also stressed that the programmes used should have an evidence base, be followed consistently and with 'fidelity to the programme'. In terms of content, approaches are recommended that teach beginner readers:

- grapheme–phoneme (letter–sound) correspondences (the alphabetic principle) in a clearly defined, incremental sequence;

- to apply the highly important skill of blending (synthesizing) phonemes all through a word in order to read it;

- to apply the skills of segmenting words into their constituent phonemes to spell;

- that blending and segmenting are reversible processes (Rose 2006: 20).

The report acknowledges uncertainties in research findings, but suggests that the systematic approach, referred to as 'synthetic' phonics, represents the best approach for the vast majority of young children in developing skilled reading and writing. Synthetic phonics involves focusing on the phonemes associated with particular graphemes which are pronounced in isolation and blended together (synthesized) (Torgerson *et al.* 2006). 'For example, children are taught to take a single-syllable word such as *cat* apart into its three letters, pronounce a phoneme for each letter in turn /k, æ, t/, and blend the phonemes together to form a word' (Torgerson *et al.* 2006: 13) Synthetic phonics is contrasted with analytic phonics in which children analyse whole words to identify the common phoneme in a set of words. 'For example, teacher and pupils discuss how the following words are alike: *pat, park, push* and *pen*' (Torgerson *et al.* 2006: 13).

The recommendation of synthetic phonics has been criticized, for example by Wyse and Styles (2007), who cite the findings of systematic reviews from the USA and UK in support of their criticisms. In the USA the National Reading Panel (2000) did not find evidence that teaching programmes focused on small units in words (phonemes) were any more effective than those focusing on larger units (onset/rime, e.g. sh/op, st/op, dr/op), or that synthetic approaches focused on blending were more effective than analytic approaches focused on word families. In the UK, Torgerson *et al.* (2006) concluded that the evidence was weak and inconclusive. Only three well-designed studies could be found and none of them reported a statistically significant difference in effectiveness between synthetic and analytic phonics instruction.

The framework for teaching literacy in a multilingual society

The guidance documents provided with the revised PNS Framework for literacy advise that planning, teaching and learning for children learning EAL should be underpinned by three key principles:

- Bilingualism is an asset and the first language has a continuing and significant role in identity, learning and the acquisition of additional languages.

- Cognitive challenge can and should be kept appropriately high through the provision of linguistic and contextual support.

- Language acquisition goes hand in hand with cognitive and academic development, with an inclusive curriculum as the context.

Advice is given on the implementation of these principles in practice and frequent cross-references are made to the extensive guidance available in the PNS more generally on supporting children learning EAL (DfES 2006a). In particular, it is noted that EAL learners have to learn a new language while learning through the medium of that new language, and it is recommended that in order to achieve both sets of objectives learning and teaching approaches need both to ensure access to the curriculum at a cognitively appropriate level and offer opportunities for maximum language development.

On the one hand, appropriate scaffolding to enable access to the curriculum will be important. Well-structured teaching contexts will also be valuable for assessment. When the Literacy Hour was first introduced, Cline and Shamsi (2000) suggested that for pupils at the very early stages of learning EAL, its regular routines provided teachers with important opportunities to observe and evaluate in detail these pupils' strengths and difficulties. But those routines involved some risks for this group too. For example, when a teaching routine focuses on isolated words during word-level teaching, some pupils who are learning EAL may need to see and hear key words in meaningful contexts if they are to make connections with their possible use in continuous text (Ofsted 2005a).

On the other hand, it will also be important to identify the academic and cognitive language demanded by the curriculum and to use strategies such as modelling by adults and peers to demonstrate appropriate use of the language. The provision of language support within the curriculum wherever possible is recommended, as withdrawal from subject lessons for additional language tuition is likely to mean that learners will fall further behind in those curriculum areas. However, it is recognized that new arrivals who are beginners in English may benefit in the short term from a programme that incorporates some teaching in small withdrawal groups alongside teaching within a whole class. The desirability of providing opportunities to learn with peers who provide good models of language and learning is emphasized and placement in lower-ability sets and groups discouraged.

In addition to learning a new language while learning through the medium of that language, a third need is identified for children learning English as an additional language – maintaining their first language. The guidance notes:

> Often parents from minority communities feel ill equipped to support their children's learning in school if English is not their strongest language but again they should be encouraged to understand that rich communication using their strongest language is the best way to support their children's learning in school. Parents should be confident that the school values their child's bilingualism and that research shows that this has the potential to confer an intellectual advantage as providing children with opportunities to continue to use their first language for cognitively demanding tasks supports the development of their additional language. Concepts, knowledge and skills developed in one language transfer readily to additional languages.
>
> (DfES 2006k: 14)

There is evidence of positive transfer across languages in the development of both phonological and reading skills (see Siegel 2004) However, high levels of word reading accuracy in a child's first language will not necessarily mean that reading in English will come easily to them. Seymour *et al.* (2003) found that the rate of literacy skills acquisition relates to the consistency of letter-sound correspondences in the language. In most languages the relationships between letters and sounds are more straightforward than they are in English, where they are notoriously inconsistent. However, the best evidence of positive transfer is from more regular languages to English.

In contrast to the recent, clear, inclusive guidance available to primary schools, more concerns are expressed about the situation in secondary schools. The Key Stage 3 section of the NLS, introduced in 2000, had been incorporated into the Secondary National Strategy and extended to Key Stage 4 in 2005. Cline *et al.* (2002) found that the NLS was not perceived as supporting multicultural education and teachers expressed unease about the lack of 'any recent development at national level encouraging a focus on this area of work'. The report of the curriculum review on diversity and citizenship (DfES 2007a) expressed concern that English is often seen solely as a utilitarian and skills-based subject. It was argued that English should also include 'the key concept of cultural understanding, with reference to how literature in English is rich and influential, reflecting the experiences of people from many countries across the centuries to contribute to "our sense of cultural identity"' (DfES 2007a: 49). The Secondary Curriculum Review was identified as providing an opportunity whereby teachers could be supported in providing a culturally responsive, skills-based English curriculum.

The framework for teaching literacy and pupils with SEN

From the inception of the NLS there was a strongly inclusive philosophy for pupils with SEN:

> Many mainstream children with special educational needs, with help and encouragement, will be able to achieve at the level for their age in the

National Literacy Strategy, and most will benefit significantly from being involved in classwork with their peers. Where children need to work to different objectives, they should nevertheless be taught with their own class and year group . . . Pupils with identified special educational needs should normally work with their peers within the Literacy Hour. They should only be taken out of the hour to work in parallel when extra support within the Literacy Hour or outside this time is not enough.

(DfEE 1998c: 115)

Guidance issued with the revised Framework for Literacy for planning across the literacy strands (DfES 2006c), advised that, where possible, learning objectives should be chosen for children with SEN and/or learning difficulties and disabilities that are related to the aspect on which the whole class is working. If this is not possible even with appropriate access strategies and support, it is suggested that teachers use the new electronic planning tool available on the PNS Literacy Strategy website to track back along a progression strand and locate earlier learning objectives. While the emphasis is on children with SEN working on objectives that are within the same aspect as those on which the whole class is working, it is recognized that sometimes the need to concentrate for a period on key skills central to the learning of a particular child may be judged to take priority. This advice builds on previous publications, such as the DfES (2002d) publication on including all children in the Literacy Hour and daily mathematics lesson which provides information on teaching strategies as well as planning approaches, including tracking back to choose appropriate learning objectives. Among the strategies analysed and discussed are the use of additional adults in the classroom and alternatives to written recording.

In all discussion of the literacy strategy and pupils with SEN frequent reference is made to the three 'waves' of provision. These were introduced to address the requirements of the SEN *Code of Practice* (DfES 2001a) and offer a continuum of provision for children with literacy difficulties ranging from 'good quality teaching and differentiated curriculum' to provision under the headings of 'School Action' and 'School Action Plus':

- Wave 1 – the effective inclusion of all children in daily, high-quality teaching.

- Wave 2 – Wave 1 plus additional interventions to enable children to catch up and work at age-related expectations or above.

- Wave 3 – Wave 1 plus additional, highly personalized interventions, for example, specifically targeted approaches for children identified as requiring SEN support (on School Action, School Action Plus or with a statement of special educational needs).

High-quality phonic work, as defined by the Rose review, is advocated as a key feature of literacy provision in all the 'waves' of intervention. At all three levels also, the use of approaches that carry a strong evidence base of success and that are implemented with fidelity are advised as essential.

Schools are encouraged to consider problems with their Wave 1 or Wave 2 provision before concluding that the relatively expensive Wave 3 provision is required. So DfES (2003f) advises that where a child is experiencing significant literacy difficulties, schools should consider whether:

- they may not have had consistent high quality teaching at Wave 1;

- they have missed an opportunity to take part in a Wave 2 intervention;

- they have not yet had access to Wave 3 intervention or the Wave 3 intervention selected has not been effective in accelerating their rate of progress.

Wave 2 interventions are not primarily intended to be SEN interventions and include NLS Early Literacy Support, Additional Literacy Support and Further Literacy Support programmes, booster classes and other school-based programmes for children who can be expected to 'catch up' with their peers as a result of the intervention. These interventions are intended to be tight, structured programmes of small-group support, carefully targeted and delivered by teachers or teaching assistants. Normally of short duration with built-in review and exit procedures, they can be delivered in addition to whole-class lessons, or can be built into mainstream lessons as part of guided work. However, it is critical in either case that pupils are supported to apply their learning in mainstream lessons. Wave 2 programmes include:

- Early Literacy Support, designed for teaching assistants to use with children identified as needing additional support at the end of the first term in Year 1;

- Additional Literacy Support, targeted at children in Year 3 and also Year 4 who achieved at Level 1 or 2c at the end of Key Stage 1;

- Further Literacy Support, targeted at children in Year 5 who are working at Level 3;

- Booster units, mainly directed to improving achievement in Key Stage 2 tests.

The Early Literacy Support (ELS) programme was designed to identify and support pupils who are not making the expected progress during the first term of primary school. There is some good evidence that the ELS can be effective in enabling 6-year-olds to 'catch up' to an average level of reading. Hatcher *et al.* (2006a) examined the ELS and a modified version of Reading Intervention (RI) programme (Hatcher *et al.* 1994). Both programmes targeted phoneme and grapheme linkage skills and letter knowledge, included guided reading and writing and were delivered by teaching assistants. While the content of the ELS programme is tightly structured and scripted, the RI programme provides a framework for teaching within which the content is tailored to assessment information collected on each child at the start of the programme. Both intervention programmes were implemented over a 12-week period during the children's fourth term in school. In the ELS programme children worked in groups of six for 60 daily 20-minute teaching sessions. In the RI programme children worked on alternate days in groups of six, for a total of thirty 20-minute sessions, and on the intervening days they worked individually with the teaching assistant for a total of thirty 20-minute sessions. The results showed few differences between the two groups of children, both of whom made significant gains in letter identification, reading and spelling which led to them catching up with their classmates. A check three months later demonstrated that they had not slid back.

Whereas Wave 2 interventions are designed for those who are falling behind as a result either of weaknesses in the teaching they have received or of issues relating to their personal, social and economic circumstances, Wave 3 provision is intended for those who have specific neurodevelopmental or other problems (Rose 2006). Rose (2006) considered that some of those in receipt of Wave 3 provision may be able to make progress but were unlikely to be able to 'catch up' with their peers. However, DfES (2003f) advises that schools should review their Wave 3 literacy interventions if children receiving them do not, on average, make at least twice the normal rate of progress. This advice is based on a DfES-commissioned study (Brooks 2002) which reviewed British studies on intervention approaches conducted with lower-achieving (but apparently non-dyslexic) children in Years 1–4. Eighteen of the types of intervention investigated were identified as providing evidence that they produced at least twice the normal rate of progress. It should be noted that this review did not attempt to screen or weight studies using quality criteria, although this is generally considered important in reviews of this kind (e.g. National Reading Panel 2000; Petticrew and Roberts, 2006). While its recommendations should therefore be treated with some caution, the emphasis placed by DfES (2003f) on ongoing evaluation by schools of interventions employed will offer a check on effectiveness.

From the outset the NLS was widely adopted by special schools, including schools for pupils with SLD and PMLD, with appropriate modifications to address pupils' specific needs (Berger *et al.* 1999). The modelling of strategies and provision of explicit instruction are features that would be expected to be beneficial to pupils who have SEN in both special and mainstream schools. The DfES (2003e) training publication on teaching the Literacy Hour and daily mathematics lessons in special settings suggests that the materials may also be valuable in securing curriculum access for children who are individually included in mainstream. Video case studies are presented from special schools for children with severe or profound learning difficulties, moderate learning difficulties, physical disabilities and behavioural, social and emotional difficulties. Further discussion of the teaching of pupils with SEN during the Literacy Hour can be found in Byers (1999b), Dehaney (2000), Lee and Eke (2004), Miller *et al.* (2003) and Pietrowski and Reason (2000).

Understanding difficulties in literacy

Illustrations such as the extract in Activity 13.2 have often been used to argue that reading may be conceived of as a 'psycholinguistic guessing game' (Goodman 1967; Smith 1978). In this approach the features of a printed word were not seen as a primary source of hypotheses about its identity but were used to test hypotheses generated from the grammatical context and the meaning of the passage. Even as a model of skilled reading the assumptions of the 'psycho-linguistic guessing game' approach were quickly found to lack empirical support. Skilled adult readers were only able to predict 25 per cent of the words in connected prose, and prediction took longer than just looking at the word (Gough *et al.* 1981). Reading for meaning proved to be dependent on good word decoding skills, rather than the other way round (see Adams and Bruck 1993).

Unfortunately the approach had great appeal with teachers and proved very influential. It was argued that through exposure to print and the use of semantic and syntactic cues in the context of meaningful stories, children would develop the knowledge required to decode print with minimal explicit teaching of

Activity 13.2   Primary cues in decoding text

Hw cn u rd ths? 'It muts be fairyl obvouis to aynone rding ths lettre that raedres draw on thier konwledeg of how lagnuaege wroks, their abitily to recgonise wrods on sihgt and ther capacity to ues contextual cleus to enabel them to maek senes of what has goen befor and perdict what is cmoing next.'

(Extract from a letter to the *Times Educational Supplement*, March 1991)

What are the most important sources of information you are drawing on in identifying the words in this letter? Are there some words that could be replaced with a line and you would still know what they are? How many? Are there some that could be replaced with a line and just one letter? How many? Are you sure? What about 'uses contextual c____ to enable' – could it be cues, rather than clues?

letter–sound correspondences. By contrast, all the recent reviews and meta-analyses of the effectiveness of different methods for teaching reading have consistently highlighted a need for explicit and systematic teaching of letter–sound correspondences in reading alongside a focus on reading for meaning (Snow and Juel 2005).

There is also evidence to indicate that children at risk of reading failure and those with specific reading difficulties/dyslexia require reading development programmes that have a stronger, additional focus on the explicit and systematic teaching of letter–sound correspondences. Hatcher *et al.* (2004) carried out a study in the UK with children aged 4–5 in their first year at school. They were divided into four matched groups and randomly assigned to one of three experimental teaching programmes (delivered to groups of 10–15 children for three 10-minute sessions per week):

- reading with rhyme;

- reading with phoneme;

- reading with rhyme and phoneme;

- reading control condition – usual literacy curriculum with teaching as a class, in groups and as individuals).

In each programme there was a strong phonic component and the same amount of time was devoted to reading instruction. Normally developing children did equally well in all four groups. However, for children identified as being at risk of reading failure, additional training in phoneme skills resulted in greater gains in phoneme awareness and in reading skills. These findings suggest that any reading programme that contains a highly structured phonic component is sufficient for most 4–5-year-old children to learn to read effectively, but for young children at risk of reading delay, additional training in phoneme awareness and linking phonemes with letters is required.

Further evidence comes from a US study by Torgesen *et al.* (2001) of interventions with children aged 9–10 who had been receiving special education services for dyslexia for at least 16 months and whose reading attainments were at a 5–6 year age equivalent level. The interventions were highly intensive, providing individual teaching in two 50-minute sessions each day for around 8 weeks. They provided supportive and explicit teaching on phomemic awareness and phonemic-based decoding strategies and included activities for building fluency with high-frequency words and reading words in meaningful context with teacher support. During the previous 16 months, while they had been receiving special education services, the children had made some improvements in their reading performance so that they had not fallen any further behind their peers, but neither had they 'caught up' at all. At the start of the study they were scoring in the bottom 7 per cent of children of their age. Following the 8-week intervention the children were scoring above 30 per cent of children of their age, so they had caught up significantly. An important caveat is that these are group averages and the interventions were not equally successful with all children. In addition, despite improvements in reading accuracy, reading fluency remained substantially below average, a common finding from intervention programmes for children with dyslexia (Torgesen 2005).The importance of explicit, intensive and highly structured phonics programmes for children with dyslexia can be understood by reference to the literature on the central role of phonological difficulties in dyslexia. A wide range of different theories have been put forward to account for learning difficulties in literacy.

Theories of dyslexia

A report by the Division of Educational and Child Psychology of the British Psychological Society (BPS 1999) on *Dyslexia, Literacy and Psychological Assessment* identified ten different types of hypothesis (see Table 13.1). The causal modelling framework (Morton 2004; Morton and Frith 1995) was used to represent and compare these different approaches. Some of the hypotheses included comprehensive description at each level in the framework and, in addition, modelled causal links between the features included at different levels. Others focused on description at one level of explanation only. A number of these will be discussed further to illustrate some of the most important general considerations in understanding learning difficulties in literacy. Information about the other hypotheses can be found in the BPS (1999) report.

The *phonological delay/deficit* hypothesis was identified in the BPS (1999) report as being particularly important, both because of the broad empirical support which it commands and because of the important role phonology is given in a number of the other hypotheses also. Figure 13.4 shows the core phonological delay/deficit hypothesis. Phonological processing is broadly defined as the ability to process sounds in spoken language. Phonology is that part of language that concerns the sounds of words, rather than their meanings or grammatical structures. The phonological hypothesis has gained particular prominence in recent years and many of its predictions are supported by a wide range of research evidence.

The hypothesis depicted in Figure 13.4 assumes a problem in some aspect of the way in which information is processed by the brain. At the cognitive level it is hypothesized that the processing problem will cause a weakness in a cognitive component of the phonological system. Frith (1997) points out that such a consequence, although likely, is not inevitable. There may be protective factors or redundancy in the system which allow normal phonological processing to be maintained.

Table 13.1 Understanding learning difficulties in literacy: theoretical accounts described in the British Psychological Society (1999) report

Theoretical account	Reference source to consult for further information	Phonological difficulties implicated
Phonological delay/deficit hypothesis	Frith (1997), Snowling (1998), Stanovich (1988)	Yes
Temporal processing hypothesis	Tallal *et al.* (1997)	Yes
Skill automatization hypothesis	Nicolson and Fawcett (1995)	Yes
Working memory hypothesis	Rack (1994)	Yes
Hypotheses that involve visual processing	Lovegrove (1994), Stein (1994)	No
Syndrome hypothesis	Miles (1993)	Yes
Hypotheses involving intelligence	Turner (1997)	No
Subtype hypotheses	Boder (1973), Bakker (1979)	Yes
Learning opportunities and social context hypothesis	Solity (1996a)	No
Emotional factors hypothesis	Ackerman and Howes (1986), Rourke (1988), Biggar and Barr (1996)	No

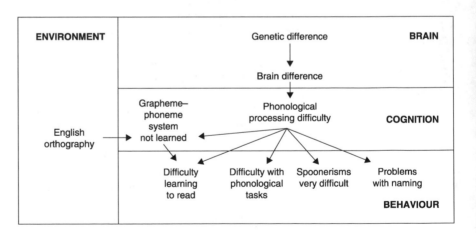

Figure 13.4 Phonological delay/deficit hypothesis
Source: British Psychological Society (1999).
NOTE: See Table 13.2 for a description of a range of phonological tasks.

If a weakness in phonological processing does result, this may affect aspects of speaking. Scarborough (1990) showed that children who were later identified as dyslexic showed subtle language difficulties when they were 3 years old. It is also likely to be more difficult for children who have phonological processing problems to establish grapheme–phoneme links and so their acquisition of literacy skills will probably be affected. This is represented at the behavioural level where the model predicts poor reading skills. However, phonological weaknesses are also found to have a number of other effects (see Snowling 1995 for a review). Some of these, like poor phoneme awareness (e.g. being able to tell which sound comes at the beginning of the word 'cat' or in the middle of the word 'pig'), will also be influenced by knowledge of grapheme–phoneme correspondences and hence by reading skill. Other areas of poor performance resulting from weaknesses in phonological processing, such as poor short-term auditory memory and slow naming speed, are not likely to be directly influenced by reading ability.

The majority of researchers now agree that phonological difficulties are the pre-eminent cause of literacy difficulties in dyslexia. From a review of research on dyslexia over the past four decades Vellutino *et al.* (2004: 2) conclude:

> The evidence suggests that inadequate facility in word identification due, in most cases, to more basic deficits in alphabetic coding is the basic cause of difficulties in learning to read. We next discuss hypothesized deficiencies in reading related cognitive abilities as underlying causes of deficiencies in component reading skills. The evidence in these areas suggests that, in most cases, phonological skills deficiencies associated with phonological coding deficits are the probable causes of the disorder rather than visual, semantic, or syntactic deficits, although reading difficulties in some children may be associated with general language deficits.

It is thought that many children with dyslexia form mental representations of the sounds of language that are poorly specified or 'fuzzy' which makes it difficult to develop an awareness of the internal sound structure of words and to learn letter–sound relationships (Snowling 2000).

A number of studies have shown differences in brain functioning between children with dyslexia and normally developing readers, using different methods (Simos *et al.* 2000; Shaywitz *et al.* 2002). Simos *et al.* (2000) used magnetic source imaging (MSI), which detects changes in magnetic fields surrounding electrical discharges from neurons. They found a sequence of activation across three areas of the left hemisphere of the brain when normally developing children read. By contrast, in children with dyslexia the brain areas activated in the final stage are in the right rather than the left hemisphere (see Figure 13.5). This has been interpreted as follows:

> These findings support the notion that following visual processing of printed stimuli (which takes place in complex visual processing areas), poor readers do not use their left temporoparietal region for phonological processing of the visual symbols, but ineffectively employ their inferior frontal and right posterior temporal cortices.
>
> (Simos *et al.* 2007a: 38)

It has been suggested that this different pattern may reflect compensatory processing, where parts of the brain not normally used for these tasks are conscripted to try to get round problems in the brain areas normally used. The results of such compensatory processing are generally less effective and efficient.

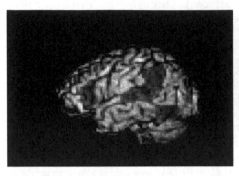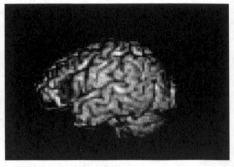

Typical readers   Dyslexic readers

Figure 13.5   Brain regions engaged during reading and reading-related tasks in typically developing readers (left inferior frontal gyrus, left temporoparietal cortex and left inferotemporal cortex) and readers with dyslexia (left inferior frontal gyrus only) *Source:* Goswami (2006).

A number of other theories identify different types of difficulty and causative factors, while agreeing that the problems experienced with reading and spelling are due to phonological difficulties. A good example is the *skill automatization hypothesis* (Nicolson and Fawcett 1995). This hypothesis proposes that dyslexic children have difficulties across a range of skills, including phonological skills, when they are required to perform at a fluent, automatic level and are prevented from employing conscious compensation to overcome their difficulties (see Figure 13.6). For example, Nicolson and Fawcett (1995) reported that dyslexic children had difficulty in balancing without wobbling when they were prevented from consciously compensating for their difficulties (either by being given a distracting task or by being blindfolded). At the biological level Nicolson and Fawcett (1994) suggested that a dysfunction in the cerebellum in the brain could give rise to difficulties in areas as balance, estimating time and speech fluency. A speech fluency problem could disrupt phonological processing, which would, in turn, affect reading and spelling.

There is a continuing lively debate within the literature on dyslexia about the merits of different theories. For example, White *et al.* (2006) tested the cerebellar and pure phonological hypotheses along with two further hypotheses. In this study children with dyslexia and matched normally developing children, aged 8–12 years, were compared on a range of measures. Comparisons were made between groups, but in addition, and of particular relevance for practitioners, clustering of difficulties were examined for individual children. Despite the weight of evidence supporting the phonological deficit approach in group-based research, a sizeable minority of the children with dyslexia in the White *et al.* (2006) study did not have a significant phonological deficit. Many of the children in the study had received specialist phonologically-based intervention which is likely to have improved their phonological skills. It is important to be aware of other possible causes of dyslexia, particularly as around 20 per cent of children

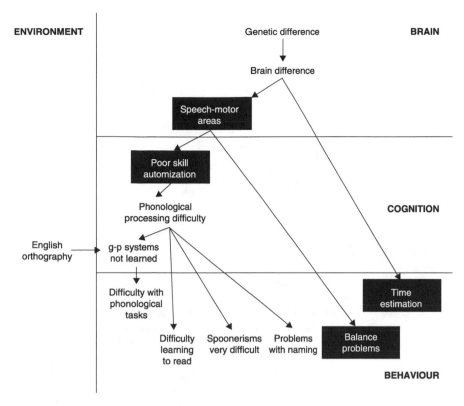

Figure 13.6   Skill automatization hypothesis
Source: BPS (1999).
Key: g-p systems = grapheme–phoneme systems.

identified by educational psychologists as having dyslexia but who have not received specialist intervention do not show phonological impairments (Frederickson and Frith 1998).

Of course, the absence of specialist intervention is increasingly seen as a counter-indication to a diagnosis of dyslexia. We have seen that the national framework for literacy places emphasis on considering hypotheses about absence of Wave 2 interventions, or even poor quality of Wave 1 interventions, prior to considering that the child might have a significant literacy difficulty. This emphasis would seem to relate in particular to the *learning opportunities and social context hypotheses* (see Figure 13.7). These are based on the assumption that poor literacy skills may result primarily from limited or inappropriate learning opportunities and experiences, rather than individual processing differences (Solity 1996a). Poor learning progress is attributed to children's school- and home-based experiences in learning to read, and attention is focused on environmental interventions which alter aspects of the social context, the learning opportunities and the instruction provided. The assumption is that, whatever their individual differences, children will learn given appropriate teaching.

It is argued that some of the individual differences that are ascribed causal significance in other theories may simply be indicators of consistent and important

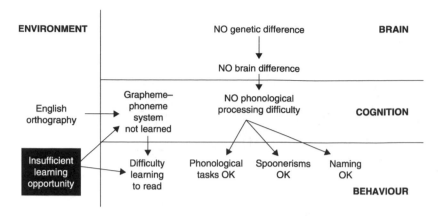

Figure 13.7   Learning opportunities and social context hypotheses
Source: BPS (1999).

differences in children's social contexts. Solity (1996a) suggests that the preschool differences in phonological awareness may well reflect differences in parental input, while differences in progress with learning to read could also reflect differences in the effectiveness of the teaching received. While this hypothesis on its own would not be widely accepted as providing a complete account of available research findings, increasing importance has been given in recent years to evaluating the availability of learning opportunities both inside and outside school in understanding children's learning difficulties in literacy. This is particularly evident in the literature on dyslexia.

Defining dyslexia

At least one of the early exclusionary definitions of dyslexia (see Figure 13.8) did show rudimentary awareness of the need to consider the instruction received. The first of these definitions would 'rule out' a child who had never attended school,

---

A disorder manifested by difficulty in learning to read despite conventional instruction, adequate intelligence and sociocultural opportunity. It depends on fundamental cognitive disabilities which are frequently of constitutional origin.

(World Federation of Neurology 1968,
quoted in Critchley and Critchley, 1978)

A disorder in one or more of the basic psychological processes in understanding or using language, spoken or written . . . does not include learning problems which are primarily the result of visual, hearing or motor handicaps, or mental retardation or emotional disturbance, or environmental, cultural or economic disadvantage.

(United States Education for All Handicapped Children Act,
PL94–142, 1975)

Figure 13.8   Exclusionary definitions of dyslexia

and clearly it would not be necessary to invoke a concept like dyslexia to understand why such a child might not be able to read.

However, both of these definitions also excluded sociocultural factors and this may have placed a hurdle in the way of bilingual children's access to specialist provision. A number of studies have drawn attention to the under-representation of bi- and multilingual children in provision for dyslexic children (Cline and Frederickson 1999; Deponio *et al.* 2000).

A variety of explanations have been advanced to account for this underidentification:

- distortions in the referral process (Graf 1992);

- sources of bias in the content of tests (Miller 1984; Lam 1993);

- inappropriate test administration and interpretation procedures (Desforges *et al.* 1995);

- failure to contextualize the assessment (Cline 1993).

Cline and Frederickson (1999) have argued that traditional ways of defining specific reading difficulties and dyslexia may have contributed to the under-representation in provision for pupils with specific learning difficulties/dyslexia of children from minority linguistic or cultural backgrounds, not just through the use of sociocultural factors as a basis for exclusion, but also through the use of intelligence test scores.

Both of the early exclusionary criteria shown in Figure 13.8 contain reference to general intellectual factors, one requiring 'adequate intelligence' and the other excluding children whose intelligence fell within the range designated as indicating 'mental retardation'. Until very recently such exclusionary definitions have been either explicitly or implicitly incorporated in special education assessment policy and practice both in the UK (Frederickson and Reason 1995) and the USA (Gresham 2002). It is possible to calculate the discrepancy between a child's actual reading test score and the reading test score which would be predicted for them on the basis of the correlation between reading and IQ test scores in the general population. Tables are available (e.g. Wechsler 2003) that show the statistical probability of different sizes of discrepancy and the percentages of the population in which discrepancies of different sizes occur. This 'IQ–achievement' discrepancy approach to defining dyslexia, apparently based on the assumption that intelligence defines potential for reading attainment, has attracted increasing criticism.

The notion that an IQ score indicates a child's 'potential' for reading achievement has been challenged by studies of children with low IQs who are good readers (Siegel 1992). Stuebing *et al.* (2002) conducted a meta-analysis of 46 studies to assess the validity of classifying poor readers into those who demonstrated an IQ–achievement discrepancy (and qualified for special help) and those who did not. They concluded that large overlaps between the two groups and negligible to small differences on variables closely related to the reading process cast serious doubt on the validity of the approach. The utility of the approach has also been challenged by findings that poor readers with and without a discrepancy do not differ in their response to intervention (Stage *et al.* 2003). An equity issue is thereby also raised where a child is denied access to intervention from which they are likely to benefit because of the application of an irrelevant criterion score on an IQ test. Without intervention the child's reading, relative to their classmates, is likely to get worse over time and may eventually fall to the point where it is significantly discrepant from their IQ, whereupon they would qualify for special help. This 'wait to fail model' (Stuebing *et al.* 2002) has caused particular concern and led to calls for its replacement with an approach which instead encourages early intervention.

In some cases the position may be even worse than that. While IQ may influence reading achievement, there is evidence of influence in the other direction also. Children with reading problems read less and are therefore less likely to gain the knowledge required by verbal IQ tests (Snowling *et al.* 2007). The verbal IQ of children with reading difficulties therefore often decreases with age (Bishop and Butterworth 1980), so that they may never achieve the level of discrepancy needed to qualify for support. By contrast Arnold *et al.* (1987) found that this drop in IQ could be prevented when an intensive intervention programme was provided. These results illustrate that the popular notion of IQ as a measure of innate potential that can set a level of expectation for reading achievement is not supported by the research evidence and may well have been damaging in depriving children of appropriate intervention and in setting inappropriately low levels of expectation for them.

Defining dyslexia through response to intervention

Although conventional instruction was listed as one of the exclusionary criteria in early definitions of dyslexia, Clay (1987) argued convincingly that virtually all studies of reading difficulties failed to control for the potentially confounding effects of inadequate instruction or prereading experience, which could produce effects very similar to those arising from organically-based learning disabilities. This has continued to be a problem with the literature on dyslexia until very recently when emphasis has been placed on study selection criteria that include failure to respond adequately to interventions validated as effective for most children of comparable age/stage of reading development (see Vellutino *et al.* 2004).

In recent years response to intervention has also been embraced at a national level in the USA and the UK. The US Department of Education, Office of Special Education Programs (2002) recommended the elimination of discrepancy criteria from identification of learning disabilities and the use instead of response-to-intervention approaches using interventions that are supported by research. In the UK, the Parliamentary Office of Science and Technology (POST 2004: 3) reported:

> In the past, people were not identified as dyslexic unless their reading ability was found to be lower than expected, given their IQ. . . . However most experts now doubt that IQ can be used as a meaningful indicator of reading potential. In most cases, a person who encounters severe difficulties in learning to read, write and spell will now be identified as dyslexic, regardless of IQ.

The expert view cited by POST (2004) is the BPS report on *Dyslexia, Literacy and Psychological Assessment*. This report (BPS 1999: 5) provides the following working definition of dyslexia:

Dyslexia is evident when accurate and fluent word reading and/or spelling develops very incompletely or with great difficulty. This focuses on literacy learning at the 'word level' and implies that the problem is severe and persistent despite appropriate learning opportunities. It provides the basis for a staged process of assessment through teaching.

The report proceeds to spell out the implications – that the problem is severe and persistent and has resisted usual teaching methods and additional help at the school-based stages of assessment and teaching advised by the *Code of Practice*. As this definition of dyslexia requires persistent difficulties, notwithstanding appropriate learning opportunities, children whose reading problems are due to inadequate learning opportunities (Solity 1996a) would be expected to make progress when given appropriate help and therefore would not be identified as dyslexic.

This working definition has no exclusionary criteria. Rather, positive identifying characteristics focus on severe and persistent problems with accurate and fluent word identification and spelling. It also allows for cases where literacy performance, particularly in older pupils, may appear relatively normal in some respects but where development is, or has been, achieved 'with great difficulty'. Where problems are identified, it is recommended that hypotheses are explored in areas involving phonological and orthographic awareness and memory and that account should be taken of compensatory styles such as heavy reliance on context when reading.

Literacy difficulties: assessment for intervention

It is widely advocated that assessment and teaching should be linked in a continuous cycle of action and evaluation in order to prevent reading failure (Clay 1987; DfES 2003f; Good *et al.* 1998). The BPS (1999) report recommends that assessment of learning difficulties in reading address the following questions:

- How well has the pupil learned accurate and fluent word reading and/or spelling?

- What possible hypotheses about the pupil's difficulties can be investigated to help understand their problems and how to help them?

- Have appropriate learning opportunities been provided?

- Has progress been made only as a result of much additional effort/instruction and does it show that difficulties are persisting?

A number of steps can be taken to collect appropriate assessment information in relation to each of these elements.

Assessing reading accuracy and fluency

The first question to address is: 'How well has the pupil learned accurate and fluent word reading and/or spelling?' In order to judge whether the pupil's learning has been 'very incomplete' or 'satisfactory', comparisons will need to be made between the levels achieved by the pupil and those required or expected of them. The pupil's level of achievement may be compared to typical performance of other pupils of the same age. End-of-key-stage tests serve this purpose. A number of standardized tests of reading and spelling are available which enable more detailed comparisons to be made as needed (for a review, see Hurry and Doctor 2007). Tests of reading accuracy require pupils to read aloud either a list of single words or a number of sentences/prose passages. The Wechsler Individual Achievement Test (WIAT) II UK for Teachers (Wechsler 2006) provides both types of materials. The sentence/prose passage materials can be used to assess reading fluency and comprehension in addition to oral reading accuracy. The Neale Analysis of Reading Ability (Neale *et al.* 1997) also provides a measure of accuracy, fluency and comprehension using prose passages as stimuli. It has been evaluated by Cain and Oakhill (2006) as an effective instrument for researchers and practitioners who need to assess both word reading accuracy and reading comprehension and to identify children with relative difficulties in one of these areas.

Rather than comparing the pupil's level of achievement to that of other pupils of their age, it may be compared with performance criteria that define realistic accuracy/fluency levels for particular tasks. The objectives of the PNS Framework for Literacy represent a set of performance criteria. Detailed observation and analysis of a child's reading performance on texts of known difficulty will indicate what levels of challenge the child can cope with. As we showed in Chapter 7, assessment for learning can help to establish whether knowledge in particular areas has been accurately learned and can be used fluently in reading and spelling. Good *et al.* (1998) explain how monthly measures of reading which require only 1 minute per child to administer can be used to chart progress at individual and class level across the school year.

There are advantages to drawing upon multiple sources of evidence, and reliable assessment of children learning EAL may require greater efforts to secure multiple sources of evidence than are needed with monolingual children. This may be done in a variety of ways: using multiple indicators to assess progress over time (Carrasquillo and Rodriguez 1996); or sampling the child's performance and behaviour in different situations (Hernandez 1994). It will be important to investigate reading comprehension as well as reading accuracy since, as noted above, children learning EAL may develop good decoding skills while remaining confused about much of what they read (Hutchinson *et al.* 2003). A further question to explore is whether there is a gap between a child's comprehension of a passage that is spoken aloud ('listening comprehension') and their comprehension of a similar passage in print ('reading comprehension'). There is a small gap for most children, but if a child learning to read in their second or third language shows a substantial gap with very much better listening comprehension than reading comprehension, it may indicate that the difficulties that the child is experiencing are not with processing and comprehending verbal information but with processing print (Geva 2000). When a child of school age who has recently arrived from overseas appears to be making slow progress in developing word attack skills with printed English, it will be important to collect evidence of their reading skills in the language of the school system where they lived previously.

Testing hypotheses: phonological processing, attitudes and attributions

If the conclusion is reached that acquisition of accurate and fluent reading and spelling skills is not satisfactory, this will trigger an investigation of hypothesized factors that may be important in understanding the nature of the difficulties being experienced and in identifying ways of overcoming them. The BPS report suggests that:

> observations start from a determination of the severity and persistence of problems with word reading and spelling. Reasons are then explored in areas involving phonological and orthographic awareness and memory and take account of compensatory styles, such as heavy reliance on context when reading, and coping strategies, such as the avoidance of frustrating learning opportunities.
>
> (BPS 1999: 53)

This is very similar to the approach recommended by leading researchers in the USA which also emphasizes an ongoing cycle of assessment, intervention and evaluation: 'Obviously assessment of reading skills would be the first order of business if one uses early intervention as a first cut approach to diagnosing reading disability. Assessment of cognitive abilities might then help to confirm or reject diagnostic impressions based on the child's ability to profit from remediation' (Vellutino *et al.* 1998: 392). It is apparent from the variety of different theories outlined above that very many different hypothesized factors could be selected for investigation. In this chapter particular attention is given to two sets of factors: phonological skills, and children's self-perceptions and evaluation in relation to literacy. These have been selected because there is good research evidence on the effectiveness of targeting these variables in intervention programmes.

Several tests have been developed to assess phonological competencies shown by research to be closely associated with the development of literacy skills. Table 13.2 outlines the phonological processing skills assessed by standardized tests. Some of the tests listed also assess other cognitive abilities in addition to the phonological skills shown in the table. For example, the Dyslexia Screening Test, developed by Fawcett and Nicolson (2004), whose work was outlined above, assesses reading, writing and spelling fluency, motor skills, balance, temporal processing and semantic fluency in addition to the phonological measures. It should also be noted that, despite considerable overlap, no two measures assess exactly the same skills. Furthermore, it appears that performance on some measures, such as tasks involving phoneme awareness, is influenced by the pupils' reading skills – in this case their knowledge of grapheme–phoneme correspondences. It would therefore be possible for a pupil to be assessed as having phonological difficulties on one test but not on another. Even when the tests are assessing the same phonological skill, if they do so in different ways different results may be obtained. For example, if two methods of assessing the same phonological skill place different demands on memory, the child may be able to utilize compensatory strategies only when the assessment method having the lighter memory load is used. Highly relevant though they are, tests of phonological processing on their own are best regarded as indicative, rather than definitive.

A number of studies have reported positive findings using these assessment measures. Marks and Burden (2005) reported a small-scale longitudinal

Table 13.2   Phonological processing skills assessed by tests standardized and published in the UK

Phonological processing skill	Test
Alliteration detection	CoPS, PhAB[1]
Alliteration production	PhAB[1]
Auditory discrimination	CoPS
Naming speed	DEST/DST, PhAB[1]
Non-word reading	GNRT, PhAB[1]
Phoneme deletion	PAT
Rhyme detection	DEST/DST, PAT, PhAB[1]
Rhyme production	CoPS, PAT, PhAB[1]
Spoonerisms	PhAB[1]
Speech rate	PAT
Word completion	PAT
Working memory	DEST/DST, CoPS
Auditory/verbal associative memory	CoPS
Visual/verbal associative and sequential memory	CoPS

Key:
CoPS: Cognitive Profiling System (Singleton 1995)
DEST: Dyslexia Early Screening Test (Nicolson and Fawcett 2004)
DST: Dyslexia Screening Test (Fawcett and Nicolson 2004)
GNRT: Graded Nonword Reading Test (Snowling *et al.* 1996)
PAT: Phonological Abilities Test (Muter *et al.* 1997)
PhAB: Phonological Assessment Battery (Frederickson *et al.* 1997)

[1] See below for illustrative descriptions of phonological measures, from PhAB:

Alliteration detection: The Alliteration Test is designed to assess children's ability to isolate the initial sounds in single-syllable words. On each trial they listen to three words and say which two of the three start with the same sound (e.g. ship, fat, fox).

Alliteration production: The Alliteration Fluency Test is designed to assess retrieval of phonological information from long-term memory. Children are asked to say as many words as they can in 30 seconds beginning with a particular sound (e.g. words beginning with /m/).

The Naming Speed Tests are designed to assess speed of phonological production. The Picture Naming Speed Test uses line drawings of five common objects: a table, a door, a ball, a hat and a box. The Digit Naming Speed Test uses numbers 1–9. The children are shown a visual display of randomly presented digits and asked to name them in sequence as quickly as they can.

The Nonword Reading Test is designed to tap the phonological processing involved in reading nonwords. There are two parts: one-syllable items (e.g. 'tib') and two-syllable items (e.g. 'haplut').

Rhyme detection: The Rhyme Test is designed to assess the ability to identify the rhyme in single-syllable words (e.g. the 'ate' in 'gate, plate'). On each trial the children listen to three words and say which two of the three end with the same sound (e.g. made, hide, fade).

Rhyme production: In the Rhyme Fluency Test children are asked to say as many words as they can in 30 seconds that rhyme with a particular sound (e.g. words that rhyme with 'bat').

The Spoonerisms Test is designed to assess whether children can segment single-syllable words and then synthesize the segments to provide new words or word combinations. The test consists of two parts. In the easier Part 1 the child is asked to replace the first sound of a word with a new sound (e.g. 'cot' with a /g/ makes 'got'). In Part 2 the child is asked to exchange the initial sounds of two words (e.g. 'sad cat' makes 'cad sat').

investigation using CoPS to predict literacy attainment at the end of Key Stage 1. Positive associations were found between many of the CoPS scores at age 5 years and literacy assessments conducted almost 2 years later. Simpson and Everatt (2005) reported that the 'at risk' quotient on the DEST predicted literacy difficulties 1–2 years later, with some of the individual tests (sound order and rapid naming) identified as stronger predictors than the others. From a longitudinal study of children learning to read in the UK, Hutchinson *et al.* (2004) positively evaluated the usefulness of the PhAB in identifying reading accuracy difficulties in both monolingual and bilingual children. However, scores on alliteration, rhyme and non-word reading were found to be higher than the standardization sample, suggesting that the norms of such measures have been affected by the introduction of the Literacy Hour. It appears that beyond Year 2 norms may no longer be sufficiently sensitive to identify all significant difficulties with phonological skills.

A range of studies, for example Torgesen *et al.* (2001) which was reviewed earlier in this chapter, have shown that children who are found to have phonological difficulties require intensive, explicit and highly structured teaching to develop phoneme awareness and letter–sound knowledge in reading. Evidence was also reviewed that both commercially available programmes (e.g. Sound Linkage: Hatcher 2000) and the UK Early Literacy Support programme, described earlier in this chapter, can provide effective intervention (Hatcher *et al.* 2006b). In a further rigorously designed study, Hatcher *et al.* (2006a) identified around 20 per cent of children who show reading delays at the end of their first year in school and found that three-quarters of these made significant gains in response to a 10-week reading intervention programme delivered on a daily basis by trained teaching assistants. However, this study also highlighted the need for further attention to the children who did not respond to this intervention, comprising around 5 per cent of pupils, who are likely to require intervention that is more intensive or of longer duration.

Attitudes and attributions

It has been argued that finding out how children perceive the reading task and how they evaluate their own progress will be important in any assessment. The relationship between attitude and attainment is not a simple one and Pumfrey (1997) points out that in some cases pupils' attitudes to reading and their reading attainments are not found to be positively correlated. It is suggested that two kinds of threshold effect may be operating. First, children whose attitudes or motivation are below some threshold level may be prevented from engaging with the intellectual challenges of literacy learning and make poor progress. However, increases in enthusiasm and commitment above the threshold level may not automatically lead to improvements in attainment. Second, once children have attained a threshold level of basic competence in reading and writing they will not lose those skills, even if there is a loss of interest and reduced motivation as they move through school (Davies and Brember 1995).

Pumfrey (1997) has provided a short introduction to the range of techniques that are available for assessing attitudes to reading. Among others he lists:

- observations using checklists of reading-related behaviours from which the pupil's attitudes towards reading can be inferred;

- self-report techniques;

- scaling of various types (e.g. paired comparisons);

- projective techniques;

- semantic differential techniques;

- repertory grid techniques.

Other cognitive constructs that have been investigated in understanding reading difficulties are self-concept/self-perception and attribution. The Reading Self-Concept Scale (Chapman and Tunner 1995) can be used by a class teacher or SENCO to explore with 5–10-year-olds their perceptions of reading competence and reading difficulty as well as their attitudes towards reading. The Burnett Self Scale (Burnett 1994) provides a global measure of self-concept and also assesses eight specific aspects including reading self-concept. The other seven areas relate to physical appearance, physical ability, peer relations, relations with mother, relations with father, mathematics and learning generally. The Reading Self-Concept Scale and the Burnett Self Scale are both widely available to schools in the *Children's Self-Perceptions* booklet of the *Psychology in Education Portfolio* (Burden 1999).

The Self-Perception Profile for Children (Harter 1985), which is described in more detail in Chapter 14, assesses a child's general self-worth/esteem and their judgement of their competence across a number of specific domains, including scholastic competence – the others being social, behavioural and athletic competence, and physical appearance. Frederickson and Jacobs (2001) used the Harter Profile to compare 20 children with dyslexia and 20 typically developing classmates. They found that the children with dyslexia had significantly lower scholastic self concept, but their scores in the other domains, including general self-worth, were not significantly different from those of their classmates. A review of self concept studies using a variety of assessment measures with children who have specific learning disabilities more generally reported similar findings (Zeleke 2004).

Where pupils are experiencing difficulties with some aspect of literacy it can be valuable to find out why they think they are having problems. Research has shown that the type of cause to which a child attributes their difficulties or their successes can have an effect on their motivation and subsequent achievement. Weiner (1985) suggested that common attributions made by children for success and failure in school could be classified along three dimensions – whether they are generally seen by children as internal or external to them, as stable or unstable, and as controllable or uncontrollable. For example, if children think they did well in an examination because of luck with the questions (an external factor) rather than through their own hard work (a factor that is internal to them), it will make a difference to their future approach to school activities. Table 13.3 summarizes the research findings on these issues that apply to most children. But there are developmental and individual differences. For example, it is not until about age 9 that children begin to see effort and ability as distinct (Nicholls 1978). Also, some children who experience repeated failure can develop the perception that achieving success in learning is completely outside their control, no matter what they do.

Table 13.3 Attributions for success and failure in school

Attribution	Dimensions		
	Internal/external	Stable/unstable	Controllable/uncontrollable
Ability (> 9 years)	Internal	Stable	Uncontrollable
Effort	Internal	Unstable	Controllable
Task difficulty	External	Stable	Uncontrollable
Luck	External	Unstable	Uncontrollable
Poor teaching	External	Unstable	Uncontrollable
Strategy used	Internal	Unstable	Controllable

Source: Developed from Weiner (1985).

Weiner thought that stability was particularly important in influencing future expectations. He suggested that if a pupil attributed academic success to a supposedly stable factor (such as ability) and failure to a transitory one (such as use of an incorrect strategy), they would come increasingly to expect successful outcomes. On the other hand, if a pupil attributed success to unstable factors and failure to stable factors, this would be likely to lead to increasing expectations of failure and reduced motivation to engage in academic tasks. However, other authors have argued that controllability is more important than stability in influencing future expectations and motivation. The link between attributions and motivation is of particular relevance to pupils who experience difficulties at school. In one longitudinal study (Kistener *et al.* 1988), the progress of children with specific learning difficulties was monitored over a two-year period through use of achievement test scores and teacher ratings of classroom performance and behaviour. Those children who attributed failure to unstable, controllable causes, such as their own level of effort, made the greatest achievement gains and received the most positive behaviour ratings.

Locus of control – whether people believe that they mainly control events, as opposed to being at the mercy of other people and outside forces – is one factor of a scale specifically designed to explore the developing sense of identity of young people with dyslexia. The other factors that comprise the Dyslexia Identity Scale (Burden 2005) are: self-efficacy, learned helplessness and feelings of being understood. Initial trialling of this measure with boys aged 11–16 at a special residential school for pupils with dyslexia indicated that it was helpful, alongside broader qualitative information, in generating relevant information that had useful education implications.

A number of affective areas, such as self concept and attributions, have been targeted for intervention. In the area of self concept, Elbaum and Vaughn (2003) warn that it is a mistake to think that pupils with dyslexia will necessarily have low self concept and require support with it. As we have seen, it is often only academic self concept that is affected, and even then not necessarily so. Elbaum and Vaughn (2003) analysed the outcomes of a large number of school-based intervention studies aimed at enhancing the self concept of students with specific learning difficulties. They found that only students with low self concept benefited significantly from intervention and highlighted the importance of good assessment.

Promising results have been obtained from attribution retraining programmes involving children who have SEN. For example, Borkowski *et al.* (1988) designed and evaluated an attribution retraining programme on reading comprehension for older primary children with specific reading difficulties. Some children received attribution retraining alone, some received reading comprehension strategy training alone and some received a combined programme of attribution retraining and reading comprehension strategy training. Only the combined programme group showed significant improvements in reading comprehension skills both on the special programme materials and on a standardized reading test. Borkowski *et al.* (1988) argue that teaching reading comprehension strategies alone or emphasizing the role of effort in isolation will be less effective than a systematically

---

Activity 13.3   Case study: Michael

Read the following case study and decide:

(a)   What hypotheses might prove useful in understanding Michael's difficulties?

(b)   What assessment approaches would you plan to use to collect more information and test out each of these hypotheses?

Michael (aged 14) is the second of two children of professional parents with high educational aspirations. He attends a successful comprehensive school in a prosperous suburb of a small county town in the South of England. He received speech therapy as a preschooler but now talks fluently and shows a lively curiosity, notably in relation to scientific topics. But, with the exception of mathematics, his educational attainments are poor because he is very slow at reading and has difficulty expressing his ideas in writing. In fact, his written work is so full of mistakes that some subject teachers underestimate his understanding.

As a small child he enjoyed being read stories at bedtime with his sister but took little interest in the books. In primary school he made very slow progress in reading, committing common words to memory but failing to develop strategies for working out words with which he was unfamiliar. He found this frustrating and began to use all kinds of tactics to avoid having to read or refer to books. His parents were not seriously concerned about this at first, because his father had been slow to learn to read as a child but had grown out of it and his paternal grandfather had a similar history. To some extent his parents' optimism was justified in that, with the help of an excellent learning support teacher, he did eventually learn how to overcome his problems with reading new material (though he still struggles sometimes when he comes across a text with a large proportion of unfamiliar vocabulary – e.g. in a new topic in history).

What is still undermining his educational performance (and his self-confidence) is that he can only write very slowly indeed, making many errors of spelling and syntax. He does not seem to recognize when he is going wrong, although his form tutor feels that he takes insufficient care in checking his work and could do better if he applied himself. Normally quite self-contained, he recently became angry when his history teacher criticized the amount of written work he had produced and its untidy presentation. An argument ensued with Michael saying that writing was a waste of time and that when he was a scientist he would talk into a computer and wouldn't be bothered with old-fashioned stuff like that.

linked programme which can cue and motivate pupils to apply what they have learned.

Providing appropriate learning opportunities

The next question in the BPS (1999) sequence is: 'Have appropriate learning opportunities been provided?' 'Appropriate learning opportunities' can be defined as those approaches and methods known to be generally successful in increasing pupils' rate of progress in acquiring reading and spelling skills. Pietrowski and Reason (2000) reviewed theory and research on learning, literacy development and motivation and compiled eight questions that can be asked in assessing the appropriateness of the learning opportunities in literacy that have been provided:

1 *A comprehensive model* – do the materials that are used in the classroom reflect a comprehensive model of reading and/or spelling development – (e.g. including comprehension of the text as a whole as well as providing instruction in phonics)?

2 *Progression* – do the materials show a clear progression of targets (e.g. starting from phonological awareness and moving gradually to more advanced phonic structures)?

3 *Speaking and listening* – are children exploring and reinforcing the learning of phonological regularities through both speaking and listening?

4 *Reading and writing* – are children exploring and reinforcing the learning of phonological regularities through both reading and writing?

5 *Assessing to teach* – do the materials provide guidance on 'assessing to teach' or 'assessment for learning' (i.e. on assessing what the children know in order to plan, in appropriately small steps, what should be learned next)?

6 *Mastery learning* – are the materials based on 'mastery learning' (i.e. on planned repetition and revision that ensures retention of what has been learned)?

7 *Role of the learner* – in terms of motivational influences, is there explicit guidance on the involvement of the children themselves in setting their own targets and monitoring progress?

8 *Home–school links* – is there clear guidance on how parents can help their children at home?

Pietrowski and Reason (2000) used these questions to compare three kinds of commercially published materials with a strong emphasis on the teaching of phonics: first, those developed for all children as meeting the requirements of the NLS at the word level; second, those intended for learners making slower progress in literacy; and third, those targeted at learners regarded as having difficulties of a dyslexic nature. The comparison undertaken involved four programmes in each of the three categories. A number of interesting similarities and differences were reported. Explicit guidance for parents appeared in the text of only four of the 12 programmes – in two of the programmes for all children and in two of those for learners making slower progress. Possibly the dyslexia orientated materials surveyed were considered too specialized for parental involvement? Likewise an explicit emphasis on the active involvement of learners in monitoring their own targets to enhance motivation was generally absent, only appearing in two of the programmes for learners making slower progress.

All programmes were reported to provide a progression of targets for teaching phonics. However, the materials developed for all children were more likely to teach through speaking and listening, whereas the dyslexia-orientated programmes were more likely to utilize repetitive reading and writing. Both the dyslexia-orientated programmes and those designed for learners making slower progress placed major emphasis on mastery learning. A focus on assessing to teach was also present in both these approaches, being particularly strongly emphasized in programmes for learners making slower progress. This was less likely to feature in materials that had been developed for all children.

It does seem that the provision of appropriate learning opportunities for pupils with learning difficulties in literacy can be assisted by the use of commercially developed programmes. However, on their own these are unlikely to address the full range of factors that have been shown to be important in enhancing progress and in most cases IEPs will need to incorporate other measures, depending on the programme used and the additional needs of the individual pupil. The preventive impact of programmes developed for all children might be enhanced through incorporation of more emphasis on mastery learning.

Reading comprehension

On the other hand, the materials developed for all children were more likely to fully incorporate elements of literacy other than phonics and this could be problematic for children with SEN. Children who have been struggling with word recognition may well have been given fewer opportunities to develop comprehension-fostering strategies. Padron (1992) suggests that pupils who fall behind their peers for whatever reason may increasingly be denied the opportunity to learn higher-level thinking or comprehension skills, as effort is focused on skills assumed to be more basic, such as decoding skills. Indeed, in some cases they may have lost sight of 'getting meaning' from the text as a core purpose of reading. Explicit instruction in strategies for comprehension will therefore often be appropriate. This may be particularly important for children learning EAL who are experiencing difficulties in literacy learning (Hutchinson *et al.* 2003).

Reciprocal teaching (Palinscar and Brown 1985) is a well-researched approach to the development of reading comprehension skills that has been successfully used in many classrooms. It involves a teacher working with a small group who are instructed in four specific comprehension monitoring strategies:

1   summarizing what has happened so far;

2   self-questioning about the passage before it is read, so that reading can be a purposeful seeking of answers to the questions posed;

3   clarifying and rehearsing any difficult, unusual or technical words in the passage;

4   predicting what is likely to happen or what information is likely to be gained.

The teacher begins by explaining what strategies will be learned, why, and when to apply them. The strategies are then modelled for the pupils through questions, generated initially by the teacher. The pupils summarize and add their own predictions, clarifications and responses to questions. The passage is then read (usually silently) by members of the group and the teacher leads a discussion, referring back to the questions asked before the passage was read. Through guided practice, responsibility for leading the process is gradually transferred to the pupils who take it in turns to assume the role of the teacher and generate the questions while the teacher takes on a supporting role. Figure 13.9 provides an example of a teaching session from a reciprocal teaching programme involving 6–7-year-old pupils.

This process can be used by teachers and classroom assistants not only to teach generic comprehension skills but also to prepare pupils who have reading comprehension difficulties for particular lessons so that they are able to access meaning from curriculum materials with which they would otherwise have problems. However, Le Fevre *et al.* (2003) noted that there are barriers to participation in reciprocal teaching for pupils who also have decoding difficulties in reading the texts. They found that poor decoders were unable to apply the four cognitive and metacognitive strategies during a conventional reciprocal teaching intervention. As a consequence they developed a modified intervention, tape-assisted reciprocal teaching (TART). This strategy, which involved listening to an audiotaped recording while following the text, was found to be successful in improving reading comprehension for readers who had poor comprehension skills whether or not they also had poor decoding skills. It is suggested that TART may provide a form of 'cognitive bootstrapping' which helps to ensure that children with poor word reading skills are not denied opportunities to develop higher-order thinking and comprehension skills.

Padron (1991) reported that this reciprocal teaching can also be very useful when teaching students who are learning EAL. If at the early stages of learning to decode, the teacher reads the text aloud to the pupils, the process can provide opportunities to place emphasis on reading for meaning from the outset. The

---

Activity 13.4   Providing appropriate learning opportunities

Consider the eight areas in which Pietrowski and Reason (2000) identify questions that can be asked about the learning opportunities that have been provided. Apply them either (a) to a published reading programme of your choice or (b) to the literacy programme being provided for a pupil with SEN or EAL with whom you are working.

- *A comprehensive model*

- *Progression*

- *Speaking and listening*

- *Reading and writing*

- *Assessing to teach*

- *Mastery learning*

- *Role of the learner*

- *Home–school links.*

Text which the teacher read to the children: 'Behind the front legs, there are two odor glands. They look like two extra eyes. To protect itself, a daddy longlegs can give off a smelly liquid from these glands. Birds, toads, and large insects don't like it at all. It makes them feel too sick or too weak to try to catch the daddy longlegs'.

Child B is taking responsibility for acting as the teacher in this session and the group of 6–7-year-old pupils manage the dialogue independently for most of the time. The teacher mainly intervenes to restore direction when there is misunderstanding and the dialogue begins to go off course.

1 *Child B*: [question] What does the daddy longlegs do when something comes around it? J —— ?

2 *Child A*: Use that odor and . . . [not audible]

3 *Child B*: Yeah, C.

4 *Child C*: When an animal comes along, he puts out his odor and they get too sick to catch him.

5 *Child B*: Yeah, M.

6 *Child M*: Or too weak.

7 *Child D*: They feel too weak and too sick.

8 *Child B*: Everybody gave me good answers.

9 *Teacher*: Very good.

10 *Child B*: [summary] I will summarize. When an animal comes around, it gives out its bad smell, and they get weak and too old to catch it.

11 *Child A*: [clarification] Who does?

12 *Child B*: That's the daddy longlegs.

13 *Child A*: [clarification] Who does?

14 *Child D*: The animals.

15 *Child A*: [clarification] Which animals?

16 *Child D*: All kinds of animals.

17 *Child B*: Yeah, different kinds.

18 *Child A*: Different kinds of animals put out a spray?

19 *Child D*: [clarification] Um, it might be the same kind of animal as tries to catch the daddy longlegs.

20 *Teacher*: Okay, I think you are talking about two different things. He's talking about the animals that come around to the daddy longlegs and he's trying to get you to say who puts out the odor. Is it all animals?

21 *Child A*: No, the daddy longlegs.

Figure 13.9 Example of a reciprocal teaching dialogue
Source: Palinscar (1986).

importance of this for promoting the reading progress of pupils learning EAL is discussed further in the final part of this section of the chapter. First language assisted reciprocal teaching has also been positively evaluated for EAL learners (Fung *et al.* 2003).

Recognizing that the majority of pupils with dyslexia will spend the majority of their time in ordinary classrooms in mainstream schools, the 'Dyslexia Friendly Schools' campaign of the British Dyslexia Association (BDA) was aimed at raising awareness and developing capacity to support pupils there. Of particular relevance at classroom level are professional development materials produced by the BDA to support teachers in understanding the difficulties experienced by pupils with dyslexia and adjusting their teaching style to minimize difficulties and promote achievement (Johnson 2004). The DfES (2005a) resources for school-based professional development on teaching and learning for dyslexic children draws on the BDA materials and adopts a very similar approach. Much of the advice, for example to avoid copying from the board, while essential for most pupils with dyslexia, is also desirable for most pupils generally.

The use of technology is often advocated in promoting the access and participation of pupils with dyslexia, although provision of a laptop, for example, is unlikely to assist with writing unless training in keyboard skills is provided and a reasonable typing speed attained (Ofsted 1999b). From a review of the literature, McArthur *et al.* (2001) drew similar conclusions, identifying positive effects on writing when instruction on word-processing/keyboard skills, writing strategy and writing process was provided. Spell-checking and word-predicting software was also found to be helpful in compensating for severe spelling problems.

Monitoring and evaluating progress: behavioural and biological level changes

The final question to address is: 'Has progress been made only as a result of much additional effort/instruction and does it show that difficulties are persisting?' Fine-grained progress monitoring can be carried out by means of well-established techniques such as precision teaching (Lindsley 1992) which is described in Chapter 9. Such techniques offer opportunities to:

- fine-tune the learning opportunities offered to pupils so that they are as appropriate as possible to their assessed strengths and needs and consistent with research evidence on effective teaching approaches;

- monitor the fluency of pupil's performance and the extent to which their difficulties persist across interventions and over time.

In work on spelling, Brooks and Weeks (1999) showed how a precision teaching framework can be used to monitor progress on a daily basis for pupils with dyslexic difficulties. Each week for three weeks a different systematic teaching strategy was used to help the pupils learn ten new words. Each day a teacher, classroom assistant or parent tested pupils on the words. When an error was made, the pupil was taught by the strategy being used that week. The number of words spelled correctly each day was graphed. By comparing the graphs obtained in different weeks the most effective strategy for teaching that pupil spellings could be identified. Initial selection of the three strategies to try out was made by analysing the types of errors the pupil made when spelling, and/or drawing on research and experience of successful teaching of spelling. However, if none of the strategies that were trialled produced a satisfactory rate of learning then additional strategies would need to be tried out until this was achieved. The most important advantage of this kind of fine-grained progress monitoring for pupils who have learning difficulties in literacy is that it clearly shows which intervention strategies work best for each individual. Also, it quickly shows up whether a change in strategy is working and so avoids wasting teaching time on approaches that are not helping a particular pupil accelerate their rate of learning progress. As Adams (1990: 90) points out, 'For these children we have not a classroom moment to waste'.

The SEN *Code* of Practice (DfES 2001a) emphasizes that the key test of how far pupils' learning needs are being met, and whether further action is required, is whether they are making *adequate progress*. It is suggested that the adequacy of pupils' progress can be defined in a number of ways:

- against progress made by their peers (i.e. progress is adequate which closes the gap between them and their peers, prevents the gap growing wider or maintains their position relative to peers starting from the same attainment baseline);

- by comparing pupils' progress in areas of difficulty with their progress in areas of relative strength (i.e. progress is adequate if the gap between their areas of difficulty and strength is closing or is not widening);

- in terms of other success criteria for that pupil (i.e. it matches or betters the pupil's previous rate of progress, ensures access to the full curriculum, is likely to lead to accreditation and to participation in further education, training or employment).

Where pupils' progress is not adequate it will always be important to review the strategies currently being used for assessment, planning and review, for grouping for teaching purposes, for utilizing additional human resources and for selecting alternative curricula and teaching methods. Schools are advised that overcoming specific learning difficulties may call for carefully targeted interventions using particular teaching techniques (such as a focus on phonological awareness or multi-sensory approaches). Whether an approach is right for a particular pupil can only be determined by fine-grained monitoring of that pupil's rate or trajectory of progress. As Good *et al.* (1998: 68) argue: 'No matter how great an intervention sounds, no matter how much it costs, no matter how much research has been published, and no matter how many criteria or belief systems it satisfies, if the intervention does not change the child's trajectory, then it is not effective for that child and a change is indicated'.

Changes in brain functioning

It has recently emerged that evidence-based phonological interventions can not only improve reading scores but also produce a shift towards typical brain functioning in children with dyslexia (Simos *et al.* 2002; Shaywitz *et al.* 2004). Simos *et al.* (2002) provided an intensive, phonologically-based intervention to eight children aged 7–17 years with severe dyslexia. Reading accuracy scores rose into the average range and there was a significant increase in left hemisphere activation of those areas typically activated in normally developing readers.

Simos *et al.* (2007b) provided a two-stage intensive intervention to pairs of pupils with dyslexia, aged 6–8 years. Stage 1 focused on phonological decoding skills for 8 weeks (two 50 minute sessions per day) while stage 2 focused on rapid word recognition ability for a further 8 weeks (1 hour per day). The 15 children in this study had previously been identified as inadequate responders to reading instruction that was effective for most children. Statistically and educationally significant improvements in reading test scores were noted for eight of the children who also showed 'normalizing' changes in brain activity. The other seven children did not show an adequate response to intervention or normalizing changes in brain functioning. A control group of normally developing readers did not show systematic changes in brain activity during the study. This suggests that the changes observed were associated with the special programme as opposed to developmental changes or normal classroom teaching.

Pugh *et al.* (2005) argue that functional neuroimaging techniques have a potential contribution to make to identifying EAL learners who have dyslexia. Existing cross-language research suggests commonalities in the brain organization for speech and reading in monolingual and bilingual populations, although the rate of acquisition may differ. While there is little current research in this area, it is also suggested that it may in future be possible to identify neurobiological measures that can help evaluate the success of different approaches to teaching reading in English to pupils learning EAL.

Home–school support for literacy learning

There is evidence that the literacy needs experienced by pupils learning EAL are qualitatively different from those of pupils who have SEN (Cline and Shamsi 2000). For example, the 'literacy eco-system' in which they live at home may encompass print sources in other languages in which different family members have varying levels of skills (Kenner 2005). Those pupils learning EAL who also have SEN are likely to require support in relation to both sets of needs. Frederickson and Frith (1998) studied the performance on reading tests and the Phonological Assessment Battery of 50 children aged 10–12 years whose first language was Sylheti and who had been educated in English since the age of 5. They were compared with two groups of monolingual children – children assessed as having specific learning difficulties/dyslexia and normally developing readers matched for age and IQ. The children with dyslexia showed considerable degrees of phonological impairment compared both to the normally developing readers and the bilingual pupils. The results suggested that the phonological skills assessed were similarly developed in bilingual children whose exposure to English had been sufficient to develop surface competencies, as in monolingual English-speaking children. The children learning EAL performed less well in reading comprehension than in reading accuracy, while the reverse was true for the children with specific learning difficulties. This was presumably because those with specific learning difficulties were able to use their semantic knowledge to compensate for their poor phonological processing and decoding skills, while those learning EAL were able to develop good decoding skills even when they did not understand what they were reading.

Cline and Cozens (1999) used miscue analysis to identify the sources of information children used when they found words difficult to read. They compared a group of monolingual Key Stage 2 children with a group of bilingual children from a Pakistani/Kashmiri community who were of the same age and level of reading achievement. All the children made most use of grapho-phonic cues and the two groups made equal use of grapho-phonic and syntactic cues. However, the bilingual children made less use of semantic cues. The authors hypothesize that 'after struggling to read culturally unfamiliar material with a limited English vocabulary in the early stages, some of the children become habitual users of the surface and syntactic cues in print and, in effect, learn not to read for meaning' (Cline and Cozens 1999: 27).

So, available evidence suggests that most children learning EAL do not encounter particular problems in decoding print at the word level, even in their second language. Similar proportions of monolingual children and those learning EAL appear to experience the difficulties associated with phonological dyslexia (Frederickson and Frith 1998; Geva 2000). But children learning EAL do potentially face challenges with reading material at school at the sentence and text levels as linguistic and cultural differences can become obstacles which they will need help to negotiate.

Schools need to give consideration to cultural discontinuities that children learning EAL in the UK may experience between their home community and the local authority school over the development of literacy. Gregory (1994) compared the experiences of children aged 5–7 from six East London Bangladeshi families in their local authority primary schools and in the community schools that they attended at the end of the day. Table 13.4 shows that children studied reading for longer in the community school, were expected to read for different purposes, used different types of reading material and were taught by different methods.

An important implication for assessment is that if children who are learning EAL are making poor progress in learning to read English and are known to attend a religious or community class where reading is part of the curriculum, there are additional assessment questions to be addressed, such as: how do they respond to the different literacy demands made of them in that setting, and what impact does that experience have on their perception of the reading task in school? In general, teachers need to consider carefully how they can assess in an individual case of apparent learning difficulty whether discontinuities between home and school are inhibiting reading progress.

There are parallels here in terms of the successful outcomes that have been obtained through parental involvement programmes for pupils who experience literacy learning difficulties. MacLeod (1996: 382) had expressed concern about approaches where 'parents would be expected to accommodate to the school without the school being expected to accommodate to them'. She argued that parental involvement should build on parents' own resources and abilities rather than imposing school practices in an attempt to 'compensate for perceived deficits in community literacy practices'. Some of the approaches that have proved most successful are indeed characterized by attempts to accommodate to the needs of the parents involved (Crawford and Zygouris-Coe 2006). The Parents, Children and Teachers (PACT) project in Haringey produced gains in literacy learning which were still apparent three years later (Hewison 1988). In this project, where parents were asked to hear their child read on a regular basis, home visits from

Table 13.4 Learning to read in LEA primary schools and Bangladeshi community schools

LEA primary school	Community school
Extent:	
2–5 hours a week	6–9 hours a week
Length:	
20 minutes (often interrupted)	2–3 hours (usually without a break)
Purpose:	
To improve chances of employment (parents)	To strengthen cultural identification
To gain enjoyment (teacher)	To learn religion
To play (child)	To learn
Materials:	
Storybooks on high-quality paper with coloured illustrations and complex language	Reading primers on low-quality paper with black and white print and simple language
Can be changed when child pleases	Must be completed before changing
Bought by school and unfamiliar to parents	Bought by and familiar to parents
Method:	
Teacher reads to child, encourages, does not correct and does not test	Teacher demonstrates instructs, corrects, tests
Child experiments, 'pretends', guesses	Child repeats, practises, is tested

Source: Adapted from Gregory (1994).

project staff were provided to offer support. Where children are experiencing significant literacy learning difficulties, where parents lack confidence and experience of educational success or where there are difficulties in the parent–child relationship, concern has been expressed that these additional parental needs will also have to be accommodated if a parental involvement programme is not to produce detrimental rather than beneficial effects.

A number of more structured methods were developed to support positive and failure-free parent–child engagement with books. Paired reading (Morgan and Lyon 1979; Topping and Lindsay 1991) is probably the best known of these techniques. It allows children to read at home with a parent whatever books interest them, provided that the books can be read by the parent who is working with them. If the text is too difficult for the child to read unaided they are supported by 'reading together' when parent and child read all the words out loud together. The parent adjusts speed to match the child whom they ensure says every word correctly. If the child makes an error, the parent simply repeats the word until the child reads it correctly. When the child comes to an easier section that they think they can read themselves, they give the parent some prearranged non-verbal signal, such as a nudge or a tap on the book, to tell them to be quiet. The child then continues reading alone until an error is made which is not self-corrected within five seconds. The parent then joins in again, says the word for the child to repeat, and they continue reading together until the child gives the next signal that they want to try reading alone. The parent gives the child lots of praise throughout for reading well, whether together or alone, and for signalling to read alone. They also spend time with the child discussing the story or information about which they are reading.

Topping and Lindsay (1992: 222) report on a comprehensive review of the research on paired reading. They identified the following criteria for community interventions against which paired reading could be evaluated: (i) simple, (ii) inexpensive, (iii) effective, (iv) compatible with the existing values and need structures of the population, (v) flexible, (vi) decentralized, and (vii) sustainable. The research on paired reading reviewed was judged to be encouraging – a view that has been confirmed by subsequent research (e.g. Fiala and Sheridan 2003). In addition Overett and Donald (1998) conducted a study of paired reading in a disadvantaged community in South Africa and reported positive effects on family relationships and parent–school interactions, in addition to reading accuracy, comprehension and attitudes.

Conclusions

In this chapter the discussion of SEN in literacy has been set within the context of the national framework for teaching literacy. The origins and implementation of the literacy framework were briefly outlined, and particular considerations relating to the participation of pupils who have SEN and who are learning EAL were discussed. The causal modelling framework which was introduced in Chapter 5 was used to represent the range of theories that have been advanced to account for learning difficulties in literacy. Recent research evidence has consistently supported the particular importance of problems with phonological processing in understanding difficulties with literacy learning.

Issues and problems in defining dyslexia were discussed. In particular, the problems associated with IQ–achievement discrepancy definitions of dyslexia were explained. We suggested that the definition of dyslexia developed by the British Psychological Society (1999) was to be preferred. It separates description from explanation and provides a framework for assessment through intervention. Within this framework hypotheses about the reasons for a pupil's difficulties can be tested, and we reviewed a range of assessment techniques which can be used to investigate two types of hypotheses in particular – hypotheses about a pupil's phonological processing skills and hypotheses about their attitudes to reading and attributions for success and failure.

We considered appropriate literacy learning opportunities that should be provided for pupils experiencing difficulties in word reading and comprehension. Promoting access and participation through staff training and the use of ICT are also considered. The importance of monitoring and evaluating the progress in each individual case was highlighted. Changes in brain functioning in children with dyslexia in response to evidence-based interventions that are strongly phonological were outlined. The potential was noted for neuroimaging techniques to contribute to identifying EAL learners who have dyslexia. Finally, the additional needs of those pupils who are also learning EAL were considered. Parallels were drawn between positive action to address home–school discontinuities for pupils learning EAL and features of successful parental involvement in reading programmes for pupils who have SEN, including paired reading initiatives.

14

Mathematics

Objectives

When you have studied this chapter you should be able to:

- outline in summary current issues relating to the mathematics curriculum and the social context of mathematics learning and teaching;
- explain how problems of understanding, procedural skill, anxiety and language may contribute to learning difficulties in mathematics;
- analyse the impact that specific learning difficulties and SEN may have on mathematics learning;
- describe the main approaches to assessment in mathematics and suggest what methods might be appropriate for different purposes.

Contents

The mathematics curriculum

- The aims and scope of mathematics education
- Multicultural mathematics
- School mathematics and home mathematics

Learning difficulties in mathematics

- Mathematical understanding
- Anxiety and motivation
- 'Reading' mathematics
- Specific learning difficulties
- Learning difficulties in mathematics associated with other SEN

Learning difficulties in mathematics: assessment for intervention

- Assessment in the context of educational reform
- Assessment in the service of teaching
- Individual diagnostic assessment in mathematics

Conclusions

The mathematics curriculum

The aims and scope of mathematics education

Following the Cockcroft Committee (DES 1982), successive official statements about the aims of education in mathematics emphasized that mastery of the subject:

- is needed for adult life and employment;
- is a valuable means of communication;
- is important as a tool for studying other subjects;
- can be an aesthetically pleasing element of our cultural experience.

For example, the report of the National Curriculum Council Working Group on Mathematics set out a vision of the nature of mathematics which at the time appeared to command a wide measure of consensual support (DES 1988: Chapter 2). This vision stressed that mathematics is a means of organizing, communicating and manipulating information with a language consisting of diagrams and symbols plus associated conventions and theorems. While it was to be taught because it is useful, the Working Group was also committed to the idea that it should at the same time be a source of delight and wonder. This might arise, for example, in discovering relationships or in achieving elegant solutions.

They saw it as important that pupils should master the special language of maths (including numbers, graphs and algebraic expressions) because this language is a powerful means of communication that can simplify and clarify a message. The use of symbols in maths makes for dense, concise and precise statements – a source of power but also, they pointed out, one reason why many children find it difficult.

'Arithmetic' or 'number' was even then seen as central and fundamental to school maths. While number was to be pervasive, maths was seen as much wider in scope. However, the balance of different aspects of the maths curriculum is subject to regular 'swings of the pendulum' (Brown 1999). Following political concern about a perceived gap in maths attainments between children in the UK and in some overseas countries (Reynolds and Farrell 1996; DfEE 1998a: paras 28–9), an increasing emphasis was placed on numeracy targets and on the teaching of number and of fluency in calculation. It was perceived that schools in countries with higher standards of performance in mathematics tended to give more time to developing oral and mental work at an early stage and to whole-class teaching. The National Numeracy Strategy (NNS) aimed to ensure that teachers would spend 'less time in mathematics lessons working and trouble-shooting with individuals' and would 'provide appropriately demanding work for pupils with limited differentiation around work common to all pupils in one class' (DfEE 1998a: 22). This strategy had only limited success so that by 2005 nearly a quarter of 11-year-olds were 'still not confidently attaining level 4 or above in mathematics by the time they leave primary school' (DfES 2006c: 2). Reporting a study that was conducted over a period before and after the national strategy was introduced, Brown and Millett (2003: 202) noted that 'both observation of lessons . . . and interviews with children suggest that low attaining pupils derive little benefit from the whole-class teaching episodes, and the topic of the lesson does not always correspond to their areas of greatest need'.

In a revised Primary National Strategy, mathematics learning objectives in primary schools in England were reorganized into seven strands:

- using and applying mathematics;

- counting and understanding number;

- knowing and using number facts;

- calculating;

- understanding shape;

- measuring;

- handling data (DfES, 2006c: 65)

Eight years earlier the Numeracy Task Force had stated that 'the national drive for early, high quality intervention in both literacy and numeracy is intended to reduce the number of children who need long term provision for SEN'. At the same time they acknowledged that including pupils with SEN in the daily maths lesson in mainstream primary schools would pose particular challenges for teachers (DfEE 1998b: paras 122 and 124). The negative stance on differentiation that was noted above was modified in the 2006 Guidance on the new National Primary Framework:

> For children working significantly below the level of their class or group, learning objectives related to the aspect on which the whole class is working should be chosen as much as possible. However, they should be right for each child at each stage of their learning and development. If, with appropriate access strategies and support, a child cannot work towards the same learning objective as the rest of the class, teachers may want to track back to an earlier objective.
>
> (DfES 2006c: 14)

In Activity 14.1 you are invited to examine the specific recommendations that have been made at different times and reflect on them in the light of your own experience of work with children who have learning difficulties.

Activity 14.1 Recommendations for work with children who have learning difficulties

Below you will find a number of statements about how pupils with SEN may be helped within the framework of the NNS. Where you have worked with children in the relevant age range and setting, reflect on your own experience with either one or two children who have experienced serious learning difficulties in school. Consider what aspects of the recommended strategies might work well with them and what aspects might present problems. How could those problems be overcome? Discuss these issues with a colleague.

> Our recommended strategy envisages that children would be taught together as a whole class right from the beginning of Year 1, and for some of the time in Reception . . . It is quite possible to accommodate a range of

attainment at this stage, with children learning about mathematical ideas and language through a broad range of stimulating, interactive activities. The experience of the National Numeracy Project has been that children who know less about mathematics than others when they enter a Reception class can derive great benefit, and make considerable progress, by listening to, and watching, their peers engage in mathematical activities for part of their time. This is an important stage of learning, which gradually allows them to participate successfully in the activities. (DfEE 1998b: para. 156)

We have been particularly encouraged by the progress of pupils with SEN, including some with statements, in schools taking part in the National Numeracy Project. Teachers have generally aimed to keep children with SEN up with the general pace of teaching in the class, rather than to offer a high degree of differentiated work . . . There may, however, be a small proportion of children in mainstream schools who suffer from severe difficulties that seriously hamper their progress in mathematics . . . All these children should participate in at least part of the daily mathematics lesson with other members of their class. In the middle part of the lesson, children with severe difficulties with mathematics should follow an individualized programme with appropriate support, but would benefit from being included in the oral work with the whole class at the beginning of the daily lesson. (DfEE 1998b: paras 122–3)

Where special educational needs have been identified, it is important that the child's individual education plan (IEP) includes suitable objectives for numeracy, that are challenging but realistic. It is common at the moment for IEPs to refer to literacy only. If these numeracy objectives are linked to the school's framework or scheme of work, teachers can bear them in mind when planning lessons. Pupils with statements may to some extent be working on individual programmes based on their statements, but it would also be appropriate for their IEPs to mention numeracy. (DfEE 1998a: para. 109)

The National Numeracy Task Force expressed the hope that as many special schools as possible would be involved in the implementation of the National Numeracy Strategy. Indeed, aspects such as a high proportion of oral work, thorough consolidation of learning, structured lessons, good diagnosis of children's misconceptions, and regular assessment and target setting for all pupils have long been recognised as best practice in special schools. (DfEE 1998a: para. 111)

Special schools will need to adapt these methods in some cases. Some pupils, for example, may find the physical and mental effort involved in concentration for, say, 50 minutes of mathematics, too great, and need a much shorter lesson of, say, 30 minutes, with a supplementary time later in the day. (DfEE 1998a: para. 111)

If, with appropriate access strategies and support, a child cannot work towards the same learning objective as the rest of the class, teachers may want to track back to an earlier objective. The structure and the new electronic format of the renewed Framework for literacy and mathematics support multi-level curriculum planning, and allow teachers to easily track back and forward through a progression strand to locate earlier and later learning objectives. It also makes direct links to a wealth of other useful materials which will help to plan teaching and children's learning. Planning for individual children or groups of children based on informed observation and assessment for learning will be informed by knowledge of their priorities. For the majority of the time it will be appropriate for children to work on objectives that are similar and related to those for the whole class. However, at other times you will also have to consider whether the children have other priority needs that are central to their learning, for example a need to concentrate on some key skills. (DfES 2006c: 14)

Research on school effectiveness has shown that performance in maths is more strongly influenced by differences between schools than performance in reading (Reynolds and Muijs 1999: 18). There have been concerns about specific weaknesses in maths teaching for many years. In a review of 355 primary school visits between 1982 and 1988, Her Majesty's Inspectorate of Schools (HMI) reported that shortcomings in maths teaching identified ten years before had persisted in many schools: 'It is evident and unsurprising that the children's confidence and competence in learning mathematics is closely associated with the confidence and competence of their teachers' (HMI 1989: 27). A key factor locally in England and Wales may have been the shortage of staff who were well qualified and confident to teach the subject (A. Smith 2004). For some years school inspections continued to identify shortcomings in the teaching of mathematics in a significant minority of schools (Ofsted 1996b, 1997b). The National Numeracy Strategy and the National Primary Strategy represented energetic attempts to address these issues (DfEE 1998b; DfES 2006c). But for the foreseeable future staff shortages and the quality of maths teaching will remain possible contextual factors when seeking to understand children's learning difficulties in maths. A careful assessment of the classroom learning environment may be particularly important for this reason.

Multicultural mathematics

Maths is sometimes described as 'abstract' or 'international' or 'universal'. The implication is that there is one form of mathematical representation of human experience that is uniform across cultural groups. Such assumptions have been contradicted by research in both developing and developed countries over the last 30 years. For example, investigators have identified diverse skills and approaches to calculation among particular groups of workers such as weavers or market traders and among children in different countries. They have shown that the same children may adopt different approaches to mathematical tasks depending on whether they are working at school or in a family or street enterprise. The sociocultural organization of the maths practices was a crucial factor (Nunes *et al.* 1993), as was the social value given to different forms of practice (Abreu and Cline 2007). Comparative studies have shown that the content and structure of mathematics curricula vary a great deal across the world (Sutherland 2007).

In a multicultural society it is beneficial if the school maths curriculum draws upon and refers to the diverse mathematical traditions that are represented in the cultural heritage of the various ethnic groups in the school population. This will enable maths teaching to contribute to the achievement of broader educational aims of inclusiveness, mutual respect and intellectual flexibility. An example of how that aspiration might be realized is the GARP resource – Integrating Global and Anti-Racist Perspectives within the Primary Curriculum – developed in Nottingham with national support. Its core principles are that:

- The cultural diversity of Britain and the world should be reflected across the curriculum.

- The achievements of individuals and cultures are universal and not only Western.

- All children need to be able to talk about and challenge unfair generalisations and racism as well as to examine prejudices and different perspectives.

(Nottingham City Council 2005)

Applied to mathematics, these principles lead to teaching that:

- highlights the culturally diverse historical roots of mathematical ideas and techniques when introducing them to pupils;

- supports pupils to develop a positive understanding of their own multicultural society and of contemporary cultures elsewhere through the choice of content in mathematics lessons – for examples, applying new mathematical skills to statistics of language use or household occupation and to data that challenges stereotypical views of particular groups of people;

- employs classroom strategies that encourage collaborative learning and partnership rather than competitive effort and rivalry (Alladina 1985; Nelson *et al.* 1993; Schiro 2004; Nikolay 2006).

For an example of a teaching strategy of this kind, see the project designed by teachers in Portsmouth for use in Key Stage 3 (Portsmouth EMAS 2005). This project looks at mathematics around the world, focusing on different number systems and how the four basic operations are carried out. It also introduces pupils to different writing systems. This perspective may be contrasted with that of the working party who developed the original National Curriculum framework for maths, who were sceptical of the value of such approaches (DES 1988: paras 10.18–23). See Activity 14.2.

Activity 14.2   The implications of different perspectives on multicultural mathematics

Examine the quotations below and suggest three differences that you think might be observed between the classroom practices in mathematics of two teachers who adopt these contrasting perspectives. There will be differences in their work with all children, but you are asked to focus specifically on differences that might emerge in how they work with a child from an ethnic or linguistic minority with which you are familiar, who has learning difficulties in mathematics.

> It is sometimes suggested that the multicultural complexion of society demands a 'multicultural' approach to mathematics with children being introduced to different numeral systems, foreign currencies and non-European measuring and counting devices. We are concerned that undue

emphasis on multicultural mathematics, in these terms, could confuse young children. While it is right to make clear to children that mathematics is the product of a diversity of cultures, priority must be given to ensuring that they have the knowledge and understanding and skills which they will need for adult life and employment in Britain in the twenty-first century. We believe that most ethnic parents will share this view. (DES 1988: para. 10.20)

The mathematics curriculum must provide opportunities for all pupils to recognise that all cultures engage in mathematical activity and no single culture has a monopoly on mathematical achievement. All pupils must be given the opportunity to enrich their mathematical experience by selection of appropriate materials to stimulate and develop the knowledge, understanding and skills which they will need for adult life and employment in Britain in the twenty-first century. Mathematical experience may be enriched by examples from a variety of cultures – e.g. Vedic arithmetic enhances understanding of number, Islamic art patterns are based on complex geometric construction, and the Chinese had a rod numeral method of solving simultaneous equations that leads naturally to methods used in higher mathematics. (Joseph 1993: 19)

When children from an ethnic or linguistic minority community experience learning difficulties in maths at school, one factor in the frustrations they encounter may be not so much the curriculum as the way it is taught. For example, Zevenbergen *et al.* (2004) observed pupils from diverse backgrounds in Australian schools and concluded that those from some ethnic groups would have benefited from more time being devoted to talking through tasks before any attempt was made to commit solutions to writing. There was also evidence of individuals resisting their best work being displayed to the rest of the class. The research team argued that it is not just the content of mathematics that needs to be responsive to the needs of different groups but also its pedagogy. Similarly, in the report of a study conducted in Catalonia, Gorgorió and Planas (2005) argued that it is necessary to negotiate classroom norms afresh when students from immigrant families join a mathematics class. The implication of such findings is that, when a pupil from an ethnic minority community displays apparent learning difficulties in mathematics, it may be important to analyse the match between what happens in their classroom and their culturally sanctioned learning style. A mismatch between existing learning style and the teaching strategies adopted in the classroom may explain initial difficulties more accurately than a traditional attribution of the problem to a deficit of learning ability within the child.

School mathematics and home mathematics

There is general agreement that it is important to involve parents and carers in their children's education, including their maths education (Merttens *et al.* 1996; DfEE 1998b: paras 172–8). This may require three kinds of activity on the part of the school:

- informing parents about their children's progress and about the maths curriculum and how it is taught;

- encouraging and supporting parents to engage in mathematical activities with their children at home;

- creating opportunities for parents to become actively involved in maths work with their children at school.

For practical suggestions under each of these headings, see Fitzgerald (2004), Merttens *et al.* (1996) and Merttens (1999).

The task is not straightforward, as there is often a significant gap to be bridged between school and home (Aubrey *et al.* 2003). Table 14.1 shows Merttens's (1999) summary of the differences between 'school maths' and 'home maths'. These lists probably give too little attention to parents' participation in assisting their children at home with school maths – or with the best approximation they can make to school maths (Abreu and Cline 2005). However, it is helpful that the lists highlight basic differences in the way mathematics is generally practised in the two settings. These differences are associated with different perceptions of what tools are to be used and what skills are involved. More fundamentally, they are associated with different perceptions of the social value of what is done (Abreu 1995).

In a series of case studies of maths learning in multiethnic primary schools Abreu and Cline (2005) illustrated the complex issues that parents and children can face:

- In recounting their experiences with their own children, parents often described themselves as being confronted with alternative tools that could perform the same mathematical function. They might be faced with new strategies or different methods, or, in the case of bilingual parents, different linguistic codes. A difference in strategies could lead to debates about 'who owns the proper knowledge': was it the parent or the teacher? Or it might lead to parents questioning their own competence or to a child offering resistance to their parents' help, or to the parents being selective in what knowledge they presented to the child. In each case the basis of the action was a value judgement about home and school mathematics that was rooted in a wider set of

Table 14.1   Differences between 'school maths' and 'home maths'

Maths at home	Maths at school
Occurs contingently, as a result of what is happening at the time.	Is usually planned, and follows the teacher's agenda
Is often initiated by the child who is the prime mover in the questioning process.	Is often initiated by the teacher who is the prime mover in the questioning process.
Numbers are always in a real-life context, but are only occasionally matched to a physical representation.	The physical or concrete representation of numbers will often be emphasized.
Follows no formal curriculum and is bounded only by the child's interest and the parent's time/expertise.	Follows a formal curriculum and is bounded by professionally defined notions of what is appropriately taught at each stage.

Source: Merttens (1999).

values. For example, a child might assert that they should not follow their parents' practices because they ought to give priority to what is contemporary and modern in mathematics over what is old and outdated. Or a father who was a first-generation immigrant might express confidence in the underlying efficiency of tried and tested approaches to life, even in a new environment.

- Where children learned maths in English at school and spoke a different language at home, parents were compelled to take a position regarding the role of language in their children's maths learning. Perhaps some parents who spoke the language of the school as their own first language faced a linguistic challenge in relation to changes in maths vocabulary since they were at school but did not recognize it as a serious problem. At least one monolingual English-speaking mother showed an awareness of the issue, calling for courses for parents on, among other things, the 'jargon ... teachers use' (Abreu and Cline 2005: 717). The importance of helping parents to bridge the gap between school and home was emphasized by the finding that across ethnic groups those who had a strategy for doing so were more likely to have a child who was succeeding in maths at school. One example was a mother who made it her business to ask in detail about the method taught in school for tackling a particular type of maths problem that featured in homework.

- Another parent simply taught a different and parallel form of maths at home, making clear to the child that the school approach and the home approach were both valid but should be practised in the setting for which they were designed.

Partnership with parents should not always involve a one-way traffic in which professionals provide support (Civil and Andrade 2002). Many parents are the fount of hard-won wisdom on how to bridge the gap. Teachers will have much to learn from them, especially when the two groups come from different cultural backgrounds. 'Careful listening is the most critical aspect for anyone working with parents' (Wheale 2000: 2). Particular care may be needed when preparing 'parent information sheets' about maths for families whose children have learning difficulties in the subject and require understanding and support (Hannell 2005).

Learning difficulties in mathematics

Within the school curriculum, learning maths is uniquely challenging in that it is highly organized, sequential and progressive. Simpler elements must be learned successfully before moving on to others:

It is a subject where one learns the parts; the parts build on each other to make a whole; knowing the whole enables one to reflect with more understanding on the parts, which in turn strengthens the whole. Knowing the whole also enables an understanding of the sequences and interactions of the parts and the way they support each other so that the getting there clarifies the stages of the journey.

(Chinn and Ashcroft 1998: 4).

Because of the interrelating nature of the subject, children who have learning difficulties in maths may sometimes appear to feel even more lost and disempowered than those who encounter problems in other subjects.

In this chapter learning difficulties in maths will be analysed first in terms of what children understand about maths and second in terms of the emotional significance that the subject has for many children and adults. We will then examine the language that is used in maths and the challenges it poses for many learners. Finally, there will be short accounts of specific learning difficulties in maths (a complex topic that has received less attention than specific learning difficulties in reading), and of the learning difficulties in maths that are associated with other SEN.

Mathematical understanding

Skemp (1976: 20) pointed out that the word 'understanding' has been used in two different senses in relation to mathematics – *relational understanding* which means 'knowing both what to do and why' and *instrumental understanding* which means 'knowing rules without reasons'. As examples of 'rules without reasons' Skemp quoted the formulae for getting the area of a rectangle (multiply the length by the breadth), subtracting one large number from another (use the 'borrowing' method), and dividing by a fraction (turn it upside down and multiply). He argued that children's learning difficulties often arise because of a mismatch between what they are expecting (e.g. help towards instrumental understanding) and what the teacher offers (e.g. teaching of basic generalizable concepts) – or vice versa. Fashions in the teaching of maths shift over time between emphasizing procedures and emphasizing concepts (Hiebert and Lefevre 1986; Brown 1999). It is now generally accepted that, in addition to conceptual understanding and procedural efficiency, children need to learn to think about mathematical problems strategically (formulating and representing problems in ways that lead to a logical solution). They also need to develop a 'productive disposition' towards the subject, that is, 'a habitual inclination to see mathematics as sensible, useful and worthwhile, coupled with a belief in diligence and one's efficacy' (Baroody 2003: 26).

Activity 14.3   Conceptual understanding and procedural knowledge

John and Peter are aged 8. They both like mathematics, but while John has good conceptual understanding of the mathematics he has learned as well as an ability to reproduce the procedures he has been taught, Peter has a good memory for the procedures but is uncertain about some of the concepts. Consider how the two boys might differ in their approaches to the following mathematical problems that were read out to them by their teacher:

(a)   The Smith family went to the fair. At one stall Mr Smith won two goldfish, at another stall the children won four balloons and at a third stall Mrs Smith won a stuffed animal. How many things did the family win altogether?

(b)   Mrs Smith had a bag with 12 sweets in it. She had four children. If she shared the sweets fairly between her children, how many sweets would each child get?

Recent research has suggested that, in any case, children's understanding of mathematical concepts is positively correlated with their ability to execute procedures. At the same time it is commonly found that children who fall behind in maths across the board show a particular weakness in processes that are normally automatic. Examples of the processes involved are:

- recognizing small numerical quantities without delay – for example, when 2–4 stars are displayed in an array on a screen (Koontz and Berch 1996);

- rapid recall of basic number facts – for example, 3×4 (Russell and Ginsberg 1984);

- solving simple addition problems without a visual prompt (Ostad 1997).

The failure of automatic processes appears to have a further consequence. Ostad showed that the mathematically weak children in their sample did not broaden the range of strategies they used over a two-year period. Although the group was assumed to be heterogeneous in terms of intelligence, language skills, etc., there was a striking degree of similarity in the strategies used for these tasks across the group as a whole. In contrast, the children they described as 'mathematically normal' continued to experiment with new strategies even after finding methods that were successful: their approach was seen as showing 'strategic flexibility'.

Anxiety and motivation

Many children and adults who take other intellectual challenges in their stride panic about maths. Buxton (1981) quoted adults saying things like 'A string of figures and my brain seizes up' and 'I can't think precisely enough for this sort of thing'. A survey carried out for the Cockcroft Committee (DES 1988) showed that such feelings were widespread in the adult population and that they were not without justification: many of those interviewed showed serious gaps in their competence when faced with mathematical problems in everyday life. In Activity 14.4 you will read what a university tutor thought the implications of such attitudes might be.

Activity 14.4 'Maths phobia'

The following extract from the University of Hull Study Advice website (http://www.hull.ac.uk/studyadvice/MathsResources/Mathsphobia.doc, accessed 22 December 2006) aims to outline what a fear of maths might mean in the everyday life of an adult:

> The fear of maths may not seem as scary as a fear of snakes or tarantulas; but think about it – when was the last time you encountered a snake in the checkout queue at the supermarket, on your phone bill, or in your homework (biologists excepted from the latter). People who fear maths have to deal with that fear on a daily basis.
>
> Clearly it can be a major problem, and can seriously affect people's lives. Maths phobia affects people's lives by making them:
>
> - lose confidence in themselves and in their academic abilities

- trust blindly any bills they receive, because they daren't question the figures

- shy away from helping their kids with their homework

- avoid courses in case they contain maths

- leave courses when they encounter the maths element

- run up credit card bills as they can't keep track of how much they've spent

Reflect on how a fear of maths might affect a school child. What aspects of mathematics do you think would have the greatest impact in terms of raising anxieties, and how would those anxieties affect children's learning across the curriculum and their lives outside school?

Quilter and Harper (1988) interviewed a group of 15 graduates of other subjects who described themselves as having a negative attitude to maths. The reasons they cited most frequently were categorized by the researchers as:

- lack of relevance or applicability to real-world experience;

- exposure to instrumental learning at school leading to disaffection;

- personality characteristics and/or teaching style of maths teachers.

Thus the problems were attributed not to the subject itself nor to personal inadequacy but rather to deficiencies in the way maths was taught. A similar emphasis was found when trainee primary school teachers were interviewed about maths anxiety (Haylock 1995: Chapter 1; Bibby 2002).

Sepie and Keeling (1978) differentiated between anxiety about maths, anxiety about school and general (trait) anxiety. With a sample of 246 children aged 11–12 in New Zealand they showed that anxiety about maths correlated significantly with maths achievement, while the other two types of anxiety did not. Similar results were obtained by Suinn *et al.* (1988) and Gierl and Bisanz (1995) with North American groups that included younger children. In the second of these studies, maths anxiety was differentiated into *mathematics test anxiety* ('feelings of nervousness associated with past, present and future mathematical testing situations') and *mathematics problem-solving anxiety* ('feelings of nervousness associated with situations both in and out of school that require students to solve math problems and use the solutions in some way'). They found that between the ages of 9 and 12 average scores on measures of maths test anxiety increased relative to average scores for maths problem-solving anxiety. It seemed that, as children progress through school at this stage, they become relatively more anxious about maths testing than about using maths to solve problems in contexts other than testing.

That point may helpfully be kept in mind when examining the results of a systematic review of the effectiveness of various treatments for test anxiety. Hembree (1990) found that individuals who had scored high on measures of maths anxiety improved their scores on standardized maths achievement tests immediately after behavioural and cognitive-behavioural interventions that had brought down their levels of anxiety about the subject. This suggested to Ashcraft *et al.* (1998) that their abilities had previously been underestimated because anxiety had disrupted their test performance. Further work by that team indicated that anxiety disrupts maths performance selectively. The greatest impact is experienced when the maths tasks that are set involve close concentration and a challenge to working memory. In contrast, high levels of anxiety did not disrupt performance on the recollection of simple number bonds or the completion of straightforward addition and subtraction sums. When working with individuals who show high levels of anxiety about maths it is important to investigate how exactly their learning is affected. It may be that they will show depressed performance across the board, but they may only underperform on tasks that make high demands on working memory where their concentration is disrupted by thoughts of anticipated failure (Ashcraft 2002). For a fuller account of these issues and of research on gender as a factor in maths anxiety, see the chapter on mathematics learning in Frederickson *et al.* (2008).

'Reading' mathematics

Some have argued that communication is at the core of the subject and that maths should be seen 'as a "language" in the same way that Italian is a language' (Rowland 1995: 54). But there are some important differences too. In everyday life many of the concepts we use most often are imprecise, contradictory and ambiguous. We tend to qualify what we say and put our thoughts forward tentatively. Mature adults like to express uncertainty and feel it is important to be able to tolerate ambiguity. When we talk, our comments are often repetitive, circular, imperfectly structured and full of redundancy. It is often claimed that mathematical thought is very different so that mathematical language is abstract, unambiguous, precise and without redundancies. This may be one reason why some people find the subject intimidating.

A specific source of difficulty in learning the language of maths is its reliance on special symbols. First, the speech forms used for '+', '−', etc. vary a great deal. Teachers have to decide when to employ one form consistently in order to aid understanding in their own classroom and when to vary the forms they use in order to aid generalization to other settings. (Misunderstanding is commonplace. Kerslake (1982) found that 29 per cent of a sample of 194 London pupils aged 12–14 had an accurate view of what $3 \div 4$ means, but 52 per cent read it the other way round – as 4 divided by 3.) Second, the same symbol may be used in ways that appear intuitively different. For example, the symbol '×' causes integers such as 3 to increase (as in $2 \times 3 =$) or decrease (as in $\frac{3}{4} \times 3 =$), depending on whether the multiplier is greater than or less than 1. Third, the abstract character of mathematical symbols creates difficulties for children who may understand a concept in context but not when contextual cues are removed. In a useful chapter on the language of testing, Davis (1991) quotes the example of a 4-year-old boy who answered accurately the question 'How many is two elephants and one elephant?' but gave the wrong answer immediately afterwards to 'How many is two and one more?'. Fourth, the organization of mathematical symbols in writing or print presents a challenge to children who are confused about left and right, or have problems over sequencing, or have visual-perceptual difficulties. For example, a child may read 34 as 43, or may tackle a decimal sum from the wrong direction, or may make frequent mistakes when reading down a column of figures.

Many of these problems arise because in a decimal system place value is crucial: the same digit (e.g. 3) means *three* if it appears in the right-hand *units* column and *thirty* if it appears in the left-hand *tens* column. Children in English-speaking countries often struggle to appreciate this (Jones and Thornton 1993). There is evidence that place value difficulties may be less acute for children in some other language communities, notably in Asia. Children appear to achieve higher standards of accuracy and speed in place value judgements in countries where the language reflects place value in a more systematic and consistent way than English (e.g. saying the equivalent of 'ten and four' instead of 'fourteen'). This has been shown in a number of comparative studies – for example, focusing on children from Japanese and Anglo-American backgrounds (Miura 1987; Miura and Okamoto 1994) and children in Korea (Fuson and Kwon 1992).

There is evidence that the language factor has been over-interpreted by some commentators to explain national differences in other aspects of maths achievement that almost certainly have a broader cultural basis. For example, Towse and Saxton (1998) have shown in a series of experimental studies that there may be non-linguistic explanations for some of the specific findings on place value. Similarly, a study of school entrants in Hong Kong has shown that their superior results were not due to counting methods that exploited the structure of the language (Cheng and Chan 2005). However, the fundamental conclusion remains in place: where the language of number is inconsistent in its structure, children are more likely to experience difficulties in learning to use it for maths and to transform it into its two written forms – number words and Arabic numerals. I. Thompson (2000) reported evidence that children are likely to find it easier to move between those two forms if they have a good deal of experience of decimal calculations through mental maths before they are required to set out the numbers in columns in their written form. He subsequently argued that the key aim should be to help children develop not just knowledge of place value but a broad grasp of how numbers work and what they mean, an 'overall number sense' (Thompson 2003: 189).

Mathematicians' claims that the language of their subject is exact and concise appear to be undermined also by the ambiguous ways in which everyday terms are often used in maths education (see Table 14.2). It is words in the right-hand column that cause most confusion (Otterburn and Nicholson 1976).

There is an additional dimension of linguistic complexity and ambiguity for bilingual children. In a report on a GCSE paper set in Wales, Jones (1993) analysed the effect of translating the general English word 'similar' (in a phrase about 'similar triangles') into a Welsh word, *cyflun*, which is used only in maths. In a sample of Welsh and English speakers who were matched for overall maths achievement, the Welsh speakers did almost twice as well as the English speakers on that item. Wiliam (1994) showed how the technical and non-technical uses of terms for 'speed' and 'velocity' in the two languages could work in the opposite direction, making items more difficult in the Welsh version.

It is not just the vocabulary of maths that causes difficulty. The syntax in which mathematical ideas are expressed is often more complex than children are accustomed to in other areas of the curriculum. This may present particular challenges to pupils who are learning EAL. Examples include:

- the use of the passive voice – as in 'Each side of the equation is divided by 3' (Shuard and Rothery 1984);

Table 14.2 Categories of words used in the teaching of mathematics

Words that have the same meaning in mathematical English as in ordinary English	Words that have a meaning only in mathematical English	Words that have different meanings in mathematical English and ordinary English
cat	hypotenuse	difference
dog	parallelogram	product
because	coefficient	parallel
it		odd
taxi		mean
shelves		value
climb		

Source: Shuard and Rothery (1984: Chapter 3).

- conditional clauses – 'if . . . then' (Shuard and Rothery 1984);

- describing relationships – as in 'as the height increases, the weight increases in proportion' (Driver 2005);

- hypothetical language – as in 'I think that boys' heights would be on average greater than the girls' heights' (Driver 2005).

On the basis of work with bilingual pupils in Bradford, Burwell *et al.* (1998: 22) advocated that teachers use the following checklist when communicating about maths to children, whether in written or spoken form:

Teachers should aim to use:

1 simple sentence structure;

2 one fact per sentence;

and ensure that:

3 any extra information given is useful;

4 questions are split into sections, as appropriate;

5 the first part of the question can successfully engage the whole group;

6 the question tests the mathematical skills of the child, not their English comprehension.

Elbers and de Haan (2005) showed that, when collaborative learning was encouraged in a multicultural primary school classroom in the Netherlands, pupils' discussions of unfamiliar vocabulary became part of their exploration of the mathematical tasks and they solved language problems through their growing knowledge of the mathematical discourse.

Sometimes, however, the content of what is intended to be a down-to-earth, everyday problem is itself the source of difficulty for some pupils. For example, Virani-Roper (2000: 70) tells the story of a Ugandan boy who could not solve a simple word problem that required a calculation involving fractions, not because he did not understand the fractions but because he had no knowledge of the fruit that was the subject of the question. He was asked: 'I ate half an apple and half of what was left. What was left?' As an answer he wrote down 'seeds'. When the teacher asked what would happen if she had an orange instead, the boy's reply was to ask what an apple is. This fruit did not then grow in Uganda. If teachers attempt to contextualize mathematical ideas with examples that are outside the experience of some pupils, they make the mathematics more difficult rather than more transparent (Barwell 2005). For a classroom activity that enables pupils in Years 5 and 6 to analyse this phenomenon and become more conscious of it see Scott (2004), and for more detailed analyses of the specific challenges that pupils learning EAL may face in mathematics lessons and of strategies for overcoming them see DfES (2002e), Barwell (2004) and Driver (2005).

It should not be assumed that these issues only affect children learning EAL: Jordan *et al.* (2003b) have shown that the linguistic challenges of mathematical problem-solving may lead to underperformance by children from low-income families as well, even if their first language is the language of school instruction.

One initiative within the NNS was to try to standardize the mathematical vocabulary that is introduced to each year group through Key Stages 1 and 2 (DfEE 1999b). It was anticipated that that would have many advantages, particularly when children move between schools. However, a small case study has suggested that, while class teachers in primary schools do use the recommended vocabulary, they do not prioritize it in their lesson planning or ensure that it is used consistently by pupils (Raiker 2002). In any case prompting and rehearsal alone will not ensure that all pupils can fully understand the vocabulary, and many will be helped to achieve that through undertaking tasks that involve focused collaborative discussion in which they are required to talk through problems and puzzles and explain what they think to each other (Higgins 2003: 64). But, whatever strategies have been used by previous teachers, those working with children with SEN and children learning EAL cannot assume that they will be familiar and competent with all the words listed in the NNS Guidance.

Specific learning difficulties

> Dyscalculia is a condition that affects the ability to acquire arithmetical skills. Dyscalculic learners may have difficulty understanding simple number concepts, lack an intuitive grasp of numbers, and have problems learning number facts and procedures. Even if they produce a correct answer or use a correct method, they may do so mechanically and without confidence.
>
> (DfES 2001c)

It is relatively rare for a child to experience specific learning difficulties solely in maths (Chinn and Ashcroft 1998). One estimate based on a survey of over 1,200 children in Lancashire primary schools suggested that 1.3 per cent had 'specific arithmetic difficulties', less than half the proportion found to have 'specific reading difficulties' (Lewis *et al.* 1994). The incidence figure that research teams report for dyscalculia seems to vary with the definition they adopt for the phenomenon. In addition, there is evidence that many of those assessed as having maths problems in the early years of schooling catch up with their peers within

2–3 years (Mazzoco and Myers 2003), though if a student is identified later (e.g. at the age of 11), the problem seems much more likely to persist (Shalev *et al.* 2005).

The debate on definitions of dyscalculia has echoed the debate on dyslexia in some respects. For example, there has been extensive discussion of an IQ–performance discrepancy, and attempts have been made to identify subtypes of dyscalculia with different patterns of difficulty (Gifford 2005; see also Chapter 13). Geary and Hoard (2001) have argued that there may be a common under-lying neurological deficit in dyslexia and dyscalculia, perhaps relating to the retrieval of information from memory. However, a number of investigators have challenged this claim. In a longitudinal study that involved detailed analysis of performance on a range of mathematics tasks, Jordan *et al.* (2003a) showed that children with maths difficulties but not reading difficulties (MD only) had a different profile of success and failure from children with maths difficulties who also had reading difficulties (MD/RD). Fuchs *et al.* (2004) studied the impact of a 16-week special teaching programme in mathematical problem-solving and showed that children with MD/RD had a different pattern of improvement from those with MD only and control groups.

Landerl *et al.* (2004) pursued a different line of argument, presenting evidence that children with MD alone and those with MD/RD could be differentiated from normal achievers and those with RD alone on counting tasks and tasks in which they had to compare the magnitude of numbers. Thus the children with MD/RD showed a pattern of numerical disability similar to that of those with MD alone. There were 'no special features consequent on their reading or language deficits. We conclude that dyscalculia is the result of specific disabilities in basic numerical processing, rather than the consequence of deficits in other cognitive abilities' (Landerl *et al.* 2004: 99).

On the basis of findings of this kind, Butterworth (2003) published a screening test to identify children with dyscalculia. It is based on the premise that an appreciation of 'numerosity' is fundamental to understanding numbers:

> Broadly, a child will understand the concept of numerosity if she or he:
>
> - understands the one-to-one correspondence principle;
>
> - understands that sets of things have numerosity and that some manipulations of these sets affect the numerosity – combining sets, taking subsets away, and so on – and that one set has the same numerosity as another, or a greater numerosity, or a smaller numerosity;
>
> - understands that sets need not be of visible things; they can equally be audible things, tactile things, abstract things (like wishes);
>
> - can recognise small numerosities – sets of up to about four objects – without verbal counting.
>
> (Butterworth 2005a: 4)

The screening test is computer-based and requires children to process arrays of dots rapidly ('subitizing') and compare the value of numerals. Their response times are measured as well as the accuracy of their answers. The aim is to identify innate difficulties in basic number comprehension and avoid the risk that previous teaching will affect children's results. There have been no large-scale studies so far to demonstrate the predictive value of this as a screener. Its underlying argument is supported by some reviewers of the psychological evidence (e.g. Gersten *et al.* 2005), though critics have expressed concern that it samples a narrow range of mathematical knowledge.

> If dyscalculia is related to difficulties in number understanding, this needs to be assessed. It follows that timed tests should not be the sole form of assessment for dyscalculia. The various possible causes, including experiential and emotional factors, indicate the need for more probing, diagnostic assessment.
>
> (Gifford 2005: 49)

Butterworth and his colleagues (e.g. Landerl *et al.* 2004) would respond that dyscalculia is the result of specific disabilities in basic numerical processing, rather than the consequence of deficits in other cognitive abilities. Assessment strategies are discussed in more detail later in the chapter.

Mathematics is a complex activity, and it is not surprising that many different aspects of psychological functioning have been implicated in mathematics learning difficulties, including language difficulties, spatial difficulties, memory difficulties and specific difficulties in processing numbers (Gifford 2005). However, neuropsychological research has attempted to identify the fundamental mental activities that might be involved and to show how the failure of a particular processing module or of interactions between modules might lead to specific difficulties with counting and the manipulation of numbers. This is seen as the crucial feature of the highly specific learning difficulties that are involved in *dyscalculia* (Butterworth 2005b; Geary and Hoard 2001).

Learning difficulties in mathematics associated with other SEN

Children who have sensory or physical difficulties often experience related problems in maths. For example, children with dyspraxia may have difficulties in analysing and organizing what they see in terms of visuospatial relationships – as when estimating the dimensions of a two-dimensional figure on a page or trying to understand a three-dimensional figure (Dixon and Addy 2004: Chapter 8). In addition, they may have difficulty in writing numbers accurately or may become confused because they are not able to set out two- or three-digit numbers neatly in the necessary columns. Moreover, just as some children with physical difficulties experience problems with maths learning when it involves visuospatial skills, some children with specific language impairment experience maths problems when it involves language skills. This effect is greater in some maths tasks than in others, presumably because of variations in how crucial a role is played by language competence in each task (Crown *et al.* 2005).

The complex relationship between maths performance, language skills and special needs has been investigated further by Paterson *et al.* (2006) in relation to two genetic disorders. Williams syndrome (WS) is associated with a distinctive facial appearance, a sociable manner and severe learning difficulties. Typically individuals with WS develop language skills that are more mature than would have been predicted from their overall cognitive ability. However, there is often a specific weakness in the visual systems of the brain in WS, with poor depth perception and an inability to visualize how different components can be put together to make larger objects (e.g. when doing a jigsaw puzzle). The better-known genetic disorder, Down's syndrome (DS), also involves some impairment of cognitive ability as well as a distinctive facial appearance. Cognitive development varies a good deal, but DS does not normally involve visual difficulties to the same extent as WS. Paterson *et al.* (2006) predicted that children and adults with WS and those with DS would show a different profile of strengths and weaknesses in mathematics. They matched the two groups in their study for chronological age and overall cognitive ability. The results showed that, while the DS group did less well on the maths tasks in infancy, the performance of the older children and adults with DS was superior to that of the WS group on all the tests. The performance of the DS group improved with age, following a developmental path similar to normally developing groups but consistently behind them. The developmental path of the WS group was different: they could manage the simple processing of numerosity involved in the infant tasks, but at a later stage the relative strengths of their language skills did not appear to compensate for the impact of their weak visuospatial skills on all aspects of maths learning. The authors stressed the importance of differentiating between simple delay (as shown by the DS group) and 'deviant cognitive processing' (as shown by the WS group). Detailed assessment is essential at each stage if the implications of an individual's distinctive pattern of special needs are to be fully understood.

Many children with special needs show compensatory strengths. For instance, some pupils with visual disabilities surprise their teachers in mainstream schools by particular success in mental computation. This appears to arise because they regularly rely on their memories rather than checking in books for what they need to know (Chapman and Stone 1988). But the same children will be handicapped if they are provided with the kind of textbook that is designed to make maths accessible and attractive for most children – visually stimulating in design, packed with illustrations, diagrams and graphs with fragments of text squeezed between them. If they are given materials designed to be accessible to them, such as shapes made of cardboard that they can examine tactually, they will explore them in distinctive ways and may name them through tactile recognition without, for example, counting the angles or sides (Argyropoulos 2002).

In the case of hearing impairment, a programme of research by Nunes (2004) and her colleagues has challenged the notion that the disability as such is a 'cause' of difficulties in learning maths because of the lack of some supposedly essential process in development. They pointed out that there is only a weak relationship between degree of hearing loss and maths test performance (Powers *et al.* 1998). They investigated children's success and errors with materials designed to minimize communication problems. With that approach they found evidence that the hearing-impaired and hearing children in their sample were progressing along the same developmental path. There was no sign of a qualitative difference in their approaches to learning how to tackle more difficult problems, but there were extra hurdles for the children with hearing impairment. For example, they found it more difficult to learn the counting string and to use it to solve problems. For a brief account of Nunes' intervention programme, see Activity 14.5.

Activity 14.5   Analysing the reasons for an intervention programme's success

The intervention programme developed by Nunes (2004) was designed to supplement the normal mathematics curriculum, not to replace it. It aimed to help the pupils to develop their informal mathematical understanding to 'a level where it could offer a solid basis for learning the curriculum that they are taught in school' (Nunes 2004: 159). They were required to work through booklets that contained pictures but no text. The information was presented through drawings, diagrams, number lines, tables and graphs. Story problems were presented as temporal sequences on the page from left to right. Figure 14.1 shows an extract from a teacher's booklet that includes the instructions, which they would give to the pupils in the language they were most comfortable with. Discussion among pupils about the way they solved the problems was encouraged, and additional explanations were offered by the teachers too. All the problems were given to all the pupils, even if their teachers thought that some might be too easy or too difficult for them.

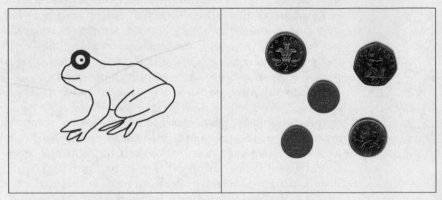

The frog costs 11p. Tick the coins you need to pay the exact money.

Figure 14.1   An additive composition item using 10p and 1p coins
Source: Nunes (2004: 101).

The intervention programme, which lasted one year, generally took place once (sometimes twice) a week, with the usual maths programme being delivered in the normal way for the rest of the week. Twenty-three pupils participated in the project in six different classrooms across the age range 7–11, and 68 control pupils in the same year groups who were also deaf did not receive the intervention but were given the same maths tests at the beginning and end of the year. All the pupils spent the same amount of time on mathematics in total. The only difference was that they spent part of that time differently. The project pupils obtained similar scores to the control pupils at the beginning of the year but significantly outperformed them at the end.

Here are some of the reasons that Nunes (2004: 161–2) puts forward as possible factors in the success of the programme:

1   Communication was supported through visuospatial means.

2   Deaf children were exposed to concepts systematically that hearing children often pick up informally and incidentally.

3   The programme booklets provided drawings and diagrams to illustrate key concepts. The children did not have to invent these for themselves.

4   The programme consisted exclusively of activities that involve reasoning. No time was taken up with the teaching of algorithms.

5   Less reliance was placed on language than in a traditional mathematics lesson.

6   Teachers and pupils may have been energized by the novelty of the programme.

7   Pupils found it fun.

Reflect with a partner on which of those factors seem likely to have had the greatest impact on the deaf pupils' learning. Note that Nunes suggested that both *cognitive* effects and *motivational* effects should be taken into account.

There is a need for more work of this kind which bases intervention strategies on a rigorous analysis of how the thinking processes involved in maths performance interact with the cognitive profiles that are characteristic of children with different forms of special needs. For further examples based on a review of research, see Dowker (2004); for specific guidance relating to pupils with dyslexia see Kay and Yeo (2003), and pupils with dyspraxia see Dixon and Addy (2004).

Learning difficulties in mathematics: assessment for intervention

Assessment in the context of educational reform

In most education systems, including the UK, systematic national or regional assessment arrangements are now in place that make it possible to monitor the overall progress of large groups of children on core elements of the curriculum, including maths. The introduction of a tighter testing regime is intended to ensure that schools and teachers are accountable for the results they achieve with their pupils. It is hoped that 'high-stakes testing' will improve standards by focusing instruction on the required curriculum and enhancing the motivation of both teachers and pupils. The evidence to support these aspirations is nebulous, and the impact on approaches to teaching may be more complex than anticipated (and sometimes negative). For example, there may be excessive teaching to the test, resulting in a narrowing of the received curriculum, and there may be a lack of faith in the validity of the test, resulting in feelings of dissonance and alienation (Smith 1991, analysed by Gipps 1994: Chapter 3). There may be increased pressure to set maths lessons on the basis of 'ability' (McSherry and Ollerton 2002), and this may lead to 'its own miniature forms of elitism in terms of class, gender, race and birth date' (Ollerton 2005: 150). However, there is an international trend towards the strategy of high-stakes testing, and it is likely to remain in place for some time before the usual cycle of further reform replaces or modifies it.

Large-scale systems of assessment are not usually sufficiently fine-tuned to make it possible to analyse the learning difficulties of individual children, but they provide a clear framework of expected achievement against which individual progress can be monitored. Traditionally this has led to detailed diagnostic assessment which underpins careful differentiation in teaching. In the rest of this section we will describe strategies that are available to identify individual learning needs in maths. Many of the strategies are based on a teach–assess–teach cycle. With some children it will only be possible for teachers to follow through the implications of what they observe in such a strategy if the organization of the classroom and the school allows some degree of effective differentiation.

Assessment in the service of teaching

Traditionally children's mastery of mathematical knowledge and mathematical techniques has been the main focus of assessment. But, as noted earlier, there are other important aspects of performance that have a crucial impact on long-term results – thinking processes, problem-solving strategies, creativity, confidence and attitudes towards maths – and assessment can be broadened to cover these features (Foxman *et al.* 1989). Classroom learning is a social process, and a rounded picture of the potential strengths and learning needs of children with difficulties will also include observations on their ability to work autonomously and to work collaboratively in pairs or in teams. QCA guidance takes account of these factors in its emphasis on the value of self assessment and peer assessment (QCA 2003b). It is essential that the detailed monitoring and assessment that is carried out when children are identified as being at risk investigate the possibility that problems in working autonomously or working collaboratively are exacerbating their learning difficulties.

A central aim of classroom assessment must be to help teachers to plan their teaching. This happens all the time, not just through formal testing. Throughout a lesson children will be observed closely to check their level of understanding. Teachers will look out for clues such as a change in demeanour, an ability to modify what has been heard rather than simply copy it, an ability to explain something to other children (Reynolds *et al.* 1995). The pace of the lesson and the use of concrete illustrations or textual materials will be adapted in the light of these insights. Unfortunately, sensitivity to relevant clues may be blunted when a pupil who comes from a different cultural background is not comfortable with the conventions of the classroom or gives non-verbal signals of comprehension or puzzlement that are unfamiliar to the teacher (Tharp 1989; Gorgorió and Planas 2005). In these circumstances the lesson may not be planned in an adaptive way that takes account of the pace of children's learning and provides scaffolding when it is needed. Children are more likely to opt out and refuse to attempt a task if it is presented in a way that they find difficult or challenging. Varying the level of difficulty, the mode or the required method of calculation may enable pupils to overcome their resistance (Houssart 2005a). In the case of children learning EAL and those with language difficulties, an assessment of their understanding of mathematics may be more valid if non-verbal methods of testing are used – for example, through practical tasks using objects or gestalt images such as Numicon or number lines (Gifford 2005: 52). (Numicon is a multi-sensory approach to arithmetic teaching for children aged 3–7 and older pupils with special needs (Tacon *et al.* 2004). Patterns are used to represent each numeral, and the patterns are structured to encourage the understanding of number and number relationships.)

In the past, formal assessment procedures have often consumed a great deal of resources and effort with remarkably limited feedback to those involved. The Numeracy Task Force was aware of the danger of this and gave more attention to what is to be done with the findings from assessment than to the detailed content of assessment tasks and tests. The justification for this was that evidence has accumulated that when pupils are given frequent and detailed feedback about their learning, they often make substantial learning gains. In a thorough review of the available research, Black and Wiliam (1998a) showed that the nature of the feedback is crucial. They argued that feedback is more likely to have a positive impact on subsequent learning when, among other things, it:

- is designed to stimulate pupils to think further about the original learning task in the light of whatever additional information has now been provided (Bangert-Drowns *et al.* 1991);

- goes beyond informing pupils how far short their response was of a required standard and seeks also to suggest to them what they need to do to close the gap.

There are good reasons for believing that children with learning difficulties will be particularly reliant on feedback being explicit on such points. For a fuller account of the use of assessment that will support learning by children who have learning difficulties see Chapter 8, and for a commentary on the role of effective formative assessment of mathematics within the national strategies see Hafeez (2003).

Individual diagnostic assessment in mathematics

Ascertaining how the gap may be bridged requires *diagnostic* assessment. A variety of techniques may be employed:

1 the analysis of errors in written work;

2 published diagnostic materials;

3 informal observation;

4 questioning pupils and discussing their concepts and methods of work with them.

Often some combination of (1), (2) and (3) may be followed up by (4). These processes will generate hypotheses about what is going wrong, but the value of the conclusions that are drawn can only be assessed by implementing teaching strategies based on the information and evaluating the outcome.

In the past *analysis of errors* has often been advocated as the key approach. For example, West (1971: 467) wrote: 'Diagnostic teaching is teaching that looks at the errors children make and subsequently structures the learning experiences so that the errors will be eliminated'. When analysing errors in written work, West advocated that at the simplest level an attempt is made to distinguish between systematic (conceptual/process) errors and random (careless) errors. Is there any pattern to the careless errors? Do they occur in particular kinds of work or at a particular stage (e.g. after working for some time, suggesting a fatigue or boredom effect)? Where there are systematic errors, can one infer how they occurred – that is, what misconceptions or faulty line of reasoning lay behind them? Stakes and Hornby (1996: 75) suggested that the key points in any assessment of difficulties are as follows:

- What did the child get wrong?

- Why did they get it wrong?

- Is it a problem of the perception of how to address the task?

- Can children complete the task with the use of concrete examples?

- Can children explain the process which they are required to do? At which point are they not able to do this?

Teachers may attempt a more detailed categorization of the causes of a child's errors through inspecting written work and via structured questioning. Newman (1983) devised materials to explore whether errors chiefly arose during one of the following processes:

- reading the question;

- comprehending the question (specific terminology or general meaning);

- translating the question into an appropriate mathematical form (not all questions require transformation);

- process skills – that is, working out the answer using an effective method (for numerical items errors might include random response, using an incorrect operation such as subtraction instead of addition, using the correct operation but in an incorrect way, faulty computation, no response);

- encoding the answer – that is, writing it down incorrectly;

- carelessness (e.g. gives correct answer on second try and shows good understanding when questioned);

- motivation or attitude;

- task form (e.g. source of error appears to lie in ambiguous wording or poor presentation of the item).

Alternative approaches to analysing and categorizing children's errors may be found in Koshy (2000), Chinn (2004) and Hansen (2005). It is possible for the analysis of errors to be carried out on computer. A computer-administered test can adapt its questions systematically to the child's responses, identifying and probing areas of difficulty as the test proceeds.

Such strategies develop hypotheses about children's difficulties solely on the basis of an analysis of their errors. But it may be worthwhile probing even when no error has been made. This can lead to a fuller appreciation of pupils' understanding of the task and the concepts involved in it (Foxman *et al.* 1989). It may enable the teacher to gain information about the methods pupils have used to reach their solutions and suggest the best way to help them develop further on the basis of their existing knowledge and problem solving style. Published materials designed to facilitate this process include the the *Quest* materials (Robertson *et al.*

2000), Mathematics Assessment for Learning and Teaching (*MaLT*; see www.hoddertests.co.uk) and a diagnostic procedure designed for children with dyslexia (Chinn and Ashcroft 1998). The adaptation of standardized tests for diagnostic purposes is advocated by Kay and Yeo (2003).

Published materials such as these can make a significant contribution to diagnostic assessment in extreme cases, but the first and most important contribution will be made by *informal classroom observation* during the course of everyday maths sessions, including the Numeracy Hour. It is valuable to observe the child in a range of situations, both when maths is the ostensible subject and when mathematical concepts or procedures are being used in the course of other work. This is probably the most effective way of checking some hypotheses that you may have formed after examining children's written work and deciding that they are underperforming in maths (Charles *et al.* 1987; Sawyer 1995). You might check whether:

- they do not read the instructions fully before tackling a problem or they do not act on what they read;

- they do not take time to work out what a problem is about before starting work on it;

- they adopt ineffective strategies when attempting a new task or when faced with a task on which they have previously made errors;

- they employ unsystematic problem-solving strategies when tackling a task or frequently change their approach without allowing time for one strategy to bear fruit;

- they stick to a single strategy and do not try a different approach when it is unsuccessful;

- they seek help appropriately when faced with a difficulty;

- they lose concentration quickly when they find something difficult;

- they work at a very slow pace, losing track of what they are doing;

- they race through their work making many careless mistakes without noticing that there are errors;

- they are frequently off task and take avoidance action such as making frequent trips to the toilet or interfering with other children;

- they do not check their work when it is finished;

- when working with others on a joint task, they adopt a passive role, contribute little to any discussion or wait for others to take the initiative and then follow;

- they could make effective use of concrete support materials such as interlocking cubes, a number track or a number line;

- they adopt a defeatist or hostile attitude when working in maths.

Informal observation will not be effective in facilitating pupils' progress unless the teacher's findings and conclusions are recorded systematically. This can be done with a minimum expenditure of time through the use of small 'free comment' cards that are prepared in advance, or structured checklists, or a simple rating scale (Charles *et al.* 1987). In some classrooms, where teamwork is encouraged, learning support assistants may make a crucial contribution (Houssart 2005b).

There are some assessment questions which cannot be answered by examining children's test results or written products, or by observing them while they are working. For example, there are limits to what can be inferred about their thinking processes and about *why* they work as they do. So additional assessment information may be gleaned by *questioning pupils* about maths informally (and, in extreme cases, through a structured interview). It is helpful to have in mind the stems with which informal questions might begin. A teacher needs to be aware of what each type of question might achieve in terms of illuminating a child's areas of mastery and weakness. Random questioning achieves little. Time is at a premium both because other pupils require attention and because the concentration span and length of recall of many children with learning difficulties is limited. So the aim should be to probe systematically in order to find out what a child has and has not mastered in the target area of maths. A further, and perhaps even more important, goal will be to identify the emerging skills and knowledge that they can only demonstrate securely with support from another person. Charles *et al.* (1987) suggested the following possible list of question stems:

1 How did you . . .?

2 Why did you . . .?

3 What did you try . . .?

4 How do you know that . . .?

5 Have you . . .?

6 How did you happen to . . .?

7 How did you decide whether . . .?

8 Can you describe . . .?

9 Are you sure that . . .?

10 What do you think . . .?

11 How do you feel about . . .?

You may find that the wording in some of these question stems needs to be adapted for children with learning difficulties. A child may be asked to explain how they worked out their answer, to draw a picture to help the teacher to understand what they mean or to describe what the task reminds them of (cf. Swan 2003). An example of the value of such questioning for the planning of future teaching may be seen in their study. When asked to find the time interval between 7.40 a.m. and 8.20 a.m., one pupil said: 'I imagined the face of a clock and worked out that 7.40 was 20 to 8, then up to 20 past is 40 minutes' (Foxman *et al.* 1989: 202). This pupil evidently found it helpful to use visual imagery to solve such problems. A teacher who was aware of this could suggest an imagery-based strategy when the pupil faced a mathematical problem they were finding very difficult.

Wiliam (1999: 18) has discussed the role of 'rich questioning' in work with a whole class (cf. Askew and Wiliam 1995: 12–13):

> It has become abundantly clear that students' naïve conceptions are not random aberrations, but the result of sophisticated and creative attempts by students to make sense of their experience. Within a normal mathematics classroom, there is clearly not enough time for the teacher to treat each student as an individual, but the good news is that the vast majority of the naïve conceptions are quite commonly shared, and as long as the teacher has a small battery of good questions it will be possible to elicit the most significant of these misconceptions. If the teacher then does have any time to spend with individual students, this can be targeted at those whose misconceptions are not commonly shared. After all, teaching is interesting because students are so different, but it is only possible because they are so similar.

In a classroom where *all* pupils can expect to have their mathematical thinking probed in an exacting way, those who have learning difficulties are more likely to feel comfortable with an approach that focuses separate individual questioning on their particular areas of uncertainty and failure. The teacher's diagnostic information (as well as the pupil's confidence) will be enhanced if the questioning also probes how they achieve success in the tasks they complete satisfactorily. (For further discussion and ideas on questioning strategies, see Watson and Mason 1998; DfES 2002d.)

Questioning strategies and other diagnostic procedures enable teachers to investigate hypotheses about what a child who seems to have difficulties is doing. They can then develop inferences about the possible effects on the child's learning of teaching them new strategies or employing different methods to teach the same strategies. To test out these hypotheses and develop an accurate understanding of maths difficulties it would be necessary to undertake trial teaching along the new lines and evaluate its impact. This cycle of assessment, planning, action and review is in line with the general pattern recommended to schools in the draft revised *Code of Practice* (e.g. DfES 2001a: para. 5.3). It was noted above that children with learning difficulties are particularly likely to benefit when any feedback they are given about the outcomes of assessment is explicit about what they need to do next. The same is true in relation to their teachers: an assessment–planning–action–review cycle will help them to set realistic but challenging targets for pupils with learning difficulties in maths and to develop clear ideas about how to work towards them.

Conclusions

Learning difficulties in maths must be seen in the context of the aims and scope of the school maths curriculum – which in the UK has evolved rapidly in recent years. In a multicultural society it is beneficial if the curriculum draws upon and refers to the diverse mathematical traditions that are represented in the wider society. When this is achieved, maths teaching can contribute to the achievement of broader educational aims of inclusiveness, mutual respect and intellectual flexibility. In maths, as in literacy, there is scope for deep misunderstanding in the interaction between home and school. But there is also the possibility of strong and mutually beneficial interaction and support. The national strategies are transforming the learning environment for numeracy, but there are still significant weaknesses in the learning environment for maths in many classrooms.

We analysed learning difficulties in maths first in terms of what children understand about maths and second in terms of the emotional significance that maths has for many children and adults. We then examined the language that is used in maths and the challenges it poses for many learners, notably bilingual learners. Finally, there was a short account of specific learning difficulties in maths (less common than specific learning difficulties in literacy and also less well understood), and of learning difficulties in maths associated with other SEN. We highlighted that a particular challenge for many children with SEN in mainstream maths classes is the *pace* of teaching and learning. The essential maths may be within their grasp, but they may need longer than others to plan and produce a response or to consolidate a new concept.

The last section of the chapter concerned assessment for intervention. Assessment may take many forms and have many different purposes. Fullest attention was given here to individual diagnostic assessment and questioning. These processes are most effective when they occur within a well-established cycle of assessment, planning, action and review. Diagnostic assessment need not concentrate on failure and problems. It may also make a powerful contribution to the effectiveness of teaching when the teacher also explores how pupils achieve success in the tasks that they complete satisfactorily.

Behavioural, emotional and social difficulties

Introduction

Definitions and distinctions

While many concepts in the special needs arena are contested, disagreement in this area of disturbed and disturbing behaviour is more widespread than in any other. Since 1944 terminology used in government publications to describe the area has included: maladjustment; emotional or behavioural disorders; emotional and behavioural difficulties (EBD); and behavioural, emotional and social difficulties (BESD). The Challenging Behaviour Research Project (2005: 10) report describes definitional difficulties in the area as 'chronic' and points to a 'debate that has persisted through many generations over who pupils with BESD are, where they should be placed and what interventions are beneficial.'

The 1944 Education Act introduced the term 'maladjustment' to describe pupils who show evidence of psychological disturbance or emotional instability and who would require special education treatment to become readjusted – personally, socially and educationally. While early conceptualizations of BESD have frequently been characterized as exclusively 'within child', there was some acknowledgement of the role of environmental factors. For example, in the Underwood Report on maladjusted children (Ministry of Education 1955) one of the defining characteristics of maladjusted, as opposed to disaffected, delinquent or merely naughty pupils, was failure to respond to ordinary discipline. The Warnock Committee endorsed the use of the term 'malajusted' for this reason: 'Indeed, we consider that the implication of this term (namely that behaviour can sometimes be meaningfully considered only in relation to the circumstances in which it occurs) is an advantage rather than a disadvantage. This consideration in our opinion outweighs the possible harm of stigmatization' (DES 1978: 44). While the Warnock Report adopted the term 'emotional or behavioural disorders', it recommended that 'malajusted' also be retained as a 'servicable form of description'. However, concern about possible stigmatization appears to have triumphed and reference to children as 'maladjusted' effectively ceased post-Warnock.

By 1989 the Warnock Committees's term, 'emotional or behavioural disorders', had become 'emotional and behavioural difficulties' (EBD) and the Elton Committee drew a number of distinctions between pupils who could be described by this term and 'other difficult pupils'. 'Children with EBD tend to present behaviour problems earlier in their school career than other difficult pupils and to behave in a disturbed and disturbing way regardless of which teacher or class they are with' (DES 1989c: 150). The Department for Education Circular 9/94 (1994b) further elaborated distinctions between different types of problem behaviour (see Figure 15.1)

This continuum-based approach to definition was supported by the EBD sub-group of the National Advisory Group on SEN and its continuing use recommended (Daniels *et al.* 1999a). However, when staff in schools identified as having effective practice with pupils who present EBD were interviewed, some (subject specialists and heads of department) did not make a distinction between EBD and general naughtiness in thinking about pupils presenting behavioural problems, whereas others (senior pastoral staff, SENCOs, headteachers) did (Daniels *et al.* 1999b). In discussing pupils known to them, staff who made the distinction

Behaviour that 'is simply disruptive or naughty'

- results from a child 'experiencing some emotional stress within normal and expected bounds'

- 'challenges teachers but is within normal, albeit unacceptable, bounds'

Emotional and behavioural difficulties

- 'are persistent (if not necessarily permanent) and constitute learning difficulties'

- 'range from social maladaption to abnormal emotional stresses'

- 'may become apparent through withdrawn, passive, depressive, aggressive or self-injurious tendencies'

- 'may be associated with school, family or other environments or physical or sensory impairment'

- mean a child will 'generally behave unusually or in an extreme fashion to a variety of social, personal, emotional or physical circumstances'

Serious mental illnesses

- 'may be episodic, but are generally indicated by significant changes in behaviour, emotions or thought processes which are prolonged and/or so severe that, taking into account the child's development and the social and cultural background, they interfere profoundly with everyday life and are a serious disability for the child, the family, friends or those who care for or teach the child'.

Figure 15.1 A continuum of problem behaviour
Source: Department for Education (1994c: 7).

described children who present EBD as engaging in difficult behaviour that is more persistent over time and pervasive across different settings. Some also characterized the behaviour exhibited as more unusual for the child's age: odd or idiosyncratic. This is consistent with the further advice offered in Department for Education Circular 9/94 (1994b: 8): 'Whether the child is judged to have emotional and behavioural difficulties will depend on the nature, frequency, persistence, severity or abnormality and cumulative effect of the behaviour, in context, compared to normal expectations for a child of the age concerned'. Activity 15.1 invites you to consider how to place a number of real case studies on the continuum.

Activity 15.1   Continuum case studies (DfEE, 2000c, 2001)

Consider the following case studies and decide where would you place them on the continuum shown in Figure 15.1, and why.

Nadia is in Year 7. Her behaviour has caused difficulties throughout her school life. She has poor social skills, is very egocentric, finds it difficult to accept praise, is reluctant to comply with teacher requests and is difficult for her parents to manage at home. She displays some aspects of autistic spectrum disorders and of specific learning difficulties. Nadia's reading and spelling lag over 3 years behind her chronological age, so that she has limited literacy skills. Psychological and speech and language assessments suggest that she has limited verbal skills and some specific phonological difficulties.

James is a Year 1 pupil in a medium-sized primary school. He has difficulties interacting with other pupils, has coordination problems, poor muscle tone, finds it difficult to sit still and is in the habit of making noises at inappropriate times. His mother is concerned about his difficulties and unsuccessfully sought additional provision from the LEA preschool service. Baseline information pointed to poor language skills, and he is having difficulty with the early stages of reading.

Mohammed is aged 13, and has always been a slightly anxious child. On entering a large comprehensive school, he seemed to withdraw totally into himself, finding it increasingly difficult to communicate with other children and with teaching staff. His parents have visited the school on numerous occasions to discuss their worries about Mohammed with his form teacher and year head, and a range of strategies have been put in place in order to support Mohammed in school. These have included peer support schemes, a social skills programme and a mentoring programme to help him develop confidence within school and attend after-school activities. Yet he is increasingly reluctant to attend school, preferring to remain alone in his room. He is withdrawn and unable to communicate to anyone what is worrying him. On occasions, he can be extremely aggressive.

Ewan is 10, and has been described as being difficult for most of his school life. He is academically a very able child, yet he does not appear to understand basic classroom rules. Teachers often describe his behaviour as being 'wilfully naughty', especially when he fails to respond to their requests, and carries on completing his own projects or games when expressly told not to. He can become very distressed in these situations. He sometimes appears to have a slight nervous tick, finds it difficult to maintain eye contact with teaching staff and always prefers to work alone – being shunned by and shunning others when requested to become involved in joint project work. Ewan always seems to play alone at breaktimes – and spends hours playing complex computer games in the school library. His parents have visited the school on a number of occasions and expressed concern about Ewan's difficult behaviour at home and at school. They say that they have run out of ways of trying to discipline Ewan – and are keen to find new ways of trying to improve his behaviour. They are concerned that Ewan often appears to be unhappy – and that his isolation at school often causes him real distress.

Here is where the needs of the children described in Activity 15.1 are located by relevant government guidance:

- 'Nadia currently has her needs met through *School Action Plus* but her progress is limited. The SENCO is monitoring the situation so as to decide whether to refer her for statutory assessment' (DfEE 2000c: Section 6).

- 'James currently has his needs met through *School Action*, but his progress is being monitored half-termly by the SENCO with a view to deciding whether more specialist assessment of his associated difficulties may be necessary' (DfEE 2000c: Section 6).

- 'For some children like Mohammed, their mental health problems will be such that may require intensive support in the community or periods of in-patient treatment' (DfEE 2001: 23)

- 'Children such as Ewan ... may require a fuller assessment of their needs from educational psychologists, or other child and adolescent mental health specialists, often working in partnership with other professionals such as social workers who may be involved with the child and their family' (DfEE 2001: 18)

Circular 9/94 asserted that it is important to make a distinction between the three points on the continuum shown in Figure 15.1 because each needs to be treated differently. This was reinforced in the Green Paper on meeting SEN (DfEE 1997: 80) which stated that 'boundaries between EBD, ordinary unruliness, disaffection and various clinical conditions are not always clear cut but have a major bearing on the solution required'. However, the relevance of the distinctions made in Figure 15.1 has been questioned. For example, Daniels and Williams (2000) questioned the value of distinguishing between behaviour problems felt to be due to naughtiness, as opposed to SEN. Their focus is very much on early intervention aimed at optimizing the learning environment to support positive behaviour. The crucial role of the environment in defining EBD was also recognized in government guidance: 'Perceptions of whether a child's behaviour constitutes an emotional and behavioural difficulty are likely to differ according to the context in which it occurs as well as the individual teacher's management skills, tolerance levels, temperament and expectations (DfE 1994b: 9).

The *Special Educational Needs Code of Practice* (DfES 2001a) cautioned against the use of exclusive categories of need and instead argued that multiple needs may be present. Behaviour, emotional and social development was one of four broad areas of need identified. Under this heading consideration was given to the types of additional support that may be required by 'Children and young people who demonstrate features of emotional and behavioural difficulties, who are withdrawn or isolated, disruptive and disturbing, hyperactive and lack concentration; those with immature social skills and those presenting challenging behaviours arising from other complex special needs' (DfES 2001a: 87). Further guidance was given on indicators of significant emotional or behavioural difficulties: 'clear recorded examples of withdrawn or disruptive behaviour; a marked and persistent inability to concentrate; signs that the child experiences considerable frustration or distress in relation to their learning difficulties;

difficulties in establishing and maintaining balanced relationships with their fellow pupils or with adults; and any other evidence of a significant delay in the development of life and social skills' (DfES 2001a: 83). Hence the definition had broadened to include disruptive behaviour, persistent concentration difficulties and problems in the development of social skills.

Guidance on recording pupils' needs in the Pupil Level Annual Schools Census (DfES 2005b: 7) has provided a definition of BESD that is broader still:

> Pupils with behavioural, emotional and social difficulties cover the full range of ability and a continuum of severity. Their behaviours present a barrier to learning and persist despite the implementation of an effective school behaviour policy and personal/social curriculum. They may be withdrawn or isolated, disruptive and disturbing, hyperactive and lack concentration, have immature social skills or present challenging behaviours. Pupils with a range of difficulties, including emotional disorders such as depression and eating disorders; conduct disorders such as oppositional defiance disorder (ODD); hyperkinetic disorders including attention deficit disorder or attention deficit hyperactivity disorder (ADD/ADHD); and syndromes such as Tourette's, should be recorded as BESD if additional or different educational arrangements are being made to support them.'

Although constrained by the additional requirements that only pupils with a statement or at School Action Plus and those for whom BESD is considered to be their primary or secondary SEN should be included in this category in the annual returns made by schools to the DfES, it does seem that the new term, BESD, is intended to include the 'serious mental illness' end of the continuum shown in Figure 15.1. This is unlikely to be welcomed by authors such as Thomas and Loxley (2001) who expressed concern at the 'infiltration' of concepts from psychology and psychiatry and argued against the validity of the EBD category, much as Tomlinson (1982: 51) had argued against the earlier concept of 'maladjustment', on the grounds that it served primarily a social control function by translating 'the *school's* needs for order, calm, routine and predictability to the *child's* needs – supposedly for stability, nurture, security, one-to-one help, or whatever'.

However, the change in emphasis clearly reflects a new focus on the role of schools in identifying and supporting children and young people who have mental health problems. In this chapter we will focus on the school inclusion of pupils who have emotional and behavioural difficulties across the broad continuum now included in BESD and will start with a consideration of the relationship between BESD and mental health problems. In the next chapter we will consider the area of social skills, the new component to receive explicit consideration in the 2001 revision of the *Special Educational Needs Code of Practice*. We will also look in the next chapter at preventive initiatives in the areas of social and emotional development, promoting well-being and raising staff awareness of children's mental health issues, an area for action identified in the government's strategy for SEN (DfES 2004c).

BESD and mental health problems

Even prior to the change from EBD to BESD, the guidance on promoting children's mental health within early years and school settings (DfEE 2001) recognized that the group of children so identified would include many who experienced, or were at risk of developing, mental health problems. The guidance describes these pupils as those whose behavioural difficulties often have a significant emotional element, and 'may be so intertwined with their inability to concentrate, to learn and to get on with their peers, that an approach which does not include attention to the educational alongside their emotional, social and behavioural needs will fail to provide the range of support that they need' (DfEE 2001: 3). Such children may be defined both as having an emotional and behavioural problem within an educational context and, within a medical context, as having a mental health problem, such as conduct disorder.

It is also acknowledged that some children and young people may have mental health problems which require intervention but which do not result in a special educational need, requiring additional or different educational provision. For example, a young person with an eating disorder might be high achieving and socially included in a school with an effective pastoral system. Conversely, pupils may have a BESD but not a mental health disorder. For example, a child with a very disrupted history of schooling may present with levels of anxiety, fear of failure, antagonism towards teachers and aggression towards classmates that do not constitute a definable mental health problem but do significantly interfere with their learning and participation in school.

Schools are advised that the extra support needed by the majority of children who experience mental health problems should be provided within the school setting, often with support from educational psychologists or other specialist professionals from child and adolescent mental health services (CAMHS) (DfEE 2001). Likewise, a strengthening of the support provided by CAMHS to schools is seen as essential in bringing about desirable improvements in the care delivered to vulnerable children and young people (Pettit 2003). While the government objective of establishing a comprehensive CAMHS in all parts of England by the end of 2006 was not fully achieved, these services have expanded substantially in recent years (Appleby *et al.* 2006).

A comprehensive CAHMS consists of four tiers of provision (DfEE 2001):

Tier 1. A primary level of services focused on mental health promotion, prevention, early identification, general advice and intervention for less severe problems. It can include interventions by GPs, health visitors, school nurses, social services, voluntary agencies, teachers, residential social workers and juvenile justice workers.

Tier 2. A network of professional groups providing services such as training and consultation to Tier 1 professionals and families, assessment and outreach service provision. The professional groups involved include educational psychologists, clinical child psychologists, paediatricans, child psychiatrists and community psychiatric nurses.

Tier 3. This is usually a multi-disciplinary team working in a community mental health clinic or child-psychiatry outpatient service, and including: child psychiatrists, social workers, clinical psychologists, community psychiatric nurses, child psychotherapists, occupational therapists, art, music and drama therapists. The focus at this level is on assessment and treatment of the more severe, complex and persistent disorders and referral, as appropriate, to Tier 4.

Tier 4.   Access to infrequently used tertiary-level services such as day units, highly specialized outpatient teams, and inpatient units for older children and adolescents who are severely mentally ill or presenting a suicide risk.

It is expected that most children and young people with mental health problems will be helped through services at Tiers 1 and 2.

Guidance for schools (DfEE 2001) outlines the most common mental health problems that teachers may encounter (see Table 15.1 for a summary), together with advice on useful approaches that schools can implement to support pupils experiencing these difficulties. A summary of available evidence on the most effective interventions for CAMHS, Tier 2 and above, is provided by Wolpert *et al.* (2006). While seeking to inform practice, the authors caution against any blanket applications of the findings to all children who have similar problems. There are a number of reasons for this, important ones relating to complexity and diversity issues. Most controlled trials are conducted with participants who fall into a clear diagnostic category and complete the intervention. Yet many children have multiple problems and personal or social circumstances that militate against sustained engagement with treatment. In addition, very little is known about the appropriateness of most treatments for children from minority ethnic groups in the UK. Hence it is recognized that choice of approach will involve a decision-making process guided by a range of factors including the characteristics of the child/young person, their family and social circumstances, as well as the available research.

The prevalence estimates in Table 15.1 come from a national survey of the mental health of children and young people in Great Britain in 2004 (Green *et al.* 2005). By contrast, prevalence figures on BESD tend to be based on statistical returns from schools about children already identified. So they are likely to underestimate numbers in the population as a whole and to be influenced by the availability of support services and special provision. In 2006 in England 0.45 per

Table 15.1   Types of mental health problems common in schools and prevalence estimates (percentage of 5–16 year olds)

	Boys	Girls	Total
Conduct problems	7.5	3.9	5.8
Emotional problems			
Anxiety disorders	2.9	3.8	3.3
Depressive disorders	0.6	1.1	0.9
Attention deficit/hyperactivity disorder	2.6	0.4	1.5
Autistic spectrum disorders	1.4	0.3	0.9
Less common disorders*	0.5	0.4	0.5

* including eating disorders (anorexia nervosa and bulimia nervosa), tics (motor and verbal, Tourette's syndrome) and selective mutism (see Chapter 10).

cent of the school population aged 5–16 years had a statement on which BESD was the primary or secondary need and a further 1.25 per cent were identified at School Action Plus (DfES 2006d). Cole *et al.* (2003) estimated 0.3–0.4 per cent of the school population were placed in special schools or in pupil referral units. EBD are not evenly distributed within the school population, or across England but are more prevalent in inner cities, socially deprived families, boys, children who have other language learning, health or developmental difficulties, and among those who come from homes where there is or has been parental discord or divorce, mental health problems or neglect, significant parental coldness or irritability towards the child (DfE 1994a).

BESD across settings

Given the role of environmental demands and others' perceptions in defining both BESD and many childhood mental health problems, it is not surprising that both estimates of incidence and the ratings given to individuals can depend on the infomant. Parents and teachers may have very different perceptions. In the Isle of Wight study (Rutter *et al.* 1970), parents and teachers completing the same schedule identified almost completely different groups of 'problem' children. Tizard *et al.* (1988) reported an overlap of around 33 per cent between 7-year-olds identified as having a behaviour problem by parents and teachers. Similar results have been obtained in a number of studies carried out in different countries (e.g. McGee *et al.* 1983 in New Zealand; Verhulst and Akkerhuis 1989 in Holland), thus indicating the cross-cultural applicability of these findings.

There are many important differences between home and school environments that might be expected to influence a child's behaviour. Therefore differences in ratings may reflect real differences between behaviour in the two settings. This receives some support from Wright and Torrey (2001) who found stronger relationships between teacher and classmates' ratings of problem behaviours than between teacher and parent ratings. Furthermore, parents' and teachers' expectations are likely to differ in ways that will lead them to rate the same behaviours differently. A 6-year-old who finds it difficult to sit still and concentrate on a task for more than five minutes is more likely to be expected to do this regularly at school than at home and would therefore be more likely to receive negative ratings for these aspects of their behaviour from teachers than from parents. It is of interest that Angtrop *et al.* (2002) found little agreement between parent and teacher ratings of ADHD, but moderate agreement on behaviours characteristic of conduct problems, where there may be fewer home–school differences in expectations and perceptions.

Differences between teacher and parent expectations of behaviour and differences between children's behaviour at home and at school may also be culturally influenced. Keller (1988) compared parent and teacher ratings of the social behaviour of 7-year-old black, Hispanic and white children in the USA. As in other studies, significant low to moderate correlations were found between parent and teacher ratings for white pupils only. For black and Hispanic children there were no significant associations between the behaviour ratings given by teachers and parents. Stevens *et al.* (2003) compared parent and teacher ratings of Dutch native children and Turkish and Moroccan immigrant children aged 4–18 years in Holland. Dutch and Moroccan parents reported similar levels of problem, while

Turkish parents reported more. However, teachers reported substantially more conduct problems in Moroccan pupils than in the other two groups. These studies suggest that great caution should be exercised in interpreting ratings of a pupil's behaviour when information is provided by a single rater in relation to a single setting. This is particularly so for pupils from minority ethnic groups.

Exclusion from school

The early 1990s saw a steep rise in permanent exclusion from schools in England, from an annual rate of 2,910 in 1990–1 to 11,181 in 1993 4 (Parsons 1996). A steady high rate was then maintained through to 1997–8 (see Figure 15.2). In 1999 the number of permanent exclusions started to fall for the first time since 1990, with government statistics showing a decrease of 15 per cent between 1998 and 1999. Possible reasons for this decrease, and potential repercussions in terms of teacher stress and discipline in schools, have been debated between ministers and teaching unions (Thornton 2000). Among the factors that appear relevant to an examination of this fall in the number of exclusions are: targets set by government, the identification of local authorities where particularly high numbers of black pupils were excluded and the provision of additional funding for school-based support to pupils at risk of exclusion. Of particular importance were the requirements placed on local authorities in 1999 to ensure access to full-time education for pupils excluded for more than three weeks, which were amended from September 2007 to require the provision of full-time education from day 6 of a permanent exclusion.

Differences have been reported in the incidence of exclusion in different groups:

- *Exclusions and gender.* Overall, around four boys are excluded for every girl (DfES 2006k), while in primary schools a ratio of 10 to 1 has been reported (Ofsted 2005f).

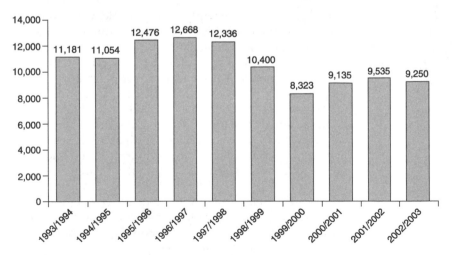

Figure 15.2   Permanent exclusions from schools in England.
Source: from Ofsted (2005f).

- *Exclusions and age.* In 2004–5 government figures showed that 12% of those excluded were in primary schools and 3% in special schools, with 85% of exclusions from school being at secondary level. The peak age for exclusion was 13 and 14 years, with 46% of exclusions occurring at this point (DfES 2006j).

- *Exclusions and ethnicity.* Gillborn and Gipps (1996) reported that African-Caribbean pupils were between four and six times more likely to be excluded than are white pupils. Statistics for 1999 suggested that exclusions of black pupils were falling, although rates continue to be disproportionately high. In 2004–5 black pupils were still twice as likely to be excluded as white pupils (DfES 2006j). The highest rates of exclusion were found among Travellers, of both Irish and Gipsy/Roma origin.

- *Exclusions and social disadvantage.* It has been reported that children excluded from school are more likely to have experienced poverty, homelessness, parental illness and bereavement (Ofsted 1996a; Hayden 1997). Disproportionate numbers of children in care are also excluded (Brodie and Berridge, 1996). In 2005 pupils in care were nine times more likely to be permanently excluded than their peers (DfES 2006j).

- *Exclusions and SEN.* In the mid-1990s the rate of permanent exclusions was seven times higher for pupils who had a statement compared to those without statements (DfEE 1999a). In 2004–5 it was reported that the differential rate had decreased in each of the previous three years, although the exclusion rate among pupils with statements was still three times higher than among the school population generally (DfES 2006j).

Reducing the disproportionate exclusion of black pupils has been a particular focus over the last 10 years. Among the measures that have been advocated are: ethnic monitoring of achievement; community mentoring schemes; the development of a black perspective in the school curriculum; and effective links between mainstream and supplementary schools. Grant and Brooks (1996, 2000) emphasized the role that the black community can play and have described how an LEA can energize and support initiatives such as those advocated in government guidance (DfEE 1999a). Current figures suggest that the measures taken have enjoyed some success, but need to be extended to other cultural groups. Derrington (2005) investigated the disproportionate exclusion of Gipsy Traveller pupils, following a group of 44 pupils over a period of three years. While positive behavioural reports were received from primary teachers, problems began to emerge during the first year in secondary school. Over the next two years a third of the pupils received at least one fixed-term exclusion, although only one was permanently excluded. However, by the age of 14 years half the group had self-excluded. While conflicting cultural expectations as the pupils grew older played a part, this study found that bullying and racism were also influential.

Some success also appears to have been achieved in reducing exclusion rates among pupils who have SEN. Examination of the high rates of exclusion of pupils with statements in the mid-1990s indicates that a large number of these exclusions were from special schools for pupils with EBD. Government guidance (DfEE 1999a) was issued advising schools that, unless the circumstances are exceptional, they should avoid excluding pupils with statements or those whose SEN are being assessed by the local authority. Where efforts to maintain a placement had been exhausted, schools were asked to liaise with the local authority to arrange an interim review of the pupil's statement so that proper planning for their future education could take place. However, there is concern for those pupils with SEN still excluded as provision is likely to be made in a pupil referral unit and an investigation by Ofsted (2006) found that the quality and outcomes of education for pupils with learning difficulties and disabilities were less likely to be successful in pupil referral units than in either mainstream or special schools.

The reduction in the differential rate of exclusion of children and young people in care – from 14:1 in 2000 to 9:1 in 2005 (DfES 2006i) – suggests that further work is needed here. In addition, Brodie (2000) highlighted a number of unofficial pathways to exclusion, including exclusion by non-admission, where schools refused admission to looked-after children living in local authority homes, sometimes explicitly because they were looked after. In other cases children were admitted following protracted negotiations between care staff and schools, which resulted in a considerable period of lost education. However, admission without adequate preparation was also problematic, with some pupils being excluded within days of joining their new school. Best results were obtained when school and care staff worked collaboratively to devise admissions programmes, phased as necessary, to ensure the child was supported to succeed in school. The government has announced its intention of strengthening guidance to encourage schools not to exclude children in care other than in the most exceptional circumstances and asking Ofsted to investigate examples of both good and poor practice (DfES 2006i).

Understanding behavioural, emotional and social difficulties

There are a number of different approaches that can be adopted in understanding and managing pupil behaviour in schools. Given the range of the behaviour and the influences involved, we will argue that a multi-level approach will usually be most useful. In the first part of this section the interactive factors (IF) framework, which is based on the work of Morton and Frith (1995) and was introduced in Chapter 5, will be used to summarize different theoretical approaches to understanding BESD. The IF framework uses three levels of description to explain developmental problems – the biological level, the cognitive level and the behavioural level – and, in addition, recognizes the operation of environmental factors at all three levels. At the biological level we record information about the brain and about sensory processes such as hearing and vision. Hypothesized within-child factors, including affective factors, are located at the cognitive level, while directly observable behaviours are placed at the behavioural level. The major theoretical approaches that have been developed to understand BESD are represented in Figure 15.3 using the IF framework which can help to clarify similarities and differences between them. Further information about these approaches and the assessment and intervention approaches developed from them can be found in Ayers *et al.* (2000) and Farrell (2006).

ENVIRONMENT/MANAGEMENT

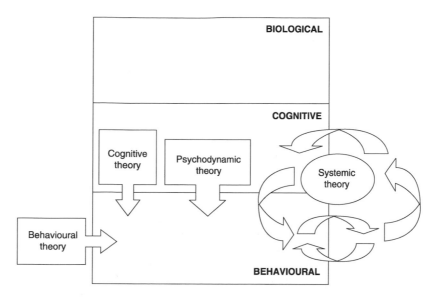

Figure 15.3 The major theoretical approaches that have been applied to understanding BESD

Behavioural approaches

In behavioural approaches the primary focus is on behaviour that can be directly observed. It is assumed that behaviour is learned through what happens in a child's environment, so that well-established patterns of behaviour can be changed by changing environmental consequences or other related events. There are a number of different learning theories – for example, Pavlovian classical conditioning, Hull's operant conditioning, Skinner's neo-behaviourism and Bandura's social learning theory. They all share the basic assumptions of the behavioural approach but differ in the detailed mechanisms through which behaviour is thought to be learned. Behavioural approaches make no reference to pupils' thoughts or feelings. The relationship between the environment and pupil behaviour which they embody is represented in Figure 15.3. In understanding emotional and behavioural difficulties the focus is on clarifying the specific behaviours regarded as undesirable and identifying the features of the environment that support the undesirable behaviour or can be used to help the pupil unlearn it.

From a behavioural perspective the undesirable behaviour characteristic of BESD develops when children learn to engage in it because it is associated with outcomes that are positive for them. For example, screaming in the supermarket may become associated with being given sweets. Even though they may not be able to articulate the relationships between their behaviour and contingent environmental events and conditions, children are sensitive to them from a young age, as are many animals. Screaming in the supermarket may occur with one parent, but not the other. It may not occur when both are there together as the child will have learned to discriminate the conditions under which screaming is associated with getting the sweets. The child may begin to generalize the behaviour – screaming in the supermarket to get other things, screaming at home to get sweets, screaming at nursery to get toys they want, etc. Whether the behaviour becomes established in each of these new situations will depend on whether or not it is reinforced by being linked with a desirable outcome. However, a child who screams in nursery when they do not get what they want is not necessarily one whose preschool reinforcement history has taught them this response. It might be that they have learned it in the nursery: they may have observed the screaming behaviour of another child being reinforced in this way, or their own screaming might have initially occurred accidentally – in response to a fall, for example.

In the behavioural approach intervention involves changing the environmental conditions to help the child unlearn the undesirable behaviour and learn desirable behaviour instead. The more securely learned the undesirable behaviour is the more difficult it is to unlearn. The consistency with which the new environmental conditions are applied will also influence the child's progress in unlearning the undesirable behaviour. For example, the parent with whom the child has learned to scream for sweets in the supermarket might try to help the child unlearn the screaming behaviour by not giving them sweets when they scream. If the parent sticks to this plan the child, although initially likely to redouble their efforts, will quickly learn that screaming no longer 'works' and will stop. However, if the parent gives in after a couple of visits the learning for the child will be that screaming still works, not every time, but sometimes, so it is always worth giving it a try. This is likely to make the behaviour even harder to unlearn in future as it will take much longer to establish that screaming really no longer works and that the parent really is not going to change their mind again next time.

Cognitive approaches

In cognitive approaches the primary focus is on cognitive processes – how the individual perceives events, thinks about them, plans, and solves problems. It is assumed that the relationship between environmental events and a child's behaviour will depend on the child's interpretation of events. If two children are reprimanded by the teacher they may each interpret this same event differently and attribute responsibility accordingly. One may feel that they deserved the reprimand and that they are to blame, while the other may feel that the teacher was picking on them unfairly and blame the teacher. An important factor in their response will be the way in which they *perceive* events. It is argued that in order to change the behaviour of children who present BESD it is important to help them change the way in which they think about themselves and the world. Different cognitive theories focus on different processes. Examples include:

- children's perception of themselves and their self-esteem;
- their attributions for the causes of their difficulties – for example, to themselves or others
- their attitudes and how these develop and change;

- their skills in problem-solving, applied to situations that arise in their every-day interactions with other people.

From a cognitive perspective the undesirable behaviour that is characteristic of BESD develops when children misperceive and misconstrue situations, so that they respond in a way that seems appropriate and rational to them, but inappropriate to other people who see the situation differently. For example, if a pupil is bumped into in a corridor by another, most teachers and pupils would regard a physical attack as an unreasonable response. Most people would not attribute negative intent to this action but would assume that it was an accident. If hostile intent is attributed feelings of anger or anxiety are likely to result and can lead to the pupil hitting out at their unwitting assailant.

Traumatic life events may predispose children to interpret the world as a hostile place. Dodge *et al.* (1995) followed up children who had suffered physical abuse in the preschool years. They found that these children were four times as likely to be rated as aggressive by teachers at 8–10 years of age. The children rated as aggressive were also found to be experiencing a number of associated cognitive processing difficulties. They misperceived social situations because they tended to focus disproportionately on any hostile cues that were present (a tendency that doubtless had protective significance in the past but which was counterproductive in the present). They also showed strong hostile attribution biases about the intentions of others and held beliefs that aggressive behaviours lead to positive outcomes for the perpetrator. Traumatic violence that can lead to hostile attributional biases is not confined to out-of-school contexts but can also be experienced in schools, as the literature on bullying illustrates (MacDonald 1996). Furthermore, vicious cycles are often set up where children who react in ways that seem unpredictable and unreasonable become rejected by the peer group and regarded negatively by teachers. In this way their belief that the world is a hostile place can become a self-fulfilling prophecy in each new situation they encounter.

Cognitive approaches to intervention involve working with the child or young person to challenge their misperceptions, faulty beliefs or attributions and to help them learn more adaptive ways of perceiving and interpreting themselves and their world. Pupils may be helped to improve their self-esteem by substituting rewarding and supportive self-talk for defeatist and undermining self-statements. Cognitive mediation of biological-level influences may also be targeted, for example by anger and anxiety management programmes where children are taught to recognize physiological indicators of these emotions at an early stage (e.g. pounding heart, sweaty palms) and to engage in relabelling and other self-talk strategies in order to stay calm and not be panicked into 'fight' or 'flight' behaviour (see Table 15.4 for sources of information on these strategies).

However, cognitive changes resulting from intervention are not always accompanied by changes in behaviour. A pupil's difficult behaviour will often be well established and exacerbated by responses from peers which will not be changed by a cognitive approach that focuses on the target child alone. Cognitive interventions are therefore often combined with behavioural interventions designed to address other influences on the behaviour.

Psychodynamic approaches

Psychodynamic approaches are based on the assumption that many of the wishes, drives, anxieties and fantasies that determine our behaviour are unconscious. Children's behaviour problems are seen as 'outward and visible symptoms of internal and invisible conflict' (Davie 1986: 6). But the individual concerned may not be aware of the conflict that is expressed in this way, they may simply have intense feelings for which they cannot easily find a cause. Perhaps, when their teacher sets them work that they find difficult, the scenario recaptures unconsciously a repeated sequence of events from earlier in their life. It may be that, whenever they tried to please one of their parents, there was a pattern in which whatever they did was not good enough and they were subjected to harsh criticism or punishment. Perhaps this did not always 'really' happen, but it seemed to them that this was how it was, because they came to expect to fail every time. Now, some years later, when work is set in the classroom the teacher is unconsciously treated as that parent through a process of *projection*. So the teacher too is seen to be expecting failure from the outset.

Psychodynamic approaches focus on understanding and resolving such internal conflicts rather than working directly to reduce the undesirable behaviour that results from them. In fact, tackling the behaviour problem without resolving the inner conflict is seen as likely to have only a short-term impact. The underlying problem is expected to manifest itself again in a different way. So psychodynamic approaches have a quite different focus from behavioural approaches. In Figure 15.3 they are shown as involving cognitive-level processes in the same way that cognitive approaches do. But, whereas cognitive theories focus on interpretations and perceptions of concurrent environmental events, classic psychodynamic theories focus on unconscious conflicts and fantasies that may have deep-seated roots in the early history of the individual concerned. These approaches thus give more attention to how a pattern of behaviour has developed. They are based on *developmental* theories in which emotional and behavioural difficulties are seen as emerging out of personal experience over time.

An important feature of psychodynamic approaches is that all of this is seen as applying not only to pupils and their parents but also to the teachers and carers. Just as a child may project unresolved and intense feelings onto adults, the adults may respond by becoming caught up in the distressing feelings themselves:

> Given the potency of some of the projections experienced when working with children experiencing emotional and behaviour difficulties, the adult needs to be keenly aware of the feelings aroused in him/herself, and what happens to those feelings. To what extent are we able to observe ourselves and recognise feelings being aroused by others? To what extent can we manage those feelings? To what extent do such feelings become unconsciously part of our interaction?
>
> (Greenhalgh 1994: 90)

Attachment theory

Just as there are different types of behavioural and cognitive theories, so too there are different types of psychodynamic theories. One of the most influential contemporary psychodynamic theories is attachment theory (Shaver and Mikulincer

2005; Target 2005). This has been developed from the theoretical work of Bowlby (see Bowlby 1988) and associated experimental work of Ainsworth (Ainsworth *et al.* 1978). Ainsworth *et al.* devised the Strange Situation Procedure in which 10–24-month-old infants were briefly separated from their parent in an unfamiliar setting. When reunited with the parent three patterns of behaviour were observed which were regarded at indicative of different types of infant–parent attachment:

- Secure – these infants were happy to see the parent, and if they had been distressed when the parent had left they settled on the parent's reappearance and re-engaged in absorbed play or exploration.

- Insecure-avoidant – these infants typically showed little distress on separation and when the parent reappeared they moved or turned away, engaging in play and ignoring the parent.

- Insecure-resistant/ambivalent – these infants were very distressed on separation, and when the parent returned they tended both to seek contact and reject it when offered.

Bowlby hypothesized that these early patterns of interaction generated mental representations (working models of others and the self) which guided subsequent relationships and so could have long-term effects. An 'insecure' pattern of attachment was indeed found to be a risk factor for later development, with avoidant patterns tending to be associated with later antisocial behaviour and ambivalent patterns with social withdrawal in middle childhood and anxiety in late adolescence (Green and Goldwyn 2002). However, the high base rate of these patterns of attachment in the normal population (about 40 per cent) limited their predictive value. By contrast, about 10 per cent of normal population samples showed behaviour in the Strange Situation Procedure that could not be classified as a consistent pattern of behaviour with a predictable caregiver. These infants showed a variety of unusual and contradictory responses, which subsequently gave rise to a fourth category, 'disorganized'. Among high-risk (especially maltreated) groups as many as 50 per cent may show disorganized attachment and signs of pervasive fear.

Strong associations are reported between disorganized attachment and later BESD in school and psychopathology in adolescence (Green and Goldwyn 2002). However, where there are two caregivers, disorganization in one relationship is not significantly associated with disorganization in the other (Steele *et al.* 1996), and it has been suggested that compensatory effects may be possible, provided the infant has at least one relationship to provide a 'secure base'. Increasing attention is also being given to the extent to which teachers may play an important role as an 'attachment figure of convenience' in providing a secure base and promoting positive school adjustment for children with BESD who exhibit a disorganized attachment style (Zionts 2005). However, Zionts also urges caution to avoid misinterpretation of attachment behaviour when there are cultural differences between home and school. For example, in cultures where growth in interdependence, rather than independence, is seen as a desirable developmental outcome for family members, behaviours that would be seen as overprotective of children or indicative of parent–child role reversal in the majority culture may be considered appropriate and adaptive.

Psychodynamic approaches to intervention involve bringing to the child's conscious awareness unconscious defences and fantasies, interpreting them and building the child's positive resources and sense of security so that they feel strong enough to give up negative behaviour that was previously serving important purposes for them in defending the self. Individual psychodynamic psychotherapy with children is generally carried out by child psychotherapists employed by the NHS, and the work of art, music and educational therapists is often informed by psychodynamic perspectives. Applications of attachment theory can found in the work of educational therapists (Barrett and Trevitt 1991; Geddes 2006) and in nurture groups (Bennathan and Boxall 2002).

Systemic approaches

In systemic approaches the focus is on reciprocal interaction between individuals and their environment. The core features of a systems approach are summarized by Gorrell-Barnes (1985): 'Systems thinking derives principally from the concept of mutual causality and from the familiar notion that the whole is greater than the sum of its parts'. Two main strands of systems thinking may be identified. The first (general systems theory) stems from the work of von Bertalanffy (1968) and is derived from the study of biological organisms. Systemic family therapy (Palazzoli *et al.* 1978) and the joint family–school approach of Dowling and Osborne (1994) developed in this tradition. The second strand of systems thinking (systems analysis) was derived from the study of computer systems. Both 'hard' and 'soft' systems methodologies for addressing problems in organizations developed in this tradition and have been applied in schools (Burden 1981; Frederickson 1990c). Systemic theory is represented on the IF framework in Figure 15.3 which illustrates the reciprocal interactions and circular causality that are characteristic of this approach.

The first stage in a systems analysis of a pupil behaviour considered problematic by a teacher is to undertake a holistic investigation which attempts to build up a picture of the behaviours, knowledge, feelings, beliefs and attitudes of both teacher and pupil that might be relevant to the problematic situations arising between them. Initial discussion with the teacher would not be narrowly focused on pupil behaviour, its antecedents and consequences (ABC). Rather, the emphasis is more likely to be placed on finding out on a broad level what the behaviours mean to all involved – both teacher and pupil, in looking for reciprocal interactions and circular sequences. For example Figure 15.4 shows how a behavioural ABC analysis is extended by adopting a systemic perspective.

From a systemic perspective undesirable behaviour that is characteristic of BESD arises from mismatches in the goals and expectations of the different people who are involved. Even when the goals of different people and groups are not in conflict with each other, ineffective or inconsistent processes for achieving key goals may undermine, rather than support, pupils in learning socially acceptable behaviour.

Systemic approaches to intervention involve identifying and recognizing the different perspectives held by different groups and individuals in a situation and developing plans for improvement, usually involving interrelated action at a number of levels, that can be supported by all involved (see the account in Chapter 9 of the application of soft systems methodology in schools). Systemic approaches

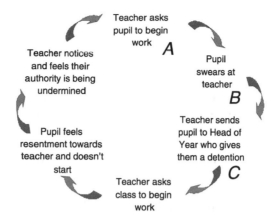

Figure 15.4 A systemic perspective

to intervention will often utilize techniques and strategies from other theoretical approaches. What is characteristic is a recognition that both problem behaviour and intervention strategies have knock-on effects for everyone involved in the situation. Hence consultative staff support groups represent a systemic approach to problem behaviour in schools that can be informed either by psycho-dynamic concepts (Hanko 2001) or by cognitive behavioural concepts (Monsen and Graham 2001).

Activity 15.2   Circular causality

Most behaviour that causes concern is not a 'one-off' but represents an entrenched pattern of responding. Think about the behaviour of a child or adult you know which falls into this category. First, record the problematic behaviour. Secondly, complete a behavioural analysis, thinking about several instances and adding the typical antecedents and consequences. Thirdly, look at the example systemically, considering the perspectives of everyone involved and mapping out possible circles of causality that may be maintaining the behaviour. Finally, consider what action might be recommended to improve the situation if it is analysed (a) behaviourally and (b) systemically.

Many behavioural interventions focus on rewarding a pupil with praise when they follow classroom rules. A systemic perspective is likely to highlight the importance of considering the possible impact on other members of the class group. As a consequence, strategies may be incorporated to encourage peer support for the pupil's appropriate behaviour. Similarly, recognizing the importance of parent/carer and pupil commitment to school and class rules may lead to their involvement, within clearly stated boundaries, in devising them. Miller (2003) highlights the ways in which the involvement of an educational psychologist working with a teacher on a behavioural programme for a pupil experiencing BESD can create a new temporary system. Such a system overlaps the boundaries of home and school and embodies norms that allow pupils, parents and teachers to construe each other in a different way from that usually dictated by school policy and staff culture. Within such systems exceptions can be made and flexible approaches adopted that allow participants to break out of entrenched and unhelpful patterns of interaction.

Biological-level influences

So far nothing has been said about biological-level influences on behaviour, or about formulating and testing hypotheses at this level. While biological-level influences will be important in some cases, their investigation is outside the scope of the professional qualification and expertise of teachers and educational psychologists. Close interdisciplinary collaboration with medical staff will be important in these cases, of which ADHD represents a good example.

Figure 15.5 uses the IF framework to summarize possible influences on ADHD reviewed by a British Psychological Society (1996) working party. From the behavioural level we can see that children described as having ADHD tend to be impulsive, overactive and inattentive to a degree that causes serious concern. At the cognitive level are listed a number of the many psychological mechanisms that have been put forward to understand the problems these children experience. At the biological level consideration is given to:

- factors that may result in types of neurological damage known to be associated with behaviour of this kind (e.g. head injuries, epilepsy, the metabolic disorder phenylketonuria);

- possible genetic factors which have been suggested in a number of studies carried out with twins (Pennington and Ozonoff 1996);

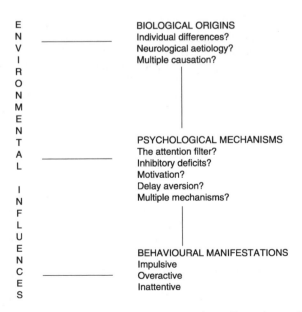

Figure 15.5 Possible influences on the behavioural manifestations of ADHD
Source: British Psychological Society (1996).

● neuroanatomical and neurochemical factors implicating reduced blood flow or levels of key chemicals in particular areas of the brain.

It is recognized that there will be considerable individual differences in the effects such factors may have and that multiple influences may also be present.

In England and Wales a range of interventions are recommended by the National Institute for Health and Clinical Excellence (NICE 2008), depending on the severity of the problems experienced. For moderate difficulties parent training is recommended, either alone or alongside a group intervention programme (such as cognitive behavioural therapy and/or social skills training) for the child or young person. Where the problems are severe, drug treatment, an environmental intervention which impacts at the biological level, is recommended as the first-line treatment. However, it is also recommended that a group-based parent-training programme should be offered. The guidance states that 'Drug treatment for children and young people with ADHD should always form part of a comprehensive treatment plan that includes psychological, behavioural and educational advice and interventions' (NICE 2008). In reviewing school-based intereventions for children with ADHD, DuPaul and Weyandt (2006) emphasize the need to individualize the treatment programmes delivered in school. As illustrated in Table 15.2, even the same behaviour may call for different approaches, depending on the function the behaviour is serving for the pupil. DuPaul and Weyandt highlight the importance of sustained programmes, involving parents, teachers and peers that also directly address the academic and social difficulties experienced by pupils with ADHD, in addition to the management of disruptive and off-task behaviour. This is because success in reducing disruptive and off-task behaviour does not necessarily lead to spontaneous improvements in other areas.

Professional guidance for work with children who have ADHD closely

Table 15.2   Classroom interventions linked to behavioural function

Behavioural function	Antecedent-based intervention	Consequent-based intervention
Obtain teacher attention	Remind of class rules and state connection between appropriate behaviour and receipt of teacher attention	Provide attention contingent on appropriate behaviour while ignoring disruptive behaviour; time out from positive reinforcement contingent on disruptive behaviour
Obtain peer attention	Remind of class rules and encourage classroom peers to ignore disruptive behaviour	Provide peer attention contingent on appropriate behaviour (e.g. peer tutoring)
Avoid/escape effortful tasks	Increase stimulation value of task; reduce size of task	Provide brief 'attention breaks' when sub-units of task are completed

Source: DuPaul and Weyandt (2006).

parallels the four guiding principles for work with pupils who present BESD in an educational context identified by Rizzo and Zabel (1988):

● commitment to an integrative framework;

● emphasis on an ecological/systemic orientation;

● belief in the necessity of interdisciplinary approaches in intervention;

● inclusion of parents as key resources in the educational process.

These principles are reflected in the following discussion of approaches to assessment and intervention with pupils displaying BESD.

Assessment methods

Different theoretical approaches lead to different questions being asked. The same assessment method may be used within different theoretical perspectives to collect different information. For example, the importance of involving the child's parents or carers has been highlighted. However, interviews with parents and carers conducted from different theoretical perspectives would seek different information, as shown in Table 15.3.

Often, because different information is considered relevant in different theories, different assessment methods will be used. Direct detailed observations in the situation where the problems occur will be considered very important from a behavioural perspective in order to identify the specific behaviour that causes concern and the environmental events that control its occurrence. From a cognitive perspective the actual sequence of environmental events will be considered less important than the pupil's perception and interpretation of what happened. So interviewing the pupil is likely to be prioritized over direct observation.

Table 15.3 Information collected in interviews conducted from different theoretical perspectives with parents/carers

Theoretical perspective	Information collected
Behavioural	Information about the frequency and duration of target problematic behaviours at home and the environmental events surrounding their occurrence. The child's 'reinforcement history' for similar behaviours.
Cognitive	Information about the parents' perceptions, interpretations and feelings about the child's behaviour and the actions being taken by the school.
Psychodynamic	Information about the child's early development and family relationships, paying particular attention to experiences that are seen as having had crucial emotional significance.
Systemic	Information about the parents' perceptions and their interpretation of the perceptions of others, such as the child and their teachers. Their hypotheses about ways in which everyone involved would be affected by particular changes.

Outlined below are some of the assessment methods most commonly used to gain an understanding of BESD and to guide positive action. The methods are categorized according to the theoretical framework with which they are most closely associated. Further details about many of these methods and their implementation in schools can be found in Ayers *et al.* (2000) and Farrell (2006).

Behaviourally-based methods

Systematic observation is particularly characteristic of behaviourally-based assessment. It may be carried out by teachers, the pupil or support professionals such as behaviour support teachers or educational psychologists. Information may be collected on:

- the frequency and/or duration of identified problematic behaviour or of the positive behaviour which it is hoped to encourage;

- the events or conditions in the environment that occur prior to and following the behaviour and which may therefore be acting to encourage or reinforce it.

A number of systematic observation techniques are available. A crucial requirement of all of these is that the observer must define the behaviour they are observing clearly before they start. If an observer is not familiar with the classroom and pupil(s) concerned they are likely to need to spend some time talking with the teacher and/or conducting unstructured observations first. Time sampling and interval sampling are two observational methods that are often considered together. For both you must first identify one or more target behaviours (e.g. working, sitting, calling out, inappropriate talking).

Time sampling involves observing, say for 10 seconds, and on the tenth second recording whether or not the pupil at that moment is engaging in any of the target behaviours. The observation period might last in total for 20 minutes, with spot observations being made at the end of each 10-second period.

Interval sampling involves observing, say for 20 seconds, and at the end of that time spending 10 seconds recording whether or not the pupil has engaged in any of the behaviours during the preceding 20 seconds. The observation period may last in total for 20 minutes, with observations being made for the first 20 seconds of each half minute and the final 10 seconds of each half minute being spent recording those behaviours which had occurred at least once during the preceding 20 seconds.

Interval sampling makes good use of a visiting observer's time in that more time is spent observing than is the case with time sampling. However, the number of pupils that can be observed is limited and it is not really practical for teachers and pupils to use. With time sampling the use of a quiet timer can allow teachers and pupils to sample behaviours such as 'in seat' and 'on task' throughout a lesson at longer intervals, such as 1-minute intervals. Both time and interval sampling are appropriate only for behaviours that occur frequently. If the behaviour occurs less than once in 15 minutes, event sampling (see below) should be selected.

Realistic intervention targets can be set by collecting information on the frequency of key behaviours for comparison pupils in the same teaching group who are making satisfactory progress. This recognizes, for example, that it would probably be unreasonable to expect a pupil *never* to call out without raising their hand. The importance of using systematic observation is reinforced by the finding that once teachers are concerned about the disruptive behaviour of particular pupils they will tend to overestimate its frequency. By collecting observations on a regular basis it is possible to obtain an indication of the success of interventions designed to reduce problem behaviour and increase positive behaviour. Scherer (1990) provides a clear and practical account of how this process of 'assessment by baselines' can be used by subject teachers in secondary schools to count and graph the number of disruptive incidents occurring with particular pupils while a series of intervention strategies are tried.

Event sampling involves recording each occurrence of a specified behaviour during a particular time period. For example, you might want a record of each time a pupil complies or fails to comply with a request from the teacher. This approach can be used whether or not a behaviour occurs frequently, and it is possible to collect information on other pupils at the same time. Provided the number of behaviours and pupils to be observed is kept to a manageable number (and this will depend on the frequency of occurrence of the behaviour) this is a highly feasible approach for ongoing use by staff and pupils. Observations collected across different sessions may help to identify certain lessons or times of day the pupils find difficult and inform action planning.

Event sampling may also provide information about the environmental events surrounding the behaviour of concern. An 'ABC' outline is frequently used where the observer records:

A: antecedent events that precede the pupil's behaviour (e.g. 'teacher asks pupil to begin work');
B: behaviour engaged in by the pupil on that occasion (e.g pupil shouts and swears at teacher);
C: consequences for the pupil that result from the behaviour (e.g. pupil is sent out of class to the head of year).

One problem with observational approaches is that both children and the adults interacting with them may behave differently when being observed or when asked to carry out self-recording. If only a limited number of lessons are being observed a further concern is that these may not be representative and conclusions may be drawn that will not apply more generally.

Documentary sources such as report cards, records of attendance, detentions or other sanctions can be useful where they are sufficiently specific about the behaviour concerned. These sources can also be useful for monitoring the success of interventions over longer periods than is usually feasible with direct observations.

A wide variety of *questionnaires, checklists and rating scales* are available which provide behavioural descriptors on which key informants can rate a particular child. The Strengths and Difficulties Questionnaire (Goodman 1997) is a measure of adjustment and BESD in 3–16 year olds which is increasingly widely used. It consists of five scales (of five items each): Emotional Symptoms Scale; Conduct Problems Scale; Hyperactivity Scale; Peer Problems Scale; and Prosocial Scale. Parallel versions are available for completion by teachers, parents/carers and children/young people. The applicability of items over the last six months to the child in question is rated using a 3-point scale: 'not true', 'somewhat true' or 'certainly true'. The questionnaires and scoring instructions are available free on the web (http://www.sdqinfo.com) for all these informants in a large number of languages. The teacher and parent versions have been found to produce results consistent with established behaviour rating scales, such as Achenbach's Child Behaviour Checklist and Rutter's Child Behaviour Rating Scale (Goodman 1999), and with psychiatric diagnoses (Goodman 2001). Although the self-report version was originally designed for young people aged 11–16, there is evidence that it is applicable from 8 years (Muris *et al.* 2004).

Cognitively-based methods

A variety of questionnaires and other techniques are available for use with pupils to assess particular cognitive constructs, such as self-perception (see Burden 1999), attributions (see Indoe 1999) and personal constructs (see Beaver 1996; Ravenette 1999).

For example, the Self-Perception Profile for Children (Harter 1985) is a paper-and-pencil questionnaire which was developed to assess the self-perception of children aged 8–14 years. It includes 36 items and covers five specific domains of competence: scholastic competence (assessing how clever the children think they are, how well they believe they are performing at school); social acceptance (assessing how popular the children feel they are and if they believe they have a lot of friends); athletic competence (assessing the children's perception of their athletic ability); physical appearance (assessing how attractive the children feel they are); and behavioural conduct (assessing how well the children feel they behave and if they like the way they behave). In addition, there is a global self-worth subscale, which assesses the extent to which children like themselves as people. For each item there are two statements which the child reads, or which can be read to them, 'Some children often do not like the way they behave *but* other children usually like the way they behave'. The child is first asked to decide which statement is most like him/her. Then the child is asked to decide if the statement selected is 'really true' or 'sort of true' for him/her. These responses are scored from 1 to 4, where a score of 1 indicates low perceived competence and a score of 4 indicates high perceived competence.

As Gibbs and Huang (1989) point out, cultural groups may differ in the value attached to the different characteristics and abilities that become the sources of self-concept and self-esteem for the child. They highlight the importance of finding out about these differential values in order to properly interpret a pupil's criteria for self-evaluation. In this respect an advantage of the Harter measure is that an additional questionnaire is provided where the pupil rates the importance they attach to competence in each of the areas where self-perception is assessed. Children's priorities in self-evaluation are likely to change over time. These developmental changes may occur not only because of increasing psychological maturity but also when their personal circumstances change. This is perhaps seen most dramatically with those refugee children who have been exposed to traumatic life events before their migration (Hodes 2000).

One problem with self-report scales for children is that there is often a tendency for children to select the most socially desirable option, even if it is not really true for them. The structure of the Harter questionnaire attempts to overcome this by suggesting that each statement is chosen by some children and that both are therefore acceptable. Other questionnaires tackle the problem in a different way by including a 'social desirability' scale containing items such as 'I always tell the truth' and 'I am never unhappy'. That is a way of checking if the person completing the questionnaire is trying to give a good impression. The problem is that it does not eliminate the effects of that distortion from the other scales and the type of approach used by the Harter questionnaire is usually preferred.

Other problems sometimes encountered with pupil self-report scales relate to the pupil's understanding of the language used, and their perceptiveness and capacity for self-analysis. Approaches such as those based on personal construct psychology generally lack the data on reliability typically provided with standardized questionnaires. However, they offer some relative advantages in that they use the child's own language and ways of categorizing their experience. This may be of particular value in the case of children whose cultural experience differs from that of the scale's authors. For further information about these techniques, see Stoker and Walker (1996) and Ravenette (1997).

Psychodynamically-based methods

An individual interview is central to most psychodynamic approaches, sometimes deriving support from the use of projective techniques. The projective hypothesis is based on the assumption that when we respond to something outside ourselves our reactions are partly a reflection of our private inner world. When interviewers employ a projective technique they generally seek open-ended responses to stimuli designed to evoke inner conflicts of interest. For example, the Children's Apperception Test (Bellak and Bellak 1949) consists of black and white pictures of 'adult' and 'child' animals depicting scenes relating to various aspects of family life, such as food and mealtimes, toileting and bedtime. The child is asked to tell a story about each picture and their stories are interpreted as a projection of their inner conflicts. A child's perceptions of relationships within their family may be explored using a kinetic family drawing (Burns and Kaufman 1970). Children are asked to draw a picture showing themselves and everyone who lives at home with them in their family. Inferences about children's perceptions of their role in the family may be drawn on the basis, for example, of where they locate themselves in the picture or how large they draw themselves in relation to other family members.

One criticism of early uses of projective techniques was that insufficient attention was given to testing out in other ways the interpretations generated. It has been argued that the techniques may offer an interesting source of hypotheses but these should not be accepted at face value. A further criticism is that the assessment information provided has only very limited applicability in generating practical intervention strategies for use in schools. On the other hand, these techniques may sometimes highlight an aspect of a child's problems that is otherwise likely to be ignored. The case study of Lesley (see Activity 15.3) illustrates this point. She completed another form of projective technique – a sentence completion task. In this method the child is presented with a series of sentence stems and asked to complete each sentence with the first words they think of. They are encouraged to work quickly and sometimes, if they do not write fluently

Activity 15.3   Lesley's sentence completions

Lesley (aged 9) had severe difficulties with reading and writing. She seemed constantly sad and subdued in school and rarely played with other girls during breaktimes. For these reasons she was referred to an educational psychologist. At the time she was living in accommodation for the homeless with her mother. She had no siblings. There had not been any contact with her father since shortly after she was born. Her mother rarely visited the school but had agreed to the referral to the educational psychologist because she shared the teacher's concern about Lesley's poor progress with reading. The sentence completion task was one of a number of exercises that the psychologist employed to explore her wide-ranging difficulties. In the text below the words in italics in each sentence are the stem provided by the psychologist and the rest is what Lesley dictated in response.

Consider these questions:

(a)   What, if anything, do you think Lesley's sentence completions indicate about her mood, state of mind, concerns and interests?

(b)   What hypotheses might be formed about her feelings about key figures in her early life?

(c)   Why do you think she kept coming back to the same themes – e.g. the dog, being nice? What purposes might this perseveration (excessive repetition) be serving for Lesley in this situation?

1   *I like* the dog.

2   *Father* sees the dog.

3   *I wish* I had a dog.

4   *When I am older* I will be by myself.

5   *My school work* is great.

6   *I hate* meat.

7   *I dream that* of fairies.

8   *I became shy when* uncle came.

9   *I love* father very much but I wish that he wouldn't die.

10   *Other children* are playing.

11   *I try to get* out.

12   *In the dark* it is cold.

13   *What makes me angry is* boys.

14   *My brothers and sisters* is nice.

15   *School* is nice.

16   *Grown ups* are nice.

17   *I need* a father.

18   *Mother* cooks.

> 19 *I can't* read.
>
> 20 *I* love my mother very much but I wish she wouldn't die.
>
> 21 *I hope* uncle comes.
>
> 22 *My greatest worry is* that mummy isn't here.
>
> 23 *I secretly* hide in a hiding place.

themselves, dictate their responses to the interviewer. That is what Lesley did, as she had difficulty with all forms of literacy.

Systemically-based methods

Systemic assessment methods may be used to collate different perceptions about either organizational- or individual-level issues (see Chapter 9 for more information about the use of one such approach – soft systems methodology). At the organizational level, information about school rules and sanctions will generally be given in the school brochure. However, interviews with pupils, teachers and parents will often be necessary to identify the ways in which these rules and sanctions are perceived to operate in practice by different individuals. At the individual level, different perceptions of the behaviour of a particular pupil, perhaps collected by means of a round robin of their secondary school teachers, may be a starting point for identifying combinations of factors that are especially problematic for the pupil and those factors that are more successful in supporting appropriate behaviour.

The importance of the peer group social system in either supporting or undermining appropriate behaviour has also been recognized. Sociometric assessment questionnaires collect information from classmates (see Chapter 16) about the child's level of acceptance or rejection in the peer group. More recent questionnaires for monitoring bullying behaviour in school collect information from pupils not just about engagement in bullying or experience of victimization, but also about the range of roles that other members of the peer group play in relation to bullying incidents, roles such as assistant of the bully, defender of the victim and outsider (see Sharp 1999). Because of the hidden nature of much bullying, assessment approaches such as this are very important in assisting headteachers to discharge their legal duty to introduce measures to prevent all forms of bullying (School Standards and Frameworks Act 1998).

Systemic assessment approaches typically collect information at a number of levels and may use cognitive or behavioural assessment strategies to do so. Information is also collected about interactions between different levels and different individuals' perceptions. Techniques such as 'circular questioning' may be used to obtain information about relationships and differences in the perceptions of pupils, parents and teachers. Each person present may be asked to consider the thoughts, feelings and behaviour of the others and ways in which they may interact. For example, each person might be asked to choose, and give reasons for their choice of, the person who would be most pleased and the person who would be most disappointed if the pupil suddenly stopped presenting behavioural difficulties. Dowling and Osborne (1994: 23) point out that this style of questioning is 'intended to explore connections and effects rather than look for causes of behaviour' and makes 'it possible for the participants in the interview to develop a different view of the situation'.

'Reframing' involves putting forward an alternative interpretation of a situation. The use of circular questioning can indirectly lead participants to reframe events. Reframing may also be used directly to try out different possible interpretations of events that may enable all involved to shift their positions slightly and agree on action to move the situation on. For example, more opportunities for constructive action are likely to result if a parent's angry refusal to support a school's homework policy can be reframed as strong concern for their child's progress and worry that the child may be disadvantaged if the parent is unable to help them. It is generally possible to challenge some constructions of events because they are inconsistent with aspects of the information that is available. Usually however, a number of alternative constructions of events are plausible so several 'reframes' are possible. This may be particularly important to acknowledge where different constructions of events relate to cultural differences. Ultimately we can only evaluate the success of this kind of systems analysis by asking whether it leads to improved outcomes, and this generally involves collecting data at the behavioural level.

Assessment measures: some conclusions

Each of the commonly used assessment methods reviewed above has particular strengths, weaknesses and potential sources of bias. Greater confidence can be placed in conclusions reached when the results of different methods point in the same direction. This may be particularly important for pupils from certain cultural groups. Gray and Noakes (1994) stress the importance of checking out the accuracy of all information. For example, school staff may make inferences about the reasons for frequent family moves which become accepted within the school as fact. It is important to ask 'How do we know this?', 'How much reliance can we place on this source of information?' and 'Do we have supporting information from other sources?'

Given the identified importance of a multi-level systemic approach and an integrative orientation, the IF framework offers a means of representing assessment information about a particular pupil and their situation that has been collected using different assessment methods. The framework can accommodate a wide range of types of assessment information, irrespective of the theoretical perspectives employed. The framework can also be used to model the hypothesized effects of intervention strategies. Where problem behaviour is thought to be maintained by a number of interacting factors, it generally follows that a multi-pronged intervention approach will be required. This is a conclusion which emerges strongly from the following review of commonly-used intervention approaches for problem behaviour in schools.

Intervention strategies

The intervention strategies for BESD that are most commonly used in schools are drawn from behavioural, cognitive and systemic theories. Table 15.4 shows

Table 15.4   Percentages of each type of strategy recommended by educational psychologists in one LEA in one school term

Strategy	Frequency (%)		
	High	Medium	Low
Behavioural Based on behavioural approaches with the aim of increasing desirable behaviour and/or decreasing undesirable behaviour:	25.8	18.4	6.4
• Behavioural management work with school staff/involving pupil			
• Family work on behavioural programmes with parent			
Cognitive Based on a cognitive model addressing a child's problem-solving skills, poor self-image etc. For example:	3.5	20.6	4.3
• Social problem solving and skills training (see Chapter 16)			
• Anger management – a set of approaches which helps clients analyse events that trigger anger for them, identify yearly signs in themselves, remain calm, think differently about the triggers, develop impulse control, learn adaptive strategies for expressing anger in an effective way (see Faupel *et al.* 1998)			
• Counselling – a collaboration between a helper and a client where clients, 'through client–helper interactions, are in better positions to manage their problem situations and/or develop the unused resources and opportunities of their lives more effectively' (Egan 1994:5)			
• Brief solution-focused therapy – consists of finding out where clients want to get to and helping them appreciate and build on what they are already doing which is likely to help them get there. The emphasis is on working towards solutions rather than exploring problems, and on helping clients find their own solutions or routes to their goals (see Rhodes and Ajmal 1995; Ajmal and Rees 2001)			
Systemic Focusing on contextual interactions within the classroom (teacher and peer group), within the school at different levels, concerning home–school links, within the family/home environment. For example:	8.5	5.0	5.0
• Circle of Friends – this approach attempts to support children who present BESD and other SEN by enlisting the help of the other pupils in their class and setting up a special group or 'circle' of friends. The special group helps to set, monitor and review weekly targets in a meeting facilitated by an adult. Group members also provide agreed support to facilitate the focus child's inclusion and to help them achieve their targets (see Newton *et al.* 1996; Frederickson and Turner, 2003)			
• Family systems work – this is a model for working jointly with both families and schools which draws on applications of systems theory to the fields of family therapy and consultative work in schools (see Dowling and Osborne 1994)			
• Conferencing with staff – this involves group consultation with teachers where the consultant acts as a non-directive interventionist who generates valid information that highlights the underlying issues; enables the teacher to make autonomous free and informed choices about the nature of the intervention; and fosters a climate of commitment to its implementation (see Hanko 2001)			
Suggested involvement of other agencies (e.g. pupil referral units, child guidance, play therapist)	0.7	0.7	2.1

the frequency with which different types of strategies for pupils with BESD were recommended or implemented by educational psychologists in one county in a single term. A diverse range of strategies were also reported to have been employed by the multi-agency behaviour and education support teams formed in local authorities as part of behaviour improvement projects in areas where there were high crime rates:

> There were positive examples of case study work with individual children and their families, of the outcome of anger management groups, Continuing Professional Development (CPD) for school staff, changes in school policies, approaches to thinking about behaviour, and transition work.
>
> (Hallam 2007: 109)

In order to compile Table 15.4, educational psychologists were first asked to identify all the strategies they had recommended in the past term and then to indicate the frequency (high, medium or low) with which each strategy had been recommended. It can be seen that behavioural strategies were the most frequently used, with almost half the psychologists reporting at least medium frequency of use. The use of behavioural strategies was reported about three times more often in primary than secondary schools, while counselling and other cognitive interventions were more frequently implemented in secondary schools. This is consistent with the finding of a national survey of educational psychologists' work which reported that counselling and therapeutic work in relation to behaviour had been provided in 50 per cent of secondary schools in the year of the survey but in only 15 per cent of primary schools (DfEE 2000b). A predominance of interventions based on behavioural and cognitive behavioural approaches were also apparent in the systematic review of effective strategies to support pupils with BESD in mainstream primary schools conducted by Evans *et al.* (2004). Systematic reviews apply stringent quality criteria in excluding studies which have weaknesses in design or execution, and the first conclusion reached in this review was that there was a dearth of good-quality research. The other conclusions of the review will be reported below.

Behavioural strategies

A brief outline of the range of behavioural strategies commonly used with pupils who present BESD is provided below. The reader is referred to Ayers *et al.* (2000) and Farrell (2006) for more detailed accounts.

Strategies aimed at increasing desirable behaviour include:

- *Positive reinforcement.* This is something which is given following the desirable behaviour and which increases the occurrence of the behaviour in future. For many pupils an opportunity to use the computer upon finishing their work would be an effective tangible reinforcer, while for most pupils a quiet word of praise from the teacher is an important social reinforcer. Houghton *et al.* (1988) found that a complimentary letter home to parents was regarded even by secondary pupils as a significant incentive. However, different things are experienced positively by different pupils. So it is advisable to consult the pupil concerned and to monitor the frequency of the desirable behaviour being targeted to ensure that it actually does increase.

- *Negative reinforcement.* This is something that increases a pupil's behaviour if it is removed as a result of the behaviour. Apologizing for disruptive behaviour is likely to be negatively reinforced by the lessening of teacher displeasure. While positive reinforcement is more commonly and appropriately used, teachers should be aware of ways in which they may unwittingly use negative reinforcement with the effect of increasing undesirable behaviour. For example, this may happen when a teacher removes or reduces work requirements because the pupil complains about them.

Strategies aimed at reducing undesirable behaviour include:

- *Extinction.* This involves withdrawing reinforcement from an undesirable behaviour. For example, the teacher may decide to withdraw their attention and start ignoring pupils who shout out answers instead of raising their hands.

- *Time out.* This involves removing the pupil for a brief period from all sources of reinforcement. There may be a chair in a screened-off section of the classroom or the pupil may be sent out of the classroom to a specially designated place supervised by a senior member of staff. This may be necessary when the disruptive behaviour is reinforced by other pupils or is behaviour which cannot be reasonably or safely ignored by the teacher.

- *Punishment.* For most pupils teacher reprimands or detentions are a form of punishment. One of the problems with punishments are the negative emotions that they often arouse. Unless carefully handled, there is the risk that they may damage the pupil–teacher relationship and make the teacher a less potent source of positive reinforcement and motivation for the pupil in future. These risks can be minimized by ensuring that the 'rules' relating to the use of punishments or sanctions are well known to all pupils, that they are applied consistently and in a way that is seen to be fair, and that they are administered in a calm and unemotional way by the teacher.

A problem with all approaches to reducing undesirable behaviour is that if they are used on their own there is no guarantee that the pupils will learn what they should be doing instead. It is important, therefore, that they are only used in combination with approaches to increase the desirable behaviour that is wanted instead.

Behavioural techniques can be used with groups or whole classes as well as individuals, and Merrett and Houghton (1989) reported a number of studies carried out in the UK in which they have been successfully implemented in secondary schools in a wide variety of interesting ways. For example, some studies have used novel game-type formats and some have utilized pupil self-recording. In their systematic review of strategies for which there was good evidence of effectiveness in primary schools, Evans *et al.* (2004: 7) report:

> Behavioural strategies using token systems for delivering rewards and sanctions to either the whole class or individuals within a whole class are effective for reducing behaviour which is disruptive to children's own or others' learning in the mainstream classroom. Positive effects are immediate and restricted to the period of intervention delivery. Such strategies should attempt to incorporate some element of peer support and pressure.

Examples of the rewards for on-task and non-disruptive behaviour used in these studies were minutes of free time for play (either alone or with chosen peers) or listening to music. Off-task and disruptive behaviour typically led to loss of rewards. Graphs or symbols (e.g., smiley faces, ribbons) were used to chart progress towards receiving a reward.

It is important to bear in mind that a particular pupil's reactions to a particular reinforcer will depend on their previous experience. Teachers and other professionals should be cautious in making assumptions about what will constitute reinforcement for an individual pupil. This is particularly so when the pupil's background or culture differs from their own. From a behavioural perspective, problem pupils may be thought of as those for whom the reinforcers normally used in the school are less effective for whatever reason or who have more difficulty in learning the associations between their behaviour and the events that follow as consequences. In identifying a more personalized approach for these pupils behavioural contracts are often negotiated, sometimes involving parents/carers and other professionals as well. They specify clearly what everyone will and will not do, and identify specific consequences that make success more likely for the individual pupil. Figure 15.6 shows an example of a contract for Carl.

In negotiating a behavioural contract it is important that everyone has a say in it and develops a commitment to it, recognizing that it will probably not be possible to get everything right at once and that some aspects may need to be renegotiated at the review meetings which are written into the contract. Similarly, the behaviours identified for the pupil need to be realistic and achievable. Where a pupil needs to make significant changes to their behaviour these will probably have to be achieved on a step-by-step basis over a number of contracts, each being reviewed after two to three weeks. When a satisfactory level of behaviour has been achieved it is important that the additional supports that have been put in place are phased out gradually. This will enable the need for any ongoing level of support to be accurately identified.

DfEE (1999a) introduced 'pupil support programmes' which are school-based interventions for pupils who do not respond adequately to the approaches generally employed in school to combat disaffection and who are therefore likely to be at risk of exclusion. They share a number of features with the behavioural contracting approach reviewed above: 'The programme should set targets broken down into fortnightly tasks. It should identify the rewards that can be achieved for meeting the targets and the sanctions that will apply if certain behaviour occurs' (DfEE 1999a: 29). In addition to involving parents, schools are encouraged to involve other relevant agencies including voluntary agencies and ethnic minority community groups, who may be able to support schools with mentoring programmes as well as offering advice and guidance.

At the whole-school level behavioural approaches have informed the development of behaviour policies, involving the specification of consistent expectations and reinforcement of these with recognition systems and sanctions. Some schools have supported this by introducing structured whole-school behavioural programmes such as 'assertive discipline' (Canter and Canter 1992). The focus is on making classroom rules and procedures clear and following through with associated rewards and sanctions. Nicholls and Houghton (1995) have shown that for some classes at least the introduction of assertive discipline can result in an

---

Contract

A From today, 9 June, Carl agrees:

1   To arrive at lessons on time

2   To ensure that he has the equipment that he needs

3   To complete the tasks set by the teacher, without complaint

B Carl's teachers agree:

1   To provide support and positive comments when Carl is punctual and appropriately equipped

2   To check Carl's understanding of instructions and task demands with him individually

3   To tick Carl's contract card for each task successfully completed

C Mr Williams, form tutor, will meet with Carl at the end of each school day to monitor his successes:

1   He will arrange for Carl to spend a session in the computer room for every ten ticks achieved on his contract card

2   When Carl achieves an 80% task completion rate in a week, Mr Williams will inform Mr and Mrs Peters

3   He will arrange for incomplete work to be sent home along with relevant instructions as homework

D Mr and Mrs Peters agree:

1   To ensure Carl completes any tasks he brings home

2   Mr Peters will take Carl to watch City play at home when he achieves an 80% task completion rate

This contact will be reviewed by all concerned at 2 p.m. on 7 July.

Signed:

_____ Carl Peters

_____ Mr Williams

_____ Mr Peters

_____ Mrs Peters

Figure 15.6   An example of a behavioural contract

increase in on-task behaviour and a decrease in the frequency of disruptive behaviour. However, assertive discipline is one of the behavioural strategies identified by Evans *et al.* (2004) as requiring further evaluation, along with daily report cards and training teachers to use praise.

Cognitive strategies

Cognitive strategies may be used to help children change their self-perceptions, the ways in which they attribute meaning to events in their environment or their ability to think and solve problems effectively about the situations they encounter. Some of the approaches listed in Table 15.4, such as counselling and solution-focused therapy, require the development of an extended repertoire of skills, discussion of which is outside the scope of this book. Elliott and Place (1998) point out that counselling and solution-focused approaches are generally based on the premise that the pupil recognizes that they have a problem and wish to work with another to seek a solution. This may not necessarily be true where the disruptive behaviour is serving other purposes, such as securing status in the peer group. Hence, the appropriateness of these approaches to a particular situation requires careful consideration. For detailed consideration of the application of these approaches in schools readers are referred to Rhodes and Ajmal (1995) and Ajmal and Rees (2001) in the case of solution-focused work, while in the case of counselling skills and approaches Cowie and Pecherek (1994) and Hornby (2003) are recommended for further reading.

Anger management, self-instruction training and social skills training all receive some support from the rigorous review of research evidence for effective strategies for primary school pupils conducted by Evans *et al.* (2004). In the rest of this section we consider an area that has become controversial in recent years – strategies used to enhance children's self-esteem – defined as 'how much individuals value themselves as a person' (Harter 2006: 314). Three types of approach to improving self-esteem were identified by Beane (1991):

- personal development activities such as individually focused self-esteem courses;

- curriculum programmes that focus directly on improving self-esteem;

- structural changes in schools that place greater emphasis on cooperation, student participation, community involvement and ethnic pride.

Beane (1991) argued that the third of these elements is crucial. He queried the relevance of interventions which are exclusively focused at the individual level and ignore 'the fact that having positive self-esteem is almost impossible for many young people, given the deplorable conditions under which they are forced to live by the inequities in our society' (Beane 1991: 27). Covington (1989) summarized research showing that programmes designed to promote self-esteem at an individual level alone, by making students feel better about themselves, are unlikely to improve academic outcomes. Such findings have readily been picked up by the media in articles such as 'Education: doing bad and feeling good' (Krauthammer 1990).

Several reviews that examined the relationship between self-esteem and other outcomes for children and young people (Baumeister *et al.* 2003; Emler 2001) have concluded that among the exaggerated claims that have been made for causative effects of self-esteem, there are some findings of note. Emler (2001) concluded that relatively low self-esteem is a risk factor for suicide, suicide attempts and depression, for teenage pregnancy, and for victimization. However, relatively low self-esteem was not found to be a risk factor for delinquency, violence towards others, drug use, alcohol abuse, or racism. Baumeister *et al.* (2003) cautioned that while high self-esteem may result from recognition and acceptance by an individual of their good qualities, it may also result from self-delusion by narcissistic, defensive and conceited individuals. They advise against attempting to boost self-esteem in the hope that this by itself will lead to improved outcomes. 'Instead, we recommend using praise to boost self-esteem as a reward for socially desirable behavior and self-improvement' (Baumeister *et al.* 2003: 1).

Returning to the three types of approach for improving self-esteem, Beane (1991: 29) was a little more positive about curriculum programmes: 'there is a place for some direct instruction regarding affective matters, but this is not enough either'. In England and Wales, approaches utilizing the curriculum became more formalized following the introduction of the national framework for personal, social and health education and citizenship (DfEE/QCA 1999a, 1999b). Key components of self-esteem are included, although not as isolated components, but tied in with areas of achievement – for example, it is recommended that pupils should be taught:

- to think about themselves, learn from their experiences and recognize what they are good at (Key Stage 1);

- to recognize their worth as individuals by identifying positive things about themselves and their achievements, seeing their mistakes, making amends and setting personal goals (Key Stage 2);

- to reflect on and assess their strengths in relation to personality, work and leisure (Key Stage 3);

- to be aware of and assess their personal qualities, skills, achievements and potential, so that they can set personal goals (Key Stage 4).

Kahne (1996) agreed with the importance of a structural focus at the level of the school and classroom and argued that major threats to self-esteem are the narrow range of competencies that are valued in many schools and the focus on competition, where students make external comparisons of their achievements with those of other students. Attempting to boost self-esteem at an individual level through positive, affirming feedback might be unlikely to have a long-term impact on a pupil who has SEN in a school context where recognition and rewards focus on the highest levels of achievement, with effort or relative improvement being recognized in a more marginal or tokenistic way.

This has become an increasingly important issue as more pupils who have SEN have been included in mainstream classes. Renick and Harter (1989) found that pupils with learning difficulties who were included in mainstream classes tended to have lower academic self-esteem than those who were educated in separate special classes, while self-esteem in other areas (e.g. social, physical) did not show a difference across placements. However, they account for this finding by referring to social comparison theory, hypothesizing that individuals do not employ absolute standards in evaluating their own performance, but engage in a process of comparing their performance with an available reference group. In the case of the included pupils they appeared to be basing their self-evaluations on the performance of their mainstream peers, whose academic achievement was considerably higher. As an alternative to social comparison theory it could be argued that the special class pupils might have their self-esteem boosted by being in a selected special group. Pupils who are withdrawn to participate in special programmes for gifted pupils provide a test of these different explanations. In support of a social comparison theory interpretation, Marsh *et al.* (1995) found that such pupils tended to show declines in academic self-esteem compared to similar pupils who remained in mainstream classes, although self-esteem in other areas did not change.

Harter (2006) has reported that self-worth can also vary in different relationship contexts; for example, some adolescents may appraise self-worth positively in relationships with peers but not parents. The level of self-worth in a relationship context was strongly related to the level of approval in that context. It would seem therefore that an integrative focus on both individual- and organizational-level factors and strategies will be important in raising pupils' self-esteem, or at least in ensuring that school practices do not undermine the self-worth of diverse students. Woolfolk (2004) reviews a range of strategies supported by research that can be used to develop children's self-esteem. All of these relate to Beane's (1991) structural level in that they apply to pupils generally and would be appropriate to include in a school's behaviour policy for implementation within and across classrooms. However, a number of the strategies are also particularly applicable at the individual level in that they could be individualized for use with a particular student as part of an IEP. In Activity 15.4 you are asked to consider the

---

Activity 15.4 Developing self-esteem

Listed below is a range of strategies (from Woolfolk 2004: 75) which are supported by research and can be used to develop children's self-esteem.

(a) Consider the applicability of each of these strategies in a school with which you are familiar.

(b) Identify those which would appear particularly appropriate for use with individual pupils where low self-esteem has been identified as a significant influence on the BESD they are presenting.

1 Value and accept all pupils for their attempts as well as their accomplishments.

2 Create a climate that is physically and psychologically safe for students.

3 Make sure that your procedures for teaching and grouping students are really necessary, not just a convenient way of handling problem students or avoiding contact with some students.

4 Make standards of evaluation clear and help students learn to evaluate their own accomplishments.

5 Model appropriate methods of self-criticism, perseverance and self-reward.

6 Avoid destructive comparisons and competition; encourage students to compete with their own prior levels of achievement.

7 Accept a student even when you must reject a particular behaviour or outcome. Students should feel confident, for example, that failing a test or being reprimanded in class does not make them 'bad' people.

8 Remember that positive self-concept grows from success in operating in the world and from being valued by important people in the environment.

9 Encourage students to take responsibility for their reactions to events; show them that they have choices in how to respond.

10 Set up support groups or 'study buddies' in school and teach students how to encourage each other.

11 Help students set clear goals and objectives; brainstorm about resources they have for reaching their goals.

12 Highlight the value of different ethnic groups, their cultures and accomplishments.

applicability of these strategies in a school with which you are familiar and to identify those which appear particularly appropriate for use with individual pupils who are presenting BESD.

Strategies derived from psychodynamic theory

School-based strategies derived from psychodynamic theory can be illustrated with the example of nurture groups.

Nurture groups

The importance of secure and trusting relationships with adults in attachment theory has provided the basis for the development of nurture groups (Bennathan and Boxall 2000). These groups are designed to meet the needs of children who are seen as having missed crucial preschool experiences of adequate and attentive early nurturing care needed to build a secure base from which they can explore the world with confidence and relate to others in an autonomous but caring manner. Early nurture

> is a many-stranded, intermeshing, forward-moving, unitary learning process that centres on attachment and trust and has its foundations in the close identification of parent and child, and the interaction and participation in shared experiences that stem from this. It is the first stage of a developmental process through which the child builds up adequate concepts and skills, learns to interact and share with others and feel concern for them.
>
> (Bennathan and Boxall 2000: 23)

'Nurture groups' were originally developed as small special classes in primary schools of up to 12 children with a teacher and a special support assistant. Pupils do not normally attend for more than four terms. The aim is to provide 'a structured and predictable environment in which the children can begin to trust adults and to learn' (DfEE 1997: 80). The nurture group team of a teacher and a special support assistant attempt to recreate the processes of adequate parenting within school. Creating a classroom setting in which elements of 'home' and 'school' interact is intended to give children the opportunity to go through the early learning experiences they may have missed. In the home area of the classroom there is 'food, comfort, consistent care and support, and close physical contact seen in cradling, rocking, sensory exploration and communication by touch' (Bennathan and Boxall 2000: 23).

Early basic experiences are offered within clear structures and routines that the teacher and assistant control. In contrast to the mainstream classroom, activities are taken slowly with a much greater emphasis on repetition, order and routine than is necessary for most children of this age. In contrast to the homes of the majority of children in the groups, strategies for managing their often uncontrolled behaviour emphasize consistency and clarity, as is needed by a younger child. Through these means it is intended that the child's experiences in the group will establish 'growth-promoting patterns' which were not encouraged in their earlier lives. Lucas *et al.* (2006) offer detailed practical guidance on the operation of nurture groups, following the principles established by Boxall.

Evidence of effectiveness for nurture groups has been limited by the design of the evaluation studies conducted to date. Holmes (1995) reported follow-up information on over 200 children who had attended nurture groups in London: 71 per cent had transferred to mainstream class without difficulty, while 17 per cent had transferred with additional support. The remaining 12 per cent transferred to special educational provision. O'Connor and Colwell (2002) followed 68 children who had attended nurture groups in Enfield, and reported significant improvements over three terms on the Boxall developmental diagnostic profile, albeit completed by the nurture group teachers.

While these results appear encouraging, in the absence of well-matched comparison groups it is possible that many of these young children would have improved anyway as they became accustomed to the school context. Iszatt and Wasilewska (1997) offered some comparison data at a school level. They reported that more than four out of five children entering nurture groups in the London Borough of Enfield returned to their mainstream classes after an average stay in a nurture group of just three terms. In two comparable schools where nurture group provision was not available the proportion of children requiring statutory assessments and special provision was almost three times greater, and 'the proportion of pupils requiring BESD school provision was almost seven times greater' (Iszatt and Wasilewska 1997: 69). From a pilot of the approach in Glasgow, Gerrard (2005) reported that 100 out of 108 children attending nurture groups showed significantly improved scores on the Boxall profile and 110 out of 133 showed significantly improved scores on the Goodman (1997) Strengths and Difficulties Questionnaire (SDQ). Two comparison schools provided data for 11 children, none of whose scores showed significant improvements over the course of the study. Gerrard acknowledges the limitations of these comparison data and recommends that they be addressed in future studies.

Cooper *et al.* (2001) reported preliminary findings from an evaluation study which was comparing the progress of 216 children with BESD attending 'nurture groups' with that of two comparison groups from mainstream classrooms in the nurture group schools. The first comparison group consisted of 64 children matched with the nurture group pupils for age, gender, educational attainment and level of BESD, while the second group consisted of 62 children who were also matched for age and gender with the nurture group children but did not have emotional and behavioural difficulties. It is not clear from the preliminary report how the children with BESD were selected for or excluded from the nurture group nor how the matching was carried out. Mainstream class teachers' ratings of the children at the start and end of the year, using the SDQ, showed that while both groups of children with SEBD improved, significantly greater improvements were found for those attending nurture groups. The proportion of children in the nurture groups in the abnormal or borderline range on the SDQ decreased from 92% to 63%, while the proportion of matched mainstream pupils with SEBD decreased from 85% to 75%. So results to date appear promising, although convincing evidence of the effectiveness of nurture groups is still awaited (Evans *et al.* 2004).

Systemic approaches to intervention and combating bullying

Systemic approaches are increasingly advocated by both researchers and practitioners. Reid (1993) reported that most of the more promising interventions for children who display antisocial behaviour focused on the *social interactional fabric* in which the child's behaviour problems were embedded, dealing with the *behaviour* itself, the *social environment's reaction* to that behaviour, *social cognitions*, and/or *skills*. Bear (1998) concluded from a review of the literature that effective teachers can be characterized by their integrated use of three sets of strategies:

- classroom management and positive climate strategies for preventing behaviour problems;

- operant learning strategies for the short-term management and control of behaviour problems;

- decision-making and social problem-solving strategies for achieving the long-term goal of self-discipline.

In an evaluation of projects supported under the Standards Fund category 'Truancy, Disruptive and Disaffected Pupils', Hallam and Castle (1999) reported that projects successful in reducing exclusions incorporated three levels of intervention: whole-school development work, class-based work and work with individual pupils. Elliott and Place (1998) argued that a whole-school behaviour policy is unlikely to be sufficient for children who present particularly challenging behaviour. In these cases it is likely that additional measures will be needed, such as: an analysis of interpersonal interactions at home and school; consideration of behavioural approaches; and analysis of the suitability of the educational tasks with which the child is being presented. It is argued that intervention should operate at all three levels and there are examples of programmes such as 'Building a Better Behaved School' (Galvin *et al.* 1990) where classroom management approaches and behavioural approaches for managing the most disruptive pupils are considered as part of a comprehensive whole-school approach.

The 'Framework for Intervention' has been developed as a systemic approach based on the understanding that 'problems in behaviour in educational settings are usually a product of complex interaction between the individual, school, family, community and wider society' (Daniels and Williams 2000: 222). The Framework offers an approach for tackling behaviour problems at a series of levels analogous to the stages of the *Code of Practice*. However, at level 1, rather than developing individual programmes, intervention is focused on addressing environmental factors in the classroom and school by developing behaviour environment plans. The power of this approach is illustrated in the systematic review of effective strategies for BESD in primary schools conducted by Evans *et al.* (2004) which reported that changes in the seating arrangements in classrooms from groups to rows had a positive impact on time on task, in particular for the most easily distracted pupils. In the Framework for Intervention at levels 2, 3 and beyond, individual behaviour plans are introduced in addition to, not instead of, the behaviour environment plans which continue.

Bullying in school

Systemic approaches have been identified as particularly important in dealing with bullying following research that has highlighted its serious repercussions, its disproportionate impact on minority groups, the extent to which it is usually hidden from staff, the complex influences of school ethos and peer group characteristics and the positive impact whole-school approaches can have in tackling it (Pepler *et al.* 2004). There is substantial consensus on the key characteristics of bullying behaviour (DfES 2002a; Orpinas and Horne 2006):

- it is intentional;

- it involves an imbalance of power;

- it is repeated over time.

These facets are apparent in the definition of bullying offered by Sharp (1999: 1) as 'any behaviour which is deliberately intended to hurt, threaten or frighten another person or group of people. It is usually unprovoked and is often repeated and can continue for a long period of time. It always reflects an imbalance and abuse of power.' They also feature prominently in the government definition:

> The UK Government defines bullying as:
>
> - Repetitive, wilful or persistent behaviour intended to cause harm, although one-off incidents can in some cases also be defined as bullying;
>
> - Intentionally harmful behaviour, carried out by an individual or a group; and
>
> - An imbalance of power leaving the person being bullied feeling defenceless.
>
> Bullying is emotionally or physically harmful behaviour and includes: name-calling; taunting; mocking; making offensive comments; kicking; hitting; pushing; taking belongings; inappropriate text messaging and emailing; sending offensive or degrading images by phone or via the internet; gossiping; excluding people from groups and spreading hurtful and untruthful rumours.
>
> (House of Commons Education and Skills Committee 2007a: 7–8)

Hawker and Boulton (2001) identified different types of bullying:

- Physical – hitting, kicking, taking or damaging belongings.

- Verbal – name calling, insulting, making offensive remarks, sending threatening e-mails or text messages on mobile phones.

- Relational – spreading nasty stories about someone, exclusion from social groups, being made the subject of malicious rumours.

The guidance offered to schools in *Social Inclusion: Pupil Support* highlighted different foci of bullying that may lead to diverse pupils groups being particularly targeted: 'racial, or as a result of a child's appearance, behaviour or special educational needs, or related to sexual orientation' (DfEE 1999a: 24). It makes clear schools' responsibilities: 'Headteachers have a legal duty to prevent all forms of bullying among pupils' (DfEE 1999a: 25). The DfES (2002a) anti-bullying pack for schools included specific advice on prevention and intervention with respect to racist and homophobic bullying and that directed against pupils with SEN.

There is evidence that lesbian, gay and bisexual young people are more likely to be targets of bullying behaviour (Bontempo and D'Augelli 2002; Ellis and High 2004) and that many teachers feel less competent in dealing with incidents of this kind (House of Commons Education and Skills Committee 2007a). Turning to ethnicity, it appears that minority status rather than ethnicity *per se* is associated with victimization (Graham and Juvonen 2002; Verkuyten and Thijs 2002). Pupils who belong to a numerical-minority ethnic group in a particular school or classroom are more likely to be identified by classmates as victims. The government has recently issued further specialist guidance to assist schools in preventing and responding to prejudice-driven bullying in these areas:

- bullying around racism, religion and culture (DfES, 2006h);

- homophobic bullying (DCSF, 2007b).

The proportion of children with SEN who report that they are targets of bullying is higher than for their classmates without SEN: 68% as opposed to 46% in primary school, 59% as opposed to 11% in secondary school (Whitney *et al.* 1994). However, the percentage reporting that they bully others is also higher: 35% of pupils with SEN as opposed to 24% without SEN in primary, and 30% with SEN as opposed to 11% without SEN in secondary. Among children with BESD, behavioural difficulties are more likely to be associated with bullying behaviour and emotional difficulties with victimization. Some pupils (known as bully-victims) get high scores as both bullies and victims. In some contexts they are targeted by older or stronger pupils while in other contexts they bully children younger or weaker than themselves. It appears that they may represent an especially high-risk group and they have been found to experience higher levels of depression than either bullies or victims (Swearer *et al.* 2001).

As can be seen from Figure 15.7, Sharp (1999) highlights the influences on bullying of social dynamics at a range of environmental levels. Sharp argues that intervention at the individual level, focused on assertiveness, self-esteem, social skills or coping strategies, for example, is unlikely by itself to be sufficient in the long term. Rather it is recommended that bullying should be tackled through quite intense intervention at organizational, group and individual levels, such as:

- Staff and students working together to develop a clear set of guidelines for everybody which specify what bullying is and what they should do when they know or suspect it is going on.

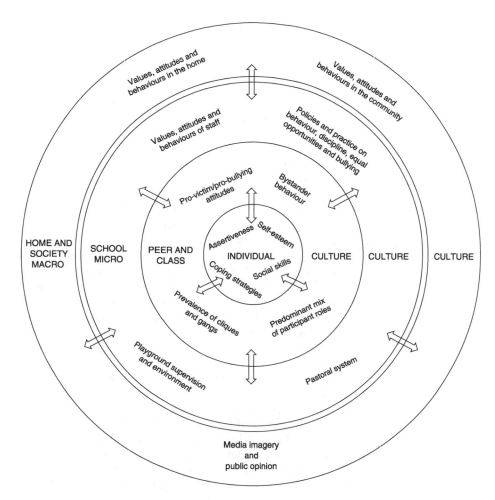

Figure 15.7 Bullying as a complex social phenomenon incorporating multiple sources of influence
Source: from Sharp (1999).

- Long-term curriculum work about bullying and other forms of antisocial behaviour, including teaching students how to manage personal relationships assertively and constructively.

- Peer-led approaches, such as peer counselling and buddying, to offer support to pupils who are new to the school or who are feeling lonely, rejected or victimized.

- Direct intervention strategies when bullying has occurred or is suspected of occurring. Problem-solving approaches which involve all students, including those who have been indirectly involved, are most effective. Early involvement of parents is recommended. Follow-up over time is always needed to check that the bullying has not resumed (Sharp 1999: 5).

International research indicates that this kind of multi-level intervention usually leads to reductions of around 5–20 per cent in victimization rates (P.K. Smith 2004). The varying success rate appears to be influenced by the extent to which schools take ownership of the issue and show commitment in supporting and following through on the approaches implemented. It is not clear to what extent different ingredients contribute to the overall success. Some evaluative research has been conducted on particular direct intervention strategies, and the evaluation of interventions to address bullying has been identified as an important area where much further research is needed.

Examples of systemic direct intervention strategies that involve not just a victim and bully (or bullies) but others who are part of the context in which the bullying occurs are the support group approach (see DfES 2002a; Young 1998) and the method of shared concern (Pikas 2002; Rigby 2005). These approaches are essentially solution-focused, placing the emphasis on getting those present when incidents have occurred to identify with the victim and commit to positive action in the future. Objections by some to these approaches on the grounds that bullies appear to be 'counselled and let off', rather than punished, have been countered by arguments that punishment is ineffective in stopping the bullying in the longer term and may even make matters worse.

A related approach with potential to address the concerns on both sides is restorative justice. This is an approach developed in the criminal justice system which is being used in schools increasingly to address instances of bullying and other serious infractions of the rules of the school community (Hopkins 2004; Morrison 2006). An essential basis of the approach is a school ethos in which there is a commitment to build and nurture relationships. When conflict occurs and harm is done a process of restorative conferencing may be undertaken with the primary objective of seeking to repair the damage done to the relationships. A restorative conference brings together those involved in a particular problematic situation, to talk through issues and find ways of making amends, 'developing a plan for restoration of the situation, especially the relationships that have been impoverished by the offence' (Drewery 2004: 335). All are encouraged to contribute in pooling ideas about what might be most helpful from here, for all concerned. However, 'particular attention is paid to meeting the needs of victims and providing them with a voice; ensuring the community is heard in matters that affect them; and emphasizing restoration rather than punishment' (Drewery 2004: 336). While there is some evidence of effectiveness for the approach in reducing school exclusion in New Zealand of students from Maori and low socioeconomic status backgrounds (Drewery 2004), specific outcome evidence of its effect on bullying in schools has yet to be obtained.

Ofsted (2003a) produced the following recommendations to improve the way in which bullying is tackled. Schools, supported by LEAs, are encouraged to:

● maintain the momentum on action against bullying through initiatives to improve attitudes and behaviour in schools generally;

● regularly collect and analyse information on the incidence of bullying, taking full account of pupils' views;

● arrange systematic training for staff on managing behaviour, counselling pupils and working with parents in difficult situations;

- ensure that training to help teachers identify and deal with bullying tackles cases where bullying focuses on race and sexuality;

- check that follow-up action on confirmed allegations of bullying is appropriate in its range and is sustained;

- consider the use of positive peer pressure, the involvement of pupils in befriending and mentoring schemes, and the support of outside agencies;

- use other professionals to work alongside teachers, pupils and parents in overcoming the extreme effects of bullying.

The recommendation that schools regularly collect and analyse information on the incidence of bullying would provide an important means of evaluating the effectiveness of strategies employed to combat bullying. A number of methods for identifying perpetrators and targets of bullying are available, including self-report, peer nomination, teacher questionnaire and observation (Cornell *et al.* 2006; Rigby, 2002). While self-report has been the most commonly used method to date, peer nomination is increasingly recommended, in particular where children who have SEN are concerned. Activity 15.5 describes an example of each approach and provides an opportunity to consider their strengths and limitations.

Activity 15.5 Methods for identifying perpetrators and targets of bullying

Here are seven features of assessment methods for identifying perpetrators and targets of bullying:

1 Data are collected from the actual participant-observers of peer social interactions.

2 There may be effects of social desirability bias as pupils may resist endorsing responses that involve admitting to an unfavourable self-presentation.

3 Information is provided about behaviour in situations where there is little adult supervision and where bullying is particularly likely to occur (Astor *et al.* 1999).

4 Such methods are particularly suitable for obtaining information about bullying of some children with SEN who may lack awareness of bullying interactions or have difficulties in reporting incidents.

5 Children may well have different sensitivity to bullying behaviour and their well-being or distress is likely to be more closely related to their perception of what they are experiencing – irrespective of the views of other pupils in their class.

6 The power of the assessment procedure is increased since many informants are involved.

7 It is not easy to obtain information about relational, as opposed to physical or verbal, bullying.

Read the descriptions of each of the four types of method outlined below and decide which features apply to which methods. What other features can you identify that represent strengths of some methods but not others?

Self-reports. Typically children are presented with a definition of bullying and asked to rate the frequency with which they have been involved over a specified period in either bullying or being bullied. For example the Peer Relations Questionnaire (Rigby 1998) contains a six item bully scale and a five item victim scale. Items such as 'I am part of a group that goes around teasing others' and 'I get picked on by others' are rated on a four-point scale ranging from 'never' to 'very often'.

Peer assessments. These methods generally involving surveying a classroom of pupils, asking each to tick the names of any classmates who meet behavioural descriptions characteristic of bullies and victims. For example:

- a bully – someone who often picks on other children or hits them, or teases them or does other nasty things to them for no good reason;

- a bullying victim – someone who often gets picked on or hit or teased or has nasty things done to them by other children for no good reason (Nabuzoka and Smith 1993).

Teacher questionnaires. Monks *et al.* (2003) asked teachers of 4–6-year-olds to nominate pupils for roles in four bullying situations: physical, verbal, social exclusion and rumour spreading. For the physical situation teachers were asked 'Do any of the children in your class hit/kick or push others? If so, who?' and 'Are any children in your class hit/kicked or pushed by others? If so, who?' (Monks *et al.* 2003: 459).

Observation. These methods involve trained observers noting the emission of defined behaviours by focus children, sampled in a predefined sequence for a predefined time period. In the study by Pellegrini and Bartini (2000: 362), 'Victimisation was defined as a youngster being the target of either physical or verbal aggression and responding submissively (no retaliation, crying), which is indicative of a power differential'.

Conclusions

In this chapter we have highlighted the extent to which definitions of BESD must take account of interactions between the expectations, perceptions and behaviour of all those involved in a situation where a child's behaviour is considered to be problematic. There is evidence that there are often disparities in expectations and perceptions of parents and teachers – disparities that can be magnified by differences in culture. It is argued that an integrative framework is needed to properly understand the range and complexity of the interactive influences on behaviour. The IF framework which was introduced in Chapter 5 can be used to represent in an integrated way the theoretical approaches that are most commonly applied in attempting to understand situations in which BESD are identified.

Of the four commonly applied theoretical approaches, systemic approaches have proved particularly useful as they encompass influences at the cognitive, behavioural and environmental levels of the IF framework and interactions between factors at these different levels. However, each of the theoretical approaches can offer insights that may be valuable in particular situations. They each have also given rise to a range of assessment techniques and intervention approaches that have been described in this chapter. A final consideration must be evaluation, which is particularly highlighted in relation to bullying behaviour. It is only through careful analysis of changes in the outcome measures specified in the objectives of the intervention programme that the appropriateness and success of the action taken can be judged. If the objectives are not satisfactorily achieved the evaluation information that has been collected will be crucial in helping all involved to look again at their understanding of the factors operating in the situation and to revise the intervention programme accordingly.

16

Promoting emotional and social competence and well-being

Objectives

When you have studied this chapter you should be able to:

- explain the range of terms used to denote components of emotional and social competence and well-being;
- describe the most influential theoretical models of relevance to educational settings;
- select appropriate techniques for assessing different aspects and evaluating interventions;
- analyse different types of intervention programmes and suggest ways of improving their effectiveness.

Contents

Introduction

In recent years there has been an increasingly strong and explicit focus on promoting the social and emotional competence, mental health and psychological well-being of children and young people (Appleby *et al.* 2006). This has been particularly marked in schools as the result of a new emphasis on investment in universal services, prevention and early intervention. In 1999 a national framework was provided for the first time from Key Stage 1 for the teaching of personal, social and health education, and citizenship (DfEE/QCA 1999a, 1999b). From September 2002 citizenship became part of the statutory curriculum for secondary schools. The government's strategy for SEN (DfES 2004c) identified raising staff awareness of children's mental health issues as an area for action. Since September 2005 the criteria for school inspections have covered the contribution schools make to pupil well-being (Ofsted 2005b). The Social and Emotional Aspects of Learning (SEAL) materials have been rolled out in primary (DfES 2005d) and secondary (DfES 2007d) schools in England. The National Healthy Schools programme has been given increased prominence and resources and all schools are expected to be working towards achievement of national Healthy School status (NHSS) by 2009 (DfES/DH 2005a). Achieving NHSS involves demonstrating the attainment of standards in eight areas, one of which is emotional health and well-being (and includes bullying). However, a survey conducted by Ofsted (2005c) revealed that only a little over a half of the schools involved were aware that the NHSS existed and only a very small minority were working towards or had met the criteria for emotional health and well-being.

The focus on universal provision and prevention is seen as complementing the provision of individualized, often multi-agency, support for those with particular difficulties in this area. Such interventions for individuals with statements for social, emotional and behavioural difficulties or mental health problems, located towards the point of the inverted triangle shown in Figure 16.1, were considered in Chapter 15. In this chapter the focus will be on the universal provision shown in the top section, on the early intervention initiatives shown in the middle section provided for groups 'at risk', and on individualized interventions recommended for pupils at School Action and School Action Plus of the Code of Practice.

Why is it important to promote social and emotional competence and well-being?

Two sets of reasons have been presented to support the development of this work. The first set of reasons has to do with avoiding the negative consequences of deficiencies in social and emotional competence and well-being. Prevalence estimates obtained from national surveys in Great Britain in 1999 and 2004 (Green *et al.* 2005) indicated that as many as one in ten children and young people experience a mental health disorder. Effective provision for all children (at the top level in Figure 16.1) is seen as an important means of reducing the numbers at the bottom who will need more individual support (DfES 2005d).

The second set of reasons has to do with reaping positive benefits associated with well-developed competencies. Weare and Gray (2003: 6) report that there is sound research evidence, primarily from the USA, 'that work on emotional and

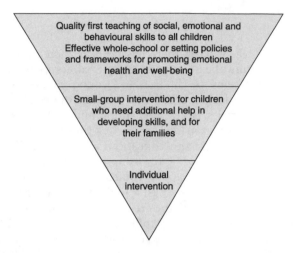

Figure 16.1 Relationship between universal provision, early intervention and individualized support
Source: DfES (2005d).

social competence and well-being has a wide range of educational and social benefits, including greater educational and work success, improved behaviour, increased inclusion, improved learning, greater social cohesion, increased social capital and improvements to mental health'. For elaboration of these headings see Activity 16.1.

Activity 16.1 Achieving the Every Child Matters outcomes through promotion social and emotional competence and well-being

In the first column below we have listed outcomes of social and emotional competence programmes identified by Weare and Gray (2003) from a review of the literature. In each case decide to which, if any, of the Every Child Matters outcomes they relate. Share your conclusions with a colleague.

	Be healthy	Stay safe	Enjoy and achieve	Make a positive contribution	Achieve economic well-being
Greater educational and work success					
• Improved school attendance					
• Higher motivation at school					
• Workplace teamwork skills					
• Workplace communication skills					
• Management skills					
Improvements in behaviour					
• Improved classroom behaviour					

	Be healthy	Stay safe	Enjoy and achieve	Make a positive contri- bution	Achieve eco- nomic well- being
• Reduced aggression					
• Decreased early behaviour problems					
Increased inclusion					
• Improved self-control					
• Increased peer tolerance					
• Increased peer support					
Improved learning					
• Managing 'blocking' emotions					
• Utilizing facilitative emotions					
Greater social cohesion and capital					
• Decrease in hostile beliefs					
• Better conflict resolution strategies					
• Decrease in violent acts					
• Reduced police involvement					
• Decline in alcohol use					
Improvements in mental health					
• Reduced depression and anxiety					
• Lowered incidence of suicide					
• Reductions in eating disorders					
• Lower levels of stress					

Concepts and terminology

In this section we introduce and define the concepts and terms that will be used in this chapter. Weare and Gray (2003) report that many find the proliferation of terminology in this area confusing. In some cases terms such as 'well-being' are given very different meanings by different authors. In other cases terms such as 'emotional intelligence' and 'emotional literacy' are used by different groups to refer to essentially the same phenomenon. We will examine three areas:

● psychological well-being;

● social competence/skills;

● emotional competence/intelligence.

These areas are conceptually related within the overarching framework of positive psychology, defined as the 'science of positive subjective experience, positive individual traits, and positive institutions ... that will come to understand and build the factors that allow individuals, communities, and societies to flourish' (Seligman and Csikszentmihalyi 2000: 5). Proponents argue that psychology, until recently, has focused on fixing problems, rather than enhancing achievement. While this has been contested as too sweeping a generalization, which ignores some established areas of psychologists' work, for example with gifted pupils, the shift in emphasis advocated by positive psychology has attracted considerable support and interest (Boniwell 2006; Gable and Haidt 2005). Three 'pillars' of positive psychology have been identified (Seligman 2002), and these are represented in Figure 16.2, along with five example aspects of each.

Psychological well-being

This is the term used in the National Service Framework for Children, Young People and Maternity Services (Department of Health 2004). It includes 'emotional well-being' which is used in National Healthy Schools Theme 4 and 'social and emotional wellbeing' used in the SEAL materials. However, it is clearly located in the 'subjective experience' pillar of the positive psychology framework and so distinct from physical or economic well-being, for example. Martin and Huebner (2007) present a multi-dimensional model of psychological well-being among US adolescents, which includes:

- positive affect – the extent to which a person typically feels positive emotions (e.g. enthusiasm, activeness, and alertness);

- negative affect – the extent to which negative emotions (e.g., distress, anger, nervousness) are experienced;

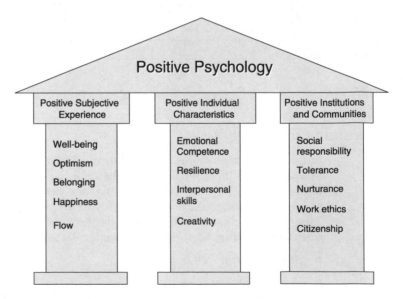

Figure 16.2   The three pillars of positive psychology

● life satisfaction – the cognitive appraisal of the quality of one's life across the five domains of family, friends, school, living environment and self.

The validity of distinguishing these three aspects was supported by the finding that being a victim of relational bullying (see Chapter 15) and pro-social experiences in school had different effects on the different aspects. Physical and verbal bullying had a negative impact on all three aspects of well-being.

Konu *et al.* (2002) assessed well-being using the General Subjective Well-being Indicator which consists of items assessing:

● positive mood

● future orientation

● success

● satisfaction

● global self-esteem

● specific self-esteem (appearance)

● decision making

● sleeping

● energy

● appetite

● anxiousness.

They investigated the association between well-being and the school environment factors shown in Figure 16.3 and reported significant relationships with many of the factors, suggesting strong links between characteristics of the school context and psychological well-being.

From a review of studies with children and adolescents, Park (2004) identified a range of additional factors that are significantly associated with the development of psychological well-being: supportive parenting, engagement in challenging activities, positive life events, and high-quality interactions with significant others. In addition, attention is drawn to cultural differences in the bases for life satisfaction. For Korean youth, satisfaction with school was found to be a more important predictor than satisfaction with self, whereas the reverse was found with American adolescents. These findings may be considered to reflect the relative positions of Korean and American societies on a collectivistic–individualistic dimension. As Park (2004) pointed out, they have implications for the design of programmes to develop psychological well-being in a society of increasing diversity where they will need to take account of the cultural backgrounds of their participants.

A longitudinal study among adolescents by Suldo and Huebner (2004) highlighted the moderating role played by life satisfaction in the relationship between stressful life events and subsequent outcomes. Young people with high psychological well-being developed fewer problems following stressful events. This suggests that a process might be operating where individuals with high life satisfaction and positive affect are likely to appraise stressful life events in ways that enable them to display more effective coping behaviours or resilence.

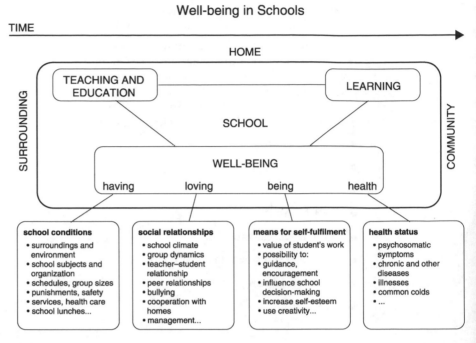

Figure 16.3   A conceptual model of well-being in schools
Source: Konu and Rimpelä (2002: 83).

Social competence (skills)

Social skills or competencies are defined in terms of the way in which others react to them. For example, Gresham and Elliott (1993: 139) defined social skills as 'socially acceptable behaviours that enable a person to interact effectively with others and avoid socially unacceptable responses from others'. This means that there are no absolute criteria that can be applied. Different societies, cultures and subcultures may approve of, and sanction, different behaviours. The relative, interactional, context-dependent nature of social competencies, which are depicted in Figure 16.4, makes them particularly challenging for many children with SEN to acquire, and the adoption of a multicultural perspective particularly important.

The model shown in Figure 16.4 also helps to clarify terminology in this area. Children's social behaviour (stage 3) is conceptually separated from social cognitive competencies (stage 2) such as social perception, problem-solving, knowledge and understanding. Sometimes the term 'social skills' is used to refer only to the performance of appropriate behaviours and 'social competence' to knowing what to do and how to do it. These are separable as is illustrated by the following examples where the child knows what to do and really wants to do it, but just cannot seem to get it right. Emma may know that 'asking nicely' is the best way to be let into a game but when she tries to 'ask nicely' she comes across to the other children as stuck up and bossy and is told she cannot play. Lucy may know that apologizing when reprimanded by a teacher is the best way to avoid getting into further trouble, but may often find herself in detention for insolence. Behavioural

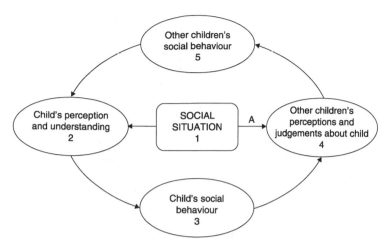

Figure 16.4   A model of social interaction in children
Source: Adapted from Dodge *et al.* (1986).

social skills training can help these pupils change what they say and the way they communicate – both verbally and non-verbally – so that they can more skilfully convey to other people what they *want* to convey.

However, in many cases the term 'skills' is used to refer to cognitive as well as behavioural components, for example 'problem-solving skills'. Likewise 'competence' may be used to include successful performance of behavioural sequences, for example those involved in joining a game. In this chapter we will use the term 'social competence' to encompass both cognitive and behavioural aspects and will distinguish more specifically between them as appropriate. A description of each of the stages of this model is now provided.

Stage 1 at the centre of the model draws attention to the importance of the social situation in influencing children's perceptions of and judgements about each other's behaviour. This was well illustrated by a study conducted by Dodge *et al.* (1982) which found that children who were well accepted by peers made more social approaches than other children – but only in the playground, not in the classroom. On the other hand, children who were less well accepted made more social approaches in the classroom where they were likely to disturb children who were trying to work and hence attract the teacher's disapproval.

Stage 2 highlights the importance of the child's perception and understanding of the situation in which they find themselves. Crick and Dodge (1994) review a range of studies which show that children who have low social competence tend to interpret situations in a different way from their classmates; in particular, they tend to attribute hostile intent to others. In one study children aged 5–10 years were shown a video containing a number of ambiguous situations in which one child did something that upset another. For example, in one scene two children were painting and one spilled paint on the other's picture. Compared to their classmates, children who had low social competence were more likely to jump to the conclusion that this had been done on purpose, rather than by accident.

Problem-solving skills are also important at Stage 2. Children who have low social competence are less likely to be proficient in one or more of the steps involved in processing information about a social situation and producing an effective response. These steps include: generating a range of possible responses (children who have low social competence tend to be able to think of fewer alternative possibilities for action) and evaluating the probable consequences of the responses generated (children who have low social competence tend to be inappropriately optimistic about the likely outcomes of aggressive behaviour) (Crick and Dodge 1994).

At *Stage 3* the child produces the social behaviour selected at Stage 2. It may be skilfully or unskilfully executed, but the effect on the child's acceptance or rejection by their classmates will depend on how their classmates interpret the behaviour at *Stage 4*. This will be influenced by:

- whether the behaviour is perceived as fitting in with or offending peer-group norms (Boivin *et al.* 1995). These may vary in groups with different cultural values (Cartledge and Milburn 1996).

- whether the behaviour is perceived as being appropriate to the situation. Coie and Benenson (1983) conducted a study where children were shown a video of child actors behaving aggressively. While unprovoked aggressive behaviour led to social rejection, aggressive behaviour in response to provocation led to social acceptance.

- judgements which have been made about the child by their classmates. These may be based on prejudicial stereotypes with children giving higher acceptance ratings to same-sex classmates and, to a lesser extent, same-race classmates (Boulton and Smith 1992).

There is some evidence that prejudicial stereotypes can be influenced by situational factors (arrow A in Figure 16.4). Johnson *et al.* (1983) have demonstrated that cooperative learning experiences can lead to greater cross-ethnic acceptance in the classroom. However, Cowie *et al.* (1994) suggested that the effectiveness of cooperative group work may be lower outside special projects, when teachers are left to implement it with comparatively little support. These considerations are also relevant in trying to ensure that children who have SEN do not suffer severe social rejection because they lack competence in key areas accorded disproportionate status in school. Thus intelligence, academic achievement and skill at sport are all frequently associated with social acceptance. Yet these effects can be weakened and acceptance more equitably distributed if teachers act to ensure that a range of other skills and contributions are also valued.

The way in which classmates interpret a child's behaviour is also influenced by their previous social experience with the child in question. Asarnow (1983) found that when boys with positive reputations behaved negatively towards others they were likely to receive a neutral response. But when boys with negative reputations behaved negatively towards others they were likely to receive a negative response. This suggests that children respond in a biased way to negative behaviour depending on the reputation of the child concerned. This helps to explain why teaching rejected children social skills is usually not enough to ensure their social acceptance. It is necessary also to change the perceptions and responsiveness of those rejecting them. The final stage in the cycle of social interaction shown in this model is the peers' behavioural response to the pupil (*Stage*

5). The peers' response in turn acts as a cue, which the pupil will process within the context of the ongoing social situation.

So current theory and research suggest that a pupil's social acceptance and competence are the result of an interaction between individual and environmental factors in a particular social situation at a particular time (Newcomb *et al*. 1993). Practical application in schools of the full range of implications arising from the model in Figure 16.4 usually involves creating a situation:

- in which rejected children and their classmates can interact positively;

- where prejudices can be broken down;

- where differences in competence can be minimized by ensuring that everyone can make some valued contribution;

- where rejected children can be taught new skills;

- where their classmates can be helped to attend to change in the behaviour of the rejected child and interpret it positively.

Later in this chapter we will describe a range of programmes and strategies which can be used by teachers in helping children who are rejected in school settings.

Social competence and acceptance in school have been found to be linked to school achievement (Wentzel 1991; Wentzel and Asher 1995), and low social acceptance in primary school has been linked with problems in adolescence and adulthood. When pupils who experienced social rejection by their peer group in primary school were followed up in secondary school they were found to have more academic problems, to present more discipline problems and to engage in more truancy (Coie *et al*. 1995; Kupersmidt *et al*. 1990). Over 30 years ago Cowen *et al*. (1973) established that 8–9-year-old pupils who had received negative ratings from peers were more likely to experience mental health problems in adulthood. So the promotion of social adjustment is both an important educational objective in itself and a potentially important factor in raising achievement and reducing exclusions.

To date the majority of studies have been conducted in the USA, and it must be acknowledged that there may be dangers in generalizing research findings between countries. For example, Chen *et al*. (1992) carried out a comparative study between Canada and China with 8- and 10-year-old children. In both samples sociability-leadership characteristics were associated with social acceptance in the peer group, and aggression-disruption characteristics with peer rejection. However, shyness-sensitivity was negatively associated with measures of peer acceptance in the Canadian sample but positively associated with peer acceptance in the Chinese sample. The authors reported that in China children were encouraged to be dependent, cautious, behaviourally inhibited and self-restrained, as these behaviours were positively valued in Chinese culture. But they were negatively valued in Western culture where they were seen as reflecting social immaturity and fearfulness. Of course, we cannot assume that similar findings would be found if Chinese children in Canada had been studied, particularly for those living in highly acculturated communities.

What is more, longitudinal research carried out in China by Chen and colleagues has demonstrated that any gross generalizations about cultural differences may quickly become out of date given ongoing changes in cultural and social conditions. China has undergone radical cultural and social change in the last 10–15 years related to widespread adoption of Western-style market economics. When the data collection carried out in 1990 was repeated in China in 1998 and again in 2002, a very different picture emerged from that presented by Chen *et al.* (1992). In the 1998 data the clear positive relationship of shyness to good peer relationships and school adjustment, apparent in 1990, had disappeared. By 2002 the Chinese data resembled the Canadian data of 1990: shyness was negatively associated with peer acceptance and school adjustment and positively associated with peer rejection and depression (Chen *et al.* 2006).

Alongside our developing understanding of the importance of social and cultural influences there is also increasing evidence that specific brain systems have an important role in social functioning. Blakemore *et al.* (2004: 216) acknowledge that 'it may once have seemed foolhardy to work out connections between fundamental neurophysiological mechanisms and highly complex social behaviour', but go on to review a number of neuroimaging studies in which monitoring of brain activation during highly complex sociocognitive processes such as moral reasoning, deception and fairness has already produced promising results in adult samples. In some studies the role of specific brain areas has also been implicated in development. For example, Anderson *et al.* (1999) compared two groups of patients in which the medial frontal cortex had been damaged; in one group the damage had occurred in adulthood and in the other it had occurred at a young age. Defective social and moral reasoning was only found when the damage had occurred in childhood, suggesting that this brain area appears to be critically involved in moral development.

Emotional competence (intelligence)

The concept of emotional intelligence was introduced by Salovey and Mayer (1990) and popularized by Goleman (1995) who defined it as:

- knowing one's own emotions;

- managing emotions;

- motivating oneself;

- recognizing emotions in others;

- handling relationships.

If these five domains of emotional intelligence are compared with the five most commonly identified dimensions of social skills shown in Table 16.1, it is clear that there is considerable overlap. In particular, 'peer relationship skills' map closely onto 'handling relationships'; and 'self-management skills' onto 'motivating oneself'. The concept of emotional intelligence was initially criticized on the grounds that it added little to the concept of social skills and, in addition, that it was vague and loosely defined and there was no convincing reason for using the term 'intelligence'.

In response to these criticisms, Salovey and Sluyter (1997: 10) revised the definition of emotional intelligence as follows: 'Emotional intelligence involves the ability to perceive accurately, appraise, and express emotion; the ability to

Table 16.1   The five most commonly occurring dimensions of social skills and the percentage of studies in which they occurred

Social skills dimension	Percentage of total sample
Peer relationship skills (positive, prosocial behaviour with peers, empathy, sociability, and peer reinforcement and support)	52
Self-management skills (temper control, follows rules and limits, accepts criticism, reaches appropriate compromises and shows self-restraint)	52
Academic skills (shows independent and productive work habits in the classroom social context)	48
Compliance skills (gets on with others by appropriately sharing things and following rules and expectations)	38
Assertion skills (shows outgoing behaviour and exercises appropriate independence and social assertion)	33

Source: Caldarella and Merrell's (1997) analysis of 21 studies of social skills involving over 22,000 children and adolescents.

access and/or generate feelings when they facilitate thought; the ability to understand emotion and emotional knowledge; the ability to regulate emotions to promote emotional and intellectual growth'. This definition focuses on 'emotional contributions to intelligence or intellectual understanding of emotion' (Salovey and Sluyter 1997: 16) and separates these processes from the collection of social skills and behavioural predispositions which had been included in earlier definitions. Salovey and Sluyter have elaborated their new definition into the two-dimensional cognitive model shown in Figure 16.5. The four branches of the model are organized in increasing order of psychological complexity, so that the lowest branch, 'Perception, appraisal and expression of emotion', is thought to contain the most basic processes, while 'Reflective regulation of emotions to promote emotional and intellectual growth' involves higher, more psychologically integrated processes. Along each branch there is a hypothesized developmental progression from left to right, with the earlier emerging and more discrete skills in level 1 on each branch best illustrating the distinctions between the branches.

However, this more narrowly focused 'ability' model of emotional intelligence has not replaced the original broader conceptualization of the construct which has become known as 'trait' emotional intelligence (EI). The facets of trait EI are emotion-related dispositions and self-perceived abilities and are shown in Activity 16.2. A key difference between ability and trait models of EI lies in the way they are measured. Ability EI is measured by assessing performance on test items. For example, the Kusché Affective Inventory – Revised (KAI-R), a measure for pupils aged 6–11 years, includes a number of items which involve defining feeling words and identifying facial expressions. However, it also contains items (e.g. 'Tell me about a time when you felt guilty') which are scored 'appropriate' or 'inappropriate' in the judgement of the tester. A key problem is that there is no way of distinguishing between an answer that is incorrect because the child does not understand the emotion and an answer that is true for that child in terms of

EMOTIONAL INTELLIGENCE

Reflective regulation of emotions to promote emotional and intellectual growth

LEVEL 1:	LEVEL 2:	LEVEL 3:	LEVEL 4:
Ability to stay open to feelings, both those that are pleasant and those that are unpleasant	Ability to reflectively engage or detach from an emotion depending upon its judged informativeness or utility	Ability to reflectively monitor emotions in relation to oneself and others, such as recognizing how clear, typical, influential or reasonable they are	Ability to manage emotion in oneself and others by moderating negative emotions and enhancing pleasant ones, without repressing or exaggerating information they may convey

Understanding and analysing emotions: employing emotional knowledge

LEVEL 1:	LEVEL 2:	LEVEL 3:	LEVEL 4:
Ability to label emotions and recognize relations among the words and the emotions themselves, such as the relation between liking and loving	Ability to interpret the meanings that emotions convey regarding relationships, such as that sadness often accompanies a loss	Ability to understand complex feelings – simultaneous feelings of love and hate, or blends such as awe as a combination of fear and surprise	Ability to recognize likely transitions among emotions, such as the transition from anger to satisfaction, or from anger to shame

Emotional facilitation of thinking

LEVEL 1:	LEVEL 2:	LEVEL 3:	LEVEL 4:
Emotions prioritize thinking by directing attention to important information	Emotions are sufficiently vivid and available that they can be generated as aids to judgement and memory concerning feelings	Emotional mood swings change the individual's perspective from optimistic to pessimistic, encouraging consideration of multiple points of view	Emotional states differentially encourage specific problem approaches, such as when happiness facilitates inductive reasoning and creativity

Perception, appraisal and expression of emotion

LEVEL 1:	LEVEL 2:	LEVEL 3:	LEVEL 4:
Ability to identify emotion in one's physical states, feelings and thoughts	Ability to identify emotions in other people, designs, artwork etc. through language, sound, appearance and behaviour	Ability to express emotions accurately and to express needs related to those feelings	Ability to discriminate between accurate and inaccurate, or honest versus dishonest expressions of feelings

Figure 16.5   A model of emotional intelligence
Source: Salovey and Sluyter (1997).

Activity 16.2   Trait emotional intelligence

Here is a list of the facets of trait emotional intelligence on which there is general consensus (Petrides *et al.* 2004).

Facets	High scorers perceive themselves as
Adaptability	flexible and willing to adapt to new conditions
Assertiveness	forthright, frank and willing to stand up for their rights
Emotion expression	capable of communicating their feelings to others
Emotion management (others)	capable of influencing other people's feelings
Emotion perception (self and others)	clear about their own and other people's feelings
Emotion regulation	capable of controlling their emotions
Impulsiveness (low)	reflective and less likely to give in to their urges
Relationship skills	capable of having fulfilling personal relationships
Self-esteem	successful and self-confident
Self-motivation	driven and unlikely to give up in the face of adversity
Social competence	accomplished networkers with excellent social skills
Stress management	capable of withstanding pressure and regulating stress
Trait empathy	capable of taking someone else's perspective
Trait happiness	cheerful and satisfied with their lives
Trait optimism	confident and likely to 'look on the bright side' of life

Consider which of these facets:

(a) could be categorized under the five most commonly occurring dimensions of social skills (listed in Table 16.1).

(b) fit within the multi-dimensional model of psychological well-being presented earlier in this chapter: positive affect, the extent to which a person typically feels positive emotions (e.g., enthusiasm, activeness, and alertness); negative affect, the extent to which negative emotions (e.g., distress, anger, nervousness) are experienced; and life satisfaction, the cognitive appraisal of the quality of one's life across the five domains of family, friends, school, living environment and self.

(c) are left unclassified.

their emotional and life experience but simply unusual or atypical in the experience of the tester who is scoring the answer. This issue is underlined when we look at ability EI tests for adults. Instead of using expert judgement to decide if answers are correct, consensus scoring is often used, where the correct answer for each item is that endorsed by the majority of respondents. This is very different from conventional IQ tests. By contrast, trait EI is assessed by asking children to complete a questionnaire where, for example, they would rate on a five-point scale from 'very much true of me' to 'not true of me' items such as 'I get angry easily' (Bar-On and Parker 2000). Petrides *et al.* (2004) argue that this approach, more akin to personality assessment, better encapsulates the primarily subjective nature of EI. They suggest 'emotional self-efficacy' as a more accurate description of the area than 'emotional intelligence'.

In addition to boundary disputes with social skills and psychological well-being, this area itself is rife with debates about terminology: 'emotional intelligence', 'emotional literacy' and 'emotional competence' all have their supporters. In recent years all three terms have been advocated by different UK authors: 'intelligence' (Humphrey *et al.* 2007), 'literacy' (Faupel 2003) and 'competence' (Weare and Gray 2003). Arguments against 'intelligence' have tended to focus on concerns that the term may suggest a fixed entity, not amenable to development, although as Humphrey *et al.* (2007) have pointed out, this reflects a rather outdated conceptualization of intelligence. Certainly programmes aimed at schools have tended to use the term 'emotional literacy', whether developed in the US and based on an 'ability' model (Maurer *et al.* 2004) or developed in the UK and based on the broader 'trait' approach (Faupel 2003). However, the term 'literacy' also has pre-existing connotations which could be quite misleading – for example, the idea that it will not be developed unless explicitly taught does not reflect the very substantial implicit component in emotional learning during normal development. It has also been criticized as suggesting a unitary construct when many subcomponents have been identified. Weare and Gray (2003) advocate use of the term 'competence' on the basis that other terms (intelligence and literacy) are generally defined in terms of competencies in any case. They additionally argue that the use of 'competence' focuses attention on the cognitive, affective and behavioural components that are needed for success, and this is helpful in an educational context. In this chapter we will use the term 'emotional competence' to parallel the term 'social competence', recognizing that each encompasses a range of subcomponents.

There has been a rapid growth in recent years in knowledge about the ways in which emotional competencies may mediate important academic or social outcomes for children and young people. Much of this has focused on specific, well-defined components, identified with particular areas and processes in the brain. For example, Eisenberg *et al.* (2006) collate findings from a range of studies which indicate that the ability to consciously regulate emotion is positively related to measures of social competence and peer group acceptance. Furthermore, this applies in a similar way across cultures that differ considerably and is particularly strong for children prone to negative emotions. It is suggested that this is likely to involve the strong connections found to exist in adulthood between the 'emotional brain' – the set of structures in the limbic system of the brain (OECD 2002) – and the parts of the brain responsible for executive functions or top-down control – prefrontal cortex and anterior cyngulate gyrus. Blakemore and Frith (2005) describe how this connection also has importance for learning, for example in managing emotions such as anxiety, fear and stress that disrupt attention and in controlling impulses or delaying gratification which facilitate engagement with learning tasks.

Developing interest in emotional intelligence has also stimulated more broadly conceptualized research on associations between assessed EI and social or academic outcomes. Working within an ability model of EI, Trinidad and Johnson (2002) found that high EI was associated with decreased tobacco and alcohol use in adolescence. Petrides *et al.* (2006) investigated the relationship between trait EI and social behaviour in primary school as rated by peers and teachers. Pupils with high trait EI scores received more peer nominations for 'co-operation' and 'leadership' and fewer nominations for 'disruption', 'aggression' and 'dependence'. Teachers rated high EI pupils higher on prosocial descriptors and lower on antisocial descriptors, than pupils who had low EI scores.

Petrides *et al.* (2004) found that trait EI moderated the relationship between cognitive ability and academic performance in secondary school in the UK. Furthermore, there were particular implications for pupils at risk of school failure. Among pupils with high cognitive abilities there was little difference in academic attainment between those with high EI and those with low EI. However, among pupils with low cognitive abilities, those with high EI did significantly better academically than those with low EI. This study also found that pupils with high EI scores were less likely to have unauthorized absences from school or to have been excluded. Parker *et al.* (2004), working in the USA, also found trait EI to be a significant predictor of academic success in secondary school.

Social and emotional competence and well-being: an integration

The three areas reviewed in this section cover a spectrum of personal and interpersonal aspects. While social competence is the longest established, there has been increasing recognition of a need to consider the other two areas. In reviewing the model of social interaction in children shown in Figure 16.4, Crick and Dodge (1994) acknowledged that 'affect' or emotion had generally been overlooked in discussions of social competence and argued that emotions need to be considered as an integral part of each social information-processing step described in Stage 2 of the model. Figure 16.6 shows the integrated model subsequently produced by Lemerise and Arsenio (2000).

The importance of considering psychological well-being has also been highlighted. Park (2004) noted that unless this is specifically targeted, individuals may continue to experience dissatisfaction and unhappiness even when successful behaviour change has been achieved through intervention. This in turn may have implications for maintenance of intervention effects and the emergence of other problem behaviours. The three areas complement each other and can readily be coherently aligned. As Activity 16.2 illustrates, the facets of emotional competence span a range of emotion-related dispositions that shade into psychological well-being (trait happiness and trait optimism) at one end and self-perceived abilities that shade into aspects of social competence at the other. It is not surprising that universal programmes embrace the spectrum and focus on Social and Emotional Learning (SEL; Weissberg and O'Brien 2004) in the USA or Social and Emotional Aspects of Learning (SEAL; DfES 2005d) in the UK.

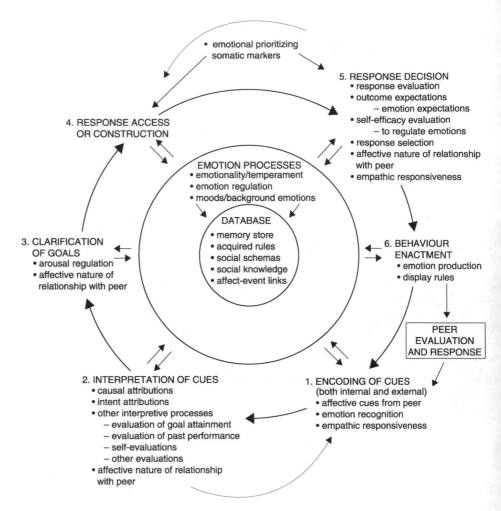

Figure 16.6 An integrated model of emotion processes and cognition in social information processing
Source: Lemerise and Arsenio (2000).

In such programmes emphasis is placed on a multi-level, integrated approach involving a number of key components (Conduct Problems Prevention Research Group 2002; Weissberg and O'Brien 2004). The approach adopted by the Conduct Problems Prevention Research Group (2002) is one of the best-researched and contains all the key components most commonly included. Three levels of prevention activities are involved from the early years through to the end of primary school:

● universal preventive programmes at school;

● standard prevention initiatives for children identified through initial screening as high risk – these include parenting skills groups and child social skills groups;

● individualized preventive support as needed (indicated by criterion-referenced assessments).

These will be discussed in turn in the following sections, together with available evidence of effectiveness. First the assessment measures that are most commonly used in evaluating the effectiveness of these programmes will be briefly described.

Assessing social and emotional competence and evaluating interventions

There is no standard battery of assessment methods or tests in this area. 'Rather, hypotheses dictate the direction of assessment, the questions to be answered and the methods to be used' (Elliott and Busse 1991: 67). The interactive model shown in Figure 16.4 is the basis for hypothesis generation. It is important in each case to consider the different facets of social and emotional competence, and the assessment techniques described below are categorized according to the stage in this model on which they mainly focus. It is also important to collect further information over time about any aspects of a pupil's skills that are identified as problematic so that the success of any individualized intervention programme can be evaluated. Do bear in mind that even the 'best evidenced' interventions for children and adolescents do not work in as many as a third of individual cases and that some children get worse in response to intervention (Carr 2000). There is a duty of care to carefully monitor and evaluate individual progress as well as general programme effectiveness.

Activity 16.3   Assessment techniques case study

As you read about the types of assessment technique described in this section of the chapter, consider and note their potential advantages and disadvantages in assessing the needs of the child featured in the following case study, Ben.

Ben is 11 years old. He is one of seven children from a school for children with physical difficulties who were integrated 12 months ago into a mainstream middle school (for 8–12-year-old children). Ben was originally admitted to the special school with asthma, language delay, poor articulation and clumsiness – difficulties in each of these areas persist. In addition, he has learning difficulties. His mathematics and spelling skills are at the equivalent level of a 7-year-old, although reading accuracy and comprehension are at a 9½–10-year level.

The mainstream school feel that they are able to provide for Ben's learning needs from the resources which have been provided to support the integration programme. However, the school is seriously questioning the appropriateness of Ben's placement because he does not seem able to cope socially in mainstream. He is said to find peer relationships very difficult, tantruming when unable to get his own way.

Figure 16.7 describes available techniques for assessing each of the stages in the model of social interaction in children, with the exception of Stage 4 which is considered separately below. Those marked with an asterisk are available to educational psychologists and schools in the *Psychology in Education Portfolio* (Frederickson and Cameron 1999).

Stage 1: Assessing the social situation

*Taxonomy of Problematic Situations (TOPS)** (Dodge *et al.* 1985): a teacher-completed rating scale which identifies the social situations that a pupil finds difficult.

Observations of the Classroom and School Environment: see Chapter 8 for approaches and techniques.

Stage 2: Assessing the child's perception and understanding

Multidimensional Students' Life Satisfaction Scale (Huebner 1994): a self-report scale for pupils aged 8–16 that assesses satisfaction across five domains (school, self, family, friends and living environment).

Positive and Negative Affect Scale – Children (Laurent *et al.* 1999): a self-report scale where pupils rate the extent to which they have experienced various positive (e.g. happy, strong, excited) or negative (e.g. nervous, scared, guilty) feelings or moods over the previous few weeks.

*Kusché Affective Interview – Revised (KAI-R)** (Kusché *et al.* 1988): an interview that taps two of Salovey and Sluyter's (1997) branches of ability emotional intelligence: identifying the cues pupils use to recognize emotion, their under-standing of simultaneous and changing emotions and their knowledge of display rules for emotions.

Bar-On Emotional Quotient Inventory: Youth Version (Bar-On and Parker 2000): a self-report measure of trait emotional intelligence that consists of four scales: intrapersonal, interpersonal, adaptability and stress management. Additional scales assess general mood, positive impression and inconsistency in responding.

Emotional Literacy, Assessment and Intervention (Faupel 2003): checklists for pupils, teachers and parents assess the five components of emotional intelli-gence identified by Goleman and featured in the SEAL materials (self-awareness, self-regulation, motivation, empathy and social skills).

Perceived Competence Scale for Children (Harter 1985): a self-report question-naire which has been widely used to assess children's global self-worth and their perception of their competence in the following areas: scholastic competence, social acceptance, athletic competence, physical appearance and behavioural conduct (assessing how well the children feel they behave and if they like the way they behave).

*Burnett Self Scale** (Burnett 1994): a self-report questionnaire which provides information on pupils' thoughts and feelings about significant aspects of their lives – self-esteem, physical appearance, physical abilities, relationships with peers, reading, maths, learning.

*Children's Shyness Questionnaire** (Crozier 1995): this self-report questionnaire for 8–11-year-olds asks about feelings of shyness and embarrassment, about being nervous and quiet in social situations, about whether the child has a tendency to blush and whether they enjoy performing in front of others.

Loneliness and Social Dissatisfaction Questionnaire (Asher *et al.* 1990): this assesses pupils' perception of loneliness and their dissatisfaction with their peer relationships at school. It has been used in a number of studies in inclusive settings with pupils who have SEN.

Wally Social Skills and Problem Solving Game (Webster-Stratton *et al.* 2001): an interview using pictures of hypothetical problem situations related to object acquisition and friendship skills to assess quantity and quality of social problem-solving strategies. Available at http://www.son.washington.edu/centers/parenting-clinic/forms.asp.

Stages 3 and 5: Assessing children's social behaviour

Observations in natural settings such as the classroom or playground: see Merrell and Gimpel (1997) for descriptions of different types of observational procedures, such as event recording, interval recording, time-sample recording, duration and latency recording and copies of forms that can be used to record observations.

Child Role-Play Measure* (Dodge *et al.* 1985): assesses pupils' social skills by asking them to imagine themselves in a number of social situations and to role-play their responses.

Strengths and Difficulties Questionnaire (SDQ) (Goodman 1997): rates behaviour on five scales – emotional symptoms, conduct problems, hyperactivity, peer problems, prosocial. Teacher, parent and pupil versions are available in many languages at http://www.sdqinfo.com.

Social Skills Questionnaires (Spence 1995) and *Social Skills Rating System* (Gresham and Elliott 1990): questionnaire measures of children's social behaviour that contain versions for teachers, parents and the pupils themselves.

Guess Who Technique* (e.g. Hartshorne *et al.* 1929; Coie *et al.* 1982): descriptions (e.g. of cooperative and disruptive behaviour) are presented to a class who are asked to 'guess who?' from their classmates fit each description.

Figure 16.7 Assessment techniques appropriate to different stages in the model of social interaction in children (Figure 16.4)

Assessing other children's perceptions and judgements

This is a particularly important aspect as it is pupils' social adjustment and acceptance in school, resulting in part from their social skills, that are associated with other important short- and long-term outcomes. A variety of sociometric (social measurement) techniques are available to assess the perceptions and judgements of members of the peer group. Much of the research on the long-term effects of poor social competence in childhood has used one of the following kinds of sociometric measure.

Peer nomination. This type of approach was developed by Moreno (1934). Children are asked to nominate a certain number of classmates according to a specified criterion (e.g. best friend, especially liked). The majority of studies have used positive criteria but negative ones have also been employed (name three classmates you don't like much). The reliability of peer nomination measures over time is similar to that obtained for achievement tests and is found to increase throughout the primary age range. The approach can be adapted by using pictures of classmates for preschool children.

Rating scale measures. Here children are provided with a list of all their classmates and asked to rate (on a scale from 1 to 5, for example) how much they like to play with them at school (Asher, 1985). Versions for younger children include smiling, frowning and neutral faces instead of numbers and can include photos instead of names.

Forced choice group preference records. These methods appear similar to rating scale techniques but present and treat the alternative responses open to the child as separate categories that are totalled but not averaged. The Social Inclusion Survey (Frederickson and Graham 1999) is an example of a forced choice group preference record which can be used with whole classes of children aged 7 years and above. The method involves making up a worksheet like that shown in Figure 16.8, where a class of 9-year-olds are being asked about how much they like to play with each of their classmates. For older children it may be more appropriate

How much do you like to ___*play*___ with each person at school?

James	(?)	☺	😐	☹
Richard	(?)	☺	😐	☹
David	(?)	☺	😐	☹
Samantha	(?)	☺	😐	☹
Catherine	(?)	☺	😐	☹
Lucy	(?)	☺	😐	☹
	(?)	☺	😐	☹
	(?)	☺	😐	☹
	(?)	☺	😐	☹

Figure 16.8   A forced choice group preference record: The Social Inclusion Survey
Source: Frederickson and Graham (1999).

to phrase the question in terms of who they like to 'go around with at breaktimes'. A second version of the questionnaire asks pupils to tick the face which shows how much they like to 'work with' each person at school: the smiling face to indicate classmates with whom they like to work, the straight-mouthed face to indicate classmates with whom they don't mind whether they work or not and the frowning face to indicate classmates with whom they prefer not to work. Pupils are asked to use the question mark category to indicate any classmates they do not know well enough to decide how much they like to work with them. Good reliability and validity data on these measures are reported from studies carried out in schools in England with pupils who have SEN and their mainstream peers in inclusive school contexts (Frederickson and Graham 1999).

Teachers sometimes express concern about the possibility that sociometric assessment activities may implicitly sanction making negative statements about others or may influence children's attitudes towards classmates in undesirable ways. Connolly (1983) has argued that the dangers of highlighting unpopular children may be particularly pronounced in classes where children with learning difficulties are included. A number of studies have investigated this question but failed to find evidence of any negative effects (Iverson and Iverson 1996; Iverson *et al.* 1997). Nevertheless, it is advisable to design procedures so as to minimize any possible risk, for example by stressing confidentiality and including buffer or distractor activities at the end of the assessment session. Frederickson and Furnham (1998a) argue that the forced choice group preference record approach can be particularly suitable for assessing the social acceptance or inclusion in mainstream schools of children with SEN because it avoids singling out the included children in any way and does not require negative responses to be made. It also allows classmates to say if they do not know someone well enough to decide how much they like to play with them, which is important if children with SEN are integrated on a part-time basis.

It is important to appreciate that sociometric acceptance is also influenced by personal factors such as physical attractiveness, intelligence and academic success and by interactive factors such as similarities in gender and race (Hartup 1992; Foster *et al.* 1996). Within-race choice is less pronounced than is within-gender choice. The few studies that have examined the behaviours associated with high peer rejection in predominantly white and predominantly black groups have reported similar findings, indicating that verbal and physical aggression and disruptive/inappropriate behaviour are similarly implicated in both populations.

Multi-method assessment in multiethnic contexts

Different assessment techniques have different advantages and limitations. A potential advantage of carrying out observations in natural settings is that comparison data from other pupils in the same situation can be collected and used to provide helpful context in interpreting the behaviour of the pupil targeted for observation. Where there are other pupils from the same ethnic or cultural group as the target child, comparative data can usefully be collected from them. However, observational approaches also have potential problems such as observer reactivity, where the presence of the observer has the effect of altering pupil behaviour. This is less likely to occur in a classroom if the observations are being carried out by a teaching assistant who is often present rather than by someone who is a stranger to the pupils.

Peer assessment is also sometimes preferred to direct observation because it is less intrusive, particular out of the classroom. The social behaviour of older pupils, in particular, is relatively complex and private, making it difficult for adult observers to make reliable and representative observations. Peers may have better access to low-frequency but psychologically meaningful events that lead to the establishment of social reputations.

Role-play measures can be economical of time and can provide useful information for intervention planning, alongside other approaches. However, there are concerns about validity. In a role-play, pupils may act out what they know they are supposed to do, even if this is not what they would actually do in a real-life situation. So, a role-play test will show whether pupils know what behaviour is expected and whether they have the competencies to carry it out, but it cannot be assumed that the behaviour they choose to role-play is what they would actually do if the situation were real.

Because different approaches to assessment have different strengths and limitations it is desirable to have convergent evidence from a variety of approaches. Assessment of a number of different stages in the model of social interaction will provide a better understanding of the process overall. The advisability of obtaining information from different respondents has also been highlighted by research findings. Whereas teacher ratings have been found to match closely with pupil self-report and observational data, parental reports tend not to correlate highly with other assessments (Cartledge and Milburn 1996). This probably reflects differences between children's behaviour at home and at school, and provides some support for the view that there is considerable situational specificity in social behaviour.

However, studies in the USA consistently report lower correlations between teacher and parent ratings when children are from racial and ethnic minority populations. For example, Keller (1988) found higher correlations between parents' and teachers' social skill ratings of white 7-year-olds than of Hispanic or African-American children. This suggests the possibility of culturally or ethnically based differences in expectations and highlights the importance of parental involvement, if not in completing their own rating scale, then in discussing the assessment information collected in school and in contributing to the resulting intervention planning.

Cartledge and Milburn (1996) argue that the use of a variety of respondents and assessment procedures is particularly important when working with pupils from racial and ethnic minority groups. They report findings which suggest that culturally different behaviours by African-American and Asian-American pupils may be misperceived by teachers. A need is identified for educationists to seek advice and improve their cultural understanding so that they are able to accurately distinguish acceptable and problematic social skills, notwithstanding cultural differences in behavioural expression. Adding assessment information from parents and from classroom peers (with cultural backgrounds similar to and different from those of the target child) may be valuable to teachers both in improving the appropriateness of their assessments and in developing their cultural understanding.

Programmes to promote social and emotional competence and well-being

Universal preventive programmes at school

These are programmes which are accessed by all pupils. They involve a curriculum component delivered by classroom teachers, alongside a whole-school emphasis on promoting social, emotional and behavioural skills which involves strategies for effective home–school collaboration. Existing research informed the SEAL initiative in the UK in primary (DfES 2005d) and secondary (DfES 2007d) schools. In this section we will look in more detail at the primary initiative. Further information can be obtained from the SEAL website (http://www.bandapilot.org.uk/). From the following list of resources provided to primary schools it can be seen that all of the components listed above have been incorporated:

- an assembly to launch each of the seven themes and a whole-school resource file;

- teaching ideas and materials for class-based work in each age group;

- a set of activities for families to use at home during each theme;

- staff development activities and information sheets;

- differentiated resources for small group work with children who need extra support.

The seven SEAL themes (new beginnings; getting on and falling out; saying no to bullying; going for goals; good to be me; relationships; and changes) have been constructed to address the social and emotional aspects of learning shown in Figure 16.9. Within the SEAL guidance emphasis is placed on exploring cultural differences with interest and respect, recognizing that expected social behaviours

Figure 16.9 Social and emotional aspects of learning
Source: DfES (2005d).

and rules about displaying emotion may vary considerably. It is suggested that discussion of differences in expectations, for example between home and school, can helpfully be set in the context of the 'culture-jumping' between contexts expected of all children, in understanding for example that acceptable behaviour differs between classroom and playground.

In an initial qualitative and quasi-experimental evaluation of the SEAL pilot, Hallam *et al.* (2006) reported positive impacts of the programme on staff understanding of social and emotional aspects of learning, confidence in their interactions with pupils and thoughtful management of behaviour incidents. In addition, staff perceived a positive impact on the children's behaviour and well-being and reported that classrooms and playgrounds were calmer. Because of the absence of a control group it was difficult to draw any firm conclusions from questionnaire data collected from the children before and after the pilot. It is regrettable that government rhetoric concerning evidence-informed practice in recent years has rarely been matched by funding to allow innovations to be evaluated in ways that meet accepted quality standards (e.g. see Rutter 2006). Notwithstanding the limitations of the SEAL pilot evaluation, careful analysis produced some evidence to suggest that the programme was most probably responsible for positive changes in social skills and relationships and awareness of emotion in others. Gender differences were apparent in many areas, with girls demonstrating more positive responses.

While the materials were generally perceived as excellent, there was considerable variability across schools in implementation of the SEAL programme. Hallam *et al.* (2006) report that it was most effective where:

- it fitted in with existing PHSE work or circle time;

- it was complementary to the school ethos;

- it was adopted across the whole school;

- appropriate training and time for planning implementation were provided;

- there was commitment from the senior management team.

Overall these conclusions fit well with those drawn from those from more rigorously evaluated programmes designed to promote social and emotional learning. Wells *et al.* (2003) conducted a systematic review of well-controlled evaluations of universal programmes to promote mental health in schools and concluded that important features of successful programmes were:

- the adoption of a whole-school approach;

- continuous implementation for more than a year;

- a focus on the promotion of mental health rather than the prevention of mental illness.

PATHS

One of the programmes positively reviewed by Wells *et al.* (2003), the Promoting Alternative Thinking Strategies (PATHS) curriculum (Kusché and Greenberg 1994) is of particular interest for three reasons. First, its efficacy for children with special needs has been specifically evaluated. Second, it focuses in particular on emotional competence and is one of the few intervention approaches to have been evaluated in relation to a measure of emotional intelligence (the Kusché Affective Inventory). Thirdly, there is initial evidence that it can promote neurocognitive functioning important in behavioural regulation. Finally, although developed in the USA, its use has been successfully evaluated in a number of different contexts in the UK.

The PATHS Curriculum consists of a Teacher's Manual and all the pictures, scripts, and stories for 131 lessons designed to be used in a flexible manner across the primary school years. In addition to daily (three times per week minimum) teaching sessions, generalization is encouraged throughout the classroom day and throughout the school environment, and materials are provided for use with parents. The conceptual domains targeted in PATHS include 'emotional awareness of self and others, increased self-control over impulses and behavior, use of empathy, improved relationship skills, enhanced self-esteem, use of analytic thinking, and mature interpersonal problem solving skills' (Kusché 2002: 285).

A well-controlled, large-scale evaluation of the PATHS curriculum in the USA (Common Problems Prevention Research Group 1999) reported significant reductions in peer ratings of aggression and hyperactive-disruptive behaviour at 7 years in the intervention schools. Observer ratings of classroom atmosphere were also more positive in the intervention schools than in control schools serving similar diverse populations which had not used the programme. Greenberg *et al.* (1995) described an evaluation of the 35-lesson unit on 'Feelings and Relationships'. Pupils were taught that all feelings are OK to have but that not all behaviours are OK. They were taught to attend to what their feelings are telling them and to use information from feelings in deciding what to do next. Labelling feelings was seen as an important basis for facilitating self-control and resolving problems effectively. Instruction was also provided on the use of cues in recognizing feelings in oneself and others, in managing feelings and deciding whether to show or keep them private and in gaining an empathetic realization of how one's behaviour can affect other people. The evaluation study found that the programme was effective for both mainstream and special needs pupils in Years 3 and 4 in:

- improving their vocabulary and fluency in discussing emotional experiences;

- enhancing their belief in their ability to manage emotions;

- developing their understanding of a number of aspects of emotions.

These aspects, evaluated using the KAI-R, can be seen to map on to two of Salovey and Sluyter's (1997) four branches of emotional intelligence. Greenberg *et al.* (1995: 134) reported that, to their knowledge, this study provided the first clear demonstration that 'aspects of emotional fluency and understanding can be successfully taught in a school environment by classroom teachers'.

In an evaluation of effects on neurocognitive functioning underpinning emotional regulation, Riggs *et al.* (2006) report findings which suggest the effectiveness of the PATHS Curriculum in promoting inhibitory control and verbal fluency in pupils aged 7–9. In addition, inhibitory control was found to be related to externalizing behaviour, while both inhibitory control and verbal fluency were related to internalizing behavior. In special education classes also a three-year study found significant effects of PATHS on teacher reports of internalizing and externalizing behaviour problems as well as child self-reported depression (Kam *et al.* 2004).

The efficacy of the PATHS curriculum with deaf children has been investigated in the USA and UK. In the USA, Greenberg and Kusché (1998) found significant improvement in students' social problem-solving skills and emotional recognition skills. Teacher and parent-rated social competence also improved and follow-up assessments indicated maintenance of effects for as long as two years after the programme ended. A study in the UK (Hindley *et al.* 1998) showed significant improvement in emotional understanding, behaviour, self-image, and emotional adjustment after one year of PATHS.

Other implementations of the PATHS curriculum in the UK involved a class of 9–10 year olds in Scotland and classes of 5–8 year olds in the South of England. In the study by Kelly *et al.* (2004) the PATHS curriculum was rated positively by class teachers, pupils and other staff. Seven target pupils were selected for individual assessment and monitoring on account of impulsive, confrontational and oppositional behaviour. While no control group was involved and the results must therefore treated with caution, statistically significant improvements from pre-intervention to post-intervention were found on emotional competence as assessed by the KAI-R. In addition, assessment by both the learning support teacher and the home/school worker using the Taxonomy of Problematic Social Situations indicated significant improvements in situations involving peer group entry, response to provocation, response to failure, response to success, social expectations and teacher expectations.

Curtis and Norgate (2007) evaluated the PATHS curriculum with Year 1 to Year 3 classes in schools in the South of England. They found significant improvements on all dimensions of the SDQ for children in the intervention schools, but not in the comparison schools. They describe the PATHS programme as more structured and rigorous than the curriculum component of the SEAL approach, but highlight their compatibility and suggest that schools following PATHS can use the SEAL materials as a source of supplementary ideas and resources.

Standard prevention initiatives for high-risk groups

At this level the approach adopted by both the Conduct Problems Prevention Research Group (2002) in the USA and the Primary Behaviour and Attendance Strategy in the UK (see Hallam *et al.* 2006) focused on parenting skills groups and child social skills groups. These twin foci are well supported by available evidence, with Wolpert *et al.* (2006) reporting problem-solving skills training for children, combined with parent training, as an effective intervention for conduct problems in children aged 8–12 years.

Parenting skills groups

Gibbs *et al.* (2003) summarized some of the findings that led to the development of parenting programmes, reporting that as much as 30–40 per cent of the variation in child antisocial behaviour may be attributable to parenting and family interaction factors. Particularly implicated in negative behavioural and emotional outcomes are harsh and inconsistent discipline, high levels of criticism, poor supervision, low involvement, and a lack of warmth in the parent–child relationship. Research conducted within a behavioural and cognitive-behavioural tradition has furthered our understanding of the mechanisms linking parenting approaches and child outcomes, and this in turn has formed the basis for the development of successful intervention programmes.

In a review for the DfES of international evidence on 'what works' in parenting support, Moran *et al.* (2004) reported that interventions with a strong theory base were more effective than those that were atheoretical. For changing parenting and child behaviours the use of behavioural components that focus on specific parenting skills and practical approaches for implemention at home were recommended. Cognitive components were recommended for changing beliefs, attitudes and self-perceptions about parenting. In addition, better evidence of effectivieness was reported for interventions using a number of different methods of delivery and interventions that provide detailed manuals and materials so staff are well supported in delivering the programme that has been evaluated, as opposed to making it up as they go along.

Very similar conclusions were reached by the National Institute for Clinical Excellence (NICE) and the Social Care Institute for Excellence (SCIE) in guidance issued in July 2006. The implementation of group-based parenting programmes for children with conduct disorder was recommended as evidence-based and cost-effective (except in families with particularly complex needs, where individual programmes are recommended). The guidance states that these programmes should:

- be structured and have a curriculum informed by principles of social learning theory;

- include relationship-enhancing strategies;

- offer a sufficient number of sessions, with an optimum of 8–12, to maximize the possible benefits for participants;

- enable parents to identify their own parenting objectives;

- incorporate role-play during sessions, as well as homework to be undertaken between sessions, to achieve generalization of newly rehearsed behaviours to the home situation;

- be delivered by appropriately trained and skilled facilitators who are supervised, have access to necessary ongoing professional development, and are able to engage in a productive therapeutic alliance with parents;

- adhere to the programme developer's manual and employ all of the necessary materials to ensure consistent implementation of the programme.

Activity 16.4 Analysing an exemplar parenting programme

For this activity you may either select a parenting progrmme which you are interested in implementing, or you can use the information presented here on the Webster-Stratton programmes. Information on a wide range of parenting programmes can be found in Appendices 1 and 2 of the report produced by Moran *et al.* (2004). This report also contains a link to an on-line database (at http://www.prb.org.uk) that provides systematic descriptions and evaluations of studies of effectiveness of parenting programmes up to 2006).

The Webster-Stratton parent training programmes were reported by Hallam *et al.* (2006) to be the most widely implemented parent training approach in the Primary Behaviour and Attendance Pilot and they have been extensively positively evaluated. Read the following description and consider the extent to which the UK trial programme meets the NICE guidelines summarized above.

Webster-Stratton parenting programmes: an overview. Adapted from Moran *et al.* (2004)

The Webster-Stratton programmes are a comprehensive set of interventions using videotape modelling, group discussion, role-playing and rehearsal techniques, homework activities and supportive telephone calls to prevent, reduce and treat conduct problems, and increase social competence in children aged 2–10 years. They are based on social learning theory and research on links between parental discipline and child aggression.

Programmes include the 'Incredible Years Basic parent training series' (ten videotapes/250 video vignettes) which teaches parents of 2–7 year old children interactive play and reinforcement skills, non-punitive disciplinary techniques, and problem-solving strategies over a 12-week period (see Figure 16.10). The 'Incredible Years School Age parent training series' (three videotapes for parents of 5–12-year-old children) is a multicultural programme emphasizing parental monitoring, problem-solving with children and family problem-solving techniques. The 'Incredible Years Advanced parent training series' (six videotapes) is a 10–12-week supplement to the 'Basic' programme, which focuses on family risk factors including depression, marital conflict, poor coping skills, poor anger management and inadequate support. Finally, the 'Incredible Years Supporting Your Child's Education' (two videotapes) complements the 'Basic' programme

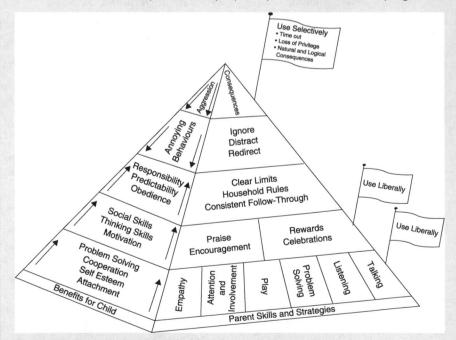

Figure 16.10   Parenting pyramid.
Source: Webster-Stratton and Hancock (1998)

by addressing ways in which parents can foster academic competence in their children, including enhancing child reading skills and academic readiness, and promoting strong home–school connections.

Example of a UK trial (From Gibbs *et al.* 2003)

The parents of 90 children met in small groups for 2 hours per week over 13–16 weeks. Each group consisted of parents of 6–8 children. A detailed training manual was used, and included topics such as play, praise, incentives, setting limits, discipline, and handling misbehaviour.

Video clips of parents with children were used with constant reference to the parents' own experiences and predicaments. Parents were helped to practise new approaches during sessions and at home, and were given written feedback after every session.

Difficulties were shown to be normal, and humour and fun encouraged. A crèche, good-quality refreshments and transport were provided. Group leaders were supervised weekly to ensure treatment fidelity and to develop skills, using video-tapes of the sessions to rehearse therapeutic approaches. The therapists held jobs across a range of disciplines in their local services and were trained over a 3-month period.

While providing overwhelmingly positive conclusions, reviews of the outcomes and implementation of parent effectiveness training programmes also highlight a number of areas where further research and development work are indicated. Moran *et al.* (2004) highlights diversity issues, pointing out that most of the knowledge base has been established with mothers rather than fathers and with white families. Wolpert *et al.* (2006) reports that on average two-thirds of children under 10 years whose parents participate, show improvement. However, greater effectiveness (fewer drop-outs, greater gains and better maintenance) is associated with younger children, higher IQ, less co-morbidity, less severe conduct problems, less socioeconomic disadvantage, lower parental discord, higher parental global functioning and absence of antisocial behaviour in parents. Parents from these groups may also be more difficult to recruit to the programmes and Hallam *et al.* (2006) reports that, overall, local authorities did not find recruitment easy. There is some agreement on elements likely to increase programme attractiveness (Common Problems Prevention Research Group 2002; Scott and Sylva 2003):

- a recruitment process that maximizes opportunities to forge a positive relationship between workers and parents and adopt a partnership to identifying needs;

- including an element focused on helping to promote success in school learning and presenting the programme as being universally relevant and providing a 'boost', rather than being designed for 'failing parents'.

Hallam *et al.* (2006) reported that programmes called 'The Incredible Years' or 'Getting Ready for Big School' were felt to recruit better than those called 'parenting programmes'. It is worth noting that there is as yet little evidence on the effectiveness of compulsory training programmes, where parenting orders have been used to compel parents to attend (Gibbs *et al.* 2003).

Child social skills groups

A range of approaches are available for running social skills groups, and these will be discussed in the next section on individualized programmes. However, among the standard prevention initiatives being discussed in this section, the Webster-Stratton small-group social skills programme for children is often the programme of choice, as was the case in the Primary Behaviour and Attendance Pilot (Hallam *et al.* 2006). A key advantage is that it is designed to run alongside the Webster-Stratton 'Incredible Years' parent training programme. This is advantageous where problems are more severe and long-standing. While small-group social skills training and anger management skills training have been found to be effective with primary-aged children with mild SEBD, use of these approaches on their own is not recommended in more severe cases and parent training should then also be offered where possible (Wolpert *et al.* 2006).

The Webster-Stratton approach, called the 'Dina Dinosaur' programme, contains the following components (Webster-Stratton and Reid 2003):

- How to do your best in school: group rules and compliance training using behavioural techniques of reward and time out.

- Understanding and detecting feelings: regulation of own emotions, identification and understanding of others' emotions.

- Problem-solving steps: seven-step problem-solving process and anger management strategies to facilitate calm implementation of problem-solving strategies.

- How to be friendly: positive conversational, collaborative and play skills important in forming and maintaining friendships.

The programme stresses the integration of cognitive, affective and behavioural components. Teaching methods include videotape modelling, use of puppets, role-play, practice activities, games, fantasy play, children's books, feedback, reinforcement and strategies to encourage generalization of acquired skills.

The programmed is delivered by trained staff in a clinic or small-group withdrawal setting on school premises. Webster-Stratton *et al.* (2001) describe the implementation and evaluation of a clinic-based programme comprising 20 weekly sessions in a group of five or six with two therapists. Children aged 4–8 diagnosed with oppositional defiant or conduct disorder were allocated to treatment or no-treatment control groups. Parents and teachers of children in the intervention group received weekly letters about session content and good behaviour charts to reinforce targeted social skills. The evaluation revealed statistically and clinically significant improvements in aggressive behaviour and cognitive social problem-solving strategies. Comparison with results from parent training programmes suggested that parent training was more effective in reducing children's aggressive behaviour, but that the social skills programme was more effective in improving child social problem-solving skills. Both independent observations and reports from parents and teachers indicated generalization of skills from the clinic to home and school while a one-year follow-up indicated maintenance of improvements over time. Children with ADHD and those from stressed families did as well as others, but negative parenting styles (criticism and physical punishment) were linked with fewer significant improvements. The main recommendation for improvement identified was for school-based delivery and general curriculum incorporation, that is, for the development of a universal preventive version of the programme. This is now available and has been implemented both in the USA (Webster-Stratton and Reid 2004) and the UK (Hutchings *et al.* 2004).

The integration of small-group work into the classroom also emerged as an issue in the Primary Behaviour and Attendance Pilot where a multi-agency approach involved CAMHS staff delivering the intervention in schools in most areas (Hallam *et al.* 2006). Issues were identified in relation to:

- the need for some children to have one-to-one attention;

- limited reinforcement of work from the small group in the classroom;

- inadequate time for teachers and small-group workers to communicate.

The second and third of these issues were partially addressed by the involvement of teaching assistants to support the small-group work. The development of more individualized approaches for children who need them is considered in the next section.

Individualized intervention programmes

A range of well-researched intervention approaches are available for developing social competence and behaviour and promoting social inclusion. The following commonly used intervention procedures will be outlined:

- reinforcement, shaping and modelling;

- coaching;

- social problem-solving.

These are also to be found in the standard prevention initiatives described in the previous section. However, they are examined at this level where a more detailed understanding is needed of when and how they should be used in devising or selecting specific individualized programmes to meet the needs of particular pupils. Gresham *et al.* (2004) conclude from a research synthesis that different strategies are required for:

- acquisition problems (can't do), when modelling, coaching and direct instruction are indicated;

- performance problems (won't do), when prompting, shaping and direct reinforcement are indicated.

Nonetheless, appropriately devised social skills programmes are found to be effective across a broad range of behaviour difficulties, such as aggression, externalizing behaviours, internalizing behaviours, antisocial behaviour patterns (Carr 2000; Gresham *et al.* 2004).

Although targets and programme elements at this level of preventive intervention are individualized, delivery in groups or involvement of peers will usually be a key aspect in order to provide social contexts in which to observe and practise social behaviour. However, cautions have been raised about the use of group approaches in adolescence. Dishion and Andrews (1995) evaluated alternative interventions to reduce problem behaviour in high-risk 11–14-year-olds: parent training groups, youth training groups, parent and youth training groups or materials (newsletters and videos). They found that the two interventions involving youth training groups showed escalation in tobacco use and problem behaviour at school, the groups having the effect of providing a readily accessible deviant peer group which reinforced undesirable behaviour.

Reinforcement, shaping and modelling

Reinforcement involves the use of praise or other rewards when the child engages in the socially desirable behaviour being targeted (see Gresham and Elliott 1993). Shaping involves rewarding the child in a step-by-step fashion for increasingly close approximations to the target behaviour. Such approaches have been successfully used with isolated pupils by using adult attention as a reward, first for playing near peers, then for talking near them, then for participating in potential cooperative situations, and finally for engaging in cooperative play. Praise or other rewards may also be given to peers for interacting with the target pupil. This approach, which has been widely used with preschool children, has also been applied with older pupils.

When modelling is used the target pupil is provided with a step-by-step demonstration of all the behavioural components required. This may involve the person giving the demonstration 'thinking aloud' about what they are doing while they are doing it. Modelling may be either videotaped or live. With live modelling the pupil can be paired up with a socially skilled classmate for assistance in areas such as playing with peers, resisting aggression and engaging in conversations. The peer is trained in modelling techniques for the behaviours to be developed and in techniques for prompting and reinforcing the target pupil. The target pupil is told to observe the peer model and do as he or she does.

Coaching

Whereas in modelling you show the pupil what is required, in coaching you tell them in a step-by-step manner what to do. Oden (1986) provides a good example of a coaching approach to teaching social interaction concepts which might make playing games with other pupils more fun. The coaching procedure used is outlined in Figure 16.11

Research has shown that the opportunity to practise with classmates is crucial to the success of coaching programmes in reducing social rejection (Bierman and Furman 1984). This also allows classmates to 'notice' the rejected child's different behaviour. In this way coaching can have an impact on other pupils' perceptions and judgements at Stage 4 of the Dodge *et al.* (1986) model, as well as the target child's understanding of the concepts being taught (Stage 2) and the social behaviour needed to put their ideas into practice (Stage 3). In some cases a class teacher may initially need the help of another member of staff to release them to spend time on Steps 1–5 of the coaching process and to set up the small-group

Step 1 Teacher suggests a relevant social concept to child – e.g. 'Jamie, I want to talk about some ideas that make games more fun to play [or that help groups work better together]. Let's talk about cooperating.'

Step 2 Teacher probes child's understanding of concept by asking for specific examples: 'Do you know what cooperating means? Give me some examples.'

Step 3 Teacher repeats/rephrases child's example, or provides one if the child can't: 'Yes, sharing out the crayons and letting everyone have a turn with the bat are good examples of cooperating.'

Step 4 Teacher asks for specific counter-examples of the concept: 'Now give me some examples of not cooperating. What sort of things do children do when they are not cooperating?'

Step 5 Teacher asks child to evaluate whether each type of example (from Steps 3 and 4) should help make a game more fun to play: 'OK, suppose you share out the crayons, will that help to make the game more fun? Why's that? Suppose you won't stick to the rules, like you won't stand still when you are tagged, will that help to make the game more fun? Why's that?'

Step 6 Teacher asks the child to try out some of the ideas they have discussed. Especially when coaching is first used with the child, the teacher may set up an educational game for the child to play with a small group of classmates. This provides the child with an immediate opportunity to try out the ideas, observed by the teacher from a distance and to receive feedback at Step 7. Oden envisaged this small-group work being done outside the classroom and advised that once the child had got used to the procedure they should be asked to identify class-room or playground activities where the ideas could be tried out later. They would then be asked to try out the strategies which they had thought of and during the subsequent session a week later they would be asked if they had tried out the strategies and what the results had been.

Step 7 Teacher reviews with the child the helpfulness of the ideas: 'Did you try sharing during that game you've just played/when your group finished off their collage? How did things work out? Why do you think that happened?' If things have gone well: 'Well done for sharing, that was a good idea of yours.' If things have not gone well: 'What could you try next time? OK, give that a try and then tell me how it works.'

Figure 16.11 The coaching procedure
Source: Adapted from Oden (1986).

opportunities at Step 6. The case study description included in Activity 16.5 is typical of the inventive way in which class teachers have adapted the procedure so as to integrate it into ongoing group work in the classroom.

Coaching techniques can be adapted for use with any group, of whatever size, at any time that the group is about to engage in an activity that involves social interaction. Steps 1–5 can be run through by a teacher in a few minutes prior to starting the activity. For example, for a class about to engage in a group activity which involves discussion, the teacher could focus on the concept 'paying attention' in the following way:

Now it is very important during this discussion to pay attention to whoever

Activity 16.5   Case study: Kelly's classroom coaching programme

This programme, described by Frederickson (1991), was implemented with Kelly, an attention-seeking, domineering 9-year-old, by Mark, her class teacher. Mark first noted down a list of social concepts and skills which he felt that Kelly needed to learn in order to improve her social acceptance. He also thought about the complaints which he frequently received from the other girls: 'Do we *have* to have Kelly in our group? She's so bossy/stuck up/nasty.' He reasoned that even if *he* didn't see Kelly as 'stuck up', work might have to be done to help the other children to see her in a different way.

At the start of each day Mark would review the activities involving a teaching input with a group containing Kelly and, if possible, would select one which lent itself to work on a relevant social concept. During his time with the group he would spend five minutes working through Steps 1–5 of the coaching procedure with the whole group, making sure that Kelly was actively involved. He would then ask the children to try out their ideas during the group work, letting them know that the implementation of the ideas would be reviewed briefly with the whole group when he came back to review their work on the activity with them.

Because Mark wished to discourage Kelly from being boastful, and encourage her to be positive and complimentary towards others, he asked pairs of children to try to notice each other using the ideas. In the feedback session children could only give positive examples, and only ones which involved others, not themselves. The children labelled this 'telling nice tales', and it proved a very effective way of getting the other children to notice positive behaviour in Kelly. On the first few occasions that Mark used this approach he made sure before leaving the group to work on the activity that Kelly's partner would have something to say during the feedback. This was achieved by subtle prompting.

On days when there was no suitable teaching session with a group containing Kelly, Mark planned to prompt the group she was working with to apply ideas which had been worked on previously, and to ask them briefly how things had gone at the end of the session. As this took little more than the time required to walk past the group, the only difficulty was remembering to do it. In practice it often proved easier to do this with Kelly individually. Just before the start of each session Kelly would almost invariably come up to Mark to ask about something, despite his best efforts to discourage her. He now turned this to his advantage by asking her what idea(s) she was going to try out in the following session.

Mark chose to develop a coaching programme to help Kelly:

(a)   Could he have used reinforcement and shaping, or modelling instead?

(b)   If he had done so how might he have gone about it?

(c)   What do think would have been the pros and cons of using each technique in this situation?

is speaking. What does paying attention mean? . . . Good. Can you give me an example of what you would be doing if you were paying attention? . . . Good. Paying attention means looking at a person, not interrupting, nodding and saying something about what they have said when they have finished speaking. Can you give me examples of what you might do if you were not paying attention? . . . Good. Examples of not paying attention are interrupting, reading, chatting to someone else. Which of these examples would make a discussion more interesting and enjoyable? . . . Now let's start the discussion, remembering the things that will help.

Many teachers have found that the coaching procedure provides a useful way of ensuring that the practical implications of school or class rules for acceptable social behaviour are clearly understood by all the children. Some children offer surprising examples of what they would be doing if they were 'being sensible' or 'being responsible'. Class rules are usually clearer and the children will ideally have been involved in developing them. However, it may be that most contributions to class discussion of rules are made by a small number of the most articulate children. It cannot simply be assumed that all the children really understand all the rules. This is a particularly important consideration in relation to children who have SEN and those from minority language communities. The coaching procedure offers a flexible and efficient means of checking practical understanding and remedying any misunderstanding.

Social problem-solving

Social problem-solving (SPS) programmes focus on Stage 2 of the Dodge *et al.* (1986) model – on the target child's social perception and cognition. The primary use of such programmes has been for preventive/developmental purposes. A number of studies have attempted to evaluate the effectiveness of programmes of this kind, particularly with children who show early signs of social difficulties. While most studies report gains in trained problem-solving skills, some have not found corresponding gains in broader adjustment measures such as changes in social behaviour or social acceptance in the peer group (Pellegrini and Urbain 1985).

In the UK, Thacker (1982) devised an SPS programme aimed at supporting transition to secondary school, which has also been used extensively by educational psychologists with groups and individuals in primary schools (e.g. Daniels 1990). Thacker's programme involves the following components:

- instructions in the use of the problem-solving sequence using cartoons and discussion;

- modelling of the steps involved, either live or videotaped;

- role-play, through which the group was able to explore alternatives and provide each other with feedback as to the consequences which might attach to the alternatives considered.

Pupils are taught to see problems as a normal part of life and are given an eight-point plan for dealing with them:

1 *Problem identification* – watch out for signs of upset feelings.

2 *Impulse delay* – stop and think before you act.

3 *Problem definition* – pinpoint the problem and decide on your goal.

4 *Generation of alternatives* – think of as many solutions as you can.

5 *Consideration of consequences* – think ahead to what might happen next.

6   *Implementation* – when you have a really good solution, try it.

7   *Persistence* – if your solution does not work, be sure to try again.

8   *Planning for success* – do you need to work out a step-by-step plan?

One advantage of SPS programmes is that most of the content and the examples used are drawn from the children themselves. Foster *et al.* (1996) challenge the idea that socially competent behaviours can be identified independently of the racial and ethnic context in which the child interacts. They highlight the necessity of considering the 'cultural fit' of the content of SPS programmes and advocate a flexible approach which enables diverse cultural perspectives to be represented.

If the advantages of SPS programmes are to be realized it is important that the problem-solving approach to social skills training is used within a non-judgemental classroom ethos where all alternatives suggested are accepted, pending evaluation of their consequences by the pupils. Teachers may find this difficult as it sometimes means acknowledging as a possible solution behaviour that is not sanctioned by the school. For example, if a class are discussing a situation where Peter is teasing and laughing at Simon, they will usually identify beating Peter up as one of the possible options open to Simon. If the teacher expresses disapproval the pupils are likely to close down discussion of the consequences of this alternative from their point of view. However, if the teacher accepts the pupils' suggestion neutrally as one possibility and supports them in evaluating its consequences everyone may learn a great deal more. For example, in this kind of situation teachers have reported learning that:

● Children can usually identify more negative consequences of beating someone up than teachers can. (These include consequences that did not occur to the teachers, such as 'Your clothes might get torn, then your mum will be really angry and stop your pocket money'.)

● Although schools typically have rules and sanctions against fighting, inconsistent application by staff can create an ethos where pupils feel they can get away with it. (If pupils do not identify 'You get into trouble with the teachers' as an important negative consequence of beating someone up at school, then this is uncomfortable but important information for a school to have in reviewing the implementation of its behaviour policy.)

● In one school some boys from a particular group had been told by their fathers that they were to resolve their differences in a 'manly' way and not bring negative staff attention to their ethnic group by 'telling on' each other. (In this situation the teacher was able to help the boys identify a number of 'manly' ways in which they could resolve their differences that had more positive consequences than fighting with each other.)

At the same time it is also important to appreciate that a problem-solving approach is not culturally neutral. Rotheram-Borus (1993) points out that SPS training is grounded in a world view that regards individuals as active shapers of their world. This contrasts with a 'wait and see' or 'trust to a higher power' type of philosophy that characterizes some cultures. One of the four dimensions along which Foster *et al.* (1996: 138) locate ethnically related differences in children's social behaviour is 'active, outcome orientated versus passive, accepting coping styles'. We might anticipate that problem-solving approaches would be more congruent with the predominant approach in cultural groups located at the 'active, outcome orientated' end of this dimension.

Spivack and Shure (1974) describe ways in which teachers can use 'problem-solving dialogues' to intervene in problem situations and help children resolve their difficulties for themselves. This approach can also be applied to incidents that the teacher has not seen, through having the children stage a re-enactment. Although this sounds potentially time-consuming, it can in fact save much of the time which is typically wasted in fruitless interrogation of children involved in playground incidents. If the children involved in a playground incident are upset, first wait until they are calm enough to talk. Then ask them to act out exactly what happened, the only proviso being that they must not actually make physical contact with each other. If rekindling of angry contact appears likely the children can be asked to replay the event 'in slow motion'. Primary-aged children tend to find it difficult to 'stick to a story' when required to act out what happened with others. It is important at this stage that the teacher maintains a narrow and neutral focus on sorting out the practical detail of what happened. Sometimes a child will refuse to take part. In this case an onlooker can be asked to play their part and in practice most children soon start to join in, indignantly correcting inaccuracies in the acting.

Having quickly established what has happened, the teacher can then take the children through the SPS steps, establishing:

- how each child perceived and interpreted the behaviour of others;

- how each child felt about it;

- what else they could have done and how things would then have been different;

- what can be done now and what consequences are likely to follow.

There are advantages to working through this process in the classroom, involving classmates in order to sensitize them to issues of fairness and increase their supportiveness towards children who are experiencing difficulties.

The potential advantages of involving school support staff in training are indicated from the evaluation of the SEAL pilot which reported a change in the way in which incidents were dealt with: 'They tended to shout at the children less and understood that the children needed to calm down, have time out to talk to an adult about the incident, work through why it happened and what the consequences of their actions would be. Schools reported that changes in lunchtime behaviour had a major impact on school life' (Hallam *et al.* 2006: 74).

Integrated social skills training programmes

As with social skills assessment, multi-method training programmes are generally recommended. Erwin (1994) examined 43 studies in order to evaluate the relative effectiveness of three methods: modelling, coaching and problem-solving. He concluded that social skills training produced significant improvements in pupils' levels of social interaction, sociometric status and problem-solving abilities, but that no particular training technique produced a significantly greater improvement than either of the others. It is generally recommended that intervention programmes combine different approaches in order to capitalize on the particular effects produced by each.

Spence (1995) provides a session by session guide to implementing individualized programmes with children and adolescents which incorporates a number of different methods:

- training in performance of specific basic social skills (e.g. eye contact) – techniques include instructions and discussion, modelling, role-playing, giving feedback and setting homework tasks;

- social perception skills training – components include learning about feelings, understanding and use of non-verbal social cues, relaxation training;

- training in social problem-solving skills;

- training in the use of self-instructions to guide behaviour;

- replacement of unhelpful thoughts with positive, helpful thinking;

- application of these skills to specific social problems (e.g. making friends, dealing with teasing or dealing with disagreements).

The selection of situations and skills on which to focus is important to encourage generalization or application of newly developed competencies across different situations. Elliott and Busse (1991) suggest that generalization can be facilitated by including as many of the following strategies in the programme as possible:

- teach behaviours that are likely to be valued in everyday settings and so be naturally reinforced when they occur there;

- train across people and settings that the child encounters every day;

- gradually phase out any special rewards until they blend in with those generally available in the classroom or school;

- reinforce applications of skills to new and appropriate situations;

- include peers in training.

Interventions focused on the peer group

The importance of systematically considering and targeting for intervention each of the stages of the Dodge *et al.* (1986) model has been highlighted by other studies which also found that even when low-accepted pupils show changes in their behaviour following social skills training, classmates may be slow to grant them higher social status. Pellegrini and Urbain (1985) point out that well-established friendship networks and a prior history of negative contact with the target pupil may both reduce the generalization of training effects from a social skills group to the classroom or playground. Because of this it has been suggested that other approaches, in addition to social skills training with the target pupil, may need to be implemented in order to change the perceptions, judgements and behaviour of their classmates.

Activity 16.6   Intervention programme case study

Read the following account of a social skills training programme that combined cognitively based SPS approaches and behavioural social skills training (Frederickson and Simms 1990).

(a) Think about the five stages of the Dodge *et al.* (1986) model shown in Figure 16.4 and decide which stages are targeted by the programme and which are not.

(b) How could you change the programme so that the other stages are also targeted?

The programme involved a series of eight after-school sessions each lasting 1½ hours. It was run by psychologists in an out-of-school centre for a group of eight children from seven different schools. The children had all been referred by their schools to the educational psychology service, and difficulty in relationships with other children was a major area of concern in each case. During the sessions both behavioural social skills and problem-solving strategies were taught to the children through games, discussion and role-play activities. Meetings were also held with parents and teachers to inform them about the programme, the skills that would be taught, and follow-up work which could be done at home and school.

At the end of the programme, assessment of children's SPS skills showed substantial gains, and both parents and teachers noted improvements in the specific social skills that had been taught to their children. In addition, measures of social adjustment were completed by teachers, and sociometric measures were completed by classmates. These measures were completed on three occasions: before the programme started; just after it finished; and six months later (when most of the children had changed teacher). There was clear evidence of an improvement in teacher ratings of social adjustment following the programme that was maintained six months later. However, the children's acceptance by their classmates did not improve – despite their improved adjustment and newly learned social skills.

Circle of Friends (Newton *et al.* 1996) is an inclusive approach to supporting children experiencing emotional, behavioural or social difficulties in the educational setting by enlisting the help of the other children in their class and setting up a special group or 'circle' of friends. The special group helps to set, monitor and review weekly targets in a meeting facilitated by an adult. They also provide agreed support to facilitate the focus child's inclusion and to help them achieve their targets. Encouraging results were initially reported by a number of studies using qualitative case study methodologies (Newton *et al.* 1996; Pearpoint and Forest 1992; Taylor 1996) or illuminative analysis of participant perspectives and impressions (Taylor and Burden 2000; Whitaker *et al.* 1998). More recently a small-scale controlled trial (Frederickson and Turner 2003) provided evidence for the positive impact of the approach on social acceptance by classmates at stages 4 and 5 of the model shown in Figure 16.4. However, no effect of the intervention was apparent at stages 1–3.

Frederickson *et al.* (2005) investigated the impact of different components of the circle of friends (CoF) intervention. They replicated the finding of improvements in social acceptance but not behaviour (this time peer-rated) and found that the improvements in social acceptance were produced by the whole-class meeting but gradually diminished with time. The weekly meetings of the circle of friends appeared to contribute little and it was suggested that consideration should be given to shifting the focus of the small-group meeting from general befriending and support to delivery of a structured programme to improve social behaviour and problem-solving skills. This complementary emphasis on developing both individual competencies and peer acceptance might be expected to promote maintenance of gains and further improvements. It would seem also to address some of the concerns that have been expressed about techniques such as Circles of Friends, namely, 'a clear lack of reciprocity has been one of the major problems in such relationships, with the child with disabilities consistently being the one helped or supported' (Sapon-Shevin *et al.* 1998: 105).

Interventions focused on the social situation

Interventions targeted on the social situation (Stage 1) have also received attention. For example, Johnson and Johnson (1991) have reported greater social acceptance of included special needs pupils if the classroom has been structured around cooperative group learning situations, and Siner (1993) describes a cooperative group-work approach to improving the social competence of Year 2 pupils. Cartledge and Milburn (1996) review evidence that cooperative classroom learning activities contribute to positive peer interactions, acceptance of SEN and racial differences, and academic achievement. They suggest that cooperative learning methods are particularly appropriate for ethnic groups such as African-Asian and Hispanic-Americans whose cultural roots are in collectivist rather than individualistic societies. It could equally be argued that such methods are urgently needed where children have been prepared at home and in their community only for a competitive and individualistic model of behaviour.

Frederickson and Furnham (1998b) have demonstrated that both personal and environmental factors are associated with peer-group acceptance of integrated pupils who have MLD and that these factors differ when acceptance is assessed in relation to a play as opposed to a work context. Findings such as these suggest that the design of social skills programmes for particular pupils needs to be informed by knowledge both of their individual skills and peer-group interactions, and of broader situational factors such as the ethos and social organization of the classroom and school environment. Such factors were considered in detail in Chapter 8 on the learning environment.

Conclusions

A growing appreciation of the importance of education in promoting children's social and emotional development, well-being and mental health is apparent in the new emphasis placed on these areas in government policy on SEN, the national strategies and the Ofsted inspection framework. In this chapter we have reviewed research on emotional and social competence in childhood which has been developed from different theoretical bases. A model of social interaction in children was adopted as an integrating framework, within which different theoretical strands and assessment approaches can be located. This framework was also found to be useful in analysing the multi-level integrated intervention programmes common in this area. This was particularly so for programmes of individualized support at School Action Plus, although these programmes shared many components with universal preventive programmes, such as SEAL, or standard initiatives for groups of high-risk children and their parents, such as those developed by Webster-Stratton.

17

Sensory needs

Objectives

When you have studied this chapter you should be able to:

- describe the main causes of sensory impairments and their impact on children's psychological development;
- analyse environmental factors at school that can inhibit or facilitate the inclusion of children with sensory impairments;
- outline a range of teaching strategies designed to meet the needs of pupils with sensory impairments.

Contents

Hearing impairment

- Forms and causes of hearing impairment
- Improving the conditions for effective hearing
- A social/cultural perspective on deafness
- Development of communication
- Deaf children from ethnic and linguistic minorities

Visual impairment

- Forms and causes of visual impairment
- Education

Conclusions

Hearing impairment

In this chapter we will examine the major obstacles that are encountered when there is impairment in a child's ability to use one of the two major sensory channels that underpin learning – hearing and vision. It was emphasized in Chapter 10 that children who are not proficient in their school's main language of instruction cannot easily access the full curriculum. For children with hearing impairment the development of oral language is particularly challenging. Sound is a key channel of communication for human babies from birth. In daily activities such as feeding, bathing and dressing, adults interact with babies in a lively and structured way. They notice where the baby's attention is directed and comment on it, or they say something about what they think the baby is experiencing or feeling. For hearing babies, the sounds of the speech of those around them are a constant feature of their environment – a feature which, over time, reveals itself as having pattern and meaning. The speech they hear helps them to interpret regularities in their experience and make sense of them. At the same time the sounds that they themselves make, gurgling and babbling, are treated by others as a form of communication and reinforce those around them to maintain contact. The exchange of sounds plays a crucial role in infants' cognitive and social development. These achievements depend on a very fragile and vulnerable physiological system: the ear and the hearing system, illustrated in Figure 17.1.

In the outer ear soundwaves travel along the external auditory canal and hit the eardrum (the tympanic membrane) which lies across the canal, causing it to vibrate. The vibrations are transmitted through the middle ear, an air-filled space, and greatly amplified in the process by the ossicular chain of tiny bones. The inner ear is a fluid-filled space containing the cochlea which turns the mechanical vibrations from the middle ear into electrical nerve impulses, activating fibres of the auditory nerve. Now that the sound has been detected, it must be processed and analysed in the central nervous system.

Forms and causes of hearing impairment

In order to understand hearing impairment it is necessary to appreciate two key features of sounds and how they are measured – level and frequency. *Sound level*

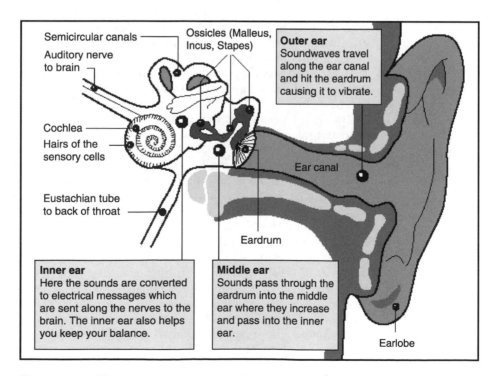

Figure 17.1 The structure of the ear and the hearing system
Source: Ridley (1991).

is the volume of a sound: it is measured in decibels (dB). At a standard distance of three feet whispered speech measures 30 dB, normal speech 60 dB and a loud shout 90 dB. *Sound frequency* is the main physical basis of our subjective impression of the pitch of a sound. Frequency largely determines whether we hear sounds as 'high' or 'low': it is measured in hertz (Hz). The lowest C on a piano is 32 Hz, the highest is just over 2000 Hz or 2 kilohertz (kHz). The normal hearing range for human beings is between 18 Hz and 18 kHz. The normal speech range is between 100 Hz and 10 kHz.

Hearing may be impaired in terms of the range of frequencies one can hear or the volume of sound or both. As far as frequency is concerned, unless a person can hear within the vital range 500 Hz–2 kHz, it is likely that their speech development will be affected. As shown on an audiogram (see Figure 17.2), a hearing loss may be 'flat' – that is, roughly equivalent for each frequency. Alternatively, it may be uneven in one or both ears. For example, there may be normal hearing for low frequencies but a loss for high frequencies (so that the graph on the right-hand side of the audiogram dips low). With that profile a child will hear vowel sounds clearly but will miss many or most consonant sounds – a pattern that may affect how they learn to read.

As far as volume is concerned, hearing impairment may involve a quite limited or very considerable level of decibel loss (see Table 17.1). It is typically described in terms of the average loss, even though the loss may vary between the two ears. A unilateral loss affecting one ear will be less severe in its psychological consequences than a bilateral loss affecting both ears. It should be noted also that the impact of any loss on development and psychological functioning will depend in part on the age of onset. A congenital loss that the child has from birth or a loss that occurs before language develops (say, before the age of 18 months) will have a greater impact than a loss that is sustained in the 'postlingual' period (i.e. after the child has developed speech and language). With all these provisos, it remains helpful to be aware of the normal impact of a characteristic overall level of hearing loss.

It has been estimated that about a fifth of all children will experience some degree of fluctuating hearing loss during their first two to three years at school (Bamford and Saunders 1991: 78). Of course, the number with permanent and severe or profound hearing loss is much smaller. A national survey in the UK reported by Fortnum *et al.* (2002) indicated that, when postnatal onset of deafness is taken into account (see Table 17.2), the prevalence of permanent hearing impairment greater than 40 dB rises to a plateau at age 9 years of at least 1.65 per 1,000 live births and may be as high as 2.05 per 1,000. At least 30 per cent of hearing-impaired children (slightly more boys than girls) were reported to have an additional disability. Incidence has declined over an extended period (Davis *et al.* 1995). Advances in medicine are partly responsible for this (e.g. following effective immunization campaigns that have led to fewer children in Western countries becoming deaf because of maternal rubella during pregnancy). However, medical advances have not had an entirely positive impact on the statistics. Among the increased numbers of children who survive after very early premature birth there is a significant proportion who experience serious hearing loss.

Hearing impairment is usually categorized in terms of the main site of the damage, as this is what normally determines the nature of the impairment:

- *Conductive*. Physical transmission of sound in the outer or middle ear is interrupted.

- *Sensorineural*. Damage to neural transmission in inner ear or auditory nerve. Also called perceptive or nerve deafness, this is less common and more serious.

- *Mixed*. Both conductive and sensorineural loss are involved.

- *Central*. Damage to the auditory nerve in the brain stem or hearing centres of the cortex. This is also known as cortical deafness.

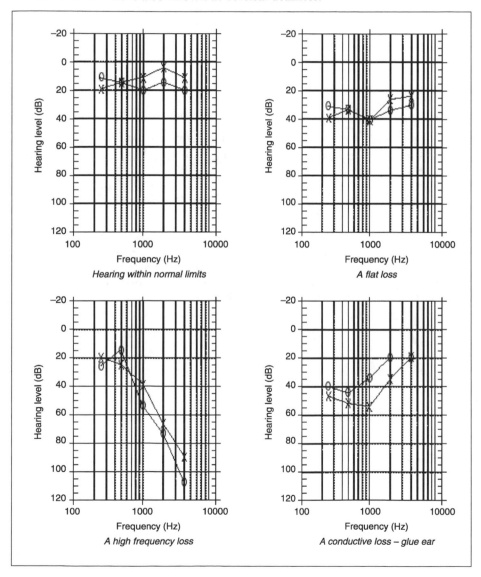

Figure 17.2 Examples of pure tone audiograms.
Source: Watson (1996).

Table 17.1 Impairment characteristic of particular levels of hearing loss

Decibel loss	Impairment*	Understanding of speech
0	None	
Up to 40	Slight–mild	Some difficulties
41–70	Moderate (53%)	Difficulty with normal speech (41–55) and loud speech (56–70)
71–95	Severe (21%)	Limited/very limited understanding of speech
96+	Profound (25%)	Rarely show understanding of speech

* Figures in parentheses show the proportion each group forms within the total UK population of hearing impaired children at school as estimated by Fortnum *et al.* (2002).

These forms of loss may be accompanied by:

- *Tinnitus*. Noises without source 'heard' in the ear/head.

- *Recruitment*. Sensorineural sufferers may experience increased volume from loud sounds.

- *Vertigo*. Giddiness experienced because the cochlea are linked to organs of balance.

The main causes of hearing impairment are summarized in Table 17.2. Overall in the past about 40 per cent of cases of hearing impairment were linked to hereditary causes. But the relative importance of different causes changes over time. For example, as noted above, maternal rubella is now very much less common in the West as a prenatal source of risk leading to childhood deafness.

Table 17.2 Main causes of hearing impairment

Type of hearing loss	Stage	Examples
Conductive	Congenital	Physical abnormality of the ear
	Acquired	Otitis media (middle ear infection)
		Glue ear
		Obstruction with wax or a small object such as a bead
Sensorineural	Prenatal	Hereditary (e.g. Usher's syndrome)
		Infections (e.g. rubella contracted by the mother)
	Perinatal	Lack of oxygen, jaundice
	Postnatal	Infections (of which the most common is meningitis)
		Damage from noise, accident, drugs and poisons

It has been estimated that 35 per cent of children with severe or profound hearing impairment have some form of impairment to their vision (Armitage *et al.* 1995). A small proportion of these will have Usher's syndrome, a genetic condition which causes both sensorineural hearing loss and progressive visual impairment. The eye condition is not evident at birth but becomes slowly worse as the child grows older. The outcome is variable, with some adults losing vision totally and others retaining central vision throughout their lives. There has been significant progress in understanding the genetics of Usher's syndrome: many of the disease-causing genes have been identified, and with further study of the pathological processes associated with these genes it is hoped that therapy will be possible in the future (Ahmed *et al.* 2003).

The impression has been given so far that a hearing loss is a stable feature of an individual's experience and that, once a person's hearing is impaired, an assessment can be made and the position summarized in a single graphical representation as an audiogram. In fact, the most common form of hearing impairment in childhood, *otitis media with effusion* (OME), fluctuates over time. If a child catches a cold with symptoms such as a runny nose, coughs and sneezes, the infection can spread into the middle ear via the Eustachian tube which leads there from the back of the throat. While the middle ear is affected, the mechanisms that enable it to conduct sound are blocked, so that the child's hearing is impaired (sometimes eventually becoming 'glue ear'). In most cases, as soon as the infection is overcome, hearing is recovered. Since some children have repeated infections, they can experience bewildering fluctuations in their ability to make sense of what is being said around them. Their language development may be affected, though the effects may be more limited than was sometimes thought in the past (Roberts *et al.* 2004). The results of studies of the impact on later educational progress (e.g. in learning to read) have been inconsistent, possibly because of variations in the socioeconomic status of the populations being assessed or differences in the sensitivity of the assessment instruments that were used (Winskel 2006). For a practical guide with a particular focus on OME and reading difficulties see Peer (2005).

It is, therefore, essential that teachers are alert to signs of unidentified hearing loss that they can look for in the classroom. All such signs can have another explanation, but they may indicate that a child has hearing difficulties. Some are particularly associated with 'glue ear'. The following list, which has been collated from a number of sources, including Webster and Wood (1989) and Watson (1996), may be helpful. It is worth raising a query about possible hearing loss if it is observed in the classroom that a child:

- is often slow to react to instructions or repeatedly asks what to do even though they have just been told;

- watches others to see what they do and then follows;

- constantly asks others to repeat what they have said;

- hears sometimes and not others, for example when standing on one side of the room and not the other;

- often misinterprets information and questions, or responds to only part of what has been said;

- is unable to locate a speaker or the source of a sound, especially in noisy conditions;

- has a tendency to daydream or shows poor concentration, especially during group discussions or when a story is being read aloud;

- makes inappropriate comments sometimes, as though not having followed the topic of conversation;

- has delayed language development (e.g. immature use of syntax, limited vocabulary);

- finds it difficult to repeat words or sounds or to remember the names of people and places;

- sometimes shouts without apparently realizing that they are being noisy;

- makes speech errors (e.g. omitting the consonants from the end of words, missing out s, f, th, t, ed, en);

- confuses words that sound similar (e.g. that, fat, vat);

- fixes their eyes on the speaker as though lip-reading;

- sometimes becomes disruptive during lessons in which children are required to listen;

- experiences difficulties with reading, spelling or writing;

- seems to have colds and coughs frequently.

Improving the conditions for effective hearing

There are three ways in which the physical conditions for effective hearing can be improved for children with hearing impairment. First, better acoustic conditions can be created in the environment. For example, if a room has a carpet, curtains and soft furnishings, the amount of background noise will be reduced so that it is easier for a person with moderate hearing impairment to detect the sound signals they need to hear. An individual deaf child can be helped by seating them in a relatively quiet part of the classroom, away from radiators, noisy equipment or windows which overlook a busy area (National Deaf Children's Society 2007). But, as so often, there is evidence that strategies designed to help a child with particular special needs in school are likely to benefit others too. In an experiment conducted in a sound booth, Blandy and Lutman (2005) showed that 7-year-old children with normal hearing thresholds did not yet have a fully developed ability to recognize speech in a noisy environment. In a study with a realistic classroom-based design, Dockrell and Shield (2006) showed that the ordinary babble of a primary class may be particularly distracting to children with a wide range of SEN – not just hearing impairment. They suggested that this result could best be explained by assuming that the children had difficulties with verbal processing which might be exacerbated in acoustically marginal classrooms.

Second, children with many (though not all) forms of hearing impairment can be helped by wearing a hearing aid. Technical improvements to these aids are being achieved all the time. It is possible to adjust aids to suit the individuals who wear them. For example, a child with high-frequency hearing loss may best be helped by an aid that amplifies those frequencies more than others. Radio hearing aids are increasingly common. With these systems the teacher wears a transmitter which is turned on when addressing the class as a whole or a group with the target child in it. The child wears a receiver which is connected to their own regular hearing aid. A system of this kind reduces the problems caused by background noise. However, new developments are typically tested initially in use with adults, and it is important to evaluate any benefits that may be experienced by children separately (e.g. McCracken 2003). For example, the potential benefits of new aids may be devalued in the minds of potential users if they feel them to be stigmatizing and 'abnormal'. Kent and Smith (2006) found that among adolescents perceptions of this kind overrode such factors as the age at fitting, the length of time since fitting, or the extent of deafness in determining whether aids were used regularly at school or not. They recommended that, when an individual fails to use their aids regularly, intervention should focus on their social context and relationships and specifically on peer group acceptance of their identity as hard of hearing.

The third (and newest) way of improving the physical conditions for hearing is a form of aid that can be fitted surgically for people with profound hearing impairment who cannot be helped with conventional hearing aids as they have irretrievable damage to their inner ear. A cochlear implant is an electronic device which bypasses the damaged area altogether, stimulating the nerve of hearing directly. For adults who have become deaf through illness or accident an implant can restore an auditory channel of communication which enables them to make use of their previously established language base. In working with most children the challenge is greater because the artificial channel of communication has to enable them to develop aural language from the basics. However, by 2007 nearly 3,000 children had received implants in the United Kingdom, and over half the profoundly deaf children starting school had a cochlear implant (Wheeler *et al.* 2007). There had been positive reports of the impact of cochlear implantation on hearing ability and on speech perception and production, but the results were highly variable, and many factors seemed to contribute to the relative success of the outcomes in an individual case. Notable among these was the child's age when the operation was carried out (Connor *et al.* 2006). Evidence on educational outcomes remains mixed but indicates, on balance, a significant improvement in core attainments compared to profoundly deaf pupils who do not have cochlear implants. Children with implants also make greater use of mainstream school provision (Thoutenhoofd 2006; Fortnum *et al.* 2007).

However, cochlear implantation remains controversial. While medical expertise and technology have improved and support and follow-up services have evolved, a separate cause for concern has continued to be expressed by some members of the deaf community. They were anxious not just that cochlear implantation programmes would raise false hopes for some parents and deaf teenagers but also that they would encourage the belief that 'getting rid of deafness' is a desirable objective (Lane 1992). This line of argument is based on a social/cultural perspective on deafness which is discussed in the next section.

Activity 17.1   Case study: John

John (aged 5) is the only child of his devoted mother who is bringing him up alone after separation from his father when he was a year old. He had meningitis at age 2 and became severely deaf. He attends a unit in an ordinary primary school where he spends about a third of his time in the mainstream Reception class. Many of the children there have learned that he is good at lip-reading and automatically turn towards him when they speak to him. But, while he understands spoken language quite well, John's own speech is halting and indistinct and his expressive language is limited. He lacks confidence in the classroom and is at his best when there are regular routines with which he is familiar. His command of number concepts is immature, and he tends to be restless during storytime. He has made only minimal progress in the underlying skills of reading.

Recently it has been suggested that he might be assessed for a cochlear implant operation. His mother is enthusiastic about this and is investing great hopes in it. The specialist teachers directly involved with John feel that she should move on from hoping for 'magical solutions'. The family doctor is cautioning her that most of the patients considered for the operation are found not to be suitable.

Draw up a balance sheet of the advantages and disadvantages of a cochlear implant operation for John from an educational and developmental perspective, assuming that the specialist advice is that the operation is medically possible.

A social/cultural perspective on deafness

The account of cochlear implants given above, which is based on advances in the medical understanding of hearing loss, inevitably makes it appear that what we are dealing with is mainly a mechanical problem. It arises because hearing is a rather fragile physiological system that can go wrong in various complex ways. As we have seen, some solutions and remedial approaches tackle the mechanical breakdown directly: a hearing aid or a cochlear implant aims to improve the efficiency of the impaired physiological system. The value of recent medical advances should not be underestimated. At the same time this should not lead us to assume that the medical perspective is the only one that has valuable insights and practical measures to offer. As with other forms of SEN, it is important to consider the role that social and communal attitudes play in the development of people with hearing impairment. In recent years increasing attention has been paid to a social/cultural perspective on deafness.

The medical/deficit perspective on deafness is based on the ideal image of an unimpaired, healthy person: to be deaf is simply to be without the ability to hear. An alternative perspective on what it means to be deaf focuses on the social and cultural status of the person in society as a whole and as a potential member of a community of deaf people. The central differences between these two perspectives are summarized in Table 17.3 which is adapted from Cline (1997a) and draws on notes in Pickersgill (1994) and discussions in Gregory (1993) and Gregory and Hindley (1996). It is possible to trace different perspectives on deafness in the words that institutions concerned with deaf people use to describe the condition (Rosen 2003). For example, those with a social/cultural perspective on deafness will distinguish between deaf persons with a small letter 'd' and Deaf persons with

Table 17.3 Alternative perspectives on deafness

	Medical/deficit perspective on deafness	Social/cultural perspective on deafness
What are the implications of deafness for the individual's independent identity?	Deafness is an inherited or acquired deficit of the sensory apparatus which inevitably leads to dependence on the hearing.	Deafness gives a person the potential for autonomous membership of a community of deaf people with a shared language, culture and heritage.
What are the implications for the development of communication skills?	Attention is focused on limitations to communication through spoken and written English; the term 'bilingualism' is little used.	Attention is often focused on a form of bilingualism in which the individual makes use of a sign language as a first language with spoken or written English as an additional language.
What are the best conditions for effective communication with others?	Successful compensatory strategies are required to overcome the hearing impairment suffered by one party in a conversation (e.g. hearing aids).	Effective communication is achieved when both parties use a wholly visual mode of communication such as British Sign Language.
What are the implications for a child's cognitive development?	Deaf children have specific and important deficits compared to hearing children.	Deaf children will show the normal range of ability to learn if they are given an effective means of access to what other children access through hearing.

a capital letter 'D'. People who are 'deaf' share the condition of not being able to hear and do not take on board the knowledge, beliefs, and practices that make up the culture of Deaf people. People who are 'Deaf' share a language, British Sign Language in the UK, as a key means of communication. They also share a culture of beliefs and practices, and participate in their society's Deaf community.

The value of the social/cultural perspective can be illustrated by considering the situation of those deaf children (5–10 per cent) who are born to parents who are themselves deaf. A research finding that has been influential in the development of current thinking has been the recognition that this small group of deaf young people fare better in their psychological development in many ways than the deaf children of hearing parents. Surveys have indicated that they tend to attain higher standards of academic achievement, report a more positive self-image and show greater self-reliance (Marschark 1993). They may also develop superior skills in predicting the behaviour of other people (Edmondson 2006). Note, though, that a distinction should be made between situations where only one parent is deaf and those where both parents are deaf. There are also differences where parents have a less substantial hearing impairment rather than being severely or profoundly deaf (Mitchell and Karchmer 2004).

The key factor in the more positive outcome for deaf children who are born to deaf parents appears to be that their family is likely to communicate using a sign language such as British Sign Language (Mitchell and Karchmer 2004). Deaf children of hearing parents will sometimes be well beyond the normal age of early language acquisition before they encounter a fluent speaker of a visual language – the only kind in which they can easily and quickly become fluent. This is bound to have an adverse effect on the child's development of communication skills. Compared to hearing parents, deaf parents of deaf children may report a more positive emotional response when their child's deafness is identified (Gregory and Hindley 1996). They tend to:

● give more frequent positive facial expressions when interacting with the child as an infant, expressions that can be considered the visual equivalent of the warm tone of voice that hearing parents typically employ with their infants;

● ensure that their infant is located where they can see the parent's hands, face and eye gaze during conversation;

● maintain their infant's attention more effectively during joint play (Gregory and Hindley 1996; Harris and Chasin 2005).

Thus the parents' response to the child's deafness is a key factor in the early development of deaf children. At least in part, this response is determined by general attitudes towards and awareness of deafness and sign language in society. Deaf parents are more likely to see their child as a potential full member of the community – the Deaf community.

In this context an important development over recent years in England has been the introduction of a Newborn Hearing Screening programme. This was intended to bring the median age when congenital deafness is identified down from 20 months to 3 months. Clinical diagnosis and the prescription of hearing aids will occur at a younger age, and crucially an initiative has been taken to increase the provision of professional support services to families after a deaf baby is identified (DfES 2003c). Previous studies in the USA had shown a significant positive impact on language development when hearing loss was identified and intervention services introduced at a younger age (Yoshinaga-Itano 2003). An important change is that, instead of deafness being diagnosed on the instigation of parents who had noticed 'something wrong', it was now identified as the result of a routine, medical screening procedure that was not reliant on the observations of those close to the child. In addition, because it occurs very early in the development of a relationship between parents and child, information about the child's deafness may be more easily integrated into their experiences of getting to know each other. Young and Tattersall (2007) who made that observation interviewed a small sample of hearing parents whose infants had been correctly identified as deaf during the first phase of the English screening programme. They reported that the parents were pleased to have learned about their child's deafness at an early stage but that they still faced complex challenges when adjusting to the unexpected reality of having a deaf baby in a hearing family.

Development of communication

Early years

There are differences in language development between deaf and hearing children from the outset. Although the speech sounds they make when babbling are initially similar, by 7–10 months of age the babbling of hearing babies has become significantly more complex while that of children with severe or profound prelinguistic hearing loss has become more limited (Stoel-Gammon and Otomo 1986). Their continuing development will be influenced by the forms of communication to which they are exposed. Within a deaf family where sign language is the normal mode of communication, they may develop simplified, playful hand movements with primitive elements of sign language – a form of 'manual babbling' (Petito and Marentette 1991). Within a hearing family, hearing mothers speak as much to their deaf child as they do to hearing children of the same age, and they modify their speech in similar ways (Gallaway and Woll 1994). In fact, they may adapt to the visual needs of their children, using visual communication more than mothers of hearing children and using touch more often to get the child's attention (Lederberg and Everhart 1998). But giving deaf infants this input does not mean that they understand it or even that they perceive it. The mothers in Lederberg and Everhart's study made little use of sign language with the children, even when they had attended signing classes. As is universally found in such studies, the deaf children's oral language development was severely delayed from an early stage.

Wood *et al.* (1986) analysed in some detail the preverbal stages of development that lead a deaf child to achieve effective involvement in a two-way conversation. They emphasized the changing nature of the child's participation and suggested strategies that adults can use to support a child with mild to moderate hearing loss towards fuller participation. For example, if a child appears disengaged and unaware that they are being addressed, the adult may follow the child's line of gaze and comment on what they are looking at; if the child begins to

---

Activity 17.2   Analysing a child's communication skills

Marschark (1993: vii) describes an incident when he was first becoming interested in the psychology of deaf children. A 4-year-old girl who was deaf visited the centre where he was working. He was asked to look after her for an hour or so in a preschool observation room while her mother and grandmother were taking part in a research project elsewhere in the building:

> My signing skills were just below beginner level then, and it did not take long for my companion to discover that fact. At one point we were looking through the observation mirror at a dramatic play center that included a 'kitchen'. My companion pointed into the room, turned to me, and made a sign. When I failed to respond, she took it (quite correctly) as a lack of comprehension. She then pantomimed putting bread into a toaster, pushing it down, taking out the finished toast, and taking a bite. Then she repeated the sign, TOAST. I was awestruck. . . .

Why do you think Marschark was awestruck? What might he have concluded from the episode about the child's communication skills?

attend to what is being said, the adult may respond contingently to the child's glances, gestures or vocalizations; if the child offers vocalizations that are word-like though not easily intelligible, the adult may take up the child's utterances and respond to the apparent intended meaning.

Hearing children acquire a significant proportion of their concepts, vocabulary and knowledge of the structure of language incidentally through overhearing adults and other children, through the media and through partici-pating in group conversations. Opportunities for incidental learning of this kind are much more limited for those with hearing impairment (Gregory *et al.* 1995). All too often, deaf learners are in the position of asking what is being said in a group conversation (or a lesson) and being told: 'It's not important'. Sub-sequently, as with younger children, surveys of deaf adolescents have found that their oral language skills, use of syntax and vocabulary are depressed on average compared to those of hearing peers. For example, teachers of two samples of 16-year-old deaf pupils in mainstream schools in England informed Powers (1996, 1998) that almost one quarter of each group were unable to communicate easily through speech (while over 80 per cent were unable to communicate easily through sign language). The debate on school policies on sign language education and 'bilingual education' is discussed below.

School years

It is clear, then, that the primary challenge in educating deaf children lies in help-ing them to develop effective means of communication with others. A wide range of strategies has evolved for this purpose, and there has been intense controversy on the subject for more than a century. An influential International Congress for the Deaf in 1880 resolved that: 'considering the incontestable superiority of speech over signs in restoring the deaf-mute to society and giving him a more perfect knowledge of the language, the Congress declares that the oral method ought to be preferred to that of signs for the education and instruction of the deaf and dumb' (quoted in Markides 1991).

Very slowly over the last 30 years the downgrading of manual communication has been overturned. Finally, in the UK, after a struggle lasting well over a century, the Deaf community achieved one of its key objectives: in 2003 the government granted official recognition to BSL as a language. This change was partly motiv-ated by persuasive group advocacy and partly by convincing research evidence. Psychological studies had shown that the cognitive and social development of deaf children suffers if they are not given access to visually mediated forms of communication (Marschark 1993). In addition, linguists had recognized that the various national sign languages have all the main characteristics of an oral language (Kyle and Woll 1983). Finally, educational research had shown that oral methods do not enable most deaf pupils to keep up with their peers in basic aspects of the school curriculum (Powers *et al.* 1998).

At the same time, pressure from within the deaf community had built up to facilitate the official use of signing. A young deaf woman in an adult education group in Manchester expressed the feelings of many:

> My family don't like me to sign because they say I will lose my voice. They don't want me to go to the Deaf Club very often. My Gran thinks I have wasted her time because when I was young she tried very hard to teach me . . .

I know my Gran tried to do what's best for me, but she doesn't realise I need some friends who are Deaf. If I get friendly with hearing people we can understand each other but I often feel left out because hearing friends can talk to each other and not me. It feels like I'm wasting my time. I need to sign to talk to Deaf people. It can make me very happy and understand more. Sometimes I have fun with them and I am never left out with Deaf people.

(Cripps 1996)

Educators have not found it easy to develop an approach to the teaching of communication that takes account of all this evidence, builds on the skills of existing teachers and also meets the needs of the deaf community. American Sign Language, British Sign Language and other sign languages do not follow the structure of an oral language but have a completely different kind of syntax. This means that a child learning American Sign Language or British Sign Language is not at the same time directly laying the basis for oral communication in English. So a variety of supplementary communication strategies have been developed to support the learning of English by deaf people. These are shown in Figure 17.3.

Such approaches all emphasize the use of a visual/gestural system to facilitate an ultimate goal of using oral English fluently. Educational methods that employ visual and oral methods together with that aim ('total communication' methods) may be contrasted with 'oral' approaches in which language is developed through lip-reading and the use of residual hearing, together with amplification. Total

Cued speech	Many phonemes look similar when we mouth them. As a result, lip-reading is fraught with ambiguities and confusions. In cued speech different hand positions are employed together with speech to facilitate lip-reading.
Finger spelling	The 26 letters of the English alphabet are represented by 26 hand positions. These can be used (rather laboriously) to spell out words in English. This system appears to be used most often in schools for the deaf to support work on literacy skills (Baker and Child 1993).
Manually Coded English	American term for Sign Supported English (see below).
Signed English	A system that represents the English language grammatically in a manual, visual form. The signs for most words are based on signs used in British Sign Language, but these are supplemented by a set of specially devised grammatical signs and markers. The speaker speaks and signs simultaneously. Signed English is intended to help a deaf listener to interpret ambiguities in the oral language that arise because of limited hearing.
Sign Supported English	Signed English without the grammatical markers. Only key words are signed in the expectation that this alone will be sufficient to facilitate comprehension.

Figure 17.3 Supplementary communication strategies to support deaf people in learning English

communication approaches became increasingly popular in UK schools for the deaf during the late 1970s and the 1980s compared to exclusively oral methods (Child 1991). But over the last 20 years there has been increasing pressure to take the possibility of bilingualism more seriously and to plan education on that basis. In this context in the UK bilingual education means teaching British Sign Language as a first language while English is taught as a second language. Key features of what has become known as *sign bilingual education* include the following (Knight and Swanwick 2002; Gregory 2004):

- Equal status is given to BSL and English as the languages of teaching and learning.

- Preschool support is given to enable a child and their family to develop both BSL and English at an age-appropriate point. For families who mainly speak a language other than English at home that language will also be a focus for preschool support.

- At school the teaching of BSL aims to develop children's skills to the point where they can use it to access complex ideas within the curriculum, as is done for hearing children with English.

- Early attention is given to writing since this allows a deaf child whose first language is sign language 'to think in their first language and control the use of the second as they choose the elements to be written down. Reading on the other hand means that they have to work from their second language where they have no direct control over the material and then translate back into their first language' (Gregory 2004: 116).

- Curriculum assessments are conducted in the child's first language.

- Native users of both BSL and English contribute fully to the child's education.

After the earlier suppression of sign languages there has been an understandable reaction in the form of high hopes of bilingual education. It is not a panacea, and there are many outstanding challenges. For example, Gregory *et al.* (cited in Gregory and Hindley 1996) found that deaf children in bilingual education programmes do usually become competent communicators in sign language. But the children in these programmes who develop relatively complex signing are mainly those with a signing background from a deaf family. The authors suggested that in such programmes children may sometimes receive inconsistent models of signing. Some of the hearing adults who work with them are still learning to sign themselves, and the deaf adults may modify their own language to accommodate the hearing people with whom they work. The passionate debate between those advocating oral methods and those favouring bilingual approaches continues.

In any case, bilingual approaches have only been available for a minority. There is a much more powerful trend in deaf education, as in SEN provision generally, that has nothing to do with the development of language or communication *per se*. That trend is for an increasing proportion of the children to be placed in mainstream schools and for the pupils of special units to spend more of their time in ordinary classrooms. By 2006 75 per cent of children with hearing impairment in England who had SEN statements were being educated in primary or secondary schools rather than in special schools (DfES 2006d). There is a risk that their particular communication needs will be overlooked in these settings. Observational studies have shown that there is a temptation for the children to adopt undemanding strategies in order to get by – for example copying another child or nodding instead of answering a question orally (Gregory and Bishop 1991). A major challenge for teachers is to ensure that a deaf child in a mainstream class is a full and active participant. Some studies have reported positive evaluations by specialist teachers of the outcomes for children with hearing impairment in mainstream settings both in terms of academic progress and social inclusion – for example, an Australian study by Power and Hyde (2002). Studies in the UK have indicated that pupils with hearing impairment in special schools achieve weaker academic results than those in mainstream schools, but, since there is a tendency for the special schools to have children with more severe and complex forms of impairment, we cannot draw conclusions about educational effectiveness from this comparison (Powers 2002).

Wherever they are educated, children with hearing impairment face major challenges in developing basic academic skills that are not experienced by their hearing peers: they must find alternative routes to reading and spelling that avoid the reliance that hearing pupils place on phonological skills (Kyle and Harris 2006), and they require a systematic approach to learning mathematics that compensates for their lack of experience of some forms of incidental learning that are encountered by hearing children in everyday life (Nunes 2004). A shift to mainstream schooling does not reduce the need for pupils with hearing impairment to receive specific support that is tailored to meet their very particular educational needs. Powers (2002: 237–8) argued that good practice in inclusion for deaf pupils requires the following:

1 a whole school approach to special needs where all staff in a school share responsibility for all students and where the school promotes an ethos of acceptance of disability and difference; specifically where the school promotes positive attitudes to deafness and deaf people, ensuring that deaf students feel valued members of the community;

2 regular opportunities for successful interaction between deaf students and hearing students whether in mainstream schools and classes or in other contexts;

3 regular opportunities for deaf students to interact with other deaf students and to make deaf friends;

4 an effective communication environment, according to the competencies and needs of the student;

5 access for deaf students to the formal curriculum through a flexible response to individual need, including in mainstream contexts effective strategies by teachers to meet the needs of all students, but also where there are appropriate opportunities for small group or individual tutorial work;

6 teachers (mainstream and specialist) and learning support assistants who have the necessary knowledge, skills, and attitudes to effectively teach and support deaf students;

7 the involvement of deaf students in extracurricular activities, providing them with opportunities to develop leisure interests and social skills and to make friends with hearing and deaf students;

8 access for deaf students to Deaf culture;

9 access for deaf students to d/Deaf adult role models;

10 the involvement of deaf students in decisions that affect them, for example, over educational placement and curriculum;

11 the involvement of parents in decisions that affect their deaf children, for example, over educational placement and curriculum;

12 the involvement of deaf adults, including members of the Deaf community, in policy making for deaf children;

13 high academic and nonacademic achievement for deaf students.

Activity 17.3   Evaluating the Classroom Participation Questionnaire for children with hearing impairment

A research team in Arizona and New York State has developed a questionnaire for children with hearing impairment that is designed to assess the degree to which students who are placed in mainstream classrooms are enjoying full participation there (Antia *et al.* 2007). Items from the short form of their questionnaire are listed below. Review these items in the light of your studies of the development and education of deaf children.

● Is each of these items necessary and important?

● Are there any issues that you regard as important that have been omitted from this questionnaire?

Understanding Teachers

I understand my teacher

I understand my teacher when she gives me homework assignments

I understand my teacher when she answers other students' questions

I understand my teacher when she tells me what to study for a test

Understanding Students

I understand the other students in class

I join in class discussions

I understand other students during group discussions

I understand other students when they answer my teacher's questions

Positive Affect

I feel good about how I communicate in class

I feel relaxed when I talk to my teacher

I feel happy in group discussions in class

I feel good in group discussions in class

Negative Affect

I feel frustrated because it is difficult for me to communicate with other students

I get upset because other students cannot understand me

I get upset because my teacher cannot understand me

I feel unhappy in group discussions in class

Deaf children from ethnic and linguistic minorities

The education of deaf children from ethnic and linguistic minorities presents particular challenges. This group is growing fast, but there has been relatively little systematic research on its size and characteristics. A survey of children under 5 with sensorineural hearing loss in England found that 18.8 per cent of that population were from ethnic minority backgrounds, of which the largest group (12.2 per cent) were from the Indian, Pakistani and Bangladeshi communities. In the area covered by the 12 inner London boroughs over half the affected population was from ethnic minority backgrounds. These proportions are markedly higher than would be expected from the communities' numbers in the general population (Turner 1996). Over-representation was particularly marked in the case of children from South Asian communities. In studies in which the over-inclusive category 'South Asian' has been analysed further, it has emerged that it is the Pakistani and Bangladeshi groups who show the highest rate of over-representation (Powers 1996; DfES 2005c).

There have been serious concerns about the ability of existing services to respond to the specific needs of deaf children from ethnic minority communities (Sharma and Love 1991). In the services covering the areas surveyed by Turner (1996) the number of qualified staff able to converse in a minority language was very small indeed. For example, 10 of the 12 inner London boroughs had no such staff at all, although over half the children they served came from ethnic minority communities. This is an issue often highlighted by South Asian parents when asked to evaluate the services offered to them – for example, the parent interviewed by Meherali and quoted in Gregory and Bishop (1991: 58). Many teachers of the deaf shared the parents' frustration and would have liked to see specialist interpreting services shared across local authority areas (Turner and Lynas 2000). However, there is no evidence that services of this kind have increased since then.

Surveys in both the UK (Powers 1996) and the USA (Holt and Allen 1989) have shown that deaf children from black and ethnic minority communities perform significantly less well on some measures of academic achievement than white deaf children. Powers's (1996: 114) analysis of English GCSE results suggested that it was 'not quite ethnic background itself that is the significant factor but rather the language used in the home'. But commentators have identified a wider range of factors that may disadvantage these groups of deaf pupils. A key issue for some appears to be that the early development of communication skills may be even more difficult when deaf children are exposed to different languages inside and outside the home (Mahon 2003). But tensions around the negotiation of personal identity may be a central factor for many (Atkin *et al.* 2002). Factors that relate specifically to education include the predominance of white teachers in specialist work with the deaf, the impact of the low socioeconomic status of some ethnic minority communities and the impact of language differences (Powers *et al.* 1998). In seeking appropriate measures to meet the challenge, analysts have drawn equally on insights deriving from specialists in deaf education and specialists in EAL and multicultural teaching.

In addition to tackling the staffing and discrimination issues noted earlier, the following elements have been suggested as important to a strategy for the future:

- measures to reverse negative teacher attitudes and expectations;

- improvements to parent–teacher communication as a basis for partnership;

- the introduction and celebration of the cultural traditions of ethnic minorities in the curriculum;

- the clarification of difficult issues in school language policy, such as whether greater emphasis should be placed on English or on a community language as a child's first oral language and what guidance to give parents on the use of language(s) with their child at home (Chamba *et al.* 1998);

- support for teachers to foster sensitivity and commitment in helping children to develop a strong dual personal identity as black *and* deaf;

- information materials on deaf education in community languages and information materials on minority religions and cultures in British Sign Language (Cohen *et al.* 1990; Meherali 1994).

The list focuses on school measures. There are many social factors outside school that may also have the effect of depressing the children's educational performance. The most important of these are probably the obstacles that deafness places in the way of what Meherali (1994) has called the 'immunization' provided by familiar and positive relationships within the family and immediate ethnic group against the threats posed outside in the broader society. Many children in ethnic minority communities experience sociocultural dissonance – stress and a sense of incongruity caused by belonging to two cultures: a minority culture and the dominant culture of the society where one lives (Chau 1989). For deaf children in hearing families in minority communities the balm of communicating about those stresses with others who share them may not be easily available.

Activity 17.4   Deaf children from ethnic minority communities

Zehra, aged 15

Zehra is 15 and comes from a Turkish-speaking Muslim family. There is no family history of hearing impairment. She is profoundly deaf and uses Sign Supported English in school. She is also exposed to British Sign Language which is used by the majority of her peers in school. She lives in a large city where she is able to attend a day school for the deaf and continue living at home. Her school employs a total communication strategy.

Recently the school staff and her parents identified small changes in the way Zehra performs everyday tasks. After a further medical examination she was identified as having Usher's syndrome, which means she is progressively losing her sight.

Zehra's parents do not speak English. They are described by a family member as a very traditional Turkish family with a strong Muslim faith. Zehra's older sister Sibel attends all the meetings in school regarding Zehra's progress. Sibel works in a bank and speaks fluent English.

At a recent review meeting in school all the professionals were concerned that Zehra should be helped to lead as independent a life as possible as a teenager for as long as her condition allows.

Imagine that you are a teacher contributing to this review. How would you respond to the following questions and challenges?

● What factors would you suggest need to be taken into account in planning Zehra's educational future?

● What further information would you seek during the review in order to ensure that any decisions that are made have a firm basis?

● Are there any stereotypes which you might expect to influence the views expressed by professionals or the family in this situation?

● What could you do to minimize the impact of stereotyped thinking?

Thaeba, aged 10

Thaeba comes from an Urdu-speaking family. She has severe bilateral sensori-neural hearing loss which has recently been identified as having swiftly deteriorated to profound levels of loss in both ears. She is a member of a unit for partially hearing pupils using oral/aural approaches to communication. Her speech, which was previously quite good, is gradually deteriorating too. Thaeba has started to learn a few signs in Sign Supported English with her speech and language therapist to support her communication. It has now been agreed that Thaeba will transfer to a local school for the deaf at the start of the next academic year, where she will learn Sign Supported English as part of a total communication approach.

Thaeba attends a community school every Saturday to learn to read and write in Urdu. Thaeba's mother asks for your opinion as to whether she should let Thaeba continue attending Saturday school. She also wants to know what to do about learning to sign and if all the family should learn and attend classes.

Consider the following:

● What factors do you think should be taken into account in answering the questions Thaeba's mother wishes to pose?

● What further information would be needed in order to give sound advice?

Visual impairment

For sighted people seeing is virtually the same as consciousness. For most of the time, to be conscious is to have one's eyes open, and thus to see. There are exceptions: sighted people tend to close their eyes for a moment when they are deep in thought, or in order to concentrate on music, or when kissing. Usually however we return to consciousness from sleep with the opening of our eyes, and we prepare for sleep as our eyelids become heavy.

John Hull, the teacher educator who wrote that, had lost his sight himself some 20 years earlier. He argued that the equation of consciousness with vision means that a sighted teacher must make a challenging leap of imagination and empathy to cross the barrier between their world and that of a pupil who has severely impaired vision (Hull 2004). That leap is probably the more formidable because public attitudes towards visual impairment have mixed fear and awe for a very long time (Wagner-Lampl and Oliver 1994).

The connotations of the word 'blind' in English also include concealment (as in 'blind experiment' and 'blind corner') and ignorance (as in 'blind stupor' and 'blind prejudice') (Bolt 2004). But just as some Deaf people and organizations have argued for the continued use of the term 'Deaf' to describe them, organizations such as the National Federation of the Blind in the United States have resisted the use of person-first terms to describe blindness. The Federation resolved at its 1993 annual convention:

> We believe that it is respectable to be blind, and although we have no particular pride in the fact of our blindness, neither do we have any shame in it. To the extent that euphemisms are used to convey any other concept or image, we deplore such use. We can make our own way in the world on equal terms with others, and we intend to do it.
>
> (Jernigan 1993)

In this chapter, as throughout the book, we have tried to use phrases such as 'children with visual impairment' and 'blind children' carefully in ways that reflect their connotations as clearly as possible. You may judge as a reader how far we have succeeded and make your own decisions on what terminology to use to refer to this and other forms of special educational need.

Children with visual impairment form a small proportion of the overall population of those who have SEN – 1.8 per cent of those with SEN statements in England in 2006 according to DfES (2006d). There is some evidence that children from Bangladeshi and Pakistani backgrounds are over-represented in this population (Schwarz *et al.* 2002; Lindsay *et al.* 2006). The official prevalence data are difficult to interpret because of variations in the definitions used and in service provision. A major review of the UK literature by Tate *et al.* (2005) concluded by using 'a broad and pragmatic definition of visual loss sufficiently bad as to mean a child is identified as being in need of special educational or social services'. This led to an estimated prevalence across the UK of visual impairment in the region of 10–20 per 10,000 children. For severe visual loss, this team placed greatest reliance on a study by Rahi and Cable (2003) which estimated that the cumulative incidence of blindness or severe visual impairment by the age of 16 years was 5.9 per 10,000 children.

Forms and causes of visual impairment

Light enters the eye at the cornea, is refracted (bent) there and passed back to the retina (see Figure 17.4). The light-sensitive cells in the retina generate an electrical message that is sent through the optic nerve to the visual centre in the cerebral cortex. There the information is processed and turned into an image. Different areas of the visual cortex are devoted to different aspects of vision – colour, the shape of objects, movement, and so on. A major achievement of the visual system is that it instantaneously analyses these separate aspects and integrates them so that we see the world about us as a coherent and seamless whole, something we can make sense of and negotiate our way around.

Problems can occur in each stage of this process because of a malformation or malfunctioning of the eye, the optic nerve or the visual system within the cerebral cortex:

- Vision may become blurred.

- The system may work well with objects that are close but not with those that are more distant (short-sightedness or myopia), or vice versa (long-sightedness or hyperopia).

- There may be gaps in the visual field (affecting peripheral vision or central vision).

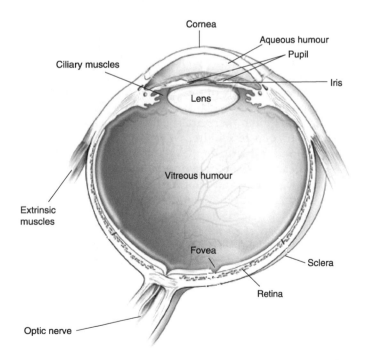

Figure 17.4   Structure of the eye
Source: R.F. Thompson (2000).

- There may be excessive sensitivity to light.

- There may be confusion over colour discrimination.

- The processing of visual information in the brain may be defective.

Some common childhood problems should normally be treated before a child comes to school – for example, strabismus (or squint) which may lead to weak binocular vision if left untreated. However, if a child's preschool years were spent in a developing country or a war zone, there may be outstanding visual problems that teachers would not normally see in a Western country.

Causes of problems in the visual system include genetic factors such as albinism, infectious diseases during pregnancy, and diseases and injury during birth or during childhood. The specific cause of some eye conditions may vary in different cases. For example, a *cataract* (which leads to loss of transparency in the lens of the eye) may be inherited or may be caused by infection during pregnancy or through an accident during childhood. Another example of a severe condition that may have different causes is *optic nerve atrophy* (ONA). In this condition the optic nerve is not able to carry information from the eye to the cortex for processing. A quantity of the nerve fibres (axons) are damaged so that the brain does not receive full vision information and sight becomes blurred. ONA can affect one or both eyes. It may also be progressive. Among the causes of ONA are tumours of the visual pathways, inadequate blood or oxygen supply before or shortly after birth, trauma and heredity. If the cause is a tumour, the process may be halted by removing the tumour, but otherwise it is normally irreversible.

Many of the problems of the eye are now prevented or treated in developed countries (e.g. through the vaccination programme that has made maternal rubella during pregnancy a rare disease). The effect of this is that one of the most frequent causes of visual difficulties in childhood in these societies is damage or malfunctioning of the visual cortex. It was the cause of blindness in 50 per cent of pupils at a Scottish special school for the blind surveyed by Alagaratnam *et al.* (2002), and there are suggestions that the prevalence may be even higher in the subgroup of children who have multiple disabilities (Frebel 2006). In *cortical visual impairment* (CVI) the child's problems may not be recognized quickly because the eyes are not damaged. This complex condition is not currently well understood, and efforts to classify its different forms continue. For example, its current name may come to be replaced by *cerebral visual impairment* to reflect the finding that the damage is often in cerebral areas outside the cortex (Frebel 2006). A range of problems has been reported with CVI – 'problems with clarity of vision, colour vision, contrast perception, field of vision, movement detection, visual memory, crowding, dealing with complex visual scenes, visual fatigue, recognition, orientation and mobility in the three-dimensional world'. From the meeting with parents and relatives at which that list was generated, McKillop *et al.* (2006) reported that 'every child exhibited a range of these problems to a varying degree and many of the problems diminished with age, but all had associated social problems'. They noted that the parents had developed many coping strategies to improve their child's everyday life and highlighted the value of drawing on family observations and experiences to help develop expertise in a challenging area of work.

Visual impairment is often associated with other disabilities, especially when the visual loss is severe (Rahi and Cable 2003). In the special school surveyed by Alagratnam and his colleagues three-quarters of the children had an additional impairment – severe or profound learning difficulties (27%), epilepsy (22%), physical disabilities (19%) and hearing loss (7%). Many of the children had multiple impairments because of brain injury, for example with a combination of visual impairment, cerebral palsy, learning difficulties and epilepsy (Alagaratnam *et al.* 2002: 559). A national survey covering children with less severe levels of visual impairment found that of the 23,860 pupils reported by local authority specialist visual impairment services:

- 49.8% had visual impairment without additional disabilities;

- 18.4% had visual impairment with additional disabilities such as sensory, physical and/or mild to moderate learning difficulties;

- 30.3% were 'multi-disabled, visually impaired', that is, had visual impairment alongside multiple difficulties including severe or profound learning difficulties;

- 1.4% were deafblind, that is, had visual and hearing impairment of sufficient severity to warrant substantial curriculum intervention/differentiation but without severe or profound learning difficulties (derived from Keil and Clunies-Ross 2003: Table 1).

Complex and severe special needs may sometimes be treated as a priority in a child's care and education, masking significant visual impairments.

The conventional measurement of degree of loss of vision focuses on a person's ability to resolve fine detail when reading a chart at a standard distance (the Snellen chart). The point of reference is what a person with normal vision can read at a distance of 6 metres or 20 feet:

6/6–6/18   *Normal vision.*
<6/18   *Low vision.* The person can read at 6 m what a normally sighted person can read at more than 18 m. At the more severe end of this range they will require low-vision aids and special text.
<3/60   *Blind.* The person can read at 3 m what a normally sighted person can read at 60 m or more. Eligible for registration as blind. Special teaching methods and materials will be required.

This classification provides a useful basis for medical description and administrative registration, but for the purposes of educational planning their *functional vision* is of greater relevance. Key questions concern their likely needs in school, such as those listed by Miller and Ockelford (2005: 5):

- Is the child likely to need additional help with dressing and eating skills?

- Is there a need to give specific consideration to lighting conditions either to reduce light/glare or to customize task lighting?

- Will the child need specialist mobility training to learn her way around?

- Should special consideration be given to stimulating vision?

- Is the child likely to need opportunities to learn through touch rather than vision?

- Should particular attention be paid to helping the child develop effective listening skills?

The answers to those questions may not map exactly onto a simple measure of visual acuity.

Education

Identification

This chapter is mainly concerned with children whose serious problems of vision will have been identified well before they start school. But some less severe problems may have been overlooked until they emerge under the pressure of the close, detailed tasks of the classroom. Signs that a child may need a vision test include:

- physical symptoms such as clouding in the eyes, frequently swollen, sore or inflamed eyes, watery eyes, erratic eye movements, frequent rubbing of the eyes after periods of close work;

- indicators of problems with eye–hand coordination such as unusual difficulty in throwing or catching a ball;

- indicators of problems with gross motor skill coordination such as unusual care in climbing or descending stairs or when moving about in an unfamiliar room;

- indicators of strain or effort when examining something visually such as frowning a good deal, screwing the eyes up, squinting at the material, moving the head a good deal or tilting it, holding the material very close to the eyes or a long way from them, becoming fatigued more quickly than most children when working on a task involving visual attention and concentration;

- adapting classroom routines to make them more convenient, for example copying from a neighbour rather than the whiteboard;

- presenting written work that is regularly untidy, where writing is not on the line when using lined paper or is poorly spaced perhaps with occasional omissions.

Of course, there may be another explanation, but if the signs persist and, in particular, if there are several of them in combination, it is worth exploring the possibility that the child has an unidentified visual defect (Bostock 1988; Kenefick 2002).

The school environment

From birth infants learn by exploring the world around them through their senses. Vision plays a substantial role in most of their incidental and spontaneous learning and is crucial to the development of mobility and independence. A child with impaired vision will not be able to integrate information that impinges on other senses from a distance (e.g. a sound heard at a distance). They will learn best from what they can reach or put in their mouths, but their difficulties in directing their hands to where they think things are in space will limit the range of objects that are brought within touch. Their concept development may be fragmented and delayed. The environment around them may play a particularly critical role in the development of blind children in facilitating learning (Pérez-Pereira and Conti-Ramsden 1999).

In schools there will be two major objectives in planning the environment when pupils with visual impairment are admitted – safety and access. It is important to encourage independence. Around the school children with visual impairment may need particular consideration at times when areas such as corridors or stairways are crowded with pupils. Decorating in bold, contrasting colours will be helpful and may be supplemented by simple measures like surrounding a light switch with brightly coloured tape. Extensive shiny surfaces on walls or floors may create glare. We have already noted that carpeting which keeps the ambient noise level down is helpful to children with hearing impairment. It is also of value for children with visual impairment as they are dependent on listening carefully both for learning purposes and to check their position within a room. Detailed guidance on further points such as the lighting of staircases and the textured marking of the edge of an outdoor path may be found in a very helpful chapter on environmental issues in Arter *et al.* (1999). Guidance on auditing the school environment where children have multiple disabilities and visual impairment may be found in Naish *et al.* (2004).

In the classroom teachers need to position demonstrations and presentations against a contrasting background and away from any glare (e.g. taking care not to stand by a window where they might appear in silhouette). They need to ensure that children with visual impairment are given reading and writing materials on paper that is not shiny or glossy so that it is non-reflective. Accommodations such as adjustable desk tops or book stands may be of value so as to make it possible to study work at a close distance without adopting an awkward sitting position. However, Arter *et al.* (1999) point out that some pupils may resist any arrangement that makes them feel different from others. If the layout of the classroom and arrangements for storage are clear and are maintained consistently, it can be very helpful.

Curriculum support

Arter *et al.* (1999) emphasized the time pressures on pupils with visual impairments in mainstream schools. They are likely to take longer to complete many classroom tasks and to experience fatigue in the process. When they are being taught in mainstream classrooms, teachers also need to bear in mind a number of factors that may impact on their access to the general curriculum that is being studied by all pupils. Firstly, they are likely to experience fatigue if using low-vision aids and looking at things from an unusual position for any length of time. Secondly, they will only develop a sense of independence in school that can transfer outside if staff make a conscious effort to facilitate that and insist on it. Children should have responsibility for organizing and taking care of their own belongings. When they are offered any support from a learning support assistant, it should be given in a manner that maximizes their ability to find their own way and manage self-care skills themselves. In addition, careful attention needs to be given to the provision of appropriate resources. There is some evidence, for example, that the provision of school textbooks in Braille and large print in England, Wales and Northern Ireland is unsatisfactory and that blind and partially sighted pupils do not always have equal access to school textbooks in alternative formats (Keil *et al.* 2006).

In addition, the children have additional learning needs over and above their peers and outside the National Curriculum. The following list includes areas highlighted by Arter *et al.* (1999) and Douglas and McLinden (2005):

- They need to develop, practice and generalize orientation, mobility and independence skills (Pavey *et al.* 2002).

- They need to learn how to use any residual vision that they have to maximum effect, for example through adaptive technology and low-vision aids such as magnifiers.

- They need to develop the use of other senses to maximum effect too, for example listening and tactual skills.

- They need to learn to use ICT to its fullest potential (Douglas 2001).

- They need to develop literacy skills with print or with special codes such as Moon or Braille.

The teachers who are responsible for a child with a visual impairment in a mainstream classroom will reasonably expect to receive specialist support and guidance. Arranging this may be a particular problem because of the low frequency of visual impairment which means that specialist services may be a considerable distance away. The support may be provided by a qualified teacher of the visually impaired who may be employed by a local authority peripatetic advisory service and visit the school on a regular basis or may work out of a resource base for the visually impaired within a school. The specialist teacher is likely to work both directly with the pupil (undertaking specialist teaching of key skills that are specifically associated with visual impairment) and also with the mainstream teachers (helping them to improve their confidence and knowledge in teaching the rest of the curriculum with this child). Examine Activity 17.5 in which you are asked to reflect on what is needed in each of those aspects of support.

Teachers have found working with pupils who are deafblind particularly challenging, because they cannot employ the normal strategy of helping children to develop special skills in the use of one major sense modality in order to compensate for weakness in the other. The extent of a child's difficulties with communication, mobility and understanding will depend on their age when impairment in each sense was established and the severity of the impairment in each area. They are a very small group: 340 in total up to the age of 16 across England, Scotland and Wales in the survey by Keil and Clunies-Ross (2003). For detailed discussions of the education of children who are deafblind see McLinden and McCall (2002) and Miller and Hodges (2005), and for a paper that focuses on their early care and education see Murdoch (2004).

Activity 17.5 What is needed from specialist teachers of children with visual impairment working to support mainstream schools

Examine the account that is given below of the role of specialist teachers in mainstream settings. Reflect on which aspects of the role would be particularly important if a specialist teacher was working in a school known to you and aimed to provide support when one of the following children were placed in the school:

(a) Jane (aged 4), a child with low vision who is comfortable when playing or working on her own but lacks confidence in the company of her peers and tends to avoid popular areas of the classroom in her early years setting. She has a hereditary condition which meant she has had very limited vision since birth. Both gross and fine motor coordination are impaired.

(b) Vasily (aged 9), a child who is at the early stages of learning English after arriving in the UK from Russia (via Poland) two years ago. He now has no vision in either eye but did not lose his sight until developing retinoblastoma, a cancer of the retina, in both eyes at the age of 5.

(c) Sam (aged 13), a congenitally blind child who was described by his previous teachers as 'quick thinking, confident, sociable and motivated to do well but still struggling with aspects of Braille'. Latterly he has appeared more withdrawn and passive in his interactions with others and has 'slipped back' in his academic work, according to all his subject teachers in the mainstream secondary school that he attends.

In their textbook on children with visual impairment in mainstream settings Arter *et al.* (1999: 4–5) described the support roles of specialist teachers as follows:

Direct support for teachers

- explaining the effects of visual impairment, and how it can affect the child's daily functioning, to individual teachers or to the whole school, through in-service training;

- assessing the child's needs and advising the class/subject teachers on setting objectives and planning individual educational plans (IEPs);

- advising on:

  - resource materials, e.g. large print, raised work surfaces, low vision aid and devices (LVA/Ds), personal computers;

  - positioning of the child in the classroom and lighting conditions;

- liaising with external examination boards for additional time and resources;

- advanced preparation of materials, e.g. tactile diagrams, enlarged/adapted print copies;

- working with parents and other agencies involved.

Direct support for pupils

- assessing visual functioning and providing training in the use of residual vision including visual discrimination and perception;

- monitoring visual conditions and if necessary, referring the child to other agencies, e.g. Low Vision Clinic;

- helping with:
  - organisational and study skills;
  - acceptance of impairment, social skills, self-confidence and independence;
- developing:
  - tactile and other sensory skills to complement vision;
  - communication skills including listening, Braille and print reading, spelling and writing and keyboard skills;
  - orientation and mobility skills within the school;
  - Low Vision Aid user skills.

If there is a Resource Base within the school then the pupils may attend discrete lessons to develop particular skills which need to be acquired quickly to enable inclusion. The mastery of some new piece of technological equipment or the development of Braille literacy skills when eyesight is rapidly deteriorating are two common examples. The Resource Base will be the place where pupils collect adapted materials or the equipment they need to access the curriculum, and it may provide a quiet place where they can catch up on class work, receive extra help and relate to other youngsters who have a visual impairment.

Conclusions

The first part of this chapter analysed hearing impairment – a form of SEN in which the primary barriers to access to the curriculum are serious problems of communication. The most common forms and causes of hearing impairment were described, and we examined their potential impact on children's participation in school. A major challenge for architects, equipment designers and teachers is to find ways of improving the conditions for effective hearing while maintaining an appropriate learning environment for all children. Only if this is achieved will the majority of children with hearing impairment benefit from inclusive education.

The traditional medical perspective on deafness was contrasted with a social/cultural perspective. In illustrating this analysis we outlined some of the differences that have been identified between the experience of the 5–10 per cent of deaf children who are born to deaf parents and that of the majority of deaf children who have hearing parents. We outlined the development of communication by deaf children and discussed the passionate debate that surrounds the choice of a medium of communication for deaf children in school.

The last section of that part of the chapter concerned the particular situation of deaf children from ethnic and linguistic minorities. It appears that a full response to the needs of this group of deaf children should have three prongs – respecting their hearing impairment, their family's cultural and religious values and language, and their unique and vulnerable identity as black and deaf, an identity that may be threatened by discrimination equally within the black community and within the deaf community. In every context educating for bilingualism must confront issues of personal and group identity. In the context of work with children who are black and deaf these issues are presented in an exceptionally complex and challenging form.

The second part of the chapter focused on visual impairment. The various forms and degrees of visual impairment have a relatively low incidence but present a major challenge to teachers. Visual impairment is often associated with other disabilities such as learning difficulties and epilepsy. It is conventionally measured in terms of visual acuity, but for the purposes of educational planning an understanding of a child's functional vision may be of great importance.

For children with severe visual impairment detailed attention needs to be paid to the planning of the school and classroom environment and of appropriate learning materials. The curriculum for this group of children, as for those with additional disabilities, will extend beyond the National Curriculum and encompass extra learning tasks around mobility, independence and access.

18

Physical needs

Objectives

When you have studied this chapter you should be able to:

- describe the range of physical needs and medical conditions that require special arrangements for access or support in school;
- explain the implications of an analysis of physical needs for teaching methods in inclusive education;
- outline the possible impact of exceptional physical needs and medical conditions on children's psychosocial and emotional development and suggest school-based strategies for reducing any negative effects.

Introduction

There is a very wide range of physical needs that may mean that a child requires additional help to have access to a broad and balanced education. One subset of physical needs is the range of sensory needs that were covered in the previous chapter. This chapter is concerned with:

- physical impairments which do not affect a child's learning but could hinder appropriate access to educational facilities and equipment;

- physical impairments which are associated with more complex learning and social needs;

- medical conditions that, if not properly managed, could hinder access to education (DfES 2001a: paras 7:62–7:64).

The DFES *Code of Practice* makes it clear that impaired mobility or a medical condition will not necessarily lead to a child requiring a statement of special educational needs. That will only be necessary if additional provision or support is required to facilitate their work on the school curriculum. A medical condition may have a direct impact on children's educational progress through cognitive or physical disabilities or indirectly by disrupting their school attendance because of medical treatment or through its emotional impact on them or their family (DfES 2001a: para. 7:65). The impact on education will also vary over time because the physical and psychological effects of a medical condition may be intermittent depending on the course of the illness, and the physical demands that school life makes on a child will change as they grow older.

Almost a third of children with statements of SEN relating to physical needs are educated in mainstream schools in England (DfES 2006d: Table 9). Teachers tend to be positive about the prospects for inclusion with this group, and surveys suggest that these views are strengthening over time. Thus a survey conducted by Croll and Moses (2000) in 48 primary schools showed 25% of headteachers and 20% of classroom teachers seeing a continuing role for special schools in the education of children with physical handicaps. These were much lower than the figures for children with emotional and behaviour difficulties (67% and 69%, respectively). Five years later, when Bloom (2005) reported a similar survey for the *Times Educational Supplement*, only 15% of mainstream headteachers and 12% of classroom teachers wanted to see children with impaired mobility educated in special schools. Only 3% of heads and 5% of classroom teachers thought that pupils with dyspraxia would best be educated in special schools. In contrast, half the heads and classroom teachers who were questioned thought that autistic pupils should not be taught with other children in a mixed-ability classroom. A commentator was quoted as saying:

> Teachers are concerned about disruptive behaviour in the classroom. There's the fear that certain pupils will be unmanageable. With physical disabilities, as long as you've solved the basic access issue, there's no other problem. But for all children, you have to have the right resources, or they can become as isolated in the mainstream as in special schools.
>
> (Bloom 2005)

The idea that 'there's no other problem' would be treated with scorn by many children who have disabilities. Reporting a study that involved participant observation and interviewing in 14 schools, Shakespeare (2005: 17) noted:

> Disabled children, according to many of our respondents, all have one thing in common: as one of the children told us, when asked what disability meant, 'we all get picked on'. Children told us about experiences of physical, emotional and verbal bullying, for example being called names such as 'spastic',

being excluded from peer groups, or being kicked and hit, and we observed all these processes. Even those who had not actually experienced bullying personally, were aware of the possibility, and it therefore shaped their sense of self and their social relationships.

It was reflecting on the personal experience of physical disability that led to the development of the social model of disability which has become a central influence on thinking about inclusion and special educational needs (Abberley 1987). In this model disability is seen as resulting from the interaction between individuals and their environments rather than as simply arising within the individual. A person's participation in the life of their society is seen as determined not by their physical (or other) impairments alone but by the social, attitudinal and physical environment in which they find themselves. When individuals are seen as highly dependent on others, their dependency 'is not an intrinsic feature of their impairments but is socially created by a disabling and disablist society' (Oliver 1990: 85). The social model of disability does not deny the reality of physical impairments and difficulties but analyses their impact in the lives of individuals with additional physical needs in terms of how society responds to those needs. The disadvantages experienced are not an inevitable result of their personal impairments, but the outcome of a failure by those around them and by society in general to accommodate differences. Disability is analysed in terms of oppression and discrimination rather than impairment (Swain *et al.* 2004). The social model of disability is now applied to the full range of additional needs, but its roots were in the analysis of physical disabilities.

Activity 18.1   Applying the social model of disability

There are very few teachers at any level who have significant physical disabilities. Here is a brief account from a teacher who has cerebral palsy:

> When I first started teaching I felt the need to hide my impairment and stress on application forms that it did not affect my teaching at all. I have, however, always talked to pupils about my disability and now recognize how vital it is to promote the positive roles disabled pupils and teachers can play in schools. Over the years I have grown tired of the discrimination I face in various areas of my life and have come to identify myself as someone disabled by the mindset of the vast majority of society. I am disabled by inaccessible buildings and systems – a situation which can only be effectively addressed through ensuring the full civil rights of disabled people. (From National Union of Teachers training materials on teachers with disabilities)

Reflecting on this account, discuss how the staffing and the physical environment of a school that you know might be interpreted in the light of the social model of disability.

Vignettes of physical needs

Paul, who is 6 years old, was taken to the family doctor by his mother when he was aged 3. He is the younger of two boys and, by comparison with his brother, he had been late in sitting up, late in beginning to crawl, and very late in walking.

In each case he had eventually mastered the milestone and moved on, but his coordination was poor so that he could not manage to dress himself. He constantly bumped into furniture about the house and knocked things over when the family was sitting at a meal. She was worried that he would not fit in at nursery school and would be bullied. The doctor predicted that he would catch up and told her that there was 'nothing medically wrong with him'. However, three years later he continues to show significant difficulties at home and at school. He is described by his teacher as 'forever falling off his chair, never sitting still, not focusing on tasks that are set, not organizing himself to work through a series of activities when we have a "rotation", and, in particular, failing to get the hang of forming letter shapes and organizing his writing on a page'. She is not sure whether he can see what is wrong and cannot put it right or if he does not actually notice that there is a mismatch between his attempt and the model from which he is copying. His mother still dresses him, notices that he bumps into things and tries hard to keep him away from his brother's railway set because he is liable to cause damage if he tries to play with it. Both the teacher and his mother emphasize that he is sweet-natured and well liked by others most of the time – except when they become frustrated by the accidents he causes.

Jerzy, who is 10 years old, came to the UK from Poland with his mother and older sister two years ago. They joined his father who had established the family home initially as an illegal immigrant and latterly as an official migrant worker from a new EU state. Jerzy has a moderate degree of cerebral palsy. His limb movements are stiff and poorly controlled, but he can walk without assistance. He has difficulty in coordinating the muscles of his mouth, and therefore eats very slowly with some gagging. In the classroom he presents as a quick learning child with a wide curiosity about the world around him, but his abilities are not fully reflected in his educational attainments there. One reason for this is that his progress in spoken English has been slow because of articulation and pronunciation problems. Another reason in the past was that, despite detailed advice and regular support teaching, he continues to experience severe difficulties in handwriting. He can, however, produce good-quality content if allowed to use a laptop and encouraged to rely on the spell-check facility in its word-processing software. Jerzy is not unpopular among his classmates but remains quite isolated for much of the time – except when the talk turns to football which he watches avidly on TV.

Sandra, who is 14 years old, suffered severe burns in a house fire six months ago. The damage to her skin in some parts of her body was superficial and healed within two weeks, but there was full-thickness burning to her left shoulder and part of the left side of her face which destroyed all skin layers. She was away from school for an extended period, spending much of that time in hospital. The overall shape of her face has not been affected, but the skin graft on one side gives her an atypical appearance. She does not experience physical pain or discomfort, but feels acutely embarrassed when meeting people who do not know her well and when entering a crowded area such as the school canteen. During her time in hospital she received regular tuition from teachers who were briefed on the work she was missing at school. She enjoyed the hospital school and says they used to have a laugh there. However, on returning to her local school she became much quieter and more reticent. At one point she made excuses not to go to school, explaining that she could not bear 'everyone looking at me all the time'.

Michael, who is 16 years old, is from a black British family. His grandparents came to England from Jamaica during the wave of Caribbean immigration shortly after the Second World War. Like three other members of his family he suffers from sickle cell disease, a genetic disorder that affects haemoglobin in the blood. Most of the time he is well, but every two weeks or so there is inflammation of the blood vessels in one part of the body or another which causes him long periods of pain. There is a good deal of knowledge about the disease in his family, and he understands that it is a chronic condition that will be with him throughout his life. One of his uncles died from a stroke that was a side-effect of the disease, and Michael becomes impatient because his mother is very protective of him and constantly worried that he will become ill. Although he can usually manage his pain crises without going into hospital, his treatment over the years has included relatively frequent blood transfusions. An effect of this is a build-up of excessive iron in the body. This can be treated with chelation therapy, an overnight drug treatment which he can manage himself. But he finds the chelation routine tedious, especially as he has to keep up with it even when he is feeling perfectly healthy.

Activity 18.2   Reviewing the vignettes of physical needs

Review the brief accounts that are given above of Paul, Jerzy, Sandra and Michael.

1   For each child draw up a list of their *special educational needs* and their *additional educational needs*, as described in Chapter 3 (see Activity 3.2). Do you have enough information from these brief vignettes for this purpose?

2   For each child attempt to draw an interactive factors framework figure as shown in Chapter 5 (Figure 5.4). You will probably find that you do not have enough information to complete the diagrams in full. Identify key questions that you would need answered in order to be able complete each diagram.

The range of physical needs

Severe physical disabilities

Severe motor impairment may arise from a range of medical conditions, including cerebral palsy, spina bifida and muscular dystrophy. There may be additional factors affecting the child's educational needs, such as associated visual or hearing impairments, neurological problems or learning difficulties. For example, a common cause of additional physical needs in school is *cerebral palsy*. This term describes a group of brain disorders that affect the development of movement and posture. Children may show a range of symptoms that can vary in severity, such as convulsive muscular contractions, a range of involuntary movements, unsteady gait, poor balance and impaired coordination. Some risk factors for cerebral palsy have been identified, but in many cases no single cause is identified. Its origin does not appear to be genetic, and in many cases there may have been brain trauma during pregnancy or birth. It is not a progressive disease but the brain damage is permanent (Bax *et al.* 2005). Because of its early onset, cerebral palsy may have a substantial influence on many aspects of a child's development, both through associated visuo-perceptual impairments or learning difficulties and through the child's normal patterns of experience being restricted through the way in which their basic motor impairment is managed.

Dyspraxia and developmental coordination disorder

Many children who do not have a medical condition such as cerebral palsy nonetheless show marked impairment in motor coordination. In the past they were described as *physically awkward* or *clumsy* or having *perceptuo-motor dysfunction* (Henderson 1995). The term that has been used most often in the UK recently is *dyspraxia*, though internationally the term that now has widespread formal acceptance is *developmental coordination disorder* (DCD; Chambers *et al.* 2005).

The primary problem for children who have DCD is a marked impairment in the development of motor coordination which will show itself in different ways as a child develops. In its diagnostic manual the American Psychiatric Association gives these examples: 'younger children may display clumsiness and delays in achieving developmental motor milestones (e.g. walking, crawling, sitting, tying shoe laces, buttoning shirts . . .). Older children may display difficulties with the motor aspects of assembling puzzles, building models, playing ball'. Their performance in daily activities that require motor coordination is substantially below what would be expected given their age and intelligence to a degree that 'significantly interferes with academic achievement or activities of daily living' (American Psychiatric Association 2000: 56–7).

Follow-up studies have indicated that DCD can have a long-term impact on educational progress and social development. However, Cantell *et al.* (2003) showed that a proportion of children who were originally identified with DCD at the age of 5 improved significantly in relation to their peers by late adolescence. Some of the research that showed poor academic outcomes may have failed to control for socioeconomic status or overall intelligence (Cousins and Smyth 2005). However, it is clear that many of the children continue to show specific areas of difficulty in aspects of non-verbal functioning such as visuospatial organization or psychomotor skills or abstract thinking involving perceptual concepts (Portwood 2005).

Chronic and severe illness

Chronic and severe illness may interfere with children's education because their medical needs prevent them from attending school or because their medical condition has an adverse effect on their learning while in school. A serious illness such as cancer may develop at any age and, initially at least, will have an uncertain prognosis. Some chronic conditions, such as sickle cell disease and thalassaemia, may be hereditary and will show themselves very early in life. Those examples represent very serious threats to development and sometimes even to survival. The extent and nature of special educational needs that are associated with a medical condition are not necessarily correlated with its severity. Thus, for instance, conditions which cause visible differences in the face and head may not have a poor prognosis in themselves but may have a substantial adverse impact on a child's psychosocial development (Walters 1997) and on their inclusion in school (Frances 2004); see Figure 18.1

Education of children with physical needs

The trend to inclusion

Dunsdon (1952) conducted a meticulous study for the then Ministry of Education and concluded that 60 per cent of children with cerebral palsy were not 'educable in the usual sense of the word'. Nearly 20 years later in another official report Wilson (1970: 3) reported that only 8 per cent of the 343 children with cerebral palsy whom she had studied 'were eventually found to be unsuitable for education in school. All had at least a year's trial, or longer, in school.' In the same year, however, Parliament passed the Education Act (Handicapped Children), which was enacted in 1971. This deleted the concept of ineducability from UK law. Along with all other children, those who had not only severe physical disabilities but also profound learning difficulties and/or communication difficulties became entitled to education. They would no longer be the responsibility of health authorities and looked after in 'junior training centres' and 'special care units'.

Subsequently there was growing acceptance of the idea that there should be a continuum of provision for children with physical disabilities. While those with severe difficulties might attend special schools, those with moderate difficulties might be partially integrated in mainstream schools. Steadily, as noted above, opinion moved in the direction of accepting greater inclusion for this group. By the turn of the century Fox (2003) concluded that successful inclusion of children with physical disabilities was not determined by within-child factors but by the school environment: structured teaching, appropriate support and a positive school ethos for inclusion would enable children with a range of disabilities to benefit academically and socially.

Developing children's ability to access the school environment

For some parents whose children have severe and complex special needs the first step in maximizing their potential for growth is to reject professional judgements that place a limitation on what they might be able to achieve. Developing the child's ability to access normal environments comes to be seen as a key goal. One strategy for working towards this end has been Conductive Education, an intensive training programme that was originally developed in Hungary in the 1940s:

> The object of Conductive Education is not to accommodate the severe dysfunctional patients in an institute, or to send them to a special school, but to accomplish a basic task to render possible a normal education, traveling in the streets, self-supporting and work. In order to bring about an equilibrium between child and environment, we do not change the environment, but the adaptation of the child's constitution.
>
> (Hari 1968, quoted in Oliver 1990: 55–6)

Extracts from Statutory Guidance issued to LEAs, schools, headteachers and governors by the DfES in April 2002 (DfES, 2002f)

Section 19 of the Education Act 1996 provides that 'Each local authority shall make arrangements for the provision of suitable . . . education at school or otherwise than at school for those children of compulsory school age who, by reason of illness, exclusion from school or otherwise, may not for any period receive suitable education unless such arrangements are made for them'.

The statutory guidance issued by the DfES (2002f) emphasizes the following principles:

- *Access to education*. All pupils should continue to have access to as much education as their medical condition allows so that they are able to maintain the momentum of their education and to keep up with their studies, for example through a hospital school or hospital teaching service, home teaching or an integrated hospital/home education service. LEAs have to ensure that pupils are not at home without access to education for more than 15 working days. Pupils educated at home should receive a minimum entitlement of 5 hours teaching per week, more as needed to enable them to keep up with their studies. The education should be of 'similar quality to that available in school, including a broad and balanced curriculum'.

- *Clear policies, procedures and standards of provision*. All parties should be aware of their rights and responsibilities and be clear about the standards of service that are expected of them. Policies should be clear, transparent and easily accessible to all.

- *Early identification and intervention*. When a student is unable to attend school because of medical needs steps should be taken to identify their educational needs and provide educational support quickly and effectively.

- *Continuity of educational provision*. The aim should be to provide continuity of education similar to that provided at the pupil's home school, and there should be liaison to support that.

- *Working together*. Achieving these goals will require close partnership between education, health and other agencies.

- *Successful reintegration into school*. There should be an individually tailored reintegration plan when they are ready to return to school.

- *Partnership with parents and pupils*. Parents hold key information and knowledge and have a crucial role to play. They should be full collaborative partners and should be informed about their children's educational programme and performance. Children also have a right to be involved in making decisions and exercising choice.

- *High-quality educational provision*. The curriculum and educational opportunities offered to pupils in this situation should be equal to what they would have received in their home school.

- *Accountability*. Arrangements should be in place to ensure adequate monitoring and evaluation.

Figure 18.1 The rights of pupils with medical needs in terms of access to education

Evaluation studies have had mixed results, and there is no unequivocal evidence for the method achieving group outcomes that are better than those achieved through traditional methods. The original programme insisted that children should learn to walk because in that period the available schools in the region were not wheelchair accessible and had only very basic assistive technology. As efforts have been made to adapt the programme to different cultural and educational settings, great variation has been introduced around the original concept, occasionally diluting key features. Darrah *et al.* (2004) noted that an attraction of the approach to many families may be that it focuses on activities of daily living and preparing children for schooling. At the same time, like many such programmes, it makes very considerable demands in terms of cost, time, access and the effect of the intervention on family dynamics. These may be key issues, they concluded, in the absence of strong evidence of its effectiveness.

Preparing a child to access the school environment may be a key task with other, apparently less severe forms of physical need. A child in pain cannot focus on classroom learning tasks. Effective pain management may be a crucial step towards the child enjoying full access to the curriculum and to the social experiences of school. In some chronic illnesses, such as sickle cell disease, medical treatment may not be able to achieve this so that children continue to face frequent episodes of pain. Cognitive behavioural approaches can help in this situation. For example, in one study Gil *et al.* (2001) trained 46 African-American children with sickle cell disease to use three coping strategies – deep breathing relaxation, pleasing imagery and calming self-talk. At the end of the training session the children were provided with audiotaped instructions for the techniques, a tape player and a daily assignment to practise the new strategies. From their daily diaries up to a month later it became evident that, compared to control patients who received routine medical care, the children in the coping intervention group were significantly more active in their approach to managing pain. 'Daily diary data indicated that on pain days when children practiced their strategies, they had fewer health care contacts, fewer school absences, and less interference with household activities than on days when they did not practice' (Gil *et al.* 2001: 163). There is evidence that cognitive behaviour therapy techniques may have a contribution to make in enabling young people with other persistent health conditions such as chronic fatigue syndrome to persist with their education (Stulemeijer *et al.* 2005). Where techniques of this kind are incorporated into a self-management strategy, teachers may have a role to play in supporting its implementation (Chalder and Hussain 2002).

Ultimately, however, the key factor in enabling children to access the school environment will not be changes within the child but developments in the school's ability to facilitate access. There is now a legal duty 'not to treat disabled pupils less favourably and to take reasonable steps to avoid putting disabled pupils at a substantial disadvantage' (DfES, 2002g: para. 1.2). All schools are required to produce an 'accessibility plan' for:

- increasing the extent to which disabled pupils can participate in the school curriculum;

- improving the physical environment of schools to increase the extent to which disabled pupils can take advantage of education and associated services; and

- improving the delivery to disabled pupils of written information which is provided to pupils who are not disabled.

(DfES 2002g: para. 2.3)

It is important to note that 'The curriculum covers not only teaching and learning but the wider curriculum of the school such as participation in after school clubs, leisure, sporting and cultural activities or school visits' (DfES 2002g: para. 3.2).

The process by which a school develops its accessibility strategy may be almost as important as the detail of the strategy itself. Firstly, the planning process can ensure that all those involved in the school – governors, staff, parents and pupils – develop their awareness of disability and of the part they personally can play in exacerbating or ameliorating the effects of physical impairment within the school. Secondly, the planning process can determine the attitude of those involved – how far they see the plan as a necessary, 'politically correct' outcome in which they have no sense of ownership or, alternatively, a valuable extension of what the school stands for, something with which they are proud to identify. Fox (2003) has described how a specially designed consultation process ('MAPS') may be used for this purpose.

From 2007 the provisions of a new Disability Equality Duty came into force in England and Wales. This requires public authorities, including schools and local authorities, to involve disabled people structurally in their planning.

> The Disability Equality Duty does not give individuals more rights; instead it is about improving public authorities' policies and services as a whole for all disabled people. It is also not focused on removing physical barriers solely; instead it is focused on removing those barriers within policy and the design of services or initiatives which have a negative impact on the lives of all disabled people . . . The duty reflects the social model of disability. This takes the approach that what stops or hinders a disabled person doing something are barriers that society has put in place or chosen to ignore. It is society that disables a person, not their impairment. The Disability Equality Duty takes the social model and applies it to the functions of a public authority. It does this by recognising the negative impact on disabled people of a society designed for nondisabled people. It also recognises that active steps are needed to promote equality for disabled people.

(See http://www.drc.org.uk)

Ensuring that teachers know what they need to know about pupils' physical needs

For many teachers who work in mainstream schools there can be something rather formidable about the medical labels that are attached to children with physical needs. It has been suggested that understanding a child's diagnosis will help a teacher to:

- liaise with other professionals who will use this label;

- discuss issues with the parents in a knowledgeable way;

- be more aware of why certain activities are beneficial and why others are not;

- be sensitive to secondary problems, for example tiredness.

(Fox 2003: 25)

At the same time there are risks in relying on a general diagnostic label and the general information about it that can be found on the internet and from medical dictionaries. Statistical association with learning difficulties may be misleading in an individual case. In addition, labelling may lead teachers to develop negative expectations which can then affect children's performance. Frances (2004), who emphasized those risks, suggested the checklist in Figure 18.2 for obtaining information about a child with facial disfigurement. It could be adapted without difficulty for children with other physical needs.

There is no substitute for close observation of an individual child's functioning in the school together with an awareness of possible signs of change in the condition. The focus should be on physical skills that will directly impact on learning in the classroom and for which adaptations or allowances may need to be made by the teacher. Examples (adapted from Fox 2003: Table 2.2) might include:

- mobility and walking;

- head control for shorter and longer periods of time;

- sitting with and without support;

- use of hands, e.g. when dressing or holding a pencil or reaching out and grasping an object;

- Who is this child? What has happened to her face?

- How does this affect her? (Speech? Breathing? Swallowing? Hearing? Sight? Sensitivity to heat or cold?) How does she manage?

- Is her condition stable or will it/could it alter? Gradually or suddenly?

- Does she have any special medical needs related to this disfigurement?

- Does she have any special educational needs (which may or may not be related to the injury or condition that affects her appearance)?

- Is she having/going to have any treatment?

- How does/will this affect her? (Many health professionals and parents report a period of 'regression', particularly for younger children, following traumatic or invasive treatments such as surgery, or time in hospital. A pupil may be less able, less independent, or more needy, for a while.)

- If school attendance may be affected, how can teachers, parents and health professionals work together to ensure the child's continued sense of belonging in the school, and how will the continuity of her education be safeguarded?

- How is she likely to be affected longer term?

- How does she get on socially – with strangers? with adults? with other children or young people?

Figure 18.2   A checklist for obtaining information about a child with facial disfigurement (Frances 2004)

- speech articulation;

- control of unwanted movements such as a tremor or muscle spasms.

Focused observation will only be of value if it leads to changes in teaching and management that that are specifically designed to meet the child's individual pattern of abilities and needs. Where there are indications that more detailed school-based assessment for DCD will be helpful, the Movement Assessment Battery for Children Checklist may be considered (Chambers *et al.* 2005). This checklist is a criterion-referenced questionnaire which requires teachers to rate pupils' performance on 48 items that reflect motor activities that are common in the everyday school lives of children aged 4–12. It has been shown to meet expected standards of reliability and those for most aspects of validity in a school context (Schoemaker *et al.* 2003). (A review of instruments for assessing functional motor abilities of children with cerebral palsy may be found in Ketelaar *et al.* 1998).

Ensuring that all children are offered a broad and balanced curriculum

One of the perceived disadvantages of special schools in the past was that their size and specialist focus meant that they did not offer a broad and balanced curriculum to the pupils. Looking back at his education Phil Friend, one of the informants who helped Davies (1993) write a 'mutual biography' of disabled people, recalled:

> looking back from the age of nine to sixteen, the primary concern of that school was to 'therap' me. It was nothing to do with education, really. I had drama-therapy, art-therapy, you name it, I had it coming out of my ears. No academic work at all. I mean we did do academic work, but it was meaning-less – copying, dictation and pathetic handwriting. I think the staff decided these kids were largely unemployable, largely ineducable and therefore thought, 'what was the point?' So they would go through the motions of an education. I mean, rug-making as an education? C'mon! I can remember sitting for f'ing hours, making all these f'ing Readi-cut Rugs. I mean, what was going on? And this is at, sort of, fourteen, you know. When most people are getting ready to take 'O' levels, I was making Readi-cut Rugs!
>
> (Davies 1993: 37).

By the time Friend was giving that account the legal rights of all children to a broad and balanced curriculum, including the National Curriculum, had been enshrined in law. This will be illustrated briefly with examples from two areas of the curriculum – Science and Physical Education.

It has sometimes been suggested that problems of access for pupils with physical disabilities must be particularly acute in Science because effective learning involves complex practical tasks. Such notions have been challenged by the inclusion of practical science in the curriculum of home-based teaching sessions for preschool children with disabilities (Bennington 2004) and by the use of settings such as a special school's multi-sensory room and hydrotherapy pool for Science investigations (Fisher 2002). Strategies have been developed to ensure that children with disabilities participate in National Curriculum assessments on an equal basis with others (QCA 2007a). The motto that 'every teacher is a teacher of English' has to be adapted in the case of pupils with physical needs: for them 'every teacher is a teacher of access skills'. Thus teachers of Science, along with others, may adapt for their purposes the principles of methods developed by occupational therapists to help support parents. In one cognitively oriented approach children who have DCD are taught explicit thinking strategies as a method of solving motor performance problems and in order to acquire and practise motor skills (Mandich and Polatajko 2005).

Like Science, PE and Games present major problems for many of the children with whom this chapter is concerned. Firstly, simply adapting teaching strategies and learning objectives that are designed for other children in a mainstream class may not meet their needs. Secondly, if adaptations are not made, they are likely to feel particularly exposed and frustrated not only by the activities themselves but also by the routines associated with them, such as getting changed within a restricted time, following group instructions designed for the rest of the class and working as part of a competitive team. But it is clearly important that they are not deprived of the opportunities that PE provides. Children with DCD, for example, have been shown in a number of studies to prefer leisure pursuits that do not involve physical activity, and there are negative health risks associated with a sedentary lifestyle in childhood and subsequently. Schooling should help pupils to find satisfaction in more active ways of enjoying their leisure. Cairney *et al.* (2005) have suggested that it may not be DCD in itself that leads children to resist participation in physical activities, but rather the feelings about themselves that they have as a result of DCD (see Figure 18.3). They argued for the development of psychosocial interventions aimed at improving coping skills and quality of life. The first step is to set short-term goals that take account of the child's current motor abilities. Evidence in support of this strategy, they say, comes from clinical trials designed to increase motor proficiency in children with DCD. The gains appeared to be due to increased confidence and willingness to participate in physical tasks, rather than actual improvement in motor skills. 'Therapists and others (parents and teachers) need to carefully consider a child's motor abilities, assist the child in finding a suitable vigorous activity and environment, and work incrementally toward improving the child's mastery of the task' (Cairney *et al.* 2005: 519). This type of strategy was supported when Smith and Thomas (2006) reviewed studies of the views of PE teachers on including pupils with SEN and disabilities in National Curriculum PE.

Schools' response to pupil illness

The first priority for a child who is ill or has physical disabilities is to attend to their medical and physical needs. In the early years of universal education schools were often seen as a major weapon in the armoury of preventive medicine. When children in crowded industrial towns were prone to pulmonary tuberculosis, a preventive measure for the most vulnerable was to expose them to healthy doses of fresh air and exercise in 'open air schools'. Some of these schools helped to lay the basis for the development of a holistic care philosophy which underpinned evolving ideas about education welfare (Hughes 2004). This thinking eventually led to the inclusion of 'being healthy' as one of the strands of the recent *Every*

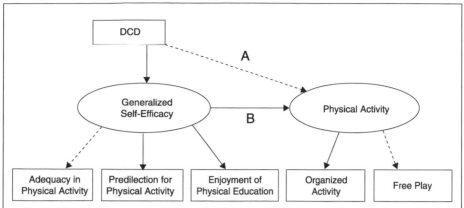

Figure 18.3 Why are children with DCD less likely to participate in physical activities than their peers?
Source: Adapted from Cairney *et al.* (2005).

This figure shows a model based on data from a study of 564 students in primary schools in the Niagara region of Ontario, Canada. It is partly concerned with self-efficacy, which is the belief that one is capable of performing something successfully or attaining certain goals. In this study DCD was identified through a motor proficiency test. Students' generalized sense of self-efficacy in physical exercise was assessed through a questionnaire that examined their confidence in, preference for, and enjoyment of physical education classes. Finally, they completed a questionnaire on physical activity which asked them to report their actual participation levels in the areas of free-time play, seasonal recreational pursuits, school sports, community sports teams and clubs, and sport and dance lessons over the past year. The figure is based on structural equation modelling, a statistical technique for testing and estimating causal relationships. The children with DCD had much lower generalized self-efficacy than children without the disorder and lower rates of participation in physical activity. But the direct relationship between DCD and physical activity (arrow A) was not statistically significant. Instead the effect of DCD on physical activity was mediated through generalized self-efficacy (arrow B). In the model, 28 per cent of the variance in children's physical activity can be predicted by generalized self-efficacy and DCD.

Child Matters initiative. Meanwhile the number of children assessed as needing an open air school declined. Swann (1985) showed that there was a 13 per cent reduction in the proportion of children assessed as being 'delicate' between 1978 and 1982. General improvements in medical care and in social conditions might be expected to lead to this trend. A survey in inner London a few years later indicated that, while the schools for delicate pupils still had children with a wide range of health problems such as asthma, eczema and bronchial and heart conditions, they also included more who had 'emotional and behavioural difficulties of the less aggressive kind' and 'many with a combination of different special educational needs'. The Fish Committee, who had commissioned the survey, concluded that it was 'often this combination rather than the degree of any one need which cause[d] them to be placed in such schools' (ILEA 1985: 93).

With the disappearance of such schools and the development of new medical techniques new questions have arisen about what forms of medical support it is reasonable to expect from staff in mainstream schools where there is no nurse on site. A child may return to school after a short illness and still need to finish a course of antibiotics, or a child with a chronic condition may need to take medicines regularly during the day on a long-term basis, for example to control epilepsy. School staff who have not had experience of this before may feel anxious and confused about what is expected of them in the situation. In order to allay concerns of this kind, which have the potential to undermine moves towards inclusion, the Department for Education and Skills and Department of Health (2005b) issued joint guidance on managing medicines in schools and early years settings. This was designed to help schools and the other organizations involved to:

- review their current policies and procedures involving children with medical needs in order to make sure that everyone, including parents, is clear about their respective roles;

- put in place effective management systems to help support individual children with medical needs;

- make sure that within early years and school settings medicines are handled responsibly;

- help ensure that all school staff are clear about what to do in the event of a medical emergency (DfES/DH 2005b: 2).

Effective learning may not be possible when a child is ill, but it is necessary to maintain a balance between medical treatment and education. One challenge is to maintain continuity when children are absent from school for medical treatment or for periods of hospitalization. The official guidance on this in England was outlined in Figure 18.1. Two years after the new regulations had been issued, Ofsted surveyed 12 LEAs to evaluate the effectiveness of the provision. The inspectors found that, while the guidance had helped almost all the authorities to improve parts of their service, 'in over half policies and procedures do not yet reflect all aspects of the guidance. Providers, schools, parents and outside agencies are unclear about the service available and their respective roles and responsibilities within it' (Ofsted 2003c: 2).

The challenges go beyond clarifying and communicating policies. It was acknowledged that the task of providing education in these circumstances is not easy:

The challenge facing providers is how to provide effective education for pupils who may differ considerably in terms of their age, ability, length of stay, medical condition and the setting within which they require education. Providers may be teaching pupils as young as four or working with 18 year olds; some pupils may be working towards Advanced Level (A level) qualifications whilst others have severe learning difficulties. Some pupils may require education in hospitals for only one or two days, but others may remain in units for over two years as a result of their mental health difficulties. Some may have illnesses that result in regular support from providers; others might require short-term support while recovering from operations or accidents. Pupils may require home tuition as a result of their physical or mental illnesses, some may attend schools and units every day, while others may require regular teaching in their hospital beds while they receive treatment for recurring illnesses. A wide range of provision and well-qualified, adaptable staff are needed to meet the needs of this diverse group.

(Ofsted 2003c: 5)

The schools that pupils normally attend have a role to play in facilitating good practice. The inspectors noted that few pupils had personal education plans that detailed all aspects of their education and that this had a negative impact on the continuity of learning. They recommended, among other things, that schools should

work closely with the hospital and home tuition service and, in particular:

- take responsibility for drawing up personal education plans which outline all aspects of pupils' education and the person responsible for each aspect

- provide the hospital and home tuition service with information about the pupils' curriculum, their achievements and any special educational needs

- provide appropriate work and materials promptly and regularly

- ensure pupils are re-integrated into their own schools smoothly.

(Ofsted 2003c: 4)

Activity 18.3   Review of the case studies

Look back at the brief descriptions of Paul, Jerzy, Sandra and Michael above. Choose two of them whose situation and challenges interest you. As a teacher working with the child in question, what considerations would you bear in mind when:

- organizing seating arrangements in the classroom?

- planning, presenting and marking homework?

- meeting with the child and parents for an annual review?

Conclusion

This chapter has been concerned with physical impairments and medical conditions which could hinder appropriate access to education. The inclusion of children with physical disabilities generates less opposition from teachers than is the case with some other forms of SEN. However, the experience that people with disabilities had of oppression and discrimination led to the development of the social model of disability. Four vignettes illustrated the broad range of physical needs, which includes severe physical disabilities, developmental coordination disorder, and chronic and severe illness. While special measures may be taken to help a child prepare for the school environment, the most important initiatives do not concern changes within the child but developments in the capacity of schools to facilitate access and to meet special needs. This will include ensuring that teachers know what they need to know about pupils' physical needs, are able to offer them a broad and balanced curriculum while taking full account of those needs, and are able to respond appropriately to problems and interruptions to their education caused by illness and hospitalization. If some teachers have had the impression that the inclusion of this group of learners would pose few challenges, they have underestimated the challenges – and the potential satisfactions – of effective educational inclusion.

References

Abberley, P. (1987) The concept of oppression and the development of a social theory of disability. *Disability and Society*, 2(1): 5–19.

Abbott, D., Townsley, R. and Watson, D. (2005) Multi-agency working in services for disabled children: what impact does it have on professionals? *Health and Social Care in the Community*, 13(2): 155–63.

Abreu, G. de (1995) Understanding how children experience the relationship between home and school mathematics. *Mind, Culture and Activity: An International Journal*, 2(2): 119–42.

Abreu, G. de and Cline, T. (2005) Parents' representations of their children's mathematics learning in multiethnic primary schools. *British Educational Research Journal*, 31(6): 697–722.

Abreu, G. de and Cline, T. (2007) Social valorization of mathematical practices: the implications for learners in multicultural schools. In N.S. Nasir and P. Cobb (eds) *Improving Access to Mathematics: Diversity and Equity in the Classroom* (pp. 118–31). New York: Teachers College Press.

Ackerman, D. and Howes, C. (1986) Sociometric status and after-school activity of children with learning disabilities. *Journal of Learning Disabilities*, 2: 416–19.

Adams, C. (2001) Clinical diagnostic and intervention studies of children with semantic-pragmatic language disorder. *International Journal of Language & Communication Disorders*, 36(3): 289–305.

Adams, M.J. (1990) *Beginning to Read: Children Thinking and Learning about Print*. Cambridge, MA: MIT Press.

Adams, M.J. and Bruck, M. (1993) Word recognition: the interface of educational policies and scientific research. *Reading and Writing: An Interdisciplinary Journal*, 5: 113–39.

Adey, P., Csapo, B., Demetriou, A., Hautamäki, J. and Shayer, M. (2007) Can we be intelligent about intelligence? Why education needs the concept of plastic general ability. *Educational Research Review*, 2(2): 75–97.

Ahmed, Z.M., Riazuddin, S. and Wilcox, E.R. (2003) The molecular genetics of Usher syndrome. *Clinical Genetics*, 63(6): 431–44.

Ainley, J. (2006) Developing interdependence: an analysis of individual and school influences on a social outcome of schooling. *Educational Psychology*, 26(2): 209–27.

Ainscow, M. (1988) Beyond the eyes of the monster: an analysis of recent trends in assessment and recording. *Support for Learning*, 3(3): 149–53.

Ainscow, M. (1995) Education for all: making it happen. *Support for Learning*, 10(4): 147–54.

Ainscow, M. (2007) From special education to effective schools for all: a review of progress so far. In L. Florian (ed.) *The Sage Handbook of Special Education*. London: Sage.

Ainscow, M. and Tweddle, D. (1979) *Preventing Classroom Failure: An Objectives Approach*. Chichester: Wiley.

Ainscow, M. and Tweddle, D. (1988) *Encouraging Classroom Success*. London: David Fulton.

Ainscow, M., Booth, T. and Dyson, A. (2006a) *Improving Schools, Developing Inclusion*. London: Routledge.

Ainscow, M., Booth, T. and Dyson, A. (2006b) Inclusion and the standards agenda: negotiating policy pressures in England. *International Journal of Inclusive Education*, 10(4–5): 295–308.

Ainsworth, M., Blehar, M., Waters, E. and Wall, S. (1978) *Patterns of Attachment*. Hillsdale, NJ: Erlbaum.

Ajmal, Y, and Rees, I. (2001) *Solutions in Schools: Creative Applications of Solution Focused Brief Thinking with Young People and Adults*. London: BT Press.

Alagaratnam, J., Sharma, T.K., Lim, C.S. and Fleck, B.W. (2002) A survey of visual impairment in children attending the Royal Blind School, Edinburgh using the WHO childhood visual impairment database. *Eye*, 16(5): 557–61.

Albers, C.A., Glover T.A. and Kratochwill, T.R. (2007) Introduction to the special issue: How can universal screening enhance educational and mental health outcomes? *Journal of School Psychology*, 45(2): 113–16.

Ali, S. and Frederickson, N. (2006) Investigating the evidence base of Social Stories. *Educational Psychology in Practice*, 22(4): 355–77.

Alladina, S. (1985) Second language teaching through maths – learning maths through a second language. *Educational Studies in Mathematics*, 16: 215–19.

Allyn, B.A. and Boykin, A.W. (1992) African-American children and the educational process: alleviating cultural discontinuity through prescriptive pedagogy. *School Psychology Review*, 21: 586–96.

Alves, A.J. and Gottlieb, J. (1986) Teacher interactions with mainstreamed handicapped students and their nonhandicapped peers. *Learning Disabilities Quarterly*, 8: 77–83.

American Association on Intellectual and Developmental Disabilities (2002) *Definition of Mental Retardation*. Washington, DC: American Association on Intellectual and Developmental Disabilities. Available online at: http://www.aaidd.org/Policies/faq_mental_retardation.shtml (accessed 12 December 2007).

American Psychiatric Association (2000) *Diagnostic and Statistical Manual of Mental Disorder, Fourth Edition, Text Revision (DSM-IV-TR)* Washington: American Psychiatric Publishing.

Anderson, A., Hamilton, R.J. and Hattie, J. (2004) Classroom climate and motivated behaviour in secondary schools. *Learning Environments Research*, 7: 211–25.

Anderson, L.W., Ryan, D.W. and Shapiro, B.J. (eds) (1989) *The IEA Classroom Environment Study*. Oxford: Pergamon.

Anderson, S.W., Bechara, A., Damasio, H., Tranel, D. and Damasio, A.R. (1999) Impairment of social and moral behaviour related to early damage in human prefrontal cortex. *Nature Neuroscience*, 2: 1032–7.

Angtrop, I., Roeyers, H., Oosterlaan, J. and Van Oost, P. (2002) Agreement between parent and teacher ratings of disruptive behaviour disorders in children with clinically diagnosed ADHD. *Journal of Psychopathology and Behavioral Assessment*, 24(1): 67–73.

Anning, A., Cottrell, D., Frost, J. and Robinson, M. (2006) *Developing Multiprofessional Teamwork for Integrated Children's Services*. Maidenhead: Open University Press.

Antia, S.D., Sabers, D.L. and Stinson, M.S. (2007) Validity and reliability of the Classroom Participation Questionnaire with deaf and hard of hearing students in public schools. *Journal of Deaf Studies and Deaf Education*, 12(2): 158–71.

Appleby, L., Shribman, S. and Eisenstadt, N. (2006) *Promoting the Mental Health and Psychological Well-Being of Children and Young People. Report on the Implementation of*

Standard 9 of the National Service Framework for Children, Young People and Maternity Services. London: DH Publications.

Arce-Ferrer, A.J. (2006) An investigation into the factors influencing extreme-response style: improving meaning of translated and culturally adapted rating scales. *Educational and Psychological Measurement*, 66, 374–92.

Arens, L. and Molteno, C. (1989) A comparative study of postnatally acquired cerebral palsy in Cape Town. *Developmental Medicine and Child Neurology*, 31: 246–54.

Argyropoulos, V.S. (2002) Tactual shape perception in relation to the understanding of geometrical concepts by blind students. *British Journal of Visual Impairment*, 20(1): 7–16.

Armitage, I.M., Burke, J.P. and Buffin, J.T. (1995) Visual impairment in severe and profound sensorineural deafness. *Archives of Disease in Childhood*, 73: 53–6.

Armstrong, D. (2003) *Experiences of Special Education*. London: RoutledgeFalmer.

Arnold, L.E., Barnaby, N., Macmanus, J. *et al.* (1987) Prevention by specific perceptual remediation for vulnerable first-graders. *Archives of General Psychiatry*, 34: 1279–94.

Arter, C., Mason, H.L., McCall, S., McLinden, M. and Stone, J. (1999) *Children with Visual Impairment in Mainstream Settings*. London: David Fulton.

Arter, J.A. and Jenkins, J.R. (1979) Differential diagnosis – prescriptive teaching: a critical appraisal. *Review of Educational Research*, 49(4): 517–55.

Artiles, A.J. (2003) Special education's changing identity. Paradoxes and dilemmas in views of culture and space. *Harvard Educational Review*, 73(2): 164–202.

Asarnow, J.R. (1983) Children with peer adjustment problems: sequential and non-sequential analysis of school behaviours. *Journal of Consulting and Clinical Psychology*, 51: 709–17.

Ashcraft, M.H. (2002) Math anxiety: personal, educational, and cognitive consequences. *Current Directions in Psychological Science*, 11(5): 181–5.

Ashcraft, M.H., Kirk, E.P. and Hopko, D. (1998) On the cognitive consequences of mathematics anxiety. In C. Donlan (ed.) *The Development of Mathematical Skills*. Hove: Psychology Press.

Asher, S. (1985) An evolving paradigm in social skills training research with children. In B. Schneider, K. Rubin and J. Ledingham (eds) *Peer Relationship and Social Skills in Childhood: Issues in Assessment and Training*. New York: Springer Verlag.

Asher, S.R., Parkhurst, J.T., Hymel, S. and Williams, G.A. (1990) Peer rejection and loneliness in childhood. In S.R. Asher and J.D. Coie (eds) *Peer Rejection in Childhood*. Cambridge: Cambridge University Press.

Ashton, R. (2007) Learning from writing to students. *DECP Debate*, 122: 27–33.

Askew, M. and Wiliam, D. (1995) *Recent Research in Mathematics Education 5–16*. London: HMSO.

Assessment Reform Group (1999) *Assessment for Learning: Beyond the Black Box*. Cambridge: University of Cambridge School of Education. (www.assessment-reform-group.org.uk)

Association for All Speech-Impaired Children (AFASIC) (1990) *Checklists of Language Disability*. London: AFASIC.

Astor, R.A., Meyer, H.A. and Behre, W.J. (1999) Unowned places and times: Maps and interviews about violence in high schools. *American Educational Research Journal*, 36(1): 3–42.

Atkin, K, Ahmad, W.I.U. and Jones, L. (2002) Young South Asian deaf people and their families: negotiating relationships and identities. *Sociology of Health and Illness*, 24(1): 21–45.

Attwood, A., Frith, U. and Hermlin, B. (1998) The understanding and use of interpersonal gestures by autistic and Down's syndrome children. *Journal of Autism and Developmental Disorders*, 18: 241–57.

Aubrey, C., Bottle, G. and Godfrey, R. (2003) Early mathematics in the home and out-of-home contexts. *International Journal of Early Years Education*, 11(2): 91–103.

Audit Commission (1992) *Getting in on the Act. Provision for Pupils with Special Educational Needs: The National Picture*. London: HMSO.

Audit Commission (2002a) *Special Educational Needs: A Mainstream Issue*. London: Audit Commission.

Audit Commission (2002b) *Statutory Assessment and Statements of SEN: In Need of Review?* London: Audit Commission.

Avramadis, E. and Bayliss, P. (1998) An inquiry into children with emotional and behaviour difficulties in two schools in the south west of England. *Emotional and Behaviour Difficulties*, 3(3): 25–35.

Ayers, H., Clarke, D. and Murray, A. (2000) *Perspectives on Behaviour: A Practical Guide to Effective Interventions for Teachers*, 2nd edition. London: David Fulton.

Baca, L.M. and Cervantes, H.T. (1989) *The Bilingual Special Education Interface*. Columbus, OH: Merrill Publishing.

Baird, G., Simonoff, E., Pickles, A., Chandler, S., Loucas, T., Meldrum, D. and Charman, T. (2006) Prevalence of disorder orders of the autistic spectrum in a population cohort of children in South Thames: the Special Needs and Autism Project (SNAP). *Lancet*, 368: 210–15.

Baker, C. (2006) *Foundations of Bilingual Education and Bilingualism*, 4th edition. Clevedon: Multilingual Matters.

Baker, C. and Child, D. (1993) Communication approaches used in schools for the deaf in the U.K. – a follow-up study. *Journal of the British Association of Teachers of the Deaf*, 17(2): 36–47.

Baker, C. and Hinde, J. (1984) Language background classification. *Journal of Multilingual and Multicultural Development*, 5(1): 43–56.

Baker, E.T., Wang, M.C. and Walberg, H.J. (1994–5) The effects of inclusion on learning. *Educational Leadership*, 52(4): 33–5.

Baker, J.M. and Zigmond, N. (1995) The meaning and practice of inclusion for students with learning disabilities: themes and implications from the five cases. *Journal of Special Education*, 29(2): 163–80.

Bakker, D.J. (1979) Hemispheric differences and reading strategies: two dyslexias? *Bulletin of the Orton Society*, 29: 84–100.

Ball, E.W. and Harry, B. (1993) Multicultural education and special education: parallels, divergences and intersections. *The Educational Forum*, 57: 430–7.

Ball, M.J. (2000) Problems of pragmatic profiling. In N. Muller (ed.) *Pragmatics in Speech and Language Pathology: Studies in Clinical Applications*. Philadelphia, PA: John Benjamins Publishing.

Ball, S.J. (1993) Education markets, choice and social class: the market as a class strategy in the UK and the USA. *British Journal of the Sociology of Education*, 14(1): 3–19.

Bamford, J. and Saunders, E. (1991) *Hearing Impairment, Auditory Perception and Language Disability*, 2nd edition. London: Whurr.

Bandura, A. (1977) *Social Learning Theory*. Englewood Cliffs, NJ: Prentice Hall.

Bangert-Drowns, R.L., Kulik, C.L.C., Kulik, J.A. and Morgan, M.T. (1991) The instructional effect of feedback in test-like events. *Review of Educational Research*, 61: 213–38.

Baranek, G. T. (2002) Efficacy of sensory and motor interventions for children with autism. *Journal of Autism and Developmental Disorders*, 32(5): 397–421.

Barden, R. (2003) Whither mother tongue assessment? *NALDIC News*, 29: 9–11.

Barnes, C. (1996) Theories of disabilities and the origin of oppression of disabled people in Western society. In L. Barton (ed.) *Disability and Society: Emerging Issues and Insights*. London: Longman.

Barnett, D.W., Daly, E.J., III, Jones, K.M., and Lentz, F.E., Jr. (2004) Response to intervention: empirically-based special service decisions from increasing and decreasing intensity single case designs. *Journal of Special Education*, 38(2): 66–79.

Bar-On, R. and Parker, J.D. (2000) *Bar-On Emotional Quotient Inventory: Youth Version*. Newbury: NHS. Toronto: Multi-Health Systems.

Baron-Cohen, S., Leslie, A.M. and Frith, U. (1985) Does the autistic child have a 'theory of mind'? *Cognition*, 4: 37–46.

Baroody, A.J. (2003) The development of adaptive expertise and flexibility: the integration of conceptual and procedural knowledge. In A.J. Baroody and A. Dowker (ed.) *The Development of Arithmetic Concepts and Skills: Constructing Adaptive Expertise* (pp. 1–32). London: Lawrence Erlbaum Associates.

Barrados, O. (1996) A study of the oral language proficiency of Portuguese bilingual children in London. In T. Cline and N. Frederickson (eds) *Curriculum Related Assessment, Cummins and Bilingual Pupils*. Clevedon: Multilingual Matters.

Barrett, M. and Trevitt, J. (1991) *Attachment Behaviour and the Schoolchild: An Introduction to Educational Therapy*. London: Routledge.

Barwell, R. (2004) *Some Issues Concerning EAL in the Mathematics Classroom*. Unit within the ITTSEAL Website. http://www.naldic.org.uk/ITTSEAL2/teaching/Maths1.cfm (accessed 29 December 2006).

Barwell, R. (2005) Working on arithmetic word problems when English is an additional language. *British Educational Research Journal*, 31(3): 329–48.

Bates, J.E., Deater-Deckard, K., Dodge, K.A. and Pettit, G.S. (1996) Physical discipline among African American and European American mothers: link to children's externalizing behaviors. *Development Psychology*, 32(6): 1065–72.

Batten, A., Corbett, C., Rosenblatt, M., Withers, L. and Yulle, R. (2006) *Make School Make Sense. Autism and Education: the Reality for Families Today*. London: National Autistic Society.

Baumann, G. (1996) *Contesting Culture: Discourses of Identity in Multiethnic London*. Cambridge: Cambridge University Press.

Baumeister, R.F., Campbell, J.D., Krueger, J.I. and Vhos, K.D. (2003) Does high self-esteem cause better performance, inter-personal success, happiness or healthier lifestyles? *Psychological Science in the Public Interest*, 4(1): 1–44.

Bauminger, N. (2002) The facilitation of social-emotional understanding and social interaction in high functioning children with autism: intervention outcomes. *Journal of Autism and Developmental Disorders*, 32(4): 283–98.

Bax, M., Goldstein, M. *et al.* (2005) Proposed definition and classification of cerebral palsy, April 2005. *Developmental Medicine & Child Neurology*, 47: 571–6.

Beane, J.A. (1991) Sorting out the self-esteem controversy. *Educational Leadership*, 49(1): 25–30.

Bear, G.G. (1998) School discipline in the United States: prevention, correction and long term social development. *Educational and Child Psychology*, 15(1): 15–39.

Beaton, A.E., Mullis, I.V.S., Martin, M.O., Gonzalez, E.J., Kelly, D.L. and Smith, T.A. (1996) *Mathematics Achievement in the Middle School Years*. Boston, MA: Boston College.

Beaver, R. (1996) *Educational Psychology Casework: A Practical Guide*. London: Jessica Kingsley.

Beech, J.R. and Keys, A. (1997) Reading, vocabulary and language preference in 7–8 year old bilingual Asian children. *British Journal of Educational Psychology*, 67: 405–14.

Bellak, L. and Bellak, S. (1949) *The Children's Apperception Test*. New York: CPS Co.

Benjamin, S. (2003) Gender and special educational needs. In C. Skelton and B. Francis (eds) *Boys and Girls in the Primary Classroom* (pp. 98–112). Maidenhead: Open University Press.

Bennathan, M. and Boxall, M. (2000) *Effective Intervention in Primary Schools: Nurture Groups*, 2nd edition. London: David Fulton.

Bennett, J., Gash, H. and O'Reilly, M. (1998) Ireland: Integration as appropriate, segregation where necessary. In T. Booth and M. Ainscow (eds) *From Them to Us*. London: Routledge.

Bennington, A. (2004) Science and pre-school children with special educational needs: aspects of home-based teaching sessions. *British Journal of Special Education*, 31(4): 191–8.

Beresford, B. (1995) *Expert Opinions: A National Survey of Parents Caring for a Severely Disabled Child*. Bristol: The Policy Press.

Berger, A., Henderson, J. and Morris, D. (1999) *Implementing the Literacy Hour for Pupils with Learning Difficulties*. London: David Fulton.

Berk, R.A. (1984) Conducting the item analysis. In R.A. Berk (ed.) *A Guide to Criterion-Referenced Test Construction*. Baltimore, MD: Johns Hopkins University Press.

Berliner, D.C. (1987) Knowledge is power: a talk to teachers about a revolution in the teaching profession. In D.C. Berliner and B.V. Rosenshine (eds) *Talks to Teachers*. New York: Random House.

Bettle, S., Frederickson, N. and Sharp, S. (2001) Supporting schools in special measures: the contribution of educational psychology. *Educational Psychology in Practice*, 17(1): 53–68.

Beveridge, M. and Conti-Ramsden, G. (1987) *Children with Language Disabilities*. Milton Keynes: Open University Press.

Bhopal, R. (2004) Glossary of terms relating to ethnicity and race: for reflection and debate. *Journal of Epidemiology and Community Health* 58: 441–5.

Bibby, T. (2002) Shame: an emotional response to doing mathematics as an adult and a teacher. *British Educational Research Journal*, 28(5): 705–21.

Bickel, W.E. (1999) The implications of the effective schools literature for school restructuring. In C.R. Reynolds and T.B. Gutkin (eds) *The Handbook of School Psychology*, 3rd edition (pp. 959–83). New York: Wiley.

Bierman, K. and Furman, W. (1984) The effects of social skills training and peer involvement on the social adjustment of pre-adolescents. *Child Development*, 55: 151–62.

Biggar, S. and Barr, J. (1996) The emotional world of specific learning difficulties. In G. Reid (ed.) *Dimensions of Dyslexia*, Vol. 2. Edinburgh: Moray House.

Binder, C. (1993) Behavioural fluency: a new paradigm. *Educational Technology*, October: 8–14.

Bishop, D.V.M. (1997) *Uncommon Understanding: Development and Disorders of Language Comprehension in Children*. Hove: Psychology Press.

Bishop, D.V.M. (1998) Development of the Children's Communication Checklist (CCC): a method for assessing qualitative aspects of communicative impairment in children. *Journal of Child Psychology and Psychiatry*, 39(6): 879–92.

Bishop, D.V.M. (2003) *Test for Reception of Grammar*, 2nd edition. London: NFER-Nelson.

Bishop, D.V.M. (2006) What causes specific language impairment in children? *Current Directions in Psychological Science*, 15(5): 217–21.

Bishop, D.V.M. and Butterworth, G.E. (1980) Verbal-performance discrepancies: relationship to birth risk and specific reading retardation. *Cortex*, 16: 375–90.

Black, P.J. and Wiliam, D. (1998a) Assessment and classroom learning. *Assessment in Education: Principles, Policy and Practice*, 5(1): 7–73.

Black, P.J. and Wiliam, D. (1998b) *Inside the Black Box: Raising Standards through ClassRoom Assessment*. London: King's College London School of Education.

Black, P. and Wiliam, D. (2006) The reliability of assessments. In J. Gardner (ed.) *Assessment and Learning* (pp. 119–32). London: Sage.

Black, P.J., Harrison, C., Lee, C., Marshall, B. and Wiliam, D. (2002) *Working Inside the Black Box*. London: King's College London Department of Education and Professional Studies.

Blakemore, S. and Frith, U. (2005) *The Learning Brain. Lessons for Education*, Oxford: Blackwell.

Blakemore, S., Winston, J. and Frith, U. (2004) Social cognitive neuroscience: where are we heading? *Trends in Cognitive Sciences*, 8(5): 216–22.

Blandy, S.E. and Lutman, M.E. (2005) Hearing threshold levels and speech recognition in noise in 7-year-olds. *International Journal of Audiology*, 44(8): 435–43.

Blatchford, P., Russell, A., Bassett, P., Brown, P. and Morton, C. (2007) The role and effects of teaching assistants in English primary schools: years 4–6, 2000–2003. Results from the class size and pupil-adult ratios (CSPAR). K.S.2 Project. *British Educational Research Journal*, 33(1): 5–26.

Bloom, A. (2005) Teachers shy away from hyperactivity and autism. *Times Educational Supplement*, 14 October: 4.

Board of Education (1943) *Curriculum and Examinations in Secondary Schools* (Norwood Report). London: HMSO.

Boder, E. (1973) Developmental dyslexia: a diagnostic approach based on three atypical reading patterns. *Developmental Medicine and Child Neurology*, 75: 663–87.

Boivin, M., Dodge, K.A. and Coie, J.D. (1995) Individual-group behavioural similarity and peer status in experimental play groups of boys: the social misfit revisited. *Journal of Personality and Social Psychology*, 69(2): 269–79.

Bolt, D. (2004) Terminology and the psychosocial burden of blindness. *British Journal of Visual Impairment*, 22(2): 52–4.

Bondy, A.S. and Frost, L.A. (1994) The Picture Exchange Communication System. *Focus on Autistic Behavior*, 9: 1–19.

Boniwell, I. (2006) *Positive Psychology in a Nutshell*. London: Personal Well-Being Centre.

Bontempo, D.E. and D'Augelli, A.R. (2002) Effects of at school victimisation and sexual orientation on lesbian, gay or bi-sexual youths. *Journal of Adolescent Health*, 30: 364–74.

Booker, R. (2005) Integrated children's services: implications for the profession. *Educational and Child Psychology*, 22(4): 127–42.

Booth, S.R. and Jay, M. (1981) The use of precision teaching technology in the work of the educational psychologist. *Journal of the Association of Educational Psychologists*, 5(5): 21–6.

Booth, S.R. and Jewell, T. (1983) Programmes for slow learners. *Journal of the Association of Educational Psychologists*, 6(2): 58–62.

Booth, T. and Ainscow, M. (eds) (1998) *From Them To Us: An International Study of Inclusion in Education*. London: Routledge.

Booth, T. and Ainscow, M. (2002) *Index for Inclusion: Developing Learning and Participation in Schools*. Bristol: CISE.

Booth, T., Ainscow, M., Black-Hawkins, K., Vaughn, M. and Shaw, L. (2000) *Index for Inclusion: Developing Learning and Participation in Schools*. Bristol: CSIE.

Borkowski, J.G., Weyhing, R.S. and Carr, M. (1988) Effects of attributional retraining on strategy-based reading comprehension in learning-disabled students. *Journal of Educational Psychology*, 80: 46–53.

Bostock, A. (1988) *Eyes: Children with Impaired Vision*. London: Inner London Education Authority.

Botting, N., Crutchley, A. and Conti-Ramsden, G. (1998) Educational transitions of seven-year-old children with specific language impairment in language units: a longitudinal study. *International Journal of Language and Communication Disorders*, 33(2): 177–219.

Boulton, M.J. and Smith, P.K. (1992) Ethnic preferences and perceptions among Asian and white British middle school children. *Social Development*, 1: 55–66.

Bourne, J. (2001) Discourses and identity in a multilingual primary classroom. *Oxford Review of Education*, 27(1): 103–14.

Bourne, J. (2005) Constructing 'ability' through talk. *NALDIC Quarterly*, 2(3): 3–9.

Bowlby, J. (1988) *A Secure Base: Parent–Child Attachment and Healthy Human Development*. New York: Basic Books.

Braden, J.P. and Athanasiou, M.S. (2005) A comparative review of nonverbal measures of intelligence. In D.P. Flanagan and P.L. Harrison (eds) *Contemporary Intellectual Assessment: Theories, Tests and Issues*, 2nd edition (pp. 557–78). New York: Guilford Press.

Brand, C. (1996) *The g Factor: General Intelligence and its Implications*. New York: Wiley.

Brennan, W.K. (1982) *Changing Special Education*. Milton Keynes: Open University Press.

Brettingham, M. (2007) Delays hit SEN support. *Times Educational Supplement*, 27 April: 1.

Briskman, J., Happé, F. and Frith, U. (2001) Exploring the cognitive phenotype of autism: weak 'central coherence' of parents and siblings of children with autism II. Real life skills and preferences. *Journal of Child Psychology & Psychiatry*, 42: 309–16.

Bristow, J., Cowley, P. and Daines, B. (1999) *Memory and Learning: A Practical Guide for Teachers*. London: David Fulton.

British Psychological Society (1996) *Attention Deficit Hyperactivity Disorder (ADHD): A Psychological Response to an Evolving Concept* (Report of a working party of the British Psychological Society). Leicester: BPS.

British Psychological Society (1999) *Dyslexia, Literacy and Psychological Assessment*. Leicester: BPS.

Broadfoot, P. and Black, P. (2004) Redefining assessment? The first ten years of assessment in education. *Assessment in Education: Principles, Policy and Practice*, 11(1): 7–26.

Brodie, I. (2000) Children's homes and school exclusion: redefining the problem. *Support for Learning*, 15(1): 25–9.

Brodie, I. and Berridge, D. (1996) *School Exclusion: Research Themes and Issues*. Luton: University of Luton Press.

Bronfenbrenner, U. (1979) *The Ecology of Human Development*. Cambridge, MA: Harvard University Press.

Bronfenbrenner, U. (1986) A generation in jeopardy: America's hidden family policy. Testimony presented to the Committee on Rules and administration, Washington, DC, 23 July.

Bronfenbrenner, U. and Morris, P.A. (2006) The bio-ecological model of human development. In R.M. Lerner (ed.) *Handbook of Child Psychology*, 6th edition, Vol. 1, *Theoretical Models of Human Development* (pp. 793–828). Hoboken, NJ: Wiley.

Brooks, G. (2002) *What Works for Children with Literacy Difficulties?* DfES Research Report RR380. London: DfES.

Brooks, P. (1995) A comparison of the effectiveness of different teaching strategies in teaching spelling to a student with severe specific difficulties/dyslexia. *Educational and Child Psychology*, 12 (1): 80–8.

Brooks, P. and Weeks, S. (1999) *Individual Styles in Learning to Spell: Improving Spelling in Children with Literacy Difficulties and All Children in Mainstream Schools*. London: DfEE Publications

Brown, A. and Campione, J. (1996) Communities of learning and thinking, or a context by any other name. In P. Woods (ed.) *Contemporary Issues in Teaching and Learning*. London: Routledge.

Brown, A.L., Campione, J.C., Webber, L.S. and Winnikur, D.W. (1992) Interactive learning environments: a new look at assessment and instruction. In B.R. Gifford and M.C. O'Connor (eds) *Changing Assessments: Alternative Views of Aptitude, Achievement and Instruction*. New York: Kluwer Academic.

Brown, J.R. and Rogers, S.J. (2003) Cultural issues in autism. In S. Ozonoff, S.J. Rogers and R.L. Hendren (eds) *Autistic Spectrum Disorders: A Research Review for Practitioners*. Washington, DC: American Psychiatric Publishing.

Brown, M. (1999) Swings of the pendulum. In I. Thompson (ed.) *Issues in Teaching Numeracy in Primary Schools*. Buckingham: Open University Press.

Brown, M. and Millett, A. (2003) Has the National Numeracy Strategy raised standards? In I. Thompson (ed.) *Enhancing Primary Mathematics Teaching* (pp. 198–209). Buckingham: Open University Press.

Brown, R., Hobson, R.P., Lee, A. and Stevenson, J. (1997) Are there 'autistic-like' features in congenitally blind children? *Journal of Child Psychology and Psychiatry*, 38: 693–703.

Brownlow, C. and O'Dell, L. (2002) Ethical issues for qualitative research in on-line communities. *Disability and Society*, 17(6): 685–94.

Budoff, M. (1987) The validity of learning potential assessments. In C.S. Lidz (ed.) *Dynamic Assessment: An Interactional Approach to Evaluating Learning Potential*. New York: Guilford Press.

Building Schools for the Future (2004) *Transforming Schools, Inspiring Learning*. Available online at: http://www.bsf.gov.uk/ (accessed 4 December 2007).

Burden, R. (1978) School systems analysis: a project centred approach. In B. Gillham (ed.) *Reconstructing Educational Psychology*. Beckenham: Croom Helm.

Burden, R. (1981) Systems theory and its relevance to schools. In B. Gillham (ed.) *Problem Behaviour in the Secondary School*. London: Croom Helm.

Burden, R. (1999) Children's self perceptions. In N. Frederickson and R.J. Cameron (eds) *Psychology in Education Portfolio*. Windsor: NFER-Nelson.

Burden, R. (2005) *Dyslexia and Self Concept. Seeking a Dyslexic Identity*. London: Whurr.

Burden, R.L. and Fraser, B.J. (1993) Use of classroom environment assessments in school psychology: a British perspective. *Psychology in the Schools*, 30: 232–40.

Burnett, P.C. (1994) Self-concept and self-esteem in elementary school children. *Psychology in the Schools*, 11: 164–71.

Burns, R. and Kaufman, S. (1970) *Kinetic Family Drawings (K-F-D): An Introduction to Understanding Children through Kinetic Drawings*. New York: Brunner/Mazel.

Burt, C. (1917) *The Distribution and Relations of Educational Abilities*. London: King and Son.

Burt, C. (1937) *The Subnormal Mind*, 2nd edition. London: Oxford University Press.

Burwell, J., D'Sena, P. and Barrett, F. (1998) Accessing GCSE maths for 'bilingual' pupils. In P. D'Sena and F. Barrett (eds) *Raising Educational Achievement for All*, LMU Education Papers No. 3. Leeds: Leeds Metropolitan University.

Butler, I. (2006) *Viewpoint Looked After Children Report 2006*. Bridgend: The Viewpoint Organisation.

Butterworth, B. (2003) *Dyscalculia Screener*. London: NFER-Nelson. .

Butterworth, B. (2005a) The development of arithemetical abilities. *Journal of Child Psychology and Psychiatry*, 46(1): 3–18.

Butterworth, B. (2005b) Developmental dyscalculia. In J.I.D. Campbell (ed.) *Handbook of Mathematical Cognition* (pp. 455–67). New York: Psychology Press.

Buxton, L. (1981) *Do You Panic About Maths?* London: Heinemann.

Byers, R. (1999a) Experience and achievement: initiatives in curriculum development for pupils with severe and profound and multiple learning difficulties. *British Journal of Special Education*, 26(4): 184–8.

Byers, R. (1999b) The National Literacy Strategy and pupils with special educational needs. *British Journal of Special Education*, 26(1): 8–11.

Byers, R. and Fergusson, A. (2003) Policies for promoting literacy: including pupils with severe and profound and multiple learning difficulties. In C. Tilstone and R. Rose (eds) *Strategies to Promote Inclusive Practice* (pp. 134–50). London: RoutledgeFalmer.

Caesar, G., Parchment, M. and Berridge, D. (1994) *Black Perspectives on Services for Children in Need*. London: Barnardo's/National Children's Bureau.

Cain, K. and Oakhill, J. (2006) Assessment matters: issues in the measurement of reading comprehension. *British Journal of Educational Psychology*, 76(4): 697–708.

Cairney, J., Hay, J.A., Faught, B.E. Wade, T.J., Corna, L. and Flouris, A. (2005) Developmental coordination disorder, generalized self-efficacy toward physical activity, and participation in organized and free play activities. *Journal of Pediatrics*, 147: 515–20.

Caldarella, P. and Merrell, K.W. (1997) Common dimensions of social skills of children and adolescents: a taxonomy of positive behaviours. *School Psychology Review*, 26(2): 264–78.

Cameron, L. and Bygate, M. (1997) Key issues in assessing progression in English as an additional language. In C. Leung and C. Cable (eds) *English as an Additional Language: Changing Perspectives*. Watford: National Association for Language Development in the Curriculum.

Cameron, R.J. and Monsen, J.J. (2005) Quality psychological advice for teachers, parents/carers and LEA decision-makers with respect to children and young people with special needs. *Educational Psychology in Practice*, 21(4): 283–306.

Cameron, R.J. and Reynolds, A.R. (1999) Learning style and metacognition. In N.L. Frederickson and R.J. Cameron (eds) *Psychology in Education Portfolio*. Windsor: NFER-Nelson.

Campione, J.C. (1989) Assisted assessment: a taxonomy of approaches and an outline of strengths and weaknesses. *Journal of Learning Disabilities*, 22(3): 151–65.

Cantell, M.H., Smyth, M.M. and Ahonen, T.P. (2003) Two distinct pathways for developmental coordination disorder: persistence and resolution. *Human Movement Science*, 22: 413–31.

Canter, L. and Canter, M. (1992) *Assertive Discipline*. Santa Monica, CA: Lee Canter Associates.

Carr, A. (2000) *What Works with Children and Adolescents? A Critical Review of Psychological Interventions with Children, Adolescents and Their Families*. London: Routledge.

Carr, J. (1988) Six weeks to twenty one years old: a longitudinal study of children with Down's syndrome and their families. 29(4): 407–32.

Carrasquillo, A.L. and Rodriguez, V. (1996) *Language Minority Students in the Mainstream Classroom*. Clevedon: Multilingual Matters.

Cartledge, G. and Milburn, J.F. (1996) *Cultural Diversity and Social Skills Instruction: Understanding Ethnic and Gender Differences*. Champaign, IL: Research Press.

Causey, V.E., Thomas, C.D. and Armento, B.J. (2000) Cultural diversity is basically a foreign term to me: the challenges of diversity for preservice teacher education. *Teaching and Teacher Education*, 16: 33–45.

Center for Effective Collaboration and Practice (2006) Problem behavior pathway. http://cecp.air.org/fba/problembehavior2/appendixg.htm.

Chakrabati, S. and Fombonne, E. (2001) Pervasive developmental disorders in pre-school children. *Journal of the American Medical Association*, 285: 3093–9.

Chalder, T. and Hussain, K. (2002) *Self Help for Chronic Fatigue Syndrome: A Guide for Young People*. Witney, Oxon: Blue Stallion Publications.

Challenging Behaviour Research Project (2005) *A Study of Children and Young People who Present Challenging Behaviour*. University of Birmingham/Ofsted.

Chamba, R., Ahmad, W.I.U., Darr, A. and Jones, L. (1998) The education of Asian deaf children. In S. Gregory *et al.* (eds) *Issues in Deaf Education*. London: David Fulton.

Chambers, M.E., Sugden, D.A. and Sinani, C. (2005) The nature of children with developmental coordination disorder. In D.A. Sugden and M.E. Chambers (eds) *Children with Developmental Coordination Disorder* (pp. 1–18). London: Whurr.

Chapman, E.K. and Stone, J.M. (1988) *The Visually Handicapped Child in Your Classroom*. London: Cassell.

Chapman, J.W. and Tumner, W.E. (1995) Development of young children's reading self-concepts: an examination of emerging sub-components and their relationship with reading achievement. *Journal of Educational Psychology*, 87(1): 154–67.

Chapman, S.S., Ewing, C.B. and Mozzoni, M.P. (2005) Precision teaching and fluency training across cognitive, physical and academic tasks in children with traumatic brain injury: a multiple baseline study. *Behavioural Interventions*, 20: 37–49.

Charles, R., Lester, F. and O'Daffer, P. (1987) *How to Evaluate Progress in Problem Solving*. Reston, VA: National Council for Teachers of Mathematics.

Charlop-Christy, M.H., Le, L. and Freeman, K.A. (2000) A comparison of video modeling with invivo modeling for teaching children with autism. *Journal of Autism and Developmental Disorders*, 30(6): 537–52.

Charman, T. and Howlin, P. (2003) Research into early intervention for children with autism and related disorders: methodological and design issues. *Autism*, 7(2): 217–25.

Charman, T., Baron-Cohen, S., Swettenham, J., Baird, G., Cox, A. and Drew, A. (2001) Testing joint tension, imitation and play as infant precursors to language and theory of mind. *Cognitive Development*, 15: 481–98.

Chau, K.L. (1989) Sociocultural dissonance among ethnic minority populations. *Social Casework: The Journal of Contemporary Social Work*, 224–30.

Chaudhury, A. (1986) *ACE Special Education Advice Service for the Bangladeshi Community Annual Report 1986*. London: Advisory Centre for Education.

Chazan, M. (1964) The incidence and nature of maladjustment among children in schools for the educationally subnormal. *British Journal of Educational Psychology*, 35: 292–304.

Chazan, M. (1974) Children with learning difficulties. In M. Chazan, T. Moore, P. Williams and J. Wright (eds) *The Practice of Educational Psychology*. London: Longman.

Checkland, P.B. (1981) *Systems Thinking, Systems Practice*. Chichester: Wiley.

Checkland, P.B. (1986) A basic introduction to systems thinking. Unpublished paper, University of Lancaster.

Checkland, P.B. and Scholes, J. (1990) *Soft Systems Methodology in Action*. Chichester: Wiley.

Chen, J.-Q. and Gardner, H. (2005) Assessment based on multiple-intelligences theory. In D.P. Flanagan and P.L. Harrison (eds) *Contemporary Intellectual Assessment: Theories, Tests and Issues*, 2nd edition (pp. 77–102). New York: Guilford Press.

Chen, X., Rubin, K.H. and Sun, Y. (1992) Social reputation and peer relationships in Chinese and Canadian children: a cross cultural study. *Child Development*, 63: 1336–43.

Chen, X. Wang, L. and DeSouza, A. (2006) Temperament, socio-emotional functioning and peer relationships in Chinese and North American children. In X. Chen, D.C. French and B.H. Schneider (eds) *Peer Relationships in Cultural Context*. Cambridge: Cambridge University Press.

Cheng, Z.J. and Chan, L.K.S. (2005) Chinese number-naming advantages? Analyses of Chinese pre-schoolers' computational strategies and errors. *International Journal of Early Years Education*, 13(2): 179–92.

Chiesa, N. and Roberston, A. (2000) Precision teaching and fluency training: making maths easier for pupils and teachers. *Educational Psychology in Practice*, 16(3): 297–310.

Child, D. (1991) A survey of communication approaches used in schools for the deaf in the U.K. *Journal of the British Association of Teachers of the Deaf*, 15(1): 20–4.

Chinn, S. (2004) *The Trouble with Maths: A Practical Guide to Helping Learners with Numeracy Difficulties*. London: RoutledgeFarmer.

Chinn, S.J. and Ashcroft, J.R. (1998) *Mathematics for Dyslexics: A Teaching Handbook*. London: Whurr Publishing.

Chrispeels, J. (1996) Effective schools and home-school-community partnership roles: a framework for parent involvement. *School Effectiveness and School Improvement*, 7(4): 297–323.

Civil, M. and Andrade, R. (2002) Transitions between home and school mathematics: rays of hope amidst the passing clouds. In G. de Abreu, A.J. Bishop and N.C. Presmeg (eds) *Transitions between Contexts of Mathematical Practices*. (pp. 149–69). Dordrecht, The Netherlands: Kluwer Academic.

Clark, A. and Moss, P. (2005) *Spaces to Play: More Listening to Young Children Using the Mosaic Approach*. London: National Children's Bureau.

Clark, C., Dyson, A., Millward, A. and Robson, S. (1999) Theories of inclusion, theories of schools: deconstructing and reconstructing the inclusive school. *British Educational Research Journal*, 25(2): 157–77.

Clarke, A.M. and Clarke, A.D.B. (1976) *Early Experience: Myth and Evidence*. Shepton Mallett: Open Books.

Clarke, S. (2003) *Enriching Feedback in the Primary Classroom*. London: Hodder and Stoughton.

Clarke, V. (2002) Sameness and difference in research on lesbian parenting. *Journal of Community & Applied Social Psychology*, 12, 210–22.

Clay, M. (1998) *By Different Paths to Common Outcomes*. York, ME: Stenhouse.

Clay, M.M. (1987) Learning to be learning disabled. *New Zealand Journal of Educational Studies*, 22: 155–73.

Cline, T. (1991) Professional constructions of the concept of moderate learning difficulties. In P.L.C. Evans and A.D.B. Clarke (eds) *Combatting Mental Handicap: A Multidisciplinary Approach*. Bicester: A.B. Academic.

Cline, T. (1992) Assessment of special educational needs: meeting reasonable expectations? in T. Cline (ed.) *The Assessment of Special Educational Needs: International Perspectives*. London: Routledge.

Cline, T. (1993) Educational assessment of bilingual pupils: getting the context right. *Educational and Child Psychology*, 10(4): 59–68.

Cline, T. (1997a) Educating for bilingualism in different contexts: teaching the deaf and teaching children with English as an additional language. *Educational Review*, 49(2): 145–52.

Cline, T. (1997b) Special educational needs and language proficiency. In C. Leung and C. Cable (eds) *English as an Additional Language: Changing Perspectives*, pp. 53–64. Watford: National Association for Language Development in the Curriculum.

Cline, T. (1998) The assessment of special educational needs for bilingual children. *British Journal of Special Education*, 25(4): 159–63.

Cline, T. (ed.) (2005) *Assessing Children's Knowledge and Use of Community Languages for Educational Purposes: Report of a Workshop Held at the University of Luton*. Luton: National Association for Language Development in the Curriculum.

Cline, T. and Baldwin, S. (2004) *Selective Mutism in Childhood*, 2nd edition. London: Whurr.

Cline, T. and Cozens, B. (1999) The analysis of aspects of classroom texts that challenge children when learning to read in their second language: a pilot study. In H. South (ed.) *Literacies in Community and School* (NALDIC occasional publications series). Watford: National Association for Language Development in the Curriculum.

Cline, T. and Frederickson, N. (eds) (1991) *Bilingual Pupils and the National Curriculum: Overcoming Difficulties in Teaching and Learning*. London: University College London, Department of Psychology.

Cline, T. and Frederickson, N. (eds) (1996) *Progress in Curriculum Related Assessment for Bilingual Pupils*. Bristol: Multilingual Matters.

Cline, T. and Frederickson, N. (1999) Identification and assessment of dyslexia in bi/multilingual children. *International Journal of Bilingual Education and Bilingualism*, 2(2): 81–93.

Cline, T. and Reason, R. (1993) Specific learning difficulties (dyslexia): equal opportunities issues. *British Journal of Special Education*, 20(1): 30–4.

Cline, T. and Shamsi, T. (2000) *Language Needs or Special Needs? The Assessment of Learning Difficulties in Literacy among Children Learning English as an Additional Language: A Literature Review*, Research Report RR184. London: DfEE.

Cline, T., De Abreu, G., Fihosy, C., Gray, H., Lambert, H. and Neale, J. (2002) *Minority Ethnic Pupils in Mainly White Schools*, Research Report RR365. London: The Stationery Office.

Coard, B. (1971) *How the West Indian Child is Made Educationally Subnormal in the British School System*. London: New Beacon Books.

Coffield, F.C., Moseley, D.V.M., Hall, E. and Ecclestone, K. (2004) *Should We Be Using Learning Styles? What Research Has to Say to Practice*. London: Learning and Skills Research Centre.

Cohen, O.P., Fischgrund, M.A. and Redding, R. (1990) Deaf children from ethnic, linguistic and racial minority backgrounds: an overview. *American Annals of the Deaf*, 135: 67–73.

Coie, J.D. and Benenson, J.F. (1983) A qualitative analysis of the relationship between peer rejection and physically aggressive behaviour. Unpublished manuscript. Duke University, Durham NC.

Coie, J.D., Dodge, K.A. and Coppotelli, H. (1982) Dimensions and types of social status: a cross-age perspective. *Developmental Psychology*, 18(4): 557–70.

Coie, J., Terry, R., Lenox, K., and Lochman, J. (1995) Childhood peer rejection and aggression as predictors of stable patterns of adolescent disorder. *Development and Psychopathology*, 7: 697–713.

Cole, B.A. (2004) *Mother-Teachers: Insights into Inclusion*. London: David Fulton.

Cole, T., Daniels, H. and Visser, J. (2003) Patterns of provision for pupils with behavioural difficulties in England: a study of government statistics and support plan data. *Oxford Review of Education*, 29(2): 187–205.

Collishaw, S., Pickles, A., Messer, J., Rutter, M., Shearer, C. and Maughan, B. (2007) Resilience to adult psychopathology following childhood maltreatment: evidence from a community sample. *Child Abuse and Neglect*, 31(3): 211–29.

Commission for Racial Equality (1986) *Teaching English as a Second Language: Report of a Formal Investigation in Calderdale Local Education Authority*. London: CRE.

Condry, J. and Condry S. (1976) Sex differences: a study of the eye of the beholder. *Child Development*, 47: 812–19.

Condry, J. and Ross, D.F. (1985) Sex and aggression: the influence of gender label on the perception of aggression in children. *Child Development*, 56: 225–33.

Conduct Problems Prevention Research Group (1999) Initial impact of the Fast Track prevention trial for conduct problems: II. Classroom effects. *Journal of Consulting and Clinical Psychology*, 67: 648–57.

Conduct Problems Prevention Research Group (2002) Evaluation of the first three years of the fast track prevention trial with children at high risk for adolescent conduct problems. *Journal of Abnormal Child Psychology*, 30: 19–35.

Connolly, J.A. (1983) A review of sociometric procedures in the assessment of social competencies in children. *Applied Research in Mental Retardation*, 4: 315–27.

Connor, C.D., Craig, H.K., Raudenbush, S.W., Heavner, K. and Zwolan, T.A. (2006) The age at which young deaf children receive cochlear implants and their vocabulary and speech-production growth: is there an added value for early implantation? *Ear and Hearing*, 27: 628–44.

Connor, M. (2005) Autistic spectrum disorders, South East Region: a survey of provision. In S. Dunsmuir and N. Frederickson (eds) *Autistic Spectrum Disorders* [CD]. London: Educational Psychology Publishing, University College London. Originally published on the National Autistic Society website in 2001.

Conti-Ramsden, G., Simkin, Z. and Botting, N. (2006) The prevalence of autistic spectrum disorders in adolescents with a history of specific language impairment (SLI). *Journal of Child Psychology and Psychiatry*, 47(6): 621–8.

Cook, G., Jerrish, K. and Clark, C. (2001) Decision making in teams: issues arising from two UK evaluations. *Journal of Inter Professional Care*, 15(2): 141–51.

Cooper, D.H. and Valli, L. (1996) Designing classrooms for inclusion: beyond management. In D.L. Speece and B.K. Keogh (eds) *Research on Classroom Ecologies: Implications for Inclusion of Children with Learning Disabilities*. Hillsdale, NJ: Lawrence Erlbaum Associates.

Cooper, P. (1997) The myth of attention deficit/hyperactivity disorder. *British Psychological Society Education Section Review*, 21(1): 3–14.

Cooper, P., Arnold, R. and Boyd, E. (2001) The effectiveness of nurture groups: preliminary research findings. *British Journal of Special Education*, 28(4): 160–6.

Corbett, J. (1995) *Bad-Mouthing: The Language of Special Needs*. London: Falmer Press.

Corbett, J. (1998) *Special Educational Needs in the Twentieth Century: A Cultural Analysis*. London: Cassell.

Cornell, D.T., Sheras, P.L. and Cole, J.C.M. (2006) Assessment of bullying. In S.R. Jimerson and M. Thurlong (eds) *Handbook of School Violence and School Safety: From Research to Practice*. Mahwah, NJ: Lawrence Erlbaum.

Coupe, J. and Porter, J. (eds) (1986) *The Education of Children with Severe Learning Difficulties: Bridging the Gap between Theory and Practice*. London: Croom Helm.

Cousins, M. and Smyth, M.M. (2005) Progression and development in developmental coordination disorder. In D.A. Sugden and M.E. Chambers (eds) *Children with Developmental Coordination Disorder* (pp. 119–34). London: Whurr.

Covington, M.V. (1989) Self-esteem and failure in school: analysis and policy implications. In A. Mecca, N.J. Smelser and J. Vasconcellos (eds) *The Social Importance of Self-Esteem*. Berkeley: University of California Press.

Cowen, E.L., Pederson, A., Babigian, H., Izzo, L.D. and Trost, M.A. (1973) Long-term follow up of early detected vulnerable children. *Journal of Consulting and Clinical Psychology*, 41: 438–46.

Cowie, H. and Pecherek, A. (1994) *Counselling Approaches and Issues in Education*. London: David Fulton.

Cowie, H., Smith, P., Boulton, M. and Laver, R. (1994) *Cooperation in the Multiethnic Classroom*. London: David Fulton.

Cox, T. and Jones, G. (1983) *Disadvantaged Eleven Year Olds*. Oxford: Pergamon Press.

Crawford, C., Lorraine Dearden, L. and Meghir, C. (2007) *When You Are Born Matters: The Impact of Date of Birth on Child Cognitive Outcomes in England*. London: Institute for Fiscal Studies.

Crawford, P.A. and Zygouris-Coe, V. (2006) All in the family: connecting home and school with family literacy. *Early Childhood Education Journal*, 33(4): 261–7.

Creese, A. (2005) *Teacher Collaboration and Talk in Multilingual Classrooms*. Clevedon: Multilingual Matters.

Crick, N.R. and Dodge, K.A. (1994) A review and reformulation of social information-processing mechanisms in children's social adjustment. *Psychological Bulletin*, 115(1): 74–101.

Cripps, M. (1996) Sign Language and me. In *Sign Writing: Writing by a Group of Deaf People in Manchester*. Manchester: Ducie Adult Education Centre (Lloyd Street North, Moss Side, Manchester M14 4GA).

Critchley, M. and Critchley, E.A. (1978) *Dyslexia Defined*. London: Heinemann Medical.

Croll, P. and Moses, D. (2000) *Special Needs in the Primary School: One in Five?* London: Cassell.

Cross, L. and Walker-Knight, D. (1997) Inclusion: developing collaborative and co-operative school communities. *The Educational Forum*, 61: 269–77.

Crown, R., Donlan, C., Newton, E. and Lloyd, D. (2005) Number skills and knowledge in children with specific language impairment. *Journal of Educational Psychology*, 97(4): 732–44.

Crozier, G. and Davies, J. (2007) Hard to reach parents or hard to reach schools? A discussion of home-school relations, with particular reference to Bangladeshi and Pakistani parents. *British Education Research Journal*, 33(3): 295–313.

Crozier, W.R. (1995) Shyness and self-esteem in middle childhood. *British Journal of Educational Psychology*, 20: 220–2.

Crutchley, A., Botting, N. and Conti-Ramsden, G. (1997a) Bilingualism and specific language impairment in children attending language units. *European Journal of Disorders of Communication*, 32: 267–76.

Crutchley, A., Conti-Ramsden, G. and Botting, N. (1997b) Bilingual children with specific language impairment and standardised assessments: preliminary findings from a study of children in language units. *International Journal of Bilingualism*, 1(2): 117–34.

Crystal, D. and Varley, R. (1998) *Introduction to Language Pathology*, 4th edition. London: Whurr.

Crystal, D., Fletcher, P. and Garman, M. (1989) *Language Assessment, Remediation and Screening Procedure (LARSP)*, 2nd edition. London: Cole and Whurr.

Cullingford, C. (1985) Teachers, parents and the control of schools. In C. Cullingford (ed.) *Parents, Teachers and Schools*. London: Robert Royce.

Cullingford, C. (2002) *The Best Years of Their Lives? Pupils' Experiences of School*. London: Kogan Page.

Cummins, J. (1984) *Bilingualism and Special Education: Issues in Assessment and Pedagogy*. Clevedon: Multilingual Matters.

Cummins, J. (1989) A theoretical framework for bilingual special education. *Exceptional Children*, 56(2): 111–19.

Cummins, J. (1996) *Negotiating Identities: Education for Empowerment in a Diverse Society*. Ontario, CA: California Association for Bilingual Education.

Cummins, J. (2000) *Language, Power and Pedagogy. Bilingual Children in the Crossfire*. Clevedon: Multilingual Matters.

Cunningham, C. and Davis, H. (1985) *Working with Parents: Frameworks for Collaboration*. Milton Keynes: Open University Press.

Cunningham, C.C. and Sloper, P. (1984) The relationship between maternal ratings of first word vocabulary and Reynell Language scores. *British Journal of Educational Psychology*, 54(2): 160–7.

Cunningham, C.E., Cataldo, M.F., Mallion, C. and Keyes, J.B. (1983) Evaluation of behavioral approaches to the management of elective mutism. *Child and Family Behavior Therapy*, 5(4): 25–49.

Curnyn, J.C., Wallace, I., Kistan, S. and McLaren, M. (1991) Special educational need and ethnic minority pupils. In Scottish Education Department/Regional Psychological Services (eds) *Professional Development Initiatives 1989–1990*. Edinburgh: Scottish Education Department.

Curtis, C. and Norgate, R. (2007) An evaluation of the promoting alternative thinking strategies curriculum at Key Stage 1. *Educational Psychology in Practice*, 23(1): 33–44.

Dale, P. (2007) Special education at Starcross before 1948. *History of Education*, 36(1): 17–44.

Dalton, P. (1996) When words fail: a personal construct approach to children's construing. *Educational and Child Psychology*, 13(4): 21–8.

Daniels, A. (1990) Social skills training for primary aged children. *Educational Psychology in Practice*, 6(3): 159–62.

Daniels, A. and Williams, H. (2000) Reducing the need for exclusions and statements for behaviour: the framework for intervention (Part 1). *Educational Psychology in Practice*, 15(4): 220–7.

Daniels, H. (1992) Dynamic assessment: pitfalls and prospects. In T. Cline (ed.) *Assessment of Special Educational Needs: International Perspectives*. London: Routledge.

Daniels, H., Hey, V., Leonard, D. and Smith, M. (1999a) Issues of equity in special needs education from a gender perspective. *British Journal of Special Education*, 26(4): 189–95.

Daniels, H., Visser, J., Cole, T. and de Reybekill, N. (1999b) *Emotional and Behavioural Difficulties in Mainstream Schools* (Research Report 90). London: HMSO.

Darrah, J., Watkins, B., Chen, L. and Bonin, C. (2004) Conductive education intervention for children with cerebral palsy: an AACPDM evidence report. *Developmental Medicine and Child Neurology*, 46(3): 187–203.

Dart, B., Burnett, P., Bolton-Lewis, G., Campbell, J., Smith, D. and McCrindle, A. (1999) Classroom learning environments and students' approaches to learning. *Learning Environments Research*, 2: 137–56.

Davie, R. (1986) Understanding behaviour problems. *Maladjustment and Therapeutic Education*, 4(1): 2–11.

Davie, R. (1996) Raising the achievements of pupils with special educational needs. *Support for Learning: British Journal of Learning Support*, 11(2): 51–6.

Davies, C. (1993) *Lifetimes: A Mutual Biography of Disabled People*. Farnham, Surrey: Understanding Disabilities Educational Trust.

Davies, J. and Brember, I. (1995) Stories in the kitchen: reading attitudes and habits of Year 2, 4 and 6 children. *Educational Research*, 37(3): 305–13.

Davis, A. (1991) The language of testing. In K. Durkin and B. Shire (ed.) *Language in Mathematical Education: Research and Practice*. Buckingham: Open University Press.

Davis, A., Wood, S., Healy, R., Webb, H. and Rowe, S. (1995) Risk factors for hearing disorders: epidemiological evidence of change over time in the UK. *Journal of the American Academy of Audiology*, 6: 365–70.

Davis, P. and Florian, L. (2004) *Teaching Strategies and Approaches for Pupils with Special Educational Needs: A Scoping Study*. Ref. RR516. London: Department for Education and Skills.

de Wolf, I.F. and Janssens, F.J.G. (2007) Effects and side-effects of inspections and account-ability in education: an overview of empirical studies. *Oxford Review of Education*, 33(3): 379–96.

DeBlassie, R.R. and Franco, J.N. (1983) Psychological and educational assessment of bilingual children. In D.R. Omark and J.G. Erickson (eds) *The Bilingual Exceptional Child*. San Diego, CA: College-Hill Press.

DECP (2006) *Promoting Racial Equality within Educational Psychology Services: A Report from the DECP Working Party on Anti-Racism*. Leicester: British Psychological Society.

Dehaney, R. (2000) Literacy hour and the literal thinker: the inclusion of children with semantic-pragmatic language difficulties in the literacy hour. *Support for Learning*, 15(1): 36–40.

Dekker, M. (2000) *On Our Own Terms: Emerging Autistic Culture*. Retrieved 11 April 2007 from http://autisticculture.com/index.php?page=articles.

DEMOS (2005) *About Learning: Report of the Learning Working Group*. London: DEMOS. http://www.demos.co.uk.

Den Boer, K. (1990) Country briefing: Special education in the Netherlands. *European Journal of Special Needs Education*, 5(2): 136–50.

Denney, M.K., Itkonen, T. and Okamoto, Y. (2007) Early intervention systems of care for Latino families and their young children with special needs: salient themes and guiding implications. *Infants & Young Children*. 20(4): 326–35.

Deno, S.L. (1985) Curriculum based measurement: the emerging alternative. *Exceptional Children*, 52(3): 219–32.

Deno, S.L. (1989) Curriculum-based measurement and special education services: a fundamental and direct relationship. In M.R. Shinn (ed.) *Curriculum-based Measurement: Assessing Special Children*. New York: Guilford Press.

Deno, S.L. and Fuchs, L.S. (1987) Developing curriculum based measurement systems for data-based special education problem solving. *Focus on Exceptional Children*, 19(8): 1–16.

Department for Children, Schools and Families (2007a) *Extended Schools Building on Experience*. Nottingham: DCSF Publications.

Department for Children, Schools and Families (2007b) *Homophobic Bullying*. Nottingham: DCSF Publications.

Department for Children, Schools and Families (2007c) *Schools and Pupils in England: January 2007*. SFR 30/2007. London: DCSF.

Department for Education (1992) *Education (Schools) Act*. London: HMSO.

Department for Education (1994a) *Code of Practice on the Identification and Assessment of Special Educational Needs*. London: HMSO.

Department for Education (1994b) *The Education of Children with Emotional and Behavioural Difficulties* (Circular 9/94). London: HMSO.

Department for Education and Employment (1997) *Excellence for All Children: Meeting Special Educational Needs*. London: DfEE Publications.

Department for Education and Employment (1998a) *Numeracy Matters: The Preliminary Report of the Numeracy Task Force*. London: DfEE Publications.

Department for Education and Employment (1998b) *The Implementation of the National Numeracy Strategy: The Final Report of the Numeracy Task Force*. London: DfEE Publications.

Department for Education and Employment (1998c) *The National Literacy Strategy. Framework for Teaching*. London: DfEE Publications.

Department for Education and Employment (1999a) *Social Inclusion: Pupil Support* (Circular 10/99). London: DfEE Publications.

Department for Education and Employment (1999b) *The National Numeracy Strategy: Mathematical Vocabulary*. London: DfEE Publications.

Department for Education and Employment (1999c) *What the Disability Discrimination Act Means for Schools and LEAs* (Circular 20/99). London: DfEE Publications.

Department for Education and Employment (2000a) *SEN and Disability Rights in Education Bill. Consultation Documentation*. London: DfEE Publications.

Department for Education and Employment (2000b) *Educational Psychology Services (England): Current Role, Good Practice and Future Directions – The Research Report*. London: DfEE Publications.

Department for Education and Employment (2000c) *SEN Code of Practice on the Identification and Assessment of Pupils with Special Educational Needs and SEN Thresholds: Good Practice Guidelines on Identification and Provision for Pupils with Special Educational Needs*. London: DfEE Publications.

Department for Education and Employment (2001) *Promoting Children's Mental Health within Early Years and Schools Settings*. Ref. DfES/0112/2001. Nottingham: DfEE Publications.

Department for Education and Employment/Qualifications and Curriculum Authority (1999a) *The National Curriculum Handbook for Primary Teachers in England*. London: DfEE/QCA.

Department for Education and Employment/Qualifications and Curriculum Authority (1999b) *The National Curriculum Handbook for Secondary Teachers in England*. London: DfEE/QCA.

Department for Education and Employment/Qualifications and Curriculum Authority (2000) *The National Curriculum Handbook for Primary Teachers in England – Key Stages 1 & 2*. London: The Stationery Office.

Department for Education and Skills (2001a) *Special Educational Needs Code of Practice*, Ref. DfES/581/2001. London: DfES.

Department for Education and Skills (2001b) *Inclusive Schooling: Children with Special Educational Needs*. London: DfES.

Department for Education and Skills (2001c) *The National Numeracy Strategy – The Daily Mathematics Lesson: Guidance to Support Pupils with Dyslexia and Dyscalculia*. Ref. DfES 0512/2001. London: DfES.

Department for Education and Skills (2002a) *Bullying: Don't Suffer in Silence*. London: DfES.

Department for Education and Skills (2002b) *Area Special Needs Co-ordinators: Supporting Early Identification and Intervention for Children with Special Educational Needs*. Guidance for LEAS and EYDCPs. London: DfES.

Department for Education and Skills (2002c) *Autism Spectrum Disorders: Good Practice Guidance*. Nottingham: DfES. www.teachernet.gov.uk/mangement/sen.

Department for Education and Skills (2002d) *Including all Children in the Literacy Hour and Daily Mathematics Lesson*. 0465/2002. Nottingham: DfES Publications.

Department for Education and Skills (2002e) *Access and Engagement in Mathematics*. London: DfES.

Department for Education and Skills (2002f) *Access to Education for Children and Young People with Medical Needs*. Ref. DfES/0025/2002. London: DfES.

Department for Education and Skills (2002g) *Accessible Schools: Planning to Increase Access to Schools for Disabled Pupils*. Ref. LEA/0168/2002 London: DfES.

Department for Education and Skills (2003a) *Aiming High: Raising the Achievement of Minority Ethnic Pupils*. Nottingham: DfES Publications.

Department for Education and Skills (2003b) *Every Child Matters*. London: The Stationery Office.

Department for Education and Skills (2003c) *Developing Early Intervention/Support Services for Deaf Children and their Families*. Ref: LEA/0068/2003. London: DfES/RNID.

Department for Education and Skills (2003d) *Excellence and Enjoyment: A Strategy for Primary Schools*. Nottingham: DfES Publications.

Department for Education and Skills (2003e) Teaching the literacy hour and daily mathematics lesson in special settings: Video case studies. http://www.standards.dfes.gov.uk/primary/publications/inclusion/1088791/pns_spec_settings019803.pdf.

Department for Education and Skills (2003f) *The National Literacy Strategy Targeting Support: Choosing and Implementing Interventions for Children with Significant Literacy Difficulties*. Available from www.standards.dfes.gov.uk/literacy.

Department for Education and Skills (2004a) *Aiming High: Guidance on Supporting the Education of Asylum Seeking and Refugee Children*. Ref. DfES/0287/2004. London: Department for Education and Skills.

Department for Education and Skills (2004b) Excellence and Enjoyment. *Learning and Teaching in the Primary Years. Planning and Assessment for Learning: Assessment for Learning*. Nottingham: DfES Publications.

Department for Education and Skills (2004c) *Removing Barriers to Achievement: The Government's Strategy for SEN*. London: DfES.

Department for Education and Skills (2004d) *Working Together: Giving Children and Young People a Say. Ref.* DfES/0134/2004. London: DfES.

Department for Education and Skills (2005a) *Learning and Teaching for Dyslexic Children.* CD-ROM DfES1184-2005CDI. Nottingham: DCSF Publication Centre.

Department for Education and Skills (2005b) *Data Collection by Type of Special Educational Need.* DfES/1889/2005. Nottingham: DfES Publications.

Department for Education and Skills (2005c) *Ethnicity and Education: The Evidence on Minority Ethnic Pupils.* Ref. RTP01–05. London: DfES.

Department for Education and Skills (2005d) *Excellence and Enjoyment: Social and Emotional Aspects of Learning.* Nottingham: DfES Publications.

Department for Education and Skills (2005e) *Positive Behaviour and the Learning Environment.* Nottingham: DfES Publications.

Department for Education and Skills (2005f) *Leading and Co-ordinating Inclusion – Planning Effective Provision.* London: DfES.

Department for Education and Skills (2005g) *Special Educational Needs and Disability Update* 18. http://www.teachernet.gov.uk/wholeschool/sen/disabilityandthedda/istom disabled/

Department for Education and Skills (2006a) *Excellence and Enjoyment: Learning and Teaching for Bilingual Children in the Primary Years.* Ref: 0013–2006DCL-EN. DfES Publications.

Department for Education and Skills (2006b) *A Short Guide to the Education and Inspections Act 2006.* London: DfES.

Department for Education and Skills (2006c) *Primary Framework for Literacy and Mathematics.* Ref. 02011–2006BOK-EN. London: DfES.

Department for Education and Skills (2006d) *Special Educational Needs in England, January 2006.* Statistical First Release. Ref. SFR 23/2006. London: DfES.

Department for Education and Skills (2006e) *The Learning Environment as a Tool for Learning.* Nottingham: DfES Publications.

Department for Education and Skills (2006f) *Common Assessment Framework for Children and Young Children: Managers' Guide.* London: HM Government.

Department for Education and Skills (2006g) Assessment *for Learning. Guidance for Senior Leaders. Secondary National Strategy.* Nottingham: DfES Publications.

Department for Education and Skills (2006h) *Bullying around Racism, Religion and Culture.* Nottingham: DfES Publications.

Department for Education and Skills (2006i) *Care Matters: Transforming the Lives of Children and Young People in Care.* Norwich: HMSO.

Department for Education and Skills (2006j) *Permanent and Fixed Period Exclusions from Schools and Exclusion Appeals in England 2004/5.* London: DfES.

Department for Education and Skills (2006k) *Planning Resource: Learning English as an Additional Language.* http://www.standards.dfes.gov.uk/primaryframeworks/downloads/ PDF/EAL_Planning.pdf (accessed October 2008).

Department for Education and Skills (2006l) *Implementing the Disability Discrimination Act in Schools and Early Years Settings* [CD]. Ref. DFES 0160 2006.

Department for Education and Skills (2007a) *Curriculum Review: Diversity and Citizenship.* Nottingham DfES.

Department for Education and Skills (2007b) *Primary National Strategy – The Primary Framework: Ensuring Progress for Children with Literacy Difficulties in Key Stage 1.* Ref: 00064/2007LEF-EN. Nottingham: DfES Publications.

Department for Education and Skills (2007c) *Keeping Up – Pupils Who Fall Behind in Key Stage 2*. Nottingham: DfES Publications.

Department for Education and Skills (2007d) *Social and Emotional Aspects of Learning (SEAL) for Secondary Schools*. Nottingham: DfES Publications.

Department for Education and Skills/Department of Health (2003) *Together from the Start – Practical Guidance for Professionals Working with Disabled Children (Birth to Third Birthday) and their Families*. Reference no. LEA/0067/2003. London: DfES.

Department for Education and Skills/Department of Health (2005a) *National Healthy School Status. A Guide for Schools*. London: DH Publications.

Department for Education and Skills/Department of Health (2005b) *Managing Medicines in Schools and Early Years Settings*. Guidance Ref. DFES-1448–2005. London: Department for Education and Skills.

Department for Education and Skills/Qualifications and Curriculum Authority (2005) *The National Curriculum Handbook for Secondary Teachers in England – Key Stages 3 & 4*. London: The Stationery Office.

Department of Education (1981) *Education Statistics of New Zealand*. Wellington: Department of Education.

Department of Education and Science (1964) *Slow Learners at School*, Education Pamphlet No. 46. London: HMSO.

Department of Education and Science (1978) *Special Educational Needs* (Report of the Warnock Committee). London: HMSO.

Department of Education and Science (1982) *Mathematics Counts* (Report of the Cockcroft Committee of Enquiry into the Teaching of Mathematics). London: HMSO.

Department of Education and Science (1983) *Assessments and Statements of Special Educational Need* (Circular 1/83). London: DES.

Department of Education and Science (1988) *Mathematics for Ages 5–16: Proposals for the National Curriculum*. London: HMSO.

Department of Education and Science (1989a) *Assessments and Statements of Special Educational Needs: Procedures within the Education, Health and Social Services* (Circular 22/89). London: HMSO.

Department of Education and Science (1989b) *The Education Reform Act 1988: The School Curriculum and Assessment* (Circular 5/89). London: DES.

Department of Education and Science (1989c) *Discipline in Schools* (Report of the Elton Committee). London: HMSO.

Department of Health (2001) *Valuing People: A New Strategy for Learning Disability for the 21st Century*, Cm 5086. London: DH.

Department of Health (2004) *National Service Framework for Children, Young People and Maternity Services*, Ref. 40496. London: DH.

Deponio, P., Landon, J., Mulling, K. and Reid, G. (2000) An audit of the processes involved in identifying and assessing bilingual learners suspected of being dyslexic: a Scottish study. *Dyslexia*, 6: 29–41.

Derrington, C. (2005) Perception of behaviour and patterns of exclusion: Gypsy Traveller students in English secondary schools. *Journal of Research in Special Educational Needs*, 5(2): 55–61.

Desforges, M. and Kerr, T. (1984) Developing bilingual children's English in school. *Educational and Child Psychology*, 1(1): 68–80.

Desforges, M., Mayet, V. and Vickers, M. (1995) Psychological assessment of bilingual pupils. *Educational Psychology in Practice*, 11(3): 27–35.

Design Council (2005) *Learning Environments Campaign Prospectus: From the Inside Looking Out.* London: Design Council.

Dew-Hughes, D. (ed.) (2004) *Educating Children with Fragile X Syndrome.* London: RoutledgeFalmer.

Dewart, H. and Summers, S. (1995) *The Pragmatics Profile of Everyday Communication Skills in Pre-school and School-aged Children.* Windsor: NFER-Nelson.

Diamantes, T. (2002) Improving instruction in multicultural classes by using classroom learning environment. *Journal of Instructional Psychology*, 29(4): 277–82.

Dickinson, P. (2006) *Sharing Information with Disabled Children in the Early Years.* London: Scope.

Disability Rights Commission (2002) *Code of Practice for Schools: Disability Discrimination Act 1995, Part 4*, London: The Stationery Office.

Dishion, T.J. and Andrews, D.W. (1995) Preventing escalation in problem behaviours with high-risk young adolescents: immediate and one year outcomes. *Journal of Consulting and Clinical Psychology*, 63(4): 538–48.

Dissanayake, C. and Crossley, S.A. (1996) Proximity and social behaviour in autism: evidence for attachment. *Journal of Child Psychology and Psychiatry*, 37: 149–56.

Dixon, G. and Addy, L.M. (2004) *Making Inclusion Work for Children with Dyspraxia: Practical Strategies for Teachers.* London: Routledge Falmer.

Dockrell, J. (2001) Assessing language skills in preschool children. *Child Psychology and Psychiatry*, 6(2): 74–85.

Dockrell, J. and Lindsay, G. (2001) Children with specific speech and language difficulties: the teachers' perspective. *Oxford Review of Education*, 27(3): 369–94.

Dockrell, J. and Shield, B.M. (2006) Acoustical barriers in classrooms: the impact of noise on performance in the classroom, *British Educational Research Journal*, 32(3): 509–25.

Dockrell, J., Lewis, A. and Lindsay, G. (2000) Researching children's perspectives: a psychological dimension. In A. Lewis and G. Lindsay (eds) *Researching Children's Perspectives.* Buckingham: Open University Press.

Dockrell, J., Lindsay, G., Palikara, O. and Cullen, M. (2007) *Raising the Achievements of Children and Young People with Specific Speech and Language Difficulties and other Special Educational Needs through School to Work and College.* Ref. RR837. London: Department for Education and Skills.

Dodd, B., Hua, Z., Crosbie, S., Holm, A. and Ozanne, A. (2006) *Diagnostic Evaluation of Articulation & Phonology.* Oxford: Pearson Assessment.

Dodge, K.A., Coie, J.D. and Brakke, N.P. (1982) Behaviour patterns of socially rejected and neglected pre-adolescents: the roles of social approach and aggression. *Journal of Abnormal Child Psychology*, 10(3): 389–410.

Dodge, K.A., McClaskey, C.L. and Feldman, E. (1985) Situational approach to the assessment of social competence in children. *Journal of Consulting and Clinical Psychology*, 53(3): 344–53.

Dodge, K.A., Pettit, C.S., McClasky, C.J. and Brown, M.M. (1986) Social competence in children. *Society for Research in Child Development Monograph*, 51 (1, Serial no. 213).

Dodge, K.A., Pettit, G.S., Bates, I.E. and Valente, E. (1995) Social information-processing patterns partially mediate the effect of early physical abuse on later conduct problems. *Journal of Abnormal Psychology*, 104: 632–43.

Dombey, H. (1998) A totalitarian approach to literacy education? *FORUM*, 40(2): 36–41.

Donald, D. (1994) Children with special educational needs: the reproduction of disadvantage in poorly served communities. In A. Dawes and D. Donald (eds) *Childhood and*

Adversity: Psychological Perspectives from South African Research. Cape Town: David Philip.

Donaldson, M.L. (1995) *Children with Language Impairments: An Introduction*. London: Jessica Kingsley.

Douglas, G. (2001) ICT, education, and visual impairment. *British Journal of Educational Technology*, 32(3): 353–64.

Douglas, G. and McLinden, M. (2005) Visual impairment. In A. Lewis and B. Norwich (eds) *Special Teaching for Special Children? Pedagogies for Inclusion* (pp. 26–40). Maidenhead: Open University Press.

Douglas, J.W.B., Ingleby, J.D., Ross, J.M. and Tillott, J.M. (1972) Behavioural styles of four year old boys when responding to test demands. *Educational Research*, 14(3): 208–12.

Dowker, A. (2004) *What Works for Children with Mathematical Difficulties?* Research Report 554. London: DfES. (Available on the DfES Research website.)

Dowling, E. and Osborne, E. (1994) *The Family and the School: A Joint Systems Approach to Problems with Children*. London: Routledge.

Downer, A.C. (2007) The national literacy strategy sight recognition programme implemented by teaching assistants: a precision teaching approach. *Educational Psychology in Practice*, 23(2): 129–43.

Drewery, W. (2004) Conferencing and schools: punishment, restorative justice, and the productive importance of the process of conversation. *Journal of Community and Applied Social Psychology*, 14: 332–44.

Drillien, C. and Drummond, M. (1983) *Development Screening and the Child with Special Needs*. London: Heinemann Medical.

Driver, C. (2005) *Secondary Mathematics and English as an Additional Language*. Contribution to the Multiverse website. http://www.multiverse.ac.uk/viewArticle.aspx?contentId=550 (accessed 29 December 2006).

Dunlea, A. (1989) *Vision and the Emergence of Meaning: Blind and Sighted Children's Early Language*. Cambridge: Cambridge University Press.

Dunn, L.M. (1968) Special education for the mildly retarded – is much of it justifiable? *Exceptional Children*, 35: 5–22.

Dunn, L.M., Dunn, L.M., Whetton, C. and Burley, J. (1997) *British Picture Vocabulary Scale*, 2nd edition. Windsor: NFER-Nelson.

Dunsdon, M.I. (1952) *The Educability of Cerebral Palsied Children*. London: Newnes Educational.

Dunsmuir, S., and Frederickson, N. (eds) (2005) *Autistic Spectrum Disorders* [CD]. London: Educational Psychology Publishing, University College London.

Dunsmuir, S., Clifford, V. and Took, S. (2006) Collaboration between educational psychologists and speech and language therapists: barriers and opportunities. *Educational Psychology in Practice*, 22(2): 125–40.

DuPaul, G.J. and Weyandt, L.L. (2006) School based intervention for children with attention deficit hyperactivity disorder: effects on academic, social, and behavioural functioning. *International Journal of Disability, Development and Education*, 53(2): 161–76.

Dyches, T.T., Wilder, L.K. and Obiakor, F.E. (2001) Autism: multicultiural perspectives. In T. Walberg, F. Obiakor, S. Burkhardt *et al.* (eds) *Educational and Clinical Interventions* (pp. 151–77). Oxford: Elsiver Science.

Dyson, A. (1990) Special educational needs and the concept of change. *Oxford Review of Education*, 16(1): 55–66.

Dyson, A. (1991) Rethinking roles, rethinking concepts: special needs teachers in mainstream schools. *Support for Learning*, 6(2): 51–60.

Dyson, A. (2002) Special needs, disability and social inclusion: the end of a beautiful friendship? In SEN Policy Options Steering Group (ed.) *Disability, Disadvantage, Inclusion and Social Disadvantage* (pp. 12–17). Tamworth: NASEN.

Dyson, A. and Millward, A. (2002) Looking them in the eyes: is rational provision for students with 'special educational needs' really possible? In P. Farrell and M. Ainscow (eds) *Making Special Education Inclusive*. London: David Fulton.

Dyson, A., Farrell, P., Polat, F., and Hutcheson, G. (2004) *Inclusion and Pupil Achievement*, Research Report RR578. London: DfES Publications.

Earl, L., Watson, N., Levin, B., Leithwood, K., Fullan, M. and Torrance, N. (2003) *Watching and Listening 3. Final Report of the External Evaluation of England's National Literacy and Numeracy Strategies*. Nottingham: DfES Publications.

Edmondson, P. (2006) Deaf children's understanding of other people's thought processes. *Educational Psychology in Practice*, 22(2): 159–69.

Edwards, A. (1998) Research and its influence on learning. *Educational and Child Psychology*, 15(3): 86–98.

Edwards, A.D. and Westgate, D.P.G. (1994) *Investigating Classroom Talk*, 2nd edition. London: Falmer Press.

Edwards, S., Fletcher, P., Garman, M., Hughes, A., Letts, C. and Sinka, I. (1997) *Reynell Developmental Language Scales III: The University of Reading Edition*. Windsor: NFER-Nelson.

Egan, G. (1994) *The Skilled Helper*, 5th edition. San Francisco: Brooks/Cole.

Eisenberg, N., Zhou, Q., Liew, J., Champion, C. and Piaada, S.U. (2006) Emotion-related regulation, and social functioning. In B.H. Schneider, X.Chen and D.C. French (eds) *Peer Relationships in Cultural Context* (pp. 170–97). New York: Cambridge University Press.

Elbaum, B. and Vaughn, S. (2003) For which students with learning disabilities are self-concept interventions effective? *Journal of Learning Disabilities*, 36(2): 101–8.

Elbers, E. and de Haan, M. (2005) The construction of word meaning in a multicultural classroom mediational tools in peer collaboration during mathematics lessons. *European Journal of Psychology of Education*, 20(1): 45–59.

Elliott, J. (2003) Dynamic assessment in educational settings: realising potential. *Educational Review*, 55(1): 15–32.

Elliott, J. and Place, M. (1998) *Children in Difficulty: A Guide to Understanding and Helping*. London: Routledge.

Elliott, J.G. (2000) The psychological assessment of children with learning difficulties. *British Journal of Special Education*, 27(2): 59–66.

Elliott, S.N. and Busse, R.T. (1991) Social skills assessment with children and adolescents. *School Psychology International*, 12: 63–83.

Ellis, V. and High, S. (2004) Something more to tell you: gay, lesbian or bisexual young people's experiences of secondary schooling. *British Educational Research Journal*, 30(2): 213–25.

Emerson, E., Robertson, J. and Wood, J. (2004) Levels of psychological distress experienced by family carers of children and adolescents with intellectual disabilities in an urban conurbation. *Journal of Applied Research in Intellectual Disabilities*, 17: 77–84.

Emler, N. (2001) *Self-Esteem: the Costs and Causes of Low Self-Worth*. York: Joseph Rowntree Foundation.

Engelbrecht, P., Oswald, M. and Forlin, C. (2006) Promoting the implementation of inclusive education in primary schools in South Africa. *British Journal of Special Education*, 33(3): 121–9.

Erwin, P.G. (1994) Effectiveness of social skills training: a meta-analytic study. *Counselling Psychology Quarterly*, 7(3): 305–10.

Evans, I.M., Goldberg-Arnold, J.S. and Dickson, J.K. (1998) Children's perceptions of equity in peer interactions. In L.H. Meyer, H.-S. Park, M. Grenot-Scheyer, I.S. Schwartz and B. Harry (eds) *Making Friends: The Influences of Culture and Development* (pp. 133–47). Baltimore, MD: Paul H. Brooks.

Evans, J., Harden, A. and Thomas, J. (2004) What are effective strategies to support pupils with emotional and behavioural difficulties (EBD) in mainstream primary schools? Findings from a systematic review of research. *Journal of Research and Special Educational Needs*, 4(1): 2–16.

Farmer, M. (1997) Exploring the links between communication skills and social competence. *Educational and Child Psychology*, 14(3): 38–44.

Farrell, M. (2006) *The Effective Teacher's Guide to Behavioural, Emotional and Social Difficulties*. London: Routledge.

Farrell, P., Dyson, A., Polat, F., Hutcheson, G. and Gallannaugh, F. (2007) Inclusion and achievement in mainstream schools. *European Journal of Special Needs Education*, 22(2): 131–45.

Faupel, A. (2003) *Emotional Literacy: Assessment and Intervention*. Windsor: NFER-Nelson.

Faupel, A., Herrick, E. and Smith, P. (1998) *Anger Management: A Practical Guide*. London: David Fulton.

Fawcett, A. and Nicolson, R. (2004) *The Dyslexia Screening Test*. London: Harcourt.

Ferguson, P.D. and Fraser, B.J. (1999) Changes in learning environment during the transition from primary to secondary school. *Learning Environments Research*, 1: 369–83.

Fergusson, A. and Duffield, T. (2003) Multicultural inclusion for pupils with severe or profound and multiple learning difficulties. In C. Tilstone and R. Rose (eds) *Strategies to Promote Inclusive Practice* (pp. 34–47). London: RoutledgeFalmer.

Feuerstein, R. (1979) *The Dynamic Assessment of Retarded Performers: The Learning Potential Assessment Device*. Baltimore, MD: University Park Press.

Fiala, C.L. and Sheridan, S.M. (2003) Parent involvement and reading: using curriculum-based measurement to assess the effects of paired reading. *Psychology in the Schools*, 40(6): 613–26.

Finch, N. (2003) *Demographic Trends in the UK*, First Report for the Project 'Welfare Policy and Employment in the Context of Family Change'. University of York: Social Policy Research Unit.

Fisher, E. (2002) Science in a special setting: strategies from Charlton School. *Support for Learning*, 17(4): 162–7.

Fitzgerald, D. (2004) *Parent Partnership in the Early Years*. London: Continuum.

Fletcher-Campbell, F. (2005) Moderate learning difficulties. In A. Lewis and B. Norwich (eds) *Special Teaching for Special Children? Pedagogies for Inclusion* (pp. 180–91). Maidenhead: Open University Press.

Florian, L., Rouse, M., Black-Hawkins, K. and Jull, S. (2004) What can national data sets tell us about inclusion and pupil achievement? *British Journal of Special Education*, 31(3): 115–21.

Fombonne, E. (2003) Epidemiological surveys of autism and other pervasive developmental disorders: an update. *Journal of Autism and Developmental Disorders*, 33(4): 365–82.

Fombonne, E. and Chakrabati, S. (2001) No evidence for a new variant of measles-mumps-rubella-induced autism. *Pediatrics*, 108: E58.

Forest, M. (ed.) (1987) *More Education/Integration: A Further Collection of Readings on the Integration of Children with Mental Handicaps into the Regular School Systems*. Downsview, Ontario: G. Allan Roeher Institute.

Forest, M. and Lusthaus, E. (1989) Promoting educational equality for all students. Circles and maps. In S. Stainback, W. Stainback and M. Forest (eds) *Educating All Students in the Mainstream of Regular Education* (pp. 43–57). Baltimore, MD: Brookes.

Fortnum, H., Marshall, D.H., Bamford, J.M. and Summerfield, A.Q. (2002) Hearing-impaired children in the UK: education setting and communication approach. *Deafness and Education International*, 4(3): 123–41.

Fortnum, H., Stacey, P., Barton, G. and Summerfield, Q. (2007) National evaluation of support options for deaf and hearing-impaired children: relevance to education services. *Deafness and Education International*, 9(3): 120–30.

Foster, S.L., Martinez, C.R. and Kulberg, A.M. (1996) Race, ethnicity and children's peer relations. In T.H. Ollendick, and R.J. Prinz (eds) *Advances in Clinical Child Psychology No. 18*. New York: Plenum Press.

Fox, M. (2003) *Including Children 3–11 with Physical Disabilities: Practical Guidance for Mainstream Schools*. London: David Fulton.

Foxman, D., Ruddock, G. and Thorpe, J. (1989) *Graduated Tests in Mathematics: A Study of Lower Attaining Pupils in Secondary Schools*. Windsor: NFER-Nelson.

Frances, J. (2004) *Educating Children with Facial Disfigurement: Creating Inclusive School Communities*. London: RoutledgeFalmer.

Fraser, B.J. (1982) Development of short forms of several classroom environment scales. *Journal of Educational Measurement*, 19(3): 221–7.

Fraser, B.J. (1984) Differences between preferred and actual classroom environment as perceived by primary students and teachers. *British Journal of Educational Psychology*, 54: 336–9.

Fraser, B.J. (1986) *Classroom Environment*. London: Croom Helm.

Fraser, B.J. (1987) Use of classroom environment assessments in school psychology. *School Psychology International*, 8: 205–19.

Fraser, B.J. (1991) Two decades of classroom environment research. In B.J. Fraser and H.J. Walberg (eds) *Educational Environments: Evaluation, Antecedents and Consequences*. Oxford: Pergamon Press.

Fraser, B.J. (1998) Classroom environment instruments: development, validity and applications. *Learning Environments Research*, 1: 7–33.

Fraser, B.J. and Fisher, D.L. (1983a) Development and validation of short forms of some instruments measuring student perceptions of actual and preferred learning environments. *Science Education*, 67: 115–31.

Fraser, B.J. and Fisher, D.L. (1983b) Student achievement as a function of person–environment fit: a regression surface analysis. *British Journal of Education Psychology*, 53: 89–99.

Fraser, B.J. and Fisher, D.H. (1986) Using short forms of classroom climate instruments to assess and improve classroom psychosocial environment. *Journal of Research in Science Teaching*, 23(5): 387–413.

Fraser, B.J., Anderson, G.J. and Walberg, H.J. (1982) *Assessment of Learning Environments: Manual for Learning Environment Inventory (LEI) and My Class Inventory (MCI)*. Bentley: Western Australian Institute of Technology.

Fraser, B.J., Malone, J.A. and Neale, J.M. (1989) Assessing and improving the psychosocial environments of mathematics classrooms. *Journal of Research in Mathematics Education*, 20: 191–201.

Frebel, H. (2006) CVI?! How to define and what terminology to use: cerebral, cortical or cognitive visual impairment. *British Journal of Visual Impairment*, 24(3): 117–20.

Frederickson, N. (1990a) Systems approaches in educational psychology practice. In N. Jones and N. Frederickson (eds) *Refocusing Educational Psychology*. London: Falmer Press.

Frederickson, N. (1990b) Introduction to soft systems methodology and its application in work with schools. In N. Frederickson (ed.) *Soft Systems Methodology: Practical Approaches in Work with Schools*. London: Educational Psychology Publishing.

Frederickson, N. (1990c) Systems approaches in educational psychology. *Journal of Applied Systems Analysis*, 17: 3–20.

Frederickson, N. (1991) Children can be so cruel – helping the rejected child. In G. Lindsay and A. Miller (eds) *Psychological Services for Primary Schools*. London: Longman.

Frederickson, N. (1993) Using soft systems methodology to rethink special educational needs. In A. Dyson and C. Gains (eds) *Rethinking Special Needs in Mainstream Schools: Towards the Year 2000*. London: David Fulton.

Frederickson, N. (1997) Educational psychologists and the definition of dyslexia. Paper presented at the Annual Conference of the Association of Educational Psychologists, Bournemouth, 10 October.

Frederickson, N. (1999) The ACID test: or is it? *Educational Psychology in Practice*, 15(1): 3–9.

Frederickson, N. (2002) Evidence-based practice and educational psychology. *Educational and Child Psychology*, 19(3): 96–111.

Frederickson, N. and Cameron, R.J. (1999) *Psychology in Education Portfolio*. Windsor: nferNelson.

Frederickson, N. and Cline, T. (eds) (1990) *Curriculum Related Assessment with Bilingual Children*. London: Educational Psychology Publishing.

Frederickson, N. and Cline, T. (eds) (1995) *Assessing the Learning Environments of Children with Special Educational Needs*. London: Educational Psychology Publishing.

Frederickson, N. and Frith, U. (1998) Identifying dyslexia in bilingual children: a phonological approach with Inner London Sylheti speakers. *Dyslexia*, 4: 119–31.

Frederickson, N. and Furnham, A.F. (1998a) Use of sociometric techniques to assess the social status of mainstreamed children with learning difficulties. *Genetic, Social and General Psychology Monographs*, 124(4): 381–433.

Frederickson, N. and Furnham, A.F. (1998b) Sociometric status group classification of mainstreamed children who have moderate learning difficulties: an investigation of personal and environmental factors. *Journal of Educational Psychology*, 90(4): 1–12.

Frederickson, N. and Furnham, A.F. (2004) Peer assessed behavioral characteristics and sociometric rejection: Differences between pupils who have moderate learning difficulties and their mainstream peers. *British Journal of Educational Psychology*, 74, 391–410.

Frederickson, N. and Graham, B. (1999) Social skills and emotional intelligence. In N. Frederickson and R.J. Cameron (eds) *Psychology in Education Portfolio*. Windsor: NFER-Nelson.

Frederickson, N. and Jacobs, S. (2001) Controllability attributions for academic performance and a perceived scholastic competence, global self worth and achievement of children with dyslexia. *School Psychology International*, 22(4): 401–16.

Frederickson, N. and Monsen, J. (1999) The learning environment. In N. Frederickson and R.J. Cameron (eds) *Psychology in Education Portfolio*. Windsor: NFER-Nelson.

Frederickson, N. and Reason, R. (1995) Discrepancy definitions of specific learning difficulties. *Educational Psychology in Practice*, 10(4): 195–205.

Frederickson, N. and Simmonds, E. (2008) Special needs, relationship type and distributive justice norms in early and later years of middle childhood. *Social Development* 17(4): 1056–73.

Frederickson, N. and Simms, J. (1990) Teaching social skills to children: towards an integrated approach. *Educational and Child Psychology*, 7(1): 5–17.

Frederickson, N. and Turner, J. (2003) Utilizing the classroom peer group to address children's social needs. An evaluation of the 'Circle of Friends' intervention approach. *Journal of Special Education*, 36(4): 234–45.

Frederickson, N., Webster, A. and Wright, A. (1991) Psychological assessment: a change of emphasis. *Educational Psychology in Practice*, 6(5): 23–32.

Frederickson, N., Frith, U. and Reason, R. (1997) *Phonological Assessment Battery*. Windsor: NFER-Nelson.

Frederickson, N., Warren, L. and Turner, J. (2005) 'Circle of Friends': an exploration of impact over time. *Educational Psychology in Practice*, 21(3): 197–218.

Frederickson, N., Simmonds, E., Evans, L. and Soulsby, C. (2007) Assessing social and affective outcomes of inclusion. *British Journal of Special Education*, 34(2): 105–15.

Frederickson, N., Miller, A. and Cline, T. (2008) *Educational Psychology*. London: Hodder Arnold.

Frith, C.D. (2006) The value of brain imaging in the study of development and its disorders. *Journal of Child Psychology and Psychiatry*, 47(10): 979–82.

Frith, U. (1989) *Autism: Explaining the Enigma*. Oxford: Blackwell.

Frith, U. (1995) Dyslexia: can we have a shared theoretical framework? *Educational and Child Psychology*, 12(1): 6–17.

Frith, U. (1997) Brain, mind and behaviour in dyslexia. In C. Hulme and M. Snowling (ed.) *Dyslexia: Biology, Cognition and Intervention*. London: Whurr.

Frith, U. (2003) *Autism: Explaining the Enigma*, 2nd edition. Oxford: Blackwell.

Frith, U. (2005) Autism and Asperger's syndrome. In S. Dunsmuir and N. Frederickson (eds) *Autistic Spectrum Disorders* [CD]. London: Educational Psychology Publishing, University College London.

Frith, U. and Snowling, M. (1983) Reading for meaning and reading for sound in autistic and dyslexic children. *Journal of Developmental Psychology*, 1: 329–42.

Fuchs, D., Fuchs, L.S. and Fernstrom, P. (1993) A conservative approach to special education reform: mainstreaming through transenvironmental programming and curriculum-based measurement. *American Educational Research Journal*, 30(1): 149–77.

Fuchs, L.S. and Fuchs, D. (1986) Effects of systematic formative evaluation: a meta-analysis. *Exceptional Children*, 53: 199–208.

Fuchs, L.S., Fuchs, D. and Prentice, K. (2004) Responsiveness to mathematical problem-solving instruction: comparing students at risk of mathematics disability with and without risk of reading disability. *Journal of Learning Disabilities*, 37(4): 293–306.

Fung, I.Y.Y., Wilkinson, I.A.G. and Moore, D.W. (2003) L1-assisted reciprocal teaching to improve ESL students' comprehension of English expository text. *Learning and Instruction*, 13(1): 1–31.

Fuson, K.C. and Kwon, Y. (1992) Korean children's understanding of multidigit addition and subtraction. *Child Development*, 63: 491–506.

Gable, S.L. and Haidt, J. (2005) What (and why) is positive psychology? *Review of General Psychology*, 9(2): 103–10.

Gadhok, K. (1994) Languages for intervention. In D. Martin (ed.) *Services to Bilingual Children with Speech and Language Difficulties: Proceedings of the 25th Anniversary AFASIC Conference, Birmingham, 1993.* London: Association for All Speech-Impaired Children.

Galigan, J.E. (1985) Psychoeducational testing: turn out the lights, the party's over. *Exceptional Children*, 52(3): 288–99.

Gallaway, C. and Woll, B. (1994) Interaction and childhood deafness. In C. Gallaway and B.J. Richards (eds) *Input and Interaction in Language Acquisition.* Cambridge: Cambridge University Press.

Gallimore, R. (1996) Classrooms are just another cultural activity. In D.L. Speece and B.K. Keogh (eds) *Research on Classroom Ecologies: Implications for Inclusion of Children with Learning Disabilities.* Mahwah, NJ: Lawrence Erlbaum Associates.

Gallimore, R., Tharp, R. and Rueda, R. (1989) The social context of cognitive functioning in the lives of mentally handicapped persons. In D.A. Sugden (ed.) *Cognitive Approaches in Special Education.* London: Falmer Press.

Galloway, S. and Banes, D. (1994) Beyond the simple audit. In R. Rose, A. Fergusson, C. Coles, R. Byers and D. Banes (eds) *Implementing the Whole Curriculum for Pupils with Learning Difficulties.* London: David Fulton.

Galvin, P., Mercer, S. and Costa, P. (1990) *Building a Better Behaved School.* Harlow: Longman.

Garcia-Coll, C.T. (1990) Developmental outcome of minority infants: a process-oriented look into our beginnings. *Child Development*, 61: 270–89.

Gardner, H. (1993) *Frames of Mind: The Theory of Multiple Intelligences*, 2nd edition. London: Fontana Press.

Gardner, H. (1999) *Intelligence Reframed: Multiple Intelligences for the 21st Century.* New York: Basic Books.

Gardner, S. and Rea-Dickins, P. (2002) *Focus on Language Sampling: A Key Issue in EAL Assessment.* Watford: National Association for Language Development in the Curriculum.

Gavine, D., Auchterlonie, L. and Godson, J. (2006) 'Assessment for learning' and its relevance to educational psychology. *Educational and Child Psychology*, 23(3): 99–108.

Ge, X., Conger, R.D., Cadoret, R.J., Neiderhiser, J.M., Yates, W., Troughton, E. and Stewart, M.A. (1996) The developmental interface between nature and nurture: a mutual influence model of child antisocial behavior and parent behaviors. *Developmental Psychology*, 32, 574–89.

Geary, D.C. and Hoard, M.K. (2001) Numerical and arithmetical deficits in learning-disabled children: relation to dyscalculia and dyslexia. *Aphasiology*, 15(7): 635–47.

Geddes, H. (2006) *Attachment in the Classroom.* London: Worth Publishing.

Georgiou, S.M., Christou, C., Stavrinides, P. and Panaoura, G. (2002) Teacher attributions of student failure and teacher behaviour toward the failing student. *Psychology in the Schools*, 39(5): 583–95.

Gerrard, B. (2005) City of Glasgow nurture group pilot scheme evaluation. *Emotional and Behavioural Difficulties*, 10(4): 245–53.

Gersch, I. (1992) Pupil involvement in assessment. In T. Cline (ed.) *The Assessment of Special Educational Needs: International Perspectives.* London: Routledge.

Gersch, I., Kelly, C., Cohen, S., Daunt, S. and Frederickson, N. (2001) The Chingford Hall School Screening Project: Can we have some more educational psychologists' time please? *Educational Psychology in Practice*, 17(2): 135–56.

Gersch, I.S., Holgate, A. and Sigston, A. (1993) Valuing the child's perspective: a revised student report and other practical initiatives. *Educational Psychology in Practice*, 9(1): 17–26.

Gersten, R., Jordan, N.C. and Flojo, J.R. (2005) Early identification and interventions for students with mathematics difficulties. *Journal of Learning Disabilities*, 38(4): 293–304.

Geurts, H.M., Verté, S., Oosterlaan, J., Roeyers, H., Hartman, C.A., Mulder, E.J., van Berckelaer-Onnes, I.A. and Sergeant, J.A. (2004) Can the *Children's Communication Checklist* differentiate between children with autism, children with ADHD, and normal controls? *Journal of Child Psychology and Psychiatry*, 45(8): 1437–53.

Geva, E. (2000) Issues in the assessment of reading disabilities in L2 children – beliefs and research evidence. *Dyslexia*, 6(1): 13–28.

Giangreco.M.F. and Broer, S.L. (2005) Questionable utilization of para-professionals in inclusive schools: are we addressing symptoms or causes? *Focus on Autism and Other Developmental Disabilities*, 20(1): 10–26.

Gibb, C.E., Morrow, M., Clarke, C.L., Cook, G., Gertig, P. and Ramprogus, B. (2002) Trans-disciplinary working: evaluating the development of health and social care provision in mental health. *Journal of Mental Health*, 11(3): 339–50.

Gibbs, J., Underdown, A., Stevens, M., Newbury, J. and Liabo, K. (2003) Group based parenting programmes can reduce behaviour problems of children aged three to twelve years. *ESRC What Works for Children Group Evidence Nugget*, April.

Gibbs, J.T. and Huang, L.N. (1989) A conceptual framework for assessing and treating minority youth. In J.T. Gibbs and L.N. Huang (eds) *Children of Color: Psychological Interventions with Minority Youth*. San Francisco: Jossey-Bass.

Gibson, M. (2005) Opportunities and challenges: Additional Support for Learning (Scotland) Act 2004. Paper delivered at an Irish National Disability Authority conference. http://www.nda.ie (accessed 6 November 2007).

Gickling, E.E. and Havertape, J.F. (1981) Curriculum based assessment. In J.A. Tucker (ed.) *Non-Test Based Assessment: A Training Module*. Minneapolis: National School Psychology Inservice Training Network, University of Minnesota.

Gickling, E.E. and Havertape, J.F. (1981) Curriculum based assessment. In J.A. Tucker (ed.) *Non-Test Based Assessment: A Training Module*. Minneapolis, MN: National School Psychology Inservice Training Network, University of Minnesota.

Gickling, E.E. and Thompson, V.P. (1985) A personal view of curriculum based assessment. *Exceptional Children*, 52(3): 205–18.

Gierl, M.J. and Bisanz, J. (1995) Anxieties and attitudes related to mathematics in grades 3 and 6. *Journal of Experimental Education*, 63: 139–58.

Gifford, S. (2005) *Young Children's Difficulties in Learning Mathematics: Review of Research in Relation to Dyscalculia*. London: QCA.

Gil, K.M., Anthony, K.K., Carson, J.W., Redding-Lallinger, R., Daeschner, C.W. and Ware, R.E. (2001) Daily coping practice predicts treatment effects in children with sickle cell disease. *Journal of Pediatric Psychology*, 26(3): 163–73.

Gilbert, C. (2006) *2020 Vision: The Report of the Teaching and Learning in 2020 Review*. Ref: 04255–2006DOM-EN. London: DfES.

Gillborn, D. and Gipps, C. (1996) *Recent Research on the Achievements of Ethnic Minority Pupils*. London: HMSO.

Gioia, G., Isquith, F., Kenworthy, L. and Barton, R.M. (2003) Profiles of everyday executive function in acquired and developmental disorders. *Child Neuropsychology (Neuropsychology, Development and Cognition: Section C)*, 8(2): 121–37.

Gipps, C. (1994) *Beyond Testing: Towards a Theory of Educational Assessment*. London: Falmer Press.

Gipps, C. and Murphy, P. (1994) *A Fair Test? Assessment, Achievement and Equity*. Buckingham: Open University Press.

Gipps, C. and Stobart, G. (1993) *Assessment: A Teacher's Guide to the Issues*. London: Hodder and Stoughton.

Glenny, G. (2005) Riding the dragon: developing inter-agency systems for supporting inclusion. *Support for Learning*, 20(4): 167–75.

Glover, T.A. and Albers, C.A. (2007) Considerations for evaluating universal screening assessments. *Journal of School Psychology*, 45(2): 117–35.

Glutting, J.J., Oakland, T.A. and McDermott, P.A. (1989) Observing child behaviour during testing: constructs, validity and situational generality. *Journal of School Psychology*, 27: 155–64.

Goacher, B., Evans, J., Welton, J. and Wedell, K. (1988) *Policy and Provision for Special Educational Needs*. London: Cassell.

Goddard, S.J. (1988) Parental involvement in precision teaching of reading. *Association of Educational Psychologists Journal*, 4(1): 36–41.

Godfrey, N. and Skinner, S. (1995) Investigating children's discourse in the primary classroom: the linguistic demands of classroom tasks. In M.K. Verma, K.P. Corrigan and S. Firth (eds) *Working with Bilingual Children: Good Practice in the Primary Classroom*. (pp. 1–20) Clevedon: Multilingual Matters.

Goh, S. and Fraser, B.J. (1998) Teacher interpersonal behaviour, classroom environment and student outcomes in primary mathematics in Singapore. *Learning Environments Research*, 1: 199–229.

Goldstein, H. (2002) Communication intervention for children with autism: a review of treatment efficacy. *Journal of Autism and Developmental Disorders*, 32(5): 373–96.

Goleman, D. (1995) *Emotional Intelligence*. New York: Bantam Books.

Good, R.H., Simmons, D.C. and Smith, S. (1998) Effective academic interventions in the United States: evaluating and enhancing the acquisition of early reading skills. *Educational and Child Psychology*, 15(1): 56–70.

Good, T.L. and Brophy, J.E. (2008) *Looking in Classrooms*, 10th edition. New York: Pearson.

Goodlin-Jones, B.L. and Solomon, M. (2003) Contributions of psychology. In S. Ozonoff, S.J. Rogers and R.L. Hendren (eds) *Autistic Spectrum Disorders: A Research Review for Practitioners*. Washington, DC: American Psychiatric Publishing.

Goodman, K.S. (1967) Reading: a psycho-linguistic guessing game. *Journal of the Reading Specialist*, 6: 126–35.

Goodman, R. (1997) The Strengths and Difficulties Questionnaire: a research note. *Journal of Child Psychology and Psychiatry*, 38: 581–6.

Goodman, R. (1999) The extended version of the Strength and Difficulties Questionnaire as a guide to psychiatric caseness and consequent burden. *Journal of Child Psychology and Psychiatry*, 40(5): 791–800.

Goodman, R. (2001) Psychometric properties of the Strengths and Difficulties Questionnaire. *Journal of the American Academy of Child and Adolescent Psychiatry*, 40(11): 1337–45.

Gorgorió, N. and Planas, N. (2005) Social representations as mediators of mathematics learning in multiethnic classrooms. *European Journal of the Psychology of Education*, 20(1): 91–104.

Gorrell-Barnes, G. (1985) Systems theory and family therapy. In M. Rutter and L. Hersov (eds) *Child Psychiatry: Modern Approaches*. Oxford: Blackwell.

Goss, P. (2006) Meaning-led learning for pupils with severe and profound and multiple learning difficulties. *British Journal of Special Education*, 33: 210–19.

Goswami, U. (2006) Neuroscience and education: from research to practice? *Nature Reviews Neuroscience*, 7: 406–13.

Gough, P.B. and Tunmer, W.E. (1986) Decoding, reading and reading disability. *Remedial and Special Education*, 7: 6–10.

Gough, P.B., Alford, J.A. Jnr and Holley-Wilcox, P. (1981) Words and contexts. In O.J.L. Tzeng and H. Singer (eds) *Perception of Print: Reading Research in Experimental Psychology*. Hillsdale, NJ: Lawrence Erlbaum Associates.

Graf, V.L. (1992) Minimizing the inappropriate referral and placement of ethnic minority students in special education. In T. Cline (ed.) *The Assessment of Special Educational Needs: International Perspectives*. London: Routledge.

Graham, S. (1984) Teacher feelings and student thoughts: an attributional approach to affect in the classroom. *The Elementary School Journal*, 85(1): 90–104.

Graham, S. and Juvonen, J. (2002) Ethnicity, peer harassment, and adjustment in middle school: an exploratory study. *Journal of Early Adolescence*, 22, 173–99.

Grant, D. and Brooks, K. (1996) Exclusions from school: responses from the black community. *Pastoral Care in Education*, 14: 20–7.

Grant, D. and Brooks, K. (2000) School exclusion of black pupils: an LEA response. *Support for Learning*, 15(1): 19–24.

Gravelle, M (2003) 'Weighing the Turkey does not make it fat': a reappraisal of assessment of bilingual learners. *Race Equality Teaching*, 21(2): 37–41.

Gray, C.A. (1998) Social stories and comic strip conversations with students with Asperger's syndrome and high functioning autism. In E. Schloper and G.B. Mesibov (eds) *Asperger's Syndrome or High Functioning Autism? Current Issues in Autism*. (pp. 167–98). New York: Plenum Press.

Gray, C.A. (2000) *The New Social Story Book: Illustrated Edition*. Arlington, TX: Future Horizons.

Gray, C.A. and Garand, J. (1993) Social stories: improving responses of students with autism with accurate social information. *Focus on Autistic Behaviour*, 8(1): 1–10.

Gray, H., Smekal, V. and Lewis, C.A. (2003) Introduction: Inclusive education, eastern Europe and severe marginalisation. In V. Smekal, H. Gray and C.A. Lewis (eds) *Together We Will Learn: Ethnic Minorities and Education* (pp. 13–26). Brno: Barrister and Principal.

Gray, P. (2004) Categories revisited: the emergence of a new epidemiology of SEN. In B. Norwich, C. Beak, P. Richardson and P. Gray, Examining Key Issues Underlying the Audit Commission Reports on SEN Policy Paper 1 (5th Series). *Journal of Research and Special Educational Needs*, 4(2): 98–112.

Gray, P. and Noakes, J. (1994) Providing effective support to mainstream schools: issues and strategies. In P. Gray, A. Miller and J. Noakes (eds) *Challenging Behaviour in Schools*. London: Routledge.

Gray Center (2006) *How to Write Social Stories*. http://www.thegraycenter.org (accessed 20 February 2006).

Graziano, W.G., Varca, P.E. and Levy, J.C. (1982) Race of examiner effects and the validity of intelligence tests. *Review of Educational Research*, 52: 469–97.

Green, H., McGinnity, A., Meltzer, H., Ford, T. and Goodman, R. (2005) *Mental Health of Children and Young People in Great Britain, 2004*. Norwich: HMSO.

Green, J. and Goldwyn, R. (2002) Annotation: attachment disorganisation and psychopathology: new findings in attachment research and the potential implications for developmental psychopathology in childhood. *Journal of Child Psychology and Psychiatry*, 43(7): 835–46.

Greenberg, M.T. and Kusché, C.A. (1998) Preventive intervention for school-age deaf children: the PATHS curriculum. *Journal of Deaf Studies and Deaf Education*, 3(1): 49–63.

Greenberg, M.T., Kusché, C.A., Cook, E.T. and Quamma, J.P. (1995) Promoting emotional competence in school aged children: the effects of the PATHS curriculum. *Development and Psychopathology*, 7: 117–36.

Greenhalgh, P. (1994) *Emotional Growth and Learning*. London: Routledge.

Greenway, C. (2000) Autism and Asperger's syndrome: strategies to promote pro-social behaviours. *Educational Psychology in Practice*, 60: 469–86.

Greenwood, A. and Ayre, K. (2005) The impact of date of birth on placement on the Special Educational Needs Register. *DECP Debate*, 116: 15–24.

Gregory, E. (1994) Cultural assumptions and early years' pedagogy: the effect of the home culture on minority children's interpretation of reading in school. *Language, Culture and Curriculum*, 7(2): 111–24.

Gregory, S. (1993) The language and culture of deaf people: implications for education. *Deafness*, 9: 4–11.

Gregory, S. (2004) Issues in sign bilingual education. In S. Bradarić-Jončić and V. Ivasović (eds) *Sign Language, Deaf Culture and Bilingual Education* (pp. 111–20). Zagreb: Faculty of Education and Rehabilitation Sciences, University of Zagreb.

Gregory, S. and Bishop, J. (1991) The mainstreaming of primary age deaf children. In S. Gregory and G.M. Hartley (eds) *Constructing Deafness*. London: Pinter Publishers, in association with the Open University.

Gregory, S. and Hindley, P. (1996) Communication strategies for deaf children. *Journal of Child Psychology and Psychiatry*, 37: 895–906.

Gregory, S., Bishop, J. and Sheldon, L. (1995) *Deaf Young People and their Families*. Cambridge: Cambridge University Press.

Grenot-Scheyer, M., Staub, D., Peck, C.A. and Schwartz, I.S. (1998) Reciprocity and friendships: listening to the voices of children and youth with and without disabilities. In L.H. Meyer, H.S. Park, M. Grenot-Scheyer, I.S. Schwartz and B. Harry (eds) *Making Friends: The Influences of Culture and Development*. Baltimore, MD: Paul H Brooks.

Gresham, F.M. (2002) Responsiveness to intervention: an alternative approach to the identification of learning disabilities. In R. Bradley, L. Danielson and D.P. Hallahan (eds) *Identification of Learning Disabilities: Researched Practice*. Mahwah, NJ: Erlbaum.

Gresham, F.M. and Elliott, S.N. (1990) *Social Skills Rating System*. Circle Pines, MN: American Guidance Service.

Gresham, F.M. and Elliott, S.N. (1993) Social skills intervention guide: systematic approaches to social skills training. *Special Services in the Schools*, 8(1): 137–58.

Gresham, F.M. and MacMillan, D.L. (1997a) Denial and defensiveness in the place of fact and reason: rejoinder to Smith and Lovaas. *Behavioral Disorders*, 22(4): 219–30.

Gresham, F.M. and MacMillan, D.L. (1997b) Social confidence and affective characteristics of students with mild disabilities. *Review of Educational Research*, 67: 377–415.

Gresham, F.M., Cook, C.R., Crews, S.D. and Kern, L. (2004) Social skills training for children and youth with emotional and behavioral disorders: validity considerations and future directions. *Behavior Disorders*, 30(1): 32–46.

Griffith, J. (2003) Schools as organisational models: implications for examining school effectiveness. *The Elementary School Journal*, 104(1): 29–47.

Groom, B. and Rose, R. (2005) Supporting the inclusion of pupils with social, emotional and behavioural difficulties in the primary school: the role of teaching assistants. *Journal of Research and Special Educational Needs*, 5(1): 20–30.

Grosjean, F. (1985) The bilingual as a competent but specific speaker-hearer. *Journal of Multilingual and Multicultural Development*, 6(6): 467–77.

Gross, J., Jackson, S. and Atcliffe, J. (1999) Managing behaviour difficulties. In A. Berger and J. Gross (eds) *Teaching the Literacy Hour in an Inclusive Classroom*. London: David Fulton.

Gross, R.D. (1987) *Psychology: The Science of Mind and Behaviour*. London: Edward Arnold.

Grossman, H. (1998) Linguistically appropriate special education. *Advances in Special Education*, 11: 41–54.

Grove, N. and Peacey, N. (1999) Teaching subjects to pupils with profound and multiple learning difficulties: considerations for the new framework. *British Journal of Special Education*, 26(2): 83–6.

Grugeon, E. (1992) Ruled out or rescued? A statement for Balbinder. In T. Booth, W. Swann, M. Masterton and P. Potts (eds) *Policies for Diversity in Education*. London: Routledge, in association with the Open University.

Gus, L. (2000) Autism: promoting peer understanding. *Educational Psychology in Practice*, 16: 461–6.

Gutfreund, M., Harrison, M. and Wells, G. (1989) *The Bristol Language Development Scales*. Windsor: NFER-Nelson.

Guthke, J., Beckmann, J.F. and Dobat, H. (1997) Dynamic testing – problems, uses, trends and evidence of validity. *Educational and Child Psychology*, 14(4): 17–32.

Gutierrez, K.D. and Stone, L.D. (1997) A cultural-historical view of learning and learning disabilities: participating in a community of learners. *Learning Disabilities Research and Practice*, 12(2): 123–31.

Gutiérrez-Clellen, V.F. and Peña, E. (2001) Dynamic assessment of diverse children: a tutorial. *Language, Speech and Hearing Services in Schools*, 32: 212–24.

Haager, D. (2007) Promises and cautions regarding using response to intervention with English language learners. *Learning Disability Quarterly*, 30(3): 213–18.

Hadow Committee (1924) *Psychological Tests of Educable Capacity*. London: HMSO.

Haertel, G.D., Walberg, H.J. and Haertel, E.H. (1981) Socio-psychological environments and learning: a quantitative synthesis. *British Journal of Educational Research*, 7: 27–36.

Hafeez, R. (2003) Using assessment to improve teaching and learning. In I. Thompson (ed.) *Enhancing Primary Mathematics Teaching* (pp. 101–11). Buckingham: Open University Press.

Hallam, S. (2007) Evaluation of behavioural management in schools: a review of the behaviour improvement programme and the role of behaviour and education support teams. *Child and Adolescent Mental Health*, 12(3): 106–12.

Hallam, S. and Castle, F. (1999) *Evaluation of the Behaviour and Discipline Pilot Projects (1996–1999) Supported under the Standards Fund Programme*. Nottingham: DfEE Publications.

Hallam, S., Rhamie, J. and Shaw, J. (2006) *Evaluation of the Primary Behaviour and Attendance Pilot*. London: DfES.

Hamers, J.H.M., Hessels, M.G.P. and Pennings, A.H. (1996) Learning potential in ethnic minority children. *European Journal of Psychological Assessment*, 12(3): 183–92.

Hamill, P. and Clark, K. (2005) *Additional Support Needs: An Introduction to ASN from Nursery to Secondary*. Paisley: Hodder Gibson.

Hammersley, M. (1997) Educational research and teaching: a response to David Hargreaves' TTA lecture. *British Educational Research Journal*, 23(2): 141–61.

Haney, M.R. and Evans, J.G. (1999) National survey of school psychologists regarding use of dynamic assessment and other non-traditional assessment techniques. *Psychology in the Schools*, 36(4): 295–304.

Hanko, G. (2001) 'Difficult-to-teach' children: consultative staff support as an aspect of an inclusive education: sharing expertise across national and cultural boundaries. In J. Visser, H. Daniels and T. Cole (eds) *Emotional and Behavioural Difficulties in Mainstream Schools* (pp. 47–61). Amsterdam: JAI.

Hanna, G. (1986) Sex differences in mathematics achievement of eighth graders in Ontario. *Journal for Research in Mathematics Education*, 17: 231–7.

Hannell, G. (2005) *Dyscalculia*. London: David Fulton.

Hansen, A. (ed.) (2005) *Children's Errors in Mathematics: Understanding Common Misconceptions in Primary Schools*. Exeter: Learning Matters.

Happé, F. (1994) An advanced theory of mind: understanding of story characters' thoughts and feelings in able autistic, mentally handicapped and normal children and adults. *Journal of Autism and Developmental Disorders*, 24: 129–54.

Happé, F. (1995) The role of age and verbal ability in the theory of mind task performance of subjects with autism. *Child Development*, 66: 843–55.

Happé, F. (1997) Central coherence in theory of mind and autism, reading homographs in context. *British Journal of Developmental Psychology*, 15: 1–12.

Happé, F., and Frith, U. (2006) The weak coherence account: detail-focused cognitive style in autistic spectrum disorders. *Journal of Autism and Developmental Disorders*, 36(1): 5–25.

Happé, F., Briskman, J. and Frith, U. (2001) Exploring the cognitive phenotype of autism: weak 'central coherence' in parents and siblings of children with autism. One experimental test. *Journal of Child Psychology and Psychiatry*, 42: 299–307.

Hardy, C., Ogden, J., Newman, J. and Cooper, S. (2002) *Autism and ICT: A Guide for Teachers and Parents*. London: David Fulton.

Hargreaves, D.H. (1996) *Teaching as Research-based Profession: Possibilities and Prospects*. Teacher Training Agency Annual Lecture. London: Teacher Training Agency.

Hargreaves, D.H. (1997) In defense of research for evidence-based teaching: a rejoinder to Martyn Hammersley. *British Educational Research Journal*, 23(4): 405–19.

Haring, N.G. (1982) *Exceptional Children and Youth: An Introduction to Special Education*, 3rd edition. Columbus, OH: Charles E. Merrill.

Haring, T.G. and Breen, C.G. (1992) A peer-mediated social network intervention to enhance the social integration of persons with moderate and severe disabilities. *Journal of Applied Behaviour Analysis*, 25: 319–33.

Haringey Black Pressure Group on Education (1984) *Black Critics of '81 Act*. London: Haringey Black Pressure Group on Education.

Harlen, W. (1983) *Teaching and Learning Primary Science*. London: Paul Chapman.

Harris, M. and Chasin, J. (2005) Visual attention in deaf and hearing infants: the role of auditory cues. *Journal of Child Psychology and Psychiatry*, 46(10): 1116–23.

Harry, B. (2007) The disproportionate placement of ethnic minorities in special education. In L. Florian (ed.) *The Sage Handbook of Special Education* (pp. 67–84). London: Sage.

Hart, S. (1996) *Beyond Special Needs: Enhancing Children's Learning through Innovative Thinking*. London: Paul Chapman.

Harter, S. (1985) *Manual for the Self Perception Profile for Children*. Denver, CO: University of Denver.

Harter, S. (2006) Developmental and individual difference perspectives on self-esteem. In D.K. Mroczek and T.D. Little (eds) *Handbook of Personality Development*. Mahwah, NJ: Lawrence Erlbaum.

Hartshorne, H., May, M. and Maller, J. (1929) *Studies in the Nature of Character: II – Studies in Service and Self-control*. New York: Macmillan.

Hartup, W.W. (1992) Peer relations in early and middle childhood. In V.B. Van Hasselt and M. Hersen (eds) *Handbook of Social Development: A Lifespan Perspective*. New York: Plenum Press.

Hasbrouck, J.E., Wolbeck, T., Ihnot, C. and Parker, R.I. (1999) One teacher's use of curriculum-based measurement: a changed opinion. *Learning Disabilities Research and Practice*, 14(2): 118–26.

Hastings, R., Sonuga-Barke, E.J.S. and Remington, B. (1993) An analysis of labels of people with learning disabilities. *British Journal of Clinical Psychology*, 32: 463–5.

Hatcher, P.J. (2000) *Sound Linkage: An Integrated Programme for Overcoming Reading Difficulties*, 2nd edition. London: Whurr.

Hatcher, P.J., Hulme, C., and Ellis, A.W. (1994) Ameliorating early reading failure by integrating the teaching of reading and phonological skills: the phonological linkage hypothesis. *Child Development*: 65: 41–57.

Hatcher, P.J., Hulme, C. and Snowling, M.J. (2004) Explicit phoneme training combined with phonic reading instruction helps young children at risk of reading failure. *Journal of Child Psychology and Psychiatry*, 45: 338–58.

Hatcher, P.J., Hulme, C., Miles, J.N.V., Carroll, J.M., Hatcher, J., Gibbs, S., Smith, G., Bowyer-Crane, C. and Snowling, M.J. (2006a) Efficacy of small group reading intervention for beginning readers with reading-delay: a randomised controlled trial. *Journal of Child Psychology and Psychiatry*, 47(8): 820–7.

Hatcher, P.J., Goetz, K., Snowling, M.J., Hulme, C., Gibbs, S. and Smith, G (2006b) Evidence for the effectiveness of the Early Literacy Support programme, *British Journal of Educational Psychology*, 76: 351–67.

Hawker, D.S. and Boulton, M.J. (2001) Sub-types of peer harassment and their correlates: a social dominance perspective. In J. Juvonen and S. Graham (eds) *Peer Harassment in School*. New York: Guildford Press.

Haworth, M. and Joyce, J. (1996) A resource for assessing the language skills of bilingual pupils. In T. Cline and N. Frederickson (eds) *Curriculum Related Assessment, Cummins and Bilingual Children* (pp. 116–45). Clevedon: Multilingual Matters.

Hayden, C. (1997) *Exclusions from Primary Schools*. Buckingham: Open University Press.

Hayden, S. and Jordan, E. (2007) *Language for Learning: A Practical Guide for Supporting Pupils with Language and Communication Difficulties*. London: David Fulton/NASEN.

Hayes, J. (2004) Visual annual reviews: how to include pupils with learning difficulties in their educational reviews, *Support for Learning*, 19(4): 175–80.

Hayes, S.C., Nelson, R.O. and Jarrett, R.B. (1983) The treatment utility of assessment: a functional approach to evaluating assessment quality, *American Psychologist*, 62: 963–74.

Haylock, D. (1995) *Mathematics Explained for Primary Teachers*. London: Paul Chapman.

Haynes, C. (2000) The outcome of speech and language impairment. In J. Law, S. Parkinson and R. Tamhne (eds) *Communication Difficulties in Childhood: A Practical Guide*. Abingdon: Radcliffe Medical Press.

Hegarty, S. (1987) *Meeting Special Needs in Ordinary Schools*. London: Cassell.

Hegarty, S. (1993) Reviewing the literature on integration. *European Journal of Special Needs Education*, 8(3): 194–200.

Heim, A.W. (1970) *The Appraisal of Intelligence*. Slough: NFER-Nelson.

Helms, J.E. (2006) Fairness is not validity or cultural bias in racial-group assessment: a quantitative perspective. *American Psychologist*, 61(8): 845–59.

Hembree, R. (1990) The nature, effects and relief of mathematics anxiety. *Journal for Research in Mathematics Education*, 21(1): 33–46.

Henderson, S. (1995) Children with specific perceptuo-motor difficulties: where do we stand now? In I. Lunt, B. Norwich and V. Varma (eds) *Psychology and Special Needs: Recent Developments and Future Directions* (pp. 25–44). Aldershot: Ashgate Publishing.

Hensch, T.K. (2004) Critical period regulation. *Annual Review of Neuroscience*, 27, 549–79.

Hermelin, B. (2001) *Bright Splinters of the Mind. A Personal Story of Research with Autistic Savants*. London: Jessica Kingsley.

Hernandez, R.D. (1994) Reducing bias in the assessment of culturally and linguistically diverse populations. *Journal of Educational Issues of Language Minority Students*, 14: 269–300. http://www.ncela.gwu.edu/pubs/jeilms/vol14/hernand.htm (accessed 21 November 2007).

Hess, R.S., Molina, A.M. and Kozleski, E.B. (2006) Until somebody hears me: parent voice and advocacy in special educational decision making. *British Journal of Special Education*, 33(3): 148–57.

Hessels, M.G.P. (1997) Low IQ but high learning potential: why Zeyneb and Moussa do not belong in special education. *Educational and Child Psychology*, 14(4): 121–36.

Hester, H., Ellis, S. and Barrs, M. (1988) *Guide to the Primary Learning Record*. London: Centre for Language in Primary Education.

Hewett, D. (2007) Do touch: physical contact and people who have severe, profound and multiple learning difficulties. *Support for Learning*, 22(3): 116–23.

Hewison, J. (1988) The long term effectiveness of parental involvement in reading: a follow-up study to the Haringey reading project. *British Journal of Educational Psychology*, 58: 184–90.

Hickson, J., Land, A.J. and Aikman, G. (1994) Learning style differences in middle school pupils from four ethnic backgrounds. *School Psychology International*, 15(4): 349–59.

Hiebert, J. and Lefevre, P. (1986) Conceptual and procedural knowledge in mathematics: an introductory analysis. In J. Hiebert (ed.) *Conceptual and Procedural Knowledge: The Case of Mathematics*. Hillsdale, NJ: Lawrence Erlbaum Associates.

Hieronymous, A.N. and Hoover, H.D. (1986) *Iowa Test of Basic Skills: Manual for School Administrators, Levels 5–14*. Chicago: Riverside Publishing Company.

Higgins, S. (2003) Parlez-vous mathematics. In I. Thompson (ed.) *Enhancing Primary Mathematics Teaching* (pp. 54–64). Buckingham: Open University Press.

Hill, J. (1994) The paradox of gender: sex-stereotyping within the statementing procedure. *British Education Research Journal*, 20(3): 345–57.

Hill, M. (2006) Children's voices on ways of having a voice. *Childhood*, 13(1): 69–89.

Hillage, J., Pearson, R., Anderson, A. and Tamkin, P. (1998) *Excellence in Research on Schools*, Research Report RR74. London: DfEE Publications.

Hindley, P., Reed, R., Jeffs, J. and MacSweeney, M. (1998) An evaluation of a social and emotional intervention for deaf children. Unpublished manuscript, St George's Hospital, London. Reported in Kusché (2002).

Her Majesty's Inspectorate of Schools (1989) *Aspects of Primary Education: The Teaching and Learning of Mathematics*. London: HMSO.

Ho, I. (2004) A comparison of Australian and Chinese teacher's attributions for student problem behaviours. *Educational Psychology*, 24(3): 375–91.

Hoby, R. (2002) *A National Development Agenda: What Does It Feel Like to Learn in Our Schools?* London: The Hay Group. (Report available at www.transforminglearning.co.uk)

Hodes, M. (2000) Psychologically distressed refugee children in the United Kingdom. *Child Psychology and Psychiatry Review*, 5(2): 57–68.

Hodson, P., Baddeley, A., Laycock, S. and Williams, S. (2005) Helping secondary schools to be more inclusive of Year 7 pupils with SEN. *Educational Psychology in Practice*, 21(1): 53–67.

Hogg, J. (2007) Complex needs and complex solutions: the challenge of profound intellectual and multiple disabilities. *Journal of Policy and Practice in Intellectual Disabilities*, 4(2): 79–82.

Hogg, J., Cavet, J. and Lamb, L. (2001) The use of 'Snoezelen' as multi-sensory stimulation with people with intellectual disabilities: a review of the research. *Research in Developmental Disabilities*, 22(5): 353–72.

Holmes, E. (1995) Educational interventions for young children who have experienced fragmented care. In J. Trowell and M. Bower (eds) *The Emotional Needs of Young Children and their Families: Using Psychoanalytic Ideas in the Community*. London: Routledge.

Holt, J.A. and Allen, T.E. (1989) The effects of schools and their curricula on the reading and mathematics achievement of hearing impaired students. *International Journal of Educational Research*, 13: 547–62.

Hood, J. and Rankin, P.M. (2005) How do specific memory disorders present in the school classroom? *Developmental Neurorehabilitation*, 8(4): 272–82.

Hopkins, B. (2004) *Just Schools: A Whole School Approach to Restorative Justice*. London: Jessica Kingsley.

Hornby, G. (1995) *Working with Parents of Children with Special Needs*. London: Cassell.

Hornby, G. (2003) *Counselling Pupils in Schools: Skills and Strategies for Teachers*. London: Routledge Falmer.

Horner, R.H., Carr, E.G., Strain, P.S., Todd, A.W. and Reed, H.K. (2002) Problem behaviour interventions for young children with autism: a research synthesis. *Journal of Autism and Developmental Disorders*, 32(5): 423–46.

Horton, C. (ed.) (2005) *Working with Children 2006–07: Facts, Figures and Information*. London: Sage.

Houghton, S., Merrett, F. and Wheldall, K. (1988) The attitudes of British secondary school pupils to praise, rewards, punishments and reprimands: a further study. *New Zealand Journal of Educational Studies*, 23: 203–14.

House of Commons Education and Skills Committee (2006) *Special Educational Needs*. Third Report of the Session 2005–06. Ref. HC 478–1. London: Stationery Office.

House of Commons Education and Skills Committee (2007a) *Bullying*. London: The Stationery Office.

House of Commons Education and Skills Committee (2007b) *Special Educational Needs: Assessment and Funding*. Tenth Report of the Session 2006–07. Ref. HC 1077. London: Stationery Office.

House of Commons Select Committee on Education, Science and Arts (1987) *Special Educational Needs: Implementation of the Education Act 1981*. London: HMSO.

Houssart, J. (2005a) Count me out: task refusal in primary mathematics. In A. Watson, J. Houssart and C. Roaf (eds) *Supporting Mathematical Thinking* (pp. 65–73). London: David Fulton/NASEN.

Houssart, J. (2005b) Watching, listening and acting: a case study of LSAs in primary maths lessons. In A. Watson, J. Houssart and C. Roaf (eds) *Supporting Mathematical Thinking* (pp. 120–9). London: David Fulton/NASEN.

Howes, A., Farrell, P., Kaplan, I. and Moss, S. (2003) The impact of paid adult support on the participation and learning of pupils in mainstream schools. In *Research Evidence in Education Library*. London: EPPI-Centre, Social Science Research Unit, Institute of Education.

Howitt, D. and Owusu-Bempah, J. (1994) *The Racism of Psychology: Time for Change*. Hemel Hempstead: Harvester Wheatsheaf.

Howley, M. and Arnold, E. (2005) *Revealing the Hidden Social Code*. London: Jessica Kingsley.

Howlin, P. (2000) Outcome in adult life for more able individuals with autism or Asperger's syndrome. *Autism*, 4(1): 63–83.

Howlin, P. and Cross, P. (1994) The variability of language test scores in 3- and 4-year-old children of normal non-verbal intelligence: a brief research report. *European Journal of Disorders of Communication*, 29: 279–88.

Howlin, P. and Moore, A. (1997) Diagnosis in autism. A survey of over 1200 patients in the UK. *Autism*, 1(2): 135–62.

Huebner, E. S. (1994) Preliminary development and validation of a multidimensional life satisfaction scale for children. *Psychological Assessment*, 6: 149–58.

Hughes, D. (2004) Just a breath of fresh air in an industrial landscape? The Preston Open Air School in 1926: A School Medical Service insight. *Social History of Medicine*, 17(3): 443–61.

Hull, J.M. (2004) Teaching as a transworld activity. *Support for Learning*, 19(3): 103–6.

Humphrey, N., Curran, A., Morris, E., Farrell, P. and Woods, K. (2007) Emotional intelligence and education: a critical review. *Educational Psychology*, 27(2): 235–54.

Hunt, P., Alwell, N., Farron-Davies, F. and Goetz, L. (1996) Creating social supportive environments for fully included students who experience multiple disabilities. *Journal of the Association for Persons with Severe Handicaps*, 21(2): 53–71.

Hurry, J. and Doctor, E. (2007) Assessing literacy in children and adolescents. *Child and Adolescent Mental Health*, 12(1): 38–45.

Huss-Keeler, R.L. (1997) Teacher perception of ethnic and linguistic minority parental involvement and its relationship to children's language and literacy learning: a case study. *Teaching and Teacher Education*, 13(2): 171–82.

Hutchings, J., Lane, E., Owen, R.E. and Gwin, R. (2004) The introduction of Webster-Stratton incredible years classroom dinosaur school programme in Gwynedd, North Wales: a pilot study. *Educational & Child Psychology*, 21(4): 4–15.

Hutchinson, J.M., Whiteley, H.E., Smith, C.D. and Connors, L. (2003) The developmental progression of comprehension-related skills in children learning EAL. *Journal of Research in Reading*, 26(1): 19–32.

Hutchinson, J.M., Whiteley, H.E., Smith, C.D. and Connors, L. (2004) The early identification of dyslexia: children with English as an additional language. *Dyslexia*, 10: 179–95.

Indoe, D. (1999) Attribution and motivation. In N. Frederickson and R.J. Cameron (eds) *Psychology in Education Portfolio*. Windsor: NFER-Nelson.

Inner London Education Authority (1983) *A Policy for Equality: Race*. London: ILEA.

Inner London Education Authority (1985) *Educational Opportunities for All?* (Fish Report). London: ILEA.

Iszatt, J. and Wasilewska, T. (1997) Nurture groups: an early intervention model enabling vulnerable children with emotional and behaviour difficulties to integrate successfully into school. *Educational and Child Psychology*, 14(3): 63–70.

Iverson, A.M. and Iverson, G.L. (1996) Children's long term reactions to participating in sociometric assessment. *Psychology in the Schools*, 33: 104–12.

Iverson, A.M., Barton, E.A. and Iverson, G.L. (1997) Analysis of risk to children participating in a sociometric task. *Developmental Psychology*, 33(1): 103–12.

Jefferies, E. and Donlan, S. (1994) Reluctant talkers in the early years: some key issues. In J. Watson (ed.) *Working with Communication Difficulties*. Edinburgh: Moray House Publications.

Jelly, M., Fuller, A. and Byers, R. (2000) *Involving Pupils in Practice*. London: David Fulton.

Jenkins, G.M. (1969) The systems approach. *Journal of Systems Engineering*, 1(1): 19–27.

Jensen, A.R. (1969) How much can we boost IQ and scholastic achievement? *Harvard Educational Review*, 39: 1–123.

Jensen, A.R. (1980) *Bias in Mental Testing*. London: Methuen.

Jensen, M. (2003) Mediating knowledge construction. *Educational and Child Psychology*, 20(2): 100–142.

Jernigan, K. (1993) The pitfalls of political correctness: euphemisms excoriated. *Braille Monitor*, 36(8). http://www.nfb.org (accessed 28 October 2007).

Jewell, T. and Feiler, A. (1985) A review of behaviourist teaching approaches in the UK. *Early Child Development and Care*, 20(1): 67–86.

Johnson, D.W. and Johnson, R.T. (1991) *Learning Together and Alone*, 3rd edition. Englewood Cliffs, NJ: Prentice Hall.

Johnson, D.W., Johnson, R.T. and Maruyama, G. (1983) Interdependence and inter-personal attraction among hetrogeneous and homogeneous individuals: a theoretical formulation and a meta-analysis of the research. *Review of Educational Research*, 53(1): 5–54.

Johnson, M. (2004) Dyslexia friendly schools: policy and practice. In G. Reid and A. Fawcett (eds) *Dyslexia in Context: Research, Policy and Practice* (pp. 237–56). London: Whurr.

Jones, D.V. (1993) Words with a similar meaning. *Mathematics Teaching*, 145: 14–15.

Jones, G. (2002) *Educational Provision for Children with Autism and Asperger's Syndrome: Meeting their Needs*. London: David Fulton Publishers.

Jones, G. (2006) Department for Education and Skills/Department of Health good practice guidance on the education of children with autistic spectrum disorder. *Childcare, Health and Development*, 32(5): 543–52.

Jones, G.A. and Thornton, C.A. (1993) Children's understanding of place value: a frame-work for curriculum development and assessment. *Young Children*, 48(5): 12–18.

Jones, P. (2005) Teachers' views of their pupils with profound and multiple learning difficulties. *European Journal of Special Needs Education*, 20(4): 375–85.

Jones, P. (2006) Every child's parent matters: community educational psychology and the Plymouth Parent Partnership Service. *Educational and Child Psychology*, 23(1): 16–26.

Jordan, N.C., Hanich, L.B. and Kaplan, D. (2003a) A longitudinal study of mathematical competencies in children with specific mathematics difficulties versus children with comorbid mathematics and reading difficulties. *Child Development*, 74: 834–50.

Jordan, N.C., Hanich, L.B. and Uberti, H.Z. (2003b) Mathematical thinking and learning difficulties. In A. J. Baroody and A. Dowker (eds) *The Development of Arithmetic Concepts and Skills: Constructing Adaptive Expertise* (pp. 359–83). London: Lawrence Erlbaum Associates.

Jordan, R. (2001) Multi-disciplinary work for children with autism. *Educational and Child Psychology*, 18(2): 5–14.

Jordan, R. and Powell, S. (1995) *Understanding and Teaching Children with Autism*. Chichester: Wiley.

Jordan, R., Jones, G. and Murray, D. (1998) *Educational Interventions for Children with*

Autism: A Literature Review of Recent and Current Research. DfEE Research Report 77. London: Department for Education and Employment.

Joseph, G.G. (1993) A rationale for a multicultural approach to mathematics. In D. Nelson, G.G. Joseph and J. Williams (eds) *Multicultural Mathematics*. Oxford: Oxford University Press.

Juvonen, J. and Weiner, B. (1993) An attributional analysis of students' interactions: the social consequences of perceived responsibility. *Educational Psychology Review*, 5(4): 325–45.

Kahne, J. (1996) The politics of self-esteem. *American Educational Research Journal*, 33(1): 3–22.

Kalambouka, A., Farrell, P., Dyson, A. and Kaplan, I. (2005) The impact of population inclusivity in schools on student outcomes. In *Research Evidence in Education Library*. London: EPPI-Centre, Social Science Research Unit, Institute of Education. University of London.

Kam, C.M., Greenberg, M.T. and Kusché, C.A. (2004) Sustained effects of the PATHS curriculum on the social and psychological adjustment of children in special education. *Journal of Emotional and Behavioral Disorders*, 12(2): 66–78.

Kamps, D.M., Barbetta, P.M., Leonard, B.R. and Delquadri, J. (1994) Classwide peer tutoring: an integration strategy to improve reading skills and promote peer interactions amongst students with autism and general education peers. *Journal of Applied Behaviour Analysis*, 27(1): 49–61.

Kaufman, A.S. and Kaufman, N.L. (1983) *Kaufman Assessment Battery for Children*. Circle Pines, MN: American Guidance Service.

Kaufman, A.S. and Kaufman, N.L. (2004) *Kaufman Assessment Battery for Children – Second Edition*. Circle Pines, MN: American Guidance Service.

Kaufman, B. (1994) *Son-Rise: The Miracle Continues*. Tiburon, CA: Kramer.

Kaufman, M., Agard, J.A. and Semmel, M.I. (1985) *Mainstreaming: Learners and their Environment*. Cambridge, MA: Brookline Books.

Kay, J. and Yeo, D. (2003) *Dyslexia and Maths*. London: David Fulton.

Keil, S. and Clunies-Ross, L. (2003) *Survey of Educational Provision for Blind and Partially Sighted Children in England, Scotland and Wales in 2002*. London: RNIB.

Keil, S., Parris, D., Cobb, R., Edwards, A. and McAllister, R. (2006) *Too Little, Too Late – Provision of School Textbooks for Blind and Partially Sighted Pupils*. London: RNIB.

Keller, D. and Sterling-Honig, A. (1993) Curriculum to produce positive interactions in pre-schoolers with a disabled peer introduced into the classroom. *Early Child Development & Care*, 96: 27–34.

Keller, H.R. (1988) Children's adaptive behaviors: measure and source generalisability. *Journal of Psychoeducational Assessment*, 6: 371–89.

Kellett, M. (2003) Jacob's journey: developing sociability and communication in a young boy with severe and complex learning difficulties using the Intensive Interaction teaching approach. *Journal of Research in Special Educational Needs*, 3(1).

Kelley-Laine, K. (1998) Parents as partners in schooling: the current state of affairs. *Childhood Education*, 74(6): 342–5.

Kelly, B., Longbottom, J., Potts, F. and Williamson, J. (2004) Applying emotional intelligence: exploring the promoting alternative thinking strategies curriculum. *Educational Psychology in Practice*, 20: 221–40.

Kelly, G.A. (1991) *The Psychology of Personal Constructs*, vols 1 and 2; *A Theory of Personality; Clinical Diagnosis and Psychopathology*. Florence, KY: Taylor and Francis/ Routledge.

Kelly, N. and Norwich, B. (2004) Pupils' perceptions of self and of labels: moderate learning difficulties in mainstream and special schools. *British Journal of Educational Psychology*, 74(3): 411–35.

Kendler, K.S. (2005) A gene for . . .: the nature of gene action in psychiatric disorders. *American Journal of Psychiatry*, 162: 1243–52.

Kenefick, J.D. (2002) Vision. In L. Porter (ed.) *Educating Young Children with Special Needs* (pp. 81–95). London: Paul Chapman.

Kenner, C. (2005) Bilingual families as literacy eco-systems. *Early Years*, 25(3): 283–98.

Kenner, C., Wells, K. and Williams, H. (1996) Assessing a bilingual child's talk in different classroom contexts. In N. Hall and J. Martello (eds) *Listening to Children Think: Exploring Talk in the Early Years*. London: Hodder and Stoughton.

Kenner, C., Gregory, E., Ruby, M. and Al-Azami, S. (2007) *Developing Bilingual Learning Strategies in Mainstream and Community Contexts*. ESRC Research Report ref. RES-000-22-1528. http://www.esrcsocietytoday.ac.uk.

Kent, B. and Smith, S. (2006) They only see it when the sun shines in my ears: exploring perceptions of adolescent hearing aid users. *Journal of Deaf Studies and Deaf Education*, 11(4): 461–76.

Keogh, A.F. and Whyte, J. (2005) *Second Level Student Councils in Ireland: A Study of Enablers, Barriers and Supports*. Dublin: National Children's Office.

Keogh, B.K., Gallimore, R. and Weisner, T. (1997) A sociocultural perspective on learning and learning disabilities. *Learning Disabilities Research and Practice*, 12(2): 107–13.

Kerr, K.P., Smyth, P. and McDowell, C. (2003) Precision teaching with autism: helping design effective programmes. *Early Child Development and Care*, 173(4): 399–410.

Kerslake, D. (1982) Talking about mathematics. In R. Harvey, D. Kerslake, H. Shuard and M. Torbe (eds) *Language Teaching and Learning: Mathematics*. East Grinstead: Ward Lock Educational.

Kessissoglou, S. and Farrell, P. (1995) Whatever happened to precision teaching? *British Journal of Special Education*, 22(2): 60–3.

Ketelaar, M., Vermeer, A. and Helders, P.J. (1998) Functional motor abilities of children with cerebral palsy: a systematic literature review of assessment measures. *Clinical Rehabilitation*, 12(5): 369–80.

Kirman, B.H. (1972) *The Mentally Handicapped Child*. London: Nelson.

Kistener, J.A., Osbourne, M. and LeVerrier, L. (1988) Causal attributions of learning disabled children: developmental patterns and relation to academic progress. *Journal of Educational Psychology*, 80: 82–9.

Klein, P. (1997) Multiplying the problems of intelligence by eight: a critique of Gardner's theory. *Canadian Journal of Education*, 22(4): 377–94.

Klein, P. (2003) Rethinking the multiplicity of cognitive resources and curricular representations: alternatives to 'learning styles' and 'multiple intelligences. *Journal of Curriculum Studies*, 35(1): 45–81.

Knight, J. (2007) Personalised learning and technology. Speech by Minister of State for Schools and Learners delivered in February 2007 to NAACE Annual Conference. http://www.dfes.gov.uk/speeches (accessed 28 November 2007).

Knight, P. and Swanwick, R. (2002) *Working with Deaf Pupils: Sign Bilingual Policy into Practice*. London: David Fulton.

Knight, S.L. (1991) The effects of students' perceptions of the learning environment on their motivation in language arts. *Journal of Classroom Interaction*, 26(2): 19–23.

Knoff, H.M. (1984) The practice of multi-modal consultation: an integrating approach for consultation service delivery. *Psychology in the Schools*, 21: 83–91.

Kolvin, I. and Fundudis, T. (1981) Elective mute children: psychological development and background factors. *Journal of Child Psychology and Psychiatry*, 22(3): 219–32.

Konu, A.I. and Rimpelä, M.K. (2002) Well-being in schools: a conceptual modal. *Health Promotion International* 17(1): 79–87.

Konu, A.I., Lintonen, T.P. and Rimpelä, M.K. (2002) Factors associated with schoolchildren's subjective well-being. *Health Education Research*, 17(2): 155–65.

Koontz, K.L. and Berch, D.B. (1996) Identifying simple numerical stimuli: processing inefficiencies exhibited by arithmetic learning disabled children. *Mathematical Cognition*, 2: 1–23.

Koshy, V. (2000) Children's mistakes and misconceptions. In V. Koshy, P. Ernest and R. Casey (eds) *Mathematics for Primary Teachers* (pp. 172–81). London: Routledge.

Kowszun, J. (1992) *Soft Systems Methodology*. Mendip Papers 039, The Staff College, Bristol.

Kratochwill, T. (1981) *Selective Mutism: Implications for Research and Treatment*. Hillsdale, NJ: Lawrence Erlbaum Associates.

Krauthammer, C. (1990) Education: doing bad and feeling good. *Time*, 135(6): 78.

Krol, N., Morton, J. and De Bruyn, E. (2004) Theories of conduct disorder: a causal modelling analysis. *Journal of Child Psychology and Psychiatry*, 45(4): 727–42.

Kupersmidt, J.B., Coie, J.D. and Dodge, K.A. (1990) The role of poor peer relations in the development of disorder. In S.J. Asher and J.D. Coie (eds) *Peer Rejection in Childhood*. New York: Cambridge University Press.

Kusché, C.A. (2002) Psychoanalysis as prevention: using PATHS to enhance ego development, object relationships and cortical integration in children. *Journal of Applied Psychoanalytic Studies*, 4(3): 283–301.

Kusché, C.A. and Greenberg, M.T. (1994) *The PATHS Curriculum*. Seattle: Developmental Research and Programmes.

Kusché, C.A., Greenberg, M.T. and Beilke, B. (1988) The Kusché affective interview. Unpublished manuscript. University of Washington, Department of Psychology.

Kyle, F.E. and Harris, M. (2006) Concurrent correlates and predictors of reading and spelling achievement in deaf and hearing school children. *Journal of Deaf Studies and Deaf Education*, 11(3): 273–88.

Kyle, J.G. and Woll, B. (eds) (1983) *Language in Sign: An International Perspective on Sign Language*. London: Croom Helm.

Kysel, F. (1985) Characteristics of pupils in special schools and units. In F. Kysel (ed.) *Educational Opportunities for All? Research Studies for Fish Report*, Vol. 2. London: ILEA.

Labbe, E.E. and Williamson, D.A. (1984) Behavioral treatment of elective mutism: a review of the literature. *Clinical Psychology Review*, 4(3): 273–92.

Lam, T.C.M. (1993) Testability: a critical issue in testing language minority students with Standardized Achievement Tests. *Measurement and Evaluation in Counselling and Development*, 26: 179–91.

Lamborn, S.D., Dornbusch, S.M., and Steinberg, L. (1996) Ethnicity and community context as moderators of the relations between family decision making and adolescent adjustment. *Child Development*, 67: 283–301.

Laming, H. (2003) *The Victoria Climbié Inquiry: Summary Report of an Inquiry*. Norwich: HMSO.

Lamprianou, I. and Boyle, B. (2004) Accuracy of measurement in the context of mathematics national curriculum tests in England for ethnic minority pupils and pupils who speak English as an additional language. *Journal of Educational Measurement*, 41(3): 239–59.

Landerl, K., Bevan, A. and Butterworth, B. (2004) Developmental dyscalculia and basic numerical capacities: a study of 8–9-year-old students. *Cognition*, 93: 99–125.

Landon, J. (2005) First language assessment: an overview of principles. In T. Cline (ed.) *Assessing Children's Knowledge and Use of Community Languages for Educational Purposes: Report of a Workshop held at the University of Luton* (pp. 29–33). Luton: National Association for Language Development in the Curriculum.

Lane, H. (1992) *The Mask of Benevolence*. New York: Alfred A. Knopf.

Lauchlan, F. and Boyle, C. (2007) Is the use of labels in special education helpful? *Support for Learning*, 22(1): 36–42.

Lauchlan, F. and Elliott, J. (2001) The psychological assessment of learning potential. *British Journal of Educational Psychology*, 71(4): 647–66.

Laurent, J., Catanzaro, S.J., Joiner, T.E., Rudolph, K.D., Potter, K.I., Lambert, S. *et al.* (1999) A measure of positive and negative affect for children: scale development and preliminary validation. *Psychological Assessment*, 11: 326–38.

Law, G.U., Sinclair, S. and Fraser, N. (2007) Children's attitudes and behavioural intentions towards a peer with symptoms of ADHD: does the addition of a diagnostic label make a difference? *Journal of Child Health Care*, 11(2): 98–111.

Law, J. (1999) 'It's not just the pigs . . . a comment on the RDLS III. *International Journal of Language & Communication Disorders*, 34(2): 181–4.

Law, J. and Tamhne, R. (2000) The size of the problem. In J. Law, S. Parkinson and R. Tamhne (eds) *Communication Difficulties in Childhood: A Practical Guide*. Abingdon: Radcliffe Medical Press.

Le Fevre, D.M., Moore, D.W. and Wilkinson, I.A.G. (2003) Tape-assisted reciprocal teaching: cognitive boot strapping for poor decoders. *British Journal of Educational Psychology*, 73(1): 37–58.

Leahy, S., Lyon, C., Thompson, M. and Wiliam, D. (2005) Classroom assessment: minute by minute and day by day. *Educational Leadership*, 63(3): 18–24.

Learning and Teaching Scotland (2007) Assessment for learning. http://www.ltscotland.org.uk/assess/for/index.asp.

Lederberg, A.R. and Everhart, V.S. (1998) Communication between deaf children and their hearing mothers: the role of language, gesture and vocalisations. *Journal of Speech, Language and Hearing Research*, 41: 887–99.

Lee, J. and Eke, R. (2004) 'The NLS and pupils with special educational needs. *Journal of Research in Special Educational Needs*, 4(1): 50–7.

Lees, J. and Urwin, S. (1997) *Children with Language Disorders*, 2nd edition. London: Whurr.

Lemerise, E.A. and Arsenio, W.F. (2000) An integrated model of emotion processing and cognition in social information processing. *Child Development*, 71(1): 107–18.

Leung, C., Harris, R. and Rampton, B. (1997) The idealised native speaker, reified ethnicities and classroom realities. *TESOL Quarterly*, 31(3): 543–60.

Levinson, M.P. and Sparkes, A.C. (2005) Gypsy children, space, and the school environment. *International Journal of Qualitative Studies in Education*, 18(6): 751–72.

Lewin, K. (1936) *Principles of Topological Psychology*. New York: McGraw-Hill.

Lewis, A. (1995) *Primary Special Needs and the National Curriculum*. London: Routledge.

Lewis, A. and Norwich, B. (2005) Overview and discussion: overall conclusions. In A. Lewis and B. Norwich (eds) *Special Teaching for Special Children? Pedagogies for Inclusion* (pp. 206–21). Maidenhead: Open University Press.

Lewis, A. and Porter, J. (2004) Interviewing children and young people with learning disabilities: guidelines for researchers and multi-professional practice. *British Journal of Learning Disabilities*, 32: 191–7.

Lewis, A., Robertson, C. and Parsons, S. (2005) *DRC Research Report – Experiences of Disabled Students and their Families: Phase 1*. London: Disability Rights Commission.

Lewis, C., Hitch, G.J. and Walker, P. (1994) The prevalence of specific arithmetic difficulties and specific reading difficulties in 9- to 10-year-old boys and girls. *Journal of Child Psychology and Psychiatry*, 35(2): 283–92.

Light, J. (1989) Towards a definition of communicative competence in individuals using augmentative and alternative communication systems. *Augmentative and Alternative Communication*, 5(2): 137–44.

Lim, T.K. (1995) Perceptions of classroom environment, school types, gender and learning styles of secondary school students. *Educational Psychology*, 15(2): 161–9.

Limbrick, P. (2005) 'Team Around the Child': principles and practice. In B. Carpenter (ed.) *Early Childhood Intervention: International Perspectives, National Initiatives and Regional Practice* (pp. 81–96). West Midlands SEN Regional Partnership.

Lindsay, D. (2003) Inclusive education: a critical perspective. *British Journal of Special Education*, 30(1): 3–12.

Lindsay, G. (2007) Educational psychology and the effectiveness of inclusive education/mainstreaming. *British Journal of Educational Psychology*, 77–1–24.

Lindsay, G., Pather, S. and Strand, S. (2006) *Special Educational Needs and Ethnicity: Issues of Over- and Under-representation*, DfES Research Report No. 757. London: DfES.

Lindsley, O.R. (1992) Precision teaching: discoveries and effects. *Journal of Applied Behavioural Analysis*, 25(1): 51–7.

Linn, M.C., Benedictis, T.D., Delucchi, K., Harris, A. and Stage, E. (1987) Gender differences in National Assessment of Educational Progress science items: what does 'I don't know' really mean? *Journal of Research in Science Teaching*, 24: 267–78.

Lipsky, D.K. and Gartner, A. (1996) Inclusion, school restructuring, and the remaking of American society. *Harvard Educational Review*, 66(4): 762–95.

Little, L. (2002) Middle-class mothers' perceptions of peer and sibling victimization among children with Asperger's syndrome and non-verbal learning disorders. *Issues in Comprehensive Pediatric Nursing*, 25: 43–57.

Liu, A. (1995) Full inclusion and deaf education – redefining equality. *Journal of Law and Education*, 24(2): 241–66.

Lohman, D.F., Thorndike, R.L., Hagen, E.P., Smith, P., Fernandes, C., and Strand, S. (2001) *Cognitive Abilities Test*, 3rd edition. London: NFER-Nelson.

Lord, C. and Magill-Evans, J. (1995) Peer interactions of autistic children and adolescents. *Development & Psychopathology*, 7: 611–26.

Losen, D. J. and Orfield, G. (eds) (2002) *Racial Inequity in Special Education*. Cambridge, MA: Harvard Education Press.

Lovaas, O.I. (1987) Behavioural treatment and normal intellectual and educational functioning in autistic children. *Journal of Consulting and Clinical Psychology*, 55: 3–9.

Lovegrove, W. (1994) Visual deficit in dyslexia: evidence and implications. In A. Fawcett and R. Nicolson (eds) *Dyslexia in Children*. Hemel Hempstead: Harvester Wheatsheaf.

Lowe, M. and Costello, A. (1988) *Symbolic Play Test*, 2nd edition. Windsor: NFER-Nelson.

Lucas, S., Insley, K. and Buckland, G. (2006) *Nurture Group Principles and Curriculum Guidelines: Helping Children to Achieve*. London: Nurture Group Network.

Lynch, M. and Cicchetti, D. (2002) Links between community violence and the family system: evidence from children's feelings of relatedness and perceptions of parent behavior. *Family Process*, 41(3): 519–32.

MacDonald, I.M. (1996) Expanding the lens: student perceptions of school violence. In J. Ross Epp and A.M. Watkinson (eds) *Systemic Violence: How Schools Hurt Children*. London: Falmer Press.

MacLeod, F. (1996) Encouraging parents' involvement in their children's literacy development. *School Psychology International*, 17: 379–91.

Macpherson, W. (1999) *Report of the Stephen Lawrence Inquiry*, Cm. 4262. London: Stationery Office.

Madden, N.A. and Slavin, R.E. (1983) Mainstreaming students with mild handicaps: academic and social outcomes. *Review of Educational Research*, 52(4): 519–69.

Maheady, L., Mallette, B. and Harper, G.F. (2006) Four classwide peer tutoring models: similarities, differences and implications for research and practice. *Reading and Writing Quarterly*, 22, 65–89.

Mahon, M. (2003) Conversations with young deaf children in families where English is an additional language. In C. Gallaway and A. Young (eds) *Deafness and Education in the UK: Research Perspectives* (pp. 35–52). London: Whurr.

Male, D. (1996) Who goes to MLD schools? *British Journal of Special Education*, 23(1): 35–41.

Male, D.B. and Rayner, M. (2007) Who goes to SLD schools? Aspects of policy and provision for pupils with profound and multiple learning difficulties who attend special schools in England. *Support for Learning*, 22(3): 145–52.

Mallon, F. (2000) Peer and cross age tutoring and mentoring schemes. In H. Daniels (ed.) *Special Education Reformed: Beyond Rhetoric?* London: Falmer Press.

Mandich, A.D. and Polatajko, H.J. (2005) A cognitive perspective on intervention for children with developmental coodination disorder: the CO-OP experience. In D.A. Sugden and M.E. Chambers (eds) *Children with Developmental Coordination Disorder* (pp. 228–41). London: Whurr.

Mansell, W. (2007) Education without frills. *Times Educational Supplement*, 8 June. http://www.tes.co.uk.

Manset, G. and Semmel, M.I. (1997) Are inclusive programs for students with mild disabilities effective? A comparative review of model programs. *Journal of Special Education*, 31(2): 155–80.

Marchant, P., Hussain, A. and Hall, R. (2006) Autistic spectrum disorders and Asian children. *British Journal of Educational Studies*, 54(2): 230–44.

Markides, A. (1991) The teaching of speech: historical developments (extract from 1983 text). In S. Gregory and G.M. Hartley (eds) *Constructing Deafness*. London: Pinter Publishers.

Marks, A. and Burden, B. (2005) How useful are computerised screening systems for predicting subsequent learning difficulties in young children? An exploration of the strengths and weaknesses of the cognitive profiling system (CoPS 1). *Educational Psychology in Practice*, 21(4): 327–42.

Marschark, M. (1993) *Psychological Development of Deaf Children*. New York: Oxford University Press.

Marsh, H.W., Chessor, D., Craven, R. and Roche, L. (1995) The effects of gifted and talented programs on academic self concept: the big fish strikes again. *American Educational Research Journal*, 32: 285–319.

Martin, A. (2006) Assessment using the P scales: best fit – fit for the purpose? *British Journal of Special Education*, 33(2): 68–75.

Martin, D. (1994) Towards a model of service delivery. In D. Martin (ed.) *Services to Bilingual Children with Speech and Language Difficulties: Proceedings of the 25th Anniversary AFASIC Conference, Birmingham, 1993*. London: Association for All Speech-Impaired Children.

Martin, D. and Miller, C. (2003) *Speech and Language Difficulties in the Classroom*, 2nd edition. London: David Fulton.

Martin, E.W. (1995) Case studies on inclusion: worst fears realised. *Journal of Special Education*, 29: 192–9.

Martin, K.M. and Huebner, E.S. (2007) Peer victimization pro-social experiences and emotional wellbeing of middle school students. *Psychology in the Schools*, 44(2): 199–208.

Mastergeorge, A.M., Rogers, S.J., Corbett, B.A. and Solomon, M. (2003) Non-medical interventions for autistic spectrum disorders. In S. Ozonoff, S.J. Rogers and R.L. Hendren (eds) *Autistic Spectrum Disorders: A Research Review for Practitioners*. Washington, DC: American Psychiatric Publishing.

Mastropieri, M.A. and Scruggs, T.E. (1997) What's special about special education? A cautious view toward full inclusion. *Educational Forum*, 61: 206–11.

Mastropieri, M.A., Leinart, A., and Scruggs, T.E. (1999) Strategies to increase reading fluency. *Intervention in School and Clinic*, 34(5): 278–83.

Mathes, P.G., Fuchs, D., Fuchs, L.S., Henley, A.M., and Saunders, A. (1994) Increasing strategic reading practice with Peabody classwide peer tutoring. *Learning Disabilities Research in Practice*, 9(1): 44–8.

Maurer, M., Brackett, M. and Plain, F. (2004) *Emotional Literacy in the Middle School*. New York: National Professional Resources.

Mavrommatis, Y. (1997) Understanding assessment in the classroom: phases of the assessment process – the assessment episode. *Assessment in Education*, 4(3): 381–400.

Maxwell, T. (2006) Researching into some primary school children's views about school: using personal construct psychology in practice with children on the Special Needs Register. *Pastoral Care in Education*, 24(1): 20–6.

May, H. (2005) Whose participation is it anyway? Examining the context of pupil participation in the UK. *British Journal of Special Education*, 32(1): 29–34.

Mazzocco, M.M.M. and Myers G.F. (2003) Complexities in identifying and defining mathematics learning disability in the primary school years. *Annals of Dyslexia*, 53: 218–53.

McArthur, C.A., Ferretti, R.P., Okolo, C.M. and Cavalier, A.R. (2001) Technology applications for students with literacy problems: a critical analysis. *The Elementary School Journal*, 101(3): 273–301.

McBrien, J. and Foxen, T. (1981) *Training Staff in Behavioural Methods*. Manchester: Manchester University Press.

McCallum, R.S. and Bracken, B.A. (1997) The Universal Nonverbal Intelligence Test. In D.P. Flanagan, J.L. Genshaft and P.L. Harrison (eds) *Contemporary Intellectual Assessment: Theories, Tests and Issues*. New York: Guilford Press.

McConnell, S. R. (2002) Interventions to facilitate social interaction for young children with autism: review of available research and recommendations for educational intervention and future research. *Journal of Autism and Developmental Disorders*, 32(5): 351–72.

McCracken, W. (2003) Pilot study of a two-channel compression hearing aid with school age children. In C. Gallaway and A. Young (eds) *Deafness and Education in the UK: Research Perspectives* (pp. 187–204). London: Whurr.

McDowell, C. and Keenan, M. (2001) Developing fluency and endurance in a child diagnosed with attention deficit hyperactivity disorder. *Journal of Applied Behavior Analysis*, 34: 345–8.

McGee, G.G., Daly, T. and Jacobs, H.A. (1994) The Walden preschool. In S.L. Harris and J.S. Handleman (eds) *Preschool Education Programs for Children with Autism*, 2nd edition (pp. 127–62). Austin, TX: Pro-Ed.

McGee, J.J., Menolascino, F.J., Hobbs, D.C. and Menousek, P.E. (1987) *Gentle Teaching: A Non-aversive Approach for Helping Persons with Mild Retardation*. New York: Human Sciences Press.

McGee, R., Silva, P.A. and Williams, S. (1983) Parents' and teachers' of behavior problems in seven year old children. *The Exceptional Child*, 30(2): 151–61.

McIntyre, D., Pedder, D. and Rudduck, J. (2005) Pupils voice: comfortable and uncomfortable learnings for teachers. *Research Papers in Education*, 20(2): 149–68.

McKee, W.T. and Witt, J.C. (1990) Effective teaching: a review of instructional and environmental variables. In T.B. Gutkin and C.R. Reynolds (eds) *The Handbook of School Psychology*. New York: Wiley.

McKenna, P. (1990) Learning implications of field dependence-independence: cognitive style versus cognitive ability. *Applied Cognitive Psychology*, 4: 425–37.

McKillop, E., Bennett, D., McDaid, G., Holland, B., Smith, G., Spowart, K. and Dutton, G. (2006) Problems experienced by children with cognitive visual dysfunction due to cerebral visual impairment – and the approaches which parents have adopted to deal with these problems. *British Journal of Visual Impairment*, 24(3): 121–7.

McLaughlin, M.J. (1995) Defining special education: a response to Zigmond and Baker. *Journal of Special Education*, 29(2): 200–8.

McLaughlin, M.J. and Rouse, M. (eds) (2000) *Special Education and School Reform in the United States and Britain*. London: Routledge.

McLeskey, J., Skiba, R. and Wilcox, B. (1990) Reform and special education: a mainstream perspective. *Journal of Special Education*, 24(3): 319–25.

McLinden, M. and McCall, S. (2002) *Learning through Touch: Supporting Children with Visual Impairment and Additional Difficulties*. London: David Fulton.

McSherry, K. and Ollerton, M. (2002) Grouping patterns in primary schools. *Mathematics in Schools*, 31(1): 2–6.

McWilliam, N. (1998) *What's in a Word? Vocabulary Development in Multilingual Classrooms*. Stoke-on-Trent: Trentham Books.

Meadows, S. (1998) Children learning to think: learning from others? Vygotskyan theory and educational psychology. *Educational and Child Psychology*, 15(2): 6–13.

Medical Research Council (2001) *MRC Review of Autism Research Epidemiology and Causes*. London: Medical Research Council. http://www.mrc.ac.uk.

Meherali, R. (1994) Being black and deaf. In C. Laurenzi and P. Hindley (eds) *Keep Deaf Children in Mind: Current Issues in Mental Health*. Leeds: NDCS Family Services Centre.

Merbitz, C., Vieitez, D., Hansen Merbitz, N. and Binder, C. (2004a) Precision teaching: applications in education and beyond. In D.J. Moran and R.W. Malott (eds) *Evidence-Based Educational Methods* (pp. 63–78). San Diego, CA: Elsevier Academic Press.

Merbitz, C., Vieitez, D., Hansen Merbitz, N. and Pennypacker, H.S. (2004b) Precision teaching: foundations and classroom applications. In D.J. Moran and R.W. Malott (eds) *Evidence-Based Educational Methods* (pp. 47–62). San Diego, CA: Elsevier Academic Press.

Merrell, K.W. and Gimpel, G.A. (1997) *Social Skills of Children and Adolescents: Conceptualisation, Assessment, Treatment*. Mahwah, NJ: Lawrence Erlbaum.

Merrett, F. and Houghton, S. (1989) Does it work with the older ones? A review of behavioural studies carried out in British secondary schools since 1981. *Educational Psychology*, 9(4): 287–309.

Merttens, R. (1999) Family numeracy. In I. Thompson (ed.) *Issues in Teaching Numeracy in Primary Schools*. Buckingham: Open University Press.

Merttens, R., Newland, A. and Webb, S. (1996) *Learning in Tandem: Parental Involvement in their Children's Education*. Leamington Spa: Scholastic Press.

Mesibov, G. (1997) Formal and informal measures on the effectiveness of the TEACCH programme. *International Journal of Autism*, 1: 25–35.

Mesibov, G. and Howley, M. (2003) *Accessing the Curriculum for Pupils with Autistic Spectrum Disorders: Using the TEACCH Programme to Help Inclusion*. London: David Fulton.

Messick, S. (1989) Validity. In R.D.Linn (ed.) *Educational Measurement*, 3rd edition (pp. 12–103). London: Collier Macmillan.

Meyer, L.H., Minondo, S., Fisher, M., Larson, M.J., Dunmore, S., Black J.W. and D'Aquanni, M. (1998) Frames of friendship: social relationships of adolescents with diverse abilities. In L.H. Meyer, H.S. Park, M. Grenot-Scheyer, I.S. Schwartz and B. Harry (eds) *Making Friends. The Influence of Culture and Development* (pp. 189–221). Baltimore MD: Paul H. Brooks.

Midgley, C., Eccles, J.S. and Feldlaufer, H. (1991) Classroom environment and the transition to junior high school. In B.J. Fraser and H.J. Walberg (eds) *Educational Environments: Evaluation, Antecedents and Consequences*. Oxford: Pergamon Press.

Miles, T.R. (1993) *Dyslexia: The Pattern of Difficulties*, 2nd edition. London: Whurr.

Miller, A. (2003) *Teachers, Parents and Classroom Behaviour. A Psycho-social Approach*. Buckingham: Open University Press.

Miller, C., Lacey, P. and Layton, L. (2003) Including children with special educational needs in the Literacy Hour: a continuing challenge. *British Journal of Special Educational Needs*, 30(1): 14–20.

Miller, N. (1984) Some observations concerning formal tests in cross-cultural settings. In N. Miller (ed.) *Bilingualism and Language Disability*. London: Chapman & Hall.

Miller, O. and Hodges, L. (2005) Deafblindness. In A. Lewis and B. Norwich, (eds) *Special Teaching for Special Children? Pedagogies for Inclusion* (pp. 41–52). Maidenhead: Open University Press.

Miller, O. and Ockelford, A. (2005) *Visual Needs*. London: Continuum.

Mills, A.E. (1993) Visual handicap. In D. Bishop and K. Mogford (eds) *Language Development under Exceptional Circumstances*. Hove: Lawrence Erlbaum Associates.

Milroy, J. and Milroy, L. (1985) *Authority in Language: Investigating Prescription and Standardisation*. London: Routledge.

Ministry of Education (1945) *Handicapped Pupils and School Health Service Regulations*. London: HMSO.

Ministry of Education (1946) *Special Educational Treatment*. London: HMSO.

Ministry of Education (1955) *Report of the Committee on Maladjusted Children* (Underwood Report). London: HMSO.

Mischel, W. (1969) Continuity and change in personality. *American Psychologist*, 24: 1012–18.

Missiuna, C. and Samuels, M. (1988) Dynamic assessment: review and critique. *Special Services in the Schools*, 5(1–2): 1–22.

Mitchell, D. (2004) Introduction. In D. Mitchell (ed.) *Special Educational Needs and Inclusive Education. Vol 1: Systems and Contexts*. London: RoutledgeFalmer.

Mitchell, R.E. and Karchmer, M.A. (2004) When parents are deaf versus hard of hearing: patterns of sign use and school placement of deaf and hard-of-hearing children. *Journal of Deaf Studies and Deaf Education*, 9(2): 133–52.

Mittler, P. (1985) Integration: the shadow and the substance. *Educational and Child Psychology*, 2(3): 8–22.

Mittler, P. (2002) Educating pupils with intellectual disabilities in England: thirty years on. *International Journal of Disability, Development and Education*, 49(2): 145–60.

Miura, I.T. (1987) Mathematics achievement as a function of language. *Journal of Educational Psychology*, 79(1): 79–82.

Miura, I.T. and Okamoto, Y. (1994) Comparisons of U.S. and Japanese first graders' cognitive representation of number and understanding of place value. *Journal of Educational Psychology*, 81(1): 109–13.

Molteno, C., Roux, A., Nelson, M. and Arens, L. (1990) Causes of mental handicap in Cape Town. *South African Medical Journal*, 77: 98–101.

Moni, K.B., Jobling, A., van Krayenoord, C.E., Elkins, J., Miller, R. and Koppenhaber, D. (2007) Teachers' knowledge, attitudes and the implementation of practices around the teaching of writing an inclusive middle years' classrooms: no quick fix. *Educational and Child Psychology*, 24(3): 18–36.

Monks, C.P., Smith, P.K. and Swettenham, J. (2003) Aggressors, victims, and defenders in preschool: peer, self-, and teacher reports. *Merrill-Palmer Quarterly*, 49(4): 453–69.

Monsen, J. and Graham, B. (2001) Developing teacher-support groups to deal with challenging child behaviour: a staff sharing scheme. In P. Gray (ed.) *Working with Emotions: Responding to the Challenge of Difficult Pupil Behaviour in Schools* (pp. 129–49). London: Routledge Falmer.

Monsen, J.J. and Frederickson, N. (2004) Teachers' attitudes towards mainstreaming and their pupils' perceptions of their classroom learning environment. *Learning Environments Reasearch*, 7: 129–42.

Moos, R.H. (1973) Conceptualisations of human environments. *American Psychologist*, 28: 652–65.

Moran, P., Ghate, D. and van der Merwe, A. (2004) *What Works in Parenting Support? A Review of the International Evidence*. London: DfES Publications. Available at http://www.dcsf.gov.uk/research/data/uploadfiles/RR574.pdf (accessed 13 October 2008).

Moreno, J.L. (1934) *Who Shall Survive? A New Approach to the Problem of Human Interrelations*. Washington, DC: Nervous and Mental Disease Publishing Co.

Morgan, R. and Lyon, E. (1979) Paired reading – a preliminary report on a technique for parental tuition of reading-retarded children. *Journal of Child Psychology and Psychiatry*, 20: 151–60.

Morgan-Barry, R. (1988) *The Auditory Discrimination and Attention Test*. Windsor: NFER-Nelson.

Morrison, B. (2006) School bullying and restorative justice: toward a theoretical understanding of the role of respect, pride and shame. *Journal of Social Issues*, 62(2): 371–92.

Mortimore, P., Sammonds, P., Stoll, L., Lewis, D. and Ecob, R. (1988) *School Matters: The Junior Years*. Salisbury: Open Books.

Mortimore, T. (2005) Dyslexia and learning style – a note of caution. *Support for Learning*, 32(3): 145–8.

Morton, J. (2004) *Understanding Developmental Disorders: A Causal Modelling Approach*. Oxford: Blackwell.

Morton, J. and Frith, U. (1995) Causal modelling: a structural approach to developmental psychopathology. In D. Cichetti and D.J. Cohen (eds) *Manual of Developmental Psychopathology*. New York: Wiley.

Moss, H.A. and Susman, E.J. (1980) Longitudinal study of personality development. In O.G. Brim and J. Kagan (eds) *Consistency and Change in Human Development*. Cambridge, MA: Harvard University Press.

Moss, J., Deppeler, J., Astley, L. and Pattison, K. (2007) Student researchers in the middle: using visual images to make sense of inclusive education. *Journal of Research in Special Educational Needs*, 7(1): 46–54.

Moss, P., Pullin, D., Gee, J.P. and Young, L.J. (ed.) (2008) *Assessment, Equity and Opportunity to Learn*. New York: Cambridge University Press.

Mroz, M. (2006) Teaching in the Foundation Stage – how current systems support teachers' knowledge and understanding of children's speech and language. *International Journal of Early Years Education*, 14(1): 45–61.

Muijs, D. and Reynolds, D. (2003) The effectiveness of the use of learning support assistants in improving the mathematics achievement of low-achieving pupils in primary school. *Educational Research*, 45(3): 219–30.

Mulford, R. (1988) First words of the blind child. In M.D. Smith and J.L. Locke (eds) *The Emergent Lexicon: The Child's Development of a Linguistic Vocabulary*. New York: Academic Press.

Muñoz-Sandoval, A.F., Cummins, J., Alvadero, C.G. and Ruef, M.L. (1998) *Bilingual Verbal Ability Tests*. Itasca, IL: Riverside.

Murdoch, H. (2004) Early intervention for children who are deafblind. *Educational and Child Psychology*, 21(2): 67–79.

Muris, P., Meesters, M., Eijkelenboom, A. and Vincken, M. (2004) The self-report version of the Strengths and Difficulties Questionnaire: Its psychometric properties in 8- to 13-year-old non-clinical children. *British Journal of Clinical Psychology*, 43: 437–48.

Murphy, R.L.J. (1982) Sex differences in objective test performance. *British Journal of Educational Psychology*, 52: 213–19.

Murray, D. (1997) Autism and information technology: therapy with computers. In S. Powell and R. Jordan (eds) *Autism and Learning*. London: David Fulton.

Muter, V., Hulme, C. and Snowling, M. (1997) *Phonological Abilities Test*. London: The Psychological Corporation.

Myles, B.S. (2005) *Children and Youth with Asperger's Syndrome: Strategies for Success in Inclusive Settings*. Thousand Oaks, CA: Corwin Press.

Nabuzoka, D. and Smith, P.K. (1993) Sociometric status and social behaviour of children with and without learning difficulties. *Journal of Child Psychology and Psychiatry*, 34(8): 1435–48.

Naglieri, J.A. (2005) The Cognitive Assessment System. In D.P. Flanagan and P.L. Harrison (eds) *Contemporary Intellectual Assessment: Theories, Tests and Issues*, 2nd edition (pp. 441–60). New York: Guilford Press.

Naish, L., Bell, J. and Clunies-Ross, L. (2004) *Exploring Access: How to Audit Your School Environment, Focusing on the Needs of Pupils who have Multiple Disabilities and Visual Impairment*. London: RNIB.

National Association for Mental Health (1969) *The Mentally Subnormal in England and Wales*. London: National Association for Mental Health.

National Curriculum Council (1989a) *Implementing the National Curriculum – Participation by Pupils with Special Educational Needs* (Circular No. 5). York: NCC.

National Curriculum Council (1989b) *A Curriculum for All: Special Educational Needs in the National Curriculum*. York: NCC.

National Deaf Children's Society (2007) *Deaf Friendly Teacher Training Packs*. London: NDCS.

National Foundation for Educational Research (NFER) (1998) *Code of Practice for the Development of Assessment Instruments, Methods and Systems*. Windsor: NFER.

National Initiative for Autism: Screening and Assessment Working Group (2003) *National Autism Plan for Children*. London: National Autistic Society.

National Institute for Health and Clinical Excellence (2008) *Attention Deficit Hyperactivity Disorder. Diagnosis and Management of ADHD in Children, Young People and Adults*. http://www.nice.org.uk/CG072.

National Reading Panel (2000) *Teaching Children to Read: An Evidence Based Assessment of the Scientific Research Literature on Reading and its Implications for Reading Instruction*. Washington, DC: National Institute for Child Health and Human Development.

National Research Council (2001) *Educating Children with Autism*. Washington, DC: National Academy Press.

Neale, M., Christophers, U. and Whetton, C. (1997) *Neale Analysis of Reading Ability*, 2nd revised British edition. Windsor: NFER-Nelson.

Nelson, D., Joseph, G.G. and Williams, J. (1993) *Multicultural Mathematics: Teaching Mathematics from a Global Perspective*. Oxford: Oxford University Press.

Nelson, K.E. (1998) Processes of facilitating progress by language-delayed children in special language-centred school units. *International Journal of Language and Communication Disorders*, 33: 208–10.

New York State Department of Health (2000) *Review*: Clinical Practice Guidelines Report of the recommendations – Autism/Pervasive Developmental Disorders, Assessment and Intervention for Young Children (age 0–3 years). http://www.health.state.ny.us/publications/4216.pdf.

Newcomb, A.F., Bukowski, W.M. and Pattee, L. (1993) Children's peer relations: a meta-analytic review of popular, rejected, neglected, controversial and average sociometric status. *Psychological Bulletin*, 113(1): 99–128.

Newell, P. (1991) *The UN Convention and Children's Rights in the UK*. London: National Children's Bureau.

Newman, A. (1983) *The Newman Language of Mathematics Kit: Strategies for Diagnosis and Remediation*. Sydney: Harcourt Brace Jovanovich.

Newton, C., Taylor, G. and Wilson, D. (1996) Circles of friends: an inclusive approach to meeting emotional and behavioural difficulties. *Educational Psychology in Practice*, 11(4): 41–8.

Nicholls, D. and Houghton, S. (1995) The effect of Canter's Assertive Discipline Program on teacher and student behaviour. *British Journal of Educational Psychology*, 65(2): 197–210.

Nicholls, J.G. (1978) The development of the concepts of effort and ability, perception of academic attainment and the understanding that difficult tasks require more ability. *Child Development*, 49: 800–14.

Nichols, S.L., Hupp, S.D., Jewell, J.D. and Zeigler, C.S. (2005) Review of Social Story interventions for children diagnosed with autistic spectrum disorders. *Journal of Evidence Based Practices for School*, 6(1): 90–120.

Nicolson, R. and Fawcett, A. (1994) Reaction times and dyslexia. *Quarterly Journal of Experimental Psychology*, 47A: 29–48.

Nicolson, R. and Fawcett, A. (1995) Dyslexia is more than a phonological disability. *Dyslexia*, 1: 19–36.

Nicolson, R. and Fawcett, A. (2004) *The Dyslexia Early Screening Test*. London: Harcourt.

Nikolay, S. (2006) *ITE Session on Anti-racist Mathematics*. http://www.multiverse.ac.uk/attachments/d2a10fae-efd8–48bb-bc30–65e14d08782c.doc (accessed 22 December 2006).

Nind, M. and Hewett, D. (2005) *Access to Communication: Developing Basic Communication with People who Have Severe Learning Difficulties*, 2nd edition. London: David Fulton.

Nind, M., Wearmouth, J., with Collins, J., Hall, K., Rix, J. and Sheehy, K. (2004) A systematic review of pedagogical approaches that can effectively include children with special educational needs in mainstream classrooms, with a particular focus on peer group interactive approaches. In *Research Evidence in Education Library*. London: EPPI-Centre, Social Science Research Unit, Institute of Education.

Norman, R.D. (1963) Intelligence tests and the personal world. *New Mexico Quarterly*, 33: 153–84.

Norwich, B. (1999) The connotation of special education labels for professionals in the field. *British Journal of Special Education*, 26(4): 179–83.

Norwich, B. (2007) Categories of special educational needs. In L. Florian (ed.) *The Sage Handbook of Special Education* (pp. 55–66). London: Sage.

Norwich, B. (2008) *Dilemmas of Difference: Inclusion and Disability. International Perspectives and Future Directions*. London: Routledge.

Norwich, B. and Kelly, N. (2005) *Moderate Learning Difficulties and the Future of Inclusion*. London: RoutledgeFalmer.

Norwich, B. and Kelly, N. (2006) Evaluating children's participation in SEN procedures: lessons for educational psychologists. *Educational Psychology in Practice*, 22(3): 255–71.

Norwich, B., Goodchild, L. and Lloyd, S. (2001) Some aspects of the Inclusion Index in operation. *Support for Learning*, 16: 156–61.

Norwich, B., Griffiths, C. and Burden, B. (2005) Dyslexia-friendly schools and parent partnership: inclusion and home-school relationships. *European Journal of Special Needs Education*, 20(2): 147–65.

Nottingham City Council (2005) *GARP: Integrating Global and Anti-Racist Perspectives within the Primary Curriculum*. http://www.nottinghamschools.co.uk/eduweb/schools/ schools-template.aspx?id=1327 (accessed 22 December 2006).

Nunes, T. (2004) *Teaching Mathematics to Deaf Children*. London: Whurr Publishers.

Nunes, T., Schliemann, A. and Carraher, D. (1993) *Street Mathematics and Home Mathematics*. Cambridge: Cambridge University Press.

Nuttall, D., Goldstein, H., Prosser, R. and Rasbash, J. (1989) Differential school effectiveness. *International Journal of Educational Research*, 13(7): 769–76.

Nye, B. and Hedges, L.V. (2000) The effects of small classes on academic achievement: The results of the Tennessee class size experiment. *American Educational Research Journal*, 37: 123–51.

O'Connor, T. and Colwell, J. (2002) The effectiveness and rationale of the 'nurture group' approach to helping children with emotional and behavioural difficulties remain within mainstream education. *British Journal of Special Education*, 29(2): 96–100.

O'Donnell, K. (1999) Lesbian and gay families: legal perspectives. In G. Jagger and C. Wright (eds) *Changing Family Values*. London: Routledge.

Ockelford, A., Welch, G. and Zimmerman, S. (2002) Music education for pupils with severe or profound and multiple difficulties – current provision and future need. *British Journal of Special Education*, 29(4): 178–82.

Oden, S. (1986) A child's social isolation: origins, prevention, intervention. In G. Cartledge and J.F. Milburn (eds) *Teaching Social Skills to Children*. Oxford: Pergamon Press.

Odom, S.L., Vitztum, J., Wolery, R., Lieber, J., Sandall, S., Hanson, M.J., Beckman, P., Schwartz, I. and Horn, E. (2004) Preschool inclusion in the United States: a review of research from an ecological systems perspective. *Journal of Research in Special Educational Needs*, 4(1): 17–49.

Office for National Statistics (2005) *Mental Health of Children and Young People in Great Britain*. London: Palgrave Macmillan.

Office for National Statistics (2007) *Special Educational Needs in England*, January 2007. London: DfES.

Ofsted (1996a) *Exclusions from Secondary Schools 1995–1996*. London: Ofsted.

Ofsted (1996b) *Successful Teaching of Literacy and Numeracy in Primary Schools: A Starting Point*. London: Ofsted.

Ofsted (1997a) *The Assessment of the Language Development of Bilingual Pupils (97/97/ NS)*. London: Ofsted.

Ofsted (1997b) *The Teaching of Number in Three Inner-Urban LEAs*. London: Ofsted.

Ofsted (1999a) *Raising the Attainment of Minority Ethnic Pupils: School and LEA Responses*. London: Ofsted.

Ofsted (1999b) *Pupils with Specific Learning Difficulties in Mainstream Schools*. London: Ofsted.

Ofsted (1999c) *The National Literacy Strategy: An Evaluation of the First Year of the National Literacy Strategy*. London: Ofsted.

Ofsted (2000) *Evaluating Educational Inclusion: Guidance for Inspectors and Schools*. London: Ofsted.

Ofsted (2002a) *Annual Report of Her Majesty's Chief Inspector of Schools*. London: The Stationery Office.

Ofsted (2002b) *LEA Strategy for the Inclusion of Pupils with Special Educational Needs*. Ref. HMI 737. London: Ofsted.

Ofsted (2002c) *Teaching Assistants in Primary Schools: An Evaluation of the Quality and Impact of Their Work*. London: Ofsted.

Ofsted (2003a) *Bullying: Effective Action in Secondary Schools*. London: Ofsted.

Ofsted (2003b) *The National Literacy and Numeracy Strategies and the Primary Curriculum*. London: Ofsted.

Ofsted (2003c). *The Education of Pupils with Medical Needs*. Ref. HMI 1713. London: Ofsted.

Ofsted (2004) *Special Educational Needs and Disability: Towards Inclusive Schools*. Ref. HMI 2276. London: Ofsted.

Ofsted (2005a) *Could They Do Even Better? The Writing of Advanced Bilingual Learners of English at Key Stage 2: HMI Survey of Good Practice*. London: Ofsted.

Ofsted (2005b) *Framework for Inspection of Schools in England from September 2005*. London: Ofsted.

Ofsted (2005c) *Healthy Minds: Promoting Emotional Health and Well-Being in Schools*. London: Ofsted.

Ofsted (2005d) *Inclusion: the impact of LEA support and outreach services*. (Ref. HMI 2452). London: Office for Standards in Education.

Ofsted (2005e) *The National Literacy and Numeracy Strategies and the Primary Curriculum*. HMI 2395. London: Ofsted Publication Centre.

Ofsted (2005f) *Managing Challenging Behaviour*. London: Ofsted.

Ofsted (2006) *Inclusion: Does It Matter Where Pupils Are Taught?* London: Ofsted.

Okagaki, L. and Frensch, P.A. (1998) Parenting and children's school achievement: a multiethnic perspective. *American Educational Research Journal*, 35(1): 123–44.

Oliver, M. (1990) *The Politics of Disablement*. London: Macmillan.

Ollerton, M. (2005) Inclusion and entitlement: equality of opportunity and quality of curriculum provision. In A. Watson, J. Houssart and C. Roaf (eds) *Supporting Mathematical Thinking* (pp. 142–51). London: David Fulton/NASEN.

Olswang, L.B., Coggins, T.E. and Timler, G.R. (2001) Outcome measures for school-age children with social communication problems. *Topics in Language Disorders*, 22(1): 50–73.

Organization for Economic Co-operation and Development (1981) *The Education of the Handicapped Adolescent: Integration at School*. Paris: OECD.

Organization for Economic Co-operation and Development (2002) *Understanding the Brain: Towards a New Learning Science*. Paris: OECD.

Organization for Economic Co-operation and Development (2004) *Equity in Education: Students with Disabilities, Learning Difficulties and Disadvantages*. Paris: OECD.

Orpinas, P. and Horne, A.M. (2006) *Bullying Prevention: Creating a Positive School Climate and Developing Social Competence*. Washington, DC: American Psychological Association.

Ortiz, S.O. and Dynda, A.M. (2005) Use of intelligence tests with culturally and linguistically diverse populations. In D.P. Flanagan and P.L. Harrison (eds) *Contemporary Intellectual Assessment: Theories, Tests and Issues*, 2nd edition (pp. 545–56). New York: Guilford Press.

Ostad, S.A. (1997) Developmental differences in addition strategies: a comparison of mathematically disabled and mathematically normal children. *British Journal of Educational Psychology*, 67: 345–57.

Otterburn, M.K. and Nicholson, A.R. (1976) The language of CSE mathematics. *Maths in School*, 5(5): 18–21.

Overett, J. and Donald, D. (1998) Paired reading: effects of a parent involvement programme in a disadvantaged community in South Africa. *British Journal of Educational Psychology*, 68(3): 347–56.

Ozonoff, S. (1997) Components of executive function deficits in autism and other disorders. In J. Russel (ed.) *Autism as an Executive Disorder* (pp. 179–211). Oxford: Oxford University Press.

Ozonoff, S. and Rogers, S. J. (2003) From Kanner to the millennium: scientific advances that have shaped clinical practice. In S. Ozonoff, S.J. Rogers and R.L. Hendren (eds) *Autistic Spectrum Disorders: A Research Review for Practitioners* (pp. 3–33). Washington, DC: American Psychiatric Publishing.

Padron, Y. (1991) Commentary. In M. Knapp and B. Means (eds) *Teaching Advanced Skills to At-Risk Students: Views from Research and Practice*. San Francisco: Jossey-Bass.

Padron, Y. (1992) Instructional programmes that improve the reading comprehension of students at risk. In H.C. Waxman, J. Walker de Felix, J.E. Anderson and H. Prentice Baptiste (eds) *Students at Risk in At-Risk School: Improving Environments for Learning*. Newbury Park, CA: Sage.

Palazzoli, S.M., Cecchin, G., Prate, G. and Boscolo, L. (1978) *Paradox and Counter Paradox: A New Model of the Family in Schizophrenic Transaction*. London: Jason Aronson.

Palinscar, A.S. (1986) The role of dialogue in providing scaffolded instruction. *Educational Psychologist*, 21(1–2): 73–98.

Palinscar, A.S. and Brown, A. (1985) Reciprocal teaching: a means to a meaningful end. In J. Osborn, P. Wilson and R.C. Anderson (eds) *Reading Education: Foundations for a Literate America*. Lexington, MA: Lexington.

Panerai, S., Ferrante, L. and Zingale, N. (2002) Benefits of the treatment of education of autistic and communication handicapped children (TEACCH) programme as compared with a non-specific approach. *Journal of Intellectual Disability Research*, 46(4): 318–27.

Park, N. (2004) The role of subjective well being in positive youth development. *Annals of the American Academy of Policitcal and Social Science*, 591: 25–39.

Parker, J.D., Creque, R.E., Barnhart, D.L., Harris, J.I., Majeski, S.A., Wood, L.M., Bond, B.J. and Hogan, M.J. (2004) Academic achievement at high school: does emotional intelligence matter? *Personality and Individual Differences*, 37: 1321–30.

Parliamentary Office of Science and Technology (POST) (2004) Dyslexia and dyscalculia. *Postnote*, 226. http://www.parliament.uk/documents/upload/POSTpn226.pdf.

Parrish, T.B., Merickel, A., Perez, M., Linquanti, R., Socias, M., Spain, A., *et al.* (2006) *Effects of the Implementation of Proposition 227 on the Education of English Learners, K-12: Findings from a Five-year Evaluation* (Final report for AB 56 and AB 1116, submitted to the California Department of Education). Palo Alto, CA: American Institutes for Research.

Parsons, C. (1996) Permanent exclusions from schools in England in the 1990s: trends, causes and responses. *Children and Society*, 10: 177–86.

Patel, N. B. (1995) Application of soft systems methodology to the real world process of teaching and learning. *International Journal of Educational Management*, 9(1): 13–23.

Paterson, S.J., Girelli, L., Butterworth, B. and Karmiloff-Smith, A. (2006) Are numerical impairments syndrome specific? Evidence from Williams syndrome and Down's syndrome. *Journal of Child Psychology and Psychiatry*, 47(2): 190–204.

Patrick, H., Ryan, A.M. and Kaplan, I. (2007) Early adolescents' perceptions of the classroom social environment, motivational beliefs and engagement. *Journal of Educational Psychology*, 99(1): 83–98.

Pavey, S., Douglas, G., McCall, S., McLinden, M. and Arter, C. (2002) *Steps to Independence: The Mobility and Independence Needs of Children with a Visual Impairment*. Birmingham: School of Education, University of Birmingham.

Peach, C. (1982) The growth and distribution of the black population in Britain 1945–1980. In D.A. Coleman (ed.) *Demography of Immigrants and Minority Groups in the United Kingdom*. London: Academic Press.

Pearpoint, J. and Forest, M. (1992) Kick 'em out or keep 'em in. Exclusion or inclusion. In J. Pearpoint, M. Forest, and J. Snow (eds) *The Inclusion Papers* (pp. 80–8). Toronto: Inclusion Press.

Peer, L. (2005) *Glue Ear: An Essential Guide for Teachers, Parents and Health Professionals*. London: David Fulton.

Pellegrini, A.D. and Bartini, M. (2000) An empirical comparison of methods of sampling aggression and victimization in school settings. *Journal of Educational Psychology*, 92(2): 360–6.

Pellegrini, D.S. and Urbain, E.S. (1985) An evaluation of interpersonal problem solving training with children. *Journal of Child Psychology and Psychiatry*, 26(1): 17–41.

Pema, S. and Pattinson, N. (1991) Developing bilingual assessment tasks. In G. Lindsay and A. Miller (eds) *Psychological Services for Primary Schools*. London: Longman.

Pennington, B.F. and Ozonoff, S. (1996) Executive functions and developmental psychopathology. *Journal of Child Psychology and Psychiatry*, 37: 51–87.

Pepler, D., Smith, P. K. and Rigby, K. (2004) Looking back and looking forward: implications for making interventions work effectively. In P. K. Smith, D. Pepler and K. Rigby (eds) *Bullying in Schools: How Successful Can Interventions Be?* (pp. 307–24). Cambridge: Cambridge University Press.

Pérez-Pereira, M. and Conti-Ramsden, G. (1999) *Language Development and Social Interaction in Blind Children*. Hove: Psychology Press.

Perrett, G. (1990) The language testing interview: a reappraisal. In J. de Jong and D.K. Stevenson (eds) *Individualizing the Assessment of Language Abilities*. Clevedon: Multilingual Matters.

Pert, S. (2006) *Early Mirpuri-English code-switching*. Presentation to ESRC Research Seminar Series, University of Newcastle. http://www.ecls.ncl.ac.uk/ealwcis/reports/m1/Sean%20Pert%20-%20ESRC%20Nov%202006.ppt (accessed 18 December 2007).

Peterson, E.R., Deary, I.J. and Austin, E.J. (2007) Celebrating a common finding: Riding's CSA test is unreliable. *Personality and Individual Differences*, 43(8): 2309–12.

Petito, L.A. and Marentette, P.F. (1991) Babbling in the manual mode: evidence for the ontogeny of language. *Science*, 251: 1493–6.

Petrides, K.V., Furnham, A. and Frederickson, N. (2004) Emotional intelligence. *The Psychologist*, 17(10): 574–7.

Petrides, K.V., Sangareau, Y., Furnham, A. and Frederickson, N. (2006) Trait emotional intelligence and children's peer relations at school. *Social Development*, 15(3): 537–47.

Petticrew, M. and Roberts, H. (2006) *Systematic Reviews in the Social Sciences: A Practical Guide*. Oxford: Blackwell.

Pettit, B. (2003) *Effective Joint Working between Child and Adolescent Mental Health Services (CAMHS) and Schools*. Nottingham: DfES Publication.

Pickersgill, M. (1994) A bilingual policy in the education of deaf and hearing-impaired children. Paper presented at a study day at University College London, 21 June.

Pielstick, N.L. (1987) Assessing the learning environment. *School Psychology International*, 9: 111–22.

Pietrowski, J. and Reason, R. (2000) The national literacy strategy and dyslexia: a comparison of teaching methods and materials. *Support for Learning*, 15(2): 51–7.

Pijl, S.J. (1995) The resources for regular schools with special needs students: an international perspective. In C. Clark, A. Dyson and A. Millward (eds) *Towards Inclusive Schools*. London: David Fulton.

Pikas, A. (2002) New developments of the shared concern method. *School Psychology International*, 23(3): 307–26.

Pine, D.S. (2006) A primer on brain imaging in developmental psychopathology: what is it good for? *Journal of Child Psychology and Psychiatry*, 47(10): 983–6.

Pinkus, S. (2005) Bridging the gap between policy and practice: adopting a strategic vision for partnership working in special education. *British Journal of Special Education*, 32(4): 184–7.

Pollitt, A., Marriott, C. and Ahmed, A. (2000) *Language, Contextual and Cultural Constraints on Examination Performance*. Paper presented to International Association for Educational Assessment Conference, Jerusalem (May). http://www.cambridgeassessment.org.uk/ (accessed 22 November 2007).

Pomplun, M. and Capps, L. (1999) Gender differences for constructed response mathematics items. *Educational and Psychological Measurement*, 59(4): 597–614.

Porter, J. and Ashdown, R. (2002) *Pupils with Complex Learning Difficulties: Promoting Learning Using Visual Materials and Methods*. Tamworth: NASEN.

Porter, L. (2002) *Educating Young Children with Special Needs*. London: Paul Chapman.

Portsmouth EMAS (2005) *KS3 Maths Resources*. Portsmouth: Ethnic Minority Achievement Service. http://www.blss.portsmouth.sch.uk/resources/ks3maths.shtml (accessed 22 December 2006).

Portwood, M. (2005) Dyspraxia. In A. Lewis and B. Norwich (eds) *Special Teaching for Special Children? Pedagogies for Inclusion* (pp. 150–65). Maidenhead: Open University Press.

Potts, P. (1983) Medicine, morals and mental deficiency: the contribution of doctors to the development of special education in England. *Oxford Review of Education*, 9(3): 181–96.

Powell, J.J.W. (2005) *Barriers to Inclusion: Special Education in the United States and Germany*. Boulder, CO: Paradigm.

Power, D. and Hyde, M. (2002) The characteristics and extent of participation of deaf and hard-of-hearing students in regular classes in Australian schools. *Journal of Deaf Studies and Deaf Education*, 7(4): 302–11.

Powers, S. (1996) Deaf pupils' achievements in ordinary schools. *Journal of the British Association of Teachers of the Deaf*, 20(4): 111–23.

Powers, S. (1998) An analysis of deaf pupils' examination results in ordinary schools in 1996. *Deafness and Education*, 22(3): 20–36.

Powers, S. (2002) From concepts to practice in deaf education: a United Kingdom perspective on inclusion. *Journal of Deaf Studies and Deaf Education*, 7(3): 230–43.

Powers, S., Gregory, S. and Thoutenhoofd, E. (1998) *Educational Achievements of Deaf Children*. London: DfEE.

PricewaterhouseCoopers (2002) *Study of Additional Educational Needs – Phase II*. http://www.dfes.gov.uk/efsg/docs/133.doc.

Pritchard, A. (2005) *Ways of Learning: Learning Theories and Learning Styles in the Classroom*. London: David Fulton.

Pritchard, D.G. (1963) *Education and the Handicapped 1760–1960*. London: Routledge & Kegan Paul.

Pugh, G. (1988) *Services for Under Fives: Developing a Coordinated Approach*. London: National Children's Bureau.

Pugh, K.R., Sandak, R., Frost, S.J., Moore, D. and Mencl, W.E. (2005) Examining reading development and reading disability in English language learners: potential contributions from functional neuroimaging. *Learning Disabilities Research in Practice*, 20(1): 24–30.

Pumfrey, P.D. (1997) Assessment of affective and motivational aspects of reading. In J.R. Beech and C. Singleton (eds) *The Psychological Assessment of Reading*. London: Routledge.

Pyke, N. (1993) No room for blind pupils as deal ends. *Times Educational Supplement*, 23 July.

Qualifications and Curriculum Authority (2000a) *A Language in Common: Assessing English as an Additional Language*. London: QCA.

Qualifications and Curriculum Authority (2000b) *Curriculum Guidance for the Foundation Stage*, ref. QCA/00/587. London: Qualifications and Curriculum Authority.

Qualifications and Curriculum Authority (2003a) *Foundation Stage Profile Handbook*. Ref. Qualifications and Curriculum Authority/03/1006. London: QCA.

Qualifications and Curriculum Authority (2003b) *Using Assessment to Raise Achievement in Mathematics at Key Stages 1, 2 and 3*. London: QCA.

Qualifications and Curriculum Authority (2007a) *Guidance for Key Stage 1 National Curriculum Assessments: Children Who Are Working at Level 1 or Above but Are Unable to Access the Tasks and Tests*. London: QCA.

Qualifications and Curriculum Authority (2007b) *Special Educational Needs: P Scales*. London: QCA.

Quilter, D. and Harper, E. (1988) Why we didn't like mathematics, and why we can't do it. *Educational Research*, 30(2): 121–34.

Rack, J.P. (1994) Dyslexia: the phonological deficit hypothesis. In A. Fawcett and R. Nicolson (eds) *Dyslexia in Children: Multi-disciplinary Perspectives*. Hemel Hempstead: Harvester Wheatsheaf.

Rack, J.P., Snowling, M., Hulme, C. and Gibbs, S. (2007) No evidence that an exercise-based treatment programme (DDAT) has specific benefits for children with reading difficulties. *Dyslexia*, 13: 97–104.

Rae, C., Harasty, J.A., Dzendrowskyj, T.E., Talcott, J.B., Simpson, J.M. and Blamire, A.M. (2002) Cerebellar morphology in developmental dyslexia. *Neuropsychologia*, 40: 1285–92.

Rahi, J.S. and Cable, N. (2003) Severe visual impairment and blindness in children in the U.K. *Lancet*, 362: 1359–65.

Raiker, A. (2002) Spoken language and mathematics. *Cambridge Journal of Education*, 32(1): 45–60.

Rampton, B. (1990) Displacing the 'native speaker': expertise, affiliation and inheritance. *ELT Journal*, 44: 97–101.

Ravenette, A.T. (1997) *Personal Construct Psychology and the Practice of an Educational Psychologist: Selected Papers*. Farnborough: EPCA Publications.

Ravenette, A.T. (1999) *Personal Construct Psychology and Educational Psychology: A Practitioner's View*. London: Whurr.

Raybould, E.C. and Solity, J. (1982) Teaching with precision. *Special Education Forward Trends*, 8(2): 9–13.

Reay, D. (2006) 'I'm not seen as one of the clever children': consulting primary school pupils about the social conditions of learning. *Educational Review*, 58(2): 171–81.

Rehal, A. (1989) Involving Asian parents in the statementing procedure – the way forward. *Educational Psychology in Practice*, 4(4): 189–97.

Reid, B. and Batten, A. (2006) B is for bullied: experiences of children with autism and their families. http://www.autism.org.uk/bullyingengland.

Reid, G. (1997) *Dyslexia: A Practitioner's Handbook*, 2nd edition. Chichester: Wiley.

Reid, J.B. (1993) Prevention of conduct disorder before and after school entry: Relating interventions to developmental findings. *Development and Psychopathology*, 5: 243–62.

Renfrew, C. (1997) *Renfrew Language Scales: Bus Story Test*. Bicester: Winslow Press.

Renick, M.J. and Harter, S. (1989) Impact of social comparisons on the developing self-perceptions of learning disabled students. *Journal of Educational Psychology*, 81: 631–8.

Rentoul, A.J. and Fraser, B.J. (1979) Conceptualisation of enquiry-based or open class-room learning environments. *Journal of Curriculum Studies*, 11: 233–45.

Reschley, A.L., Coolong-Chaffin, M., Christianson, S.L. and Gutkin, T. (2007) Contextual influences and responses to intervention: critical issues and strategies. In S.R. Jimerson, M.K. Burns, and A.M. Van Der Heyden (eds) *Handbook of Response to Intervention: The Science and Practice of Assessment and Intervention* (pp. 148–60). New York: Springer.

Reynhout, G. and Carter, M. (2006) Social Stories™ for children with disabilities. *Journal of Autism and Developmental Disorders*, 36(4): 445–69.

Reynolds, C.R. (1980) Differential construct validity of intelligence as popularly measured: correlation of age with raw scores on the WISC-R for blacks, whites, males and females. *Intelligence*, 4(4): 371–80.

Reynolds, C.R. and Kaiser, S.M. (1990) Test bias in psychological assessment. In T.B. Gutkin and C.R. Reynolds (eds) *The Handbook of School Psychology*, 2nd edition. New York: Wiley.

Reynolds, D. (1995) The future of school effectiveness and school improvement. *Educational Psychology in Practice*, 11(3): 12–21.

Reynolds, D. (1997) School effectiveness: retrospect and prospect. *Scottish Educational Review*, 29(2): 87–113.

Reynolds, D. and Farrell, S. (1996) *Worlds Apart? A Review of International Surveys of Educational Achievement Involving England*. London: HMSO.

Reynolds, D. and Muijs, D. (1999) Contemporary policy issues in the teaching of mathematics. In I. Thompson (ed.) *Issues in Teaching Numeracy in Primary Schools*. Buckingham: Open University Press.

Reynolds, M.C. (1989) An historical perspective: the delivery of special education to mildly disabled and at-risk students. *Remedial and Special Education*, 10(6): 7–11.

Reynolds, S., Martin, K. and Groulx, J. (1995) Patterns of understanding. *Educational Assessment*, 3: 363–71.

Rezaei, A.R. and Katz, L. (2004) Evaluation of the reliability and validity of the cognitive styles analysis. *Personality and Individual Differences*, 36(6): 1317–27.

Rhodes, J. and Ajmal, Y. (1995) *Solution Focused Thinking in Schools*. London: BT Press.

Ribeiro, J.L. (1980) Testing Portuguese immigrant children – cultural patterns and group differences in response to the WISC-R. In D.P. Macedo (ed.) *Issues in Portuguese Bilingual Education*. Cambridge, MA: Evaluation, Dissemination and Assessment Center, Lesley College.

Richardson, S.A., Katz, M. and Koller, H. (1986) Sex differences in number of children administratively classified as mildly mentally retarded: an epidemiological review. *American Journal of Mental Deficiency*, 91(3): 250–6.

Riddell, S. (1996) Gender and special educational needs. In G. Lloyd (ed.) *'Knitting Progress Unsatisfactory': Gender and Special Issues in Education*. Edinburgh: Moray House Publications.

Riddell, S. and Brown, S. (1995) Special educational needs provision in the United Kingdom – the policy context. In S. Riddell and S. Brown (eds) *Special Educational Needs Policy in the 1990s*. London: Routledge.

Riddell, S., Brown, S. and Duffield, J. (1994) Parental power and special educational needs: the case of specific learning difficulties. *British Educational Research Journal*, 20(3): 327–45.

Riding, R.J. and Rayner, S. (1998) *Cognitive Styles and Learning Strategies*. London: David Fulton.

Ridley, J. (1991) The structure of the ear and the hearing system, *Education Guardian*, 25 June.

Rigby, K. (1998) *Manual for the Peer Relations Questionnaire (PRQ)*. Point Lonsdale, Vic.: The Professional Reading Guide.

Rigby, K. (2002) Bullying in childhood. In P.K. Smith and C.H. Hart (eds) *Blackwell Handbook of Childhood Social Development*. Oxford: Blackwell.

Rigby, K. (2005) The method of shared concern as an intervention technique to address bullying in schools: An overview and appraisal. *Australian Journal of Guidance and Counselling*, 15(1): 27–34.

Riggs, N.R., Greenberg, N.T., Kusché, C.A. and Pentz, M.A. (2006) The mediational role of neurocognition in the behavioural outcomes of a social-emotional prevention programme in elementary school students: Effects of the PATHS Curriculum. *Prevention Science*, 7(1): 91–102.

Rivera, H.H. and Tharp, R.G. (2004) Socio cultural activity settings in the classroom. A study of a classroom observation system. In H.C. Waxman, R.G. Tharp and R. Soleste Hilberg (eds) *Observational Research in U.S. Classrooms. New Approaches for Understanding Cultural and Linguistic Diversity* (pp. 205–30). New York: Cambridge University Press.

Rizzo, J.V. and Zabel, R.H. (1988) *Educating Children and Adolescents with Behavioral Disorders: An Integrative Approach*. Boston: Allyn & Bacon.

Roaf, C. (2002) *Co-ordinating Services for Included Children: Joined-Up Action*. Buckingham: Open University Press.

Roberts, C. and Zubrick, S. (1992) Factors influencing the social status of children with mild academic disabilities in regular classrooms. *Exceptional Children*, 59(3): 192–202.

Roberts, J.E., Rosenfeld, R.M. and Zeisel, S.A. (2004) Otitis media and speech and language: a meta-analysis of prospective studies. *Pediatrics*, 113(3): e238–e248.

Roberts, J.R. (1984) The relative development and educational achievement of ethnic minority children in a Midlands town. *Educational and Child Psychology*, 1: 14–22.

Robertson, A., Fisher, J., Henderson, A. and Gibson, M. (2000) *Quest*, 2nd edition. Windsor: NFER-Nelson.

Robinson, M., Anning, A., Cottrell, D., Frost, N. and Green, J. (2005) Service delivery through teamwork. *Public Service Review*, 10: 124–6. http://www.publicservice.co.uk/pdf/central_gov/issue10/CG10%20Mark%20Robinson%20ATL.pdf (accessed 24 June 2007.)

Robinson, V. (1993) *Problem-Based Methodology: Research for the Improvement of Practice*. Oxford: Pergamon Press.

Robson, A. (1995) The assessment of bilingual children. In M.K. Verma, K.P. Corrigan and S. Firth (eds) *Working with Bilingual Children: Good Practice in the Primary Classroom*. Clevedon: Multilingual Matters.

Robson, A. (1996) The application of Cummins' model to work with students with hearing impairment. In T. Cline and N. Frederickson (eds) *Curriculum Related Assessment, Cummins and Bilingual Pupils*. Clevedon: Multilingual Matters.

Rogers, M.R., Ingraham, C.L., Bursztyn, A. *et al.* (1999) Providing psychological services to racially, ethnically, culturally and linguistically diverse individuals in the schools: recommendations for practice. *School Psychology International*, 20(3): 243–64.

Rogers, R., Tod, J., Powell, S., Parsons, C. *et al.* (2006) *Evaluation of the Special Educational Needs Parent Partnership Services in England*. (DfES Ref. RR719). London: Department for Education and Skills.

Rogers, S.J. (2000) Interventions that facilitate socialization in children with autism. *Journal of Autism & Developmental Disorders*, 30(5): 399–409.

Rogers, S.J. and Lewis, H. (1989) An effective day treatment model for young children with pervasive developmental disorders. *Journal of the American Academy of Child and Adolescent Psychiatry*, 28: 207–14.

Rogers, U. and Pratten, A. (1996) The Cummins framework as a decision making aid for special education professionals working with bilingual children. In T. Cline and N. Frederickson (eds) *Curriculum Related Assessment, Cummins and Bilingual Children*. Clevedon: Multilingual Matters.

Rose, J. (2006) *Independent Review of the Teaching of Early Reading*. Nottingham: DfES Publications.

Rosen, R.S. (2003) Jargons for deafness as institutional constructions of the deaf body. *Disability and Society*, 18(7): 921–34.

Rotheram-Borus, M.J. (1993) Multicultural issues in the delivery of group interventions. *Special Services in the Schools*, 8(1): 179–88.

Rourke, B.P. (1988) Socio-emotional disturbances in learning disabled children. *Journal of Consulting and Clinical Psychology*, 56(6): 801–10.

Rouse, M. and Florian, L. (2006) Inclusion and achievement: student achievement in secondary schools with higher and lower proportions of pupils designated as having special educational needs. *International Journal of Inclusive Education*, 10(6): 481–93.

Rouse, M. and McLaughlin, M.J. (2007) Changing perspectives of special education in the evolving context of educational reform. In L. Florian (ed.) *The Sage Handbook of Special Education* (pp. 85–103). London: Sage.

Rowland, T. (1995) Between the lines: the languages of mathematics. In J. Anghileri (ed.) *Children's Mathematical Thinking in the Primary Years*. London: Cassell.

Roznowski, M. and Reith, J. (1999) Examining the measurement quality of tests containing differentially functioning items: do biased items result in poor measurement? *Educational and Psychological Measurement*, 59(2): 248–69.

Ruiz, N.T. (1995) The social construction of ability and disability II – optimal and at-risk lessons in a bilingual special education classroom. *Journal of Learning Disabilities*, 28(8): 491–502.

Ruiz, N.T. and Figueroa, R.A. (1995) Learning-handicapped classrooms with Latino students: the Optimal Learning Environment (OLE) project. *Education and Urban Society*, 27(4): 463–83.

Rushton, A. and Lindsay, G. (2003) Clinical education: a critical analysis using soft systems methodology. *International Journal of Therapy and Rehabilitation*, 10(6): 271–80.

Russell, R.L. and Ginsberg, H.P. (1984) Cognitive analysis of children's mathematics difficulties. *Cognition and Instruction*, 1: 217–44.

Rust, J. and Smith, A. (2006) How should the effectiveness of Social Stories to modify the behaviour of children on the autistic spectrum be tested? Lessons from the literature. *Autism*, 10(2): 125–38.

Rustemier, S. and Booth, T. (2005) *Learning about the Index and Use*. Bristol: Centre for Studies on Inclusive Education.

Rutter, M. (1989) Pathways from childhood to adult life. *Journal of Child Psychology and Psychiatry*, 30: 23–51.

Rutter, M. (1996) Autism research: prospects and priorities. *Journal of Autism and Developmental Disorders*, 26(2) 257–75.

Rutter, M. (2006) Is Sure Start an effective preventive intervention? *Child and Adolescent Mental Health*, 11(3): 135–41.

Rutter, M. (2007a) Resilience, competence and coping: commentary. *Child Abuse and Neglect*, 31(3): 205–9.

Rutter, M. (2007b) Gene-environment interdependence. *Developmental Science*, 10(1): 12–18.

Rutter, M. (2007c) *Genes and Behavior: Nature–Nurture Interplay Explained*. Oxford: Blackwell.

Rutter, M. and Maughn, B. (2002) School effectiveness findings 1979–2002. *Journal of School Psychology*, 40(6): 451–75.

Rutter, M., Tizard, J. and Whitmore, K. (1970) *Education, Health and Behaviour*. London: Longman.

Ryan, J. (1999) *Race and Ethnicity in Multiethnic Schools*. Clevedon: Multilingual Matters.

Sacker, A., Schoon, I. and Bartley, M. (2001) Sources of bias in special needs provision in mainstream primary schools: evidence from two British cohort studies. *European Journal of Special Needs Education*, 16(3): 259–76.

Saenz, L.M., Fuchs, L.S. and Fuchs, D. (2005) Peer-assisted learning strategies for English language learners with learning disabilities. *Exceptional Children*, 71(3): 231–47.

Salas, L. (2004) Individualized Educational Plan (IEP) meetings and Mexican American parents: let's talk about it. *Journal of Latinos and Education*, 3(3): 181–92.

Salmon, P. (1988) *Psychology for Teachers*. London: Hutchinson.

Salovey, P. and Mayer, J.D. (1990) Emotional intelligence, imagination. *Cognition and Personality*, 9: 185–211.

Salovey, P. and Sluyter, D.J. (1997) *Emotional Development and Emotional Intelligence*. New York: Basic Books.

Sapon-Shevin, M., Dobbelaere, A., Corrigan, C.R., Goodman, K. and Mastin, M.C. (1998) Promoting inclusive behaviour in inclusive classrooms: 'You can't say you can't play'. In L.H. Meyer, H-S. Park, M. Grenot-Scheyer, I.S. Schwartz and B. Harry (eds) *Making Friends: The Influences of Culture on Development*. Baltimore, MD: Paul H. Brookes.

Sattler, J. (1988) *Assessment of Children*, 3rd edition. San Diego, CA: J. Sattler.

Sawyer, A. (1995) Developing early numeracy skills. In G. Moss (ed.) *The Basics of Special Needs*. London: Routledge.

Scarborough, H.S. (1990) Very early language deficits in dyslexic children. *Child Development*, 61: 1728–43.

Scarr, S., Caparulo, B.K., Ferdman, M., Tower, R.B. and Caplan, J. (1983) Developmental status and school achievements of minority and non-minority children from birth to 18 years in a British Midlands town. *British Journal of Developmental Psychology*, 1: 31–48.

Scherer, M. (1990) Assessment by baselines. In M. Scherer, I. Gersch and L. Fry (eds) *Meeting Disruptive Behaviour*. London: Macmillan.

Schiff-Myers, N.B. (1992) Considering arrested language development and language loss in the assessment of second language learners. *Language, Speech and Hearing Services in Schools*, 23: 28–33.

Schiro, M. (2004) *Oral Storytelling and Teaching Mathematics: Pedagogical and Multicultural Perspectives*. Thousand Oaks, CA: Sage.

Schoemaker, M.M., Smits-Engelsman, B.C.M. and Jongmans, M. (2003) Psychometric properties of the Movement Assessment Battery for Children-Checklist as a screening instrument for children with a developmental co-ordination disorder. *British Journal of Educational Psychology*, 73(3): 425–42.

School Curriculum and Assessment Authority (1996) *Planning the Curriculum for Pupils with Profound and Multiple Learning Difficulties*. London: School Curriculum and Assessment Authority.

Schopler, E. and Mesibov, G. (1995) *Learning and Cognition in Autism*. New York: Plenum Press.

Schwarz, K., Yeung, S., Symons, N. and Bradbury, J. (2002) Survey of school children with visual impairment in Bradford. *Eye*, 16(5): 530–4.

Scott, K. (2006) International Survey (2002–2005): EAL assessment in Australia, Canada, England and USA. *NALDIC Quarterly*, 4(1): 10–29.

Scott, S. (2004) *Which Function?* http://www.collaborativelearning.org/whichfunction.pdf (accessed 29 December 2006).

Scott, S. and Sylva, K. (2003) *The 'SPOKES' Project: Supporting Parents on Kids' Education: A Preventive Trial to Improve Disadvantaged Children's Life Chances by Boosting Their Social Functioning and Reading Skills*. London: Department of Health.

Scottish Executive Education Department (2003) *Moving Forward! Additional Support for Learning*. Edinburgh: Scottish Executive Education Department.

Scottish Executive Education Department (2004) *Summary Handout on the Additional Support for Learning Act*, 2nd edition, 21 June. http://www.scotland.gov.uk/Publications/2004/06/19516/39190

Scruggs, T.E. and Mastropieri, M.A. (1994) Successful mainstreaming in elementary science classes: a qualitative study of three reputational cases. *American Education Research Journal*, 31(4): 785–811.

Seabrook, R., Brown, G.D. and Solity, J.E. (2005) Distributed and massed practice: from laboratory to classroom. *Applied Cognitive Psychology*, 19(1): 107–22.

Sebba, J. (2004) Developing evidence-informed policy and practice in education. In G. Thomas and R. Pring (eds) *Evidence-Based Practice in Education*. Maidenhead: Open University Press.

Sebba, J. and Sachdev, D. (1997) *What Works in Inclusive Education?* Barkingside: Barnardo's.

Sebba, J., Byers, R. and Rose, R. (1993) *Redefining the Whole Curriculum for Pupils with Learning Difficulties*. London: David Fulton.

Seligman, M.E.P. and Csikszentmihalyi, M. (2000) Positive psychology: an introduction. *American Psychologist*, 55(1): 5–14.

Seligman, M.E.P. (2002) Positive psychology, positive prevention and positive therapy. In C.R. Snyder and S.J. Lopez (eds) *Handbook of Positive Psychology* (pp. 3–9). New York: Oxford University Press.

Semel, E., Wiig, E.H. and Secord, W. (2006) *Clinical Evaluation of Language Fundamentals*, 4th edition – UK (CELF4^{UK}). Oxford: Pearson Assessment.

Semmel, M.I., Gerber, M.M. and MacMillan, D.L. (1994) Twenty-five years after Dunn's article: a legacy of policy analysis research in special education. *Journal of Special Education*, 27(4): 481–95.

Sepie, A.C. and Keeling, B. (1978) The relationship between types of anxiety and under-achievement in mathematics. *Journal of Educational Research*, 72(1): 15–19.

Sex Education Forum (2004) *Sex and Relationships Education for Children and Young People with Learning Difficulties*. London: National Children's Bureau

Seymour, P.H.K., Aro, M. and Erskine, J.M. (2003) Foundation literacy acquisition in European orthographies. *British Journal of Psychology*, 94: 143–74.

Shackman, J. (1984) *The Right to be Understood: A Handbook for Anyone Working with, Employing and Training Community Interpreters*. Cambridge: National Extension College.

Shah, A. and Frith, U. (1993) Why do autistic individuals show superior performance on the block design task? *Journal of Child Psychology and Psychiatry*, 34: 1351–64.

Shah, R. (1992) *The Silent Minority: Children with Disabilities in Asian Families*. London: National Children's Bureau.

Shah, T.A., Hall, W., Nelms, S., Parkes, J. and Richards, A. (1997) 'W(h)ither professionalism in assessment?' *Newsletter of the British Psychological Society Division of Educational and Child Psychology*, 79: 28–33.

Shakespeare, T. (2005) *Life as a Disabled Child: A Qualitative Study of Young People's Experiences and Perspectives*. Research Report to the Economic and Social Research Council. http://www.esrcsocietytoday.ac.uk (accessed 14 October 2007).

Shalev, R.S., Manor, O. and Gross-Tur, V. (2005) Developmental dyscalculia: a prospective six-year follow-up. *Developmental Medicine and Child Neurology*, 47: 121–5.

Shallice, T. (1998) *From Neuropsychology to Mental Structure*. Cambridge: Cambridge University Press.

Sharma, A. and Love, D. (1991) *A Change in Approach: A Report on the Experience of Deaf People from Black and Ethnic Minority Communities*. London: Royal Association in aid of Deaf People.

Sharman, C., Cross, W. and Vennis, D. (2007) *Observing Children and Young People*, 4th edition. London: Continuum.

Sharp, S. (1999) Bullying behaviour in schools. In N. Frederickson and R.J. Cameron (eds) *Psychology in Education Portfolio*. Windsor: NFER-Nelson.

Shaver, P.R. and Mikulincer, M. (2005) Attachment theory and research: resurrection of the psychodynamic approach to personality. *Journal of Research in Personality*, 39: 22–45.

Shaw, M. (2003) Unions fearful of the opinions of children. *Times Educational Supplement*, 4 July. (Available at www.tes.co.uk)

Shaywitz, S.E., Shaywitz, B.A., Fletcher, J.M. and Escobar, M.D. (1990) Prevalence of reading disability in boys and girls: results of the Connecticut Longitudinal Study. *Journal of the American Medical Association*, 264: 998–1002.

Shaywitz, B.A., Shaywitz, S.E., Pugh, K R., Mencl, W E., Fulbright, R.K., Constable, R.T. *et al.* (2002) Disruption of posterior brain systems for reading in children with developmental dyslexia. *Biological Psychiatry*, 52, 101–10.

Shaywitz, B.A., Shaywitz, S.E., Blachman, B., Pugh, K.R., Fulbright, R.K., Skudlarski, P. *et al.* (2004) Development of left occipito-temporal systems for skilled reading in children after a phonologically based intervention. *Biological Psychiatry*, 55: 926–33.

Sheil, G. and Forde, P. (1995) Profiling pupil achievement in language and literacy: current issues and trends. In B. Raban-Bisby, G. Brooks and S. Wolfendale (eds) *Developing Language and Literacy*. Stoke-on-Trent: Trentham Books.

Shepard, L., Camilli, G. and Averill, M. (1981) Comparison of procedures for detecting test item bias with both internal and external ability criteria. *Journal of Educational Statistics*, 60: 317–75.

Shields, M.M. and Steiner, E. (1973) The language of three- to five-year olds in pre-school education. *Educational Research*, 15(2): 97–105.

Shinn, M.R. and Hubbard, D.D. (1992) Curriculum based measurement and problem solving assessment – basic procedures and outcomes, *Focus on Exceptional Children* 24(5): 1–20.

Shuard, H. and Rothery, R. (1984) *Children Reading Mathematics*. London: John Murray.

Siegel, L. (2004) Bilingualism and reading. In T. Nunes and P. Bryant (eds) *Handbook of Children's Literacy* (pp. 673–89). London: Kluwer Academic.

Siegel, L.S. (1992) An evaluation of the discrepancy definition of dyslexia. *Journal of Learning Disabilities*, 25: 616–29.

Sigel, R. (2004) Reflections on my lovely deafblind daughter. *British Journal of Visual Impairment*, 22(1): 45–6.

Sigman, M., Munday, P., Shareman, T. and Ungerer, J. (1986) Social interactions of autistic, mentally retarded and normal children and their caregivers. *Journal of Child Psychology and Psychiatry*, 27: 657–69.

Sijtsma, K. (1993) Psychometric issues in learning potential assessment. In J.H.M. Hamers, K. Sijtsma and A.J.J.M. Ruilessenaars (eds) *Learning Potential Assessment: Theoretical, Methodological and Practical Issues*. Amsterdam: Swets and Zeitlinger.

Simmons, B. and Bayliss, P. (2007) The role of special schools for children with profound and multiple learning difficulties: is segregation always best? *British Journal of Special Education*, 34(1): 19–24.

Simonoff, E., Pickles, A., Chadwick, O., Gringras, P., Wood, N., Higgins, S. Maney, J.A., Karia, N., Iqbal, H. and Moore, A. (2006) The Croydon Assessment of Learning Study: Prevalence and educational identification of mild mental retardation. *Journal of Child Psychology and Psychiatry*, 47(8): 828–39.

Simos, P.G., Breier, J.I., Fletcher, J.M., Bergman, E. and Papanicolau, A.C. (2000) Cerebral mechanisms involved in word reading in dyslexic children. *Cerebral Cortex*, 10: 809–16.

Simos, P.G., Fletcher, J.M., Bergman, E., Breier, J.I., Foorman, B.R., Castillo, E.M., Fitzgerald, M. and Papanicolau, A.C. (2002) Dyslexia-specific brain activation profile becomes normal following successful remedial training. *Neurology*, 58: 1203–13.

Simos, P.G., Fletcher, J.M., Sarkari, S., Billingsley, R.L., Denton, C.A. and Papanicolaou, A.C. (2007a) Intensive instruction affects brain magnetic activity associated with reading fluency in children with persistent reading disabilities. *Journal of Learning Disabilities*, 40: 37–48.

Simos, P.G., Fletcher, J.M., Sarkari, S., Billingsley, R.L., Denton, C. and Papanicolaou, A.C. (2007b) Altering the brain circuits for reading through intervention: a magnetic source imaging study. *Neuropsychology*, 21(4): 485–96.

Simpson, J. and Everatt, J. (2005) Reception class predictors of literacy skills. *British Journal of Educational Psychology*, 75: 171–88.

Simpson, M. (1997) Developing differentiation practices: meeting the needs of pupils and teachers. *The Curriculum Journal*, 8(1): 85–104.

Sinclair Taylor, A. (1995) 'Less better than the rest': perceptions of integration in a multi-ethnic special needs unit. *Educational Review*, 47(3): 263–74.

Siner, J. (1993) Social competence and cooperative learning. *Educational Psychology in Practice*, 9(3): 171–80.

Singleton, C. (1995) *Cognitive Profiling System*. Newark: Chameleon Education.

Sireci, S.G., Yang, Y., Harter, J. and Ehrlich, E.J. (2006) Evaluating guidelines for test adaptations. *Journal of Cross-Cultural Psychology*, 37(5): 557–67.

Skårbrevik, K.J. (2002) Gender differences among students found eligible for special education. *European Journal of Special Needs Education*, 17(2): 97–107.

Skemp, R.R. (1976) Relational understanding and instrumental understanding. *Mathematics Teaching*, 77: 20–6.

Skidmore, D. (2004) *Inclusion – the Dynamic of School Development*. Maidenhead: Open University Press.

Skutnabb-Kangas, T. (1981) *Bilingualism or Not: The Education of Minorities*. Clevedon: Multilingual Matters.

Slate, J.R. and Saudargas, R.A. (1987) Classroom behaviours of LD, seriously emotionally disturbed and average children: a sequential analysis. *Learning Disabilities Quarterly*, 10: 125–34.

Slater, J. (2004) Special needs pupils barred. *Times Educational Supplement*, 10 December. http://www.tes.co.uk.

Smith, A. (2004) *Making Mathematics Count: The Report of Professor Adrian Smith's Inquiry into Post-14 Mathematics Education*. London: DfES.

Smith, A. and Thomas, N. (2006) Including pupils with special educational needs and disabilities in National Curriculum Physical Education: a brief review. *European Journal of Special Needs Education*, 21(1): 69–83.

Smith, F. (1978) *Understanding Reading: A Psycho-linguistic Analysis of Reading and Learning to Read*, 2nd edition. New York: Holt, Rinehart and Winston.

Smith, M. (2005) *Literacy and Augmentative and Alternative Communication*. Oxford: Academic Press.

Smith, M.L. (1991) Put to the test: the effects of external testing on teachers. *Educational Researcher*, 20(5): 8–11.

Smith, P. and Whetton, C. (1988) Bias reduction in test development. *The Psychologist: Bulletin of the British Psychological Society*, 7: 257–8.

Smith, P.K. (2004) Bullying: recent developments. *Child and Adolescent Mental Health*, 9(3): 98–103.

Smith, T., Eikeseth, S., Klevstrand, M. and Lovaas, O.I. (1997) Intensive behavioural treatment for pre-schoolers with severe mental retardation and pervasive developmental disorder. *American Journal of Mental Retardation*, 102: 238–49.

Smith, T., Groen, A.D. and Wynn, J.W. (2000) Randomised trial of intensive early intervention for children with pervasive developmental disorder. *American Journal of Mental Retardation*, 105: 269–85.

SMSR (2001) *Baseline Assessment for the Foundation Stage – A National Consultation*. Report to Qualifications and Curriculum Authority. London: QCA.

Smukler, D. (2005) Unauthorized minds: how 'theory of mind' theory misrepresents autism. *Mental Retardation*, 43(1): 11–24.

Snell, M.E. (2002) Using dynamic assessment with learners who communicate non-symbolically. *Augmentative and Alternative Communication*, 18(3): 163–76.

Snow, C.E. and Juel, C. (2005) Teaching children to read: what do we know about how to do it? In M.J. Snowling, and C. Hulme (eds) *The Science of Reading: A Handbook* (pp. 501–20). Malden, MA: Blackwell.

Snowling, M. (1995) Phonological processing and developmental dyslexia. *Journal of Research in Reading*, 18: 132–8.

Snowling, M. (1998) Dyslexia as a phonological deficit: evidence and implications. *Child Psychology and Psychiatry Review*, 3(1): 4–11.

Snowling, M.J. (2000) *Dyslexia*, 2nd edition. Oxford: Blackwell.

Snowling, M., Stothard, S. and McLean, J. (1996) *Graded Nonword Reading Test*. Bury St Edmunds: Thames Valley Test Company.

Snowling, M.J., Muter, B. and Carroll, J. (2007) Children at family risk of dylexia: a follow up in early adolescence. *Journal of Child Psychology & Psychiatry*, 48(6): 609–18.

Soar, K., Gersch, I.S. and Lawrence, J.A. (2006) Pupil involvement in special educational needs disagreement resolution: a parental perspective. *Support for Learning*, 21(3): 149–55.

Sodian, B. and Frith, U. (1994) Deception and sabotage in autistic, retarded and normal children. *Journal of Child Psychology and Psychiatry*, 24: 591–605.

Solity, J. (1993) Assessment through teaching: a case of mistaken identity. *Educational and Child Psychology*, 10(4): 27–47.

Solity, J. (1996a) Discrepancy definitions of dyslexia: an assessment through teaching approach. *Educational Psychology in Practice*, 12(3): 141–51.

Solity, J. (1996b) Reframing psychological assessment. *Educational and Child Psychology*, 13(3): 94–102.

Solity, J. and Bull, S. (1987) *Special Needs: Bridging the Curriculum Gap*. Milton Keynes: Open University Press.

Solity, J., Deavers, R., Kerfoot, S., Crane, G. and Cannon, K. (1999) Raising literacy attainments in the early years: the impact of instructional psychology. *Educational Psychology*, 19(4): 373–9.

Soriano, V. (2005) *Early Childhood Intervention: Analysis of Situations in Europe*. Report to European Agency for Development in Special Needs Education. http://www.european-agency.org (accessed 5 November 2007).

Southwell, N. (2006) Truants on truancy – a badness or a valuable indicator of unmet special educational needs? *British Journal of Special Education*, 33(2): 91–7.

Sparrow, S.S. and Davis, S.M. (2000) Recent advances in the assessment of intelligence and cognition. *Journal of Child Psychology and Psychiatry*, 41(1): 117–31.

Sparrow, S.S., Balla, D.A. and Cicchetti, D.V. (1984) *Vineland Adaptive Behavior Scales (Revised)*. Circle Pines, MN: American Guidance Service.

Spence, S. (1995) *Social Skills Training: Enhancing Social Competence with Children and Adolescence*. Windsor: NFER-Nelson.

Spencer, V.G. (2006) Peer tutoring and students with emotional or behavioural disorders: a review of the literature. *Behavioural Disorders*, 31(2): 204–22.

Spivack, G. and Shure, M.B. (1974) *Social Adjustment of Young Children*. San Francisco: Jossey-Bass.

Stage, S.A., Abbott, R.D., Jenkins, J.R. and Berninger, V.W. (2003) Predicting response to early reading intervention from verbal IQ, reading-related language abilities, attention ratings and verbal IQ–word reading discrepancy: failure to validate discrepancy method. *Journal of Learning Disabilities*, 36(1): 24–33.

Stakes, R. and Hornby, G. (1996) *Meeting Special Needs in Mainstream Schools: A Practical Guide for Teachers*. London: David Fulton.

Stallings, J.A. and Freiberg, H.J. (1991) Observation for the improvement of teaching. In H.C. Waxman and H.J. Walberg (eds) *Effective Teaching: Current Research*. Berkeley, CA: McCutchan.

Stanovich, K.E. (1988) Explaining the differences between the dyslexic and the garden-variety poor reader: the phonological-core variable-difference model. *Journal of Learning Disabilities*, 21: 590–612.

Statistics Commission (2005) *Measuring Standards in English Primary Schools: Report by the Statistics Commission on an Article by Peter Tymms*, Research Report 23. London: Statistics Commission. http://www.statscom.org.uk/C_402.aspx (accessed 22 June 2007).

Steele, H., Steele, M. and Fonagy, P. (1996) Associations among attachment classifications of mothers, fathers, and their infants. *Child Development*, 67: 541–55.

Stein, J.F. (1994) A visual defect in dyslexics? in A. Fawcett and R. Nicolson (eds) *Dyslexia in Children: Multi-disciplinary Perspectives*. Hemel Hemsptead: Harvester Wheatsheaf.

Stein, Z. and Susser, M. (1960) The families of dull children: a classification for predicting careers. *British Journal of Preventive Social Medicine*, 14: 83–8.

Stenhoff, D.M. and Lignugaris-Kraft, B. (2007) A review of the effects of peer tutoring on children with mild disabilities in secondary settings. *Exceptional Children*, 74(1): 8–30.

Stevens, G.W.J.M., Pels, T., Bengi-Arslan, L., Verhulst, F.C., Bolleberg, W.A.M. and Crijnen, A.A.M. (2003) Parent, teacher and self-reported problem behaviour in The Netherlands: Comparing Moroccan immigrant with Dutch and Turkish immigrant children and adolescents. *Problem Behavior, Social Psychiatry and Psychiatric Epidemiology*, 38(10): 576–85.

Stiers P., Vanneste, G., Coene, S. and Vandenbussche, E. (2002) Visual-perceptual impairment in a random sample of children with cerebral palsy. *Developmental Medicine & Child Neurology*, 44(6): 370–82.

Stobart, G. (2005) Fairness in multicultural assessment systems. *Assessment in Education: Principles, Policy & Practice*, 12(3): 275–87.

Stoel-Gammon, C. and Otomo, K. (1986) Babbling development of hearing impaired and normal hearing subjects. *Journal of Speech and Hearing Disorders*, 51: 33–40.

Stoker, R. and Walker, C. (eds) (1996) Constructivist approaches. *Educational and Child Psychology*, 13(4): 6–35.

Stone, J. (1995) *Mobility for Special Needs*. London: Cassell.

Stott, D.H. (1978) *Helping Children with Learning Difficulties: A Diagnostic Teaching Approach*. London: Ward Lock.

Stow, C. and Dodd, B. (2005) A survey of bilingual children referred for investigation of communication disorders: a comparison with monolingual children referred in one area in England. *Journal of Multilingual Communication Disorders*, 3(1): 1–23.

Strain, P.S. and Cordisco, L.K. (1994) LEAP preschool. In S.L. Harris and J.S. Handleman (eds) *Preschool Education Programs for Children with Autism*, 2nd edition. Austin, TX: Pro-Ed.

Strickland, B.R. (1972) Delay of gratification as a function of race of the experimenter. *Journal of Personality and Social Psychology*, 22: 108–12.

Stuebing, K.K., Fletcher, J.M., LeDoux, J.M., Lyon, G.R., Shaywitz, S.E. and Shaywitz, B.A. (2002) Validity of IQ–discrepancy classifications of reading disabilities: a meta-analysis. *American Educational Research Journal*, 39: 469–518.

Stulemeijer, M., de Jong, L., Fiselier, T.J.W., Hoogveld, S.W.B. and Bleijenberg, G. (2005) Cognitive behaviour therapy for adolescents with chronic fatigue syndrome: randomized controlled trial. *British Medical Journal*, 330: 14–21.

Suarez-Balcazar, Y., Redmond, L, Kauba, J., Hellwig, M., Davis, R., Martinez, L.I. and Jones, L. (2007) Introducing systems change in the schools: the case of school luncheons and vending machines. *American Journal of Community Psychology*, 39: 335–45.

Suinn, R.M., Taylor, S. and Edwards, R.W. (1988) Suinn Mathematics Anxiety Rating Scale for elementary school students (MARS-E). *Educational and Psychological Measurement*, 48: 979–86.

Suldo, S.M. and Huebner, E.S. (2004) Does life satisfaction moderate the effects of stressful life events on psycho-pathological behaviour during adolescence? *School Psychology Quarterly*, 19(2): 93–105.

Sutherland, G. (1981) The origins of special education. In W. Swann (ed.) *The Practice of Special Education*. Oxford: Blackwell.

Sutherland, R. (2007) *Teaching for Learning Mathematics*. Maidenhead: Open University Press.

Swain, J., French, S., Barnes, C. and Thomas, C. (eds) (2004) *Disabling Barriers – Enabling Environments*, 2nd edition. London: Sage.

Swan, M. (2003) Making sense of mathematics. In I. Thompson (ed.) *Enhancing Primary Mathematics Teaching* (pp. 112–24). Buckingham: Open University Press.

Swann, W. (1985) Is the integration of children with special needs happening? An analysis of recent statistics of pupils in special schools. *Oxford Review of Education*, 11(1): 3–18.

Swearer, S.M., Song, S.Y., Cary, P.T., Eagle, J.W. and Mickleson, W.T. (2001) Psychosocial correlates in bullying and victimization: The relationship between depression, anxiety and bully/victim status. *Journal of Emotional Abuse*, 2: 95–121.

Sylva, K., Melhuish, E., Sammons, P., Siraj-Blatchford, I. and Taggart, B. (2004) *The Effective Provision of Pre-School Education (EPPE) Project (Final Report)*. Nottingham: DfES Publications.

Tacon, R., Atkinson, R. and Wing, T. (2004) *Learning about Numbers with Patterns: Using Structured Visual Imagery (Numicon) to Teach Arithmetic*. London: BEAM Education.

Taggart, B., Sammons, P., Smees, R., Sylva, K., Melhuish, E., Siraj-Blatchford, I., Elliot, K. and Lunt, I. (2006) Early identification of special educational needs and the definition of 'at risk': the Early Years Transition and Special Educational Needs (EYTSEN) Project. *British Journal of Special Education*, 33(1): 40–5.

Tallal, P., Miller, S.L., Jenkins, W.M. and Merzenich, M.M. (1997) The role of temporal processing in developmental language-based disorders: research and clinical implications. In B.A. Blatchman (ed.) *Foundations of Reading Acquisition and Dyslexia: Implications for Early Intervention*. Mahwah, NJ: Lawrence Erlbaum Associates.

Target, M. (2005) Attachment theory and research. In E.S. Pearson, A.M. Cooper and G.O. Gabbard (eds) *The American Psychiatric Publishing Textbook of Psychoanalysis* (pp. 159–72). Washington, DC: American Psychiatric Publishing.

Tate, R., Smeeth, L., Evans, J., Fletcher, A., Owen, C. and Rudnicka, A. (2005) *The Prevalence of Visual Impairment in the UK: A Review of the Literature*. London: London School of Hygiene and Tropical Medicine (report commissioned by the RNIB). http://www.rnib.org.uk (accessed 28 October 2007).

Taylor, A.R., Asher, S.R. and Williams, G.A. (1987) The social adaptation of mainstreamed mildly retarded children. *Child Development*, 58: 1321–34.

Taylor, B., Miller, E., Lingam, R., Andrews, N., Simmons, A. and Stowe, J. (2002) Measles, mumps and rubella vaccination and bowel problems or developmental regression in children with autism. *British Medical Journal*, 324: 393–6.

Taylor, E. and Rogers, J.W. (2005) Practitioner review: early adversity and developmental disorders. *Journal of Child Psychology and Psychiatry*, 46(5): 451–67.

Taylor, G. (1996) Creating a circle of friends: a case study. In H. Cowie and S. Sharp (eds) *Peer Counselling in School*. London: David Fulton.

Taylor, G. and Burden, B. (2000) The positive power of friendship: an illuminative evaluation of the circle of friends approach within the primary and secondary school phases. Unpublished paper, Calouste Gulbenkian Foundation.

Taylor, S.E., Way, B.M., Welch, W.T., Hilmert, C.J., Lehman, B.J. and Eisenberger, N.I. (2006) Early family environment, current adversity, the serotonin transporter promoter polymorphism, and depressive symptomatology. *Biological Psychiatry*, 60(7): 671–6.

Tennant, G. (2007) IEPs in mainstream secondary schools: a research agenda. *Support for Learning*, 22(4): 204–8.

Terman, L.M. (1925) *Genetic Studies of Genius*, Vol. 1. Stanford, CA: Stanford University Press.

Thacker, J. (1982) *Steps to Success: An Interpersonal Problem Solving Approach for Children*. Windsor: NFER-Nelson.

Tharp, R. (1989) Psychocultural variables and constants: effects on teaching and learning in schools. *American Psychologist*, 44: 349–59.

Tharp, R. and Gallimore, R. (1988) *Rousing Minds to Life*. Cambridge, MA: Cambridge University Press.

Thomas, G. (1992) *Effective Classroom Teamwork: Support or Intrusion?* London: Routledge.

Thomas, G. and Loxley, A. (2001) *Deconstructing Special Education and Constructing Inclusion*. Buckingham: Open University Press.

Thomas, G., Walker, D. and Webb, J. (1998) *The Making of the Inclusive School*. London: Routledge.

Thomas, R.M. (1994) The meaning and significance of *ethnicity* in educational discourse. *International Review of Education*, 40(1): 74–80.

Thomas, W. and Collier, V. (2002) *A National Study of School Effectiveness for Language Minority Students' Long-Term Academic Achievement: Final Report*. Washington, DC: Center for Research on Education, Diversity and Excellence. http://repositories.cdlib.org/crede/finalrpts/1_1_final (accessed 17 December 2007).

Thompson, I. (2000) Teaching place value in the UK: time for a reappraisal? *Educational Review*, 52(3): 291–8.

Thompson, I. (2003) Place value: the English disease? In I. Thompson (ed.) *Enhancing Primary Mathematics Teaching* (pp. 181–90). Buckingham: Open University Press.

Thompson, R.F. (2000) *The Brain: A Neuroscience Primer*, 3rd edition. New York: Worth.

Thomson, P. and Gunter, H. (2006) From 'consulting pupils' to 'pupils as researchers': a situated case narrative. *British Educational Research Journal*, 32(6): 839–56.

Thorndike, R.L. (1971) Concepts of culture-fairness. *Journal of Educational Measurement*, 8: 63–70.

Thorndike, R.L., Hagen, E.P. and Sattler, J.M. (1986) *Cognitive Abilities Test (CAT)*, 2nd edition. Windsor: NFER-Nelson.

Thornton, K. (2000) Ministers claim exclusion credit, *Times Educational Supplement*, 12 May.

Thoutenhoofd, E. (2006) Cochlear implanted pupils in Scottish schools: 4-year school attainment data (2000–2004). *Journal of Deaf Studies and Deaf Education*, 11(2): 171–88.

Tindall, G.A. and Marston, D.B. (1990) *Classroom-Based Assessment: Evaluating Instructional Outcomes*. Columbus, OH: Merrill.

Tizard, B. and Hughes, M. (1984) *Young Children Learning: Talking and Thinking at Home and School*. London: Fontana.

Tizard, B., Blachford, P., Burke, J., Farquar, C. and Plewis, I. (1988) *Young Children at School in the Inner City*. Hove: Lawrence Erlbaum.

Teaching and Learning Research Programme (2005) *Neuroscience and Education: Issues and Opportunities*. http://www.tlrp.org (accessed 10 October 2007).

Todd, L. (2003) Disability and the restructuring of welfare: the problem of partnership with parents. *International Journal of Inclusive Education*, 7(3): 281–96.

Todd, L. (2007) *Partnerships for Inclusive Education: A Critical Approach to Collaborative Working*. London: Routledge.

Tomlinson, S. (1981) *Educational Subnormality: A Study in Decision Making*. London: Routledge & Kegan Paul.

Tomlinson, S. (1982) *A Sociology of Special Education*. London: Routledge & Kegan Paul.

Tomlinson, S. (1984) Minority groups in English conurbations. In P. Williams (ed.) *Special Education in Minority Communities*. Milton Keynes: Open University Press.

Tomlinson, S. (1988) Why Johnny can't read: critical theory and special education. *European Journal of Special Needs Education*, 3(1): 45–58.

Tomlinson, S. (2000) Ethnic minorities and education: new disadvantages. In T. Cox (ed.) *Combating Educational Disadvantage: Meeting the Needs of Vulnerable Children*. London: Falmer Press.

Tooley, J. and Darby, D. (1998) *Education Research: An Ofsted Critique*. London: Ofsted.

Toplis, R. and Hadwin, J. (2006) Using Social Stories to change problematic lunchtime behaviour in school. *Educational Psychology in Practice*, 22: 53–67.

Topping, K.J. and Lindsay, G.A. (1991) The structure and development of the paired reading technique. *Journal of Research in Reading*, 15(2): 120–36.

Topping, K.J. and Lindsay, G.A. (1992) Paired reading: a review of the literature. *Research Papers in Education*, 7(3): 199–246.

Torgerson, C.J., Brooks, G. and Hall, J. (2006) *A Systematic Review of the Research Literature on the Use of Phonics in the Teaching of Reading and Spelling*. Research Report RR711. Nottingham: Department for Education and Skills.

Torgesen, J.K. (2005) Recent discoveries on remedial interventions for children with dyslexia. In M.J. Snowling and C. Hulme (eds) *The Science of Reading: A Handbook*. Oxford: Blackwell.

Torgesen, J.K., Alexander, A.W., Wagner, R.K., Rashotte, C.A., Voller, K., Conway, T. *et al.* (2001) Intensive remedial instruction for children with severe reading disabilities: immediate and long term outcomes from two instructional approaches. *Journal of Learning Disabilities*, 34: 33–58.

Towse, J. and Saxton, M. (1998) Mathematics across national boundaries: cultural and linguistic perspectives on numerical competence. In C. Donlan (ed.) *The Development of Mathematical Skills*. Hove: Psychology Press.

Trinidad, D.R. and Johnson, C.A. (2002) The association between emotional intelligence and early adolescent tobacco and alcohol use. *Personality and Individual Differences*, 32(1): 95–105.

Truscott, S.D., Catanese, A.M. and Abrams, L.M. (2005) The evolving context of special education classification in the United States. *School Psychology International*, 26(2): 162–77.

Tucker, J.A. (1985) Curriculum based assessment: an introduction. *Exceptional Children*, 52(3): 199–204.

Turner, M. (1997) *Psychological Assessment of Dyslexia*. London: Whurr.

Turner, S. and Lynas, W. (2000) Teachers' perspectives on support for under-fives in families of ethnic minority origin. *Deafness and Education International*, 2(3): 152–64.

Turner, S. (1996) Meeting the needs of children under five with sensori-neural hearing loss from ethnic minority families. *Journal of the British Association of Teachers of the Deaf*, 20: 91–100.

Tutt, R. (2007) *Every Child Included*. London: Paul Chapman.

Tutt, R., Powell, S., and Thornton, M. (2006) Educational approaches in autism: what we know about what we do. *Educational Psychology in Practice*, 22: 69–81.

UNESCO (1988) *The Review of the Present Situation of Special Education*. Paris: UNESCO.

UNESCO (1994) *The Salamanca Statement and Framework for Action on Special Needs Education*. Paris: UNESCO.

Upton, G. (1990) The Education Reform Act and special educational needs. *Newsletter of the Association for Child Psychology and Psychiatry*, 12(5): 3–8.

US Department of Education, Office of Special Education Programs (2002) *Specific Learning Disabilities: Finding Common Ground*. Washington DC: Author.

Uzzell, D. (1995) Ethnography and action research. In G.M. Brakewell, S. Hammond and C. Fife-Schaw (eds) *Research Methods in Psychology*. London: Sage.

Valdes, G. and Figueroa, R.A. (1994) *Bilingualism and Testing: A Special Case of Bias*. Norwood, NJ: Ablex.

Valsiner, J. (2000) *Culture and Human Development: An Introduction*. London: Sage.

Van der Klift, E., and Kunc, N. (2002) Beyond benevolence. In J.S. Thousand., R.A. Villa and A.I. Nevin (eds) *Creativity and Collaborative Learning: The Practical Guide to Empowering Students, Teachers, and Families* (pp. 21–8). Baltimore, MD: Paul H. Brookes.

Van der Molen, M.J., Van Luit, J.E.H., Jongmans, M.J. and Van der Molen, M.W. (2007) Verbal working memory in children with mild intellectual disabilities. *Journal of Intellectual Disability Research*, 51(2): 162–9.

van Ijzendoorn, M.H. and Juffer, F. (2006) The Emanuel Miller Memorial Lecture 2006: Adoption as intervention. Meta-analytic evidence for massive catch-up and plasticity in physical, socio-emotional, and cognitive development. *Journal of Child Psychology and Psychiatry*, 47(12): 1228–45.

VanDerHeyden, A.M., Witt, J.C. and Gilbertson, D. (2007) A multi-year evaluation of the effects of a Response to Intervention (RTI) model on identification of children for special education. *Journal of School Psychology*, 45, 225–56.

Vaughan, M. (2002) An Index for Inclusion. *European Journal of Special Needs Education*, 17(2): 197–201.

Vaughn, S. and Fuchs, L.S. (2003) Redefining learning disabilities as inadequate Response to Instruction: the promise and potential problems. *Learning Disabilities Research & Practice*, 18(3): 137–46.

Vellutino, F.R., Scanlon, D.M. and Tanzman, M.S. (1998) The case for early intervention in diagnosing specific reading disability. *Journal of School Psychology*, 36(4): 367–97.

Vellutino, F.R., Fletcher, J.M., Snowling, M.J. and Scanlon, D.M. (2004) Specific reading disability (dyslexia): what have we learned in the past four decades? *Journal of Child Psychology and Psychiatry*, 45(1): 2–40.

Venter, A., Lord, C. and Schopler, E. (1992) A follow-up study of high functioning autistic children. *Journal of Child Psychology & Psychiatry*, 33: 489–507.

Verhoeven, L. and van Balkom, H. (eds) (2004) *Classification of Developmental Language Disorders: Theoretical Issues and Clinical Implications*. Mahwah, NJ: Lawrence Erlbaum Associates.

Verhulst, F.C. and Akkerhuis, G.W. (1989) Agreement between parents' and teachers' ratings of behavioural/emotional problems of children aged 4–12. *Journal of Child Psychology and Psychiatry*, 30(1): 123–36.

Verkuyten, M. and Thijs, J. (2002) Racist victimization among children in the Netherlands: The effect of ethnic group and school. *Ethnic and Racial Studies*, 25: 310–31.

Vincent, C. (1996) *Parents and Teachers: Power and Participation*. London: Falmer Press.

Virani-Roper, Z. (2000) Bilingual learners and numeracy. In M. Gravelle (ed.) *Planning for Bilingual Learners: An Inclusive Curriculum* (pp. 65–78). Stoke-on-Trent: Trentham Books.

Vlaskamp, C., de Geeter, K.I., Huijsmans, L.M. and Smit, I.H. (2003) Passive activities: the effectiveness of multi-sensory environments on the level of activity of individuals with profound multiple disabilities. *Journal of Applied Research in Intellectual Disabilities*, 16: 135–43.

Volkmar, F.R., Lord, C., Bailey, A., Schultz, R.T. and Klin, A. (2004) Autism and pervasive developmental disorders. *Journal of Child Psychology and Psychiatry*, 45: 135–70.

Von Bertalanffy, L. (1968) *General Systems Theory*. New York: Brazillier.

Von Tetzchner, S. and Grove, N. (eds) (2003) *Augmentative and Alternative Communication: Developmental Issues*. London: Whurr.

Vye, N.J., Burns, M.S., Delclos, V.R. and Bransford, J.D. (1987) A comprehensive approach to assessing intellectually handicapped children. In C.S. Lidz (ed.) *Dynamic Assessment: An Interactional Approach to Evaluating Learning Potential* (pp. 327–59). New York: Guilford Press.

Vygotsky, L.S. (1978) *Mind in Society: The Development of Higher Psychological Processes*. Cambridge, MA: Harvard University Press.

Wade, B. and Moore, M. (1993) *Experiencing Special Education: What Young People with Special Educational Needs Can Tell Us*. Buckingham: Open University Press.

Wade, J. (1999) Including all learners: QCA's approach. *British Journal of Special Education*, 26(2): 80–2.

Wadsworth, S.J., De Fries, J.C., Stevenson, J., Gilger, J.W. and Pennington, B.F. (1992) Gender ratios among reading-disabled children and their siblings as a function of parental impairment. *Journal of Child Psychology and Psychiatry*, 33: 1229–39.

Wagner-Lampl, A. and Oliver, G.W. (1994) Folklore of blindness. *Journal of Visual Impairment and Blindness*, 88(3): 267–76.

Walberg, H.J. (1995) Generic practices. In G. Cawelti (ed.) *Handbook of Research on Improving Student Achievement*. Arlington, VA: Educational Research Services.

Walker, S.O. and Plomin, R. (2006) Nature, nurture and perceptions of the classroom environment as they relate to teacher-assessed academic achievement: a twin study of nine-year olds. *Educational Psychology*, 26(4): 541–61.

Wall, K. (2003) Pupils with special educational needs and the National Literacy Strategy. *Support for Learning*, 18(1): 35–41.

Walling, A. (2005) Families and work. *Labour Market Trends*, 113(07): 275–283.

Walters, E. (1997) Problems faced by children and families living with visible differences. In R. Lansdowne, N. Rumsey, T. Carr and J. Partridge (eds) *Visibly Different: Coping with Disfigurement* (pp. 112–20). Oxford: Butterworth-Heinemann.

Wang, M.C., Haertel, G.D. and Walberg, H.J. (1994) Educational resilience in inner cities. In M.C. Wang and E.W. Gordon (eds) *Educational Resilience in Inner-City America: Challenges and Prospects*. Hillsdale, NJ: Lawrence Erlbaum Associates.

Warnock, M. (2005) *Special Educational Needs: A New Outlook*. London: Philosophy of Education Society of Great Britain.

Warwickshire County Council (2005) *An ASD Tool Kit for Teachers*. Warwickshire County Council.

Watkins, M.W., Kush, J.C. and Glutting, J.J. (1997) Discriminant and predictive validity of the WISC-III ACID Profile among children with learning disabilities. *Psychology in the Schools*, 34(4): 309–19.

Watson, A. (2006) Some difficulties in informal assessment in mathematics. *Assessment in Education: Principles, Policy and Practice*. 13(3): 289–303.

Watson, A. and Mason, J. (1998) *Questions and Prompts for Mathematical Thinking*. Derby: Association of Teachers of Mathematics.

Watson, D., Abbott, D. and Townsley, R. (2007) Listen to me too! Lessons from involving children with complex healthcare needs in research about multi-agency services. *Child: Care, Health and Development*, 33(1): 90–5.

Watson, D.L., Omark, D.R., Grouell, S.L. and Heller, B. (1987) *Nondiscriminatory Assessment Practitioners' Handbook*. San Diego, CA: Los Amigos Research Associates.

Watson, J. (2000) Constructive instruction and learning difficulties. *Support for Learning*, 15(3): 134–40.

Watson, L. (1996) *Hearing Impairment*. Tamworth: NASEN.

Waxman, H.C. (1992) Reversing the cycles of educational failure for students in at-risk school environments. In H.C. Waxman, J. Walker de Felix, J.E. Anderson and H. Prentice Baptiste (eds) *Students at Risk in At-Risk Schools: Improving Environments for Learning*. Newbury Park, CA: Sage.

Waxman, H.C. (1995) Classroom observations of effective teaching. In A.C. Ornstein (ed.) *Teaching: Theory into Practice*. Needham Heights, MA: Allyn & Bacon.

Waxman, H.C. and Huang, S-Y.L. (1996) Motivation and learning environment differences in inner-city middle school students. *Journal of Educational Research*, 90(2): 93–102.

Waxman, H.C. and Huang, S-Y.L. (1997) Classroom instruction and learning environment differences between effective and ineffective urban elementary schools for African American students. *Urban Education*, 32(1): 7–44.

Waxman, H.C. and Padron, Y.N. (2004) The uses of the classroom observation schedule to improve classroom instruction. In H.C. Waxman, R.G. Tharp and R. Soleste Hilberg (eds) *Observational Research in US Classrooms. New Approaches for Understanding Cultural and Linguistic Diversity* (pp. 72–96). New York: Cambridge University Press.

Waxman, H.C., Wang, M.C., Lindvall, M. and Anderson, K.A. (1988) *Classroom Observation Schedule Technical Manual*. Pittsburgh: University of Pittsburgh, Learning Research and Development Centre.

Waxman, H.C., Huang, S-Y.L., Anderson, L. and Weinstein, T. (1997) Classroom process differences in inner-city elementary schools. *Journal of Educational Research*, 91: 49–59.

Weare, K. and Gray, G. (2003) *What Works in Developing Children's Emotional and Social Competence and Well-Being?* Research Report no. 456. Nottingham: Department for Education and Skills Publications.

Webster, A. (1988) The prevalence of speech and language difficulties in childhood: some brief research notes. *Child Language, Teaching and Therapy*, 4(1): 85–91.

Webster, A. and Wood, D. (1989) *Children with Hearing Difficulties*. London: Cassell.

Webster-Stratton, C., and Hancock, L. (1998) Parent training: content, methods and processes. In E. Schaefer (ed.) *Handbook of Parent Training*, 2nd edition (pp. 98–152). New York: Wiley.

Webster-Stratton, C. and Reid, M.J. (2003) Treating conduct problems and strengthening social and emotional competence in young children: the Dina Dinosaur treatment program. *Journal of Emotional and Behavioral Disorders*, 11(3): 132–43.

Webster-Stratton, C. and Reid, M.J. (2004) Strengthening social and emotional competence in young children – the foundation for early school readiness and success. *Infants & Young Children*, 17(2): 96–113.

Webster-Stratton, C., Reid, J. and Hammond, M. (2001) Social skills and problem solving training for children with early-onset conduct problems: who benefits? *Journal of Child Psychology and Psychiatry*, 42(7): 943–52.

Wechsler, D. (2003) *Wechsler Intelligence Scale for Children*, 4th edition. San Antonio, TX: The Psychological Corporation.

Wechsler, D. (2006) *WIAT-II UK for Teachers*. London: Harcourt Assessment.

Wedell, K. (2003) Points from the SENCo – Forum: What's in a Label? *British Journal of Special Education*, 30(2): 107.

Weiner, B. (1985) An attributional theory of achievement motivation and emotion. *Psychological Review*, 92: 548–73.

Weiss, L.G. and Prifitera, A. (1995) An evaluation of differential prediction of WIAT achievement scores from WISC III FSIQ across ethnic and gender groups. *Journal of School Psychology*, 33: 297–304.

Weissberg, R.P. and O'Brien, M.U. (2004) What works in school-based social and emotional learning programmes for positive youth development. *Annals of the American Academy of Political and Social Science*, 591: 86–97.

Wells, J., Barlow, J. and Stewart-Brown, S. (2003) A systematic review of universal approaches to mental health promotion in schools. *Health Education*, 103(4): 197–220.

Wentzel, K.R. (1991) Relations between social competence and academic achievement in early adolescence. *Child Development*, 62: 1066–78.

Wentzel, K.R. and Asher, S.R. (1995) The academic lives of neglected, rejected, popular, and controversial children. *Child Development*, 66: 754–63.

West, T.A. (1971) Diagnosing pupil errors: looking for patterns. *The Arithmetic Teacher*, 18: 467–9.

Westling Allodi, M. (2002) A two level analysis of classroom climate in relation to social context, group composition and organisation of special support. *Learning Environments Research*, 5: 253–74.

Wheale, A. (ed.) (2000) *Working with Parents*. Lyme Regis: Russell House Publishing.

Wheeler, A., Archbold, S., Gregory, S. and Skipp, A. (2007) Cochlear implants: the young people's perspective. *Journal of Deaf Studies and Deaf Education*, 12(3): 303–16.

Wheldall K. and Lam, Y.Y. (1987) Rows versus tables II. The effects of two classroom seating arrangements on classroom disruption rate, on-task behaviour and teacher behaviour in three special school classes. *Educational Psychology*, 7(4): 303–12.

Wheldall, K., Morris, M., Vaughan, P. and Ng, Y.Y. (1981) Rows versus tables: an example of the use of behavioural ecology in two classes of eleven-year-old children. *Educational Psychology*, 1(2): 171–84.

Wheldall, K., Beaman, R. and Mok, M. (1999) Does the individualised classroom environment questionnaire (ICEQ) measure classroom climate? *Educational and Psychological Measurement*, 59(5): 847–54.

Whitaker, P., Barratt, P., Joy, H., Potter, M. and Thomas, G. (1998) Children with autism and peer group support: using 'circles of friends'. *British Journal of Special Education*, 25: 60–4.

White, D.R. and Haring, N.G. (1980) *Exceptional Children*. Columbus, OH: Merrill.

White, J. (2004) Howard Gardner: the myth of multiple intelligences. Lecture at the Institute of Education, University of London, 17 November. Downloaded on 19 September 2007 from http://www.ioe.ac.uk/schools/mst/LTU/phil/HowardGardner_171104.pdf.

White, S., Milne, E., Rosen, S., Hansen, P., Swettenham, J., Frith, U. and Ramus, F. (2006) The role of sensory motor impairments in dyslexia: a multiple case study of dyslexic children, *Developmental Science*, 9(3): 237–69.

Whitehurst, T. (2007) Liberating silent voices–perspectives of children with profound and complex learning needs on inclusion. *British Journal of Learning Disabilities*, 35(1): 55–61.

Whitney, I., Smith, P.K. and Thompson, D. (1994) Bullying and children with special educational needs. In P.K. Smith and S. Sharp (eds) *School Bullying: Insights and Perspectives* (pp. 213–39). London: Routledge.

Wiliam, D. (1994) Creating matched National Curriculum assessments in English and Welsh: test translation and parallel development. *Curriculum Journal*, 5(1): 17–29.

Wiliam, D. (1999) Formative assessment in mathematics, Part 1: Rich questioning. *Equals: Mathematics and Special Educational Needs*, 5(2): 15–18.

Wiliam, D. and Thompson, M. (2008) Integrating assessment with learning: what will it take to make it work? In C.A. Dwyer (ed.) *The Future of Assessment: Shaping Teaching and Learning* (pp. 53–82). New York: Lawrence Erlbaum Associates.

Wiliam, D., Lee, C., Harrison, C. and Black, P.J. (2004) Teachers developing assessment for learning: impact on student achievement. *Assessment in Education: Principles, Policy and Practice*, 11(1): 49–65.

Williams, A. (1996) Curriculum auditing: an accessible tool or an awesome task? *British Journal of Special Education*, 23(2): 65–9.

Williams, H. and Muncey, J. (1982) Precision teaching before behavioural objectives. *Journal of the Association of Educational Psychologists*, 5(8): 40–2.

Williams, K.R. (2006) The Son-Rise Program[fi] Intervention for autism: prerequisites for evaluation. *Autism*, 10(1): 86–102.

Williams, R.L. (1971) Abuses and misuses in testing black children. *Counselling Psychologist*, 2: 62–77.

Williams, R.L. (1975) The BITCH-100: a culture specific test. *Journal of Afro-American Issues*, 3(1): 103–16.

Williams, S.K., Johnson, C. and Sukhodolsky, D.G. (2005) The role of the school psychologist in the inclusive education of school-age children with autism spectrum disorders. *Journal of School Psychology*, 43: 117–36.

Willingham, W.W. and Cole, N.S. (1997) *Gender and Fair Assessment*. Mahwah, NJ: Lawrence Erlbaum Associates.

Willis, L. (2002) Language use and identity among African-Caribbean young people in Sheffield. In P. Gubbins and M. Holt (eds) *Beyond Boundaries: Language and Identity in Contemporary Europe* (pp. 126–44). Clevedon: Multilingual Matters.

Wilson, M.M. (1970) *Children with Cerebral Palsy*. DES Education Survey 7. London: HMSO.

Wing, L. and Gould, J. (1979) Severe impairments of social interaction and associated abnormalities in children: epidemiology and classification. *Journal of Autism and Developmental Disorders*, 9: 11–29.

Wing, L. and Potter, D. (2002) The epidemiology of autism: is the prevalence rising? *Mental Retardation and Developmental Disabilities Research Reviews*, 8: 151–61.

Winskel, H. (2006) The effects of an early history of otitis media on children's language and literacy skill development. *British Journal of Educational Psychology*, 76(4): 727–44.

Winter, K. (1999) Speech and language therapy provision for bilingual children: aspects of the current service. *International Journal of Language and Communication Disorders*, 34(1): 85–98.

Wishart, J. (2005) Children with Down's syndrome. In A. Lewis and B. Norwich (eds) *Special Teaching for Special Children? Pedagogies for Inclusion* (pp. 81–95). Maidenhead: Open University Press.

Wolfendale, S. (1989) *Parental Involvement: Developing Networks between School, Home and Community*. London: Cassell.

Wolpert, M., Cottrell, C., Fonagy, P., Fuggle, P., Phillips, J., Pilling, S., Stein, S. and Target, M. (2006) *Drawing on the Evidence. Advice for Mental Health Professionals Working with Children and Adolescents*. London: CAMHS Publications.

Wood, D., Wood, H., Griffiths, A. and Howarth, I. (1986) *Teaching and Talking with Deaf Children*. Chichester: Wiley.

Wood, R. (1978) Sex differences in answers to English language comprehension items. *Educational Studies*, 4: 157–65.

Wood, R. (1991) *Assessment and Testing: A Survey of Research Commissioned by the University of Cambridge Local Examinations Syndicate*. Cambridge: Cambridge University Press.

Wood, S. and Shears, B. (1986) *Teaching Children with Severe Learninq Difficulties: A Radical Reappraisal*. London: Croom Helm.

Woods, K. and Farrell, P. (2006) Approaches to psychological assessment by educational psychologists in England and Wales. *School Psychology International*, 27(4): 387–404.

Woolfolk, A.E. (2004) *Educational Psychology*, 9th edition. New York: Allyn & Bacon.

Woolfson, R.C. and Harker, M.E. (2002) Consulting with children and young people: young people's views of a Psychological Service. *Educational and Child Psychology*, 19(4): 35–46.

Woolner, P., Hall, E., Higgins, S., McCaughey, C. and Wall, K. (2007) A sound foundation? What we know about the impact of environments on learning and the implications for Building Schools for the Future. *Oxford Review of Education*, 33(1): 47–70.

World Health Organization (1995) *International Classification of Disability – Version 10 (ICD-10)*. Geneva: WHO.

Worrall-Davies, A. and Marino-Francis, F. (2008) Eliciting children's and young people's views of child and adolescent mental health services: a systematic review of best practice. *Child and Adolescent Mental Health*, 13(1): 9–15.

Wright, A.K. (1991) The assessment of bilingual pupils with reported learning difficulties: a hypothesis-testing approach. In T. Cline and N. Frederickson (eds) *Bilingual Pupils and the National Curriculum: Overcoming Difficulties in Teaching and Learning*. London: Educational Psychology Publishing.

Wright, A.K., Gallagher, S.P. and Lombardi, L.G. (1991) Investigating classroom environment in British schools. *Educational Psychology in Practice*, 7(2): 100–4.

Wright, D. and Torrey, K. (2001) A comparison of two peer-referenced assessment techniques with parent and teacher ratings of social skills and problem behaviors. *Behavioural Disorders*, 26(2): 173–82.

Wright, J.A. and Kersner, M. (1998) *Supporting Children with Communication Problems: Sharing the Workload*. London: David Fulton.

Wyse, D. (2000) Phonics – the whole story? A critical review of empirical evidence. *Educational Studies*, 26(3): 355–64.

Wyse, D. and Styles, M. (2007) Synthetic phonics and the teaching of reading: the debate surrounding England's 'Rose Report'. *Literacy*, 41(1): 35–42.

Yamazaki, Y. (2005) Learning styles and typologies of cultural differences: a theoretical and empirical comparison. *International Journal of Intercultural Relations*, 29: 521–48.

Yoshinaga-Itano, C. (2003) From screening to early identification and intervention: discovering predictors to successful outcomes for children with significant hearing loss. *Journal of Deaf Studies and Deaf Education*, 8(1): 11–30.

Young, A. and Tattersall, H. (2007) Universal newborn hearing screening and early identification of deafness: parents' responses to knowing early and their expectations of child communication development. *Journal of Deaf Studies and Deaf Education*, 12(2): 209–20.

Young, S. (1998) The support group approach to bullying in schools. *Educational Psychology in Practice*, 14: 32–9.

Ysseldyke, J. and Christenson, S. (1987) Evaluating students' instructional environments. *Remedial and Special Education*, 8(3): 17–24.

Ysseldyke, J. and Christenson, S. (2002) *Functional Assessment of Academic Behavior. Creating successful learning environments*. Longmont, CO: Sopris West.

Yule, W. (1975) Psychological and medical concepts. In K. Wedell (ed.) *Orientations in Special Education*. London: Wiley.

Zeleke, S. (2004) Self concepts of students with learning disabilities and their normally achieving peers: a review. *European Journal of Special Needs Education*, 19(2): 145–70.

Zevenbergen, R., Mousley, J. and Sullivan, P. (2004) Making the pedagogic relay inclusive for indigenous Australian students in mathematics classrooms. *International Journal of Inclusive Education*, 8(4): 391–405.

Zhang, C. and Bennett, T. (2003) Facilitating the meaningful participation of culturally and linguistically diverse families in the IFSP and IEP process. *Focus on Autism and Other Developmental Disabilities*, 18(1): 51–9.

Ziegler, J.C. and Goswami, U. (2005) Reading acquisition, developmental dyslexia, and skilled reading across languages: a psycholinguistic grain size theory. *Psychological Bulletin*, 131(1): 3–29.

Zigmond, N. and Baker, J.M. (1995) An exploration of the meaning and practice of special education in the context of full inclusion of students with learning disabilities. *Journal of Special Education*, 29(2): 1–25.

Zionts, L.T. (2005) Examining relationships between students and teachers. A potential extension of attachment theory? In K.A. Kerns and R.A. Richardson (eds) *Attachment in Middle Childhood* (pp. 231–54). New York: Guilford Press.

Zubrick, A. (1992) Child language impairment in Hong Kong. In P. Fletcher and D. Hall (eds) *Specific Speech and Language Disorders in Children*. London: Whurr.

Index